ARTS AND CULTURE

AN INTRODUCTION TO THE HUMANITIES

Volume I

ARTS AND CULTURE
AN INTRODUCTION TO THE HUMANITIES

JANETTA REBOLD BENTON
ROBERT DIYANNI

PACE UNIVERSITY, PLEASANTVILLE

Prentice Hall
Upper Saddle River, New Jersey 07458

Library of Congress Cataloging-in-Publication Data

Benton, Janetta Rebold
    Arts and culture: an introduction to the humanities/ Janetta
Rebold Benton, Robert DiYanni. -- Combined ed.
      p.   cm.
    Includes bibliographical references and index.
    ISBN 0-13-863192-1
    1. Arts--History. I. DiYanni, Robert. II. Title.
NX440.B46 1998
700--dc21   97-17901
                              CIP

For our children:
Alexander, Ethan, Meredith, and Leland;
Karen and Michael.

Editorial Director: Charlyce Jones Owen
Publisher: Bud Therien
Director of Manufacturing and Production: Barbara Kittle
Editorial/production supervision: Robert Shore (Calmann &
    King Ltd.)
Production liaison: Joe Scordato (Prentice Hall)
Development editor: Robert Shore
Editor-in-chief of development: Susanna Lesan
Marketing manager: Sheryl Adams
Layout: Andrew Shoolbred
Creative director: Leslie Osher
Interior and cover design: Joseph Rattan Design
Photo research: Peter Kent
Manufacturing manager: Nick Sklitsis
Manufacturing buyer: Bob Anderson
Editorial assistant: Gianna Caradonna
Cover art: *Queen Tiy*, from Kom Medinet Ghurab (near el-
    Lahun), Dynasty 18 c. 1390–1352 BCE, boxwood, ebony,
    glass, gold, lapis lazuli, cloth, clay, and wax, height
    $3\frac{3}{4}''$ (9.4 cm), Staatliche Museen zu Berlin, Preussischer
    Kulturbesitz, Ägyptisches Museum. Photo by Margarete
    Busing.

This book was set in 10/12 Janson and was printed and bound
by RR Donnelley & Sons, Inc. The cover was printed by The
Lehigh Press, Inc.

Printed in the United States of America
10 9 8 7 6 4 3

ISBN 0-13-083909-4

Prentice Hall International (UK) Limited, *London*
Prentice-Hall of Australia Pty. Limited, *Sydney*
Prentice-Hall Canada Inc, *Toronto*
Prentice-Hall Hispanoamericana, S.A., *Mexico*
Prentice-Hall of India Private Limited, *New Delhi*
Prentice-Hall of Japan, Inc., *Tokyo*
Simon & Schuster Asia Pte. Ltd, *Singapore*
Editora Prentice-Hall do Brasil, Ltda, *Rio de Janeiro*

Contents Overview

Contents

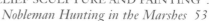

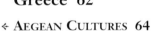

CHAPTER 10

The Civilizations of the Americas 314

CHAPTER 11

The Early Middle Ages and the Romanesque 330

CHAPTER 12

The Gothic and Late Middle Ages 362

Preface

Arts and Culture provides an introduction to the world's major civilizations—to their artistic achievements, their history, and their cultures. Through an integrated approach to the humanities, *Arts and Culture* offers an opportunity to view works of art, listen to music, and read literature, in historical and cultural contexts.

The most accomplished works of painting, sculpture, and architecture, of music, literature, and philosophy are studied for what they reveal about human life. They open doors to the past, especially to the values and belief systems from which those artworks sprang. They also tell us about human attitudes and feelings, about ideas and ideals that continue to have value today.

Works of art from different cultures reveal common human experiences of birth and death, love and loss, pleasure and pain, hope and frustration, elation and despair. Study of the humanities—history, literature, philosophy, religion, and the arts—also reveals what others value and believe, inviting each of us to consider our personal, social, and cultural values in relation to those of others.

In studying the humanities, our attention is focused on works of art in the broadest sense, works that reflect and embody the central values and beliefs of particular cultures and specific historical moments. The following questions deserve consideration:

1. *What kind of artwork is it? To what artistic category does it belong? What is its type?* These questions lead to considerations of genre. A European Renaissance painting, for example, might be a portrait or a landscape, a religious icon or an abstract design. A musical work might be a song or a symphony, a chamber instrumental work, such as a string quartet, or a religious cantata.

2. *Why was the artwork made? What was its function, purpose, or use? Who was responsible for producing it? Who paid for or commissioned it?* These questions lead to considerations of context. Many works of art were commissioned by religious institutions and wealthy patrons. Many paintings and sculptures were commissioned by the Church and were intended to be both didactic and decorative. Many eighteenth and nineteenth century string quartets and piano trios were written for performance at the home of the patrons who paid composers to write them.

3. *What does the work express or convey? What does it reveal about its creator? What does it reveal about its historical and social context?* These questions lead to considerations of meaning. Some paintings and sculptures are intended to record actual events or to encourage (or discourage) particular types of behaviour. A lyric poem written in ancient China or India may express feelings of sadness or longing, elation at seeing the beloved, grief over the death of a friend. Such poetic lyrics, whatever their age, language and country of origin, reveal not only the writer's feelings, but also cultural attitudes and social values.

4. *How was the artwork made or constructed?* This question leads to considerations of technique. Paintings made during the Middle Ages in Europe were likely to be done in egg tempera on a wooden panel. A painting from Renaissance Europe may be a fresco painted on the interior wall of a church or other building. A painting may also have been done in oil on canvas for framing and hanging in a private home. Or to take an example on a much larger scale, an Islamic mosque, a Catholic cathedral, a Greek or Japanese temple—all are constructed according to specified plans, their interior spaces designed to serve particular religious purposes.

Architectural structures such as these were also made of many types of materials and built using the technologies and tools available at the time of their construction. Developments in technology continually liberated the artistic imagination of painters, sculptors, architects, and composers, who were able to create, for example, new musical tones with the extension of the sonic range of instruments and with the invention of instruments such as the piano.

5. *What are the parts or elements of a work of art? How are these parts related to create a unified artwork?* These questions lead to considerations of formal analysis, understanding the ways the artwork coheres as a whole. Painters, sculptors, and architects work with line, form, color, composition, texture, and other aesthetic elements. In the same way, a Gregorian chant, like a Blues song or a German *Lied* or artsong, reveals a particular structural pattern or organizational design. So does an Elizabethan sonnet, a Japanese haiku, an Arabic qasida, and a Greek epic. Analysis of the form of artworks leads to an appreciation of their artistic integrity and their meaning.

6. *What social, cultural, and moral values does the work express, reflect, or embody?* Works of art bear the social, moral, and cultural values of their creators. They also reflect the times and circumstances of their creation—even when the individual artist, composer, or writer worked against the cultural ethos of the times. We

study works of art to understand the human values they embody for artworks give us insight into human experience. Unlike scientific works or creations—whether formulas, such as Newton's formula for gravitational attraction or Einstein's E=mc²—which are predictive and practical, works of art produce a creative discovery or enlightenment in viewers and readers. They appeal to the human capacity for feeling and thought through the imagination. In contrast to science, which seeks to explain what exists, art seeks to create something new—but something that bears a distinct relationship to what exists.

Balancing the social, cultural, and historical realities that works of art reflect are their uniquely personal visions of experience. Works of art are experiments in living. Through them readers and viewers can experience other imaginative perspectives, share other visions of human life. Works of art provide an imaginative extension of life's possibilities for those who remain open to their unique forms of creative expression.

MAKING CONNECTIONS

A study of the humanities involves more than an examination of the artistic monuments of civilizations past and present. More importantly, it involves a consideration of how forms of human achievement in many times and places echo and reinforce, alter and modify each other. An important aspect of humanities study involves seeing connections among the arts of a given culture and discovering relationships between the arts of different cultures.

Three forms of connection are of particular importance: (1) *interdisciplinary connections* among artworks of an individual culture; (2) *cross currents* among artworks of different cultures; (3) *transhistorical links* between past and present, then and now.

These forms of connection invite readers and viewers to locate relationships among various humanities disciplines and to identify links between and among the achievements of diverse cultures. Discovering such connections can be intellectually stimulating and emotionally stirring since the forms of human experience reflected and embodied in the works of art of many cultures resonate with common human concerns. These artworks address and answer social questions about who we are, philosophical questions about why we exist at all, and religious questions concerning what awaits us after death. These and numerous other perennial questions and the varying perspectives taken on them have been central to every culture, and find expression in their arts. Consider the following examples.

Interdisciplinary CONNECTIONS

One type of interdisciplinary connection appears in the ways the music and architecture of Renaissance Florence were influenced by mathematical proportion and ancient notions of "harmony." Mathematics played a crucial role in all the arts of the Renaissance. Architects were guided in the design of their buildings by mathematical ratios and proportions; composers likewise wrote music that reflected mathematical ratios in both its melody and harmony.

Other kinds of interdisciplinary connections are evident in the collaboration of artists, choreographers, and composers in creating producing and ballets, such as those performed by the Ballets Russes in the early twentieth century. Still other interdisciplinary connections appear in literature and music in the poems of Johan Wolfgang von Goethe that Franz Schubert set to music.

Cultural CROSS CURRENTS

Cultural cross currents reflect the ways artistic ideals, literary movements, and historical events influence the arts of other cultures. Turkish military music, for example, found its way into the symphonies and piano compositions of Viennese composers, such as Mozart and Beethoven. Japanese woodblock prints influenced the art of the Impressionist painter Claude Monet and the Post-Impressionist painter Vincent van Gogh. And the dynamic cybernetic sculpture of contemporary artist Wen-Ying Tsai weds western technology with ancient Chinese aesthetic principles.

Transhistorical Connections—THEN & NOW

Arts and Culture also considers connections between the past and present. A series of THEN & NOW boxes offers discussions of a wide range of subjects that form various types of historical bridges. Discussions range from such subjects as cities, ghettos, and legal codes to movies and monuments, revealing parallels and links between the old and the new in art and architecture, literature and music, philosophy and film.

BALANCING THE WORK AND ITS WORLD

Study of the humanities provides a balance between appreciating masterful individual works of art in themselves and understanding their social and historical contexts. *Arts and Culture* highlights the individual artistic qualities of numerous works—paintings, sculptures, architectural monuments, buildings, and other visual images, such as photographs; poems, plays, novels, and essays; songs, symphonies, and other musical compositions; philosophical and religious systems of belief—always in light of the cultural worlds in which they were created. Each work's significance is discussed in conjunction with the social attitudes and cultural values it embodies, without losing sight of its individual expression and artistic achievement.

This balancing act appears throughout the book, though it sometimes leans more in one direction than the other. In discussing ancient Chinese and Japanese sculpture and architecture, for example, explanations of the Buddhist religious ideals they reflect are accompanied by considerations of their artistic forms. In discussing Renaissance literature the focus sometimes shifts between the artistic individuality of the works examined—as with Shakespeare's *Hamlet*—and particular cultural values the works embody.

The cultural traditions included in *Arts and Culture* reflect a broad rather than a narrow understanding of the term "culture," a humanistic approach to culture rather than an anthropological or sociological study. The idea of culture presented in this book reflects the complex of distinctive attainments, beliefs, and traditions of a civilization. This sense of culture is embodied in works of art and in historical forces that reveal the social, intellectual and artistic aspects of the civilizations that produced them.

Two important questions underlie the choice of works included in *Arts and Culture*: (1) What makes a work a masterpiece of its type? (2) What qualities of a work of art enable it to be appreciated over time? These questions imply that some works of art are better, more perfect embodiments of their genre, or type, than others. The implication is also that masterpieces are worthy of more attention, more studied effort, more reflective consideration than other "lesser" works.

One of the most interesting of all questions in the humanities concerns the way in which particular works become cultural icons, enabling them to represent the cultures out of which they arose. How does the Parthenon represent Greek cultural and artistic ideals? How did Beethoven's Symphony No. 5 come to stand for the very idea of a symphony? Why does the Eiffel Tower symbolize France?

Certain works richly embody the spirit of a particular culture and yet can simultaneously transcend that culture to reflect broader universal values. It is a stunning paradox that those works that do come to speak beyond the confines of the times and places that produced them are often rooted in the local and the particular. The short stories in James Joyce's book *Dubliners*, for example, describe the lives of middle-class Irish people as they lived in early twentieth-century Dublin. Yet Joyce's stories speak to people beyond Dublin, and even beyond Europe, across time and cultures to a set of shared human concerns.

Arts and Culture includes a wide-ranging representation of the world's civilizations. In addition to Western culture, the civilizations of Africa, China, India, Japan, Latin America, and Mesoamerica are examined, along with a special chapter devoted exclusively to Russian civilization. Significant attention is accorded the contributions of women, from the eleventh-century writings of the Japanese Murasaki Shikibu, the twelfth-century music of Germany's Hildegard of Bingen, and the fourteenth-century writings of the Italian Christine de Pizan, to the Rococo art of the French Marie-Louise-Elisabeth Vigée-Le Brun, the Romantic music of Clara Schumann, and the numerous women writers, painters, architects, sculptors, and photographers of the nineteenth and twentieth centuries, European and American.

The final chapter of *Arts and Culture* brings together a broad spectrum of styles, voices, and perspectives, which, though focusing on contemporary multicultural America, reflects trends and influences from around the globe. A number of current issues in the arts are raised, including what constitutes worthwhile contemporary art, which works will endure, and how technology has globalized the arts today. The numerous and varied contributions of artists and writers include works by Native-American painters such as Lisa Fifield and Jaune Quick-to-See Smith, Latina/Latino writers such as Sandra Cisneros and Oscar Hijuelos, and Australian Aborigine artists.

Throughout the book as a whole, the authors have tried to present the arts and cultures of the world to suggest their richness, variety, and humanity. Readers of *Arts and Culture* can find in these pages the background necessary to understand not only the artistic achievements of many civilizations but also the representation of human experience in all its complexity. In a time of rapid social change when the world's cultures are becoming increasingly globalized, it has become necessary to understand the values of human beings around the world. The common humanity we share has been recorded, inscribed, and celebrated in arts and achievements of all cultures. Our survival and our happiness as human beings about to enter a new millennium warrants nothing less than understanding our human heritage as revealed in the art and cultural achievements that *Arts and Culture* brings together.

A complete package of supplementary material accompanies *Arts and Culture*.

– Student Study Guide—designed to make students' lives easier. It is carefully coordinated with the text and is thoughtfully presented to help students work their way through unfamiliar material.

– Music Compact Disk—a collection of music that contains important works discussed in the text.

– Instructors' Manual—provides chapter summaries, further topics for discussion, other activities, and a test bank. These are all carefully organized to make preparation, classroom instruction, and student testing smoother and more effective.

– Faculty Slide Set—for qualified adoptions an accompanying set of slides is available free to instructors. Contact your local Prentice Hall representative for information on ordering this supplement.

– Prentice Hall Custom Test—this computerized text item file allows you to create your own personalized exams using your own computer. Available for DOS, Windows, and Macintosh.

And finally a comprehensive website (http://www. prenhall.com/benton) has been developed to integrate many of the study guide features with many of the existing links to the arts currently found on the Internet.

Art and Humanities on the World Wide Web is a comprehensive website designed to augment *Arts and Culture*. The website is designed for professors and students teaching and studying the humanities. By utilizing the technology of "hypertext," the web allows users access to a vast array of historical, cultural, and general interest sites organized around and correlated to chapters and content found in the text.

Art and Humanities on the World Wide Web will have the following elements:
• Searchable database of worldwide museums with homepages on the WWW
• Searchable database of artist's homepages on the WWW
• Bulletin board features for professors and students
• Text specific homepages
• Links to WWW tutorials and other resources related to using the Web
• Links to resources for using the WWW in teaching art and culture
• Student toolbox with links to resources utilized by students studying art and culture.

ACKNOWLEDGMENTS

Arts and Culture represents the cooperative efforts of many people. The book originated with a suggestion ten years ago by Tony English, then of Macmillan Publishing. Work on the project began with Tony and his Macmillan colleagues and continued with Prentice Hall when Macmillan was acquired by Simon & Schuster in 1993.

At Prentice Hall we have had the good fortune to work with Bud Therien, Publisher, who oversaw the book's development in every respect, and Clare Payton, Development Editor, whose guidance and critical eye shaped the book. Important contributions were made by Bud and Clare and by their colleagues Susanna Lesan, Editor in Chief of Development; Charlyce Jones Owen, Editorial Director; Sheryl Adams, Marketing Manager; Leslie Osher, Creative Director; Joe Scordato, Production Liaison; and Gianna Caradonna, Editorial Assistant. These and other Prentice Hall staff, including the President of the Humanities and Social Sciences division, Phil Miller, offered wise counsel and made numerous helpful suggestions. The intelligence and enthusiasm Phil and his colleagues brought to their work have helped make *Arts and Culture* the book it is.

We have been fortunate as well that Calmann & King Ltd effectively handled the book's production. We have enjoyed working with Robert Shore, Editor, who not only supervised the production of *Arts and Culture*, but who also assumed responsibility for the development of Vol. I midway through the process.

Also deserving of particular mention are Sylvia Moore for her contribution to the introductory materials, Jenny Moss for her hard work on the timelines and glossary, Ailsa Heritage and Andrea Fairbrass for their imaginative work on the maps, and Simon Cowell and Pamela Ellis for their copyediting and proofreading skills.

We owe a special debt of gratitude to Henry Sayre, without whom we simply could not have completed *Arts and Culture* on schedule. Professor Sayre helped us shape the drafts of our chapters, melding our styles and recommending organizational changes that have resulted, we believe, in an integrated and compelling overview of the humanities. His engaging contributions to the historical narrative that informs the book have been of inestimable value to the project.

From readers of various drafts of *Arts and Culture* we received thoughtful criticism along with helpful suggestions for improvement. We would like to thank the following reviewers for their insight and advice: Martha G. Anderson, Alfred University; William Cloonan, Florida State University; Roger Crum, University of Dayton; Jane Anderson Jones, Manatee Community College; Kimberley Jones, Seminole Community College; Elizabeth Jordan, University of California, San Diego; Leslie Lambert, Sante Fe Community College; Virginia Pond, Catonsville Community College; Alan Pope, Albuquerque TV-I Community College; Sylvia White, Florida Community College at Jacksonville; and Judith B. Wise, Clark State Community College.

We would also like to thank each other for offering mutual support, encouragement, advice, and help throughout a long and sometimes arduous process of writing, revising, and editing. Our families, too, deserve our thanks, for without their patience and understanding we could not have completed our work with equanimity and good humor. In particular, the encouragement and loving support of our spouses, Elliot Benton and Mary DiYanni, enabled us to do our work on *Arts and Culture* with a minimum of anxiety and a maximum of pleasure.

Introduction

Arts and Culture is an introduction to the humanities and the arts, from the earliest times to the present day. The goal of the book is to familiarize readers with a fundamental body of art, history, and ideas that are a basis for understanding both Western and non-Western cultures. In demonstrating the interrelationships, obvious or subtle, between the creators of art and the historical and social forces at work in a given culture at any particular time, the text seeks to foster an understanding of the creative process and the uses of the arts.

One challenge for the reader lies in appreciating the sheer array of human creativity on display across a wide spectrum of arts and cultures. Though *Arts and Culture* focuses on Western civilization, from its ancient roots to the present, it does not limit itself to the West. Rather, Western European culture is presented within a multi-cultural global framework, represented by chapters on non-European cultures and cross-cultural features within the Western chapters.

An additional challenge for the reader is to become familiar with the vocabularies and concepts of the arts and humanities. An understanding of a wide range of artistic terms and concepts is necessary to appreciate artistic achievements. It is also essential for being able to discuss the arts knowledgeably and for the expansion of personal taste.

THE HUMANITIES AND THE ARTS

The humanities are those areas of thought and creation whose subject is human experience. They include history, philosophy, religion, and the arts. Broadly speaking, the arts are artificial objects or experiences created by human beings. Although the term "artificial" often has a negative connotation, when used to mean "phony" or "fake," it is used here in its original sense, meaning "not from nature," that is, something made by humans. The word "art" comes from the same root. The role of the human creator, therefore, is central to any study of the arts since, ultimately, the arts and humanities are a record of human experience and concerns. The arts convey information—a lyric poem can describe a summer's day, for example—yet this is not their primary function. More importantly, the arts give form to what is imagined, express human subjective beliefs and emotions, create beauty, celebrate sensual pleasure, and entertain their audiences.

The arts include visual art and architecture, drama, music, and literature, and photography and film. Seeing the arts within their historical and social context

is necessary for understanding their development. For example, the figure of the biblical giant-killer, David, was popular during the Renaissance in the Italian city-state of Florence. Michelangelo's *David* was commissioned by the Florentine city fathers (fig. 0.1; see also fig. 13.32). Florence had recently fought off an attempt at annexation by the much larger city-state of Milan. Thus, the biblical David slaying the giant, Goliath, became a symbol of Florentine cleverness and courage in defense of independence. It is a theme particular to its time and place, yet one that has been used throughout history to express the success of the "little" person against powerful exploiters.

ART AND ARTISTS OVER TIME

We study what survives, which is not necessarily all that once existed. Not all arts survive the passage of time. Art can be divided into the durable and the ephemeral, or short-lived. Surviving objects tend to be large (the

Figure 0.1 Michelangelo, *David* (detail), 1501–04, marble, height 13'5" (4.09 m), Galleria dell'Accademia, Florence.

Pyramids) or hidden (the contents of tombs). Until human beings created the means of capturing moving images and sounds, the ephemeral arts such as music and dance could be described but not reexperienced. Therefore, some of the oldest arts—music and dance of the ancient world, for example—are lost. With the development of writing, humans began the long process of liberating themselves from the tyranny of time. They began to communicate across space and time, leaving a record of their lives. In our own century, we have seen our recording abilities explode from sound recording and silent movies at the turn of the century into the digitized world of the CD-ROM and the Internet today. The result has been an unprecedented expansion in the humanities.

THE ROLE OF THE ARTIST

The functions of the artist and the artwork have varied widely during the past five thousand years. To understand these functions it may be necessary to set aside some modern assumptions about art and artists. In our time, the artist is seen as an independent worker, dedicated to the expression of a unique subjective experience. Often the artist's role is that of the outsider, a critical or rebellious figure. He or she is a specialist who has usually undergone advanced training in a university department of art or theater, or a school with a particular focus, such as a music conservatory. In our societies, works of art are presented in specialized settings: theaters, concert halls, performance spaces, galleries, and museums. There is usually a sharp division between the artist and her or his audience of non-artists. We also associate works of art with money: art auctions in which paintings sell for millions of dollars, ticket sales to the ballet, or fundraising for the local symphony.

In other societies and in parts of our own society, now and in the past, the arts are closer to the lives of ordinary people. For the majority of their history, artists have expressed the dominant beliefs of a culture, rather than rebelling against them. In place of our emphasis on the development of a personal or original style, artists were trained to conform to the conventions of their art form. Nor have artists always been specialists; in some societies and periods, all members of a society participated in art. The modern Western economic mode, which treats art as a commodity for sale, is not universal. In societies such as that of the Navajo, the concept of selling or creating a salable version of a sand painting would be completely incomprehensible. Selling Navajo sand paintings created as part of a ritual would profane a sacred experience.

Artists' identities are rarely known before the Renaissance, with the exception of the period of Classical Greece, when artists were highly regarded for their individual talents and styles. Among artists who were known, there were fewer women than men. In the twentieth century, many female artists in all the disciplines have been recognized. Their absence in prior centuries does not indicate lack of talent, but reflects lack of opportunity. The necessary social, educational, and economic conditions to create art rarely existed for women in the past.

Artists of color have also been recognized in the West only recently. The reasons for this absence range from the simple—there were few Asians in America and Europe prior to the middle of the nineteenth century—to the complexities surrounding the African diaspora. The art of indigenous peoples, while far older than that of the West, did not share the same expressive methods or aims as Western art. Until recently, such art was ignored or dismissed in Western society by the dominant cultural gatekeepers.

ART AND RITUAL

Throughout much of the history of the Western humanities, the arts have had a public function as religious or social ritual in which beauty and representation were secondary. The ritual function of art survives in the liturgical music, dance, and art of all cultures. Socially, the arts often serve to reinforce, demonstrate, or celebrate the dominant values of a society. In our own time, the arts may reflect the preferences of a large group of people—popular music and action movies, for example—or a small but influential elite—the audience for opera, or avant-garde theater, for instance.

CRITICAL THINKING AND EVALUATION OF THE ARTS

Because of their manifold functions, the arts are understood through the use of different human faculties. We know them by our senses. We can apply our intellects to analyze and describe what we see and experience. We also respond to the arts subjectively, through nonrational means such as intuition, subjective interpretation, and emotional response. Our understanding of the arts depends in part on our knowledge of the historical and social context surrounding a work. For instance, for whom was a particular work intended—a private or a public audience? What was or is its setting—public, private, accessible, or hidden? How is the work related to the economic workings of its time: for example, was it commissioned by a ruler, a religious organization, a group of guildspeople, a corporation? Was it created by nuns or monks, by peasants, or by specially trained craftspersons? Each of these considerations expands our understanding of a given work, even when we cannot know all the answers.

The branch of philosophy devoted to thinking about the arts is called "aesthetics." Aesthetic knowledge is both intuitive and intellectual; that is, we can grasp a work of art on an emotional level while at the same time analyzing it. There is no single, unquestionable body of aesthetic knowledge, although philosophers have tried to create universal systems. Each culture has its own aesthetic preferences. In addition, different disciplines and different styles within a culture reflect different aesthetic values. Today, for example, rap music coexists with country, jazz, classical, and other types of music.

Each of us is, at one time or another, a critic of the arts. For example, deciding what movie to attend, what book to read, or what recording to purchase are all critical acts, based on personal taste and judgment. Criticism in the arts takes this natural human trait and refines it.

FORM AND CONTENT DISTINCTIONS
✦

When discussing works of art, it is useful to distinguish between the form of the artwork and its content. The form of a work of art is its structural or organizing principle—the shape of its content. A work's content is what it is about—its subject matter. At its most basic, formal analysis provides a description of the apparent properties of an artwork. Artists use these properties to engineer our perception and response. In music, for example, a formal analysis would discuss the melody, the harmony, and the structure. In visual art, comparable elements would be line, color, and composition. The goal of formal analysis is to understand how an artwork's form expresses its content.

Contextual approaches to the arts seek to situate artworks within the circumstances of their creation. Historians of the arts conduct research aimed at recreating the context of a given work. Armed with this information, the historian interprets the work in light of that context. Knowing, for example, that *Guernica* (fig. 0.2; see also fig. 21.20), Pablo Picasso's anti-war painting, depicts an aerial bombing of a small village of unarmed civilians in the Spanish Civil War, drives its brutal images of pain and death home to viewers. Picasso chose black, white, and grey for this painting because he learned of the attack through the black and white photojournalism of the newspapers. Knowing the reason for this choice, which may otherwise have seemed arbitrary to modern viewers of the work, adds to the meaning of the image. Picasso's choice of black and white also intensifies the horrors he depicts.

Figure 0.2 Pablo Picasso, *Guernica*, 1937, oil on canvas, 11′5½″ × 25′5½″ (3.49 × 7.75 m), Centro de Arte Reina Sofia, Madrid.

Starter Kit

This Starter Kit provides you with a brief reference guide to key terms and concepts for studying the humanities. The following section will give you a basis for understanding, analyzing, and describing art forms.

Commonalities. We refer to the different branches of humanities—art and architecture, music, literature, philosophy, history—as the **disciplines.** The humanistic disciplines and the arts have many key terms in common. However, each discipline has defining characteristics, a distinct vocabulary, and its own conventions, so that the same word may mean different things in different disciplines. **Conventions** are accepted practices, such as the use of a frontal eye in a profile face, found in the art of the ancient Egyptians, or the use of the sonnet form by Shakespeare and his contemporaries.

Every work of art has two core components: form and content. **Form** refers to the arrangement, pattern, or structure of a work, how a work presents itself to our physical senses. **Content** is what a work is about, its nature or substance. The form might be an Impressionist painting; the content might be the beauty of nature in a particular place. To comprehend how the form expresses the content is one of the keys to understanding a work of art.

The term **artist** is used for the producer of artworks in any discipline. All artworks have a **composition,** the arrangement of its constituent parts. **Technique** refers to the process or method that produced the art. The **medium** is the physical material that makes up the work, such as oil paint on canvas. **Crafts** refers to the technical skill of the artist, which is apparent in the execution of the work.

Style. We use the term **style** to mean several different things. Most simply, style refers to the manner in which something is done. Many elements form a style. Artists working at the same time and place are often trained in the same style. In a text, historical styles are usually capitalized, as in *Classical Greek* art, referring to the arts of that particular time and place, which shared distinct characteristics. If used with lowercase letters, such as *classical* style, the term refers to works which, although not from Classical Greece, are similar in character to Classical Greek art, or to Roman art, which was largely derived from Greek forms.

Functions and Genres. In general, the functions of the arts can be divided into religious and secular art. **Religious** or liturgical art, music, or drama is used as part of the ritual of a given religion. Art that is not religious art is termed **secular** art. Secular art is primarily used for entertainment purposes, but among other functions has been its use in the service of political or propaganda ends, as films were used in Nazi Germany.

Each discipline has subsets, called **genres.** In music, for example, we have the symphony, a large, complex work for orchestra, in contrast to a quartet, written for only four instruments. In literature we might contrast the novel, with its extended narrative and complexities of character, with the compression of a short story. From the seventeenth to the nineteenth centuries, certain subjects were assigned higher or lower rank by the academies that controlled the arts in most European countries. Portrait painting, for example, was considered lower than history painting. That practice has been abandoned; today the genres are usually accorded equal respect and valued for their distinctive qualities.

THE VISUAL ARTS

The visual arts are first experienced by sight, yet they often evoke other senses such as touch or smell. Because human beings are such visual creatures, our world is saturated with visual art, in advertising, on objects from CD covers to billboards, on TV and the Internet. The visual arts occur in many varieties of two-dimensional and three-dimensional forms, from painting, printmaking, and photography, to sculpture and architecture.

As is the case with other arts, the origins of the visual arts are now lost. However, their development represents a milestone in human civilization. Drawing, the representation of three-dimensional forms (real or imagined) on a two-dimensional surface, is an inherent human ability, and failure to draw by a certain stage in a child's growth is a sign of serious trouble. Attaining the ability to draw is an important cognitive development in both babies and human history. The creation and manipulation of images was and is a first step toward mastery of the physical world itself.

The visual arts serve a variety of purposes, using different methods. **Representation** is an ancient function of visual art, in which a likeness of an object or life form is produced. There are many different conventions of representation, which have to be learned by artist and viewer alike. One important convention is **perspective,** which gives the illusion of depth and distance. Systems of perspective were perfected by artists and theorists of the Renaissance period. In **abstract** art, the artist may extract some element from the actual appearance of an object and use it for its expressive or symbolic properties. For example, an artist may use red and orange tones on a canvas to suggest a brilliant poppy. **Nonobjective** art is entirely free from representation; a nonobjective sculpture may be a group of geometric shapes welded

V·isual Arts

Line: A mark on a surface. Lines may be continuous or broken. They are used to create patterns and textures, to imply three dimensions, and to direct visual movement.

Shape: An area with identifiable boundaries. Shapes may be **organic,** based on natural forms and thus rounded or irregular, or they may be **geometric,** based on measured forms.

Mass: The solid parts of a three-dimensional object. An area of space devoid of mass is called **negative space;** while **positive space** is an area occupied by mass.

Form: The shape and structure of something. In discussions of art, form refers to visual aspects such as line, shape, color, texture, and composition.

Color: The sensation produced by various wavelengths of light. Also called **hue.** Red, blue, and yellow are the **primary colors,** which cannot be made from mixing other colors. **Secondary colors** are hues produced by mixing two primary colors.

Value: The lightness or darkness of an area of color, or as measured between black and white. The lighter, the higher in value it is; the darker, the lower in value.

Texture: The appearance or feel of a surface, basically smooth or rough. Texture may be actual, as the surface of a polished steel sculpture, or implied, as in a painting of human flesh or the fur of an animal.

Composition: The arrangement of the formal components of a work, most frequently used to describe the organization of elements in a drawing or painting.

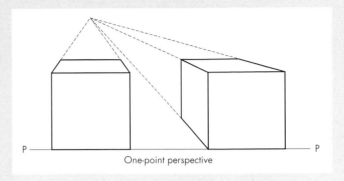

One-point perspective

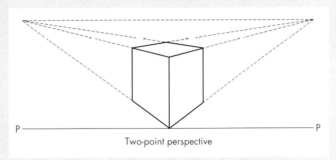

Two-point perspective

Perspective: A system of rendering three-dimensional space on a two-dimensional surface. In **single-point** perspective objects are portrayed with all lines from the picture plane (p) leading toward a single **vanishing point** on the horizon line. In **two-point** perspective there are two or more vanishing points. **Atmospheric** or **aerial** perspective uses properties of light and air, in which objects become less distinct and cooler in color as they recede into distance.

together. Abstract and nonobjective art, arising in the twentieth century, are more concerned with the elements on the **picture plane** (the paper or canvas) rather than depth of **pictorial space.** Visual art also often has a purely decorative or ornamental purpose, used to create visual pleasure or to add visual interest to a functional item, as in wallpaper, fabric, or furniture design.

Formal Analysis. To analyze a work of visual art formally, its visual elements are considered without reference to the content, whereas moving to more sophisticated levels involves the content as well. At its simplest, the content is what is represented, the subject matter, whether a person, an orange, or a flag. However, the image may not stop with the representation; there may be a symbolic element. It is useful to distinguish between signs and symbols. **Signs** convey visual information economically by means of images or words. **Symbols** are images that have resonance, or additional meaning. Works of visual art may use both signs and symbols.

Artists use symbolic systems, part of the visual language of their time. Like all languages, these must be learned. Sometimes artists create their own symbols.

The **iconography** of a work of art, that is, the meaning assigned to the symbols, is often religious in nature. For example, different representations of Jesus derive from incidents in his life. To understand the deeper levels of the work, it is necessary to understand the language of the iconography. The use of personal iconography by an artist is a relatively recent development of the past few centuries.

The following analysis of *The Scream* by Edvard Munch (fig. 0.3) will serve as an example of this process. Viewed formally, the major visual elements used by Munch in this painting are line and color. There are two kinds of lines: the geometric lines that form the sharply receding bridge contrast with the swirling organic lines of the main figure and the landscape, sea, and sky. There is little or no modelling or shading. The colors contrast bright red and yellow with rich blue, offset by neutral

Figure 0.3 Edvard Munch, *The Scream*, 1893, tempera and casein on cardboard, 36 × 29" (91.3 × 73.7 cm), Nasjonalgalleriet, Oslo.

tones. *The Scream* is a painting executed on cardboard with rapid, loose brushstrokes. The composition is dynamic; the artist has used exaggerated diagonals to suggest a dramatic perspective for the bridge. The figure at the front is the focal point. The craft is secondary to the expressive purpose of the work.

It should be obvious that in *The Scream* more is going on than the preceding analysis indicates. Three people are on a bridge at sunset. Two are walking away; one stands transfixed with his hands over his ears. The expression on his face functions as a sign to convey shock or horror. To understand the significance of his expression, we turn to the historical context and the artist's life. Munch, a Norwegian artist who worked in the late nineteenth and early twentieth centuries, was one of the artists who rejected conventions and created personal symbolic systems, based largely on his experience. *The Scream* is usually interpreted as representing a screaming person. This is not correct. As we know from the artist's diary, the work refers to the "scream of nature." The image captured is a powerful evocation of a sensitive man overwhelmed by nature's power, which his companions cannot sense. The swirling lines suggest the impact of screaming nature on this person. The blood-red sky

resonates as a symbol of savage nature oblivious to the puny humans below.

Components of the Visual Arts. The basic elements used to construct a work of visual art are line, shape, mass—a shape in three dimensions—color and value, real or implied texture, and composition, the arrangement of all the elements. While many drawings are executed in black mediums, such as pencil and charcoal, on a white ground, color is a vital ingredient of art, especially important in conveying information as well as emotion to the viewer. Color affects us both physically and psychologically and has significance to us both in our personal lives and in our cultural traditions.

There can be no color without light. In the seventeenth century, Sir Isaac Newton observed that sunlight passing through a glass prism broke up, or **refracted** the light into rainbow colors. Our perception of color depends upon reflected light rays of various wavelengths. Theorists have arranged colors on a **color wheel** (fig. 0.4) that is well-known to students of painting and even young schoolchildren. On it are the **primary colors**—red, yellow, and blue—and **secondary colors**—orange, green, and violet. Some wheels show **tertiary colors** such as yellow-green and red-violet. The primary colors cannot be created by mixing other colors, but secondary and tertiary colors are made, respectively, by mixing two primaries, or primaries and secondaries, together. **Complementary** colors are placed opposite each other on the wheel, so that red is opposite from green, orange from blue, and yellow from violet. Many artists have studied and worked with the **optical effects**

Figure 0.4 Color wheel.

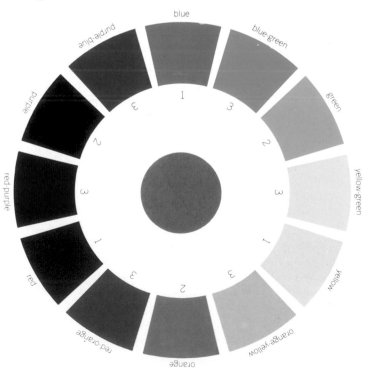

Architecture

Architect: One who designs and supervises the construction of buildings. Ideally, the architect is part builder with a sound knowledge of engineering principles, materials, structural systems, and other such practical necessities, as well as part artist who works with form, space, scale, light, and other aesthetic properties.

Scale: The relative size of one thing compared to another. The relationship of a building to another element, often the height of a human being.

Site: The location of an object or building. Care must be taken to choose a solid, attractive, and appropriate building site.

Structural System: The engineering principles used to create a structure. Two basic kinds of structural system are the **shell** system, where one or more building materials such as stone or brick provide both support and covering, and the **skeleton and skin** system, as in modern skyscrapers with steel skeletons and glass skin.

Post and Lintel: A basic structural system dating from ancient times that uses paired vertical elements (posts) to support a horizontal element (lintel).

Arch and Vault: A form perfected by the ancient Romans in which two uprights curve in toward each other, held in place by a **keystone** at top center. When many such arches are placed in a line and roofed over, they result in a **barrel vault.** When two barrel vaults are crossed at right angles, a **groin vault** is created. The resulting style of architecture is termed **Romanesque.** Later, pointed arches in the **Gothic** style were reinforced at the intersections by **ribs,** which allowed the use of large windows for more light, a step toward the skeleton and skin structural method of our day.

Column: a supporting pillar consisting of a base, a cylindrical shaft, and a decorative capital at the top. Three Classical orders, established in ancient Greece, are the **Doric, Ionic,** or **Corinthian**, identified by the capital.

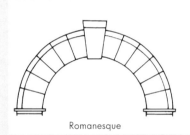
Romanesque

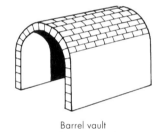
Barrel vault

Gothic

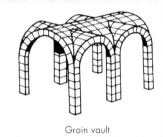
Groin vault

of color, especially the French Impressionist Claude Monet and the Post-Impressionist Georges Seurat.

Architecture. Architecture is a branch of the visual arts that combines practical function and artistic expression. The function served by a building usually determines its form. In addition to the purely useful purpose of providing shelter, architecture answers prevailing social needs. The use of architects to design and erect public and religious structures has given rise to many innovative forms throughout history. Architecture reflects the society in which it is built as it controls the actions of those who use it. Structural systems depend upon the available building materials, technological advancements, the intended function of the building, and aesthetics of the culture. The relationship between a building and its **site,** or location, is integral to architecture. The Greek Parthenon (fig. 0.5), for example, crowns a hill overlooking Athens. The elevated location indicates its importance, and the pathway one must ascend to reach the Parthenon is part of the experience.

Figure 0.5 Ictinus and Callicrates, Parthenon, Acropolis, Athens, 448–432 B.C.

LITERATURE

Speech, Writing, and Literature. Literature differs from the visual arts since it is not built from physical elements, such as paint and stone; nor is it composed of sound as is music, but from words, the basic elements of language. Paint and sound have no intrinsic meaning; words do. Speech depends on sound; words are the building blocks of meaningful communication in language. Literature presupposes language, with its multitudes of meaning (content), its **grammar** (rules for construction), and its **syntax,** the arrangement of words.

Language, essentially communicative, has many functions. We use language to make emotional contact with others: for example, a parent using baby talk to a child too young to understand the meaning of words. Through language we convey information to each other, as in the classroom, where a dialogue between teacher and student is part of the educational process. All literature is language, but not all language is literature. Distinguishing between literature and other forms of language is sometimes difficult, but refinement in language and careful structuring or ordering typically characterizes literature.

Literature, in the broadest sense, is widely apparent in everyday life. Popular songs, magazine essays, greeting card verse, hymns and prayers are all forms of literature. One meaning of the word *literature*, in fact, is what is written. Generally, however, the term "literature" is reserved for those works that exhibit "the best that has been thought and said," works that represent a culture's highest literary achievements.

Literacy and Literature.

The Development of Literature Literature predates literacy. Ancient literature was **oral**—spoken—rather than written. To make it easier to remember and recite, much of this was in the form of song or poetry. The invention of writing enabled people to communicate across space and time. It was with this invention that recorded history was born. The earliest writings of the ancient world are businesslike records of laws, prayers, and commerce—informative but not expressive. When mechanical methods of printing were developed, literacy spread. Today, universal literacy is a goal in all civilized countries.

The Functions of Literature Literature serves a variety of social functions. One of its most ancient functions is as **religious literature,** the prayers and mythology of a given culture. The myths of the Greeks and Romans have exerted a powerful influence on Western culture; their origins lie deep in the history of Egypt and Mesopotamia. **Epic literature,** such as the Greek poet Homer's *The Iliad* and *The Odyssey*, or the sagas from Norway and Iceland, combine history and imagination.

Immense bodies of literature such as these were passed down by oral tradition. Literature distinct from liturgical or epic forms was invented by the ancient Greeks. Their literary forms included history, philosophy, drama, and poetry. Novels and short stories were a later development. The novel in its modern form was named for tales popular in Italy in the late thirteenth century, though the novel is generally identified with prose narratives that developed in the eighteenth century in Europe.

Since literature is a communicative act, it is important to consider the audience and setting. Silent reading is a recent development, alien to the oral roots of literature. Most literature through the ages was meant to be recited, sung, or read aloud in groups ranging from general public gatherings to the intimate setting of the private home. Authors today may give readings from their work in libraries, bookstores, and educational institutions.

Forms of Literature. Literature can be divided into fiction and nonfiction, poetry and prose.

Poetry is distinguished by its concentrated and precise language, "the best words in the best order," as one poet defined it. **Diction** is the poet's selection of words, and **syntax** the ordering of those words in sentences. Other poetic elements include images—details that evoke sense perception—along with metaphor and other forms of comparison With its roots in song, poetry of many eras and places exhibits rhyme and other types of sound play as well as rhythm and meter, the measured pattern of accent in poetic lines. Drama, plays intended for performance, are somtimes written in verse, rhymed or unrhymed, as, for example, in **blank verse**.

Prose Language that is not poetry is **prose.** Not all prose is literature; some, such as journalism or technical writing, is purely descriptive or informative, as some visual art is purely representational. Literature can be fiction or nonfiction, or a combination of both. Fiction is a work of the imagination. Fictional forms can be long and complex, as in a novel or play, or short and concise, as in a novella or short story. Nonfiction, which deals with actual events or persons, includes expressions of opinion, such as political essays. Functions of nonfiction include explanation, persuasion, commentary, exposition, or any blend of these. Sometimes philosophic essays and works of history are included in the category of literature.

Fiction and drama, and much nonfiction as well, create their effects through elements such as the plot, or story line, characters, description of the setting, dialogue between the characters, and exposition, or explanation. The latter is presented in the voice of a narrator, who may represent the author using the third-person perspective, or may instead be a character expressing a first-person point of view.

Literature

Fiction: Literature that is imaginative, rather than descriptive of actual events. Typical fictional forms are the short story and the novel, which has greater length and complexity.

Nonfiction: An account of actual events and people. Forms of nonfiction include essays, biography and autobiography, and journalistic writing, as for newspapers and magazines.

Narrative: The telling of a story; a structured account of events.

Narrator: The storyteller from whose **point of view** the story is told. The point of view can be **first-person** or **third-person,** and may shift within the work. The narrator can be **omniscient,** knowing everything, or limited to what she or he can know personally or be told by others.

Plot: The plan or story line. To plot a story is to conceive and arrange the action of the characters and the sequence of events. Plots typically involve **rising action,** events that complicate the plot and move it forward to a **climax,** the moment of greatest intensity. This is followed by the **denouement,** the resolution of the plot.

Characters: The people in a literary work. The leading character is known as the **protagonist,** a word stemming from ancient Greek drama in which the protagonist was opposed by an **antagonist.**

Dialogue: Conversation between two or more characters. Drama is mainly rendered through dialogue; it is used in fiction to a lesser extent.

Setting: Where the events take place; includes location, time, and situation. In theatrical productions, a **set** is the scenery, sometimes very elaborate, constructed for a stage performance. In films the set is the sound stage or the enclosure where a scene is filmed.

Exposition: Explanatory material, which, especially in drama, often lays out the current situation as it arises from the past.

In common with visual art and music, literature has **themes,** or overarching ideas that are expressed by all the elements working together. The structure of a work of literature is analogous to the composition of a symphony or a painting. Writers use symbolism, much as visual artists do. A successful work of literature will likely establish a mood, hold the reader's interest through a variety of incidents or ideas with evident focus, yet possess an overall sense of unity.

Autobiography, as a separate literary and historical endeavor, began with the *Confessions* of St. Augustine (A.D. 354–430), in which he told the story of his life and the progress of his religious convictions. Autobiography is history written from a subjective point of view. The memoir, so popular in recent years, is descended from this first, spiritual autobiography.

Biography is a branch of both literature and history. The author's role is complicated because a biographer must check the facts of the subject's life, usually by interviewing both the subject and many other people. Deciding the major theme of a person's life, the relationship between that person and his or her time, and considering what is true as well as what is germane are the biographer's responsibility. Different biographers may offer quite different interpretations of a subject's life.

History is a powerful force that shapes the humanities as a whole. The writing of history varies across cultures, and as cultures change, history itself is continuously under revision. The leaders of some societies would never allow the publication of versions of history that vary from their orthodox beliefs, no matter what the facts might be. Because history is an interpretative discipline, several versions of events may coexist, with scholars arguing and defending the merits of each. This is particularly true in our multicultural and pluralist era.

MUSIC

We are surrounded by sounds at all times. The art that derives from our sense of hearing is music, order given to sounds by human intent. A temporal art, one that exists in time, music is the least material of the arts, its basic elements being sound and silence. Silence in music is analogous to a painter, sculptor, or architect's use of negative space: unoccupied but important, so that the intervals between the notes are necessary parts of a musical piece. Music permeates our daily lives—in the movies, on radio and television, in elevators and stores. The success of the Sony Walkman reflects our human desire to surround ourselves with music.

Until the development of sound recording, music was one of the **ephemeral** arts, like dance and live theater, which exist only for the duration of their performances. Until the late Middle Ages, music in the West was not written down, or **notated.** It was taught by ear, passed on from one generation to the next.

Social and Ritual Roles. Music has many different functions. It has been and remains a major element in

M·usic

Acoustics: The qualities of sound, often used to describe the relationship between sound and architecture, as in a concert hall.

Vibrations: Trembling or oscillating motions that produce sound. When singers or stringed instruments produce a wavering sound, causing a fluctuation in pitch, it is termed **vibrato.**

Pitch: The sound produced by vibrations. The speed of vibrations controls the pitch: slow vibrations produce low pitches; fast vibrations produce high pitches.

Tempo: The speed at which music is played or sung. This is shown on sheet music, usually in Italian terms, by **tempo marks** that indicate the desired speed. A device called a **metronome** can indicate tempo with precision.

Timbre: The characteristic sound or tonal quality of an instrument or voice. Also termed **color,** it can refer to the combination produced by more than one instrument's timbres, as **orchestral color.**

Tone: A sound of specific pitch and quality, the basic building material of music. Its properties are pitch, timbre, duration, and intensity.

Note: The written symbol for a tone, shown as **whole notes, half notes,** etc. These indicate the time a note is held, with a corresponding **rest** sign. **Notation** is the use of a set of symbols to record music in written form.

Melody: The succession of notes or pitches played or sung. Music with a single melodic line is called **monophony,** while music with more than one melodic line is **polyphony.**

Texture: In music, this refers to the number of different melodic lines; the greater the number, the thicker the texture.

Harmony: The combination of notes sung or played at one time, or **chords;** applies to homophonic music. **Consonance** refers to the sound of notes that are agreeable together; **dissonance** to the sound of notes that are discordant.

religious ritual. It is also used frequently in collective labor; the regular rhythm that characterizes work songs keeps the pace steady and makes the work more fun. For example, aerobics classes and workout tapes depend on music to motivate exercisers and help them keep the pace. On the other hand, parents use lullabies to lull their babies to sleep.

Since the late Middle Ages, Western music has developed many conventional types. These genres vary with the audience, the instruments, and the musical structures. **Liturgical** music was designed for churches, used sacred texts, and took advantage of church acoustics. The soaring vaults of Gothic cathedrals were perfect for the music of the Middle Ages. Music known as **chant** or **plainsong** is simply the human voice singing a religious text without instrumental accompaniment. When the voice is unaccompanied, it is known as **a cappella.** When the sound is made by specialized devices, called **instruments**, the music is termed **instrumental.**

Secular, that is nonreligious, music brought about other forms. **Chamber music,** instrumental music that was originally played in palaces for royalty and nobility, calls for more intimate spaces, a small ensemble of players, and small audiences. **Orchestral music** is the most public and complex form, involving a full orchestra and a concert hall, where the acoustics, or quality of sound, is very important. **Popular music,** often shortened to **pop,** appeals to a wide audience. It includes rock, folk, country, rap, and other types of music. **Jazz** is an improvisational form that arose in the United States from blues and ragtime. **Musical theater,** as the name

implies, is a combination of drama and music. Its songs often enter the pop repertoire as **show tunes**. **Opera,** a narrative in which both dialogue and exposition is sung, combines music with literature and drama.

Instruments. Musical instruments, which vary widely across cultures, can nevertheless be grouped in families. Probably most ancient are the **percussion** instruments, which make noise as they are struck. Drums, blocks, cymbals, and tambourines are percussion instruments. **Stringed** instruments, deriving from the hunting bow, have strings stretched between two points; sounds are produced when they are plucked, strummed, bowed, or struck. **Woodwinds** are hollow instruments that were originally made of wood, such as the flute, recorder, and panpipes. **Reed** instruments, such as the oboe, are woodwinds that use a mouthpiece created from a compressed reed. **Brasses** are metal horns like the tuba, trumpet, and cornet. In addition to their musical function, brasses were long used by the military to communicate over distances in battle or in camp. Using a prearranged trumpet call, the commander could sound "retreat" or "charge."

Musical Qualities and Structure. Musical structure ranges from a simple tune or rhythm to the intricacy of a symphony or an opera. The tone, or sound of a specific quality, is the basis of all music, using varieties of high or low pitches and timbres with varying intensity and tempos. Music appeals to our emotions through tempo, musical color or timbre, and harmonic structure. We associate different emotions with different timbres. The harp, for example, evokes gentleness or calm, whereas brasses evoke more stirring emotions.

Musical structure can be simple, such as Ravel's *Bolero*, which uses the repetition of a single melody with increased tempo and volume to build to a climax. Increases in tempo generate excitement, literally increasing the listener's heart rate and breathing speed. These qualities were used to good advantage in Blake Edwards's film *10*. Composers of movie music manipulate our emotions expertly, heightening the appeal of the action.

The comparatively uncomplicated pop songs we sing are based on melodies, a succession of notes, with accompanying words. We are also familiar with the 32-bar structure of most pop and rock music, in which **verses** alternate with repeated **choruses**. To appreciate and enjoy more complex music, some understanding of structure is important. The simple song "Row, Row, Row Your Boat," familiar to many of us from childhood, is a **round** or **canon;** the same melody is sung by each voice, but voices enter one after the other, creating overlapping notes, or **chords**. More elaborate forms stemming from such simple structures are found in **classical** music, beginning with European music of the eighteenth and nineteenth centuries.

Harmonic structure is a complex topic. Western music is written in **keys,** a system of notes based on one central note, such as the key of C Major. The different keys have their own emotional connotations. A **minor key** is often associated with sadness, a **major key** seems happier or more forceful. Notes that seem to fit together are consonant, while clashing notes are dissonant. Generally, consonance seems peaceful or happy to most people, while dissonance may be unsettling.

Listening to Music. Music is a temporal art, designed to be listened to from beginning to end without interruption. We use music as a background so much it is sometimes difficult to learn to really listen to it. If you are listening to recorded music, reduce your distractions by turning off the television or lowering the lights. At a performance, concentrate on the performers or look at a particular spot while you absorb the music. Read program notes carefully to find out all you can about the piece and the composer. Analyze your reactions to the music, keeping in mind all you have learned about the forms, the instruments, and the musical structure.

HISTORY AND PHILOSOPHY

History, the recording and explanation of events, and philosophy, the search for truth, have both influenced the arts. These subjects have themselves evolved as humanistic disciplines. **Aesthetics,** the branch of philosophy concerned with the functions, practice, and appreciation of the arts, along with their role in society, is an important part of this book and of cultural studies in general.

History. Unlike expressive literature, or fiction, history is an inquiry into and report upon real events and people. Its origins lie in the epic literature of the ancients with its creation myths. Such literature contains much that we now consider historical: stories of wars, reigns, natural disasters. However, until the Greek historian Herodotus, traveling in the Mediterranean lands of the sixth century B.C., turned his questioning and skeptical eye on the received beliefs and tales of peoples he met, history was inseparable from religious faith and folk memory. Historians have since developed methods of inquiry, questioning the likelihood of stories and delving into the motives of their informants. They learned to consider nonhistorical accounts and records as checks on the official versions of events. They began, in Byzantium, to consider the psychological motives of the people they chronicled. The artistry of their presentation became a part of the discipline.

Religion and Philosophy. Religion has played a crucial role in the development of the arts, which provide images, sounds, and words for use in worship, prayers, and religious stories. **Theology,** the theory of religious belief, prescribes religious practices, moral beliefs, and rules for social behavior. The dominant religion in a culture often controls the art, either directly by training artists and commissioning art, or indirectly. The medieval Catholic belief in the efficacy of **relics** to heal or give aid, for example, led to the practice of pilgrimage, and from that to the creation of great cathedrals. As religious orders acquired holy relics, they housed them in shrines within the churches. Problems arose when the many pilgrims who came to be healed and blessed disrupted services. Romanesque architects then developed the **ambulatory**, or walkway, that allowed pilgrims to see the relics without interrupting worshipers at a service, thereby altering religious architecture. Different religions hold different aesthetic beliefs. Nudity was acceptable in the temple statues of Classical Greece and Hindu India. Islam prohibits any figurative images in places of worship, and some Native Americans believe a permanent house of worship is itself inappropriate.

In Western culture, philosophy and religion are intertwined. Like religion, philosophy is concerned with the basic truths and principles of the universe. Both are also concerned with human perception and understanding of these truths, and with the development of moral and ethical principles for living. However, their means differ. Philosophy is based on logic; religion on faith. Like so many other humanistic inventions and advances, philosophy, along with its specialized branch of aesthetics, originated in ancient Greece.

Map 1.1   The Ancient Near East and the Fertile Crescent.

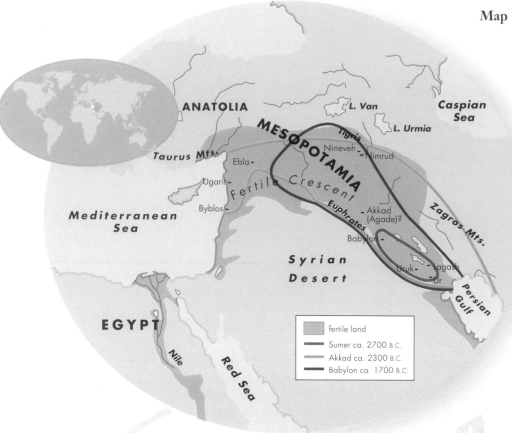

ANATOLIA

Caspian Sea

L. Van

MESOPOTAMIA

L. Urmia

Tigris

Taurus Mts.

Ebla

Nineveh

Nimrud

Ugarit

Fertile Crescent

Byblos

Akkad (Agade)?

Zagros Mts.

Euphrates

Mediterranean Sea

Babylon

Syrian Desert

Uruk

Lagash

Ur

Persian Gulf

EGYPT

Nile

Red Sea

fertile land
Sumer ca. 2700 B.C.
Akkad ca. 2300 B.C.
Babylon ca. 1700 B.C.

THE DAWN OF CULTURE

Stonehenge, Salisbury Plain, Wiltshire, England, ca. 2000 B.C.

THE EARLIEST CULTURES

A **culture** is a way of living built up by a group of people and transmitted from one generation to the next. It is, in other words, the basis of communal life. A culture expresses itself in the arts, writings, manners, and intellectual pursuits of the community, and it embodies the community's values. The ability of a culture to express itself well, especially in writing, and to organize itself thoroughly, as a social, economic, and political entity, distinguishes it as a **civilization**.

Just when the earliest cultures took form, and then subsequently transformed themselves into civilizations, is a matter of some conjecture among anthropologists, scientists who study humankind's institutions and beliefs from the earliest times. The first historical evidence of a culture coming into being can be found in the artifacts of the earliest *homo sapiens*, or "the one who knows." About 37,000 years ago, the hominid species *homo sapiens*, which had come into being about 200,000 B.C., probably in Africa, began to assert itself in the forests and plains of what is today known as Europe, gradually supplanting the Neanderthal *homo erectus* who had roamed the same areas for the previous hundred thousand years.

Both *homo sapiens* and *homo erectus* were tool makers, as even our earliest ancestors seem to have been. *Kenyapithecus* (the "Kenya ape"), for instance, which lived in the Olduvai Gorge in east-central Africa between nineteen and fourteen million years ago, made crude stone weapons or tools. *Homo sapiens* and the Neanderthals both cooked with fire, wore skins as clothing, and used tools as a matter of course. They evidently buried their dead in ritual ceremonies, which provide the earliest indications of religious beliefs and practices. These activities suggest the transmission of knowledge and patterns of social behavior from one generation to the next. But between 35,000 and 10,000 B.C.—the last part of the period known as the **Paleolithic**, or Old Stone Age, when *homo sapiens* became more and more dominant and the Neanderthal line died out—the first objects that can be considered works of art began to appear, objects that seem to express the values and beliefs of the Paleolithic people. The Paleolithic period thus represents the very earliest cultural era.

THE PALEOLITHIC PERIOD

The Paleolithic period corresponds to the geological Pleistocene era, or Ice Age. Periodically, glaciers moved south over the European and Asian continents, forcing the inhabitants of the areas to move south, around the Mediterranean and into Africa. These people lived nomadic lives, following animal herds (bison, mammoths, reindeer, and wild horses were abundant), on which they depended for food.

Wall Paintings. Long before the creation of writing, Paleolithic people began to draw and paint the animals they hunted, and what is known of Paleolithic life derives largely from paintings found in caves, particularly in the Franco-Cantabrian area of southern France and northern Spain. Many of these paintings have been discovered in relatively recent times. A cave at Lascaux, in the Dordogne region of southern France, was found by accident in 1940 by children looking for a lost dog. The entrance to the Cosquer cave near Marseilles was found under water by a diver in 1991. A cave near Vallon-Pont-d'Arc, in the Ardèche region of southern France, was found in 1994 when three explorers felt a draft coming from the ground. This cave contains wall paintings, probably made about 20,000 B.C., that provide an extraordinary inventory of the animals hunted for food and clothing in this area—woolly rhinos, bears, mammoths, and oxen are frequently depicted, but also portrayed are a hyena, a panther, and owls. The images vary in size from two to twelve feet.

The most famous prehistoric wall paintings are those in the cave at Lascaux, France (fig. 1.1), which were created between ca. 15,000 and 10,000 B.C. On the cave walls there are paintings of bison, mammoths, reindeer, boars, wolves, and horses. These images were created by people whose lives were dependent upon the animals for food. Some are shown upside down, perhaps indicating a method of killing animals in which the animals would be driven off a precipice and so fall to their deaths. A grid-like structure recurs several times in these paintings and may represent a trap.

The Lascaux paintings are extremely naturalistic and demonstrate prehistoric artists' keen observation and ability to record an image remembered after the model was no longer before the eyes. Many of the animals gracefully jump, run, and romp, conveying a remarkable sense of animation. Painting is done in blacks, browns, reds, and yellows, with most of the pigments used of mineral oxides, with deeper black from burned bones.

Questions about the meaning and purpose of these paintings will never be fully answered: only speculation is possible. The paintings at Vallon-Pont-d'Arc and Lascaux, for instance, are located deep within the caves and are often very hard to reach. There is no evidence of human habitation where the paintings are located—instead, people seem to have lived at or near the entrances to the caves, where natural light was available. How and why, then, were these paintings created? It is thought that the artists worked by the light of oil lamps. The location of the works has given rise to the so-called "mother earth" theory of the paintings' creation. By painting these animals in the "womb" of mother earth, the creators may have hoped that more animals would actually be born. Associated with this theory is the possibility that the superimposing, or layering, of animals was intended to show them mating.

Figure 1.1 Overview of the Hall of the Bulls, ca. 15,000–10,000 B.C., cave painting, Lascaux, Dordogne, France. Prehistoric artists depicted with notable realism the animals on which they depended for food. With very few exceptions, the animals represented in such paintings are identifiable.

In neither Vallon-Pont-d'Arc nor Lascaux is there evidence of an overall planned composition. Most of the animals appear randomly placed; some are shown in isolation, while others interact. Some, as noted, are superimposed on others, and scale is inconsistent. The absence of evidence of a controlling scheme suggests that the important part for the artists may have been less the finished product than the process of painting the animal, reinforcing the theory that by creating the animal in paint, the animal might be created in reality. Thus these depictions of animals may have been created for the benefit of hunters who used images to facilitate their capture.

The theory that rituals were performed in the caves to gain control over these animals is strongly supported not only by the painting of spears on the animals, but also by actual spearheads found driven into some of the painted animals who were shown to bleed as a result of their injuries. Thus, in order to ensure a successful hunt, the animal may have been killed in effigy before the hunt. Further, hand prints are found on some of the animals, suggesting the desire to have human control over, or the ability to obtain, the animals.

Sculpture. Whether painting or sculpture was developed first by prehistoric people is among the unanswered questions in the history of art. Only a fraction of the sculpture made in prehistoric times of durable materials such as ivory, bone, horn, stone, and clay is known today, and any sculpture made of a perishable material, such as wood, is lost. The many Paleolithic sculptures found in the debris on cave floors are small—easily transported mobile art, necessitated by a nomadic life style.

As in painting, the most frequently depicted subjects are highly naturalistic memory images of animals. An excellent example is offered by two bison (fig. 1.2) at Le Tuc d'Audoubert, in the Ariège region of France, carved

Figure 1.2 Two bison, ca. 13,000 B.C., clay relief on cave wall, length 25″ and 24″ (63.5 and 61 cm), Le Tuc d'Audoubert, Ariège, France. Although presumably created from memory, prehistoric depictions of animals show far greater realism than depictions of humans.

Figure 1.3 *Woman of Willendorf*, found at Willendorf, Austria, ca. 25,000–20,000 B.C., limestone, height $4\frac{3}{8}''$ (11 cm), Naturhistorisches Museum, Vienna. The so-called *Venus of Willendorf* is the most famous (but not the most physically distorted) of several extant female figurines thought to be associated with prehistoric beliefs about human fertility.

and modeled in about 13,000 B.C. from the clay of the cave, taking advantage of the wall's natural contours.

Depictions of the human figure are rare in Paleolithic sculpture, and the few known are mostly female figures. Curiously, although animals are portrayed with great realism and fidelity to nature, the same is not true of representations of humans. In spite of the greater possibility of working from a live model, depictions of humans tend to be highly abstracted. This is true of the most famous example of prehistoric sculpture, the so-called *Woman* (or *Venus*) *of Willendorf* (fig. 1.3), a stone figure small enough to be held in a hand, dated to about 25,000–20,000 B.C., and named for the place where it was found in western Austria near the Danube River.

The *Woman of Willendorf* is elementary, direct, and emphatic, able to convey expressive force in spite of its tiny scale. Highly stylized, it is voluminous and rounded. The possibility that the *Woman of Willendorf* was intended to be a portrait of a specific recognizable individual must be ruled out, because the helmet/hair covers most of the head. The greatly enlarged breasts and abdomen—which suggest pregnancy—indicate the work's possible connection to human fertility. In fact, prior to the Neolithic period, almost no other human types are known. Perhaps such figures were a type of idol and were intended to promote human fertility, much as the cave paintings of animals might have been intended to "create" animals for the hunters.

THE NEOLITHIC PERIOD

What impact the Ice Age itself had on the availability of game is difficult to say, but by about 10,000 B.C., during

Timeline 1.1 Prehistoric culture.

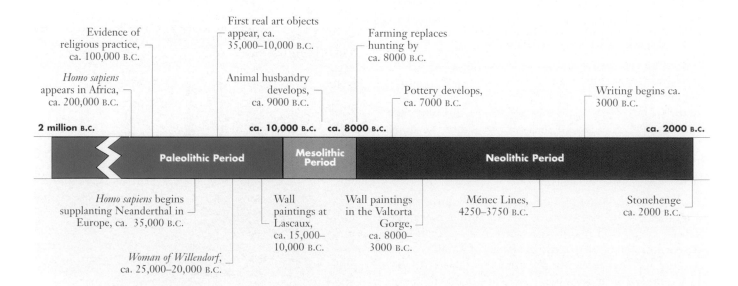

Evidence of religious practice, ca. 100,000 B.C.

Homo sapiens appears in Africa, ca. 200,000 B.C.

First real art objects appear, ca. 35,000–10,000 B.C.

Animal husbandry develops, ca. 9000 B.C.

Farming replaces hunting by ca. 8000 B.C.

Pottery develops, ca. 7000 B.C.

Writing begins ca. 3000 B.C.

2 million B.C.   **ca. 10,000 B.C.**   **ca. 8000 B.C.**   **ca. 2000 B.C.**

Paleolithic Period | **Mesolithic Period** | **Neolithic Period**

Homo sapiens begins supplanting Neanderthal in Europe, ca. 35,000 B.C.

Wall paintings at Lascaux, ca. 15,000–10,000 B.C.

Wall paintings in the Valtorta Gorge, ca. 8000–3000 B.C.

Ménec Lines, 4250–3750 B.C.

Stonehenge ca. 2000 B.C.

Woman of Willendorf, ca. 25,000–20,000 B.C.

Figure 1.4   Herd crossing river, hunters with bows and arrows, ca. 8000–3000 B.C., rock painting, Valtorta Gorge, Levant, Spain. Because humans are prominently depicted, are shown using weapons, and because this scene has a definite composition, the Valtorta Gorge paintings are believed to date later than those at Lascaux.

a short period known as the **Mesolithic**, or Middle Stone Age, the glaciers that almost covered Europe began to recede northward and dense forests began to grow. Reindeer and woolly rhinos were supplanted by elk and deer, dogs were domesticated, the wheel invented, and the arts of weaving and ceramics developed. By 8000 B.C., an even more important transition had begun to take place: around the world, in the Near East, in South and Central America, and in Southeast Asia, human beings ceased to hunt and began instead to farm, plowing and planting seeds, growing crops, and domesticating animals, using them not only as a reliable source of food and clothing but also as beasts of burden, inaugurating what is known as the **Neolithic** period, or New Stone Age. Thus, possibly the most important transformation in the history of human civilization took place. Hunters and gatherers became herders and farmers, and more permanent societies began to develop.

Wall Paintings.   Such advances were slower to arrive in Europe. In the Valtorta Gorge (fig. 1.4) on the southeast coast of Spain, paintings that date from sometime after 8000 B.C. and possibly as late as 3000 B.C. suggest that hunting remained the chief preoccupation of these peoples well into the Neolithic period. But changes

and advances are evident. Unlike the paintings of the Franco-Cantabrian area that are located deep in caves, the Valtorta Gorge paintings are on the smooth limestone walls in rock shelters and beneath cliff overhangs. The subjects portrayed differ significantly also, for here the human figure is given prominence, with humans shown hunting animals, fighting, and dancing together, as a group or community.

A degree of narrative is evident in the Valtorta wall paintings as the hunters, running from the left, attack the herd crossing a stream from the right. The composition is organized with a definite flow to the chase, a sense of action and movement conveyed by the lively postures of the figures—indeed, this appears to be a record of an actual event. A superb document of early hunting techniques, the scene shows hunters using the bow and arrow, a weapon not seen in Franco-Cantabrian art.

The paintings of the Valtorta Gorge differ from those of the Franco-Cantabrian area in additional ways. They are generally smaller in scale, and the figures are painted in solid colors—black or, more often, red. The human figures are abbreviated, abstracted, stylized, and shown in silhouette. The distinctive figure type has a small circular head, no neck, an elongated triangular torso tapering to a pinched waist, and exceptionally large legs, perhaps indicative of the importance of running quickly in the hunt. Direct and simple, these figures convey a remarkable sense of vitality and movement.

Architecture. In the Neolithic period, as cultivation of the land supplanted hunting as the chief means of obtaining food, people became increasingly tied to a single site, and permanent structures began to be built. Food storage pits have been found, indicating that, at least at times, the supply of food was more than adequate, allowing people the freedom to begin to develop social structures and specialized skills. There is evidence that people settled in communities and towns, building homes and even communal structures. Stated in the simplest terms, settled habitation plus specialization results in the earliest evidence of what may be called civilization.

Prehistoric architecture survives only from the Neolithic period, and very little survives at all. Structures made of wood, other plant material, or mud brick decayed and disappeared long ago. **Megalithic** (huge stone) arrangements and structures appear toward the close of the Neolithic period. Among them are menhirs and cromlechs. A **menhir** is a single stone or **monolith** ("mono" means one; "lith" means stone) set vertically into the ground. Menhirs were often placed at or near a burial place. A field of 1,009 menhirs known as the Ménec Lines, dated to 4250–3750 B.C., is located near Carnac, in Brittany, France. Placed on end, the tallest rising twelve feet, the stones are arranged in several rows

---

Figure 1.5 Stonehenge, Salisbury Plain, Wiltshire, England, ca. 2000 B.C., bluestone and sarsen, height of stones of outer circle 20′ (6.09 m). This enigmatic remnant of prehistoric architecture is believed to have been a monumental clock, laid out so the stones relate to the position of the sun at the summer and winter solstices.

three-quarters of a mile long. Some of the stones are unshaped, others taper toward the top, and others are carved with geometric designs. The largest menhir known is the Great Menhir, near Locmariaquer, in Brittany. It has fallen and is now broken into several pieces, but originally stood sixty-four feet high and is estimated to weigh approximately 347 tons. The purpose of the menhirs remains a subject of debate.

The most famous example of prehistoric architecture is surely the **cromlech**, or circle of stones having a religious purpose, known as Stonehenge (fig. 1.5), located on the Salisbury plain in Wiltshire, England, and built ca. 2000 B.C. A **henge** is a circle of stones or posts. Stonehenge is not the only prehistoric cromlech to have survived, but it is the most impressive and best preserved. The outer trench is approximately 150 feet in diameter, and the individual stones approximately twenty feet high. There is a definite entrance way, as well as four mounds evenly placed on the outer trench, and a central stone referred to as the altar stone. The huge upright stones form an outer circle and two inner circles or U shapes. Some of the stones are shaped into rectangles, and some also have patterns cut into them. Stonehenge is constructed using the **post and lintel** system—in its simplest form, two vertical posts support a horizontal lintel. At Stonehenge, the vertical posts have dowel pins carved into their uppermost end, which fit into circular depressions carved on the underside of the lintels at both ends, thereby locking the posts and lintels together.

Two main types of stone, bluestone and sarsen, were used to create this architectural marvel. Yet the closest site where bluestone is found is Wales. To transport stone from Wales to Wiltshire presumably required tremendous weights of stone to be moved over land, water, and then land again, by being rolled on logs and floated on rafts. Sarsen is more readily available on the Marlborough Downs, twenty miles north of Stonehenge.

What can the purpose or function of so monumental an undertaking have been? The answer seems to be connected with several "correspondences." If you stand in the center of Stonehenge and look to the so-called heelstone, you see that the top aligns with the horizon. The sun rises directly over the heelstone at the summer solstice—the longest day of the year. On each of the four mounds were other stones at horizon level—the one to the southwest is at the point of the setting sun at the winter solstice, the shortest day of the year. Stonehenge, therefore, seems to be an enormous sun clock or calendar, based upon the rising and setting sun at the summer and winter solstices. But could these simply be coincidences? That is, with enough stones in enough places, is it not probable that something is going to align with, to coincide with, something else? To resolve this question, the "coincidences" were weighed against probability by a computer; the results established that the placement of the stones must have been intentional.

MESOPOTAMIA: THE CRADLE OF CIVILIZATION

Even before Stonehenge was built in England, two far more advanced civilizations were developing in the Near East: that of Mesopotamia and that of Egypt (discussed in Chapter 2). Mesopotamian civilization developed in the valley between the Tigris and Euphrates Rivers: *Mesopotamia* is a Greek word meaning literally "the land between two rivers." Consisting of the eastern part of what is known as the Fertile Crescent, which extends northward along the eastern coast of the Mediterranean through what is today Israel and Lebanon, eastward into present-day Syria and Iraq, and south down the Tigris and Euphrates valleys to the Persian Gulf, Mesopotamia was the most fertile and arable land in the Near East, and perhaps, at the dawn of the Neolithic Age, the most fertile in the world. It was here, at any rate, that around 9000 B.C. **agriculture**—literally, the *cultura*, or cultivation, of the land, *ager*—was first fully developed.

By about 3000 B.C., two further developments had taken place that had a decisive influence on the course of civilization. Sometime after 6000 B.C. people learned to mine and use copper; by 3000 B.C., they had discovered that by combining tin with copper they could produce a much stronger alloy, bronze, which allowed tremendous innovations in the production of weapons, tools, and jewelry. This marked the beginning of the Bronze Age.

The second development marks the move from prehistory into the first historical period—that is, a period for which written records exist. By about 3000 B.C., the people of ancient Mesopotamia were using written language, known today largely from clay tablets that were first unearthed in the mid-nineteenth century. Chiefly the province of the upper class and priests, this writing was accomplished in wedge-shaped **cuneiform** characters (from the Latin *cuneus*, meaning "wedge") made with a stylus that was itself wedge-shaped and that was pressed into wet clay tablets. The original purpose of this writing seems to have been to keep agricultural records. Among the oldest examples of cuneiform writing, for instance, is a tablet from a temple complex at Uruk that lists sacks of grains and heads of cattle. Cuneiform writing began as a **pictographic** system. In its earliest form, the symbol for "cow" was an abstract "picture" of a cow's head:

But the pictographs were quickly abstracted even further, presumably in no small part because it was difficult to draw a curve with a reed stylus in wet clay. Between 2500 and 1800 B.C., the sign for "cow" was first turned ninety degrees sideways and then converted into a series of quickly imprinted wedges:

By combining pictograms, more complex ideas—or **ideograms**—and even abstract ideas could be represented. A bird next to an egg meant "fertility." Two crossed lines meant "hatred" or "enmity," and parallel lines signified "friendship":

A significant aid to our understanding the cuneiform vocabulary of Mesopotamian culture are groups of "sign lists" compiled by scribes as an aid to teaching the script to students. Sometime around 2000 B.C., another important development occurred, when pictograms began to represent not only objects but sounds—the birth of phonetic writing.

Assisted by these technical advances, three successive civilizations—those of Sumer, Akkad, and Babylon—blossomed in Mesopotamia over the following 1500 years.

SUMER

The Sumerians, who lived at the southern end of the Tigris and Euphrates Rivers, founded the Mesopotamian civilization between 3500 and 3000 B.C., contemporary with the beginning of Egyptian civilization. Sumerian culture reached its zenith by approximately 2800–2700 B.C. It was at this time that Sumer's most famous king, GILGAMESH [GIL-gah-mesh] (ca. 2700 B.C.), ruled Uruk, one of the many independent city-states that grew up in Mesopotamia.

Little or no unity ever developed among these city-states, and no concentration of wealth or population resulted. Instead, each Sumerian city-state had its own local god and its own local ruler. The kings were not thought of as gods—rather, the god was considered the owner of the city-state. Life seems to have been ruled by religion, with the king as intermediary between the god and the people. In each city-state, the buildings were clustered around the temple of the city's god. Religion focused on seasonal fertility. Agricultural mythology included the Bull of Heaven, whose fiery breath could burn crops, and Imdugud, a lion-headed eagle whose wings covered the heavens in dark clouds, a good

Figure 1.6   Ziggurat of King Urnammu (Nanna), Ur (El Muqeiyar), Iraq, ca. 2500–2050 B.C., sun-baked mud brick. The Sumerians built their temples atop ziggurats—rectangular mountains constructed of mud brick, with battered (sloping) walls.

with one another for the attention of the worshipers. The gods were human in form, and possessed human personalities and foibles—that is, they were **anthropomorphic**. The four chief gods were Anu, the heaven god; Ninhursag, the mother goddess; Enlil, the god of air; and Enki, the god of water. As human as the behavior of these gods might be, they were nonetheless clearly superior to humans, particularly by their immortality. The cuneiform sign for god is a star, which also means "on high," or "elevated," as well as "in the heavens."

Architecture.   Sumerian domestic architecture seems to have consisted largely of houses that were square or rectangular in plan and built of clay brick. Archaeologists have not been able to work out the precise layouts of Mesopotamian cities, but it seems certain that at the heart of the settlement would have been the temple. Sumerian temples were built on raised platforms known as **ziggurats**, an example of which is the Ziggurat of King Urnammu at Ur, in Iraq (fig. 1.6), constructed ca. 2500–2050 B.C. of sun-baked mud brick and, consequently, now greatly disintegrated. The lowest level is fifty feet high. The walls are **battered**, that is, sloping, making them stronger than vertical walls because they are self-supporting. The walls are constructed with **weeper holes** to allow water that collects in the masonry to run out through these small regularly placed openings. The ziggurat at Ur demonstrates the use of specific orientation in architecture, for the angles point north, south, east, and west.

creature who brought rain and ended droughts brought on by the Bull of Heaven.

Like most early religions, Sumerian and later Mesopotamian religions were **polytheistic**—that is, there were many gods and goddesses, who often competed

---

Timeline 1.2   Mesopotamian culture up to the rise of the Persian Empire.

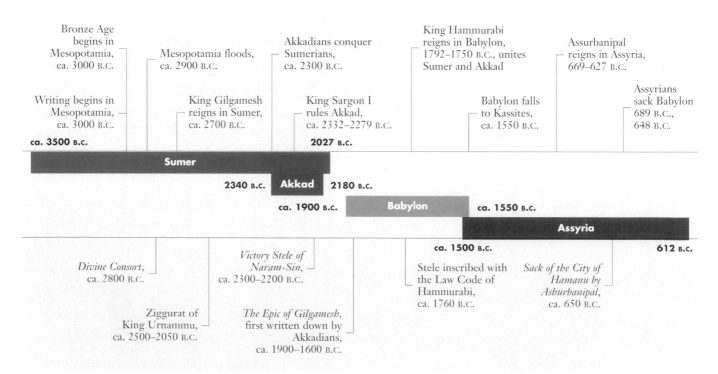

Bronze Age begins in Mesopotamia, ca. 3000 B.C.

Writing begins in Mesopotamia, ca. 3000 B.C.

ca. 3500 B.C.

Mesopotamia floods, ca. 2900 B.C.

King Gilgamesh reigns in Sumer, ca. 2700 B.C.

Akkadians conquer Sumerians, ca. 2300 B.C.

King Sargon I rules Akkad, ca. 2332–2279 B.C.

2027 B.C.

King Hammurabi reigns in Babylon, 1792–1750 B.C., unites Sumer and Akkad

Babylon falls to Kassites, ca. 1550 B.C.

Assurbanipal reigns in Assyria, 669–627 B.C.

Assyrians sack Babylon 689 B.C., 648 B.C.

Sumer

2340 B.C.   **Akkad**   **2180 B.C.**

ca. 1900 B.C.   **Babylon**   **ca. 1550 B.C.**

Assyria

ca. 1500 B.C.   **612 B.C.**

Divine Consort, ca. 2800 B.C.

Ziggurat of King Urnammu, ca. 2500–2050 B.C.

Victory Stele of Naram-Sin, ca. 2300–2200 B.C.

The Epic of Gilgamesh, first written down by Akkadians, ca. 1900–1600 B.C.

Stele inscribed with the Law Code of Hammurabi, ca. 1760 B.C.

Sack of the City of Hamanu by Ashurbanipal, ca. 650 B.C.

The actual temple was atop the ziggurat. Within the temple, a statue of the god stood in the sanctuary, a long room running the entire length of the temple. The lower levels of the ziggurat were covered with dirt and planted with trees, thus creating the effect of a mountain with a temple on top. This practice is explained by the belief that the gods lived on the mountain tops, so ziggurats brought worhipers closer to heaven.

Sculpture.   Since little stone was available naturally in Sumeria, limestone, gypsum, and marble were imported. Consequently, all Sumerian statues are small. Although Sumerian sculpture includes occasional secular subjects, most examples appear to be religious or commemorative in purpose, and to have been made for temples. The human figure is represented in a distinctive manner unique to Sumerian sculpture. The style is one of formal simplification, geometric and symmetrical. The figure type is squat in proportions, with broad hips and heavy legs.

The so-called *Divine Consort* (fig. 1.7), carved ca. 2800 B.C., is the head from a cult statue from Uruk (modern Warka). The huge eyes and single continuous eyebrows of such figures were originally inlaid with colored material. Some have their ears pierced for small gold earrings. The most expressive feature of Sumerian figures is surely the size of the wide open eyes, giving them a look of rapt devotion. They appear to be transfixed—as if they are witnessing an astounding occurrence. In fact, cuneiform texts reveal that the worshiper must fix upon the god with an attentive gaze.

Figure 1.8   Standing man, formerly thought to represent Abu, the god of vegetation, from Tell Asmar, ca. 2600 B.C., white gypsum, insets of black limestone and white shell, height ca. 11¾″ (29.8 cm), Metropolitan Museum of Art, New York. Sumerian statues are easily recognized by their large eyes, single eyebrow, and seemingly astonished facial expression.

Figure 1.7   Female head, known as the *Divine Consort*, from Uruk (Warka), ca. 2800 B.C., alabaster, height ca. 8″ (20.3 cm), Iraq Museum, Baghdad. This alabaster face was meant to be attached to a wooden background and probably wore a wig of gold.

A statue formerly thought to represent Abu (Abu means "father" in Arabic languages), the god of vegetation (fig. 1.8), comes from a group of similar statues dated ca. 2600 B.C., carved of white gypsum, with black limestone and white shell insets, found in the Abu temple at Tell Asmar. Some of these statues may represent gods. Others may represent worshipers. Curiously, it appears that Sumerian people might have a statue carved to represent themselves and do their worshiping for them—in their place, as a stand-in. An inscription on one such statue translates, "It offers prayers." Another inscription says, "Statue, say unto my king (god) ..."

The figures from the Abu temple stand erect (seated figures are rare in Sumerian art), with their hands clasped, some holding small vessels for pouring libations. Some figures are made with the head and hands of marble or other stone, and the rest of the figure of wood.

Figure 1.9 *Gudea of Lagash*, seated, ca. 2144–2124 B.C., diorite, height $17\frac{5}{16}''$ (43.9 cm), Metropolitan Museum of Art, New York. The many surviving statues of Gudea, ruler of Lagash, are stiff, rigid, frontal, and formal, the precisely carved figures intended to create an image of royalty, rather than an illusion of reality.

Their costumes consist of a skirt, perhaps made of animal skins, and they may be bearded. Otherwise, they are simple and unadorned.

Also known by name is *Gudea of Lagash* (Telloh) (fig. 1.9), carved ca. 2144–2124 B.C. of diorite, a hard stone that allows a fine finish. Gudea, ruler of Lagash, had statues of himself placed in shrines—about twenty statues of him remain, all small in scale. There is some variety to the Gudea statues, but he is always shown to be serene and forceful. Gudea's unusual attire crosses the chest and falls over one arm, and the simplified heavy skirt does not reveal the form beneath. The same squat proportions are used as with other Sumerian figures. Gudea may stand, sit, appear to worship, or offer a plan for a temple to his god, but the rigid figures do not bend, twist, or move. His hands are likely to be firmly clasped, the tension of the arms shown by the bulging muscles. The carefully rendered muscles of the arms contrast with the conventionalized face, which is fleshy and rounded, with huge eyes and one continuous eyebrow—heavy eyebrows were a racial trait. The contrast of textures of the smooth skin, eyebrows, and headdress is emphasized.

Although little or no Sumerian painting remains, decorative objects have survived. A noteworthy example is an inlaid standard (fig. 1.10), from Ur, dated ca. 2700–2600 B.C. The figures on this double-sided panel are made of shell or mother-of-pearl inlaid in bitumen, with the background formed from pieces of the blue stone, lapis lazuli, and additional bits of red limestone. The standard, on which scenes of war are portrayed, is

Figure 1.10 Inlaid Standard, from the "royal cemetery" at Ur, ca. 2700–2600 B.C., double-sided panel, shell or mother-of-pearl, lapis lazuli, and red limestone, inlaid in bitumen, ca. $8 \times 19''$ (20.3 × 48.3 cm), British Museum, London. Much like today's comic strips, a series of scenes are arranged in chronological sequence to tell a tale—in this case, that of a successful battle, the victory feast, and the taking of war spoils.

Figure 1.11 Lyre from the tomb of Queen Puabi, Ur, ca. 2600 B.C., wood with gold-leaf bull's head, inlaid gold, lapis lazuli, and shell, height ca. 12″ (30.5 cm), University Museum, Philadelphia. Akin to large-scale jewelry, this lyre represents the splendid sculpture in gold and other precious materials created in ancient Sumeria.

commemorative, with events arranged in horizontal rows. On one side, on the top row, the king steps out of his chariot to inspect his captives. The king is shown to be taller than anyone else—his head breaks through the border. On the two lower rows are scenes of battle, with fighters wearing metal helmets, cloaks, fleece kilts, and riding in four-wheeled chariots. On the other side, on the top row, the victory feast is shown. The king and his officers sit in chairs and drink. The king is, again, largest. On the two lower rows, booty taken in battle is paraded in front of them, including cows and animals of unidentifiable species.

That the crudeness of Sumerian stone sculpture is due to lack of stone on which to practice rather than to lack of skill is supported by the splendid work of Sumerian jewelers and goldsmiths. A superbly crafted wooden lyre, a stringed musical instrument similar to a harp (fig. 1.11), made ca. 2600 B.C., comes from the tomb of Queen Puabi at Ur and was ornamented with a bull's head made of gold leaf, the hair and beard of lapis lazuli. Below the head, on the sound box of the lyre, is a panel (fig. 1.12) made of wood, gold, lapis lazuli, and shell, inlaid to form a variety of images. Among these images are a man,

animals acting like people, including one who plays a harp, and monstrous combinations of humans and animals. All figures, or portions thereof, appear in one of two ways: either directly from the front or in profile, simultaneously diminishing any sensation of dimension and enhancing the decorative quality of the whole. Although seemingly amusing, and certainly engaging, these creatures played an important part in Sumerian mythology. The animals depicted here are the traditional guardians of the gateway through which newly dead Sumerians must pass, and this fantastic scene may well portray the afterlife.

Literature. The oldest major literary work in the world is *The Epic of Gilgamesh*, the earliest elements of which date from about 2500 B.C., when Gilgamesh reigned in the Euphrates city-state of Uruk. Legends about Gilgamesh were told but not recorded until hundreds of years after his death. Before about 2000 B.C., these stories were recorded on cuneiform tablets. From around 1900–1600 B.C. onward, the Gilgamesh stories were written down by the Akkadians, a people who spoke an early Semitic language related to both Hebrew and Arabic. Under the powerful military leadership of the Akkadians, who conquered the city-states of Sumer and adopted their culture, the epic work was organized into a coherent whole. The earliest known version of the epic was discovered in the seventh century B.C. in the library of the Assyrian king Assurbanipal (669–627 B.C.).

Figure 1.12 Panel from the lyre shown in fig. 1.11.

Cross Currents

SUMERIAN MYTH AND THE BIBLE

There are strong parallels between Sumerian mythology and the stories in the biblical book of Genesis. There are, for instance, surviving Sumerian texts that parallel the story of Noah and the flood, including an episode in *The Epic of Gilgamesh*—a huge flood did indeed inundate Mesopotamia about 2900 B.C. In another Sumerian myth, the story of Enki and Ninhursag, which is some three hundred verses long, Enki, the great Sumerian god of water, creates a garden paradise in Dilmun by bringing water up from the earth. In Genesis 2:6, a similar event occurs: "But there went up a mist from the earth, and watered the whole face of the ground." Ninhursag, the mother-goddess of the Sumerians, causes eight plants to sprout in this proto-Garden of Eden, and Enki, wanting to taste the plants, has another lesser god pick them. Ninhursag is furious and pronounces the curse of death upon Enki. This is a moment in the story that anticipates the biblical God's fury at Adam and Eve for eating the apple that Satan has tempted them with and their expulsion from the garden into a fallen world in which they must confront their mortality. Unlike Adam and Eve, however, Enki is eventually restored to immortality by Ninhursag, but the parallels between the two stories are striking.

Also close in spirit to the biblical Creation story is the *Poem of the Supersage*, an Akkadian text written down about 1700 B.C. Like most Akkadian texts, it is probably based on Sumerian legend. The story begins in a divine society where the gods, in order to satisfy their material needs, had to work. Some gods, the leaders, called Anunnaki, were pure consumers, but the rest were laborers. These last, called Igigu, finally revolted, creating the prospect of famine among the Anunnaki. It was Enki who resolved the crisis by proposing that the gods create a substitute labor force out of the clay of the earth, whose destiny it would be to work and whose life would have a limited duration. Thus, as in Genesis, humankind is created out of clay, must labor, and is mortal.

The earliest parts of the Bible date from about 1000 B.C. Most of the Sumerian texts date from 2000 B.C. or earlier. How these stories survived is a matter of speculation, though it is worth pointing out that the biblical Abraham was born in Ur, perhaps around 1700 B.C. It is therefore entirely possible that it was he who brought this lore with him to Palestine. Even more to the point, the language of the Akkadians, who conquered the Sumerians in about 2300 B.C., was also used throughout Palestine during the second millennium B.C., and there is little doubt that Palestinian scholars were well acquainted with Akkadian stories and texts, most of which are retellings, in one form or another, of Sumerian prototypes.

Like other ancient epics such as those of Homer (see Chapter 3), *The Epic of Gilgamesh* includes elements of folklore, legend, and myth that accrued over time. The work is compiled of originally separate stories concerning Gilgamesh; Enkidu, a primeval human figure; Utnapishtim [OOT-nah-PISH-tim], a Babylonian counterpart of Noah; and a number of other figures.

The epic begins with a kind of prologue that emphasizes Gilgamesh's wisdom as a ruler and his importance to recorded history. The prologue also characterizes him as a semi-divine figure, who, though not immortal, is courageous, strong, and beautiful. He is also described as an arrogant and oppressive ruler. When his people cry out for help to their gods for assistance, the god Anu creates Enkidu, a primitive combination of man and wild animal, a figure related to those depicted on the lyre from the tomb of Queen Puabi in Ur.

The story of the mutually positive influences Gilgamesh and Enkidu exert upon each other, of their developing friendship, and their heroic adventures occupies the bulk of the epic. An additional segment concerning Gilgamesh in the Underworld forms a kind of epilogue. In their first adventure, Gilgamesh and Enkidu confront and kill the giant Humbaba. When the goddess Ishtar proposes that Gilgamesh become her lover, he refuses, which precipitates the goddess sending the Bull of Heaven to destroy the city of Uruk by famine.

The second adventure of Gilgamesh and Enkidu involves the slaying of the destructive Bull, the punishment for which is Enkidu's death through illness. After losing his companion, Gilgamesh journeys to visit Utnapishtim, the only human ever granted immortality, but fails to learn the secret of everlasting life, though he does return home having gleaned much else from the wisdom of Utnapishtim. With this knowledge he rules as a wise king. Gilgamesh's adventures are occasions for writers to explore questions that will be raised again in later epics. What is the relationship between human beings and their deities? How are human beings linked with the world of nature and animals? What are the obligations of friendship, family, and public duty? How should one live in the face of mortality?

AKKAD

Under the leadership of King SARGON I, who ruled ca. 2332–2279 B.C., and his grandson and successor NARAM-SIN [NA-ram-sin], the Semitic people of Akkad conquered all of the city-states of Sumer. Subsequently, the governors of these cities were "slaves" to the king of Akkad, and he himself was a god to them.

Figure 1.13 *Victory Stele of Naram-Sin*, ca. 2300–2200 B.C., limestone, height 6′ 6″ (1.98 m), Musée du Louvre, Paris. This stone slab carved in relief served as a public monument to commemorate the military accomplishments of Naram-Sin. In this, it deserves comparison to the palette of the Egyptian pharaoh Narmer (see fig. 2.1).

The actual site of the city of Akkad has never been discovered, though it is thought to be near present-day Baghdad. As a result, little in the way of Akkadian art remains, and we know the culture largely through its language, which, by 2300 B.C., was spoken, as noted above, throughout the Near East.

The most celebrated example of Akkadian art is the *Victory Stele of Naram-Sin* (fig. 1.13), ca. 2300–2200 B.C. A **stele** is a vertical slab of stone that serves as a marker. The *Victory Stele of Naram-Sin*, which is six and a half feet high, is carved on one side only. At the top of the scene is a set of stars—the sign for Naram-Sin's protecting gods—and below, Naram-Sin and his army victoriously climb a mountain, as if to place themselves in closer proximity to the gods, the defeated lying slaughtered or begging for mercy at their feet. Naram-Sin himself, taller than the rest, as is always the case in Akkadian depictions of royalty, wearing the horned helmet used to identify the gods, and, standing at the very top of the battle, on the bodies of two victims, strides confidently to his place as the leader of all Mesopotamia.

BABYLON

However powerful Sargon I and Naram-Sin might have been, the Akkad kingdom lasted under two hundred years. For the next three hundred years, until about 1900 B.C., Mesopotamia was subject to constant division and conflict among its various city-states. Then a tribe of nomads, originally known as the Amorites, invaded the region from the Arab peninsula and established a royal city in Babylon. In 1792 B.C., when HAMMURABI [ham-ooh-RAH-bee] (r. 1792–1750), the first great king of Babylon, took power, the Sumerian and Akkadian city-states were unified as a single kingdom under his rule.

Sculpture. One of Hammurabi's great accomplishments was to codify the laws of the region. The stele inscribed with the Law Code of Hammurabi (fig. 1.14),

Figure 1.14 Stele inscribed with the Law Code of Hammurabi, ca. 1760 B.C., basalt, height of stele ca. 7′ (2.13 m), height of relief ca. 28″ (71.1 cm), Musée du Louvre, Paris. The significance of this legal document was made clear to the Babylonian people by the relief at the top of the stele that depicts the sun god Shamash giving these laws directly to Hammurabi, king of Babylon.

carved of basalt ca. 1760 B.C., which stands seven feet high, is both a work of art and a historic legal document. Hammurabi's law code is the earliest known written body of laws. The code consists of 282 laws arranged in six chapters: 1. Personal property; 2. Land; 3. Trade and commerce (this chapter seems strikingly modern, for it includes fixing of prices, contracts, rates of interest, promissory notes, and credit); 4. Family; 5. Maltreatment; and 6. Labor (including the fixing of wages). The death penalty is often mentioned—this is an eye-for-an-eye, tooth-for-a-tooth approach to law.

The relief at the top of the Law Code of Hammurabi shows Shamash, the sun god who controlled plant life and weather, dispelled evil spirits of disease, and personified righteousness and justice—the appropriate god for a law code. (Shamash is also represented in the *Stele of Naram-Sin* as one of the stars overlooking the scene.) Hammurabi appears to converse with Shamash, from whom he receives the laws. The difference in importance between the two figures is made clear, the king standing while Shamash is shown larger, elevated, and enthroned.

ASSYRIA

Babylon fell to the nomadic Kassite people in about 1550 B.C. This was followed by a period of relative cultural decline, before the last great ancient Mesopotamian civilization was developed by the Assyrians. The Assyrian culture began in the middle of the second millennium B.C., achieved significant power around 900 B.C., and lasted until 612 B.C. when Nineveh and Syria fell. The instability of life in ancient Assyria is reflected in the emphasis on fortifications and military subjects in art. The Assyrians took much from Sumerian and Babylonian art, such as building their temples on ziggurats at Nimrud (Calah). The Assyrians, however, had greater resources than the Sumerians, in terms of population, money, and materials.

Sculpture. Stone, in particular, was far more abundant in the northern region of the Tigris and Euphrates valleys where the Assyrians originated, permitting them to produce large-scale sculpture. Between the ninth and seventh centuries B.C., stone guardian monsters were placed at gateways and defined an Assyrian style; several examples survive, including those from the palace of ASHURNASIRPAL II [ash-er-na-SEER-pal] (r. 883–859 B.C.) at Nimrud (fig. 1.15). The headdress is peculiar to Mesopotamian deities and is similar to that worm by Shamash on the Babylonian stele with the Law Code of Hammurabi. With the body of a lion, wings of a bird, and head of a human, such guardian figures were perhaps intended to combine human intelligence with animal strength. Perhaps they were intended to be frightening as well or to impress people with the king's power.

Figure 1.15 *Human-Headed Winged Lion*, from the northwest palace of Ashurnasirpal II at Nimrud (Calah), ca. 883–859 B.C., limestone, height $10'2\frac{1}{2}''$ (3.11 m), length $9'1\frac{1}{2}''$ (2.78 m), Metropolitan Museum of Art, New York. Part human and part animal, the five-legged Assyrian gate monsters are among a vast population of early imaginary composite creatures. Later artists, in various cultures, created generations of descendants with a remarkable range of implausible physiognomies.

Alternatively, they have been said to represent the Assyrian god Nergal, whose emblem is a winged lion.

Seen from the front, only the two front legs of these creatures are visible. Seen from the side, four legs are visible and the creature appears to be walking. To make this monster appear correct both from the front and the side, the sculptor has generously given him five legs!

Other than gateway guardians, Assyrian sculpture consists mostly of **reliefs**—figures cut from a flat, two-dimensional background. **Statues in the round**—sculptures that are freestanding and made to be seen from all sides—are extremely rare. Assyrian reliefs were part of the architecture; the carved panels were set into the walls of the palaces. These reliefs show little interest in religious subjects, depicting instead scenes that provide historical documents of actual events often arranged chronologically. The subjects, which are usually royal activities that glorify the king, provide records of ancient armor, weapons, chariots, harnesses, and other accoutrements of war. Little information about ordinary life is

Connections

THE FUNDAMENTALS OF CIVILIZATION

Civilization requires many different components to function. The study of early cultures indicates what some of these things are: technology, or tools and special technical skills that give rise to trade; laws, for the regulation of society; governmental structures; cities, or permanent settlements; and writing, through which culture is transmitted.

One Sumerian text outlines the knowledge necessary to live as civilized people. An extraordinary tale, narrated by Berossos, a Babylonian scholar who, around 300 B.C., recorded in Greek the history and traditions of his country, it recalls a time when the people of Chaldea, on the Persian Gulf, in Lower Mesopotamia, "lived an irreligious life, similar to that of animals":

In the first year an extraordinary monster appeared ... on the shore of the Red Sea, and its name was Oannes. Its entire body was that of a fish, and underneath his head was a second one, as well as feet similar to those of a man—an image that is still remembered and that is still depicted up to today. This being lived among the people without eating anything and taught them writing, science, and technology of all types, the foundation of cities, the building of temples, jurisprudence, and geometry. He also revealed to them [how to cultivate] grains and how to harvest fruits. In short, he revealed to them all that constitutes civilized life. He did it so well that ever since one has found nothing exceptional in it. When the sun set, the monster Oannes plunged back into the sea to pass the night in the water, because he was amphibious. Later similar creatures appeared ...

The story is not meant to be interpreted literally. Like many of the adventures in *The Epic of Gilgamesh*, it is a **myth**, a story involving legendary heroes, gods, and creatures that explains important cultural practices or beliefs. However "true" or otherwise the story may be, the lesson is clear: No one thing guarantees civilization. It is the combination of science, technology, agriculture, mathematics, law, literature, architecture, and the arts that constitutes civilized life.

included, and women are rarely shown in these scenes of warfare and hunting.

One such relief, the depiction of *Ashurnasirpal II Killing Lions* (fig. 1.16), carved ca. 850 B.C., from Nimrud, portrays a militaristic subject commonly used to glorify the king. In fact, this event was more a ceremony than an actual lion hunt, since soldiers lined up to form a square, and the lion was released from a cage into the square. The artist has not tried to duplicate observed reality. Three horses are shown, but each receives only two legs. Although figures overlap, there is no sense of space, no setting, and everything takes place on the same ground line. The result is more a decorative surface than a realistic three-dimensional depiction.

Figure 1.16 *Ashurnasirpal II Killing Lions*, from the palace of Ashurnasirpal II at Nimrud (Calah), Iraq, ca. 850 B.C., limestone relief, 3'3" × 8'4" (0.99 × 2.54 m), British Museum, London. This precisely carved relief records a ceremony used to emphasize the power of the Assyrian king—he is shown overcoming a lion, long regarded as "king of beasts."

Figure 1.17   *Sack of the City of Hamanu by Ashurbanipal*, from the palace of Ashurbanipal at Nineveh (Kuyunjik), Iraq, ca. 650 B.C., limestone relief, 36 × 24½″ (92.7 × 62.2 cm), British Museum, London. Assyrian emphasis on narration and documentation permitted disregard for relative scale and spatial logic. Realistic representation of a military campaign in stone relief first appears on the Column of Trajan (see figs. 5.20 and 5.21) in the second century A.D.

The limestone relief depicting the *Sack of the City of Hamanu by Ashurbanipal* (fig. 1.17), from the palace of ASHURBANIPAL [ash-er-BAN-ee-pul] (r. 669–ca. 627 B.C.) at Nineveh, was carved two hundred years after the Nimrud relief, in approximately 650 B.C. Assyrian artists were the first to attempt large-scale narrative sculpture depicting specific events. The carving shown in figure 1.17 is one of a series of historical reliefs that records the defeat of the Elamites by Ashurbanipal. Here, the story of the Assyrian sack of Hamanu is clearly told. Buildings are burned; Ashurbanipal's soldiers tear down buildings with pickaxes; pieces of the structures fall through the air. Soldiers carry contraband down the hill. The little scene below shows soldiers at the campfire, eating and drinking, while one stands guard. This matter-of-fact record was no doubt intended to glorify Ashurbanipal's military achievements and to intimidate enemies wanting to challenge his authority. It should be added that the Assyrians had a real reputation for ferocity; which they earned, in part, by their practice of impaling the heads of their enemies on spikes.

NEBUCHADNEZZAR'S BABYLON

In the New Testament of the Bible, in describing Rome the author of the book of Revelation invokes the name of the great sixth-century B.C. Mesopotamian city of Babylon with at best mixed emotions: "What city is like unto this great city … that great city that was clothed in fine linen and purple and scarlet and decked with gold and precious stones and pearls! … Babylon, the Great, the Mother of Harlots and of the Abominations of the Earth." The biblical prophet tells us as much about his own Judeo-Christian morality as he does about Babylon's decadence, but of Babylon's great wealth and position in the sixth century B.C. there can be no doubt.

The Assyrians undertook a major rebuilding of the original city that Hammurabi had built a thousand years earlier, after sacking and destroying it in 689 B.C. Only forty years later in 648 B.C., its population had once again become sufficiently irritating to the Assyrian kings to cause Ashurbanipal to attack it again, killing all those who opposed him. "I fed their corpses to the dogs, pigs, *zibu*-birds, vultures, the birds of the sky and the fish of the ocean," Ashurbanipal bragged.

Figure 1.18   Reconstruction drawing of Babylon in the sixth century B.C., The Oriental Institute of the University of Chicago. In this contemporary rendering of ancient Babylon, a procession enters the Ishtar Gate. Above and to the right are the Hanging Gardens; in the distance, the Ziggurat of Marduk can be seen.

Figure 1.19 Ishtar Gate, from Babylon, ca. 575 B.C., glazed brick, Staatliche Museen zu Berlin, Preussischer Kulturbesitz, Vorderasiatisches Museum, Berlin. The appeal of animals as architectural ornament to the Babylonians is evident on this gate to Nebuchadnezzar's sacred precinct.

After the death of Ashurbanipal, when Assyrian dominance in the region collapsed, the city again rose to prominence. Referred to by scholars as Neo-Babylon, to distinguish it from the Babylon of Hammurabi, and sometimes called Chaldea as well, it was rebuilt by the architects of NEBUCHADNEZZAR II [ney-book-ad-NEZ-zahr] (r. 604–562 B.C.) to become the greatest city in the Near East (fig. 1.18). It was graced by its famous Hanging Gardens, one of the so-called "Seven Wonders of the World." Rising high above the flat plain of the valley floor, was its Marduk ziggurat—sometimes believed to be the biblical Tower of Babel, since Bab-il was an early form of the city's name. The Greek historian Herodotus, who traveled widely in the region in the fifth century B.C., described the city in some detail in his *Histories*:

Babylon lies in a wide plain, a vast city in the form of a square with sides nearly fourteen miles long and a circuit of some fifty-six miles, and in addition to its enormous size it surpasses in splendor any city of the known world. It is surrounded by a broad deep moat full of water, and within the moat there is a wall fifty cubits wide and two hundred high … The temple [of Marduk] is a square building, two furlongs each way, with bronze gates, and was still in existence in my time; it has a solid central tower, one furlong square, with a second erected on top of it and then a third, and so on up to eight. All eight towers can be climbed by a spiral way running round the outside, and about half-way up there are seats for those who make the ascent to rest on. On the summit of the topmost tower stands a great temple with a fine large couch in it, richly covered, and a golden table beside it … In the temple of Babylon there is a second shrine lower down, in which is a great sitting figure of Bel, all of gold on a golden throne, supported on a base of gold, with a golden table standing beside it. I was told by the Chaldeans that, to make all this, more than twenty-two tons of gold were used.

Figure 1.20 Vase handle in the form of a winged ibex, from Persia, fourth century B.C., silver, partly gilded, height ca. 10$\frac{1}{2}$″ (26.7 cm), Musée du Louvre, Paris. The skill of Persian metalsmiths is clearly evident in this exquisitely crafted wild moutain goat. Embellished by the addition of wings, two of Nature's creatures have been combined to create a new species.

The richness of the city is embodied in the most remarkable of its surviving parts, the Ishtar Gate (fig. 1.19), built ca. 575 B.C. by Nebuchadnezzar himself and today housed in the Berlin State Museums. Ishtar is the Sumerian goddess of love and war. Her gate is ornamented with bulls, lions, and dragons—all emblematic of her power—arranged in tiers, on a blue background, in brown, yellow, and white. The gate rose over the Processional Way, known in Babylonian as *Aibur-shabu*, the place "the enemy shall never pass." Leading up to the gate was a broad paved road lined with high walls that were decorated with the figures of 120 lions, symbols of Ishtar. The animals on both the Ishtar Gate and the wall of the Processional Way are made in relief of **glazed** (painted and fired) brick, the technique for making them probably invented in Mesopotamia during Nebuchadnezzar's reign. The glaze made the mud bricks waterproof, which accounts for their survival.

PERSIA

In 539 B.C., the King of Persia, CYRUS II [SI-rus] (r. 559–530 B.C.), entered Babylon without significant resistance and took over the city, forbidding looting and appointing a Persian governor. Cyrus offered peace and friendship to the Babylonians, and he allowed them to continue worshiping their own gods. In fact, legend quickly had it that as he advanced on the city, the Babylonian god Marduk was at his side.

The Persians originated from Elam, in modern-day western Iran. Although some sites date back to around 5000 B.C., the Persians had begun to rise to power by the sixth century B.C. and by 480 B.C. their empire extended from the Indus River in the east to the Danube in the north. Moreover, in the same period that Cyrus overran Mesopotamia, the other great Near Eastern civilization, Egypt, lost its independence to the Persians (see Chapter 2). Persian art is found across this large geographical area.

Sculpture. The earliest extant Persian art consists of portable objects characteristic of nomadic peoples. Objects buried with the dead have survived—weapons, decorative items including jewelry, containers such as jugs, bowls, and cups, and other objects. Their style is referred to as an "animal style" because the objects are characterized by the decorative use of animal motifs. Small forms are used in ornamental jewel-like concentration. Popular motifs derive from the ibex (wild goat), serpent, bird, bull, and sheep, while the human figure plays a minor role.

A later example of this animal style, and a high point in technical accomplishment, is the winged ibex (fig. 1.20), a wild mountain goat made of silver, partly gilded, and intended to serve as a handle to a vase, dating from the fourth century B.C. This ibex has been magically graced with wings. Striking a lively pose, it seems also to have been given life. Despite its supernatural characteristics, the care with which it has been crafted underscores the Persian fascination with, and love of, animals. In fact, the Persians built gardens and "paradises"—enclosed sanctuaries where birds and animals were protected.

Architecture. Because the ancient Persian religion centered on fire altars in the open air, no religious architecture was needed. However, huge palaces with many rooms, halls, and courts were constructed. The visitor to the palace at Persepolis (fig. 1.21), built 518–ca. 460 B.C. by DARIUS [DAR-ee-uss] (521–486 B.C.) and XERXES I (485–465 B.C.) who were the successors of Cyrus, is met by huge guardian monsters at the entrance towers of the Porch of Xerxes, reminiscent of

Figure 1.21 Palace of Darius and Xerxes, Persepolis, Iran, 518–ca. 460 B.C., overview. Constructed on a raised platform and impressive in its enormous scale, the palace includes large rooms filled with forests of columns. The plan—axial, formal, and repetitious— appears to have been laid out on a grid.

the Assyrian guardian monsters. The palace of Persepolis is also similar to Assyrian palaces in being set on a raised platform. At Persepolis the palace stands on a rock-cut terrace, 545 by 330 yards, approached by a broad stairway of 106 shallow steps. Beyond were the main courtyards and the Throne Hall of Xerxes, known as the Hall of One Hundred Columns. This room was a forest of pillars, filled by ten rows of ten columns, each column rising forty feet. This was a new style for Mesopotamia, based on the use of tall columns.

Relief Sculpture. The palace at Persepolis was decorated with stone reliefs, including that of *Tribute Bearers Bringing Offerings* (fig. 1.22), flanking the stairway and carved ca. 490 B.C. Such ceremonial sculpture is concentrated almost exclusively along the staircases, giving a decorative emphasis to the main approaches. Three to six figures are used to represent each of twenty-three different nations of the empire. The repetition of stylized figures—in attendance, as servants, and in processions— may be said to become monotonous. These figures are stiff, if not frozen; representations of animals in Persian art have greater life and personality than representations of humans.

Religion. Perhaps the most lasting innovation made by Persian culture was in religion. The prophet

Figure 1.22 *Tribute Bearers Bringing Offerings,* ca. 490 B.C., limestone relief, height 8′4″ (2.54 m), flanking stairway, Palace of Darius and Xerxes, Persepolis, Iran. The message conveyed by these stiff, formal, and generous gift-bearing figures, passed by the visitor when entering the palace, is hardly subtle.

Then & Now

BEER

The beer people drink today is an alcoholic beverage made by fermenting grains and usually incorporating hops, but the process of making it was discovered nearly 8000 years ago, around 6000 B.C., in Sumeria. The Sumerians made beer out of *bappir*, or half-baked, crusty loaves of bread, which they crumbled into water, fermented, and then filtered through a basket. Surviving records indicate that as much as fifty per cent of each grain harvest went into the production of beer and that in Ur, around 3000 B.C., needy persons were allotted one gallon of beer each day as part of a general social welfare program.

Literally hundreds of surviving cuneiform tablets contain recipes for beer, including *kassi* (a black beer), *kassag* (fine black beer), and *kassagsaan* (the finest premium beer). There were wheat beers, white beers, and red beers as well. One surviving tablet, which is rather reminiscent of modern advertising slogans, reads "Drink Ebla—the beer with the heart of a lion." Kings were buried with elaborate straws made of gold and lapis lazuli, designed for sipping beer. There was even a goddess, Ninkasi—"she who fills the mouth"—who looked over the production and distribution of the drink. "I feel wonderful, drinking beer," wrote one poet, about 3000 B.C., "in a blissful mood

with joy in my heart and a happy liver." But the Law Code of Hammurabi specifically banned the selling of beer for money. It could be bartered only for barley: "If a beer seller do not receive barley as the price for beer, but if she receive money or make the beer a measure smaller than the barley measure received, they shall throw her into the water."

Today there are over six hundred breweries making beer in the United States alone, each with its own unique process, producing perhaps ten times that many beers, each with its own unique flavor and color. The tradition, clearly, is as long and venerable as civilization itself.

Zoroaster, or Zarathustra, who lived around 600 B.C., rejected the polytheism of earlier Mesopotamian cultures and instead developed a **dualistic religion**, in which the universe is divided between two forces, one good and one evil. According to Zoroaster, Ahuramazda, the god of light, was caught up in an eternal struggle with Ahriman, the god of darkness. As noted earlier, the Christian Bible may have been influenced in some of its stories by *The Epic of Gilgamesh*. Similarly, there are some ideas in Zoroastrianism that may have influenced later religions, such as the idea of a "Prince of Darkness" (Satan) and a Last Judgment.

READINGS
✦

✦ THE EPIC OF GILGAMESH
Selected Episodes

The Epic of Gilgamesh *is more than likely the oldest literary work in the world, parts of it dating from as early as 2500 B.C. It describes the friendship and heroic adventures of the Sumerian ruler Gilgamesh and Enkidu, a primeval human figure. When Enkidu dies, Gilgamesh journeys to see Utnapishtim, the only human ever granted immortality. Though Gilgamesh fails to learn the secret from the old man, he returns to his kingdom having gleaned much from Utnapishtim's wisdom.*

The following extract begins with the story of the flood. Comparison with the biblical account in Genesis suggests that the author of one of these works borrowed from the other, or that both drew from an earlier common source.

The Story of the Flood

"You know the city Shurrupak, it stands on the banks of Euphrates? That city grew old and the gods that were in it were old. There was Anu, lord of the firmament, their father, and warrior Enlil their counsellor, Ninurta the helper, and Ennugi watcher over canals; and with them also was Ea. In those days the world teemed, the people multiplied, the world bellowed like a wild bull, and the great god was aroused by the clamour. Enlil heard the clamour and he said to the gods in council, 'The uproar of mankind is intolerable and sleep is no longer possible by reason of the babel.' So the gods agreed to exterminate mankind. Enlil did this, but Ea because of his oath warned me in a dream. He whispered their words to my house of reeds, 'Reed-house, reed-house! Wall, O wall, hearken reed-house, wall reflect; O man of Shurrupak, son of Ubara-Tutu; tear down your house and build a boat, abandon possessions and look for life, despise worldly goods and save your soul alive. Tear down your house, I say, and build a boat. These are the measurements of the barque as you shall build her: let her beam equal her length, let her deck be roofed like the vault that covers the abyss; then take up into the boat the seed of all living creatures.'

"When I had understood I said to my lord, 'Behold what you have commanded I will honour and perform, but how shall I answer the people, the city, the elders?' Then Ea opened his mouth and said to me, his servant, 'Tell them this: I have learnt that Enlil is wrathful against me, I dare no longer walk in his land nor live in his city; I will go down to the Gulf to dwell with Ea my lord. But on you he will rain down abundance, rare fish and shy wild-fowl, a rich harvest-tide. In the evening the rider of the storm will bring you wheat in torrents.'

"In the first light of dawn all my household gathered round me, the children brought pitch and the men whatever was necessary. On the fifth day I laid the keel and the ribs, then I made fast the planking. The groundspace was one acre, each side of the deck measured one hundred and twenty cubits, making a square. I built six decks below, seven in all, I divided them into nine sections with bulkheads between. I drove in wedges where needed, I saw to the punt-poles, and laid in supplies. The carriers brought oil in baskets, I poured pitch into the furnace and asphalt and oil; more oil was consumed in caulking, and more again the master of the boat took into his stores. I slaughtered bullocks for the people and every day I killed sheep. I gave the shipwrights wine to drink as though it were river water, raw wine and red wine and oil and white wine. There was feasting then as there is at the time of the New Year's festival; I myself anointed my head. On the eleventh day the boat was complete.

"Then was the launching full of difficulty; there was shifting of ballast above and below till two thirds was submerged. I loaded into her all that I had of gold and of living things, my family, my kin, the beast of the field both wild and tame, and all the craftsmen. I sent them on board, for the time that Shamash had ordained was already fulfilled when he said, 'In the evening, when the rider of the storm sends down the destroying rain, enter the boat and batten her down.' The time was fulfilled, the evening came, the rider of the storm sent down the rain. I looked out at the weather and it was terrible, so I too boarded the boat and battened her down. All was now complete, the battening and the caulking; so I handed the tiller to Puzur-Amurri the steersman, with the navigation and the care of the whole boat.

"With the first light of dawn a black cloud came from the horizon; it thundered within where Adad, lord of the storm was riding. In front over hill and plain Shullat and Hanish, heralds of the storm, led on. Then the gods of the abyss rose up; Nergal pulled out the dams of the nether waters, Ninurta the war-lord threw down the dykes, and the seven judges of hell, the Annunaki, raised their torches, lighting the land with their livid flame. A stupor of despair went up to heaven when the god of the storm turned daylight to darkness, when he smashed the land like a cup. One whole day the tempest raged, gathering fury as it went, it poured over the people like the tides of battle; a man could not see his brother nor the people be seen from heaven. Even the gods were terrified at the flood, they fled to the highest heaven, the firmament of Anu; they crouched against the walls, cowering like curs. Then Ishtar the sweet voiced Queen of Heaven cried out like a woman in travail: 'Alas the days of old are turned to dust because I commanded evil; why did I command this evil in the council of all the gods? I commanded wars to destroy the people, but are they not my people, for I brought them forth? Now like the spawn of fish they float in the ocean.' The great gods of heaven and of hell wept, they covered their mouths.

"For six days and six nights the winds blew, torrent and tempest and flood overwhelmed the world, tempest and flood raged together like warring hosts. When the seventh day dawned the storm from the south subsided, the sea grew calm, the flood was stilled; I looked at the face of the world and there was silence, all mankind was turned to clay. The

surface of the sea stretched as flat as a roof-top; I opened a hatch and the light fell on my face. Then I bowed low, I sat down and I wept, the tears streamed down my face, for on every side was the waste of water. I looked for land in vain, for fourteen leagues distant there appeared a mountain, and there the boat grounded; on the mountain of Nisir the boat held fast, she held fast and did not budge. One day she held, and a second day on the mountain of Nisir she held fast and did not budge. A third day, and a fourth day she held fast on the mountain and did not budge; a fifth day and a sixth day she held fast on the mountain. When the seventh day dawned I loosed a dove and let her go. She flew away, but finding no resting-place she returned. Then I loosed a swallow, and she flew away but finding no resting-place she returned. I loosed a raven, she saw that the waters had retreated, she ate, she flew around, she cawed, and she did not come back. Then I threw everything open to the four winds, I made a sacrifice and poured out a libation on the mountain top. Seven and again seven cauldrons I set up on their stands, I heaped up wood and cane and cedar and myrtle. When the gods smelled the sweet savour, they gathered like flies over the sacrifice. Then, at last, Ishtar also came, she lifted her necklace with the jewels of heaven that once Anu had made to please her. 'O you gods here present, by the lapis lazuli round my neck I shall remember these days as I remember the jewels of my throat; these last days I shall not forget. Let all the gods gather round the sacrifice, except Enlil. He shall not approach this offering, for without reflection he brought the flood; he consigned my people to destruction.'

"When Enlil had come, when he saw the boat, he was wrath and swelled with anger at the gods, the host of heaven, 'Has any of these mortals escaped? Not one was to have survived the destruction.' Then the god of the wells and canals Ninurta opened his mouth and said to the warrior Enlil, 'Who is there of the gods that can devise without Ea? It is Ea, alone who knows all things.' Then Ea opened his mouth and spoke to warrior Enlil, 'Wisest of gods, hero Enlil, how could you so senselessly bring down the flood?

Lay upon the sinner his sin,
Lay upon the transgressor his transgression,
Punish him a little when he breaks loose,
Do not drive him too hard or he perishes;
Would that a lion had ravaged mankind
Rather than the flood,
Would that a wolf had ravaged mankind
Rather than the flood,
Would that famine had wasted the world
Rather than the flood,
Would that pestilence had wasted mankind
Rather than the flood.

It was not I that revealed the secret of the gods; the wise man learned it in a dream. Now take your counsel what shall be done with him.'

"Then Enlil went up into the boat, he took me by the hand and my wife and made us enter the boat and kneel down on either side, he standing between us. He touched our foreheads to bless us saying, 'In time past Utnapishtim was a mortal man; henceforth he and his wife shall live in the distance at the mouth of the rivers.' Thus it was that the gods took me and placed me here to live in the distance, at the mouth of the rivers."

The Return

Utnapishtim said, "As for you, Gilgamesh, who will assemble the gods for your sake, so that you may find that life for which you are searching? But if you wish, come and put it to the test: only prevail against sleep for six days and seven nights." But while Gilgamesh sat there resting on his haunches, a mist of sleep like soft wool teased from the fleece drifted over him, and Utnapishtim said to his wife, "Look at him now, the strong man who would have everlasting life, even now the mists of sleep are drifting over him." His wife replied, "Touch the man to wake him, so that he may return to his own land in peace, going back through the gate by which he came." Utnapishtim said to his wife, "All men are deceivers, even you he will attempt to deceive; therefore bake loaves of bread, each day one loaf, and put it beside his head; and make a mark on the wall to number the days he has slept."

Then Utnapishtim spoke to Urshanabi the ferryman: "Woe to you Urshanabi, now and for ever more you have become hateful to this harbourage; it is not for you, nor for you are the crossings of this sea. Go now, banished from the shore. But this man before whom you walked, bringing him here, whose body is covered with foulness and the grace of whose limbs has been spoiled by wild skins, take him to the washing-place. There he shall wash his long hair clean as snow in the water, he shall throw off his skins and let the sea carry them away, the beauty of his body shall be shown, the fillet on his forehead shall be renewed, and he shall be given clothes to cover his nakedness. Till he reaches his own city and his journey is accomplished, these clothes will show no sign of age, they will wear like a new garment." So Urshanabi took Gilgamesh and led him to the washing-place, he washed his long hair as clean as snow in the water, he threw off his skins, which the sea carried away, and showed the beauty of his body. He renewed the fillet on his forehead, and to cover his nakedness gave him clothes which would show no sign of age, but would wear like a new garment til he reached his own city, and his journey was accomplished.

Then Gilgamesh and Urshanabi launched the boat on to the water and boarded it, and they made ready to sail away; but the wife of Utnapishtim the Faraway said to him, "Gilgamesh came here wearied out, he is worn out; what will you give him to carry him back to his own country?" So Utnapishtim spoke, and Gilgamesh took a pole and brought the boat in to the bank. "Gilgamesh, you came here a man wearied out, you have worn yourself out; what shall I give you to carry you back to your own country? Gilgamesh, I shall reveal a secret thing, it is a mystery of the gods that I am telling you. There is a plant that grows under the water, it has a prickle like a thorn, like a rose; it will wound your hands, but if you succeed in taking it, then your hands will hold that which restores his lost youth to a man."

When Gilgamesh heard this he opened the sluices so that a sweet-water current might carry him out to the deep-est channel; he tied heavy stones to his feet and they dragged him down to the water-bed. There he saw the plant growing; although it pricked him he took it in his hands; then he cut the heavy stones from his feet, and the sea carried him and threw him on to the shore. Gilgamesh said to Urshanabi the ferryman, "Come here, and see this marvellous plant. By its virtue a man may win back all his former strength. I will take it to Uruk of the strong walls; there I will give it to the old men to eat. Its name shall be 'The Old Men Are Young Again'; and at last I shall eat it myself and have back all my lost youth." So Gilgamesh returned by the gate through which he had come, Gilgamesh and Urshanabi went together. They travelled their twenty leagues and then they broke their fast; after thirty leagues they stopped for the night.

Gilgamesh saw a well of cool water and he went down and bathed; but deep in the pool there was lying a serpent, and the serpent sensed the sweetness of the flower. It rose out of the water and snatched it away, and immediately it sloughed its skin and returned to the well. Then Gilgamesh sat down and wept, the tears ran down his face, and he took the hand of Urshanabi; "O Urshanabi, was it for this that I toiled with my hands, is it for this I have wrung out my heart's blood? For myself I have gained nothing; not I, but the beast of the earth has joy of it now. Already the stream has carried it twenty leagues back to the channels where I found it. I found a sign and now I have lost it. Let us leave the boat on the bank and go."

After twenty leagues they broke their fast, after thirty leagues they stopped for the night; in three days they had walked as much as a journey of a month and fifteen days. When the journey was accomplished they arrived at Uruk, the strong-walled city. Gilgamesh spoke to him, to Urshanabi the ferryman, "Urshanabi, climb up on to the wall of Uruk, inspect its foundation terrace, and examine well the brickwork; see if it is not of burnt bricks; and did not the seven wise men lay these foundations? One third of the whole is city, one third is garden, and one third is field, with the precinct of the goddess Ishtar. These parts and the precinct are all Uruk."

This too was the work of Gilgamesh, the king, who knew the countries of the world. He was wise, he saw mysteries and knew secret things, he brought us a tale of the days before the flood. He went a long journey, was weary, worn out with labour, and returning engraved on a stone the whole story.

The Death of Gilgamesh

The destiny was fulfilled which the father of the gods, Enlil of the mountain, had decreed for Gilgamesh: "In nether-earth the darkness will show him a light: of mankind, all that are known, none will leave a monument for generations to come to compare with his. The heroes, the wise men, like the new moon have their waxing and waning. Men will say, 'Who has ever ruled with might and with power like him?' As in the dark month, the month of shadows, so without him there is no light. O Gilgamesh, this was the meaning of your dream. You were given the kingship, such was your destiny, everlasting life was not your destiny. Because of this do not be sad at heart, do not be grieved or oppressed; he has given you power to bind and to loose, to be the darkness and the light of mankind. He has given unexampled supremacy over the people, victory in battle from which no fugitive returns, in forays and assaults from which there is no going back. But do not abuse this power, deal justly with your servants in the palace, deal justly before the face of the Sun."

The king has laid himself down and will not rise again,
The Lord of Kullab will not rise again;
He overcame evil, he will not come again;
Though he was strong of arm he will not rise again;

He had wisdom and a comely face, he will not come again;
He is gone into the mountain, he will not come again;
On the bed of fate he lies, he will not rise again,
From the couch of many colours he will not come again.

The people of the city, great and small, are not silent; they lift up the lament, all men of flesh and blood lift up the lament. Fate has spoken; like a hooked fish he lies stretched on the bed, like a gazelle that is caught in a noose. Inhuman Namtar is heavy upon him, Namtar that has neither hand nor foot, that drinks no water and eats no meat.

For Gilgamesh, son of Ninsun, they weighed out their offerings; his dear wife, his son, his concubine, his musicians, his jester, and all his household; his servants, his stewards, all who lived in the palace weighed out their offerings for Gilgamesh the son of Ninsun, the heart of Uruk. They weighed out their offerings to Ereshkigal, the Queen of Death, and to all the gods of the dead. To Namtar, who is fate, they weighed out the offering. Bread for Neti the Keeper of the Gate, bread for Ningizzida the god of the serpent, the lord of the Tree of Life; for Dumuzi also, the young shepherd, for Enki and Ninki, for Endukugga and Nindukugga, for Enmul and Ninmul, all the ancestral gods, forbears of Enlil. A feast for Shulpae the god of feasting. For Samuqan, god of the herds, for the mother Ninhursag, and the gods of creation in the place of creation, for the host of heaven, priest and priestess weighed out the offering of the dead.

Gilgamesh, the son of Ninsun, lies in the tomb. At the place of offerings he weighed the bread-offering, at the place of libation he poured out the wine. In those days the lord Gilgamesh departed, the son of Ninsun, the king, peerless, without an equal among men, who did not neglect Enlil his master. O Gilgamesh, lord of Kullab, great is thy praise.

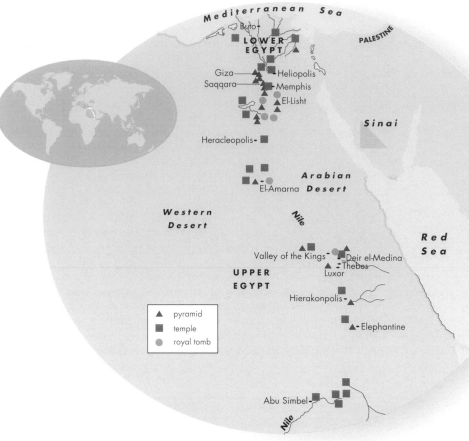

Map 2.1 Ancient Egypt.

Mediterranean Sea

Buto

LOWER EGYPT

PALESTINE

Giza — Heliopolis
Saqqara — Memphis
El-Lisht

Sinai

Heracleopolis

Arabian Desert
El-Amarna

Western Desert

Nile

Red Sea

Valley of the Kings — Deir el-Medina
— Thebes
Luxor

UPPER EGYPT

Hierakonpolis

Elephantine

▲ pyramid
■ temple
● royal tomb

Abu Simbel

Nile

ANCIENT
EGYPT

C H A P T E R   2

Great Sphinx, Giza, Egypt, ca. 2500 B.C.

THE CIVILIZATION OF THE NILE

→

Like its Mesopotamian counterpart (see Chapter 1), ancient Egyptian civilization developed slowly from about 5000 B.C. to approximately 3100 B.C. with no united or central government. There were in essence two independent Egypts: Upper Egypt and Lower Egypt ("Lower" Egypt actually lies north of "Upper" Egypt). Upper Egypt was a narrow strip of land on either side of the Nile River, extending seven hundred miles from the first cataract, or waterfall, in the south to the Nile Delta. Lower Egypt was situated in the northern lands of the fertile Nile Delta where the river branches out and runs into the Mediterranean. Then, around 3100 B.C., the two Egypts were united by the king of Upper Egypt, NARMER, also known as MENES [ME-neez], and it is with this event that Egyptian history is usually said to begin. The event is celebrated in one of the earliest surviving Egyptian stone sculptures, the so-called *Palette of Narmer* (fig. 2.1).

The decoration on the palette—which also served a practical function, since the central depression on the front was used for grinding malachite to produce face paint for ritual purposes—memorialized Narmer's victory over Lower Egypt. The composition is organized into registers or rows according to a **register system**. Each row thus contains a different idea or a separate event, and almost every figure stands on a groundline. There is no setting as such, and as in Sumerian art, Narmer is made larger than everyone else to indicate his importance. The human figure is represented in a unique, Egyptian style. Each part of the body is seen from its most characteristic angle. Thus, heads are in profile, though the eye is depicted frontally. The shoulders are also seen as if from the front, and the waist twisted so that the hips, legs, and feet are seen once again in profile. One foot is generally placed before the other on the groundline. What is particularly remarkable is that these conventions for showing the human figure persisted, especially in depictions of royalty, well into the fourth century B.C.

At the top of the front side of the *Palette of Narmer* are two images of Hathor, the cow-headed goddess who protects the city of the dead. Between the cow-heads is a hieroglyphic representation of Narmer's name (this is explained in the section on hieroglyphics below). On the top row, the King wears the crown of Lower Egypt; on the back of the palette he wears the crown of Upper Egypt. Narmer carries a club and whip, and is followed by a figure holding his sandals and a vase. In front of him is a row of standard bearers. The King is inspecting two rows of decapitated enemies—their heads are between their ankles. These are placed one above the other on the palette, as Egyptian artists indicated distance by showing things that were supposed to be further away above

Figure 2.1 *Palette of Narmer*, front and back, ca. 3100 B.C., First Dynasty, slate, from Hierakonpolis, height 25″ (63.5 cm), Egyptian Museum, Cairo. This celebrated work is simultaneously a functional palette, an exquisite relief carving, and an historical document of the uniting of Lower and Upper Egypt by Narmer, the first pharaoh of the first Egyptian dynasty.

things that were supposed to be closer to the viewer. In the center register, two feline animals with elongated necks, each held on a leash by an attendant, circle the depression used for grinding. Their intertwining probably refers to the unification of the lower and upper parts of the country. On the bottom register, a bull, whose strength probably refers to the strength of Narmer himself, menaces a fallen victim.

On the back, the King himself wears a ceremonial bull's tail. He has taken off his sandals, indicating that he is on holy ground and is about to slay an enemy as a symbol of victory. The hawk or falcon, symbol of the god Horus and of the local god of Upper Egypt, also refers to the successful war. Six papyrus buds (papyrus is a symbol of Lower Egypt) symbolize the number of Narmer's captives—six thousand. The small rectangle is the symbol for a fortified town or citadel.

Historians have traditionally viewed Narmer's victory as the beginning of Egyptian history. The Egyptian priest and historian Manetho of Sebennytos in ca. 300 B.C. was the first to divide three thousand years of Egyptian history into dynasties, or periods of ruling houses. Although subsequent historians have discovered that many of Manetho's facts were incorrect, his divisions—into about thirty dynasties, beginning with Narmer—are still in use. We know very little of the first two dynasties, but beginning with the third, the Egyptian dynasties are grouped into several major periods distinguished by their stability and achievement: the Old Kingdom (2686–2181 B.C., consisting of dynasties 3–6), the Middle Kingdom (2040–1786 B.C., consisting of dynasties 11–14), and the New Kingdom, or Empire (1552–1069 B.C., consisting of dynasties 18–20). So-called "Intermediate" periods of relative instability intervened between each of the "Kingdoms," and the last, "New" Kingdom was followed by a Late Period that concludes around 525 B.C. when Egypt finally lost its independence and was absorbed into the Persian Empire.

Despite times of relative disruption, life was unusually secure in ancient Egypt. The fertility of the Nile Valley, which swept huge amounts of fertile top soil each summer into the Valley from far upstream in the African lake region and the Ethiopian plateau, supported the establishment of a permanent agricultural society. Moreover, the surrounding deserts largely eliminated the fear of invasion. The king, later called "pharaoh," which means "great house," was the absolute ruler and was considered divine. Beneath him was a large class of priests and government bureaucrats. The permanence and stability of life and the highly centralized organization of ancient Egyptian society is reflected in the monumental and essentially permanent architecture of the pyramids. In fact, with few exceptions the art of Egypt remained remarkably consistent in style over three millennia. The unquestioning acceptance of convention is a major characteristic of ancient Egyptian culture. As a result, a sense of order and continuity pervades the history of ancient Egyptian life and art.

HIEROGLYPHICS

The Egyptians had developed a calendar, used irrigation systems, discovered the use of basic metals, and started using hieroglyphics, their writing system, all before 3000 B.C. For centuries scholars thought that the "glyphs" or characters used in hieroglyphics all represented complete ideas rather than individual units of sound. Indeed, until 1822 the actual meaning of the

Timeline 2.1   The development of writing: Sumer and Egypt.

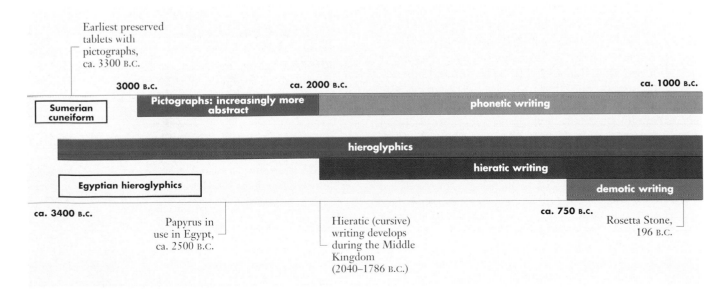

Figure 2.2 Rosetta Stone, 196 B.C., basalt, British Museum, London. The same information is inscribed in three languages: 1. Greek; 2. demotic script, a simplified form of hieroglyphic (the common language of Egypt); and 3. hieroglyphic, a pictographic script. By comparing the languages, hieroglyphics were finally translated in the early nineteenth century.

hieroglyphics was unknown. In that year, however, a Frenchman, Jean François Champollion, deciphered the Rosetta Stone (fig. 2.2). This was a large fragment of basalt that had been found during Napoleon's military campaign in Egypt near the town of Rosetta in the Nile Delta. The stone was inscribed with three languages: Greek, a common (demotic) Egyptian dialect, and Egyptian hieroglyphics. Knowledge of Greek had never been lost, and though the Greek on the stone was imperfect, Champollion was able to read it. When it became apparent that all three languages on the Rosetta Stone expressed almost the same thing—a decree in honor of Ptolemy V (196 B.C.), Champollion was able to establish that the corresponding Egyptian symbols were meant, as in Sumerian, to be read not just symbolically but phonetically as well. Thus, while a pictograph of a fish did indeed represent a "fish," combined with other pictographs it represented the sound of the word "fish," which is pronounced "nar." For instance, the name of the king of a united Egypt, Narmer, consists of the sign for a fish, "nar," and the sign for a chisel, which is pronounced "mer."

RELIGIOUS BELIEFS

Ancient Egyptian religion was polytheistic, involving belief in a profusion of gods. Among the most important gods in Egypt were the cosmic forces, including the sun, earth, sky, air, and water. The Nile was also worshiped as a deity, not surprisingly given its importance to Egyptian life. These forces and aspects of nature were depicted in various forms, often as animals, humans, or as hybrids. For example, the sun was sometimes pictured as a falcon, other times as a falcon-headed man wearing a sun-disk as a crown. Archaeologists and anthropologists have suggested that the human–animal hybrids might be "transitional" deities linking the earlier, more primitive animal cults with the later more "humanized" concept of the divine. Whatever the case may be, animals had enduring significance for the ancient Egyptians, who believed, like the Persians, that the divine was manifest in them. The animal attributes of the gods were often a shorthand for their qualities. For example, Hathor, who was the goddess of joy and love—attributes which the Egyptians viewed the cow as possessing—was depicted as a cow.

Among the most important of the Egyptian gods was Osiris, originally a local god of Lower Egypt, whose worship eventually spread throughout the country. The legend of Osiris's death at the hands of his brother Set, and the search for the corpse by Isis, Osiris's wife, plays an important part in Egyptian mythology, and is connected with Egyptian belief in the afterlife. According to the myth, after Isis discovered her husband's dead body in Phoenicia, she brought it back to Egypt and buried it there. Set came upon the buried body and, enraged, tore the dead Osiris limb from limb, scattering the pieces throughout the country. Again Isis found her dead husband's body parts and buried each where it lay.

The son of Isis and Osiris avenged his father's death by engaging Set in battle and defeating him. However, when Set was brought to Isis, instead of killing him, she set him free. According to some versions of the myth, Osiris was restored to life and became king of the underworld. This myth of Osiris's resurrection later became an important element of the cult of Isis, the most important mother goddess in Egyptian religion, and a significant influence on Egyptian belief in life after death. Egyptian religion shared this belief in an afterlife with Christianity, especially the Christian belief in the resurrection of Jesus.

The Afterlife. Much of Egyptian life appears to have been oriented toward preparing for the hereafter. The Old Kingdom Egyptians believed that the body of the deceased must be preserved if the *ka*, the indestructible essence or vital principle of each person, roughly equivalent to the Christian concept of a soul, were to live on. This is why the Egyptians embalmed and bound their dead. This process of mummification was a complex procedure that involved emptying the bodily cavities of their

Then & Now

THE NILE

"*E*gypt," the Greek historian Herodotus wrote, "is a gift of the Nile." In ancient Egypt, the Nile flooded every summer, from July to October. The floods began when the rain in the central Sudan raised the level of the White Nile, one of its tributaries, followed by the summer monsoon in the Ethiopian highlands raising the level of the Blue Nile, another of its tributaries. By August, these waters reached Egypt proper, flooding the entire basin except for the highest ground, where villages and temples were built, and depositing a deep layer of silt over the fields.

If rainfall came short of expectations, the next season's crops could be dramatically affected; and, sometimes just as disastrous, if rainfall was excessive, villages and farms had to be evacuated. To combat this, gauges, or "Nilometers," were placed upstream on the Nile, and river levels could be compared with records kept over the centuries, so that those downstream might know what to expect each August. In fact, annual taxes were levied according to the height of the river in any particular year.

In 1899, in order to gain greater control over the Nile and help local agriculture, the British financed a dam project on the Nile at Aswan, 550 miles upstream from Cairo. At Aswan, the Nile pours rapidly through steep cliffs and gorges, and it seemed a perfect spot for a dam. When the dam was finished in 1902, it regulated the flow of the river and allowed for an extra ten to fifteen percent of land to be farmed.

Originally 98 feet high, the dam was raised to 138 feet in 1933. By then a giant lake, 140 miles long, stretched behind it, submerging Nubian villages and a large number of monuments for part of the year, most famously the Temple of Isis. In the 1950s, President Nasser proposed another dam, the Aswan High Dam. The endangered Temples of Isis and Hathor were removed to higher ground for safety.

Designed to provide Egypt with predictable and sufficient water resources, as well as providing for the country's electrical needs, the Aswan High Dam has had foreseeable negative impacts as well as beneficial ones. Even the early British dam had stopped the natural flow of silt down the Nile, forcing farmers to rely on chemical fertilizers instead. But worst, perhaps, is the fact that Lake Nasser, behind the Aswan High Dam, has changed rainfall patterns in the region and significantly raised the level of the underground water table far downstream, threatening even the temples of Luxor 133 miles to the north. The Nile today never floods, but this victory has had its costs.

---

organs, refilling them with spices and Arabic gums, and then wrapping the body in layers of bandages. This took seventy days to complete, after which the mummified body was ready for the hereafter, where it would rejoin its *ka*. To be doubly sure of the survival of the *ka*, a likeness of the dead person was made in a hard stone, intended to serve as a backup, should anything happen to the mummy. One Egyptian word for sculptor translates literally as "he who keeps alive." Members of the noble class were mummified and accompanied by their personal likeness; common people were merely buried in holes, though Egyptian religion does appear to have offered them the hope of life in an afterworld, too. The belief in the necessity of housing the dead in a tomb that would endure forever, for the benefit of the *ka* of the deceased, gave rise to Egypt's monumental conception of architecture, exemplified most spectacularly in the pyramids.

THE OLD KINGDOM

The Old Kingdom (2686–2181 B.C.) was a time of political and social stability in Egypt, a stability reflected in its grandest achievements, the great pyramids. While tradition long held that slaves built these giant funerary monuments to the kings, it now seems clear that an entire class of artisans, sculptors, and builders were responsible for them. That a culture could organize such mammoth undertakings and accomplish them with what appears to be the willing cooperation of its people emphasizes the unity of the society as a whole.

ARCHITECTURE

The ancient Egyptian architecture extant today is made of stone. Stone, of many kinds, was abundantly available, and this availability must in part explain the giant proportions of these surviving buildings. Limestone and sandstone were easily quarried in nearby locations along the Nile cliffs. Harder stones such as granite, basalt, and quartzite, were obtained from more remote regions.

Although Egypt lacked timber, other plant materials could be employed instead. For instance, lotus and papyrus reeds, bundled together and matted with clay, were used as building materials. Mud brick, made by mixing mud from the Nile River with straw, shaping the resulting substance into bricks, and then allowing them to dry in the sun, was also used. Mud-brick buildings are cool in the summer, warm in the winter, and, as Egypt has little rainfall, lasted quite well. Homes of peasants were made in this way. The pharaoh's home was also made of mud brick, but was larger, lime-washed, and painted.

Ancient Egyptian architecture is based, like prehistoric Stonehenge (see Chapter 1), on the post and lintel system. Buildings constructed using this system are simple and stable, and subject only to the forces of gravity. The flat roofs produced by this method of construction are suitable for the dry Egyptian climate—a pitched roof is not needed to allow water to run off. The Egyptian builders used no cement, relying instead on the weight of the huge stones to keep the structure together.

Mastabas. The earliest burial places of the Old Kingdom Egyptian nobility were **mastabas**, flat-topped, one-story rectangular buildings with slanted walls. Faced with brick or stone, the mastabas were oriented very specifically, with the four sides facing north, south, east, and west. Surviving mastabas vary in length from 15 to 170 feet, and vary in height from 10 to 30 feet. The interiors have different layouts, but all include the following: (1) A chapel or offering room, used to make offerings to the spirit of the dead person (there are two doors to this room, one real, the other false—to be used by the spirit to collect what was offered); (2) The *serdab* or cellar, a tiny secret room in the center of the mastaba, containing a statue of the dead person (the *ka* statue) and treasure; and (3) A shaft running from the mastaba down through the earth, and into the actual burial chamber located perhaps over a hundred feet below ground level. The plan of the mastaba is believed to be an adaptation of a house plan, which seems logical since the tomb was regarded as the house of the soul.

The Stepped Pyramid of Zoser. The stepped pyramid of King Zoser [ZHO-suh] (Third Dynasty, ca. 2600 B.C.), built on the west bank of the Nile at Saqqara (fig. 2.3), makes clear how the true pyramid developed from the mastaba, as well as suggesting a possible influence from the Sumerian ziggurat (see fig. 1.6). The stepped pyramid is essentially a stack of mastabas; if the steps were filled in, the pure pyramidal form would be achieved. The stepped pyramid was built by IMHOTEP [EE-moh-tep], King Zoser's architect. Imhotep is the first artist/architect in history whose name has been recorded for posterity (his name appears on Zoser's *ka* statue in the *serdab* of the pyramid). Imhotep was also an astronomer, writer, sage, priest, and, above all, a physician who came to be deified as the god of medicine and science.

Figure 2.3 Imhotep, Stepped Pyramid of Zoser, Saqqara, ca. 2600 B.C., Third Dynasty. This stepped pyramid was transitional between the rectangular mastabas (here seemingly placed one on top of another) and the true pyramidal form.

Figure 2.4 Great Pyramids, Giza, built for the Old Kingdom pharaohs Cheops, ca. 2530 B.C., Chefren, ca. 2500 B.C., and Mycerinus, ca. 2470 B.C., Fourth Dynasty, limestone and granite, height of pyramid of Cheops ca. 450 (137.16 m). The permanence of the pyramids, built to last forever, was related to the Egyptian concept of an afterlife and the mummification of their dead.

The six levels of this stepped pyramid rise over two hundred feet high, making it the oldest sizable stone structure in the world. It was once surrounded by courts and buildings, the whole complex enclosed by a wall over thirty feet high. Zoser's *ka* statue was oriented to peer out toward an adjacent funerary temple through two peep-holes in the *serdab*, so that, in the afterlife, he could continue to observe the rituals in his honor.

The Great Pyramids. The first true pyramids—the Great Pyramids at Giza (fig. 2.4) on the west bank of the Nile—were built in the Fourth Dynasty of the Old Kingdom. The three pyramids were built by the pharaohs CHEOPS [KEE-ops], ca. 2530 B.C.; CHEFREN [KEF-run], ca. 2500 B.C.; and MYCERINUS [MIK-ur-EE-nus], ca. 2470 B.C. Because the pharaoh was considered divine and would consequently return to the

Figure 2.5   Great Sphinx, Giza, ca. 2500 B.C., Fourth Dynasty, sandstone, height 65′
(19.81 m). Although similar to the Assyrian guardian monsters in combining a human
head and an animal body (see fig. 1.15), here the facial features are those of the pharaoh,
and the monumental dimensions are intended to impress the viewer with his power.

gods when he died, the pyramids were designed to soar
to heaven. Inscribed on the walls of later pyramids are
descriptions of kings climbing the sides of the pyramids
to join the sun god Ra, and the triangular shape may
itself symbolize the falling rays of the sun.

The Great Pyramids are extraordinary accomplishments of engineering. Satisfying the Egyptian craving for
permanence, the pyramid is one of the most stable geometric forms. The Great Pyramids are built of solid
limestone masonry. The blocks were cut with metal tools
in the eastern Nile cliffs, marked by the stone masons
with red ink to indicate their eventual location, floated
across the river during the seasonal floods, and then
dragged up temporary ramps and moved into their final
position. The largest and oldest pyramid, that of Cheops,
covers thirteen acres and is made up of approximately
2,300,000 blocks, each averaging $2\frac{1}{2}$ tons in weight.
Counting the polished, pearly-white limestone encase-
ment that has now almost entirely disappeared but once
rose some 30 feet above the present apex, the pyramid
was 450 feet high.

With characteristic Egyptian mathematical precision,
the three Great Pyramids are aligned, their corners oriented north, south, east, and west. The proportions of
the base width to the height of the pyramids are eleven
to seven, a proportion that modern research has shown is
inherently pleasing to many people. Inside the pyramids
have systems of corridors that lead to the burial chamber,
where the mummified body of the pharaoh was placed,
along with the rich possessions that were to accompany
him to the afterlife.

SCULPTURE

The Great Sphinx.   Most extant Egyptian sculpture
is religious or political in purpose, and either reflects the
characteristic Egyptian desire for immortality and belief
in an afterlife or demonstrates the pharaoh's power and
divinity. The Great Sphinx (fig. 2.5), which guards the
pyramid of Chefren at Giza, is a majestic and monumental symbol of the king's strength created by combining a
human head (probably an idealized portrait of Chefren

himself, the face of which is now damaged) with the body of a lion. The Great Sphinx is 65 feet high, the scale indicative not only of the power of the pharaoh, but also of the Egyptian love of enormous proportions. The sphinx reappears in Classical Greek mythology, in particular in the story of Oedipus (see Chapter 4).

Statue of Chefren. Egyptian sculptural style is based on a handful of basic forms. With few exceptions, the human figure is shown in a very limited number of poses: sitting on a block, standing with one foot forward, sitting cross-legged on the floor (a less common pose), or kneeling on both knees (quite rare). Further, each of these poses is shown in a specific way and according to certain conventions. These standard poses were established in the Old Kingdom and continued largely unchanged through the three millennia of ancient Egyptian culture. To be original and innovative was not a goal for ancient Egyptian artists.

The seated statue of Chefren (fig. 2.6), builder of the second pyramid at Giza, was carved of diorite around 2500 B.C., during the Fourth Dynasty. It is a good example of a figure seated on a block. The pharaoh is idealized, his individual characteristics minimized, and his features carved in general terms to suggest power and immortality. He is shown to be a majestic, serene ruler.

Chefren wears a simple kilt and a linen headdress. The hawk or falcon, with wings protecting his head, is a symbol of the god Horus or Ra. This indicates that Chefren is the divine son of the god and is under this god's protection. Chefren probably held a scepter, symbol of divine royalty, in his right hand. He wears a false ceremonial beard, which derives from the idea of a pastoral chieftain carrying a crook and a goat-beard from his flock. The earliest kings are shown dressed in this way, which continued to be the ceremonial royal attire.

The carving technique used by ancient Egyptian sculptors can be deduced from unfinished statues. The front and side profiles were drawn on the block of stone. The sculptor cut along these outlines until they intersected. The angles were rounded off, the forms modeled, and the details carved. The result is a solid piece. Given this method of carving, understandably, all Egyptian statues are essentially symmetrical and **frontal** (they are carved to be viewed from one side only), with a rigid verticality to the body, no bending, no twisting, and little sense of animation.

Mycerinus and Khamerernebty. The double statue of the royal couple Mycerinus and his wife, Queen Khamerernebty (fig. 2.7), carved of slate, ca. 2470 B.C., demonstrates the conventions of representing the standing figure. This is believed to have been the first double statue of its kind made; it set a fashion for showing the pharaoh embraced by, or supported by, the queen. The Queen's revealing dress clings to her contours. The King, in addition to a wrapped linen skirt,

wears a ceremonial false beard and headdress, both symbols of rank.

Certain features seen here are characteristic of all Egyptian standing figures: the frontality, the erect stance with the left foot forward and the arms rigidly against the body, and the sense of vigor and dignity. In spite of both having a foot forward, these stiff figures do not appear to be walking, for weight is equally distributed on both feet. This is not a natural stance; people normally stand with their weight equally on both feet, placed side by side, or, more frequently, stand with their weight supported on one foot.

Because such sculpture was funerary in purpose and was placed in the tomb as a precaution against having no home for the *ka* if the mummy were destroyed, permanence was of great importance—the web of stone

---

Figure 2.6 *Chefren*, from Giza, ca. 2500 B.C., Fourth Dynasty, diorite, height $5'6\frac{1}{8}''$ (1.68 m), Egyptian Museum, Cairo. This *ka* statue portrait of Chefren gives a sense of what the face of the Great Sphinx must have looked like. His firmly anchored, seated pose is traditional in Egyptian sculpture.

Figure 2.7   *Mycerinus and Khamerernebty*, from Giza, ca. 2470 B.C., slate, height 4′6½″ (1.38 m), Museum of Fine Arts, Boston. In another common pose the figure stands, one leg forward, yet rigidly erect, weight equally distributed on both feet, and therefore seemingly immobile.

between the Queen and King is intended to prevent breakage. (This statue was actually buried with Mycerinus in his pyramid at Giza.)

Ka-Aper.   In Egyptian sculpture, class distinctions are generally made in visual terms by costume and also by physical type. The nobility are idealized and shown in their physical prime. Those of lower social status, how-ever, were evidently permitted to be depicted by artists as aged, physically imperfect, and individualized.

This is demonstrated by the figure of Ka-Aper (also called Sheikh el-Beled) (fig. 2.8), carved ca. 2500 B.C., in the Fifth Dynasty. It is made of wood. The degree of freedom evident in the pose is the result of working in this material rather than stone and of joining the arms to the torso at the shoulder. The eyes, inset with rock crystal, give a look of bright-eyed vivacity. The figure of Ka-Aper was originally covered with stucco and linen, painted, and also wore a wig. Unlike the sculptures of pharaohs and nobles, he has been individualized and given a fleshy face and full lips. His protruding abdomen shows that he is no longer in his physical prime. Such liberty was afforded to the artist only because Ka-Aper was not of the noble class. The statue was buried in the tomb of Ka-Aper's master: he would continue to serve the king in the spirit world as he had done in life.

Figure 2.8   *Ka-Aper (Sheikh el-Beled)*, from a tomb at Saqqara, ca. 2500 B.C., Fifth Dynasty, wood, height ca. 3′7″ (1.09 m), Egyptian Museum, Cairo. Sculpture such as this reveals that the Egyptians were capable of highly realistic representational accuracy, but valued more stylized forms of representation, especially in their depiction of royalty.

Figure 2.9 *Ti Watching a Hippopotamus Hunt*, ca. 2500–2400 B.C., Fifth Dynasty, painted limestone wall relief, height ca. 3′9″ (1.14 m), Tomb of Ti, Saqqara. Standard conventions of mixed perspective in ancient Egyptian art include depiction of the eye from the front though the head is shown in profile, and the shoulders from the front, though the legs are shown from the side.

RELIEF SCULPTURE AND PAINTING

Relief sculpture and painting were closely linked in ancient Egyptian art, and reliefs were often painted. Clarity in storytelling seems to have been more important to the artist than realistic representation. The style, which includes few non-essentials, is condensed and abbreviated. Figures are shown predominantly from the side, although the eye and shoulders are shown from the front. Clearly, these non-anatomical figures are not drawn directly from models but are instead memory images of a composite view of the human body, each part of the body shown from its most characteristic point of view. Egyptian art does not portray what the eye sees, but what the mind knows is there.

Ti Watching a Hippopotamus Hunt. An engaging depiction known as *Ti Watching a Hippopotamus Hunt* (fig. 2.9) was painted on the wall of Ti's tomb in Saqqara, dated ca. 2500–2400 B.C. in the Fifth Dynasty. Ti does not actually participate in the killing; instead, he stands on a small boat and directs his servants, who hold harpoons. As is traditional, Ti is distinguished from his social inferiors by being made bigger, and his pose combines both frontal and profile views. The water of the Nile River is shown as wavy lines, with fish, hippopotami, and a crocodile shown in profile. The ribbed background represents the papyrus plants along the banks of the Nile. At the top of the painting, where Egyptian artists often put background detail, there are buds and flowers, and birds of various kinds, some of which are being stalked by foxes.

A tomb painting such as this was meant to be seen only by the *ka* of the deceased—in this case the *ka* of Ti, whose position was that of "Curator of Monuments." His own final monument, like those of other high-ranking Egyptians, was painted with murals showing him in the afterlife. However, because the afterlife was believed to be a more blissful continuation of real life, it may be assumed that such tomb paintings documented daily life in ancient Egypt—at least in its more pleasant aspects.

To make such a tomb painting, which is actually a painted low relief, the composition was planned with the aid of guidelines. A grid of squares was used to assure symmetry and proper proportion. The figures were sketched and then the background cut away, leaving the design in low relief. If the stone was rough, a thin layer of plaster was applied. The pigments were probably mixed with a gum binder, and were applied with brushes made of reeds. In contrast to paintings familiar from later Western traditions, there is no illusion of light and shade, and little if any modeling or gradation of tone is used to create an illusion of dimension.

THE MIDDLE KINGDOM
←

After the collapse of the Old Kingdom, a period of political and social turmoil ensued—the first of the so-called "Intermediate" periods of Egyptian history. For over 150 years no single dynasty could reunite the country as Narmer had done a thousand years earlier. Finally, in about 2040 B.C., a prince by the name of Mentuhotep II, from Thebes, managed to subdue both upper and lower parts, inaugurating the Middle Kingdom. The subsequent government was far less centralized than that of the Old Kingdom, with only affairs of national import being left to the king, while much more authority was given to regional governors. Under these new conditions, the country prospered as never before. Large-scale waterworks were undertaken to irrigate higher ground in the Nile basin, and farming yields, which were already higher than anywhere else in the world, increased dramatically.

ARCHITECTURE

During the Middle Kingdom, most building was done in mud brick and, consequently, much of it has now disappeared. A few traces of pyramids remain—they appear to have been similar to those of the Old Kingdom but smaller, and a number of rock-cut tombs, burial places hollowed out of the faces of cliffs, survive. These are to be found at Beni Hasan, located 125 miles up the river from Giza, and were built ca. 2100–1800 B.C., during the Eleventh Dynasty.

The basic plan of these tombs is believed to be similar to that of an Egyptian home of the time. Each tomb consists of a vestibule or portico, a hall with pillars, a private sacred chamber, and a small room at the rear to contain a statue of the dead person. The interior has certain elements that appear to be stone versions of structures originally made of other materials. Thus, although the columns are of stone, the form is that of a bundle of reeds tied together. The ceiling is painted with a diapered and checkered pattern that looks much like the woven matting used to cover houses. The walls are also often painted, though there is a change from Old Kingdom styles discernible here. Instead of military exploits, the paintings now feature depictions of domestic and farm life.

SCULPTURE

During the Middle Kingdom, the traditional types of Egyptian figurative representation were perpetuated—figures sit on a block, stand with one foot forward, or sit cross-legged on the ground. In this conservative society, rigid rules, conventions, and traditions were valued more than innovation. Perhaps the most notable change found during the Middle Kingdom is that the facial expressions no longer have the calm assurance seen in the Old Kingdom; instead, faces look concerned, worried, and

Figure 2.10   Pectoral of Senwosret II, from the tomb of Princess Sithathoryunet, el-Lahun, ca. 1895–1878 B.C., Twelfth Dynasty, gold and semi-precious stones, length $3\frac{1}{4}''$ (8.2 cm), Metropolitan Museum of Art, New York. The scarab beetle that forms part of Senwosret's name is also a symbol of Ra, as well as the idea of rebirth associated with him.

introspective. Perhaps this was in response to the more troubled and uncertain times in which they lived.

One new trend is that Middle Kingdom artists seem to have been particularly adept at making small, highly crafted objects in gold and semi-precious stones. One of the most beautiful is a chest ornament, or pectoral, found at el-Lahun (fig. 2.10). Discovered in the tomb of King Senwosret II's daughter, the pectoral consists of two falcons, which represent Horus, and, above them, two coiled cobras. Between them, in an oval loop, is the hieroglyph for the king's name, consisting of a red sun

Timeline 2.2   Control of ancient Egypt, ca. 3100–1552 B.C.

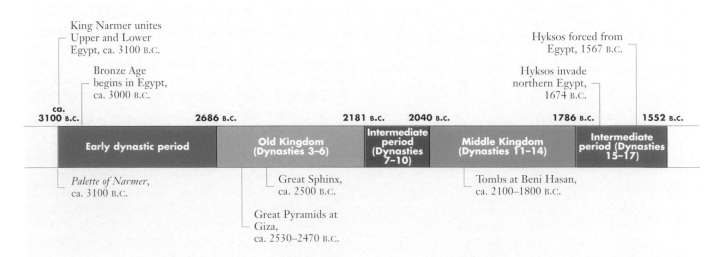

disk, made of carnelian, and below that a scarab beetle. Below this is a male figure helping the falcons support the double arch of palms, a hieroglyph meaning "millions of years." The entire pectoral image may be read, in fact, as a single message. "May Ra grant eternal life to Senwosret II."

THE NEW KINGDOM

After the Middle Kingdom collapsed and a second Intermediate period had begun, an eastern Mediterranean tribe called the Hyksos invaded northern Egypt in 1674 B.C., bringing with them bronze weapons and horse-drawn chariots. For over two hundred years, Egypt was again divided. But beginning in 1552 B.C., the old order was reestablished, perhaps by means of the new technology that the Hyksos tribes had introduced to their unwilling hosts. Certainly, it was through contact with the Hyksos that Egypt entered the Bronze Age. The New Kingdom or Empire that resulted was the most brilliant period in Egyptian history. It was a Theban king, AHMOSE I [AR-mohz], who first pushed back the Hyksos into Palestine, conquering foreign peoples along the way and bringing into being the first Egyptian empire. During the reign of THUTMOSE III [thoot-MOS-uh], (r. 1479–1425 B.C.), the first Egyptian king to be called "pharaoh," Egypt controlled not only the entire Nile basin but the entire eastern Mediterranean coast as far as present-day Syria. The great empire only fell into decline after about 1200 B.C., when it came under the successive influence of Assyria and Libya, and finally lost its independence to Persia in about 525 B.C.

ARCHITECTURE

The New Kingdom established its capital at Thebes, and a great amount of building was done there as well as up and down the length of the Nile. Much art was produced in an exuberant display of wealth and sophistication. Burial was still carried out with great care during the New Kingdom, but the futility of pyramids as places of safe preservation was now fully recognized and accepted. Pyramids, monumental advertisements of the treasures contained within, were irresistibly attractive to robbers and looters—the pyramids were not, after all, very difficult to find. Consequently, nobility and royalty were now buried in chambers hollowed deep into the cliffs on the west bank of the Nile River in the Valley of the Kings at Thebes. Here, rock-cut tombs are approached by corridors up to 500 feet long hollowed straight into the hillside. The entrances were carefully hidden, and rocks were arranged over the entrances to look as if they had fallen there. Many clever tricks and precautions were used by the ancient Egyptians to protect their tombs. In one case, their success lasted until 1922, when the shaft

tomb of Tutankhamen (sometimes referred to popularly today as King Tut) was found nearly intact. All other known tombs were looted in antiquity.

Temple of Queen Hatshepsut. The Old Kingdom has been called the period of the pyramids; the New Kingdom is the time of the temples. The concern for concealment brought about the end of monumental memorial architecture. A mortuary temple of the queen or king would now be built far from the actual tomb. The funerary Temple of Queen Hatshepsut (fig. 2.11), for instance, was built against a cliff at Deir el-Bahari, Thebes, ca. 1480 B.C., early in the Eighteenth Dynasty, by the architect SENMUT [SEN-mut].

In a culture dominated by male kings, HATSHEPSUT [hat-SHEP-sut] (r. 1478–1458 B.C.) is a figure of some significance. At the death of her husband, Thutmose II, she became regent of Thutmose III, her son-in-law. For the next twenty years, Thutmose III,

Figure 2.11 Senmut, Funerary Temple of Queen Hatshepsut, Deir el-Bahari, Thebes, ca. 1480 B.C., early Eighteenth Dynasty. In the New Kingdom, the body of the queen or pharaoh was buried in a different location from the mortuary temple. That of Queen Hatshepsut was built with terraces, ramps, sculptures, and hanging gardens.

who would later conquer so much of the Mediterranean, was at best something like her prime minister, carrying out her will. The size and magnificence of her temple reflect her political importance.

The huge temple is constructed of repeated elements—colonnaded terraces with columnar porticoes (covered walkways), halls, and private chambers. The three terraces are connected by ramps to the cliff, and chambers are cut into the cliff. These chambers are chapels to the god Amen; to the cow-headed goddess Hathor, who protects the city of the dead; to Anubis, the god of embalming, who protects the dead; and to the Queen herself.

Like all Egyptian buildings, the Temple of Hatshepsut was roofed with stone. As a result, the rooms are dense forests of statues and square or sixteen-sided support columns—the distance between these supports had to be small enough to span with a stone lintel. Sculpture was used lavishly; there were perhaps two hundred statues in Hatshepsut's funerary temple. The walls were covered with brightly painted low relief. The terraces, now bare, were once filled with gardens.

Temple of Amen-Mut-Khonsu. In the New Kingdom, many temples dedicated to the gods were built, and the priesthood remained powerful. The Temple of Amen-Mut-Khonsu (the god Amen, and his wife Mut, the goddess of heaven, were the parents of Khonsu) at Luxor (figs. 2.12 and 2.13) is one of the largest Egyptian temples. It was built over a long time

Figure 2.12   Temple of Amen-Mut-Khonsu, Luxor, major construction under Amenhotep III, ca. 1390 B.C., and Ramesses II, ca. 1260 B.C. Like all ancient Egyptian temples, this is constructed on the post and lintel system. Columns and capitals look like plant stalks and buds—perishable forms have been made permanent in stone.

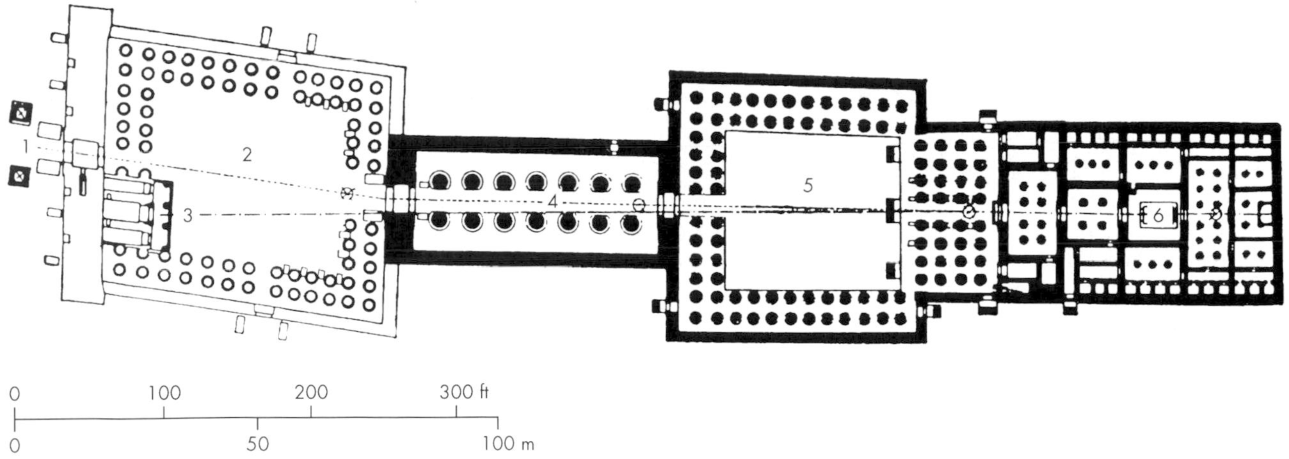

Figure 2.13 Temple of Amen-Mut-Khonsu, Luxor, plan. (1) entrance, (2) first court, (3) earlier sanctuaries, (4) great hall, (5) second court, and (6) sanctuaries of Amon, Mut, and Khonsu.

period, with major construction under Amenhotep III (r. 1390–1352 B.C.), and under Ramesses II (r. ca. 1279–1212 B.C.). The temple, which was considered the home of the god, was based on house plans, but made larger and more permanent. The entire temple complex, like many other Egyptian temple complexes, is organized around a longitudinal axis and is essentially symmetrical.

The complex at Luxor consists of a **pylon** (massive gateway), a forecourt, a hall with pillars, a court, and the actual temple, which is a square room with four columns surrounded by halls, chapels, storerooms, and other rooms. The entire structure was once enclosed by high walls. It was the interior, however, that was most important.

The columns of the temple at Luxor are used for both structure and decorative expression. They are carved in the form of many lotus and papyrus reeds bound together. The effect of the series of bulging convexities is the opposite of the concavities of a fluted Greek column (see Chapter 4). The Egyptian column capitals are bell-shaped, similar to an opening flower bud. Leaves might have been painted on—all Egyptian columns are believed originally to have been painted. In addition, papyrus, lotus, and palm leaves were carved on the walls. This choice of decorative subject may be connected with vegetable fertility and the annual resurgence of life in the Nile Valley brought by the sun and river. Archaeologists have established that there was an annual celebration in which bundles of flowers were hung from the posts of the priests' houses.

Family Homes. Much of what is known today about the ancient Egyptians derives from the study of royal tombs; consequently, knowledge of Egyptian life is largely limited to the uppermost levels of society. But at a few sites the homes of everyday people have been unearthed,

and much can be learnt about the lifestyle of average Egyptians from these excavations.

One such site is Deir el-Medina (fig. 2.14), a village that first came into being in the Eighteenth Dynasty as the permanent residence of the tomb builders and artisans who worked across the Nile at Luxor. The city existed for nearly four centuries, through the Twentieth Dynasty, and grew to contain about seventy homes within its walls and fifty outside. The interior layout of each of the houses is relatively uniform. The entrance room, which opened onto the street, was the household chapel, with niches for offerings and an image of the god Bes, a family deity associated with childbirth. Behind this was the main room, with a high roof supported by one or

Figure 2.14 Site of Deir el-Medina. The main street of the original town can be readily seen bisecting the village.

Figure 2.15 *House and Garden of the Scribe Nakte*, from Nakte's *Book of the Dead*, Eighteenth Dynasty, British Museum, London. In the New Kingdom, papyrus scrolls that would assist the dead in successfully passing their last test before Osiris prior to enjoying the afterlife were often placed among the wrappings of mummified bodies. Called *Books of the Dead*, these scrolls were often beautifully decorated.

more columns. A raised platform on one wall served as both an eating area and bed. Beneath this was a cellar. One or two smaller rooms for sleeping or storage led off the main room. At the back of the house was a walled garden, which also served as the kitchen, with an oven in one corner and, nearby, a grain silo and grinding equipment. A staircase led from this courtyard to the roof of the house, where the cool evening breezes of the Nile could be enjoyed. Furniture might have included stools, tables, wooden beds, and lamps made of pottery, containing oil and a wick.

More lavish homes, with large gardens and pools, were built by Egyptians of higher standing. A painting of the home and garden of the royal scribe Nakte (fig. 2.15), from the Eighteenth Dynasty, shows him with his wife, standing before their home, giving praise to the king and queen. Their garden pool is surrounded by trees, including a grape arbor. The house is whitewashed to reflect the heat better. High up on the wall are windows into the main room, and on the roof are two triangular vents designed to catch the evening breezes. The house is elevated on a platform to protect its mud brick from moisture and flood.

SCULPTURE

Temple of Ramesses II. The perpetuation of Old Kingdom types into the New Kingdom is demonstrated at the Temple of Ramesses II at Abu Simbel (fig. 2.16), built ca. 1260 B.C., during the Nineteenth Dynasty. The facade and inner rooms are cut into the sandstone on the

west bank of the Nile. In theory, the temple was built in honor of the sun; there is a statue of the sun god in a niche in the center of the facade. At the top of this facade is a row of dog-headed apes, sacred to the worship of the rising sun. Reliefs and hieroglyphs on the facade also have to do with the pharaoh Ramesses II's respect for the sun god. But all this is overshadowed by the four enormous statues of Ramesses II, each 65 feet high. (The much smaller figures around and between the legs of these statues are members of his family.)

Despite their giant scale, however, these four statues look very much like the statue of Chefren carved more than 1300 years earlier during the Old Kingdom (see fig. 2.6). The pose, physical type, and attire are the same. When they are compared closely, differences between sculpture of the Old, Middle, and New Kingdoms do become apparent: Old Kingdom sculpture is relatively realistic; New Kingdom sculpture is more elegant. But, in view of the enormous timespan, the differences are minor. Once again Egyptian art is seen to be characterized by remarkable uniformity. Art was, for the most part, created by adhering to and perpetuating established forms.

RELIEF SCULPTURE AND PAINTING

As in the Old and Middle Kingdoms, New Kingdom temples and tombs were decorated with reliefs and paintings. There were some innovations, however. For instance, greater freedom of pose, wider variety of movement, more complex figure groupings, and a more

Figure 2.16 *Four Seated Figures of Ramesses II*, ca. 1260 B.C., Nineteenth Dynasty, Temple of Ramesses II, Abu Simbel, facade. So completely governed by tradition and convention was Egyptian art and culture that, more than 1300 years after Chefren was carved, these figures of Ramesses II demonstrate that the seated figure continued to be depicted in almost exactly the same way.

flowing line are seen in the New Kingdom than in the Old Kingdom. But the basic conventions endure, such as the profile head with frontal eye, the impossible poses, and the arrangement of figures in zones of the register system.

Nobleman Hunting in the Marshes. *Nobleman Hunting in the Marshes* (fig. 2.17), painted around 1400 B.C., in the Eighteenth Dynasty, from a tomb at Thebes, illustrates this new freedom, as well as the perpetuation of long-established tradition in New Kingdom painting. Active and agile, the nobleman holds three birds in one hand and a wand in the other. Equally impressive is the acrobatic accomplishment of the cat sitting on the bending lotus stems, for she catches one bird with her teeth, another with her claws, and a third with her tail. One bird is catching a butterfly. All people, birds, animals, and fish are shown in profile. The birds neatly form a series of overlapping profiles.

Nobleman Hunting in the Marshes deserves comparison with *Ti Watching a Hippopotamus Hunt* (see fig. 2.9), painted a thousand years earlier in the Fifth Dynasty. The similarities are striking. Both men are long-haired and wear white skirts. Both of their boats are *on* rather than *in* the water. The water is thus not shown realistically but functions as a groundline and is rendered as a series of zigzag lines. In both, people are drawn with the heads and legs seen from the sides, but eyes and chest

Figure 2.17 *Nobleman Hunting in the Marshes*, from a tomb at Thebes, ca. 1400 B.C., Eighteenth Dynasty, wall painting on dry plaster, British Museum, London. Created a millennium after the painting of *Ti Watching a Hippopotamus Hunt*, the painting *Nobleman Hunting in the Marshes* demonstrates the remarkable consistency of ancient Egyptian style. Emphasis continued to be placed on the clarity with which information is conveyed rather than on realistic representation.

Connections

DANCE AND MUSIC IN ANCIENT EGYPT

What we know of music and dance in ancient Egypt depends upon two very different kinds of evidence: the visual record of dancers and musicians that we find in surviving reliefs and paintings; and, more problematic, present musical and dance forms that appear to have survived since ancient times. Of the first, we have, for instance, a detail of a wall painting from the tomb of Nebamun at Thebes, dating from about 1400 B.C. (fig. 2.18). It shows four seated women, three of whom are watching and apparently clapping along with music played on a double oboe by the fourth. Two nude figures dance to the music. So relaxed is the scene that most of the conventions of

traditional Egyptian representation have been abandoned.

In addition to the double oboe seen here, Egyptian music made especial use of harps, lutes, and lyres. Surviving paintings often show a blind man playing the harp, but lutes and lyres were apparently played predominantly by women. Single oboes, flutes, and clarinets were also popular, and trumpets were used in military and religious ceremonies. Religious festivals appear to have been primarily musical occasions, and participants routinely danced throughout the celebration.

Many modern Egyptians, as well as scholars, believe that contemporary belly dancing derives from dances such as that seen in the wall painting on the tomb at Nebamun. The belly dance, called the *baladi*, probably originated in

Egypt as part of both fertility and funeral rituals. Like the contemporary belly dance, the original dances may well have been designed to create a sense of physical and emotional rhapsody, and probably utilized many of the same musical effects, particularly ever-increasing rhythmic pace and provocative physical movement.

Figure 2.18 *Musicians and Dancers*, detail of a wall painting from the tomb of Nebamun, Thebes, ca. 1400 B.C., fragment, $11\frac{3}{4} \times 27\frac{1}{4}''$ (29.9 × 69.2 cm), British Museum, London. The two central figures, the one playing the reeds and the seated figure next to her, are remarkable in the way that they face the viewer, a point of view rarely seen in Egyptian painting.

from the front. The continued use of relative size to indicate importance is shown by the small figure between the nobleman's legs; she cannot be interpreted as being in the distant background, for she grasps his shin.

AKHENATEN AND TUTANKHAMEN

The sole significant challenge—and it proved only a temporary deviation—to Egypt's consistency of attitude and approach to representation and design came in the Eighteenth Dynasty under Amenhotep IV [am-EN-oh-TEP] (r. 1352–1336 B.C.). He closed the Amen temples, displaced the sun god Amen-Ra, officially dispensed with the pantheon of other Egyptian gods, and replaced them

all with a monotheistic system, worshiping the single god Aten, the sun disk. In this, his innovations seem to have anticipated the ideas of the later Hebrew and Christian religions. He moved the capital from Thebes to a new city far to the north that he called Akhetaten, "the horizon of Aten," modern-day Tell el-Amarna. He then changed his name as well, to Akhenaten [AK-uhn-AH-tan], which means "He who is effective on behalf of Aten." Just as significantly he transformed the art of Egypt, liberating it from convention. Akhenaten has been described as a mystic, a dreamer, a religious fanatic and pacifist, who was not sufficiently materialistic to be a ruler. Egypt, set in thousands of years of tradition, did not easily accept his revolutionary ideas. In particular,

Figure 2.19 *Akhenaten, Nefertiti, and Their Children Worshiping the Sun*, ca. 1348–1336 B.C., Eighteenth Dynasty, painted limestone relief, $12\frac{1}{4} \times 15\frac{1}{4}$″ (31.1 × 38.7 cm), Staatliche Museen zu Berlin, Preussischer Kulturbesitz, Ägyptisches Museum. The only significant break in the continuity of Egyptian life were the changes—political, religious, and artistic—instituted by the pharaoh Akhenaten in the Eighteenth Dynasty.

these posed a serious challenge to the influence of the priests. When Akhenaten died, Egypt thus returned to a polytheistic faith, the capital returned to Thebes, and artists began to return to the old conventions.

Akhenaten, Nefertiti, and Their Children Worshiping the Sun. This painted limestone relief (fig. 2.19), dated 1348–1336 B.C., represents an extraordinary change from traditional Egyptian art. Akhenaten and his Queen, Nefertiti, play with their three daughters, who are shown as miniature adults. Akhenaten even kisses one of his children, a rare display of affection in Egyptian art. These people are shown in easy poses. More notable, however, are their physical distortions—long necks and skulls, protruding abdomens, and large hips, presumably shown to create a likeness. Although royalty, Akhenaten and his family are not idealized, perfect physical types. This departs from the rigidity and formality of earlier Egyptian art. Royalty is now depicted in domestic situations, casually, intimately. Rather than stressing dignity, this art is playful and informal.

All depictions of Akhenaten show this peculiarly exaggerated physique, distorted to the point of caricature. But as all depictions show the same distortion, it cannot have been totally due to the artists' creativity. In fact, if the bones that archaeologists believe to be his actually are his, Akhenaten may have suffered from a rare medical condition that results in the elongated skull, broad hips, and slouching posture with which he was routinely portrayed.

Queen Nefertiti. Akhenaten's wife, the beautiful Queen Nefertiti (fig. 2.20), was recorded in a lifesize portrait in 1348–1336 B.C., carved of limestone and painted, the eyes inlaid with rock crystal. Discovered in 1912 in the studio of Thutmosis, Akhenaten's chief sculptor, this individualized portrait is characteristic of the more informal, relaxed style of Akhenaten's reign. The carving of this charming portrait is sensitive and refined, and its beauty is probably not exaggerated. Surviving texts refer to the Queen as "Fair of Face," "Great of Love," and "Endowed with Favors."

Figure 2.20 *Queen Nefertiti*, ca. 1348–1336 B.C., Eighteenth Dynasty, painted limestone, rock crystal eyes, height 20″ (50.8 cm), Staatliche Museen zu Berlin, Preussischer Kulturbesitz, Ägyptisches Museum. Although ideals of beauty have changed greatly throughout time, the appeal of Nefertiti, elegant wife of Akhenaten, endures.

Queen Tiy. Nefertiti contrasts dramatically with Akhenaten's mother, Queen TIY [TIE], whose likeness is known from a miniature portrait head (fig. 2.21). Probably the work of Yuti, her personal sculptor who had his studio within the precincts of the royal palace, her powerful and determined expression is in keeping with the realism favored by her son. Queen Tiy was, in fact, a powerful political force, who as chief wife of Akhenaten's father, Amenhotep III, exerted considerable influence throughout the Eighteenth Dynasty.

Tomb of Tutankhamen. Akhenaten's successor was TUTANKHAMEN [too-tan-KAH-moon] (r. ca. 1336–1327 B.C.), at the end of the Eighteenth Dynasty. Tutankhamen was married to one of the daughters of Akhenaten and Nefertiti. However, as king, Tutankhamen disavowed his parents-in-law and returned to the worship of Amen, reestablishing the capital at Thebes. But Tutankhamen's fame today derives from the discovery of his tomb, nearly intact and containing an extraordinary treasure, in the early 1920s by the British archaeologist Howard Carter. Tutankhamen's tomb, which was uncovered in the Valley of the Kings near Thebes, consisted of a corridor-like shaft leading to four decorated rooms.

From this tomb comes the cover of Tutankhamen's coffin, or sarcophagus (fig. 2.22), made of polished gold about a quarter of an inch thick, inlaid with enamel and semi-precious stones, $72\frac{7}{8}$ inches long, and weighing 250 pounds. This alone makes clear why tombs were sacked. Tutankhamen was probably between eighteen and twenty years old when he died from a blow to the head. Despite the brevity of his reign, this minor ruler was buried in a sarcophagus that contained three coffins, one inside another, the outer two of wood covered with gold sheets, and the innermost one made of solid gold.

Timeline 2.3   Control of ancient Egypt, 1552–525 B.C.

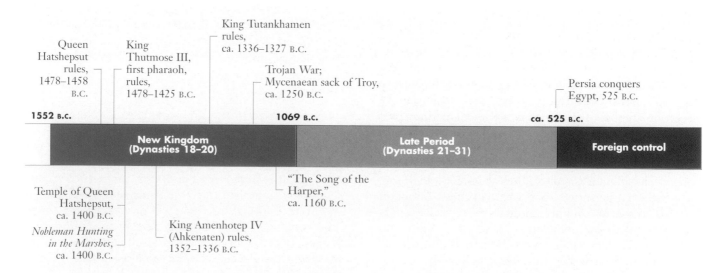

Queen Hatshepsut rules, 1478–1458 B.C.

King Thutmose III, first pharaoh, rules, 1478–1425 B.C.

King Tutankhamen rules, ca. 1336–1327 B.C.

Trojan War; Mycenaean sack of Troy, ca. 1250 B.C.

Persia conquers Egypt, 525 B.C.

1552 B.C.

1069 B.C.

ca. 525 B.C.

New Kingdom (Dynasties 18–20)   **Late Period (Dynasties 21–31)**   **Foreign control**

Temple of Queen Hatshepsut, ca. 1400 B.C.

Nobleman Hunting in the Marshes, ca. 1400 B.C.

King Amenhotep IV (Ahkenaten) rules, 1352–1336 B.C.

"The Song of the Harper," ca. 1160 B.C.

Figure 2.21 *Queen Tiy*, from Kom Medinet Ghurab, ca. 1390–1352 B.C., Eighteenth Dynasty, boxwood, ebony, glass, gold, lapis lazuli, cloth, clay, and wax, height $3\frac{3}{4}''$ (9.4 cm), Staatliche Museen zu Berlin, Preussischer Kulturbesitz, Ägyptisches Museum. Other surviving sculptures of Queen Tiy, notably a stone head found in Sinai, portray her with the same determined expression.

LITERATURE: LYRIC POETRY

The literature of the ancient Egyptians is not as readily available as their art and architecture. Less literature has survived, and most of what remains exists only in scattered fragments. The oldest Egyptian poems, dating from ca. 2650–2050 B.C., are religious. Most are incantations and invocations to the gods to aid the departed Egyptian kings. But one of the most important Egyptian religious poems is the pharaoh Akhenaten's "Hymn to the Sun." In this poem, Akhenaten presents himself as the son of Aten, and then describes the sun's rising: "At dawn you rise shining in the horizon, you shine as Aten in the sky and drive away darkness by sending forth your rays. The Two Lands [Lower and Upper Egypt] awake in festivity, and people stand on their feet, for you have raised them up. They wash their bodies, they take their garments, and their arms are raised to praise your rising. The whole world does its work."

Other ancient Egyptian poems of interest include "The Song of the Harper" (ca. 1160 B.C.) and a series of lyrics composed between ca. 2000 and 1000 B.C.,

Figure 2.22 Inner coffin of Tutankhamen's sarcophagus, ca. 1336–1327 B.C., polished gold, inlaid with enamel and semi-precious stones, height $6'\frac{7}{8}''$ (1.85 m), weight 250 lbs., Egyptian Museum, Cairo. Akhenaten's successor, popularly known today as King Tut, was a minor ruler who died young. Yet the splendor of his burial indicates the care lavished upon the burial of royalty, as well as the reason why tombs were plundered by grave robbers.

Cross Currents

ANCIENT EGYPT IN THE EUROPEAN IMAGINATION

Of the "Seven Wonders of the World" first listed by Greek authors in the second century B.C., only the pyramids at Giza survive. Perhaps because of this, they have come to symbolize in Western consciousness what is perhaps the closest thing to eternity on earth.

As a twelfth-century Arab historian put it: "All things fear time, but time fears the pyramids." When Napoleon Bonaparte attacked Egypt in 1798, in order to cut off England's lifeline to India, he inspired his troops on the day of one of the most famous battles in history, the Battle of the Pyramids, with the words: "Soldiers, forty centuries look down upon you."

The Frenchman Hubert Robert's 1760 painting *The Pyramid* (fig. 2.23) captures another of its aspects: not only was it eternal, it was colossal. Robert's painting overstates its scale: the figures that approach it are minuscule and the pyramid itself disappears off the canvas into the clouds and airy mists, like a Himalayan peak, as if the painting cannot contain it. But Robert does capture something of its emotional power. Unable to perceive its bounds, we realize we are in the presence of something that approaches, imaginatively at least, the infinite—what eighteenth-century writers would call the "sublime."

The sublime is both spiritual—an earthly manifestation of God—and terrifying, because it makes our own being seem so insignificant and ephemeral. Probably no writer in the nineteenth century summed up the ability of Egyptian art to so move us better than the English poet Percy Bysshe Shelley, whose poem "Ozymandias" is based on a statue in the mortuary temple of Ramesses II:

Figure 2.23   Hubert Robert, *The Pyramid*, 1760, oil on wood, 4 × 4 2¼≤ (1.22 × 1.28 m), Smith College Museum of Art, Northampton, Massachusetts. Robert's work was painted amidst a general revival in France of monumental Egyptian architecture, particularly of funerary monuments, many of which were proposed in competitions organized by the French government, but none of which was ever built.

I met a traveler from an antique land,
Who said: Two vast and trunkless legs of stone
Stand in the desert … Near them, on the sand,
Half sunk, a shattered visage lies, whose frown,
And wrinkled lip, and sneer of cold command,
Tell that its sculptor well those passions read
Which yet survive, stamped on these lifeless
    things,
The hand that mocked them, and the heart
    that fed,

And on the pedestal these words appear:
"My name is Ozymandias, king of kings:
Look on my works, ye Mighty, and despair!"
Nothing beside remains. Round the decay
Of that colossal wreck, boundless and bard
The lone and level sands stretch far away.

especially the love poems written during the late Rameside period (ca. 1300–1100 B.C.). The harper's song differs from Egyptian religious poetry in emphasizing the joys and pleasures of life. The spirit of the poem anticipates later Roman poetry that emphasizes the enjoyment of life's pleasures in an attitude of *carpe diem* (seize the day). As with later Greek and Roman love poetry, and the nearly equally ancient love poetry of the Hebrews (the biblical Song of Songs), ancient Egyptian love poems display a wide range of mood and feeling. Written on limestone as well as on papyrus, these ancient love poems reflect attitudes that appear strikingly modern.

Love, how I'd love to slip down to the pond

Love, how I'd love to slip down to the pond,
    bathe with you close by on the bank.
Just for you I'd wear my new Memphis swimsuit,
    made of sheer linen, fit for a queen—
Come see how it looks in the water!   *5*

Couldn't I coax you to wade in with me?
    Let the cool creep slowly around us?
Then I'd dive deep down
    and come up for you dripping,
Let you fill your eyes   *10*
    with the little red fish that I'd catch.

And I'd say, standing there tall in the shallows:
Look at my fish, love,
    how it lies in my hand,
How my fingers caress it,   *15*
    slip down its sides …

But then I'd say softer,
    eyes bright with your seeing:
        A gift, love, No words.
Come closer and   *20*
    look, it's all me.

← AKHENATEN

Hymn to the Sun

The text of the "Hymn to the Sun" was found inscribed on the walls of a tomb prepared for a courtier. It was probably chanted at fertility rituals and celebrations honoring Egypt's rulers. However, it is also something of a revolutionary statement of belief. The poem was written by the pharaoh Akhenaten himself and is regarded as the fullest expression of Atenism, the monotheistic religious system with which Akhenaten replaced earlier Egyptian polytheism and which seems to have anticipated the ideas of the later Hebrew and Christian religions.

I

When in splendor you first took your throne
    high in the precinct of heaven,
    O living God,
        life truly began!
Now from eastern horizon risen and streaming,   *5*
    you have flooded the world with your beauty.
You are majestic, awesome, bedazzling, exalted,
    overlord over all earth,
        yet your rays, they touch lightly, compass the lands
    to the limits of all your creation.
There in the Sun, you reach to the farthest of those   *11*
    you would gather in for your Son,°
        whom you love;

---

¹² *your Son:* Akhenaten.

← EGYPTIAN LYRIC POETRY

The very earliest Egyptian poems, dating from 2650–2050 B.C., are religious. However, it is the secular poems from the next millennium, 2000–1000 B.C., that are of greater interest. The "Song of the Harper" emphasizes the pleasures of life, anticipating the spirit of carpe diem of Roman poetry. A series of love lyrics from the Rameside period (ca. 1300–1100 B.C.) also survives. These ancient love poems display a wide variety of feeling and mood. In the example printed here, "Love, how I'd love to slip down to the pond," a female speaker urges her lover to take action.

Song of the Harper

I

All who come into being as flesh
    pass on, and have since God walked the earth;
        and young blood mounts to their places.

The busy fluttering souls and bright transfigured spirits
    who people the world below   *5*
        and those who shine in the stars with Orion,
They built their mansions, they built their tombs—
    and all men rest in the grave.

So set your home well in the sacred land
    that your good name last because of it;   *10*
Care for your works in the realm under God
    that your seat in the West be splendid.

The waters flow north, the wind blows south,
    and each man goes to his hour.

II

So, seize the day! hold holiday!   *15*
    Be unwearied, unceasing, alive,
        you and your own true love;
Let not your heart be troubled during your sojourn on earth,
    but seize the day as it passes!

Put incense and sweet oil upon you,   *20*
    garlanded flowers at your breast,
While the lady alive in your heart forever
    delights, as she sits beside you.

Grieve not your heart, whatever comes;
    let sweet music play before you;   *25*
Recall not the evil, loathsome to God,
    but have joy, joy, joy, and pleasure!

O upright man, man just and true,
    patient and kind, content with your lot,
        rejoicing, not speaking evil:—
Let your heart be drunk on the gift of Day   *31*
    until that day comes when you anchor.

Though you are far, your light is wide upon earth;
        and you shine in the faces of all   *15*
                who turn to follow your journeying.

II

When you sink to rest below western horizon
        earth lies in darkness like death,
Sleepers are still in bedchambers, heads veiled,
        eye cannot spy a companion;   *20*
All their goods could be stolen away,
        heads heavy there, and they never knowing!
Lions come out from the deeps of their caves,
        snakes bite and sting;
Darkness muffles, and earth is silent: *25*
        he who created all things lies low in his tomb.

III

Earth-dawning mounts the horizon,
        glows in the sun-disk as day:
You drive away darkness, offer your arrows of shining,
        and the Two Lands° are lively with morningsong.
Sun's children awaken and stand,   *31*
        for you, golden light, have upraised the sleepers;
Bathed are their bodies, who dress in clean linen,
        their arms held high to praise your Return.
Across the face of the earth   *35*
        they go to their crafts and professions.

IV

The herds are at peace in their pastures,
        trees and the vegetation grow green;
Birds start from their nests,
        wings wide spread to worship your Person;   *40*
Small beasts frisk and gambol, and all
        who mount into flight or settle to rest
                live, once you have shone upon them;
Ships float downstream or sail for the south,
        each path lies open because of your rising;   *45*
Fish in the River leap in your sight,
        and your rays strike deep in the Great Green
                Sea.°

V

It is *you* create the new creature in Woman,
        shape the life-giving drops into Man,
Foster the son in the womb of his mother,   *50*
        soothe him, ending his tears;
Nurse through the long generations of women
        to those given Air,°
        you ensure that your handiwork prosper.
When the new one descends from the womb   *55*
        to draw breath the day of its birth,
You open his mouth,

make him aware of life newly given,
        for you determine his destiny.

VI

Hark to the chick in the egg,   *60*
        he who speaks in the shell!
You give him air within
        to save and prosper him;
And you have allotted to him his set time
        before the shell shall be broken;   *65*
Then out from the egg he comes,
        from the egg to peep at his natal hour!
        and up on his own two feet goes he
                when at last he struts forth therefrom.

VII

How various is the world you have created,   *70*
        each thing mysterious, sacred to sight,
O sole God,
        beside whom is no other!
You fashioned earth to your heart's desire,
        while you were still alone,   *75*
Filled it with man and the family of creatures,
        each kind on the ground, those who go upon feet,
                he on high soaring on wings,
The far lands of Khor and Kush,°
        and the rich Black Land of Egypt.   *80*

VIII

And you place each one in his proper station,
        where you minister to his needs;
Each has his portion of food,
        and the years of life are reckoned him.
Tongues are divided by words,   *85*
        natures made diverse as well,
Even men's skins are different
        that you might distinguish the nations.

IX

You make Hapy,° the Nile, stream through the
                underworld,
        and bring him, with whatever fullness you will,   *90*
To preserve and nourish the People
        in the same skilled way you fashion them.
You are Lord of each one,
        who wearies himself in their service,
Yet Lord of all earth, who shines for them all,   *95*
        Sun-disk of day, Great Lightener!
All of the far foreign countries—
        you are the cause they live,
For you have put a Nile in the sky
        that the might descend upon them in rain—   *100*

---

30 *Two Lands:* Upper and Lower Egypt. 47 *Great Green Sea:* the Mediterranean. 53 *Air:* life.

79 *Khor and Kush:* Kush is in the Nubian region in the Sudan, which is to the south. Khor is Syro-Palestine in the northeast.
89 *Hapy:* God of the Nile's flooding.

He makes waves on the very mountains
        like waves on the Great Green Sea
    to water their fields and their villages.

X

How splendidly ordered are they,   *104*
        your purposes for this world,
    O Lord of eternity, Hapy in heaven!
Although you belong to the distant peoples,
    to the small shy beasts
        who travel the deserts and uplands,
        Yet Hapy, he comes from Below   *110*
        for the dear Land of Egypt as well.
And your Sunlight nurses each field and meadow:
    when you shine, they live,
        they grow sturdy and prosper through you.
You set seasons to let the world flower and flourish—
    winter to rest and refresh it,   *116*
        the hot blast of summer to ripen;
And you have made heaven far off
    in order to shine down therefrom,   *119*
        in order to watch over all your creation.

XI

You are the one God,
        shining forth from your possible incarnations
           as Aten, the Living Sun,
Revealed like a king in glory, risen in light,
    now distant, now bending nearby.   *125*
You create the numberless things of this world
        from yourself, who are One alone—
        cities, towns, fields, the roadway, the River;
And each eye looks back and beholds you

to learn from the day's light perfection.   *130*
O God, you are in the Sun-disk of Day,
    Over-Seer of all creation
                —your legacy
        passed on to all who shall ever be;
For you fashioned their sight, who perceive your
        universe,   *135*
    that they praise with one voice
        all your labors.

XII

And you are in my heart;
        there is no other who truly knows you
           but for your son, Akhenaten.   *140*
May you make him wise with your inmost counsels,
        wise with your power,
        that earth may aspire to your godhead,
           its creatures fine as the day you made them.
Once you rose into shining, they lived;   *145*
    when you sink to rest, they shall die.
For it is you who are Time itself,
    the span of the world;
        life is by means of you.

Eyes are filled with Beauty   *150*
        until you go to your rest;
All work is laid aside
        as you sink down the western horizon.
Then, Shine reborn! Rise splendidly!
    my Lord, let life thrive for the King!   *155*
For I have kept pace with your every footstep
    since you first measured ground for the world.
Lift up the creatures of earth for your Son
    who came forth from your Body of Fire!

Map 3.1   The Aegean world.

LEMNOS
Troy
Iolkos
Aegean
LESBOS
Mytilene
ASIA
EUBOEA
PHOCIS
MINOR
Orchomenos - Gla
- Thebes
CHIOS
BOEOTIA
CEPHALONIA
ATTICA
Ephesus
ACHAEA
Athens
ANDROS
Miletus
ZACYNTHUS
Mycenae -
- Tiryns
- Asine
PELOPONNESE
CYCLADES
Pylos Nichoria
- Menelaion
NAXOS
LACONIA
Phylakopi
Pavlopetri
MELOS
CYTHERA
Akrotiri
THERA
Mediterranean Sea

Khania
Knossos Mallia
CRETE
Gournia Zakro
Vathypetro
Ayia Triada - Phaistos Vasiliki

Aegean Culture and the Rise of Ancient Greece

Exekias, *Ajax and Achilles*, 550–525 B.C., Vatican Museums, Rome.

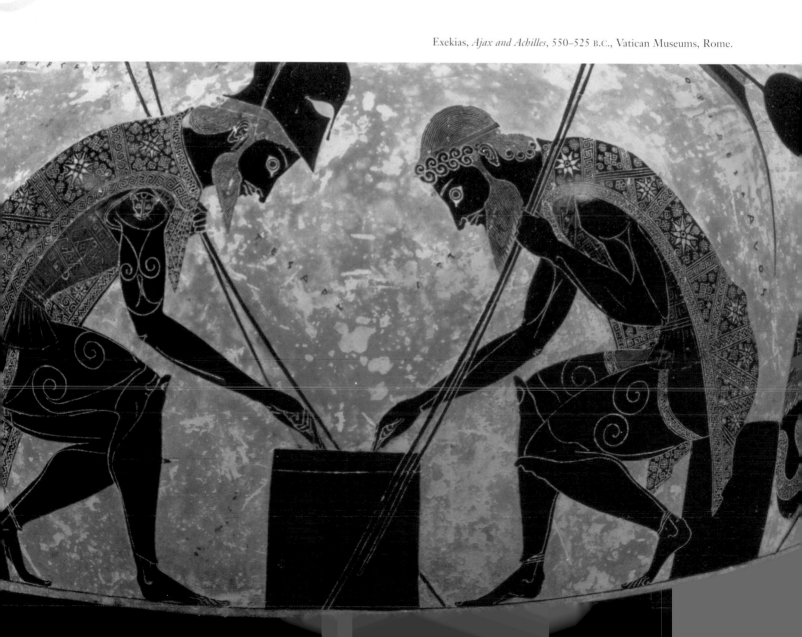

AEGEAN CULTURES

→

We now know that between approximately 3000 and 1100 B.C., prior to the rise of the Greek city-states, a number of cultures flourished along the coasts of the eastern Mediterranean and on the islands in the Aegean Sea. However, until about 1870, the existence of these cultures—Troy in Anatolia, Mycenae on mainland Greece, and Knossos on Crete—was considered more likely than not the creation of one poet's imagination. For the principal evidence for these great early cultures was to be found in Homer's Greek epics, *The Iliad* and *The Odyssey*. But when the archaeologist HEINRICH SCHLIEMANN [SHLEE-man] (1822–1890) first uncovered Helen's Troy and, subsequently, Agamemnon's Mycenae, and then, in 1899, when SIR ARTHUR EVANS (1851–1941) uncovered the labyrinth of Knossos on Crete, it became clear that the world of Homer's *Iliad* and *Odyssey* had really existed. More important still, it seemed that the stories and myths from

---

Figure 3.1   Statuette of a woman, third millennium B.C. marble, height $24\frac{3}{4}''$ (62.9 cm), Metropolitan Museum of Art, New York. This flattened physique forms a striking contrast to the bulbous body of the prehistoric *Woman of Willendorf* (see fig. 1.3). Yet this Cycladic figure, and others like it, are also thought to have been connected with early beliefs about human fertility.

these Bronze Age civilizations were, at some deep and important level, the basis of later Greek traditions and beliefs. Three civilizations rose to dominance in quick succession in this early Aegean period: the Cycladic culture on the Cyclades islands, the Minoan culture centered on the island of Crete, and the Mycenaean or Helladic culture on the Greek mainland.

Early Aegean culture was dominated by one important geographical factor, the Aegean Sea itself, which was dotted with over a thousand islands and could be sailed with confidence long before the development of sophisticated navigational equipment. What appears to have been a rich maritime culture developed. The Minoans certainly traded with mainland Greece, especially with the city of Mycenae. There is also evidence of commerce with Egypt. Surviving tablets found at Knossos on Crete are written in two different scripts known as Linear A and Linear B. The first of these remains undeciphered, although there are indications that it may have originated in Phoenicia, present-day Lebanon. Such linguistic influence again suggests trade contacts. The second script, Linear B, which has been dated to before 1460 B.C., was deciphered in 1952 by an English scholar, who discovered it to be an early version of Greek. It has also been found on similar tablets across Greece and at Mycenae itself. Two important conclusions can be drawn from this. In the first place, Mycenaeans must have occupied Crete by 1460 B.C. Second, and more important, is the suggestion that by around this date the Aegean cultures shared a common, Greek language.

CYCLADIC CULTURE

The most ancient of the Aegean civilizations developed in the Cyclades in the second half of the third millennium B.C. (2500–2000 B.C.). It continued to thrive, probably under the influence of the Minoan civilization in Crete, to the south, until the middle of the second millennium B.C. It has been suggested that the "lost" island of Atlantis may have been the Cycladic island of Thera, the majority of which disappeared into the sea in 1623 B.C. when the five-thousand-foot volcano situated on it erupted. Evidence of the eruption has recently been found in tree rings as far away as Ireland and California, as well as deep in the ice core of Greenland. On one of the remaining sections of the original island, at a site named Akrotiri, excavations that were initiated in 1967 have revealed a rich and apparently highly inventive civilization buried under fifteen feet of ash.

Until this site was explored, however, the majority of known artifacts from the Cyclades were statuettes found in tombs. Many of these figures were carved of marble in Cycladic workshops during the third and second millennia B.C. They range in size from a few inches to lifesize. The marble statuette of a nude female with her arms crossed over her body (fig. 3.1) is characteristic of most

Figure 3.2 *Landscape*, wall painting with areas of modern reconstruction, from Akrotiri, Thera, Cyclades, before 1630–1500 B.C., National Archaeological Museum, Athens. Recently discovered at Akrotiri on Thera, these murals show an affection for nature—though the subjects are by no means copied literally. Rather, nature's forms have been translated by the painters into a colorful, rhythmic decoration. The result is quite unlike anything else known from antiquity.

extant examples of Cycladic art. The only indication of attire or jewelry are lines incised at the neck. Although the legs are together and straight, the figure was not made to stand up. These Cycladic figures are presumed in general to represent the Mother Goddess, bringer of fertility and the major deity in the ancient Aegean. Since they were often buried with people, they are also presumed to have had a part in the funeral ritual.

The non-naturalistic anatomy of the carving is characteristically Cycladic. An angular torso is flattened and two-dimensional, while a cylindrical neck supports an oval head, flattened on top, with receding forehead. The eyes would probably have been painted on, and lips and ears may have been carved in relief. But the most notable facial feature is the particularly prominent nose. The proportions of the Cycladic figures vary somewhat—some are rounder, others more angular, the shoulders and hips broader or narrower. The pose, however, is unvarying. The refined geometric simplicity of these statuettes appears almost modern. A sort of minimalist approach to the body is evidenced by these extremely simple, yet extremely sophisticated, figures.

A number of wall paintings recently discovered at Akrotiri on Thera include a landscape unlike any other known to have survived from antiquity (fig. 3.2).

Swallows fly above a landscape consisting of a series of jagged peaks, with giant plumes of red lilies erupting from their tops and sides. It is thought that the art of wall painting was probably brought to the Cyclades from Crete soon after 1700 B.C., but nothing like this work is known in Minoan culture.

MINOAN CULTURE

According to later Greek myth, the Minoan civilization on the island of Crete was created by an offspring of Zeus, the chief deity in the Greek pantheon of the gods. Zeus's main characteristics include his ability to change his physical form and his attraction to mortal women. On one occasion, Zeus is said to have fallen in love with Europa, a Phoenician princess. He therefore transformed himself into a beautiful white bull and approached Europa who, entranced by the creature, climbed onto its back. In a scene depicted by the Venetian painter Titian in the sixteenth-century painting *The Rape of Europa* (see fig. 15.23), Zeus immediately flew up into the sky with his prey. According to the myth, the product of their union was King Minos, the founder of the civilization on Crete. It was after this king that the archaeologist Sir Arthur Evans later named

Minoan civilization. Evan's archaeological work established that life had flourished on the island between around 2800 B.C. and 1400 B.C., a period that Evans subdivided into three main phases—Early Minoan, Middle Minoan, and Late Minoan. It was with the beginning of the Middle Minoan phase, ca. 2000 B.C., that the civilization appeared to have developed significantly, at which time a series of large urban centers grew up on the island at Knossos, Phaistos, Mallia, and Zakro.

The Minoans were sailors and traders. Crete, which is the largest of the Aegean islands, nearly 150 miles in length, was provided with natural protection by the sea; life was secure on this idyllic island. Consequently military subjects are rarely found in Minoan painting and sculpture, and Minoan architecture is not fortified. Moreover, the extant Minoan architecture is largely domestic and secular, for although religion appears to have played an important cultural role, temples do not seem to have been a part of it. The most significant architectural remains are generally referred to as palaces, although they appear to have served a wide variety of functions beyond simply housing the ruling families.

The Palace of Minos. The major surviving Minoan architectural monument is the so-called Palace of Minos at Knossos (fig. 3.3), built between 1700 and 1300 B.C. The palace was continually modified—parts were added, demolished, and reconstructed, until the arrangement seemed to be without a plan. It was also enormous, once covering six acres and including 1300 rooms. Built around a central courtyard and several smaller courtyards, the palace is a seemingly arbitrary accumulation of rooms linked together by corridors, highly irregular and confused in layout (fig. 3.4). The Greeks later referred to

Figure 3.3   Palace of Minos, Knossos, Crete, ca. 1700–1300 B.C. Built on a site that receives cool sea breezes even in mid-summer, the palace is decorated with delicate and colorful wall-paintings that feature aquatic motifs.

Timeline 3.1   Cycladic and Minoan cultures.

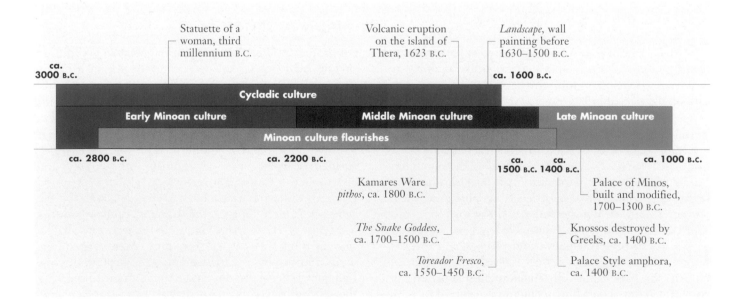

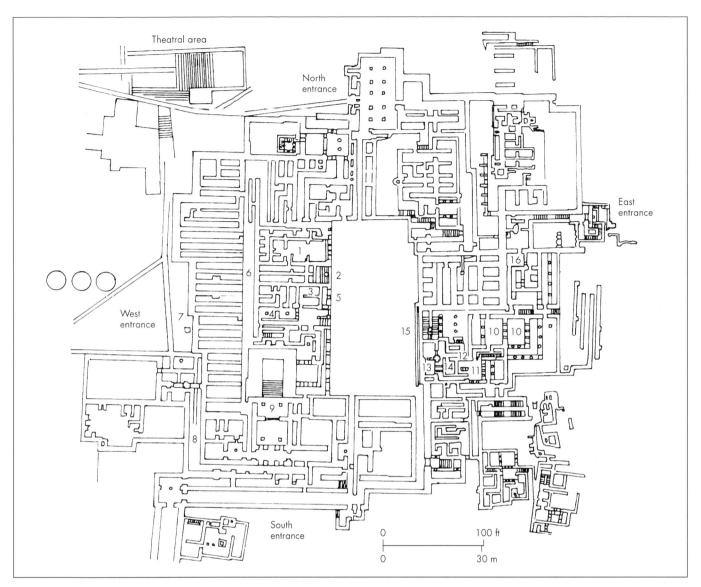

Figure 3.4 Palace of Minos, Knossos, Crete, ca. 1700–1300 B.C., plan: (1) throne room; (2) staircase; (3) temple repositories; (4) pillar crypt; (5) main shrine; (6) corridor access to magazines; (7) altars; (8) corridor of the processions; (9) staircase; (10) Hall of the Double Axes; (11) Queen's Hall; (12) bathroom; (13) lavatory; (14) storeroom; (15) Great Staircase; (16) lapidary's workshop.

it as the "Labyrinth", meaning literally the House of the Double Axes (from the Greek *labyrs*, "double ax"). Over time, however, the word *labyrinth* has taken on the meaning of "maze."

Open and airy, the palace was constructed with many porticoes, staircases, airshafts, and lightwells (uncovered vertical shafts in buildings allowing light into the lower stories), and built on several levels and in several stories—up to five stories in some areas. But the room ceilings were low and, consequently, the palace never rose very high. The wall surfaces were stuccoed and covered with frescoes.

The Minoans built with an unusual and distinctive type of column. The Minoan column is referred to as an "inverted" column because, unlike the later Greek columns, it tapers downward, the diameter being smaller at the bottom than at the top. The columns were made of wood rather than stone and were painted bright red. They stood on simple stone bases and were topped by bulging cushion-shaped capitals (fig. 3.5). Replicas now line the Great Staircase of the palace at Knossos. This impressive staircase once served as a lightwell and gave access to all five stories of the palace.

The basement of the palace was the storage area for food, supplies, and valuables. Some of the earthenware storage vases remain in place. These huge **pithoi** (singular, **pithos**) were used to store oil, grain, dried fish, beans, and olives. The palace was a self-sufficient unit

Figure 3.5 Palace of Minos, Knossos, Crete, ca. 1700–1300 B.C., staircase in east wing with "inverted" columns. Structurally as sound as the usual column shape that tapers to the top (compare the columns on the ancient Greek Parthenon, fig. 4.5), this "inverted" shape, which tapers toward the bottom, is a characteristic of Minoan architecture.

that included oil and wine presses as well as grain mills. Highly valued items, such as those made of gold and other precious materials, were stored beneath the floor of the basement. These objects were placed in carefully cut holes lined with stone slabs.

Because of today's tendency to judge other cultures on the basis of their plumbing and level of sanitation, it may also be worth mentioning that the palace had fine bathrooms with decorated terra cotta bathtubs, as well as good plumbing and an effective sewage system.

The Myth of the Minotaur. The story of the labyrinth or maze at Knossos has an honored place in later Greek mythology. According to legend, Minos's queen, Pasiphae, was seduced by a bull belonging to Poseidon, the god of the sea. The fruit of their union was the Minotaur, part man, part bull, whom Minos consigned to the maze designed by his chief artist and architect, Daedalus. The Minotaur had a huge appetite for human flesh, and to satisfy him King Minos ordered the neighboring subject city of Athens to pay a yearly tribute of seven young men and seven young women for sacrifice to the Minotaur. The Athenians were understandably

upset at the order, and so Theseus, the son of the Athenian king Aegeus, offered to accompany the fourteen to Crete, where he vowed to kill the Minotaur. As was the custom, the group set out for the island in a ship with black sails. If Theseus was successful, he vowed to his father to return flying white sails instead.

Upon his arrival in Crete, Theseus quickly won the affection of the Minoan princess Ariadne. She provided him with a sword with which to kill the Minotaur and a ball of thread to mark his path so that he would then be able to find his way out of the labyrinth. Theseus succeeded in his mission and sailed back to Athens with the relieved would-be victims. However, he forgot to replace his black sails with white ones. His father Aegeus, seeing the black sails, cast himself into the sea in despair (and by this act apparently gave the Aegean Sea its name). With the death of his father, Theseus became king of Athens himself.

The Minotaur is a characteristically Minoan mythical creature. The bull is known to have been a sacred animal on Crete, important in ceremonial and religious activities. The frequent depictions of bulls in Minoan art may be assumed to have had a religious and/or ritualistic significance. Bull's horns, some large, some small, carved of stone, were erected at the Palace of Minos. They are referred to as "horns of consecration" and are believed by archaeologists to be religious symbols, denoting sacred spots and objects.

The Toreador Fresco. The Minoans made lavish use of wall paintings. The most famous example features the sacred bull. This is the *Toreador Fresco* (fig. 3.6), which was painted around 1550–1450 B.C. in the Palace of

Figure 3.6 *Toreador Fresco*, from the Palace of Minos at Knossos, Crete, ca. 1550–1450 B.C., wall painting, height with border ca. $24\frac{1}{2}''$ (62.2 cm), Archaeological Museum, Herakleion (Iraklion), Crete. The importance of the bull in Minoan culture is evidenced by this display of bull-vaulting. In spite of extensive restoration, the delicacy and lively animation typical of Minoan wall painting remains evident.

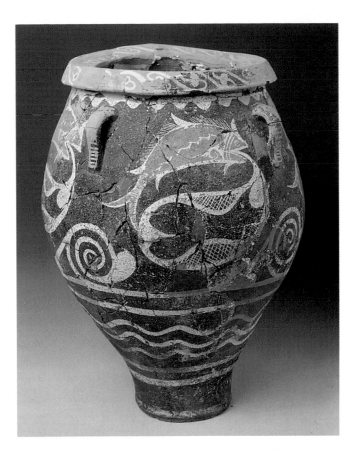

Figure 3.7 Kamares Ware spouted three-handled *pithos*, with fish, from Phaistos, Crete, ca. 1800 B.C. terra cotta, height 19⅞″ (50 cm), Archaeological Museum, Herakleion (Iraklion), Crete. Kamares Ware, identified by its color, was often decorated with aquatic motifs—in accord with the artists' island home.

Minos at Knossos. The dark areas are original; the rest is restoration. The activity depicted here is bull-vaulting, in which a person jumps over a running bull's back. As the painting illustrates, when the bull charges, the jumper must "take the bull by the horns," so to speak, vault onto its back, and hope to land standing up like the figure on the far right of this painting. Despite the fact that there are other representations of this activity, the purpose of bull-vaulting remains unclear. It may have been a means of sacrificing people or it may have been an early form of bullfighting. Whether this was a ritual or a sport remains uncertain. It has even been questioned if the acrobatic feat depicted is actually possible, but no one has come forward with an offer to prove it one way or the other.

Ceramic Ware. Painting, in several distinctive styles, was also done on Minoan ceramic objects. The most important styles of Minoan ceramic painting are known as **Kamares Ware** and the **Palace Style**. A spouted, three-handled pithos (fig. 3.7), decorated with fish and made ca. 1800 B.C., is an example of Kamares Ware,

which is distinguished by its color: a dark purplish-brown background is painted with chalk-white and touches of orange-red. Dynamic and decorative swirls, spirals, and S-shapes are typical motifs on Kamares Ware ceramics. The forms flow—wave patterns were popular with the sea-faring Minoans, as were other marine and plant forms. Kamares Ware pieces are heavy, with thick walls and asymmetrical shapes.

The Palace Style, which dates from approximately 1600 to 1300 B.C., is represented by a three-handled amphora, with naturalistic lilies and papyrus (fig. 3.8), made ca. 1400 B.C. from Knossos. Like Kamares Ware, the Palace Style is characterized by graceful forms that derive from nature. But unlike Kamares Ware decoration, the forms do not flow over the surface of the vase. Instead, the plants seem to grow up the side of the vase. Palace Style decoration is more delicate than that of

Figure 3.8 Palace Style three-handled amphora, with lilies and papyrus, from Knossos, Crete, ca. 1400 B.C., terra cotta, Archaeological Museum, Herakleion (Iraklion), Crete. In Palace Style, as in Kamares Ware, forms of nature are used as inspiration for decorations. However, rather than swirling over the surface, in Palace Style the decoration appears to grow up the vase.

Then & Now

THE SNAKE GODDESS

*T*he efforts of the Feminist movement in the United States and Europe in the late 1960s and early 1970s gave rise not only to a vast array of social and political reforms but to revisions of historical interpretation as well. Most art history texts before the early 1970s, reflecting the social balance within the society that produced them, paid little or no attention to art by women, and most works of art were viewed from a particularly male perspective. Attempting to redress the balance, Feminist historians became especially interested in the art of Aegean civilizations because it seemed that artifacts such as the Minoan *Snake Goddess* (see fig. 3.9) were the products of a matriarchal culture in which women, rather than men, played the dominant roles.

Key to this theory is a 1976 book by Merlin Stone entitled *When God Was a Woman*. "It was quite apparent", Stone wrote, describing her research into Aegean culture, "that the myths and legends that grew from, and were propagated by, a religion in which the deity was female, and revered as wise, valiant, powerful and just, provided very different images from those which are offered by the male-oriented religions of today." If it was a male, King Minos, for example, who exercised governmental authority, it was perhaps the female goddess who exercised spiritual and moral authority in Crete.

Recent scholarship suggests that the "demonization" of woman in Western thought dates from after the invasion of the Aegean basin by warlike tribes from the north who brought with them strong patriarchal traditions. This demonization is reflected in the Greek transformation of the Minoan Snake Goddess into the mythic figure of the Medusa, whose hair is a nest of vipers and whose gaze turns men into stone, as well as in the Christian story of Eve's seduction by the Devil, who, significantly, takes the form of a snake, bringing about humankind's expulsion from Paradise.

Figure 3.9 *Snake Goddess*, ca. 1700–1500 B.C., faience, height $11\frac{5}{8}''$ (29.5 cm), Archaeological Museum, Herakleion (Iraklion), Crete. Minoan religion focused on female deities. In Minoan art, both women and men were depicted with unusually tiny waists and long flowing hair.

Kamares Ware. The color, too, is different, for Palace Style decoration is painted with dark colors on a light background.

The Snake Goddess. Although the Minoans produced no large-scale sculpture in the round, they did create small-scale figures. The best-known example of Minoan sculpture is the *Snake Goddess*, or *Snake Priestess*, a statuette made of **faience**, a lustrous glazed ceramic, ca. 1700–1500 B.C. (fig. 3.9). The physical type of the statuette, with its rounded limbs and body and pinched waist, is typically Minoan. The sculptor gives great emphasis to the elaborately detailed costume. The chief deities of the Minoan religion were female—mother or fertility goddesses. The goddess portrayed here holds a snake in each hand. In many religions snakes were associated with earth deities and with male fertility. Snakes were believed to be in direct contact with the gods of the lower world, and were therefore supposed to be able to cure disease and restore life. The snakes, combined with the goddess's frankly female form and bared breasts, suggest fertility.

MYCENAEAN CULTURE

Beginning about 3000 B.C. Greek-speaking peoples began to invade the Greek mainland from the north, inaugurating the Mycenaean or Helladic Age (*Hellas* is the Greek word for "Greece"). After about 1500 B.C., when Minoan culture began to decline, these mainland peoples started to have increasing influence throughout the region. As opposed to the islanders, who relied on the sea for protection and whose palaces were, as a result, open and airy, the mainland Greeks built strong fortresses and, under continual threat of invasion from the north, were evidently much more concerned with things military. Most of these strongholds—such as Mycenae and Tiryns—were in southern Greece, the Peloponnese, although there were also settlements in the north, in particular at Athens in Attica. Among these, Mycenae was the most powerful and richest center; as a result, the entire culture takes its name from this city.

In Homer's *Iliad*, the Trojan War begins when the King of Mycenae, Agamemnon, leads the Greeks against the city of Troy. In legend, the battle was said to have

Figure 3.10 Lion Gate, entrance to Mycenae, Greece, ca. 1300–1200 B.C., limestone, height of relief ca. 9'6" (2.89 m). The lion, the animal most frequently depicted throughout the history of art, was often used as a guardian figure.

the Greeks were prompted in their aggression by their predilection for plunder, the principal target in this case being the palace of the Trojan king Priam. The Mycenaeans also conquered other territories in the Mediterranean area, including Cyprus, Rhodes, and Crete, assimilating many aspects of the defeated people's art, especially that of the Minoan civilization.

The Palace at Mycenae. The main gateway to the fortified hilltop city of Mycenae was the famous Lion Gate (fig. 3.10), built ca. 1300–1200 B.C. The Lion Gate is constructed of huge stones, with the horizontal **lintel** above the doorway estimated to weigh twenty tons. Above the lintel is a **relieving triangle**, an opening that serves to relieve the weight on the lintel. The relieving triangle is filled by a relatively thin slab of limestone on which lions are carved in relief. Symmetrical rampant guardian lions, muscular and powerful, flank a Minoan column—an "inverted" column that tapers downward and has a cushion-like capital. This relief is the oldest piece of monumental sculpture in Europe.

The Lion Gate leads to, among other structures extant at Mycenae, the so-called Treasury of Atreus (figs. 3.11 and 3.12), built ca. 1300–1200 B.C. Atreus was the

been precipitated when the Trojan prince Paris abducted Helen, the wife of Agamemnon's brother, his reward for choosing Aphrodite over Athena and Hera as the most beautiful of the goddesses. Homer's story seems to have had a basis in history, although it is more plausible that

Figure 3.12 Treasury of Atreus, Mycenae, Greece, ca. 1300–1200 B.C., stone, height of vault ca. 43' (13.11 m), diameter 47'6" (14.48 m). The final step in the construction of a corbeled dome was to cut off all projecting edges and smooth the stone surface into a continuous curve.

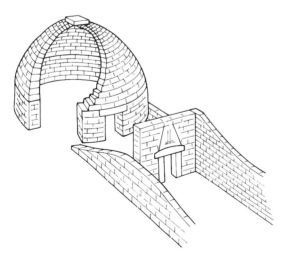

Figure 3.11 Treasury of Atreus, Mycenae, Greece, ca. 1300–1200 B.C., drawing showing the method of construction. Unlike the true dome, a dynamic structure made of wedge-shaped voussoirs, the corbeled dome is a static structure subject only to the forces of gravity. The diameter of each successive circle of stones is slightly diminished, until the central opening can be covered by a single capstone.

Timeline 3.2   Mycenaean culture.

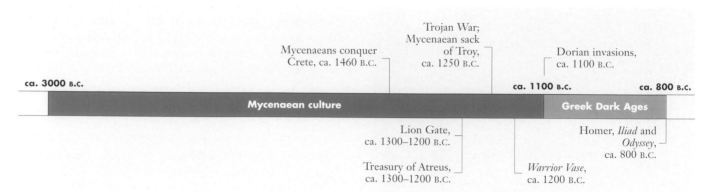

father of Agamemnon. The building was given its name by the archaeologist Heinrich Schliemann, who had a fanatical interest in Homer's heroes. It is, however, a little misleading, since it was neither a treasury nor was it associated with Atreus. It was actually a tomb.

The **dromos**, or entrance way, was cut into the hillside, and the walls were lined with **ashlar masonry**, in which each stone is carefully cut with right-angle corners. At the end of the dromos, the doorway to the tomb is surmounted by a lintel and a relieving triangle. Originally the doorway facade was elaborately decorated with carved reliefs of various colored stones, and the doorway was flanked by slender columns carved with ornamental relief, the columns tapering downward in the Minoan manner. The tomb itself is a **tholos** (plural, **tholoi**), the term for any round building, in this case a domed circular tomb shaped like a beehive about forty-five feet high. The technical name for this kind of structure is a **corbeled dome**. Such a building is constructed by first digging a circular pit in the earth. Courses of ashlar masonry are then laid in a circle around the circumference of this space, each successive course slightly overhanging the one below, gradually diminishing the diameter of the circle, until a single stone, the "capstone," covers the small remaining opening. The projecting corners of the masonry blocks are then cut off and smoothed to create a continuous curving surface.

The Treasury of Atreus is the most famous of the nine tholoi at Mycenae. All were presumably used for royal burials. They seem each to have served a royal person and the person's immediate family. The interior of the Treasury of Atreus was once decorated with bronze plaques and rosettes. Now nothing remains inside except the nails and nail holes used to hold them in place, since all the Mycenaean tholoi were pillaged in antiquity.

Also just inside the Lion Gate at Mycenae is Royal Grave Circle A (there is also a second—Grave Circle B), dated 1600–1500 B.C., which was excavated by Schliemann in 1876. Schliemann found that this double circle of stone slabs enclosed six shaft graves. In these graves

Schliemann found golden treasure. Many of the bodies buried here had been literally laden with gold. Two children were found wrapped in sheets of gold. Among the objects unearthed here were a magnificent gold diadem embossed with geometric patterns, small individual ornaments of gold plate sewn or stuck onto the clothing, a **rhyton** (drinking vessel) in the shape of a lion's head, gold cups, bronze dagger blades inlaid with gold, silver, and copper, a gold breast plate, and gold masks (fig. 3.13), some of which were found placed over the faces of the dead. These last were made of thin sheet gold and were hammered into shape over a wooden core.

Figure 3.13   Gold mask, from tomb V of Grave Circle A, Mycenae, Greece, ca. 1550–1500 B.C., gold, height ca. 12″ (30.5 cm), National Archeological Museum, Athens. The rich burials of Mycenaean nobility included a variety of sheet gold objects. Homer described Mycenae as "rich in gold."

Figure 3.14 Warrior Vase, from Mycenae, Greece, ca. 1200 B.C., terra cotta, height ca. 16″ (40.6 cm), National Archaeological Museum, Athens. Differing from the characteristic flora-and-fauna decoration of the Minoans, whose safety was insured by their island location, the war motifs of this vase reflect the more military aspect of Mycenaean life. Although not realistically drawn, the decoration of the Warrior Vase provides a document of early defensive arms and armor.

The objects found in the excavations of Grave Circle A make it easy to understand why Homer referred to the city of Mycenae as *polychrysos*—"rich in gold." These are the graves of the nobility—the Mycenaean ruling system was one of family dynasties—but they are not the graves of Atreus and Agamemnon, even though the mask illustrated here is often referred to as the "Mask of Agamemnon." In fact, the mask predates any possible Mycenaean invasion of Troy by nearly three hundred years (the Trojan War is now dated to ca. 1250 B.C.).

The Warrior Vase. Probably no surviving artifact better embodies the warlike character of the Mycenaeans than the famed Warrior Vase (fig. 3.14), made ca. 1200 B.C. Unlike the art of the earlier Cycladic and Minoan cultures, Mycenaean works tend to be concerned with war and death. Between bands of decoration, soldiers march, seemingly in single file. At the far left, a woman raises her arm to bid farewell to the troops. The execution of the painting is careless and the figures are clumsy caricatures. The vase itself is crudely constructed. The base is significantly smaller than the opening, making the shape unstable and impractical. The Warrior Vase dates from the end of the Mycenaean civilization and, in its unrefined execution and decoration, can be seen to portend the destruction of social order in Mycenae. Around 1100 B.C. the Aegean civilization died out, and the so-called "Dark Age" began, a period in which

writing seems to have disappeared, and art-making ground to a halt. Faced with Dorian invaders from the north, whose weapons were made of iron instead of bronze—perhaps the very invaders the soldiers depicted on the Warrior Vase are marching to meet—Mycenaean civilization collapsed.

THE RISE OF ANCIENT GREECE
✦

Mycenaean civilization, and with it the Bronze Age in the Aegean, came to an abrupt end around 1100 B.C. During the following century, many of the achievements of the previous millennia appear to have been forgotten. Not until around 1000 B.C. did the Greeks of the mainland begin to forge a new civilization that would culminate in the fifth century B.C. in the achievements of Classical Athens. The history of Greece in the intervening centuries is usually subdivided into several phases: the Geometric period, ca. 1000–700 B.C.: the Orientalizing period, a period of Greek colonization and contact with the East, ca. 700–600 B.C.; and the Archaic period, ca. 600–480 B.C. It was owing to the achievements of these five hundred years that Greek culture was able to flourish so spectacularly after 480 B.C. and that the artistic, cultural, and political foundations of modern Western civilization were laid.

THE PANTHEON OF GREEK GODS

According to Greek legend, before the world was created, before the division into earth, water, and sky, there was Chaos. From this Chaos there emerged a god named Ouranos [YOOR-ah-noss], representing the heavens, and a goddess named Gaea [JEE-ah], representing the earth. Their union produced a race of giants called the Titans. One of these, Kronos [KROH-nos], overthrew his father, Ouranos, and married his sister Rhea [REE-ah]. Their offspring were the Olympian gods. However, there was a prophecy that Kronos himself would be overthrown by one of his own children, and so to forestall this he decided to eat all his own progeny. Only Zeus [ZOOSS] survived, saved by Rhea. When Zeus ultimately and inevitably revolted against his father, Kronos regurgitated all the other children—Demeter [du-MEE-ter], the goddess of agriculture and fertility; Hera [HEAR-ah], goddess of marriage and stability; Hades [HAY-deez], god of the underworld; Poseidon [pu-SIGH-dun], god of the sea; and Hestia [HESS-ti-ah], goddess of the hearth and home. Zeus married Hera, and they in turn produced a second order of gods and goddesses: Apollo [a-POLL-oh], who as god of the sun and light represents intellectual beauty; Aphrodite [ah-fro-DI-tee], who as goddess of love represents physical beauty; Ares [AIR-ease], god of war; and Artemis [AR-tum-iss], goddess of the moon and the hunt. Athena [a-THEE-nuh], goddess of wisdom, and of the arts and crafts, and patron goddess of Athens, sprang full-grown from the brow of Zeus himself—a pure idea.

It was Prometheus, a Titan, who first took earth, mixed it with water, and fashioned human beings out of the resulting mud, forming them in the image of the gods. His brother fashioned the animals, bestowing on them the various gifts of courage, strength, swiftness, and wisdom, together with the claws, shells, and wings that distinguish them from one another. The first woman was Pandora, a joint creation of all the gods. According to one version of the story, each of the gods gave her something—Aphrodite gave her beauty, Hermes the gift of persuasion, Apollo musical skill. Zeus presented her to Prometheus's brother, and she brought with her a box containing all her marriage presents. When she opened the box, all the blessings escaped—except hope!

Unlike the gods of the ancient Hebrews and of India, those of ancient Greece could not be counted on for help. Traditionally inhabiting the top of Mount Olympus, in northeastern Greece, the Greek pantheon, the family headed by Zeus, supervises human society. Unlike the Christian system, there is no god who represents complete good or complete evil. Zeus is a patriarch, a father, in some sense a model for the tyrant of the Greek polis, but frequently an adulterous husband. His wife, Hera, is often jealous with good cause. Their marital relationship reflects the weakness of human relationships, and their monumental jealousies and rages were reflected not only in the devastating wars that disrupted Greek life but also in the petty animosities that spoilt civic harmony. Mirroring human frailty in exaggerated form, the ancient Greek gods represented irrational forces that were both violent and unpredictable. The ancient Greek attitude toward their gods embodied their skeptical view of human nature, and many of the more famous Greek myths reflect this. However, unlike Christianity and Judaism, Greek culture never developed a single unified account of these myths, which exist instead in many varying forms.

Apollo and Daphne.   One day Eros (Cupid), the son of Aphrodite and Hephaistos, the blacksmith god who made the gods' armor as well as Zeus's thunderbolts, was playing with his bow. Apollo, renowned for his own prowess as an archer, saw the boy and chided him: "What have you to do with warlike weapons, you saucy boy? Leave them for hands worthy of them." Eros answered back: "Your arrows may strike all things else, Apollo, but mine shall strike you." With these words, he took a golden-tipped arrow, meant to excite love, and shot Apollo through the heart with it. Then he took a second arrow, this one tipped with lead and designed to thwart love, and shot the nymph Daphne with it. Apollo was immediately enthralled by the nymph, but she was repelled by her suitor.

Apollo pursued Daphne relentlessly. But whenever he found her, she fled. The pursuit turned into an outright chase, and as Apollo gained on her, her strength fading, she pleaded with her father, Peneus, the river god, for help: "Open the earth to enclose me, or change my form, which has brought this danger on me." The moment she spoke these words, all her limbs began to stiffen, her breast was covered by bark, her feet stuck fast in the ground, and her hair was transformed into leaves. Apollo stood amazed. He realized he had lost his love forever. "Since you cannot be my wife," he exclaimed, "you will be my tree. As eternal youth is mine, you too will always be green, and your leaf shall never decay." Daphne, now a laurel tree, bowed her head with gratitude.

Athena and Arachne.   Apollo was only one of many figures in Greek mythology to bring suffering on himself through his pride, or **hubris**, as the Greeks called it. The mortal Arachne was famous for her skill in weaving and embroidery, so skilled that the nymphs would come out of the woods to watch her, and those who saw her works believed that Athena, in her role as goddess of the arts and crafts, must have taught her everything she knew. But Arachne was insulted at the idea: "Let Athena try her skill with mine," she said, "and if I am beaten, I will accept the penalty." Athena heard the challenge, and assuming a disguise she spoke to Arachne: "Challenge your fellow mortals as you wish," she warned, "but I advise you not to compete with a goddess. In fact, I suggest you ask Athena's forgiveness. She is generous, and she will forgive you." But Arachne would not take back her challenge.

And so Athena revealed herself, and the contest was engaged. Athena wove a scene in which the twelve most prominent gods were depicted, and in the four corners were illustrations of incidents in which presumptuous mortals had dared to contend with the gods. Arachne filled her weaving with subjects exhibiting the failings of the gods—Zeus's seduction of Leda when he assumed the form of a swan, his rape of Europa in the form of a bull, and his seduction of Danaë as a shower of gold.

Athena could not help but admire Arachne's skill, but neither could she accept the insult to the gods implied in her work. She struck Arachne on the forehead, causing her to feel extraordinary guilt and shame, and Arachne went and hanged herself. But Athena pitied the girl when she saw her hanging body: "You and your descendants, Arachne, shall so hang for all future times." And sprinkling Arachne with magic juices, she transformed her into a spider, hanging from the web it had woven.

Perseus.   Perseus was the son of Zeus and Danaë, the seduction of whom Arachne had condemned in the tapestry she wove in her contest with Athena. Like so many of the demi-gods in Greek legend, born of the union of god and human, and thus endowed with powers

Cross Currents

HESIOD'S *THEOGONY* AND MESOPOTAMIAN CREATION MYTHS

In his *Theogony*, Hesiod [HEH-see-ud] (ca. seventh century B.C.) presents a poetic account of the origins of the Greek gods. The *Theogony* identifies Gaia as the original divine being. Gaia is both the physical earth and a giant human-like deity who produces her own mate, Ouranos, the sky. This primal couple then spawns the first beings, the Titans, whom Ouranos tries to eliminate by stuffing them back into the recesses of their mother. One of these children, the Titan Kronos, slays his father and replaces him as Gaia's consort.

Like his father Ouranos, Kronos disposes of his offspring. However, one child, Zeus, is saved by Gaia and grows in safety until he can liberate the other devoured children, battle with the Titans, and displace his father as the chief male deity.

The Greek account of the origin of the gods is indebted to various Mesopotamian creation accounts. From Mesopotamia, Greece derived the idea of projecting a magnified version of human power onto the divine realm. Greece also borrowed the idea of the universe as a city governed by a succession of rulers, each displaced by the next in a power struggle. Moreover, with its lists of succeeding gods, Hesiod's *Theogony* echoes Mesopotamian lists of kings, which are traced back genealogically to the gods. Both Mesopotamian and ancient Greek poetry account for the order and hierarchy of the universe.

Like Homer's epics, Hesiod's works had a profound effect on succeeding generations of Greek culture. Hesiod's poems were considered repositories of wisdom and technical knowledge about a host of matters, including farming and war. The works of both Homer and Hesiod went on to form the foundation of classical Athenian education in the fifth century B.C.

---

greater than mere mortals, Perseus took on many legendary challenges. The first of these was the destruction of the monster Medusa, who had once been a beautiful maiden with gorgeous long hair before she dared to vie in beauty with Athena. In revenge Athena had transformed her hair into hissing serpents, and all that beheld Medusa in this state turned to stone. Taking care to approach her in her sleep, and looking at her only in a reflection in his brightly polished shield, Perseus cut off her head and set off to present it to Athena.

He soon arrived at the edge of the world, where he encountered Atlas, a Titan giant whose gardens bore fruit of gold. Atlas knew a prophecy that foretold that a son of Zeus would one day come to steal his golden apples, and so he attempted to throw Perseus out of his gardens. Offended, Perseus showed Atlas Medusa's head and Atlas was promptly turned to stone, whereupon he increased in bulk until he became a mountain and all the stars in heaven rested upon his shoulders.

Herakles.

Known to most contemporary readers by his Roman name, Hercules, Herakles was the son of Zeus and the mortal Alcmena. Hera, always hostile to her husband Zeus's mortal offspring, declared war on the demi-god Herakles at his birth, arranging for him a series of difficult and dangerous tasks, known as his "Twelve Labors."

First, Herakles had to fight a terrible lion in the valley of Nemea. Neither club nor arrows could subdue the lion and Herakles finally had to strangle it with his own hands. Next he was ordered to slaughter the Hydra, a creature with nine heads, the middle one of which was immortal. As Herakles struck off each head with his club, two new ones grew in its place. Finally, he burned away the Hydra's heads, and buried the ninth, immortal one under a huge rock.

Yet another labor was the cleaning of the stables of King Augeas's three thousand oxen, which had not been washed for thirty years. Herakles managed this task by diverting the rivers Alpheus and Peneus through them, cleansing the stables in a single day.

But Herakles' most difficult labor was retrieving the golden apples of Hesperides. Atlas, Hesperides' father, was best qualified to get them back, but he had been condemned to bear the weight of the heavens on his shoulders and so could not move. Hence Herakles took Atlas's place, relieving him of his heavy burden while he found the apples. Atlas was successful and returned to give them to Herakles and, somewhat reluctantly, reassumed his position beneath the weight of the sky.

Dionysos.

Yet another demi-god was Dionysos, son of Zeus and Semele. Ever jealous, Hera planted in Semele's head doubts about the paternity of her child and suggested that she ask her disguised lover Zeus to grant her a favor to prove who he was. Without bothering to ask what the favor might be, Zeus agreed, only to discover that Semele wanted to see him, not in disguise, but in all his heavenly splendor. Zeus had to comply, and when Semele saw him, her mortal being could not endure his dazzling radiance, and she was reduced to ashes.

Consequently, Zeus had to find someone to raise Dionysos, and so gave him to a group of nymphs. As a young man, Dionysos discovered grapes and perfected the means for extracting their juice and converting it to wine. But Hera, always inclined to punish Zeus's progeny, struck him mad and sent him out into the world as a perpetual wanderer. Everywhere he went, he introduced the culture of the vine, but with it he brought madness and disorder. Eventually he returned to his native Thebes, where the king, Pentheus, had him arrested. While preparations were being made for his execution, Dionysos escaped with Pentheus's mother and aunts to the nearby mountains, where they began to celebrate his freedom in a wild orgy. In a rage, Pentheus followed them, but his mother, perhaps blinded by Dionysos, mistook him for a wild boar, and, with the help of her sisters, tore her own son to pieces. The worship of Dionysos was thus established in Greece, a wild and ecstatic celebration that temporarily overpowered even the authority of the king.

For the Greeks, Dionysos, thus associated with wine and orgiastic celebration, came to represent irrational forces, including the destructive power of the emotions. Poets frequently used the figure of Dionysos to explain the irrational and violent part of human existence, while Apollo was seen as representing logic and order.

THE GEOMETRIC PERIOD

The Geometric period (ca. 1000–700 B.C.) is sometimes referred to as the Heroic Age, since it was during this time that Homer created his poetic epics, the *Iliad* and *Odyssey*, centered on the figures of the great heroes Achilles and Odysseus. The other arts are less well preserved for us now. There is very little trace of archi-

tecture and not much sculpture. Most of the evidence for the visual art of the period is derived from pottery.

Cultural development in this period appears to have been slow. After the destruction of the Mycenaean empire, mainland Greece lacked a political center. When communities began to emerge, as at Athens in Attica and at Sparta in Laconia, they took the form of independent city-states, **poleis** (singular, **polis**).

The development of the Greek polis, which provided the focus for political, artistic, and religious activities in the region, is central to the later Western ideal of democracy. However, in this early period, each polis was ruled by a council of aristocrats. It is also important to note that the polis, with its tradition of fierce independence, meant that even at its artistic and cultural height in the fifth century B.C., Greece remained politically fragmented and always on the verge of violent self-destruction. Athens and Sparta, for instance, remained hostile neighbors. Their temporary alliance in the early fifth century B.C. managed to beat off Persian invaders, but Greek civilization was delivered a fatal blow later in the same century by the Peloponnesian War between these same two city-states.

Pottery.   There was undoubtedly some cultural continuity between Mycenaean Greece and the civilization that re-emerged after 1000 B.C. However, the distinctive style of art that appears around the latter date was probably influenced by the Dorian invaders. Known as the

Timeline 3.3   Ancient Greek culture.

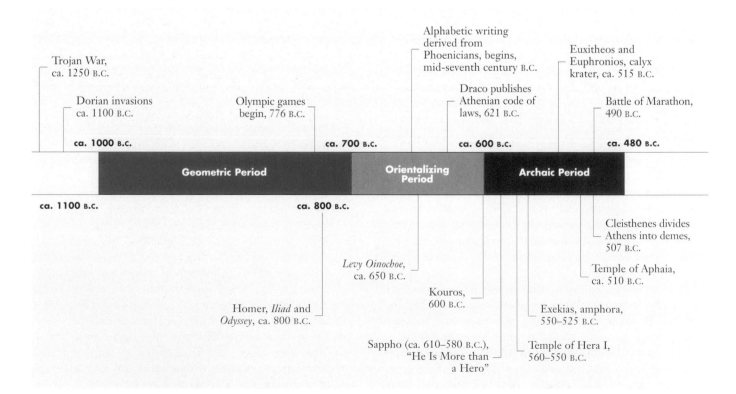

Geometric style and characterized by geometric forms, it soon dominated the art of the Greek mainland. Human and animal figures on pottery from the period are depicted in terms of simplified geometric forms, in a style reminiscent of the early sculptural forms of the Cyclades. This Geometric style in poetry was to flourish in Attica and, in particular, in its most important city, Athens.

The Geometric style is distinguished by decoration in bands covering the entire surface, and by literally geometric forms of ornament—meanders (maze patterns), checkers, zigzags, and lozenges. Whereas on Aegean pottery the decoration flows over the surface of the vessel, on Geometric pottery the painted decoration is adapted to the zones or divisions of the vase. In many ways, the Geometric system may be compared to the Egyptian register system in the horizontal divisions of the surface into defined and separated areas (see fig. 2.1). Geometric ceramics show a concern with proportion and thoughtful composition and placement of the decorative elements.

An example of the Geometric style is an eighth-century B.C. terra cotta **krater**, a large vase with a wide mouth (fig. 3.15). It comes from the Dipylon Cemetery (*di* means "two"; a *pylon* is a massive gateway; a *dipylon* is a massive double gate) in Athens. The center of the ceramics industry in Athens was here at the cemetery. Indeed, the area was also called the *Kerameikos*, the origin of our word "ceramics." Large vases, up to six feet high, were buried halfway into the ground on shaft graves as markers. Such vases have holes in the bottom or have no bottom at all. Poured in the top as offerings to the deceased, liquids would seep down into the body below.

The subject depicted on this vase is a common one: mourners lamenting for the deceased, who is shown lying on a funeral bed or bier. Funerary processions are pictured going from the home of the deceased to the cemetery, while mourners tear their hair. Other Dipylon vases include depictions of funeral processions, horse-drawn chariots, animals to be eaten at the funeral banquet, and funeral games. (It was customary to have games at funerals in honor of the deceased.) Significant to the future course of vase painting is the fact that the work here is beginning to develop narrative elements. Greek potters increasingly turned away from purely geometric decoration, giving over a greater percentage of the surface to larger and more representational figures designed to tell a tale.

However, for the moment everything is shown in strict silhouette, simplified for clarity. Figures are flat, with triangular torsos and pinched waists; humans and horses have essentially the same physique. Everything is highly stylized and simplified to a series of geometric planes. Thus, the legs on the funeral bier look like the legs on the people. More abstracted than

Figure 3.15   Krater, Geometric style, from the Dipylon Cemetery, Athens, ca. 750 B.C., terra cotta, height $3'4\frac{1}{2}''$ (1.03 m), Metropolitan Museum of Art, New York. Geometric style vases are, as the term indicates, decorated with precisely drawn, simple geometric forms. Each of the several shapes of Greek vases has a name and was used for a specific purpose; this very large krater was used as a burial marker.

realistic, this is an abbreviated or shorthand style of representation.

Sculpture.   Prior to the mid-seventh century B.C., Greek sculptors restricted their work to small-scale pieces in wood, clay, ivory, and bronze (bronze casting of sculpture seems to have started in Greece in the ninth century B.C.). All work in perishable materials has been lost, but there are a few extant ivory pieces and many fine bronzes.

The surviving examples, found in tombs and sanctuaries, are statuettes of humans and animals. Bronze cows

Figure 3.16   Horse, second half of the eighth century B.C., bronze, height ca. $6\frac{3}{8}''$ (16 cm), Staatliche Museum, Berlin. In the Geometric Period, forms of nature were simplified and made literally geometric, torsos of horses and humans (as on the Geometric vase in fig. 3.15) turned into triangles.

and rams were used as votive offerings to the gods in place of actual sacrificial animals. Because horses were associated with certain goddesses and gods, they received special attention and may have been used as votive offerings to the deities. The example shown here (fig. 3.16) dates to the second half of the eighth century B.C. This late Geometric horse is simplified, abstracted, and highly sophisticated. With its contrast between flat and rounded areas, and its crisp and sharp rendering of forms, it is clearly the work of a skilled artist. Rather than being a unique or isolated example, this horse is representative of a physical type found in sculpture and in painting—the horse looks like the horses on contemporary Geometric vases. The pinched waist is, moreover, common to both horses and humans in Geometric art, be it in sculpture or in painting.

Homer's Iliad and Odyssey.   Greek poetry in written form begins with the two most famous epics in Western literature, *The Iliad* and *The Odyssey*. Tradition credits the authorship of these poems to Homer, about whom nothing is known with certainty except his name. Early Greeks believed Homer to have been blind, and many scholars think he lived in Ionia, in Asia Minor, but none of this is sure. Both *The Iliad* and *The Odyssey* were first put in writing during the seventh century B.C., although they are based on a long oral tradition predating their written versions by hundreds of years. Despite their long genesis, each epic bears the stylistic imprint and imaginative vision of a single resourceful poet.

Both *The Iliad* and *The Odyssey* reflect their social context, a warring aristocratic society in which honor, courage, heroism, and cunning are the prime human virtues. The gods and goddesses of the Greek pantheon figure prominently in the Homeric epics. Each of the poems centers on a single heroic figure. *The Iliad* describes the wrath of Achilles and its consequences for himself and his comrades. *The Odyssey* tells the story of Odysseus, who, after long years spent wandering, returns to reclaim what is his own from a group of Greek princes who have more or less laid siege to his wife and home. Homer's *Iliad* and *Odyssey* have been enormously influential in the history of Western poetry. The Roman poet Virgil's *Aeneid* (see Chapter 5) and John Milton's *Paradise Lost* (see Chapter 14) both imitate Homer's epics in their different ways, to cite only two famous examples.

The Iliad describes a short period toward the end of the Trojan War (ca. 1250 B.C.), the ten-year siege that a band of ancient Greek military adventurers laid against the city of Troy. The work focuses on the anger and exploits of its hero, Achilles, renowned as the greatest of all soldiers. The epic begins with a quarrel between Achilles and the Greek king and military commander, Agamemnon, over the beautiful Trojan woman, Briseis. Agamemnon had taken Briseis as his royal right, even though Achilles believed he had earned her as his share of the battle spoils. Achilles expresses his disgust with Agamemnon by withdrawing sulkily and refusing to do battle with the enemy. Without Achilles' help, the Greeks are repeatedly defeated by the Trojans. Achilles returns to battle only after his friend Patroclus is killed. He kills Hector, the son of the Trojan king Priam, and abuses his corpse out of frustration and guilt at having let his friend Patroclus die through his anger. The source of the quarrel, the reason for Achilles's return to battle, and the military exploits Homer describes in vivid detail all reflect the warrior world *The Iliad* celebrates. Though the gods are present throughout to comment on the action, at the center of Homer's world are his human actors. The poet is concerned with human responsibility and motivation, and for these reasons his work stands at the very beginning of the Western literary tradition.

Although *The Iliad* glorifies great deeds performed on the battlefield, the poem also conveys a sense of war's terrible consequences. Homer vividly describes battles, with armies arrayed against one another in deadly combat. He describes with equal drama the conflicting loyalties of heroes on both sides as they take leave of their wives and families to kill one another in defense of honor and in pursuit of military glory. These heroic values are honored consistently throughout the epic, though *The Iliad*'s world-view is occasionally tempered by scenes that portray other less military virtues. For example, kindheartedness and forgiveness are exemplified in the scenes between the Trojan warrior Hector and his family, and in the scene describing Achilles' meeting with the old

Trojan king Priam, who comes to ask Achilles for the body of his son Hector.

Perhaps the most famous adventure story in Western literature, Homer's *Odyssey* contains a number of memorable episodes. Two of the most famous concern dangerous escapes. In one episode, Odysseus is captured by the giant one-eyed Cyclops. Odysseus gets the Cyclops drunk, blinds him with a stake, and escapes from the monster's cave by clinging to the belly of a sheep so that the Cyclops cannot feel him. In a second adventure, Odysseus and his men have to sail through the dangerous seas inhabited by the Sirens, whose enchanting singing causes sailors to crash their boats on the rocky shores of their island. To avoid this fate, Odysseus plugs his men's ears with wax and then has them tie him to the mast of their ship.

These and other exotic events make *The Odyssey* different in spirit from *The Iliad*. Other differences concern *The Odyssey*'s hero, Odysseus, who after a twenty-year absence from home, returns to his wife, Penelope, and his son, Telemachos. While Achilles's strength in *The Iliad* is purely physical, Odysseus also has mental fortitude. Odysseus's cunning and wit enable him to escape numerous dangerous predicaments, and he also pursues self-knowledge. Odysseus seems much more modern than Achilles, and his journeys toward understanding and toward "home" and all that that means take place in a world that is much closer to our own than is the more primitive world of *The Iliad*. Moreover, where the focus of *The Iliad* is narrowly trained on the military world, the vision of *The Odyssey* is much wider. Its values are those of home and hearth, of patience and fidelity, of filial piety, of the wisdom gained through suffering. The range and depth of its depiction of women far surpasses *The Iliad*'s image of women as the mere property of men. In addition to the clever and faithful Penelope, *The Odyssey*'s female characters include the intelligent and beautiful princess Nausicaa; the dangerously seductive witch Circe; the goddess Calypso, who offers Odysseus immortality; Athena, who serves as Odysseus's guide and protector; and Odysseus's nurse, Euryclea. Moreover, when Odysseus visits the Land of the Dead, he sees not only his mother, Anticleia, who had died in his absence, but other famous women of heroic times.

Odysseus's journey home is interrupted by his one-year stay with Circe and by the eight years he remains on Calypso's island. In total, he is absent from Penelope and home for twenty years, ten for the long siege of Troy and ten for his voyage. This long delay is due partly to Odysseus's unalterable fate and partly to his temperament. Warring within him are two contrary impulses: a wish to return to the peaceful kingdom of Ithaca, where he reigns as prince, and a desire to experience adventure and test himself against dangerous challenges. This split is echoed by the clash between Odysseus's temptation to forget his identity as husband, father, and king in his adventures, and his responsibility to resume these less exotic and more stable roles.

The Odyssey makes reference at a number of points to characters and events of *The Iliad*, most notably to the death of Achilles. In an important scene near the middle of *The Odyssey*, Homer has his hero descend to the underworld, where he meets the spirit of Achilles. Odysseus also encounters the shade of Agamemnon, whose murder by his wife serves as a warning of the fate that could befall a man who has been away too long. Homer uses the tragic story of the house of Atreus in thematic counterpoint to the duties and responsibilities of husband, wife, and son that *The Odyssey* endorses.

In essence, Homer's epics were to ancient Greece what Scripture was to the ancient Hebrews. The Homeric poems became the basis of all education and a reflection of the entire culture's values. The human characters in *The Iliad* and *The Odyssey* served as models of conduct—of heroism and pride, of cunning and loyalty—for later generations. The Homeric gods, however, were less models of ideal behavior than influences on human events. Homer gives them a secondary importance, choosing instead to emphasize men and women living out mysterious destinies. Moreover, Homer reveals the gods as subject to the same implacable fate as humans. Although they are honored and worshiped by the characters, the gods are also portrayed as worthy of blame as well as praise, of laughter as well as fear.

THE ORIENTALIZING PERIOD

In the Orientalizing period, ca. 700–600 B.C., the Greek city-states began to foster trade links, particularly across the Aegean Sea, and many built up large merchant fleets. In part, this development was the result of two factors: power and wealth remained the preserve of a small hereditary aristocracy, and the population was increasing rapidly. For this reason, the Greeks began to look overseas. Not only did they trade abroad, they also colonized. Cities were established as far east as the Black Sea, and the first settlements were made to the west in *Magna Graecia*, the Latin name for Great Greece, in southern Italy and Sicily.

The impact on the arts of this expanding commerce and colonization was immense. For the first time in three hundred years, Greece made contact with the civilizations of the Near East, in particular Egypt, Persia, and Phoenicia, and began to import objects as well as ideas. It is from the mid-seventh century B.C. that the earliest Greek stone sculptures of the human figure date, and it seems certain that the Greek sculptors were inspired by the example of the Egyptians. It is also around this time that Greece began to be unified linguistically through the introduction of a new alphabet, seemingly derived from that of the Phoenicians. The enormous impact of Near Eastern or Oriental culture on Greek art and life has led to the period being known as the "Orientalizing" period.

Pottery. Between 700 and 600 B.C. the style of Greek pottery was influenced by trade with the Near East, Asia Minor, and Egypt. An example is the seventh-century *Levy Oinochoe* (fig. 3.17) (an **oinochoe**, from the Greek word meaning "to pour out wine," is a wine jug with a pinched lip). Although the design appears to be stenciled, in fact the outlines and details are incised. In a departure from the Geometric style, the figures begin to be given much more importance. Also many Oriental motifs appear—lotuses, palmettes, rosettes—all apparently derived from Egyptian art. Winged animals similar to those found in Mesopotamia (see fig. 1.15) and sphinxes from Egypt (see fig. 2.5) appear as well.

By 600 B.C. this Orientalizing process had taken especially strong hold in Corinth, a port city with close ties to the cultures of the East. From 600 to 550 B.C. Corinth was the biggest vase-producing city in Greece. The color of Corinthian ware is distinctive: purplish-brown, reddish-brown, red, and black are painted on a lighter background. The origin of a vase may be determined by the color of the clay from which it was made. For

Figure 3.18 Pitcher (olpe), from Corinth, ca. 600 B.C., terra cotta, height 11½″ (29.2 cm), British Museum, London. Corinthian ware was made in the city of Corinth, where the clay is beige in color, differing from the orange clay found in Athens. Corinth and Athens competed in the production of vases.

Figure 3.17 *Levy Oinochoe,* Orientalizing style, east Greek, ca. 650 B.C., terra cotta, height 15½″ (39.4 cm), Musée du Louvre, Paris. The importance of figures in vase painting was gradually increased. Contact with the East resulted in the use of Oriental motifs.

instance, the clay of Corinth is beige, while that of Athens is orange.

An example of Corinthian ware is the **olpe**, or pitcher, dating from about 600 B.C. (fig. 3.18). Animals are popular motifs on Corinthian ware. Some are real animals, such as goats, panthers, lions, stags, bulls, and birds; other creatures are imaginary, such as sirens and sphinxes. Here, arranged in strict symmetry, one head is attached to two bodies, creating a monster with combined parts, something also found in the "animal" style of Mesopotamia.

THE ARCHAIC PERIOD

The Archaic period, ca. 600–480 B.C., was a time of rapid change and development in ancient Greece. The political organization of the city-states began to undergo significant alteration as the old aristocratic rulers were displaced by the vigorous new class of wealthy traders, who had profited from expanding Greek commerce and colonization overseas. Individual rulers replaced the old council of aristocrats. These powerful individuals had the title of tyrants. (The word "tyrant," however, only later came to have its modern negative connotation, for tyrants often enjoyed the broad support of the people.) These political reforms were only the first in a long and critical series that led to the establishment of what we now call the first democracy (see Chapter 4).

In other respects, the Archaic period saw the emergence of the artistic forms and skills that reached their peak in the fifth century B.C. and that have dominated the artistic history of Western civilization ever since. Central to this is the depiction of the human figure. Leaving behind the abstract decorations of the Geometric period, Greek artists took as their most important task the study of the human form and sought to depict it with ever-increasing realism. In many ways, this choice has determined the course of Western art, which, until the beginning of the twentieth century, centered on the human figure and its accurate portrayal. Sixth-century B.C. sculptors produced large-scale freestanding figures, and also began creating relief sculpture for temples. The first great architectural works were created in this period, and pottery, now dominated by Athens, showed remarkable developments.

Black-Figure Vases. One of the two most important types of Greek vase painting is the black-figure style. First developed in Corinth, the black-figure style spread from there to Athens, where it was refined in the second half of the seventh century B.C., reaching its peak between 600 and 500 B.C. In the black-figure style, painting is done with a black glaze on a natural red clay background. In essence, the artist works with silhouetted forms, drawing the outlines and then filling in the color. Once this color has been applied, details are created by scraping through the black glaze to reveal the red clay beneath. Since the artist must exert considerable pressure to make these details, the resulting lines do not flow readily. The technique thus tends to produce a decorative two-dimensional effect.

Many different black-figure workshops were active, and the distinct styles of individual artists are discernible. In fact, several black-figure artists are known by name. EXEKIAS [egg-ZEEK-yas] (active last half of the sixth century B.C.) is considered the master of the black-figure style. He was both painter and potter—two vases are signed "Exekias decorated and made me"—whereas, in other cases, different names are given for the potter and the painter. Exekias is renowned for his exquisite detailing—finely formed folds of fabric, precisely painted patterns, exquisite outlines. Many vases painted by Exekias survive.

An **amphora**—a two-handled vessel named for the Greek word meaning "to carry on both sides"—by Exekias and dated 550–525 B.C. (fig. 3.19) is a mature example of the black-figure style. It depicts Achilles and Ajax. Homer's epic *The Iliad* tells of the great warrior

Ajax and the even greater Achilles, the military heroes of the Greeks, playing checkers in their camp at Troy. Achilles eventually wins the game, but their concentration on the competition causes them not to hear Athena blowing her trumpet to call them to fight against the Trojans. This subject became popular in painting and even in sculpture after the sixth century B.C.

The figures stand on a baseline, suggesting some concept of a three-dimensional space. The composition is a perfect balance of verticals, horizontals, and diagonals. The figures, which are labeled on the vase, conform to the shape of the vase, bending with the bulge. The warriors wear their armor plus elaborate ornamental cloaks, which are used to embellish the surface decoration. Exekias paints perfect profile portraits of the protagonists, yet the eye is seen from the front in the Egyptian

Figure 3.19 Exekias, *Ajax and Achilles*, amphora, black-figure style, 550–525 B.C., terra cotta, height $26\frac{3}{8}$" (67 cm), Vatican Museums, Rome. Narrative became progressively more popular on vases, the subjects often taken from mythology. Exekias, master of the black-figure style, is especially noted for his carefully composed scenes.

Figure 3.20 Signed by Nikias as potter, Pan-Athenaic amphora, black-figure style, ca. 560–555 B.C., terra cotta, height 24⅓″ (61.7 cm), Metropolitan Museum of Art, New York. A special type of vase, routinely painted in black-figure even after the introduction of red-figure, Pan-Athenaic amphoras were given as prizes—the specific competition for which the vase was awarded is shown on the other side of the vase.

manner. Not until around 470 B.C. would artists depict the eye in profile.

Narratives dominate vase decoration over the next centuries, the subjects frequently derived from mythology as well as daily life. A special type of vase that recorded a specific aspect of ancient Greek life was an amphora representing the Pan-Athenaic Games, which were held every summer in Athens in honor of Athena. Almost always done in the black-figure technique, the type is represented here by an example (fig. 3.20) signed by NIKIAS [NEEK-i-as] (active mid-sixth century B.C.) and made ca. 560–555 B.C. Amphoras were given as prizes or awards at the games, and filled with wine, olive

oil, or water. The Greeks held various types of competitions, ranging from foot races and wrestling to chariot and horse races. The scenes on Pan-Athenaic amphoras are always much the same. The rooster on the column is a symbol of the competition. The inscription says "from the games at Athens" or "one of the prizes from Athens." Depicted on the vase is Athena, patron goddess of Athens, armed with shield and spear. On the other side the activity for which the vase was awarded is shown.

Red-Figure Vases. Around 530 B.C., under pressure from the Persians, a flood of Ionian Greek refugees came to Greece from Asia Minor, introducing Oriental and Ionic influences to mainland art. At the same time, red-figure vase painting started in Athens. As this style took hold, the black-figure style gradually disappeared. Red-figure finally replaced black-figure around 500 B.C. Only Pan-Athenaic amphoras continued to be made in the black-figure style.

The red-figure technique is essentially an inversion of the black-figure technique. In the red-figure technique the background around the figures is painted black. Details within the contours of the figures are then painted with a brush on the reddish clay. Variety of color is achieved by diluting the black, and a range from dark brown to yellowish is possible. In the red-figure

Figure 3.21 Euxitheos and Euphronios, *Death of Sarpedon*, calyx krater, red-figure style, ca. 515 B.C., terra cotta, height 18″ (45.7 cm), Metropolitan Museum of Art, New York. Although in the black-figure technique details must be scraped through the black glaze, in red-figure details are painted on with a tiny brush. Therefore, details are achieved more easily, and greater fluidity of line is possible.

Connections

LANDSCAPE AND ARCHITECTURE

According to Vincent Scully, an architectural historian, the great Greek temples can best be understood by exploring their relation to the landscape around them. Characteristically, the Greek landscape is formed by mountains of moderate size, which surround very clearly defined areas of valley and plain, and by islands, clearly demarcated land surfaces surrounded by flat blue sea. Unlike the deserts of Asia Minor and northern Africa or the Alps of Central Europe, the Greek landscape is of a scale and clarity that can be contained, so to speak, by the human eye.

With this in mind, Scully notes that each of the Cretan palaces possesses the same relation to the landscape: the palace is set in an enclosed valley on a north–south axis; there is, nearby, a gently mounded or conical hill; beyond this, on the same axis, is a higher, double-peaked or cleft mountain. This last suggests to Scully not only the horns of the bull or Minotaur, but also breasts, and even, in his words, "the *mons Veneris* of the earth"—the female principle, or earth mother.

The two temples of Hera at Paestum have an analogous relation to the landscape. Hera is not only the wife of Zeus, and thus the goddess of marriage and domestic stability, but also the earth mother. The temples at Paestum were built side by side, on the same axis, oriented toward a conical notched mountain to the east. Standing beside them, at their western end, the direction from which the viewer would naturally approach them, the perspective created by their sides points toward the mountain itself. "Once seen together," Scully writes, "both landscape and temple will seem forever incomplete without the other. Each ennobles its opposite, and their relationship brings the universe of nature and man into a new stable order."

technique, the details no longer need to be scraped into the surface as they had been in black-figure, and this facilitates the drawing of details. It is easier to paint details with a brush than to incise them.

The red-figure style put Athens in the forefront of the vase-producing industry. Athenian red-figure vases were exported, as black-figure vases had been. In the last quarter of the fifth century B.C., Athenian vase painting was at its peak of production, and the city was to maintain its monopoly on the vase industry for about two hundred years. In fact, the other vase-producing sites (Corinth, Sikyon, Sparta, the islands, the Ionian east) stopped producing vases or greatly diminished their industry.

Signed by EUXITHEOS [yoog-SITH-ios] as potter and EUPHRONIOS [yoo-FRO-nios] as painter is a **calyx krater** (fig. 3.21), dating from about 515 B.C., on which is depicted the *Death of Sarpedon* from the story of the Trojan War. As Homer tells it in *The Iliad*, Sarpedon, the son of Zeus and Europa, was a Trojan leader. He was killed by Patroclus at Troy when attacking the Greek camp, after which there ensued a battle over his body. In this scene, Sarpedon is lifted by Sleep and Death in the presence of Hermes and two Trojans. Sleep and Death are twin brothers. It is a scene of mourning—a favorite Greek subject from the Geometric period onward. Sleep and Death bring Sarpedon back to his home. Hermes is included in the scene because he is the messenger of the gods, but also because he is the guide of the dead in Hades; he conducts the souls of the dead to Hades. All the names of the figures are inscribed, sometimes written right to left.

In this active and emotional scene, the narrative element is highly developed, as is the refined style.

Sarpedon is shown from the front, with the anatomy realistically rendered. Details of the muscles, tendons, and beards are finely depicted. The scene is drawn within a rectangle, and the figures move along a baseline in typical red-figure style. Within this rectangle, the composition accommodates the shape of the vase. Decorative bands provide a border, above and below. Red-figure vases of the later Classical period show a decreased interest in the heavy borders, which become less prominent or are absent.

The Greek Temple. The monumental structures erected by ancient Greek architects have proved to be of immense importance historically, influencing much of Western architecture. Even today, the principles and "vocabulary" of the ancient Greeks continue to be an extremely significant source of inspiration for architects. Despite their continuing importance, however, the study of ancient Greek architecture is hampered by selective survival. Buildings constructed of impermanent materials—wood, for instance—no longer exist, whereas many structures built of stone still survive. The functions of these buildings also tend to be limited to public use—the history of ancient Greek architecture is largely the history of the Greek temple, although there are extant treasuries, porticoes, massive gateways, theaters, and monuments as well. Virtually nothing remains of domestic architecture, for there is no evidence of the architecture in which most of the people passed most of their lives.

The typical Greek temple consists of three basic parts: the **platform**, **colonnade**, and **entablature** (fig. 3.22). The platform is made up of the **crepidoma** or **crepis**,

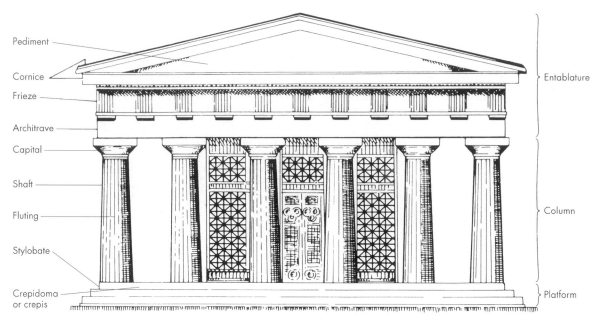

Pediment
Cornice
Frieze
Architrave
Capital
Shaft
Fluting
Stylobate
Crepidoma
or crepis

Entablature
Column
Platform

Figure 3.22 The elements of Greek temple architecture.

the three visible steps of the platform, of which the **stylobate**, or base for the columns, is the top step. The **columns** which make up the **peristyle**, or colonnade surrounding all four side of the temple, consist of a **shaft**, which tapers upward, differing from the Minoan column, which tapers downward. The columns are **fluted**, or carved with a series of parallel vertical ridges, and are topped by the **capital**. The entablature consists of the **architrave** immediately above the capitals and, in many temples, a **frieze** or band of ornamental carving. Rising above the entablature on each end of the temple and enclosed by a cornice is a triangular **pediment**.

The Temple of Hera I at Paestum. The earliest style of Greek temples is known as the **Doric**, after the tribes that invaded Mycenae from the north after about 1100 B.C. The Doric style is simple, severe, powerful in appearance, with little decorative embellishment. Some of the purest examples of the Doric style can be found in the lower third of Italy and in Sicily, regions that were considered part of Greece as early as the seventh century B.C. At Paestum in southern Italy the Greeks built three temples, side by side, the earliest of which is extremely important in the study of the development of the Doric order.

Dated 560–550 B.C., the Temple of Hera I (fig. 3.23), so called to distinguish it from the later Temple of Hera built at the same site, was constructed of local limestone. Its closely spaced columns support a high and heavy entablature that makes them appear squat. Thick heavy columns taper noticeably to the top, with an abrupt transition from shaft to capital, which projects widely beyond the shaft. Little **entasis**—a subtle convex bulge in the

middle of a column shaft—is seen in these early columns. The entire effect, while monumental, appears disproportionate and awkward.

The Temple of Aphaia at Aegina. Soon after, back on the Greek mainland, the Doric temple achieved remarkable beauty in the Temple of Aphaia at Aegina

Figure 3.23 Temple of Hera I, Paestum, Italy, 560–550 B.C., limestone. The sixth century B.C. was a time of architectural experimentation. Although the proportions used here are not harmonious, the two temples built later at Paestum have thinner columns and less overhang to the capitals.

Figure 3.24 Temple of Aphaia at Aegina, view from the southeast, ca. 510 B.C. The columns and capital of the Aeginian temple appear more graceful than those of the Temple of Hera at Paestum.

(fig. 3.24). This is accomplished by widening the spaces between the columns, making them proportionately taller in relation to the entablature, and, particularly, by narrowing the individual columns themselves. The sense of proper proportion achieved in the process became a fundamental characteristic of Greek art and architecture. Both the Temple of Hera I at Paestum and the Temple of Aphaia at Aegina utilize a 1:2 mathematical ratio. That is, at Paestum, there are nine columns on the ends and eighteen on the sides of the temple, while the Aegina temple has six columns on the ends and twelve on the sides. Soon, however, this proportion was modified. In what is now referred to as a **regular temple**, the number of columns along the sides was designed to be double the number of columns on the ends plus one. Examples of regular temples are the six-by-thirteen Temple of Athena at Paestum, and the Parthenon in Athens, which is an eight-by-seventeen temple. The desire to refine and perfect in a quest for order and harmony is seen in the continual experimentation that preoccupied the Greeks as they strived to arrive at an ideal type. The goal was to improve upon what already existed, rather than to innovate radically.

Sculpture. The history of ancient Greek sculpture is dominated by images of the human figure, particularly the **kouros** (plural, **kouroi**) [COO-ross; COO-roy] (fig. 3.25), a lifesize representation of a nude male youth, seen standing with one foot forward and arms to his sides, and the **kore** (plural, **korai**) [CO-ray], the female equivalent, but clothed.

Strictly speaking, the first large-scale sculptures of the human figure date from the Orientalizing period, although the form developed so rapidly in the Archaic period that we will concentrate on sixth-century B.C. examples. The early Near Eastern influence appears to have been decisive. The characteristic pose of the kouros is believed to have derived from Egyptian sculpture. The marble kouros (fig. 3.25), carved ca. 600 B.C., shares many of its features with Egyptian figures (see fig. 2.7): the rigid frontality, erect stance, and pose with left foot forward. However, the Greek figure is nude and has been carved to be freestanding. There are thus no webs of stone between the arms and body and between the legs, and no supporting back pillars.

The kouros reproduced here was also originally painted—all sculpture was colored with reds, yellows,

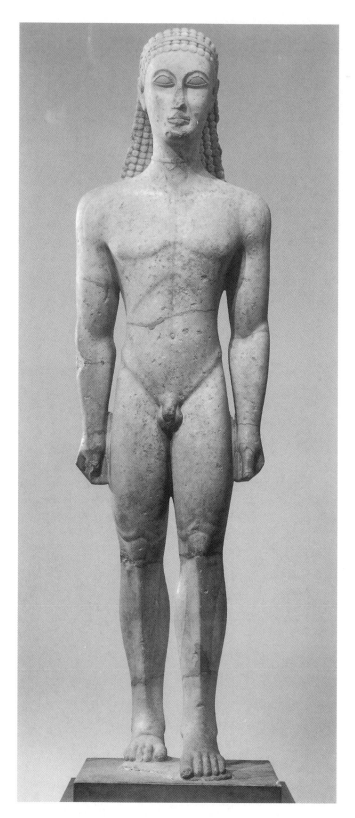

Figure 3.25 Kouros, ca. 600 B.C., marble, height 6′4″ (1.93m), Metropolitan Museum of Art, New York. A Greek kouros is a statue of a standing nude male. Details of the anatomy form a decorative surface pattern. The pose, with one foot forward yet the weight of the body equally distributed on both feet, comes from Egypt.

Figure 3.26 Kore, wearing an Ionic chiton, ca. 520 B.C., marble, height $22\frac{1}{8}$″ (56.3 cm), Acropolis Museum, Athens. The decorative chiton, made of soft, thin fabric, clings to the body. The Archaic smile is still evident here.

blues, and greens. Some pieces still retain some of their original color. Touches of red pigment remain on this kouros's hair and elsewhere.

Early kouros figures are highly stylized and character-istically have an enigmatic expression, which is often referred to as an "Archaic smile." The eyes are abnor-mally large, and the hair forms a decorative bead-like pattern. The anatomy is arranged for design rather than in strict imitation of nature; thus the abdominal muscles and knee-caps become surface decoration. The figures are not portraits of individuals; there is no evidence that they were done from models.

Over time kouros and kore figures become more real-istic and the poses more relaxed. They remain slender, but the waist gradually expands. Proportions of the vari-ous body parts become more natural and are no longer indicated by lines on the surface but rather by the sculpt-ing of the material itself. It is possible to assign approxi-mate dates to examples on the basis of these changes.

The changes that were gradually taking place are demonstrated by a late Archaic kore (fig. 3.26), carved ca. 520 B.C. Made of Island marble, this particular kore was elaborately painted. Figures like this with one hand extended may represent a goddess or donor.

Exquisitely sculpted, this delicate and dainty figure appears soft and sensual. The face still has an "Archaic smile," but the eyes are smaller than they were before, and the slanting eyes, hairstyle, and decorative treatment of the costume suggest an Eastern origin for this figure in the Ionian islands—perhaps the island of Chios.

The figure is dressed in a chiton, a belted single-piece garment for women with buttoned sleeves, which was imported to Athens from eastern Ionia just before the middle of the sixth century B.C. The sculptor gives much attention to this costume. The fabric is thin and clings to the body, the folds and draping are complex, the cut of the garment asymmetrical, and the hemlines are emphasized with colored bands. The cloak, worn over the chiton, ties on one shoulder, creating diagonal patterns and curved lines. The simplicity of earlier sculpture has given way to much more complex modeling, even as Greek culture was becoming more complex and sophisticated itself.

Philosophy. Perhaps nothing distinguishes the rise of ancient Greece as a civilization more than its love of pure thought. The Greeks were the first to practice "philosophy," literally the "love of wisdom," in a systematic way, categorizing the various aspects of the world and their relation to it in terms that were based not on faith or emotion but on logic and reasoning.

Before the ascendancy of Socrates and his pupil Plato in the late fifth century B.C. and after, Greek thinkers hotly debated the nature of the world and their place in it. There were the **materialists**, who explained the world in terms of the four elements—fire, earth, air, and water. HERAKLEITOS [hair-ah-KLY-tus] (ca. 535–475 B.C.) defined the world as being in a state of constant flux: Nothing *is*, he claimed, rather all is in a constant state of *becoming*. One can never step in the same river twice, he said, since the water will necessarily have flowed on downstream the second time, and even if one were to follow the water, the bank would have changed. Thus, every day is different, enmeshed in the flow of time.

Another group of thinkers, the **atomists**, led by DEMOCRITUS [dih-MAH-crih-tus] (ca. 460 B.C.), conceived of the world as being made up of two basic elements, atoms—small, invisible particles that cannot be divided into smaller units—and the void, the empty space between atoms. Atomism survived in a changed form in the later philosophy of the Epicureans (see Chapter 4) and had a dramatic influence on the thinking of the scientists who evolved modern atomic theory and quantum mechanics.

But perhaps the most important of these Presocratic thinkers was PYTHAGORAS [pih-THAY-guh-rus] (582–507 B.C.). For him, "number" was at the heart of all things. Today he is most often remembered for his theo-

rem in geometry—in right-angle triangles, the square of the hypotenuse is equal to the sum of the square of the other two sides. These triangles are unified by number. Pythagoras extended this principle to music. He discovered that a string of a certain length, when plucked, made a certain sound; cut in half, it played the same note, only an octave higher. Mathematical ratios, he reasoned, determined musical sounds. The entire natural world, including the movement of the planets, depended upon these same ratios, he believed. There was, underlying all things, a "harmony of the spheres."

Sappho and the Lyric Poem. As with epic poetry, there was an oral tradition of lyric poetry long before the first verse was written down. Unlike epic, which was chanted, lyric poetry was originally sung, accompanied by the lyre, the stringed instrument from which the name "lyric" derives. Also unlike epic, which flourished in Ionia, lyric flourished on the island of Lesbos, especially in the sixth century B.C. with the lyric poetry of Sappho [SAFF-oh] (ca. 610–580 B.C.). Where epic provides a somewhat distant and communal perspective on human experience, lyric offers a personal voice, an intimate expression of subjective feeling.

Sappho's fame as a poet was acclaimed by Plato, who described her as "the tenth Muse." The Early Christian Church, however, did not appreciate the sensuality of the poems, nor their lesbian subject matter. Much of Sappho's work was destroyed during the Middle Ages, with manuscripts of her poetry consigned to fires during the fourth century A.D. in Constantinople and during the eleventh century in Rome. Only a few poems remain in their entirety along with a series of fragments of others.

Little is known of Sappho's life, except that she was married and had a daughter, Cleis. Even from what little survives of Sappho's work, readers can appreciate the intensity of emotion they express and the direct and graceful way they celebrate female experience.

READINGS
✧

✧ **HOMER**
from *The Iliad*

The first of the following passages from The Iliad *describes Achilles' slaying of the Trojan hero Hector, followed by the grief expressed by Hector's wife, Hecuba, and his father, Priam. The second occurs at the very end of the epic and describes Priam's visit to Achilles to beg for the return of his son's body. Together they reveal the heroic code at work in the poem and the human sympathy that contends with it and finally works to affect even the iron-hearted Achilles.*

from BOOK XXII

Bright as that star amid the stars in the night sky,
star of the evening, brightest star that rides the

heavens,
so fire flared from the sharp point of the spear Achilles
brandished high in his right hand, bent on Hector's death,
scanning his splendid body—where to pierce it best?
The rest of his flesh seemed all encased in armor,
burnished, brazen—*Achilles'* armor that Hector stripped   *380*
from strong Patroclus when he killed him—true,
but one spot lay exposed,
where collarbones lift the neckbone off the shoulders,
the open throat, where the end of life comes quickest—*there*
as Hector charged in fury brilliant Achilles drove his spear   *385*
and the point went stabbing clean through the tender neck
but the heavy bronze weapon failed to slash the windpipe—
Hector could still gasp out some words, some last reply …
he crashed in the dust—
                              godlike Achilles gloried over him:
"Hector—surely you thought when you stripped Patroclus' armor   *390*
that you, you would be safe! Never a fear of me—
far from the fighting as I was—you fool!
Left behind there, down by the beaked ships
his great avenger waited, a greater man by far—
that man was I, and I smashed your strength! And you—   *395*
the dogs and birds will maul you, shame your corpse
while Achaeans bury my dear friend in glory!"

Struggling for breath, Hector, his helmet flashing,
said, "I beg you, beg you by your life, your parents—
don't let the dogs devour me by the Argive ships!   *400*
Wait, take the princely ransom of bronze and gold,
the gifts my father and noble mother will give you—
but give my body to friends to carry home again,
so Trojan men and Trojan women can do me honor
with fitting rites of fire once I am dead."   *405*

Staring grimly, the proud runner Achilles answered,
"Beg no more, you fawning dog—begging me by my parents!
Would to god my rage, my fury would drive me now
to hack your flesh away and eat you raw—
such agonies you have caused me! Ransom?   *410*
No man alive could keep the dog-packs off you,
not if they haul in ten, twenty times that ransom
and pile it here before me and promise fortunes more—
no, not even if Dardan Priam should offer to weigh out
your bulk in gold! Not even then will your noble mother   *415*
lay you on your deathbed, mourn the son she

bore …
The dogs and birds will rend you—blood and bone!"

At the point of death, Hector, his helmet flashing,
said, "I know you well—I see my fate before me.
Never a chance that I could win you over …   *420*
Iron inside your chest, that heart of yours.
But now beware, or my curse will draw god's wrath
upon your head, that day when Paris and lord Apollo—
for all your fighting heart—destroy you at the Scaean Gates!"

Death cut him short. The end closed in around him.   *425*
Flying free of his limbs
his soul went winging down to the House of Death,
wailing his fate, leaving his manhood far behind,
his young and supple strength. But brilliant Achilles
taunted Hector's body, dead as he was, "Die, die!   *430*
For my own death, I'll meet it freely—whenever Zeus
and the other deathless gods would like to bring it on!"

With that he wrenched his bronze spear from the corpse,
laid it aside and ripped the bloody armor off the back.
And the other sons of Achaea, running up around him,   *435*
crowded closer, all of them gazing wonder-struck
at the build and marvelous, lithe beauty of Hector.
And not a man came forward who did not stab his body,
glancing toward a comrade, laughing: "Ah, look here—
how much softer he is to handle now, this Hector,   *440*
than when he gutted our ships with roaring fire!"

Standing over him, so they'd gloat and stab his body.
But once he had stripped the corpse the proud runner Achilles
took his stand in the midst of all the Argive troops
and urged them on with a flight of winging orders: *445*
"Friends—lords of the Argives, O my captains!
Now that the gods have let me kill this man
who caused us agonies, loss on crushing loss—
more than the rest of all their men combined—
come, let us ring their walls in armor, test them,   *450*
see what recourse the Trojans still may have in mind.
Will they abandon the city heights with this man fallen?
Or brace for a last, dying stand though Hector's gone?
But wait—what am I saying? Why this deep debate?
Down by the ships a body lies unwept, unburied—   *455*
Patroclus … I will never forget him,
not as long as I'm still among the living
and my springing knees will lift and drive me on.

Though the dead forget their dead in the House of
    Death,
I will remember, even there, my dear companion.
                           Now,   *460*
come, you sons of Achaea, raise a song of triumph!
Down to the ships we march and bear this corpse on
    high—
we have won ourselves great glory. We have brought
magnificent Hector down, that man the Trojans
glorified in their city like a god!"   *465*
                     So he triumphed
and now he was bent on outrage, on shaming noble
    Hector.
Piercing the tendons, ankle to heel behind both feet,
he knotted straps of rawhide through them both,
lashed them to his chariot, left the head to drag
and mounting the car, hoisting the famous arms
    aboard,   *470*
he whipped his team to a run and breakneck on they
    flew,
holding nothing back. And a thick cloud of dust rose up
from the man they dragged, his dark hair swirling
    round
that head so handsome once, all tumbled low in the
    dust—
since Zeus had given him over to his enemies now   *475*
to be defiled in the land of his own fathers.

So his whole head was dragged down in the dust.
And now his mother began to tear her hair …
she flung her shining veil to the ground and raised
a high, shattering scream, looking down at her son.   *480*
Pitifully his loving father groaned and round the
    king
his people cried with grief and wailing seized the
    city—
for all the world as if all Troy were torched and
    smoldering
down from the looming brows of the citadel to her
    roots.
Priam's people could hardly hold the old man back,
frantic, mad to go rushing out the Dardan Gates.
He begged them all, groveling in the filth,
crying out to them, calling each man by name,
"Let go, my friends! Much as you care for me,
let me hurry out of the city, make my way,   *490*
all on my own, to Achaea's waiting ships!
I must implore that terrible, violent man …
Perhaps—who knows?—he may respect my age,
may pity an old man. He has a father too,
as old as I am—Peleus sired him once,   *495*
Peleus reared him to be the scourge of Troy
but most of all to me—he made my life a hell.
So many sons he slaughtered, just coming into
    bloom …
but grieving for all the rest, one breaks my heart the
    most
and stabbing grief for him will take me down to
    Death—   *500*
my Hector—would to god he had perished in my
    arms!

Then his mother who bore him—oh so doomed,
she and I could glut ourselves with grief."

So the voice of the king rang out in tears,
the citizens wailed in answer, and noble Hecuba   *505*
led the wives of Troy in a throbbing chant of sorrow:
"O my child—my desolation! How can I go on
    living?
What agonies must I suffer now, now *you* are dead
    and gone?
You were my pride throughout the city night and
    day—
a blessing to us all, the men and women of Troy: *510*
throughout the city they saluted you like a god.
You, you were their greatest glory while you lived—
now death and fate have seized you, dragged you
    down!"

Her voice rang out in tears, but the wife of
    Hector
had not heard a thing. No messenger brought the
    truth   *515*
of how her husband made his stand outside the
    gates.
She was weaving at her loom, deep in the high halls,
working flowered braiding into a dark red folding
    robe.
And she called her well-kempt women through the
    house
to set a large three-legged cauldron over the fire   *520*
so Hector could have his steaming hot bath
when he came home from battle—poor woman,
she never dreamed how far he was from bathing,
struck down at Achilles' hands by blazing-eyed
    Athena.
But she heard the groans and wails of grief from the
    rampart now   *525*
and her body shook, her shuttle dropped to the
    ground,
she called out to her lovely waiting women,
    "Quickly—
two of you follow me—I must see what's happened.
That cry—that was Hector's honored mother I
    heard!
My heart's pounding, leaping up in my throat,   *530*
the knees beneath me paralyzed—Oh I know it …
something terrible's coming down on Priam's
    children.
Pray god the news will never reach my ears!
Yes but I dread it so—what if great Achilles
has cut my Hector off from the city, daring
    Hector,   *535*
and driven him out across the plain, and all alone?—
He may have put an end to that fatal headstrong
    pride
that always seized my Hector—never hanging back
with the main force of men, always charging ahead,
giving ground to no man in his fury!"
                     So she cried,   *540*
dashing out of the royal halls like a madwoman,
her heart racing hard, her women close behind her.

But once she reached the tower where soldiers massed
she stopped on the rampart, looked down and saw it all—
saw him dragged before the city, stallions galloping,   545
dragging Hector back to Achaea's beaked warships—
ruthless work. The world went black as night
before her eyes, she fainted, falling backward,
gasping away her life breath …
She flung to the winds her glittering headdress,   550
the cap and the coronet, braided band and veil,
all the regalia golden Aphrodite gave her once,
the day that Hector, helmet aflash in sunlight,
led her home to Troy from her father's house
with countless wedding gifts to win her heart.   555
But crowding round her now her husband's sisters
and brothers' wives supported her in their midst,
and she, terrified, stunned to the point of death,
struggling for breath now and coming back to life,
burst out in grief among the Trojan women: "O
Hector—   560
I am destroyed! Both born to the same fate after all!
You, you at Troy in the halls of King Priam—
I at Thebes, under the timberline of Placos,
Eetion's house … He raised me as a child,
that man of doom, his daughter just as doomed—   565
would to god he'd never fathered *me*!
                                Now you go down
to the House of Death, the dark depths of the earth,
and leave me here to waste away in grief, a widow
lost in the royal halls—and the boy only a baby,
the son we bore together, you and I so doomed.   570
Hector, what help are you to him, now you are
dead?—
what help is he to you? Think, even if he escapes
the wrenching horrors of war against the Argives,
pain and labor will plague him all his days to come.
Strangers will mark his lands off, stealing his estates.   575
The day that orphans a youngster cuts him off from
friends.
And he hangs his head low, humiliated in every
way …
his cheeks stained with tears, and pressed by hunger
the boy goes up to his father's old companions,
tugging at one man's cloak, another's tunic,   580
and some will pity him, true,
and one will give him a little cup to drink,
enough to wet his lips, not quench his thirst.
But then some bully with both his parents living
beats him from the banquet, fists and abuses flying: 585
'You, get out—you've got no father feasting with us
here!'
And the boy, sobbing, trails home to his widowed
mother …
Astyanax!
                And years ago, propped on his father's knee,
he would only eat the marrow, the richest cuts of
lamb,   590
and when sleep came on him and he had quit his
play,

cradled warm in his nurse's arms he'd drowse off,
snug in a soft bed, his heart brimmed with joy.
Now what suffering, now he's lost his father—
                                        Astyanax!   595
The Lord of the City, so the Trojans called him,
because it was you, Hector, you and you alone
who shielded the gates and the long walls of Troy.
But now by the beaked ships, far from your parents,
glistening worms will wriggle through your flesh,   600
once the dogs have had their fill of your naked
corpse—
though we have such stores of clothing laid up in the
halls,
fine things, a joy to the eye, the work of women's
hands.
Now, by god, I'll burn them all, blazing to the skies!
No use to you now, they'll never shroud your
body—   605
but they will be your glory
burned by the Trojan men and women in your
honor!"

Her voice rang out in tears and the women
wailed in answer.

from BOOK XXIV

The old king went straight up to the lodge
where Achilles dear to Zeus would always sit.
Priam found the warrior there inside …
many captains sitting some way off, but two,   555
veteran Automedon and the fine fighter Alcimus
were busy serving him. He had just finished dinner,
eating, drinking, and the table still stood near.
The majestic king of Troy slipped past the rest
and kneeling down beside Achilles, clasped his knees 560
and kissed his hands, those terrible, man-killing hands
that had slaughtered Priam's many sons in battle.
Awesome—as when the grip of madness seizes one
who murders a man in his own fatherland and flees
abroad to foreign shores, to a wealthy, noble host,   565
and a sense of marvel runs through all who see him—
so Achilles marveled, beholding majestic Priam.
His men marveled too, trading startled glances.
But Priam prayed his heart out to Achilles:
"Remember your own father, great godlike
Achilles—   570
as old as *I* am, past the threshold of deadly old age!
No doubt the countrymen round about him plague him
now,
with no one there to defend him, beat away disaster.
No one—but at least he hears you're still alive
and his old heart rejoices, hopes rising, day by day,   575
to see his beloved son come sailing home from Troy.
But I—dear god, my life so cursed by fate …
I fathered hero sons in the wide realm of Troy
and now not a single one is left, I tell you.
Fifty sons I had when the sons of Achaea came,   580
nineteen born to me from a single mother's womb
and the rest by other women in the palace. Many,

most of them violent Ares cut the knees from under.
But one, one was left me, to guard my walls, my
    people—
the one you killed the other day, defending his
    fatherland,   585
my Hector! It's all for him I've come to the ships
    now,
to win him back from you—I bring a priceless
    ransom.
Revere the gods, Achilles! Pity me in my own right,
remember your own father! I deserve more pity …
I have endured what no one on earth has ever done
    before—   590
I put to my lips the hands of the man who killed my
    son."

    Those words stirred within Achilles a deep desire
to grieve for his own father. Taking the old man's
    hand
he gently moved him back. And overpowered by
    memory
both men gave way to grief. Priam wept freely   595
for man-killing Hector, throbbing, crouching
before Achilles' feet as Achilles wept himself,
now for his father, now for Patroclus once again,
and their sobbing rose and fell throughout the
    house.
Then, when brilliant Achilles had his fill of tears   600
and the longing for it had left his mind and body,
he rose from his seat, raised the old man by the hand
and filled with pity now for his gray head and gray
    beard,
he spoke out winging words, flying straight to the
    heart:
"Poor man, how much you've borne—pain to break
    the spirit!   605
What daring brought you down to the ships, all
    alone,
to face the glance of the man who killed your sons,
so many fine brave boys? You have a heart of iron.
Come, please, sit down on this chair here …
Let us put our griefs to rest in our own hearts,   610
rake them up no more, raw as we are with mourning.
What good's to be won from tears that chill the
    spirit?
So the immortals spun our lives that we, we wretched
    men
live on to bear such torments—the gods live free of
    sorrows.
There are two great jars that stand on the floor of
    Zeus's halls   615
and hold his gifts, our miseries one, the other
    blessings.
When Zeus who loves the lightning mixes gifts for a
    man,
now he meets with misfortune, now good times in
    turn.
When Zeus dispenses gifts from the jar of sorrows
    only
he makes a man an outcast—brutal, ravenous hunger 620
drives him down the face of the shining earth,

stalking far and wide, cursed by gods and men.
So with my father, Peleus. What glittering gifts
the gods rained down from the day that he was born!
He excelled all men in wealth and pride of place,   625
he lorded the Myrmidons, and mortal that he was,
they gave the man an immortal goddess for a wife.
Yes, but even on him the Father piled hardships,
no powerful race of princes born in his royal halls,
only a single son he fathered, doomed at birth,   630
cut off in the spring of life—
and I, I give the man no care as he grows old
since here I sit in Troy, far from my fatherland,
a grief to you, a grief to all your children.
And you too, old man, we hear you prospered once: 635
as far as Lesbos, Macar's kingdom, bounds to
    seaward,
Phrygia east and upland, the Hellespont vast and
    north—
that entire realm, they say, you lorded over once,
you excelled all men, old king, in sons and wealth.
But then the gods of heaven brought this agony on
    you   640
ceaseless battles round your walls, your armies
    slaughtered.
You must bear up now, Enough of endless tears,
the pain that breaks the spirit.
Grief for your son will do no good at all.
You will never bring him back to life—   645
sooner you must suffer something worse."

    But the old and noble Priam protested strongly:
"Don't make me sit on a chair, Achilles, Prince,
not while Hector lies uncared-for in your camp!
Give him back to me, now, no more delay—   650
I must see my son with my own eyes.
Accept the ransom I bring you, a king's ransom!
Enjoy it, all of it—return to your own native land,
safe and sound … since now you've spared my life."

    A dark glance—and the headstrong runner
    answered,   655
"No more, old man, don't tempt my wrath, not now!
My own mind's made up to give you back your son.
A messenger brought me word from Zeus—my
    mother,
Thetis who bore me, the Old Man of the Sea's
    daughter.
And what's more, I can see through you, Priam—   660
no hiding the fact from me: one of the gods
has led you down to Achaea's fast ships.
No man alive, not even a rugged young fighter,
would dare to venture into our camp. Never—
how could he slip past the sentries unchallenged?   665
Or shoot back the bolt of my gates with so much
    ease?
So don't anger me now. Don't stir my raging heart still
    more.
Or under my own roof I may not spare your life, old
    man—
suppliant that you are—may break the laws of
    Zeus!"

The old man was terrified. He obeyed the order.   *670*
But Achilles bounded out of doors like a lion—
not alone but flanked by his two aides-in-arms,
veteran Automedon and Alcimus, steady comrades,
Achilles' favorites next to the dead Patroclus.
They loosed from harness the horses and the mules,   *675*
they led the herald in, the old king's crier,
and sat him down on a bench. From the polished
    wagon
they lifted the priceless ransom brought for Hector's
    corpse
but they left behind two capes and a finely-woven
    shirt
to shroud the body well when Priam bore him
    home.   *680*

Then Achilles called the serving-women out:
"Bathe and anoint the body—
bear it aside first. Priam must not see his son."
He feared that, overwhelmed by the sight of Hector,
wild with grief, Priam might let his anger flare   *685*
and Achilles might fly into fresh rage himself,
cut the old man down and break the laws of Zeus.
So when the maids had bathed and anointed the body
sleek with olive oil and wrapped it round and round
in a braided battle-shirt and handsome battle-cape,   *690*
then Achilles lifted Hector up in his own arms
and laid him down on a bier, and comrades helped
    him
raise the bier and body onto the sturdy wagon …
Then with a groan he called his dear friend by name:
"Feel no anger at me, Patroclus, if you learn—   *695*
even there in the House of Death—I let his father
have Prince Hector back. He gave me worthy
    ransom
and you shall have your share from me, as always,
your fitting, lordly share."
                                        So he vowed
and brilliant Achilles strode back to his shelter,   *700*
sat down on the well-carved chair that he had left,
at the far wall of the room, leaned toward Priam
and firmly spoke the words the king had come to
    hear:
"Your son is now set free, old man, as you requested.
Hector lies in state. With the first light of day   *705*
you will see for yourself as you convey him home.
Now, at last, let us turn our thoughts to supper.
Even Niobe with her lustrous hair remembered
    food,
though she saw a dozen children killed in her own
    halls,
six daughters and six sons in the pride and prime of
    youth.   *710*
True, lord Apollo killed the sons with his silver bow
and Artemis showering arrows killed the daughters.
Both gods were enraged at Niobe. Time and again
she placed herself on a par with their own mother,
Leto in her immortal beauty—how she insulted
    Leto: *715*
'All you have borne is two, but I have borne so
    many!'

So, two as they were, they slaughtered all her
    children.
Nine days they lay in their blood, no one to bury
    them—
Cronus' son had turned the people into stone …
then on the tenth the gods of heaven interred them.   *720*
And Niobe, gaunt, worn to the bone with weeping,
turned her thoughts to food. And now, somewhere,
lost on the crags, on the lonely mountain slopes,
on Sipylus where, they say, the nymphs who live
    forever,
dancing along the Achelous River run to beds of
    rest—   *725*
there, struck into stone, Niobe still broods
on the spate of griefs the gods poured out to her.

So come—we too, old king, must think of food.
Later you can mourn your beloved son once more,
when you bear him home to Troy, and you'll weep
    many tears."   *730*

Never pausing, the swift runner sprang to his feet
and slaughtered a white sheep as comrades moved in
to skin the carcass quickly, dress the quarters well.
Expertly they cut the meat in pieces, pierced them
    with spits,
roasted them to a turn and pulled them off the fire.   *735*
Automedon brought the bread, set it out on the
    board
in ample wicker baskets. Achilles served the meat.
They reached out for the good things that lay at
    hand
and when they had put aside desire for food and
    drink,
Priam the son of Dardanus gazed at Achilles,
    marveling   *740*
now at the man's beauty, his magnificent build—
face-to-face he seemed a deathless god …
and Achilles gazed and marveled at Dardan Priam,
beholding his noble looks, listening to his words.
But once they'd had their fill of gazing at each other,   *745*
the old majestic Priam broke the silence first:
"Put me to bed quickly, Achilles, Prince.
Time to rest, to enjoy the sweet relief of sleep.
Not once have my eyes closed shut beneath my lids
from the day my son went down beneath your
    hands …   *750*
day and night I groan, brooding over the countless
    griefs,
groveling in the dung that fills my walled-in court.
But now, at long last, I have tasted food again
and let some glistening wine go down my throat.
Before this hour I had tasted nothing."   *755*
                                        He shook his head
as Achilles briskly told his men and serving-women
to make beds in the porch's shelter, to lay down
some heavy purple throws for the beds themselves
and over them spread blankets and thick woolly
    robes,
a warm covering laid on top. Torches held in hand,   *760*
they went from the hall and fell to work at once

and in no time two good beds were spread and
    made.
Then Achilles nodded to Priam, leading the king on
with brusque advice: "Sleep outside, old friend,
in case some Achaean captain comes to visit.   765
They keep on coming now, huddling beside me,
making plans for battle—it's their duty.
But if one saw you here in the rushing dark night
he'd tell Agamemnon straightaway, our good
    commander.
Then you'd have real delay in ransoming the body.   770
One more point. Tell me, be precise about it—
how many days do you need to bury Prince Hector?
I will hold back myself
and keep the Argive armies back that long."

And the old and noble Priam answered slowly,   775
"If you truly want me to give Prince Hector burial,
full, royal honors, you'd show me a great kindness,
Achilles, if you would do exactly as I say.
You know how crammed we are inside our city,
how far it is to the hills to haul in timber,   780
and our Trojans are afraid to make the journey.
Well, nine days we should mourn him in our halls,
on the tenth we'd bury Hector, hold the public feast,
on the eleventh build the barrow high above his
    body—
on the twelfth we'd fight again … if fight we must."785

The swift runner Achilles reassured him quickly:
"All will be done, old Priam, as you command.
I will hold our attack as long as you require."

With that he clasped the old king by the wrist,
by the right hand, to free his heart from fear.   790
Then Priam and herald, minds set on the journey
    home,
bedded down for the night within the porch's shelter.
And deep in his sturdy well-built lodge Achilles slept
with Briseis in all her beauty sleeping by his side.

& HOMER

from *The Odyssey*

The following passage from near the end of The Odyssey *describes
Odysseus's reunion after twenty years with his wife, Penelope. Homer
creates interest by having Penelope refuse to acknowledge Odysseus
until he can offer incontrovertible proof that he is indeed her husband.*

from BOOK XXIII

The old nurse went upstairs exulting,
with knees toiling, and patter of slapping feet,
to tell the mistress of her lord's return,
and cried out by the lady's pillow:
                                    "Wake,
wake up, dear child! Penélopê, come down,   5
see with your own eyes what all these years you
    longed for!

Odysseus is here! Oh, in the end, he came!
And he has killed your suitors, killed them all
who made his house a bordel and ate his cattle
and raised their hands against his son!"

            Penélopê said: 10

"Dear nurse … the gods have touched you.
They can put chaos into the clearest head
or bring a lunatic down to earth. Good sense
you always had. They've touched you. What is this
mockery you wake me up to tell me,   15
breaking in on my sweet spell of sleep?
I had not dozed away to tranquilly
since my lord went to war, on that ill wind
to Ilion.
        Oh, leave me! Back down stairs!
If any other of my women came in babbling   20
things like these to startle me, I'd see her
flogged out of the house! Your old age spares you
    that."

Eurýkleia said:

"Would I play such a trick on you, dear child?
It is true, true, as I tell you, he has come!   25
That stranger they were baiting was Odysseus.
Telémakhos knew it days ago—
cool head, never to give his father away,
till he paid off those swollen dogs!"

The lady in her heart's joy now sprang up   30
with sudden dazzling tears, and hugged the old one,
crying out:

        "But try to make it clear!
If he came home in secret, as you say,
could he engage them singlehanded? How?
They were all down there, still in the same crowd."   35

To this Eurýkleia said:

        "I did not see it,
I knew nothing; only I heard the groans
of men dying. We sat still in the inner rooms
holding our breath, and marvelling, shut in,
until Telémakhos came to the door and called me—   40
your own dear son, sent this time by his father!
So I went out, and found Odysseus
erect, with dead men littering the floor
this way and that. If you had only seen him!
It would have made your heart glow hot!—a lion   45
splashed with mire and blood.
                    But now the cold
corpses are all gathered at the gate,
and he has cleansed his hall with fire and brimstone,
a great blaze. Then he sent me here to you.
Come with me: you may both embark this time   50
for happiness together, after pain,
after long years. Here is your prayer, your passion,
granted: your own lord lives, he is at home,
he found you safe, he found his son. The suitors
abused his house, but he has brought them down."   55

The attentive lady said:

> "Do not lose yourself
> in this rejoicing: wait: you know
> how splendid that return would be for us,
> how dear to me, dear to his son and mine;
> but no, it is not possible, your notion   *60*
> must be wrong.
>
> Some god has killed the suitors,
> a god, sick of their arrogance and brutal
> malice—for they honored no one living,
> good or bad, who ever came their way.
> Blind young fools, they've tasted death for it.   *65*
> But the true person of Odysseus?
> He lost his home, he died far from Akhaia."

The old nurse sighed:

> "How queer, the way you talk!
> Here he is, large as life, by his own fire,
> and you deny he ever will get home!   *70*
> Child, you always were mistrustful!
> But there is one sure mark that I can tell you:
> that scar left by the boar's tusk long ago.
> I recognized it when I bathed his feet
> and would have told you, but he stopped my mouth,   *75*
> forbade me, in his craftiness.
>
> Come down,
> I stake my life on it, he's here!
> Let me die in agony if I lie!"

Penélopê said:

> "Nurse dear, though you have your wits about you,
> still it is hard not to be taken in   *80*
> by the immortals. Let us join my son, though,
> and see the dead and that strange one who killed
> them."

She turned then to descend the stair, her heart
in tumult. Had she better keep her distance
and question him, her husband? Should she run   *85*
up to him, take his hands, kiss him now?
Crossing the door sill she sat down at once
in firelight, against the nearest wall,
across the room from the lord Odysseus.

> There
leaning against a pillar, sat the man   *90*
and never lifted up his eyes, but only waited
for what his wife would say when she had seen him.
And she, for a long time, sat deathly still
in wonderment—for sometimes as she gazed
she found him—yes, clearly—like her husband,   *95*
but sometimes blood and rags were all she saw.
Telémakhos' voice came to her ears:

> "Mother,
> cruel mother, do you feel nothing,
> drawing yourself apart this way from Father?
> Will you not sit with him and talk and question him?   *100*
> What other woman could remain so cold?
> Who shuns her lord, and he come back to her
> from wars and wandering, after twenty years?
> Your heart is hard as flint and never changes!"

Penélopê answered:

> "I am stunned, child.   *105*
> I cannot speak to him. I cannot question him.
> I cannot keep my eyes upon his face.
> If really he is Odysseus, truly home,
> beyond all doubt we two shall know each other
> better than you or anyone. There are   *110*
> secret signs we know, we two."

A smile
came now to the lips of the patient hero, Odysseus,
who turned to Telémakhos and said:

> "Peace: let your mother test me at her leisure.
> Before long she will see and know me best.   *115*
> These tatters, dirt—all that I'm caked with now—
> make her look hard at me and doubt me still.
> As to this massacre, we must see the end.
> Whoever kills one citizen, you know,
> and has no force of armed men at his back,   *120*
> had better take himself abroad by night
> and leave his kin. Well, we cut down the flower of
>   Ithaka,
> the mainstay of the town. Consider that."

Telémakhos replied respectfully:

> "Dear Father,
> enough that you yourself study the danger,   *125*
> foresighted in combat as you are,
> they say you have no rival.
>
> We three stand
> ready to follow you and fight. I say
> for what our strength avails, we have the courage."

And the great tactician. Odysseus, answered:

> "Good.   *130*
> Here is our best maneuver, as I see it:
> bathe, you three, and put fresh clothing on,
> order the women to adorn themselves,
> and let our admirable harper choose a tune
> for dancing, some lighthearted air, and strum it.   *135*
> Anyone going by, or any neighbor,
> will think it is a wedding feast he hears.
> These deaths must not be cried about the town
> till we can slip away to our own woods. We'll see
> what weapon, then, Zeus puts into our hands."   *140*

They listened attentively, and did his bidding,
bathed and dressed afresh; and all the maids
adorned themselves. Then Phêmios the harper
took his polished shell and plucked the strings,
moving the company to desire   *145*
for singing, for the sway and beat of dancing,
until they made the manor hall resound
with gaiety of men and grace of women.
Anyone passing on the road would say:

> "Married at last, I see—the queen so many
>   courted.   *150*
> Sly, cattish wife! She would not keep—not she!—
> the lord's estate until he came."

So travellers'
thoughts might run—but no one guessed the truth.
Greathearted Odysseus, home at last,
was being bathed now by Eurýnomê   155
and rubbed with golden oil, and clothed again
in a fresh tunic and a cloak. Athena
lent him beauty, head to foot. She made him
taller, and massive, too, with crisping hair
in curls like petals of wild hyacinth   160
but all red-golden. Think of gold infused
on silver by a craftsman, whose fine art
Hephaistos taught him, or Athena: one
whose work moves to delight: just so she lavished
beauty over Odysseus' head and shoulders.   165
He sat then in the same chair by the pillar,
facing his silent wife, and said:

              "Strange woman,
the immortals of Olympos made you hard,
harder than any. Who else in the world
would keep aloof as you do from her husband   170
if he returned to her from years of trouble,
cast on his own land in the twentieth year?

Nurse, make up a bed for me to sleep on.
Hear heart is iron in her breast."

          Penélopê
spoke to Odysseus now. She said:

            "Strange man,   175
if man you are … This is no pride on my part
nor scorn for you—not even wonder, merely.
I know so well how you—how he—appeared
boarding the ship for Troy. But all the same …
Make up his bed for him, Eurýkleia.   180
Place it outside the bedchamber my lord
built with his own hands. Pile the big bed
with fleeces, rugs, and sheets of purest linen."

With this she tried him to the breaking point,
and he turned on her in a flash raging: 185

"Woman, by heaven you've stung me now!
Who dared to move my bed?
No builder had the skill for that—unless
a god came down to turn the trick. No mortal
in his best days could budge it with a crowbar.   190
There is our pact and pledge, our secret sign,
built into that bed—my handiwork
and no one else's!

          An old trunk of olive
grew like a pillar on the building plot,
and I laid out our bedroom round that tree,   195
lined up the stone walls, built the walls and roof,
gave it a doorway and smooth-fitting doors.
Then I lopped off the silvery leaves and branches,
hewed and shaped that stump from the roots up
into a bedpost, drilled it, let it serve   200
as model for the rest. I planed them all,
inlaid them all with silver, gold and ivory,
and stretched a bed between—a pliant web

of oxhide thongs dyed crimson.
              There's our sign!
I know no more. Could someone's else's hand   205
have sawn that trunk and dragged the frame away?"

Their secret! as she heard it told, her knees
grew tremulous and weak, her heart failed her.
With eyes brimming tears she ran to him,
throwing her arms around his neck, and kissed him,   210
murmuring:
          "Do not rage at me, Odysseus!
No one ever matched your caution! Think
what difficulty the gods gave: they denied us
life together in our prime and flowering years,
kept us from crossing into age together.   215
Forgive me, don't be angry. I could not
welcome you with love on sight! I armed myself
long ago against the frauds of men,
impostors who might come—and all those many
whose underhanded ways bring evil on!   220
Helen of Argos, daughter of Zeus and Leda,
would she have joined the stranger, lain with him,
if she had known her destiny? known the Akhaians
in arms would bring her back to her own country?
Surely a goddess moved her to adultery,   225
her blood unchilled by war and evil coming,
the years, the desolation; ours, too.
But here and now, what sign could be so clear
as this of our own bed?
No other man has ever laid eyes on it—   230
only my own slave, Aktoris, that my father
sent with me as a gift—she kept our door.
You make my stiff heart know that I am yours."

Now from his breast into his eyes the ache
of longing mounted, and he wept at last,   235
his dear wife, clear and faithful, in his arms,
longed for
          as the sunwarmed earth is longed for by
a swimmer
spent in rough water where his ship went down
under Poseidon's blows, gale winds and tons of sea.
Few men can keep alive through a big surf   240
to crawl, clotted with brine, on kindly beaches
in joy, in joy, knowing the abyss behind:
and so she too rejoiced, her gaze upon her husband,
her white arms round him pressed as though forever.

The rose Dawn might have found them weeping still 245
had not grey-eyed Athena slowed the night
when night was most profound, and held the Dawn
under the Ocean of the East. That glossy team,
Firebright and Daybright, the Dawn's horses
that draw her heavenward for men—Athena   250
stayed their harnessing.

          Then said Odysseus:

"My dear, we have not won through to the end.
One trial—I do not know how long—is left for me
to see fulfilled. Teirêsias' ghost forewarned me
the night I stood upon the shore of Death, asking   255

about my friends' homecoming and my own.

But now the hour grows late, it is bed time,
rest will be sweet for us; let us lie down."

To this Penélopê replied:

        "That bed,
that rest is yours whenever desire moves you,   *260*
now the kind powers have brought you home at last.
But as your thought has dwelt upon it, tell me:
what is the trial you face? I must know soon;
what does it mater if I learn tonight?"

The teller of many stories said:

          "My strange one,   *265*
must you again, and even now,
urge me to talk? Here is a plodding tale;
no charm in it, no relish in the telling.
Teirêsias told me I must take an oar
and trudge the mainland, going from town to town, *270*
until I discover men who have never known
the salt blue sea, nor flavor of salt meat—
strangers to painted prows, to watercraft
and oars like wings, dipping across the water.
The moment of revelation he foretold   *275*
was this, for you may share the prophecy:
some traveller falling in with me will say:
'A winnowing fan, that on your shoulder, sir?'
There I must plant my oar, on the very spot,
with burnt offerings to Poseidon of the Waters: *280*
a ram, a bull, a great buck boar. Thereafter
when I come home again, I am to slay
full hekatombs to the gods who own broad heaven,
one by one.
        Then death will drift upon me
from seaward, mild as air, mild as your hand, *285*
in my well-tended weariness of age,
contented folk around me on our island.
He said all this must come."

        Penélopê said:

"If by the gods' grace age at least is kind,
we have that promise—trials will end in peace." *290*

So he confided in her, and she answered.
Meanwhile Eurýnomê and the nurse together
laid soft coverlets on the master's bed,
working in haste by torchlight. Eurýkleia
retired to her quarters for the night,   *295*
and then Eurýnomê, as maid-in-waiting,
lighted her lord and lady to their chamber
with bright bands.

      She vanished.
      So they came
into that bed so steadfast, loved of old,
opening glad arms to one another.[1]   *300*
Telémakhos by now had hushed the dancing,
hushed the women. In the darkened hall
he and the cowherd and the swineherd slept.

The royal pair mingled in love again

and afterward lay revelling in stories: *305*
hers of the siege her beauty stood at home
from arrogant suitors, crowding on her sight,
and how they fed their courtship on his cattle,
oxen and fat sheep, and drank up rivers
of wine out of the vats.
      Odysseus told   *310*
of what hard blows he had dealt out to others
and of what blows he had taken—all that story.
She could not close her eyes till all was told.

His raid on the Kikonês, first of all,
then how he visited the Lotos Eaters,   *315*
and what the Kyklops did, and how those shipmates,
pitilessly devoured, were avenged.
Then of his touching Aiolos's isle
and how that king refitted him for sailing
to Ithaka; all vain: gales blew him back   *320*
groaning over the fishcold sea. Then how
he reached the Laistrygonians' distant bay
and how they smashed his ships and his companions.
Kirkê, then: of her deceits and magic,
then of his voyage to the wide underworld   *325*
of dark, the house of Death, and questioning
Teirêsias, Theban spirit.
      Dead companions,
many, he saw there, and his mother, too.
Of this he told his wife, and told how later
he heard the choir of maddening Seirênês,   *330*
coasted the Wandering Rocks, Kharybdis' pool
and the fiend Skylla who takes toll of men.
then how his shipmates killed Lord Hêlios' cattle
and how Zeus thundering in towering heaven
split their fast ship with his fuming bolt,   *335*
so all hands perished.
      He alone survived,
cast away on Kalypso's isle, Ogýgia.
He told, then, how that nymph detained him there
in her smooth caves, craving him for her husband,
and how in her devoted lust she swore   *340*
he should not die nor grow old, all his days,
but he held out against her.
      Last of all
what sea-toil brought him to the Phaiákians;
their welcome; how they took him to their hearts
and gave him passage to his own dear island   *345*
with gifts of garments, gold and bronze …
      Remembering,
he drowsed over the story's end. Sweet sleep
relaxed his limbs and his care-burdened breast.

Other affairs were in Athena's keeping.
Waiting until Odysseus had his pleasure   *350*
of love and sleep, the grey-eyed one bestirred
the fresh Dawn from her bed of paling Ocean
to bring up daylight to her golden chair,
and from his fleecy bed Odysseus
arose. He said to Penélopê:

          "My lady,   *355*
what ordeals have we not endured! Here, waiting

you had your grief, while my return dragged out—
my hard adventures, pitting myself against
the gods' will, and Zeus, who pinned me down
far from home. But now our life resumes: *360*
we've come together to our longed-for bed.
Take care of what is left me in our house;
as to the flocks that pack of wolves laid waste
they'll be replenished: scores I'll get on raids
and other scores our island friends will give me   *365*
till all the folds are full again.
                          This day
I'm off up country to the orchards. I must see
my noble father, for he missed me sorely.
And here is my command for you—a strict one,
though you may need none, clever as you are.   *370*
Word will get about as the sun goes higher
of how I killed those lads. Go to your rooms
on the upper floor, and take your women. Stay there
with never a glance outside or a word to anyone."

Fitting cuirass and swordbelt to his shoulders,   *375*
he woke his herdsmen, woke Telémakhos,
ordering all in arms. They dressed quickly,
and all in war gear sallied from the gate,
led by Odysseus.
                  Now it was broad day
but these three men Athena hid in darkness   *380*
going before them swiftly from the town.

✦ SAPPHO
Selected Poems

Lyric poetry, which offers a personal expression of human experience and subjective feeling, flourished in the sixth century B.C. with the female poet Sappho. It is relatively unusual to have such direct celebrations of female experience as we find in her lyrics. In "Alone" the speaker evokes feelings of passionate solitude, and in "Seizure" the speaker describes what it is like to experience attraction to another.

Alone

The moon and Pleiades
are set. Midnight,
and time spins away.
I lie in bed, alone.

Seizure

To me he seems like a god
as he sits facing you and
hears you near as you speak
softly and laugh

in a sweet echo that jolts   *5*
the heart in my ribs. For now
as I look at you my voice
is empty and

can say nothing as my tongue

cracks and slender fire is quick   *10*
under my skin. My eyes are dead
to light, my ears

pound, and sweat pours over me.
I convulse, paler than grass,
and feel my mind slip as I   *15*
go close to death.

✦ HERAKLEITOS
Maxims and Sayings

Herakleitos was known in antiquity as "the obscure" because his writings were so difficult to interpret. His extant work consists of sharply pointed and provocative maxims and sayings. Their style is compact and cryptic, partly because of Herakleitos's belief that his meaning goes beyond the limits of ordinary language. Among the most interesting sayings are those about the unity of opposites.

God is day and night, winter and summer, war and peace, satiety and hunger; but he assumes different forms, just as when incense is mingled with incense; everyone gives him the name he pleases.

If all things should become smoke, then perception would be by the nostrils.

Cool things become warm, the warm grows cool; the wet dries, the parched becomes wet.

It scatters and brings together; it approaches and departs.

You could not step twice in the same river; for other and yet other waters are ever flowing on.

War is father of all and king of all; and some he made gods and some men, some slaves and some free.

Men do not understand how that which draws apart agrees with itself; harmony lies in the bending back, as for instance of the bow and the lyre.

Opposition unites. From what draws apart results the most beautiful harmony. All things take place by strife.

Men who desire wisdom must be learners of very many things.

For woolcarders the straight and the crooked path are one and the same.

Good and bad are the same.

Thou shouldst unite things whole and things not whole, that which tends to unite and that which tends to separate, the harmonious and the discordant; from all things arises the one, and from the one all things.

All the things we see when awake are death, and all the things we see when asleep are sleep.

The name of the bow is life, but its work is death.

For to souls it is death to become water, and for water it is death to become earth; but water is formed from earth, and from water, soul.

Upward, downward, the way is one and the same.

The limits of the soul you could not discover, though traversing every path.

Life and death, and waking and sleeping, and youth and old age, are the same; for the latter change and are the former, and the former change back to the latter.

I inquired of myself.

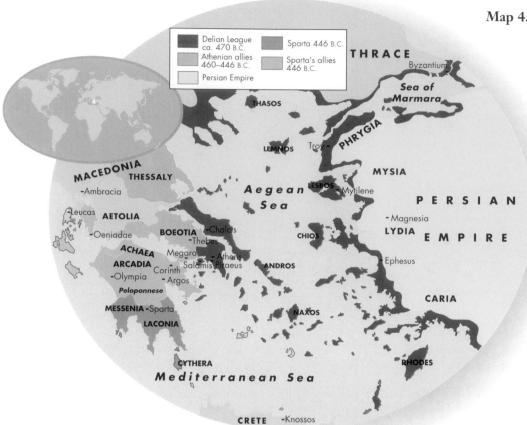

Map 4.1 Classical Greece.

Delian League
ca. 470 B.C.
Athenian allies
460–446 B.C.
Persian Empire

Sparta 446 B.C.
Sparta's allies
446 B.C.

THRACE
Byzantium

THASOS

Sea of
Marmara

LEMNOS Troy PHRYGIA

MACEDONIA THESSALY
-Ambracia

MYSIA

Aegean
Sea

LESBOS -Mytilene

PERSIAN

-Leucas AETOLIA
-Oeniadae

-Magnesia
LYDIA EMPIRE

BOEOTIA -Chalcis
-Thebes

CHIOS

ACHAEA Megara
ARCADIA Salamis -Athens
Corinth Piraeus

-Olympia -Argos

Peloponnese

-Ephesus

ANDROS

MESSENIA -Sparta

LACONIA

NAXOS

CARIA

CYTHERA

RHODES

Mediterranean Sea

CRETE -Knossos

CLASSICAL
← AND HELLENISTIC
GREECE

CHAPTER 4

⤺ *Classical Greece*

⤺ *Hellenistic Greece*

Mnesikles, Erechtheion, Acropolis, Athens, 437 or 421–406/405 B.C.

CLASSICAL GREECE

➔

In the decade between 490 and 480 B.C., something remarkable happened in Greece, and in Athens in particular, that resulted in one of the most culturally productive eras in the history of humankind. Before 490 B.C., as was explored in the last chapter, the Greeks had developed a highly sophisticated culture, but it pales by comparison to developments in the so-called Athenian Golden Age, a period of unsurpassed cultural achievement that can be said to begin with the Athenian defeat of the Persians in 479 B.C. and end nearly eighty years later, in 404 B.C., when Athens fell to Sparta. But the cultural achievement of the era was by no means exhausted with Athens's fall. This Golden Age had sparked a **Classical** period in Greece—"classical" because it forms the very basis of Western tradition down to this day—that would extend nearly another century until the death of Alexander the Great in 323 B.C. Even then, as the political power of Greece waned, its cultural preeminence carried on, through a **Hellenistic** period (from the verb "to Hellenize," or spread the influence of Greek culture), in which the basic tenets of Greek thought were perpetuated by the three dynasties that emerged after Alexander's death—the Ptolemies in Egypt, the Seleucids in Syria and Mesopotamia, and the Antigonids in Macedon—despite the competition for political dominance among them. Only after Rome captured Corinth in 146 B.C., making Greece into a province of the Roman Empire, did Greek culture begin to be absorbed into the new "Romanized" world. Even then the Hellenistic period was not truly at an end, continuing in Egypt until the death of Queen Cleopatra in 30 B.C.

Classical Greek civilization, especially that of Golden Age Athens, was crucial to the development of Western civilization as we know it today. The Greeks of antiquity developed a rich and vibrant culture, whose achievements consisted of preeminent masterpieces of pottery, sculpture and architecture, poetry and drama. Their achievements also included expertise in the practical arts of commerce and seafaring; metalwork, coining, and engraving; medicine and athletics; and philosophy, education, and government. The philosopher Protagoras [proh-TA-go-rus] (ca. 485–415 B.C.) wrote that "People are the measure of all things," a phrase that heralded the enterprise first undertaken in Classical Greece but which has been so central to Western culture ever since. Classical Greece was the first civilization to explore the human condition, recognizing the realities and constraints of human life and constantly striving to realize ideals. The Greeks invented democracy and left it as a legacy for Western Europe to emulate two millennia after the decline of Athens. Their ideal of political freedom also served as the basis for the pursuit of other ideals such as justice, truth, and beauty. Political freedom was part of the culture's belief in individual expression. The Greek system of *paideia*, or learning, was grounded in respect for individual thought, and emphasized logic, dialectic, debate, and elegance of expression. As in athletics, competition was encouraged in the arts, and the victor was celebrated as a kind of hero. The annual competition among dramatists led to the creation of Sophocles' plays, including *Oedipus the King*. Above all, against the background of warring mainland Greece in the fifth century B.C., the Greeks provided the Western world with a sense of the value, balance, and harmony in all things—in architecture, in politics, and in daily life.

FROM ARCHAIC TO CLASSICAL

Political Reform. Many things contributed to the astonishing rise of Athens as the cultural center of the world in the fifth century B.C. Chief among them is the century of political reform that preceded the Golden Age. As early as 621 B.C., the benevolent tyrant DRACO [DRAY-koh] published what is thought to be the first comprehensive code of laws in Athens. This offered a single standard of justice to all Athenians. Aristocratic judges could no longer automatically favor the landed aristocracy in their rulings, making up the law as they went along. Instead they were required to apply Draco's code uniformly to the growing commercial class and even to poor farmers.

Just as important to this process of change was SOLON [SOH-lon] (ca. 640–558 B.C.), who brought great reforms to the civil administration of Athens. He divided the citizens into four classes, all of whom had the right to take part in the debates in the political Assembly. Though Solon limited the highest offices to members of the nobility, he did allow the lower classes to sit on juries, and jury duty became a civic responsibility. He ended debt-slavery (the practice of paying off a debt by becoming the creditor's slave), employed large numbers of artisans, and promoted trade, particularly trade in pottery. PISISTRATOS [pi-SIS-truh-tus] (ca. 605–527 B.C.) went even further, redistributing the large estates of the nobility to the landless farmers, who, as a result of their improved economic status, suddenly found themselves able to vote. Like Solon, Pisistratos also championed the arts, commissioning the first editions of *The Iliad* and *The Odyssey* for students and scholars.

Shortly prior to 508 B.C. CLEISTHENES [KLICE-thuh-nees] (d. 508 B.C.) divided Athens into **demes** (neighborhoods), representing what he had labeled the ten "tribes" of Athens. Each "tribe" was allotted fifty seats on a Council of Five Hundred. The fifty representatives for each neighborhood were selected at random from a list of nominees on the theory that anyone nominated was capable of exercising judgment about affairs of state. The Council elected ten generals yearly to run the city, and at the head of them was a commander-in-chief, also elected yearly. Thus, out of the demes of Athens developed the first democracy.

The Persian Threat. This democracy was put to the test beginning in 490 B.C. when the same Darius who built the palace at Persepolis in Persia (see fig. 1.21) invaded the Greek mainland. On the plain of Marathon, north of Athens, Darius's mighty army was confronted by a mere ten thousand Greeks, led by General MILTIADES [mil-TIE-uh-dees]. In a surprise dawn attack, Miltiades' troops crushed the Persians, killing an estimated six thousand, while the Greeks suffered only minimal losses themselves. Victory was announced to the waiting citizens of Athens by the messenger PHIDIPPIDES [fi-DIP-ih-dees], who ran twenty-six miles with the news—the original "marathon" run.

To the Athenians, the Battle of Marathon symbolized the triumph of civilization over barbarian hordes, of wit and intelligence over brute strength, and of democracy over tyranny. But the Persian giant was not yet tamed, and the Athenian general THEMISTOCLES [thih-MIS-tu-klees] knew this. A rebellion in Egypt and the death of Darius in 486 B.C., following which his son Xerxes ascended the throne, preoccupied the Persians temporarily. But all the while Themistocles was preparing for what he believed to be the inevitable return of the Persian army. And come Xerxes did, in 480 B.C., with an army so large that reports had it drinking rivers dry.

It is to HERODOTUS [heh-ROD-ut-us] (484–420 B.C.), the first writer to devote himself solely to history and who is therefore known as the Father of History, that we are indebted for much of our knowledge of the Persian Wars. He estimated the Persian army at five million men, surely an exaggeration, but certainly the Persians far outnumbered the Greeks. Themistocles knew that such an army could not be defeated on land. More conservative Athenian leaders, remembering the great victory at Marathon, thought otherwise. Athens was evacuated, and a small force of three hundred Spartans led by LEONIDES [lee-ON-ih-dees] went north to Thermopylai [thur-MOP-uh-lye], a narrow pass between the sea and the mountains, where they held off the Persian advance for days. Betrayed by a local guide, who showed Xerxes a path around the pass, the Spartans were finally surrounded, but continued fighting until all were dead. With Athens now deserted, it was destroyed by the Persians, and Themistocles retreated to the island of Salamis [SAL-ah-miss]. This was a trick, however, for when the Persians boldly sailed after him, they were unable to maneuver in the narrow bay, and the Persian fleet was entirely destroyed. The playwright Aeschylus, who fought both at Marathon and at Salamis, later celebrated the victory in verse:

> Crushed hulls lay upturned on the sea, so thick
> You could not see the water, choked with wrecks
> And slaughtered men; while all the shores and reefs
> Were strewn with corpses . . .

Within a year, the Persian land forces were also driven from the mainland, and Greece was free.

Timeline 4.1 Classical Greece.

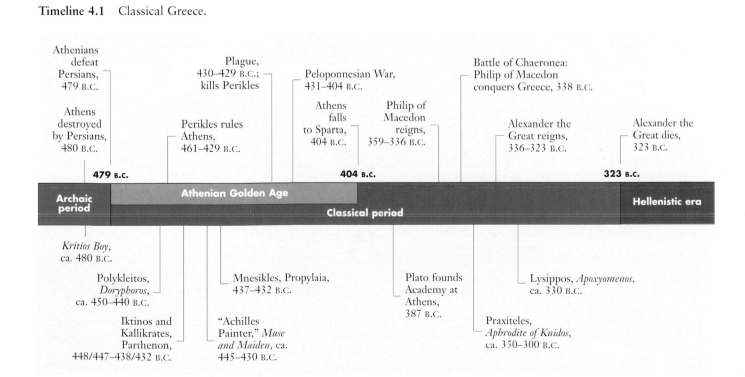

THE GOLDEN AGE OF ATHENS

Over the centuries Athens had grown and prospered, a city within strong stone walls, protected by a vast citadel on the **Acropolis** (literally, the high point of the city, from *akros*, meaning "top," and *polis*, "city"). There, temples were erected, law courts and shrines were built, and a forum for the Pan-Athenaic Games was constructed. The Persians destroyed all this and more in 480 B.C. The whole of Athens had to be rebuilt.

The first order of business was the city's walls, and the entire population was put to work restoring them. When the walls were completed, the Athenians turned their attention to the **agora**, or market place, in which shopkeepers and craftspeople made, displayed, and sold their wares. Here, at the foot of the Acropolis, they built a council chamber, a court house, several long **stoas**, or roofed colonnades, to house shops, and a smaller royal stoa in which the "Laws of Solon" were carved on stone and could be viewed by all citizens.

No attempt was made to rebuild the temples on the Acropolis. Their foundations were left bare as a reminder of the Persian aggression. But by mid-century, the restoration of the site seemed a matter of civic responsibility, an act of homage to Athena who had helped the Greeks defeat the Persians, and it was taken on by the great Athenian leader PERIKLES [PAIR-ih-klees] (ca. 500–429 B.C.). Perikles was first elected general-in-chief in 461 B.C., and, except for two years when he was voted out of office, remained in command until his death in 429 B.C. Under the artistic and administrative supervision of PHIDIAS [FI-dee-us], the best artists and artisans were hired, over 22,000 tons of marble were transported from quarries ten miles away, and vast numbers of workers were employed in a construction project that lasted until the end of the century. The Acropolis embodied, for Perikles, the Athenians' "love of beauty," as he put it in an oration delivered in 430 B.C. at a state funeral for Athenian citizens who had died in battle. Its

Figure 4.1 General view of the Acropolis. Even in relative ruin, the Athenian Acropolis remains a breathtaking sight, and a poignant reminder of past accomplishments.

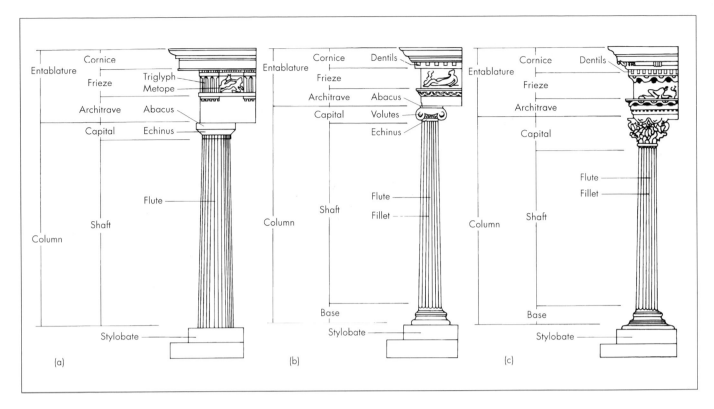

Figure 4.2 Diagram of the Doric (a), Ionic (b), and Corinthian (c) orders. The three orders of Greek architecture were developed in antiquity and continue to be used even today.

buildings were "things of the mind," he said, embodiments of the greatness of Athens itself (fig. 4.1). And it is true that when work on the citadel was completed, the Acropolis at Athens was, with the possible exception of the Egyptian pyramids, probably the most impressive visual spectacle in the world.

The achievements of the sculptors and architects on the Acropolis represent the high point of Classical Greece in the visual arts, although at the same time dramatists, philosophers, and historians were laying the foundations for their subjects for the next two millennia. However, all of this was done against a background of social and political uncertainty. It is often said that the Greeks' characteristic pursuit of balance and order in their art was a reaction to the extreme disorder of the world around them. Two major disasters struck Athens in the late fifth century B.C. The first, a devastating plague, occurred in 430–429 B.C., its most important victim being Perikles himself. The Greek historian THUCYDIDES [thyou-SID-id-ease] (ca. 460–ca. 400 B.C.) described how the "bodies of the dying were heaped upon one another" as "half-dead creatures" were "staggering about in the streets or flocking around the fountains in their desire for water." A year earlier, the longstanding Spartan resentment of Athenian power had erupted in the Peloponnesian War, which ended with Athens's defeat at the hands of the Spartans in 404 B.C.

Although the glory of Athenian civilization was effectively over, its magnificent cultural achievements in the fields of art and architecture, literature and politics, would forever influence the future of Western civilization.

ARCHITECTURE AND ARCHITECTURAL SCULPTURE ON THE ACROPOLIS

The Greek Orders. The ancient Greeks developed the three **orders** or arrangements of architecture—the Doric order, the Ionic order, and the Corinthian order (fig. 4.2). The column capital is the easiest way to determine whether the order is Doric, Ionic, or Corinthian.

As noted in Chapter 3, the **Doric** is the oldest and simplest of the three orders and was the order most frequently employed by the ancient Greek architects. By the Golden Age it had been perfected. Its capital is characterized by the square block of the **abacus** and the cushion-shaped **echinus**, usually cut from the same piece of stone. There is no base beneath the Doric column, whereas there is a base at the foot of the Ionic and Corinthian columns. The Doric **frieze** consists of alternating **triglyphs**, so called because they have three sections, and **metopes**, square or rectangular areas that may be decorated.

The **Ionic** order is characterized by the scroll/volute capital—graceful and swirling. The Ionic was Eastern in

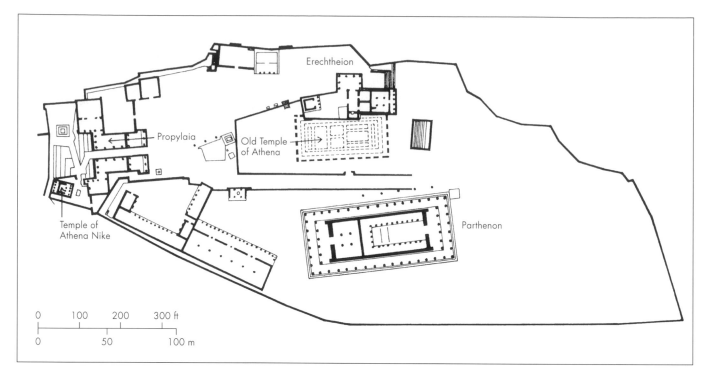

Figure 4.3 Plan of the Acropolis, Athens, after the mid-fifth century B.C. Shown here are the Propylaia, Parthenon, Erechtheion, and Temple of Athena Nike.

origin and was especially popular in Asia Minor and the Greek islands. The **entablature** has a frieze of continous decoration.

The **Corinthian** order, a development of the Hellenistic age, is characterized by the large curling acanthus

Figure 4.4 Mnesikles, Propylaia, Acropolis, Athens, 437–432 B.C., marble, seen from the west. To gain access to the Acropolis ("high city"), the visitor ascended the many stairs of the Propylaia ("front gates").

leaves that ornament the capital. The Corinthian is the most ornamental and delicate of the three orders. It was the order least used by the Greeks but most favored later by the Romans.

Both figuratively and literally, Classical Greek architecture reached its high point on the Acropolis (fig. 4.3). Here the Doric and Ionic orders came together in a stunning exhibition of architectural beauty and refinement. The four main buildings on the Acropolis are the Propylaia, the Parthenon, the Erechtheion, and the Temple of Athena Nike, all of which were built under the supervision of Phidias in the second half of the fifth century B.C.

The Propylaia. The visitor to the Acropolis must enter through the Propylaia [PROP-uh-LIE-yuh] (fig. 4.4), the front gates, constructed at the only natural access point to the Acropolis. Construction of the Propylaia was begun in 437 B.C., but due to the outbreak of the Peloponnesian War in 431 B.C., it was never finished. The architect was MNESIKLES [mee-NES-ih-klees]. On the north side of the Propylaia was a *pinakotheke* or picture gallery. The visitor passed through a porch with six Doric columns, into a hall, from which the wings of the Propylaia extended. Ascending several levels, passing between columns, the visitor emerged on the east side, exiting through another porch with six columns. The central set of columns is wider than the others—useful for processions of people and sacrificial animals.

The Parthenon. The Parthenon [PAR-theeh-none] (fig. 4.5) is the only Acropolis building that was actually finished—construction of the rest was halted by the Peloponnesian War. The Parthenon is considered the ultimate example of ancient Greek architecture, the paradigm of perfection. Dated by inscriptions to between 448/447 and 438 or 432 B.C., it is the perfect example of the Classical Doric temple and is dedicated to the goddess Athena. Located at the highest point on the Acropolis, the Parthenon is the largest building there and is also the largest Doric building on the Greek mainland. The architects were IKTINOS [ik-TIE-nus] and KALLIKRATES [ka-LIK-kra-tees]. Phidias took on the task of its sculptural decoration, and he made a gold and ivory cult image of Athena Parthenos, dedicated in 437 B.C.

The Parthenon has all the features that characterize a Classical Doric temple (fig. 4.6). The **cella**, the enclosed part of the temple, contained the cult statue of Athena Parthenos. The **pronaos** is the front porch or vestibule supported by columns (*pro* means "in front of," and *naos* means "temple"). The **opisthodomos** is the back porch, with columns. The Parthenon is surrounded by a **peristyle**, or colonnade.

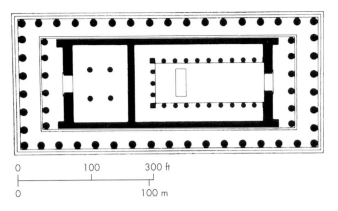

0   100   300 ft

0   100 m

Figure 4.6 Plan of the Parthenon. Because of the ratio between the number of columns on the width to those on the length, the Parthenon is referred to as a regular temple. The length (here seventeen columns) is twice plus one the width (eight columns).

Perhaps nothing better explains the overwhelming beauty of the Parthenon, still apparent even in its ruined condition today, than the perfection of its proportions. The facade is based on the so-called **Golden Section**:

Figure 4.5 Iktinos and Kallikrates, Parthenon, Acropolis, Athens, 448–432 B.C., marble, seen from the northwest. The epitome of Classical Greek architecture, the Parthenon is a regular Doric temple. All major lines actually curve slightly. Such refinements are now believed to have been intended to add to the beauty of the building rather than to correct for optical distortion.

the width of the building is 1.618 times the height, a ratio of approximately 8:5. Plato regarded this ratio as the key to understanding the cosmos. That Athena's temple, the Parthenon, should be constructed according to this proportion is hardly accidental. As the goddess of wisdom, Athena represents the ultimate wisdom of the cosmos itself.

In addition to the beauty of its proportions, the Parthenon possesses all of the "refinements"—the deviations from absolute regularity and rigidity—used by ancient Greek architects. Despite appearances, there are no straight lines to the Parthenon. The steps and the entablature both form convex curves. Each block of marble is a rectangular prism of precisely cut ashlar masonry with right-angle corners, but when the courses were laid, the blocks were positioned so as to be faceted in relation to one another. The columns have **entasis**, the slight bulge in the column shaft, and they taper to the top—that is, their diameter is less at the top than at the bottom. The columns at the corners are placed closer together than elsewhere.

Why were these refinements introduced? The columns lean inward. They would meet if they were extended, creating a pyramidal form, the most stable of geometric forms. They are fluted, we know, because, seen from a distance, they would appear as flat slabs rather than rounded columns without the pattern of light and shade created by the fluting. But why make the platform and entablature convex? It has been suggested that this was done to adjust the visual perspective, to correct optical distortion, the argument being that the human eye perceives parallel lines as coming together in the middle. However, if the refinements were intended to correct optical distortion, the argument must follow that they should go unperceived by our eyes. However, the visitor to the Parthenon finds the refinements readily visible.

Perhaps a more accurate explanation for the refinements is that they are intended to add beauty to the building. Curved lines are more appealing, satisfying, comfortable to our eyes than are rigidly straight ones. Nature creates no straight lines—only people produce perfectly straight lines and right angles. The columns, ultimately taking their form from tree trunks, are larger at the bottom than the top. And the trunks of certain types of trees do bulge along their length, as is reflected in the entasis of the stone columns.

Like the Propylaia, the Parthenon combines Doric and Ionic elements. Although the peristyle is Doric, the frieze around the top of the cella wall is an Ionic element. In addition, there were four Ionic columns inside the cella.

Parthenon Sculpture. The sculptural decoration of the Parthenon was done under the direct supervision of Phidias. Phidias himself created the now lost **chryselephantine** (gold and ivory over a wooden core) statue of the Athena Parthenos (Virgin Athena), which was housed in the cella of the Parthenon proper, and a giant bronze, also now lost, an Athena Promachus (Athena the Defender), which stood just inside the Propylaia, and which was so tall the sailors arriving at the Athenian port of Piraeus ten miles distant claimed to see the sun reflected off her helmet. It remains unclear just how much of the other Acropolis sculpture Phidias was personally responsible for, but it is generally consistent in style and is referred to as "Phidian."

There are three categories of surviving Parthenon sculpture: ninety-two squarish metopes on the entablature, carved in high relief—most of those that survive have as their subject the mythological battle between the Lapiths and centaurs (fig. 4.7); the frieze on the upper wall of the cella, carved in low relief; and the huge freestanding figures that filled the east and west pediments, carved in the round.

The west pediment depicts the competition between Athena and Poseidon for the land of Attica. The east pediment depicts the birth of Athena from the head of Zeus. The figures are badly damaged, but nonetheless demonstrate the magnificent Classical balance struck between idealism and realism. The way the sculptor suggests the folds of the drapery is at once highly realistic and governed by a sense of perfect proportion (fig. 4.8).

Figure 4.7 Lapith and centaur, metope, Parthenon, ca. 440 B.C., marble, height 4′5″ (1.34 m), British Museum, London. The struggle of the Lapiths with the centaurs served the Greeks as a metaphor for the conflict between the civilized and the barbaric.

Figure 4.8 Three seated goddesses, east pediment, Parthenon, 438–432 B.C., marble. Far from their stiff ancestors, the movements of these casual figures seem to flow easily. The drapery is contrived to reveal the body and appears almost "wet."

The frieze (fig. 4.9) was carved ca. 440 B.C. of marble. The background of the frieze was painted and so were details of the horses' bridles and reins. Other accessories were made of bronze and riveted on. Until recently, the frieze's subject was widely believed to be a procession of people at the Pan-Athenaic festival held every four years in honor of Athena. At this festival, the people of Athens walked in a long procession up the Acropolis to the Parthenon. Art historians have thus seen the frieze in the following terms: People are shown to come in chariots, on horseback, and on foot. Some move quickly, others more slowly. Some make music on flutes and kitharas.

Figure 4.9 *Procession of Women*, relief, from the Parthenon, Acropolis, Athens, ca. 440 B.C., marble, height of relief frieze 3′6″ (1.07 m), Musée du Louvre, Paris. The aesthetic principle of unity and variety is demonstrated here: the figures have enough in common to appear unified, yet sufficient variety to avoid monotony. The physical type favored in the Classical Period was strong and young, idealized rather than individualized.

Figure 4.10 *Erechtheus, Praxithea, and Their Daughters*
(?), relief, from the Parthenon, Acropolis, Athens, ca. 440
B.C., height of relief frieze 3'6" (1.07 m), British Museum,
London. This section of the frieze originally stood
immediately over the doorway giving access to the interior of
the temple and to the statue of Athena. It probably depicts
Erechtheus, dressed as a priest for the event, bestowing a
funerary dress on his daughter, who is half disrobed. Behind
him is Praxithea, who watches as her two older daughters
bring her their funerary garments.

Animals for sacrifice are also included in the procession.
However, this interpretation of the subject matter as a
"documentary" record of a contemporary festival,
though long accepted, is problematic, since on all other
Greek temples the decoration is concerned exclusively
with mythological subjects; ordinary people in scenes
from contemporary Greek life are not depicted
anywhere else.

A recent reinterpretation suggests that the Parthenon
frieze may not after all be the first representation of a
non-mythological subject in Greek art, but is instead a
version of one of the foundation myths of Athens, that of
Erechtheus and his daughters. Such an interpretation
would certainly bring the decoration of the Parthenon
into line with that of other Greek temples.

According to the 250 surviving lines of a lost play by
Euripides, the *Erechtheus*, the story runs as follows:
Athens was threatened by Eumolpos, the son of Poseidon, who was still angry at having lost the city's patronage to Athena—the battle for Athens between Athena
and Poseidon is depicted on the west pediment. The oracle at Delphi tells King Erechtheus that he must sacrifice
one of his three daughters to save Athens from destruction at Eumolpos's hands. But the daughters have long
before made a pact that if one of them dies the others will
die as well. Praxithea, Erechtheus's wife, knows this, but
when she is told that a daughter must be sacrificed, she
responds by choosing the common good over her own
children. Erechtheus sacrifices his daughter, and the
other two die, as does Erechtheus himself, swallowed up
in a chasm made by Poseidon. But Athena triumphs over
Eumolpos. In lines from Euripides' play rediscovered in
1962, Athena appears to Praxithea, and consoles her:

> And first I shall tell you about the girl whom your hus-
> band sacrificed for this land: bury her where she breathed
> out her pitiful life, and these sisters in the same tomb of
> the land, on account of their nobility ... To my fellow
> townsmen I say not to forget them in time but with
> annual sacrifices and bull-slaying slaughters to honor
> them, celebrating them with holy maiden-dances.

In light of this story, the section of the east frieze that
stood directly over the door to the temple may be seen to
show the royal family preparing their youngest daughter

Figure 4.11 Mnesikles, Erechtheion, Acropolis, Athens, 437 or 421–406/405 B.C.,
marble. The most complex of the Acropolis buildings, the highly irregular plan of the
Erechtheion covers several areas sacred to the early history of Athens. On the Porch of
the Maidens, female figures (caryatids) perform the structural role of columns.

Figure 4.12 Probably Kallikrates or Mnesikles, Temple of Athena Nike, Acropolis, Athens, 427–424 B.C., marble. Dedicated to Nike, the winged goddess of victory, this tiny Ionic temple was largely dismantled and has now been reconstructed.

for sacrifice (fig. 4.10). Dressed as a priest for the occasion, Erechtheus hands his half-dressed youngest daughter her funereal garb. Behind him Praxithea watches as their other two daughters carry funerary garments. The Parthenon itself may rest over the tombs of the three virgin daughters of Erechtheus. "Parthenoi" can be translated "place of the virgins," and thus the procession depicted on the frieze might not be a commemoration of Athena but of Erechtheus and his daughters, who gave their lives that Athens might be saved.

The Erechtheion. The most architecturally complex building on the Acropolis, the Erechtheion [er-EK-thee-on] (fig. 4.11), was begun either in 437 B.C., the same year the Propylaia was begun, or in 421 B.C., after the death of Perikles. Work continued until 406/405 B.C., but the building was never finished. The architect may have been Mnesikles, the architect of the Propylaia.

The Erechtheion is unique and extremely irregular in plan. This is not due to the fact that the building was never finished. Nor is it due to the fact that it is constructed on uneven ground—the three main rooms are on three different levels; there is a nine-foot difference between the southeast side and the northwest side. Rather, the irregularities seem to derive from functional necessity, since the Erechtheion was designed to contain several sacred sites connected with the early history of Athens.

An olive tree here relates to the legend that Athena competed with Poseidon for patronage of Athens and

won. Athens was therefore named after Athena and the goddess gave her city an olive tree. The Erechtheion certainly contained Athena's statue. The Athenians also appear to have sought to placate the defeated Poseidon, since part of the building was also dedicated to him.

In the southwest corner of the building is the Kekropium, the grave of Kekrops, the legendary founder and first ruler of Athens, who was said to be half-man and half-snake, and who judged the contest between Athena and Poseidon. Finally, the room across the west of the building is called the "Salt Sea of Erechtheus." Reputed to be a reservoir connected to the sea by an underground passageway, it is dedicated to Erechtheus, the early Athenian king under whose reign Demeter taught the Athenians the art of agriculture.

The most famous part of the Erechtheion is the Porch of the Maidens on the south side. Here there are six **caryatids**—female figures used as architectural supports. (Male figures that function in the same way are called **atlantes**.) The functional use of sculpture in architecture is a rarity in ancient Greece. However, these statues blend beautifully with the building: the figures' hair is carved so that the curls flow into the capitals. They stand in the *contrapposto* pose (see p. 110), the supporting leg hidden by the drapery of their dresses. This drapery falls in folds that simulate the fluting of a column, emphasizing their architectural role. Each figure has one arm down by her side; the other, now broken off, was extended. The figures form an obvious group, yet each of the six is slightly different—an example of the Greek aesthetic principle of "unity and variety." This porch was famous in antiquity and was used as the model for a multitude of buildings then and later.

The Temple of Athena Nike. The Temple of Athena Nike (fig. 4.12), dated between 427 and 424 B.C., was probably built from a plan by either Kallikrates or Mnesikles. In 449 B.C. a decree was issued stating that Kallikrates was to build a temple to Nike—which he may be presumed to have done, though the temple was not started until many years later.

Made in the Ionic style, it is a miniature temple with four Ionic columns on the front and four on the back. The continuous sculpted frieze on the entablature is also an Ionic feature. Between 410 and 407 B.C. a surrounding wall covered with low-relief sculpted panels depicting Athena as she prepared for her victory celebration was added—*Nike* is the Greek for "victory." The wall no longer survives, but some of its panels do.

SCULPTURE

The caryatids decorating the Porch of the Maidens on the Erechtheion, the friezes on the Parthenon, and the wall around the Temple of Athena Nike all make clear the centrality of sculpture to the architectural project on

Figure 4.13 *Kritios Boy*, ca. 480 B.C., marble, height 3′10″ (1.17 m), Acropolis Museum, Athens. This work is transitional between the Archaic and Classical periods. The rigid frontality of the Archaic era is broken by the gentle turn of the head and the slight movement in the torso.

the Acropolis. The chief subject of this sculpture, characteristically enough, is the human figure. Just as the design of the temples was determined by carefully conceived orders as well as mathematically precise notions of proper proportion and scale, the human figure was portrayed according to an equally formalized set of ideal standards. However, certain important developments are visible between Classical Greece and the mid-fourth century B.C., as sculptors first concentrated on idealized heroic figures and then passed to more realistic, emotionally charged portrayals.

The Kritios Boy. The first signs of this growing sense of an ideal human form can be seen in the kouros known as the *Kritios Boy* (fig. 4.13), which we know was damaged in the Persian sack of Athens in 480 B.C., and must, therefore, date to just before that year. The body of the figure was discovered in 1865 in the debris on the Acropolis, southeast of the Parthenon; in 1888 the head was found a bit further east. The sculpture is called the "Kritios Boy" because it was executed in a style associated with that of the sculptor KRITIOS [CRIT-i-os] of Athens, whose work is otherwise known only from Roman copies. The *Kritios Boy* differs from earlier kouroi significantly in terms of pose. The spine forms a gentle S-curve; one hip is raised slightly in apparent response to the displacement of weight onto one leg. This is the ***contrapposto*** (counterpoise) pose, introduced by the ancient Greeks at the beginning of the transition to the Classical period. The head is turned slightly to the side, the pose is relaxed and natural. The body is carved with accurate anatomical detail, and the Archaic smile has gone. A new sense of movement appears, in large part a result of his weight falling on a single leg. Although the arms are broken off, they were not placed rigidly at the sides as in earlier figures. Instead, the left arm was further back than the right arm. The sculpting of the *Kritios Boy* indicates a growing anatomical understanding of bone, muscles, tendons, fat, flesh, and skin, and the way in which they work together.

Polykleitos. The sense of naturalness and perfection hinted at in the *Kritios Boy* is fully realized in the *Doryphoros (Spear-Bearer)* (fig. 4.14). This was originally made in bronze, ca. 450–440 B.C., by POLYKLEITOS [pohl-ee-KLYE-tus], but now survives only in a marble Roman copy. At about the same time as he was working on *The Spear-Bearer*, Polykleitos developed a set of written rules for sculpting the ideal human form. These were formulated in a treatise called *The Canon* (the Greek word *kanon* means "measure" or "rule"), which, like the original *Spear-Bearer*, no longer survives. But by careful study of copies of Polykleitos's work, the basics of *The Canon* can be discerned. All parts of the body were considered. The height of the head was used as the unit of measurement for determining the overall height of the body—*The Spear-Bearer* is eight heads tall. This statue balanced. With complete understanding of the human body, Polykleitos recorded everything—down to the veins in the backs of the hands.

Praxiteles. The sculptor PRAXITELES [prac-SIT-el-ease] is known especially for Aphrodite (Venus) figures, represented by the *Aphrodite of Knidos* (fig. 4.15), another Roman copy after an original of ca. 350–300 B.C. Aphrodite is the goddess of love, born from the sea. In the sixth and fifth centuries B.C., male nudes were commonplace, as we have seen, but the female nude was a rarity. However, due to the influence of Praxiteles, whose work was considered wonderful in ancient times, the

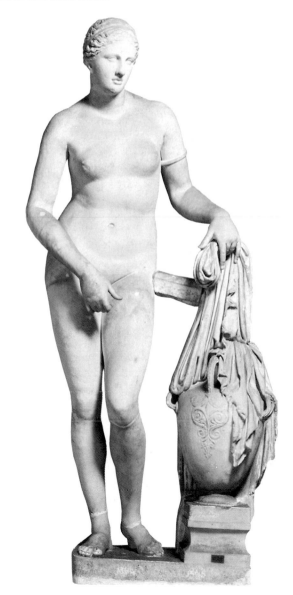

Figure 4.15 *Aphrodite of Knidos*, Roman marble copy of a Greek original of ca. 350–300 B.C. by Praxiteles, height 6′8″ (2.03 m), Museo Pio Clementino, Musei Vaticani, Rome. The female nude became a popular subject in the Hellenistic Period. An illusion of warm soft flesh is created from cold hard stone.

Figure 4.14 *Doryphoros (Spear-Bearer)*, Roman marble copy of a Greek original of ca. 450–440 B.C. by Polykleitos, height 6′6″ (1.98 m), Museo Archeologico Nazionale, Naples. In the Classical Period the relaxed and natural *contrapposto* (counterpoise) pose, with the weight on one leg, hips and shoulders no longer parallel, and spine in a gentle S-curve, became the norm.

was viewed in antiquity as the definitive word on perfect proportions and was copied many times.

The Spear-Bearer stands in a fully developed *contrapposto* pose. Because only one leg is weight-bearing, the two sides are not identical. The pelvis and shoulders are tilted in opposite directions. The spine forms a gentle S-shape. The pose is natural, relaxed, and perfectly

Then & Now

The Olympiad

The ancient Greeks had a prescription for good living that is still popular today: *"mens sana in corpore sano,"* as the Romans translated it, "A sound mind in a sound body." The Greeks celebrated the human body and physical accomplishment as no other culture had before, particularly in sporting contests. These events were an important part of the Pan-Athenaic festival in Athens, but the most enduring of all sporting contests was the Olympiad, begun in 776 B.C. at Olympia on the Greek Peloponnese. These Olympic Games were held every four years until A.D. 394, when the Roman Emperor Theodosius abolished all non-Christian events in the Empire.

From the outset, the short foot race, or *stade*, was the most important event. Held in honor of Zeus, the course was six hundred feet in length (the length of the *stadium* at Olympia), about equivalent to a modern-day two-hundred meter race. Legend has it that at the first Olympics, Herakles paced off the length himself by placing one foot in front of the other six hundred times.

The first thirteen Olympic Games consisted solely of this race, but soon the *diaulos* was added, consisting of two lengths of the stadium (or about one time around a modern track), as well as the *dolichos*, a long-distance race consisting of either twenty or twenty-four lengths of the stadium, perhaps a mile and a half. An athlete who won all three races was known as a *triastes*, or "tripler." The greatest tripler of them all was Leonidas of Rhodes, who won all three events in four successive Olympiads between 164 and 152 B.C.

Over the years, other events were added, including, in 708 B.C., the *pentathlon*, consisting of five events—discus, long-jump, javelin, running, and wrestling—all contested in the course of a single afternoon. Only two measurements of the early long-jumps survive, from the mid-fifth century B.C., both of which are over sixteen meters in length. Since the current world long-jump record is just under nine meters, it is probable that the Greek long-jump was a multiple jump event, comparable to the modern triple-jump (the modern record of which is just over seventeen meters). By the mid-fifth century B.C.

the Games had become a five-day event and had been expanded to include a chariot race and even sculpture exhibitions.

Centuries after their suppression by Theodosius, the Olympic Games were reinitiated in Athens in 1896. At this first modern Olympiad, the organizers celebrated the return of the games by introducing a new running event, the "marathon," to celebrate Phidippides's legendary run in 490 B.C. from the plain of Marathon to Athens with news of the stunning Greek defeat of the Persians.

Today the Olympic Games have become more than just an athletic contest. They are big business. The United States Olympic Committee has an annual operating budget of $388 million for funding the training and preparation of US athletes. They are also usually a major economic boon to the community that hosts the Games. When Atlanta hosted the 1996 Summer Games, for instance, 73,000 hotel rooms were filled within a ninety-minute radius of the Olympic Center, pumping over $5.1 billion into the local economy.

---

female nude became a major subject for late Classical and Hellenistic artists. His subject here is the modest Aphrodite—she covers herself—yet sensuality is not suppressed in the slightest. She stands in a slight S-curve, weight on one foot, turning her head, in a relaxed and easy pose.

Lysippos. Sculpture continued to flourish in the late Classical period between the end of the Peloponnesian War in 404 B.C. and the death of Alexander the Great in 323 B.C. The sculptor LYSIPPOS [lee-SI-pus] was active by 370 B.C. and still working ca. 310 B.C., a longevity that earned him the name "Lysippos the old man." During these many years, Lysippos is said to have produced two thousand works of art, but he is known today only through a few Roman copies. From 328 to 325 B.C. Lysippos held the position of court sculptor to Alexander the Great.

We know Lysippos's *Apoxyomenos (The Scraper)* (fig. 4.16) from a Roman marble copy of the bronze original of ca. 330 B.C. that was found in the Trastevere section of Rome. In this sculpture, an athlete is shown using a

strigil, or scraper, to clean the dirt and sweat off his body after exercising on the *palaestra*—the school where young men learned to wrestle and box under the guidance of a master. The figure's pose is relaxed and spontaneous; it looks as if he has just shifted or is just about to shift his weight from one leg to the other. Moreover, he is not only moving from left to right but is also advancing out toward the viewer as he stretches his arms forward. Lysippos makes his subject move in three dimensions.

The Scraper is a slender figure with a small head. The body is rounded, with long, loose, lithe legs. The proportions are different from those of Polykleitos's *Spear-Bearer* of 450–440 B.C. (see fig. 4.14). Indeed, Lysippos, working about a century later, created a new canon of ideal proportions for the human body. According to the Roman historian Pliny, the height ratio of head to overall figure size in Lysippos's sculpture was 1:9, whereas Polykleitos's was 1:8. This new physique was to gain favor and dominate through the end of the Hellenistic era.

The expressive face of *The Scraper*, sensitively rendered, appears somewhat nervous as he glances to the

Figure 4.16 *Apoxyomenos (The Scraper)*, Roman copy after the original bronze of ca. 330 B.C. by Lysippos, marble, height 6′9″ (2.06 m), Gabinetto dell'Apoxymenos, Museo Pio Clementino, Musei Vaticani, Rome. A little more than a century after the *Spear Bearer*, the ideal male nude has slenderer proportions and moves freely in space. No longer to be seen solely from the front, *The Scraper* is of interest from all sides.

side. This individualized face may be a portrait of the noted wrestler Cheilon of Patrai, who died in 322 B.C., of whom Lysippos is known to have made a statue after his death. This is another important development after the idealized figures and faces of the Classical period. Anonymity has been abandoned, and a new interest in individualization has arrived (see also fig. 4.19).

VASE PAINTING

White-Ground Ceramics. In the first half of the fifth century B.C., a new technique was introduced into Greek ceramic production. In this **white-ground technique**, the vase is made of the same reddish Attic clay that was used for earlier black- and red-figure pottery. However, here a white slip is painted over the surface of the vase. The figures are not then filled in, as they were in the black-figure technique, nor is the background filled in, as in the red-figure technique. Instead, the central picture and surrounding decorative patterns are painted on with a fine brush. The style is characterized by free and spontaneous lines. The white-ground technique presents the painter with no more technical problems than working on the equivalent of a white piece of paper—except that the surface of the vase curves.

The white-ground technique is associated in particular with **lekythoi** (singular, **lekythos**), small cylindrical oil jugs with a single handle, used as funerary monuments

Figure 4.17 "Achilles Painter," *Muse and Maiden*, lekythos, white-ground style, ca. 445–430 B.C., terra cotta, height 16′ (40.7 cm), Staatliche Antikensammlungen, Munich. One of the great advantages of working in the white-ground technique is that technical restrictions are reduced to a minimum. Neither the figures (as in the black-figure style) nor the background (as in the red-figure style) need to be filled in.

and offerings. They were favored in particular by fifth-century B.C. Athenians. A lekythos (fig. 4.17) by the ACHILLES PAINTER, painted ca. 445–430 B.C. in a mature Classical style, shows a muse and maiden on Mount Helikon playing a kithara, a stringed musical instrument. Mount Helikon is the mountain of the muses; the word "Helikon" is written below her seat. Muses, goddesses of the arts, excelled in song. The scene offers a comforting view of the afterlife in Elysium, Homer's beautiful blissful land at the end of the earth, where there is no pain, only happiness and constant good weather.

THE EMERGENCE OF DRAMA

Aeschylus. Greek drama developed from choral celebrations honoring Dionysos, the Greek god of wine and fertility. These celebrations included dancing as part of the religious ritual. Legend has it that the poet Thespis introduced a speaker who was separate from the chorus but who engaged in dialogue with the chorus. From this dialogue drama emerged. A second actor was then added to this first speaker and the chorus by AESCHYLUS [ESS-kuh-luss] (ca. 524–456 B.C.), who is today acknowledged as the "creator of tragedy."

Figure 4.18 Polykleitos the Younger, theater, Epidauros, ca. 350 B.C., later modified. Ancient Greek theaters were built into a hillside that provided support for the tiers of seats. Ancient Roman theaters, in contrast, were built freestanding.

Greek plays were performed in huge outdoor amphitheaters capable of seating upward of fifteen thousand people. The theater at Epidauros, for example, accommodated sixteen thousand (fig. 4.18). The audience sat in tiers of seats built into the slope of the hillside. The hills echoed the sound of the actors' voices, which were projected through large masks that further amplified them. The actors also wore elevated shoes, which restricted their movements on the stage. The shoes and masks made subtle nuances of gesture and expression impossible in this very early form of theater. The playwright's language, therefore, had to compensate for these limitations. However, the performances themselves must nonetheless have been quite spectacular. The words appear to have been mostly sung to music, and music accompanied the dances performed by the chorus.

Ancient Greek plays were performed on an elevated platform. Behind the acting area was a building (*skene*) that functioned as both dressing room and scenic background. Below the stage was the orchestra, or dancing place for the chorus. Standing between the actors and the audience, the chorus had an important part in the drama, often representing the communal perspective. One of the chorus's principal functions was to mark the divisions between the scenes of a play, by dancing and chanting poetry. These lyrical choral interludes sometimes commented on the action, sometimes generalized from it, and are an obvious remnant of Greek drama's origins in religious ritual.

Aeschylus is the earliest dramatist whose works have survived. Seven of his nineteen plays are still extant. His plays, like those of his successors Sophocles and Euripides, were all written for the twice-annual festivals for Dionysos held at Athens. Each dramatist had to submit three tragedies and a lighthearted "satyr" play for performance together at the festival. The work for which Aeschylus is best known—the trilogy called the *Oresteia* [oar-es-TIE-uh], after the central character, Orestes [oar-ES-tees]—won first prize in the festival at Athens of 458 B.C. The first play in the trilogy, *Agamemnon*, dramatizes the story of the murder of the Greek king, Agamemnon, who upon returning from the Trojan War is slain by his wife, Clytemnestra [clie-tem-NES-tra], and her lover Aegisthus [aye-GISS-this]. The second play, *The Libation Bearers*, describes the return of Agamemnon and Clytemnestra's son, Orestes, who kills his mother and her lover to avenge the death of his father. The concluding play, *The Eumenides* [you-MEN-ih-dees], describes the pursuit of Orestes by the Furies for his act of vengeance and Orestes' ultimate exoneration in an Athenian court of law.

Taken together, the three plays dramatize the growth of Greek civilization—the movement from a Homeric tribal society system, in which vengeance was the rule and individuals felt obligated to exact private vengeance, to a modern society ruled by law. The third play of the trilogy describes the establishment in Athens, under the jurisdiction of the goddess Athena, the city's patron, of a court of law to decide Orestes' case. Athena herself must render the verdict as the jury of citizens is unable to decide Orestes' guilt or innocence. Symbolically, with the establishment of the court of law in the last part of

Timeline 4.2   Classical philosophers and early tragedians.

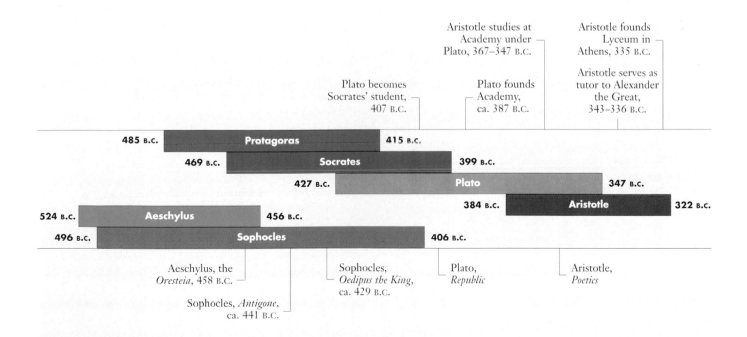

Connections

ARISTOTLE AND GREEK THEATER

Of his many achievements, Aristotle's work as the first Western literary theorist has been among his most influential. Aristotle's literary ideas are developed in his *Poetics*, a treatise on the nature of literature, focusing particularly on Sophocles' *Oedipus the King*. *The Poetics* offers a provocative and enduring set of ideas about the literary experience. Aristotle, in fact, is concerned in *The Poetics* not only with literature but with art in general.

An important idea derived from *The Poetics* concerns Aristotle's notion of "catharsis." Aristotle explains catharsis as a purging of the passions of pity and fear aroused in an audience during the tragic action of a play. Aristotle considers this catharsis the goal or end of tragedy. Aristotle's reasoning reverses conventional wisdom, suggesting that an audience's experience of pity and fear at, for example, Oedipus's tragic fate would provide pleasure and not pain. The reason is that the emotions built up during the course of the tragic dramatic action are "purged" by the end of the performance. In Aristotle's view, the purging includes both physical purging through the excitement generated and released, and a spiritual purgation analogous to the release or cleansing of the soul for religious purposes. Such purging thus contributes to the health of the society beyond the theater.

The bulk of Aristotle's *Poetics* focuses on drama, especially tragedy. Aristotle is concerned primarily with the "art" of tragedy, which he analyzes under six headings: plot, character, thought, rhythm, song, and spectacle. Aristotle's interest in tragic plots concerns how they are constructed to create particular effects leading to catharsis involving the purging of pity and fear. The action of a play is seen not in terms of isolated scenes or events but as the working out of its "motive" or "spring of action."

In Sophocles's *Oedipus the King*, for example, this motive is Oedipus's desire and attempt to find the slayer of King Laius. Like any successful tragic dramatist, Sophocles created in *Oedipus* a complete action with a beginning, middle, and end. The beginning identifies the main character's central purpose; the middle describes his passionate following through on his intention; the end reveals his perception of his tragic mistake or error. This perception on the part of the tragic hero is his recognition or *anagnorisis*, which follows the ironic reversal of his fortunes, and which leads to the pathos of his suffering inevitably to follow. Throughout *The Poetics* Aristotle refers repeatedly to Sophocles's *Oedipus* as the consummate example of tragic drama.

Aristotle also places a high premium on the literary artist's use of language, particularly metaphor. For Aristotle, mastery of metaphor is the identifying mark of a poetic genius. He writes that "the greatest thing by far is to have a command of metaphor … it is the mark of genius." Sophocles' use of imagery of light and darkness to represent knowledge and ignorance, and his metaphors of healing and disease to signify life and death, qualify him for Aristotle's highest praise.

Aristotle's insights into literary language and dramatic structure have remained influential for more than two thousand years. Throughout the Renaissance, and well into the eighteenth and nineteenth centuries, Aristotle was recognized as having set the standards for literary appreciation. At the end of the second millennium, nearly 2500 years after Aristotle wrote *The Poetics*, literary historians and critics continue to employ Aristotle's categories and terminology.

---

the trilogy, the old order passes and a new order emerges. Communal justice rather than the pursuit of individual vengeance comes to regulate civil society.

Sophocles. Of the Greek tragic dramatists, SOPHOCLES [SAH-fuh-clees] (496–406 B.C.) is perhaps the most widely read and performed today. Unlike those of his forebear Aeschylus, Sophocles' plays focus on individual human, rather than broad civil and religious, concerns. His most famous plays—*Oedipus the King* and *Antigone*—center on private crises and portray characters under extreme duress. *Antigone*, which takes place in Thebes, a city prostrated by war, turns on the difficult decisions that Antigone, Oedipus's daughter, and King Creon, his brother-in-law, must make. In *Oedipus the King*, which is set against a background of a plague-stricken city, Sophocles examines the behavior of Oedipus, who has been destined before birth to murder his father and marry his mother.

Athenian audiences watching performances of *Oedipus the King* would have been familiar with Oedipus's story from sources such as Homer's *Odyssey*. Oedipus's parents, King Laius and Queen Jocasta of Thebes, had been foretold of their son's terrible fate and therefore left him as a baby in the wilderness to die. This plan went awry when the child was taken by a shepherd to Corinth, where he was adopted by a childless couple, King Polybus and Queen Merope. Upon hearing an oracle pronounce his fate, and believing Polybus and Merope to be his natural parents, Oedipus then left Corinth to get far away from the King and Queen. Ironically, however, en route to his true birthplace, Thebes, Oedipus kills an old man who gets in his way. This old man, Oedipus only much later discovers, was his true father, Laius.

Sophocles' version of the story, *Oedipus the King*, begins at the point when Thebes has been suffering a series of catastrophes, the most terrible of which is a devastating plague. Oedipus had previously saved Thebes from the Sphinx, a winged creature with the body of a lion and the head of a woman. The Sphinx had terrorized the city by devouring anyone who crossed its path and was unable to answer its riddle correctly—"What goes on four legs in the morning, two legs in the afternoon, and three legs in the evening?" Oedipus solved the riddle by answering "Man." After slaying the Sphinx, Oedipus was given the kingship of Thebes and the hand of its recently widowed queen, Jocasta, in reward. Unknown to Oedipus, but known to the Athenian audience, was the fact that Jocasta was his mother and that her recently slain husband, Laius, had been killed by Oedipus himself. All this and more Oedipus soon discovers as he comes to self-knowledge.

Sophocles' *Oedipus the King* is one of the greatest tragedies in theatrical history—one of the definitions of **tragedy** is the representation of the downfall of a great hero. It also provides one of the best examples of **dramatic irony,** where speeches have different meanings for the audience and the speaker: the audience know much more than the speaker. Thematically, the play raises questions about fate and human responsibility, particularly the extent to which Oedipus is responsible for his own tragic destiny. Sophocles portrays his tragic protagonists heroically. These tragic heroes suffer the consequences of their actions nobly and with grandeur.

Euripides. One of the greatest and most disturbing of Greek tragic dramatists is EURIPIDES [you-RIP-id-ease] (ca. 480–406 B.C.). As Aristotle put it, where Sophocles depicts people as they ought to be, Euripides depicts them as they really are. His plays were written under the shadow of the Peloponnesian War, and they spare no one, showing humankind at its worst. While ostensibly about the enslavement of the female survivors of Troy, *The Trojan Women*, first staged in 415 B.C., is a barely disguised indictment of the women of Melos after the Athenian defeat of that city. In *The Bacchae*, Euripides depicts a civilization gone mad, as followers of Dionysos kill the king of Thebes under the drunken belief that he is a wild animal. Dionysos's followers, perhaps in part a portrait of the Athenian people, are unwilling to think for themselves and hence liable to be led blindly into the most senseless of acts.

Aristophanes. All was not tragedy on the Greek stage, however. Comedy was very popular, and the master of the medium was ARISTOPHANES [air-ihs-TOF-fan-nees] (ca. 445–388 B.C.). His plays spoofed contemporary politics and political personalities, laughing at Greek society and ridiculing the rich in particular. Aristophanes even took on Socrates, depicting him as a hopeless dreamer. In *Lysistrata*, produced in 411 B.C. in the midst of the same Peloponnesian War that so outraged Euripides, Aristophanes' title character persuades her fellow Athenian women to withhold sexual favors from their husbands until peace is declared. They carry out their plans with merriment, teasing their husbands and even occupying the Acropolis. The women win the day, judging their husbands' priorities acutely, and at the end of the play Spartans and Athenians are reconciled and dance together in joy.

PHILOSOPHY

Of all the legacies of Greece, its philosophical tradition is one of the most enduring. The Greeks believed that what distinguished human beings was their intellectual capacity, their ability to reason, and thus the philosopher held a special place in their society. It was the philosopher's business to query the nature of human existence. Is there a difference between appearance and reality? What is our relation to the divine, and how can we recognize it? What ethical principles should guide us? What happens when the individual will finds itself at odds with the will of the state, the polis? What is the nature of love? What does it mean to be free? All of these questions were posed and answered, and then posed again, as they have been ever since the Greeks first pondered them.

Socrates. SOCRATES [SOC-ra-tees] (469–399 B.C.), the most famous of Western philosophers, is known only through the exposition of his ideas in Plato's dialogues. In the earliest of Plato's writings, Socrates

Figure 4.19 Portrait bust of Socrates, Roman copy of an original bronze of ca. 350 B.C. by Lysippos, marble, lifesize, Museo Nazionale Romano, Rome. At his trial in 399 B.C. for impropriety toward the gods and corruption of the young, Socrates cheerfully admitted to causing unrest and insisted that it was his duty to seek the truth.

(fig. 4.19) appears as a figure whose supreme goal is to pursue knowledge and truth. Best known for his method of questioning others' beliefs and eliciting their assumptions in a form of dialectical inquiry, Socrates is recognized as a model of intellectual honesty and heroic equanimity in the face of death. He was executed in 399 B.C. after being put on trial for impiety and corruption of the young. The authorities appear to have offered Socrates the chance to escape, but the philosopher refused.

Socrates arrived on the philosophical scene in Golden Age Athens at a time when previous philosophy had concerned matters of cosmology. Presocratic philosophers had speculated that the world was composed of one or another substance, and that everything in existence was ultimately derivable from this original material. For THALES [THAY-lees] (fl. 585 B.C.) everything derived from and could be explained in terms of water. For Democritus it was matter; for Pythagoras number. For still others, such as ANAXAGORAS [a-nax-AG-or-us] (ca. 500–428 B.C.), the first principle was *Nous* or Mind, whereas for Herakleitos it was *Logos*, by which he meant divine intelligence or rational principle represented by fire.

Socrates would have none of this. His interest instead was in ethics, how we live in the world. Socrates was concerned with pursuing wisdom so as to know the good, the true, and the beautiful. His pursuit of right living was governed by reason, and central to this was the need to "Know thyself," as his famous maxim stated. Socrates urged a vigilant self-examination and encouraged a critical questioning of one's own and other's ideas and assumptions. Only through such efforts, Socrates believed, could one arrive at true understanding of the Good, which was necessary for the moral life and happiness.

Socrates developed his pursuit of knowledge and emphasis on virtue when the **Sophists**, who used philosophy for practical and opportunistic ends, held sway. Although Sophist philosophers such as Protagoras shared Socrates' emphasis on the immediate concerns of life in the world, their aims and practices differed sharply from his. Instead of the pursuit of an absolute standard of truth, the Sophists believed that all moral and ethical standards were matters of convention and that no such thing as absolute truth existed. Knowledge, the Sophists believed, was relative, based on individual experience, and hence could be reduced to opinion. Unlike Socrates' relentless and single-minded pursuit of truth, the Sophists would argue both sides of an issue with equal persuasiveness. Rhetoric's negative connotations, as in "mere rhetoric," and the use of the word "sophistry" to mean specious reasoning derive from the practices of the Greek Sophists.

Socrates typifies the Greek philosophical ideal developed in the writings of his pupil, Plato, who advanced and extended a number of key Socratic ideas. For

Figure 4.20   Portrait bust of Plato, 350–340 B.C., Roman copy of an original bronze of ca. 427–347 B.C. by Silanion (?), marble, Glyptothek, Munich. Though his real name was Arsitocles, Plato went by his nickname, which means "the broad one," a physical trait evident even in this portrait bust.

Socrates, the life of the mind was paramount, as evidenced by his maxim "The unexamined life is not worth living." Self-knowledge is crucial in determining how to master passion and appetite through reason. Living a virtuous life directed by a reasoned pursuit of moral perfection leads to happiness.

With this emphasis on the spiritual, the intellectual, and the moral, Socrates provided Western thought with a new philosophical direction. By living according to his principles, by making philosophy a life-long process, Socrates also provided a model and ideal of one who loves wisdom, the literal meaning, in Greek, of the word "philosopher."

Plato.   PLATO [PLAY-toh] (427–347 B.C.) and Socrates are frequently spoken of in the same breath because so many of Plato's dialogues present Socrates as a character and speaker. As a result, it is not always easy to determine where Socrates' thinking leaves off and Plato's begins. It is perhaps best to consider Plato's philosophy as extending key elements of Socratic thought. In dialogues such as *The Symposium* and *The Republic*,

Plato (fig. 4.20) developed the Socratic perspective implicit in his mentor's life and teaching.

Plato's paradigm, or model, for reality was mathematics, for Plato believed that in mathematical truth, which exists beyond time and space, perfection could be found. Plato argued, for instance, that it was the *idea* of a circle, rather than any actual example of one in nature or in a drawing, that was true and perfect. Any example of a circle only approximated the perfect idea of circularity, which existed in a special realm that transcended all particular manifestations. This realm Plato identified as the realm of Perfect Forms or Ideas. Virtues such as courage and kindness similarly transcended their everyday exemplary manifestations.

Most important, however, was Plato's postulation of ideal Goodness, Truth, and Beauty, which he argued were all One, in the realm of Ideal Forms. For if Plato's argument were true, then all actions could be measured against an ideal, and that ideal standard could be used as a goal toward which human beings might strive. This was obviously a significant departure from the relativism of the Sophists. One consequence of this idea was that, according to Plato, human beings should be less concerned with the material world of impermanence and change and more concerned with unchanging spiritual "realities." Thus, the highest spiritual principle of reason should be used to control the lower human aspects of energy and desire.

Both of these ideas are advanced in what is perhaps Plato's best-known work, *The Republic*. A complex and ambitious book, *The Republic* is concerned primarily with the concept of justice, especially with how to achieve a just society. In establishing his argument, Plato proposes the division of society into three strands or layers, each of which reflects one of the three aspects of the soul. Plato argues that people whose primary impulse is toward satisfying their physical desires are not capable of making proper judgments in accordance with reason, and that they should therefore occupy the lowest positions in society, those of servitude. Above these workers are the soldiers, whose primary force is that of energy or spiritedness. The soldiers and the workers in Plato's ideal republic work together harmoniously at their allotted tasks under the directorship of the highest social groups, the philosophers, whose decisions in governing the republic are guided by reason.

In *The Republic*, Plato explains his idea about the differences among levels of knowledge or understanding by means of two analogies. One, the analogy of the Divided Line, presents a way to distinguish between lower and higher orders of knowledge. A vertical line is divided into four segments, with the upper two representing the intellectual world and the lower two the material world. The lowest part of the line represents shadows and reflections (explained below in the Allegory of the Cave); the one above it represents material and natural things.

The two lower earthbound parts of the line are complemented by the upper segments, which represent reasoning about the world and its objects (the lower segment of the upper line), and philosophical principles arrived at without reference to objects (abstract thought, the uppermost portion of the line).

Plato supplements this visual analogy about the nature of knowledge with his famous Allegory of the Cave. In this, he illustrates his distinction between true knowledge of reality and the illusion of appearances. He describes a cave in which the only light visible to human beings chained to a wall is that reflected from a fire behind and above them. When objects are reflected as shadows on the wall, the cave inhabitants take these shadows for reality. Only those freed from the cave see that what they had previously considered real are simply shadowy reflections of their actual counterparts. Instead of being a prisoner of illusion like those still chained in the cave, the escapees have a true knowledge of reality.

For Plato, such a revelation reflects the difference between ignorance and knowledge of truth, the difference between the world of material objects and the realm of Ideal Essences, the true forms of those things. This division between the higher spiritual forms and the lower material world is echoed by other dualisms in Plato's philosophy. Foremost among the divisions are those between the philosopher and the common people, the perfect and the imperfect, and the spiritual life and the physical life.

Aristotle. Born in Stageira, in Thrace, ARISTOTLE [air-iss-TOT-ul] (384–322 B.C.) studied in Plato's school, the Academy, in Athens. He remained there for twenty years until Plato's death in 347 B.C., when he left to establish his own school, first in Assos and later in Lesbos. Aristotle's most famous pupil was Alexander the Great, whom the philosopher served as private tutor from 343 until 336 B.C., when Alexander succeeded to the Macedonian throne.

In 335 B.C. Aristotle returned to Athens to establish his own school at the Lyceum, where lectures and discussions took place under a covered walkway. Lecturers moved about among their audiences, thereby acquiring the designation "Peripatetics" (walkers). Like Socrates, Aristotle was charged with impiety and condemned by the Athenian tribunal of judges. Upon leaving Athens before a sentence of death could be carried out, Aristotle is reputed to have remarked that he would not allow Athens to commit a second crime against philosophy.

Aristotle's logic provides a framework for scientific and philosophical thinking that is still in use now. The basis of Aristotle's logic is an analysis of argument. Its central feature is the **syllogism**. In syllogistic reasoning, one proposition or statement follows from another by necessity, when the premises are true. In such a case the syllogism is considered valid, as in the following example:

All philosophers are mortal.
Aristotle is a philosopher.
Aristotle was mortal.

In the next example, the syllogism is invalid even though the conclusion is true, because one of the propositions—the first—is untrue:

All philosophers are men.
Aristotle was a philosopher.
Aristotle was a man.

Aristotle's logic also includes an analysis of the basic categories used to describe the natural world. According to Aristotle, things possess substance (their primary reality) and incidental qualities. A dog, for example, possesses something—this is its substance—that distinguishes it from other animals, making it a dog and not a cat or a horse. At the same time, the dog may be large and brown with long shaggy hair—these are incidental qualities and secondary compared to the dog's substantial reality. Another dog, which is small and white with short fine hair, nonetheless possesses the same substance as the first larger darker dog.

Aristotle disagreed with his teacher Plato on a number of important issues. For Aristotle, an object's matter and form are inseparable. Even though we can think of the "whiteness" of a dog and its "dogness," those concepts do not have independent existence outside of the things they embody. Unlike Plato, who posited an Ideal realm of Forms, where the perfect idea of a dog exists independent of any actual examples of dogs in the world, for Aristotle the idea of a dog can only exist in relation to a real canine quadruped. Aristotle held that this dependence of the form of an object on its physical matter is in effect for all things. Thus, for Aristotle, the existence of any universal concept is dependent upon empirical reality in the form of a particular physical thing. By insisting on the necessary link between form and matter, Aristotle stood Plato's thought on its head and brought Platonic ideas down to earth.

Similarly, Aristotle emphasized the way the substance of a thing becomes itself in a *process* of growth and development. With his early study of biology as an influence, Aristotle's philosophical thinking takes account of development and process in ways that Plato's more mathematically influenced philosophy does not. For example, Aristotle describes the *potential* of a seed to become a flower or a fruit, of an embryo to become a living human or animal. The oak is potentially existent in the acorn, from which it grows and toward which its growth is a natural and inevitable cause of its being.

Aristotle's philosophy is grounded in the notion of teleology, which views the end or goal of an object or being as more important than its starting point or beginning. His teleological mind explains the way all material things are designed to achieve their purpose and attain their end. This end or goal of each thing is the fulfillment of the potential it embodies from the beginning of its existence.

Aristotle arrives at a conviction about the nature of God from logic rather than from ethics or religious faith. In his *Physics* Aristotle argues that everything is in motion toward fulfilling or realizing its potential. Since everything is in motion, there must be something that provided the primary impulse (the prime mover) toward motion and that itself is not in motion. For to be in motion is to be in a potential state, and the prime mover must be in a state of completeness and thus not in motion. The prime mover must be immaterial as well as unchanging.

Finally, Aristotle differed from his Greek predecessors significantly in his approach to ethics. Ethics, for Aristotle, were a matter of contingency. For Aristotle, that is, there were no absolutely unchanging ethical norms to guide right behavior and determine right conduct. Instead, there were only approximations based on the principle of the mean between extremes. Courage, thus, exists as a balance between cowardice and rash behavior, and temperance as a balance between deprivation and overindulgence. Virtue consists of negotiating between dangerous extremes, the balance point changing according to circumstances.

Aristotle's approach to ethics is grounded in the realities and contingencies of this empirical world. Aristotle consistently emphasized the tangible, the physical materiality of concrete everyday experience. In the process of formulating his more empirically based philosophy, Aristotle thus provided a necessary counterpoint to the idealism espoused by his teacher and predecessor, Plato. Together their complementary philosophies have spurred theological and philosophical speculation for more than two thousand years. If, as one modern philosopher put it, "All philosophy is but a footnote to Plato," Aristotle's has been the richest, most complex, and most influential "footnote" of all.

MUSIC AND GREEK SOCIETY

Music is mentioned in ancient Greece as early as Homer's *Iliad*, which includes a reference to Achilles playing a lyre in his tent. It was not uncommon for a warrior to soothe his spirits with the charms of music, much as in ancient Israel David played the harp to assuage the anxieties of King Saul.

An integral part of Greek life, music was associated with festivals and banquets, religion and social ritual, including marriages, funerals, and harvest rites. It was associated with Greek drama, for which a special place, the orchestra, was set aside for dancers. Music was an essential part of the Homeric epics, which were chanted to the accompaniment of the lyre. In addition, music formed a significant part of the Olympic athletic contests. At the festivals, the ancient Greeks held contests for musicians equal to those of the athletes, awarding prizes and honors of similar measure.

Music, for the ancient Greeks, was not an isolated art. The basic elements of Greek music derived from mathematics, which served as the foundation of ancient Greek philosophy and astronomy. Music, thus, became associated with these other Hellenic achievements, largely through ideas about number, especially numerical relationships expressed as ratios. The most important of the early Greek theorists of music was Pythagoras (ca. 582–507 B.C.).

For Pythagoras, numbers provided the key to understanding the universe. He believed that music and arithmetic functioned as a single unit, with the system of musical sounds governed by mathematical laws. Pythagoras argued that since music embodies number in ratios and proportions, music exemplifies the harmony of the universe.

Music was so important to the ancient Greeks that all philosophers, including Plato and Aristotle, made a point of discussing it. Plato, for example, believed that music could influence human emotion and character. He argued that only music that encouraged bravery and emotional stability should be taught to the young. Aristotle also believed in the importance of music for building character. Like Plato, Aristotle wrote about music's power to affect the development of the inner person, particularly music's power to affect the soul. Other ancient philosophers commented on music's ethical influence. Like Plato and Aristotle, they associated certain musical modes with virtue and vice, spiritual development and spiritual danger.

The Musical Modes. For the ancient Greeks, musical scales, or modes, had particular ethical effects associated with them. Each mode used a particular sequence of intervals that established its modality. In addition, the modes of ancient Greek music differed from the scales of modern Western music in having unequal intervals. Instead of whole tones, half tones, and quarter tones of equal value or temper, ancient Greek music was more like Arabic, Chinese, and Indian music in having varying degrees of difference between intervals. Greek music was primarily a music of melody, with little concern for harmony.

Each of the Greek musical modes was considered to have a specific ethical effect on hearers, thus resulting in the various strictures placed upon them by Plato and Aristotle. The best of the modes, the one most conducive to virtue, was thought to be the Dorian mode, which, for Aristotle, represented the golden mean of music, comparable to the golden mean of his ethics.

While ancient Greek instruments can be recognized from their depiction in painting and sculpture, the melodies played on them are virtually extinct. The scraps of melody inscribed on papyrus or incised in stone do not provide much help in understanding what ancient Greek music sounded like. The best available examples of ancient Greek musical manuscripts date from the second century B.C. and are tributes to the god Apollo.

HELLENISTIC GREECE
❖

After the fall of Athens in 404 B.C., first Sparta and then Thebes controlled the Greek mainland, but neither proved very effective. And then, in 359 B.C., Macedonia, a minor Greek state on the northern end of the Aegean, beyond Mount Olympus, began to assert itself when Philip II became ruler. In 338 B.C. Macedonia defeated the Greeks decisively at Chaeronea. Ambassadors were dispatched to Athens and Thebes with terms for peace. Among the ambassadors to Athens was Philip's eighteen-year-old son, Alexander—ALEXANDER THE GREAT (356–323 B.C.), as he would come to be known (fig. 4.21). Raised to rule, he had been schooled by Aristotle to be "a leader to the Greeks and a despot to the barbarians, to

Figure 4.21   Portrait bust of Alexander the Great, Roman copy of a Greek original of ca. 330 B.C., marble, Dresden Museum, Germany. Although a womanizer, an excessive drinker, and perhaps a megalomaniac, Alexander was nevertheless a great general who astonished the world with his stunning succession of military triumphs, which gave the word "empire" a new meaning.

look after the former as after friends and relatives, and to deal with the latter as with beasts or plants." Alexander took his tutor's words to heart, and as a result came to enjoy the enthusiastic support of almost all Greek intellectuals. When Philip II was assassinated in 336 B.C.—possibly at Alexander's behest, since Philip had divorced his mother and removed his son from substantive roles in the government—Alexander took control.

On his accession, he crushed a rebellion in Thebes, destroying the city and selling the entire population into slavery. He then set out to expand the Macedonian empire and control the world. By 334 B.C. he had defeated the Persians. Soon he ruled all the territory west of the Euphrates. Next he conquered Egypt, where in 332 B.C. he founded the great port city of Alexandria in the Nile Delta. Marching back into Mesopotamia, he entered Babylon, and made a sacrifice to the local god, Marduk. Then he marched on Persepolis and burned it, seizing its royal treasure. Convinced that India was small, and that beyond it lay Ocean, as he called it, by which route he could return to Europe by sea, he set out to conquer present-day Pakistan. However, his troops were exhausted and met unexpected resistance in the form of war elephants; Alexander was thus forced to sail down the Indus River to the Indian Ocean. Along this route he founded present-day Karachi—at the time named Alexandria after himself. Returning finally to Babylon, in 323 B.C., Alexander caught a fever and died.

The Hellenistic era begins with Alexander's death at the age of thirty-three. Alexander had brought about a mingling of Eastern and Western cultures through his policies and conquests. He encouraged, for instance, marriages between his soldiers and Middle Eastern women by providing large wedding gifts and by marrying two Persian women himself. But culturally the Greek army had a greater impact on the Middle East than the Middle East had on them. In fact, the term "Hellenistic," first used in 1833 by the historian Johann Gustav Droysen, was coined to describe the impact of Greece on the Middle East—its "Hellenization"—after Alexander's death. The generals Alexander had installed as governors of the different territories in his empire set themselves up as kings. Political, artistic, social, and economic dominance shifted from the mainland of Greece to the new Hellenistic kingdoms such as those of the Seleucids in Syria and the Ptolemies in Egypt. The cities of Pergamon in Turkey and Alexandria in Egypt in particular were great centers of learning. The massive library at Alexandria contained over 700,000 papyri and scrolls, and Pergamon's library rivaled it. As if inspired by the dramatic successes of Alexander himself, the art such Hellenistic cities spawned was itself highly dramatic. Where Classical Greek art was concerned with balance and order and idealized its subjects, Hellenistic art focused on the individual, in all the individual's unidealized particularity, and on emotional states. Even the dominant philosophies of the day reflect this tendency.

Map 4.2   Alexander's empire.

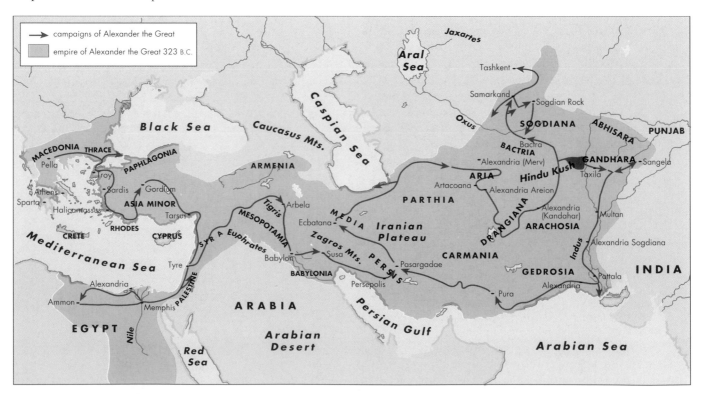

Figure 4.22 Temple of the Olympian Zeus, Athens, second century B.C.–second century A.D. This once enormous temple was the first large-scale use of the Corinthian order on the exterior of a building. The Romans would favor the ornate Corinthian order.

More important for the future of Western thought were the acts of preservation and dispersion performed by Hellenistic scholars as they collected, edited, analyzed, and interpreted the philosophical works of the past. This work of humanistic scholarship included preserving not only the works of ancient Greek philosophy and literature, especially those of Plato and Homer, for example, but the Greek translation of the Hebrew Bible as well. Moreover, the emergence of humanistic scholarship was accompanied by educational institutions established for its continued development. In the spectacular libraries at Alexandria and Pergamon, and in Athens, which was home to a great academy of its own, Greek intellectual achievements endured.

ARCHITECTURE

The Temple of the Olympian Zeus. The popularity of the Corinthian order in the Hellenistic era is demonstrated by the Temple of the Olympian Zeus in Athens (fig. 4.22). This temple was originally built in the Doric order in the sixth century B.C., but was reconstructed in

Hellenistic times, beginning in the second century B.C., with work continuing into the second century A.D. in Roman times under the Emperor Hadrian. The Corinthian capital was given greater prominence here than it ever was in Classical Greek architecture. This extraordinary structure once was an eight-by-twenty temple, the columns in the peristyle formed with double rows of twenty columns on the sides and three rows of eight columns on the ends. Today, although little remains of this monumental undertaking, there is enough to make it obvious that the Corinthian order is the most ornamental and the most luxurious of the three orders.

Pergamon's Altar of Zeus. Perhaps nothing better embodies the extravagant Hellenistic attitude to architecture and the visual arts in general than the Upper City of Pergamon in Asia Minor, built by KING ATTALOS [ah-TAL-us] (241–197 B.C.) and almost finished by EUMENES II [you-MEN-ease] (197–159 B.C.). This Hellenistic city was grand in vision, designed on a large scale and embellished with a profusion of ornament. Essentially a large complex of architecture and sculpture built in the slope of a hill, Pergamon appears as if nature

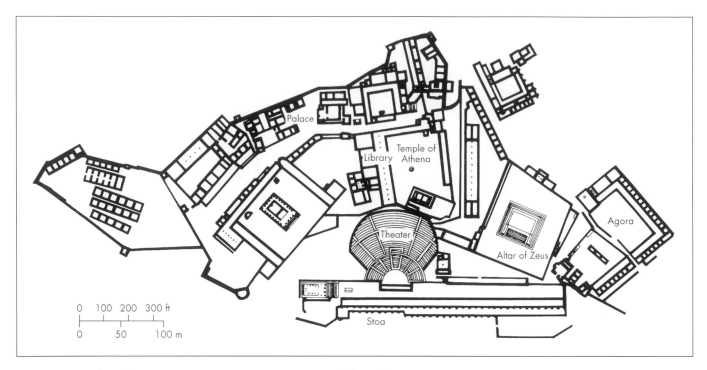

Figure 4.23 Plan of Upper City, Pergamon. In an assertion of the architect's power over nature, the steep slope of a hill had been molded into a city.

Figure 4.24 Altar of Zeus, from Pergamon, Turkey, west front, restored, built ca. 180–160 B.C., under Eumenes II, base 100′ square (30.5 sq. m), Staatliche Museen, Berlin. The subject depicted on the frieze on the Pergamon altar is highly emotional, its rendering is charged with the dramatic action and expression characteristic of Hellenistic art.

has been sculpted into several terraces occupied by splendid structures (fig. 4.23). The whole is indicative of a changed attitude toward the relationship between environment and architecture. Where Classical Greek architectural planning favored balance and order, the Hellenistic period shows a new assertiveness. Periklean restraint is a thing of the past.

The upper city included the celebrated Altar of Zeus (fig. 4.24), built 180–160 B.C. under Eumenes II, a demonstration of the dramatic theatricality and large scale favored in the Hellenistic era. In 278 B.C. the Gauls came sweeping into Asia Minor, to be conquered by Attalos I of Pergamon in 241 B.C. This monument was erected to commemorate the victory over the Gauls. The Altar of Zeus occupied a terrace all on its own on the hill at Pergamon.

SCULPTURE

The Battle of the Gods and the Giants. The Altar of Zeus at Pergamon was much celebrated in antiquity, although in the Early Christian era it was dubbed "Satan's Seat." On the sides of the podium of the altar was the relief frieze of the *Battle of the Gods and the Giants* (fig. 4.25), four hundred feet in length. The relief carving is very deep; the figures are almost carved in the round. The giants—the Titans of Greek mythology—are huge in size and terrible in appearance, with large snakes in place of legs. Legend had it that these giants of divine origin could be killed only if simultaneously slain by a god and a mortal. When the Titans revolted against the gods, attacking Zeus and Athena with rocks and flaming trees, Zeus and Athena responded with thunder-

Figure 4.25 *Battle of the Gods and the Giants*, Altar of Zeus, Pergamon, ca. 180–160 B.C., height 7′6″ (2.34 m), Staatliche Museen, Berlin. Here Athena has grabbed the hair of a winged monster who writhes in agony. His mother, identifiable by her "monstrous" curled locks, rises to help him.

Cross Currents

THE HELLENIZATION OF INDIA

By 326 B.C. Alexander the Great's forces had pushed as far east as the Punjab in northwest India. It was there that they confronted, for the first time, war elephants, two hundred strong. Though Alexander's troops defeated the Indian troops, it was rumored that the army of the Ganges, further east, was equipped with five thousand such beasts, and thus the Greek troops refused to go on. But the connection between the Greek world and India had been established.

Remnants of Alexander's forces settled in Bactria, between the Oxus River and the Hindu Kush mountains. Excavations at the Bactrian Greek city of Al Khanum have revealed Corinthian capitals and fragments of statues of various gods and goddesses. Coins with images of Herakles, Apollo, and Zeus were produced. There were portraits of the Bactrian kings on the other sides: Euthydemus, Demetrius, and Menander. However, it was not always Greek ideas that triumphed over Indian cultural traditions. Around 150 B.C. King Menander was converted to Buddhism by the monk Nagasena. The monk's conversation with the King is preserved as *The Questions of Melinda*, Melinda being the Indian version of Menander's name.

At Gandhara, on the north end of the Indus River, across the Khyber Pass from Bactria, Greek influence was especially strong. Though Gandharan art is mostly Buddhist in content, it has a Hellenistic style. In Taxila, a temple resembling the Parthenon in structure was constructed between 50 B.C. and A.D. 65. There is even evidence that the Homeric legend of the Trojan horse was known here (fig. 4.26).

Figure 4.26　Trojan horse frieze, Gandhara, second to third century a.d. Though the style shows local influences, the subject matter here is most definitely Greek as the Trojan prophetess Cassandra and the priest Laocoön (see fig. 4.28) attempt to block the entry of the Greek gift-horse into Troy.

---

bolts. Herakles, a mortal, aided them in killing the various giants in a variety of painful but picturesque ways— the giant Ephialtes, for instance, received an arrow in his left eye from the quiver of Apollo as an arrow landed in his right eye from the bow of Herakles.

Known as **gigantomachy**, the subject of the revolt of the giants against the gods was popular with Hellenistic artists. On the Altar of Zeus its treatment can be interpreted symbolically. Here the gods' triumph over the giants symbolizes the victories of Attalos I—art and politics working together for propagandistic ends. The style of this work—its action, violence, display of emotion, and windblown drapery—also defines the Hellenistic age in the arts. All restraint is gone, as Alexander had abandoned it politically at the era's outset. The scene here can stand in miniature for the Hellenistic world: sweeping, continuous, agitated movement against an ominously blank background— timeless, placeless, and spaceless.

The Nike of Samothrace.　The splendid Hellenistic *Nike of Samothrace* (fig. 4.27), also known as the *Winged Victory*, is one of the artistic treasures of the ancient world. It is related to the figures in the Pergamon frieze in the great sweeping gesture of the body, in the suggestion of movement through space, and in the treatment of the drapery. The date of the Nike is debated, but it was probably created between 200 and 190 B.C. The torso of this statue of the goddess of victory was discovered in 1863 on the island of Samothrace in the Sanctuary of the Great Gods. In 1950, further excavations uncovered the right hand and other smaller body parts. The statue was originally placed on the prow of a stone ship located in a niche cut into the mountainside above the Sanctuary of the Great Gods. The head was turned to face the sea. The composition was designed to give the impression that the goddess had just descended to the prow of the ship, her garments still responding to her movement through space. Theatrical and emotional, the statue is dynamic: the wind blows her drapery back as she appears to move forward. Far from static, the figure interacts with, and becomes part of, the surrounding space.

Laocoön and His Sons.　An expenditure of still greater energy, induced by agony, is seen in the *Laocoön*

Figure 4.27 *Nike of Samothrace*, ca. 200–190 B.C., marble, height 8′ (2.44 m), Musée du Louvre, Paris. Stone seemingly brought to life, this dynamic figure of Victory moves through space, the drapery blown against her body by her rapid movement.

group (fig. 4.28), sculpted by Hagesandros, Athanodoros, and Polydoros of Rhodes according to ancient sources. The date of this statue is debated, the possibilities ranging from 150 B.C. to the first century A.D. Whatever the case, it was only rediscovered in 1506 in Rome.

The subject of the sculpture is taken from Homer's *Iliad*. Laocoön was a priest of Apollo of Troy. He and his sons were strangled by snakes sent from the sea by Apollo when Laocoön tried to warn the Trojans against accepting the wooden horse, seemingly left as a gift to them by the retreating Greeks. In the sculpture the figures writhe violently, but all in one plane, like a relief. Laocoön and his two sons try to move apart, but are bound together by the serpent's coils, creating an extraordinary dynamism. With their wild hair and pained expressions, these figures are far removed from Classical

restraint; here, in all its full-blown glory, is the theatricality, passion, and drama of the Hellenistic age.

PHILOSOPHY

The English words "stoic," "skeptic," and "epicurean" derive from schools of Greek philosophy—Stoicism, Skepticism, and Epicureanism. Although none of these philosophical systems has had the long-term impact of Platonism or Aristotelianism, Stoicism and Epicureanism dominated Greek philosophy during the Hellenistic period. In addition, all three philosophies were embraced by the Romans, with Stoicism also later finding a home in Christian philosophy.

Stoicism. Stoicism was less concerned with formulating a systematic philosophy than with providing an approach to everyday living. Primarily ethical in impulse,

Figure 4.28 *Laocoön and His Sons*, perhaps a Roman marble copy after a Greek original by Hagesandros, Athanodoros, and Polydoros of Rhodes, variously dated between the second century B.C. and the first century A.D., height 7′ (2.10 m), Museo Pio Clementino, Musei Vaticani, Rome. In the Hellenistic Period, drama replaced the emotional restraint of the Classical Period. Laocoön and his sons, attacked by serpents, make obvious their torment through straining poses and agonized facial expressions.

it offered a basis for conduct in responding to life's misfortunes. According to the Stoic view, an intelligent spiritual force resembling reason, the *Logos*, pervades the universe. Human beings can achieve happiness only by bringing their wills into harmony with this pervasive universal reason. The individual must accept whatever fortune brings; all the individual can do is exercise control over her or his own will. Characteristic Stoic virtues are serenity, self-discipline, and courage in the face of suffering and affliction.

Epicureanism. Epicureanism is frequently thought of as a philosophy of self-indulgence and pleasure-seeking. Its primary practical impulse, however, is to escape fear and pain. The founder, EPICURUS [ep-ee-CURE-us] (341–271 B.C.), taught that fear, especially the fear of death and punishment after death, is responsible for human misery. As an antidote to what he considered religious and mythological superstition, Epicurus argued that the gods lack interest in the affairs of human beings, and that death utterly extinguishes pain. Thus, according to Epicurus, human beings have nothing to fear from it.

A materialist, Epicurus believed that the soul, like the body, was a physical substance, composed of tiny particles in motion. As such, for Epicurus the only path to knowledge was through physical sensation; consequently, the way to achieve happiness was to enhance physical pleasure and to limit physical pain. Epicurus argued that the way to achieve lasting pleasure was to avoid what he called "kinetic" pleasure in favor of "static" pleasure, which creates a state of equilibrium. Though kinetic pleasure is more intense than static pleasure, it is often accompanied by pain. For example, Epicurus recommended rejecting the pleasure of indulging in spicy or rich food for a simpler diet that prevented the pain of hunger while avoiding the dangers of indigestion. Similarly, Epicurus preferred the stability of friendship over the shifting pleasure and pain afforded by romantic passion.

Skepticism. The English word "skeptic" derives from the Greek *skeptikos*, which means "inquirer." Skepticism is not necessarily a negative perspective; rather it requires an attitude of questioning. Two early and important exponents of Skepticism were SEXTUS EMPIRICUS [em-PIR-i-cuss], who lived in the mid-second century B.C., and his intellectual ancestor, PYRRHO [PIE-roh] (ca. 360–270 B.C.). As with Stoicism and Epicureanism, Skepticism was less a philosophical system than a perspective on experience anchored in practical advice about how to live an unperturbed life. The aim of the Skeptic, like that of the Stoic and the Epicurean, was to establish and preserve a state of physical and mental composure, a condition of psychological stability and emotional equilibrium.

What distinguishes Skepticism from Stoicism and Epicureanism is its emphasis upon achieving this state of unperturbed equilibrium through suspending judgment about nearly everything. The reason for this suspension of judgment is that one cannot know anything with certainty, because for every assertion there can be a counterassertion, and all evidence is inconclusive in itself. The conflict between opposing assertions—for example, "the gods exist" and "the gods do not exist"—can only be settled by an appeal to an additional criterion, in this case, a belief. But since the criterion can be similarly called into question, there is nothing upon which finally to base knowledge. Thus, according to the Skeptics, peace of mind can only be achieved by abandoning the search for knowledge and accepting uncertainty.

Timeline 4.3   Hellenistic Greece.

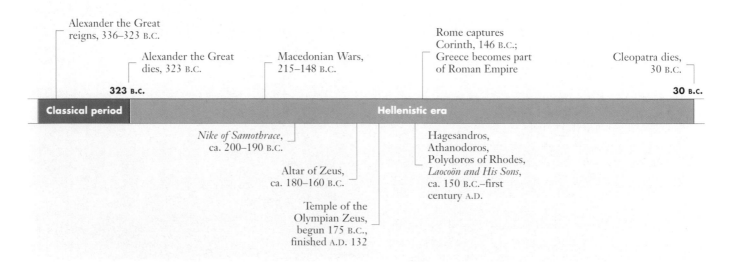

READINGS
→

✦ HERODOTUS
from the *History of the Persian Wars*

Herodotus (484–420 B.C.) was the first Greek historian. His History of the Persian Wars *describes the end of the Greek Archaic period. An outstanding storyteller, Herodotus inaugurates in Western writing a tradition of narrative history with an emphasis on action and character. In examining the ramifications of the Persian war Herodotus also initiated historical study, with war as its primary topic.*

The story he tells of the Greek battle with the Persians bears both religious and political implications. For the ancient Greeks the Persian defeat could be attributed to their excessive hubris *or pride. For others it conveys the social and political value of Greek unity in the face of a common enemy at a time when Greek city-states constantly warred against one another.*

The following passage describes the Persian advance into Greece under Xerxes in 480 B.C., and the small contingent of Greek soldiers who attempted to block the passage of the Persian army at the narrow pass at Thermopylae. Herodotus's skill as a writer is evident in both his vivid use of detail and in his building of suspense as he describes the outcome of this famous episode in Greek history.

The Persian army was now close to the pass, and the Greeks, suddenly doubting their power to resist, held a conference to consider the advisability of retreat. It was proposed by the Peloponnesians generally that the army should fall back upon the Peloponnese and hold the Isthmus; but when the Phocians and Locrians expressed their indignation at this suggestion, Leonidas gave his voice for staying where they were and sending, at the same time, an appeal for reinforcements to the various states of the confederacy, as their numbers were inadequate to cope with the Persians.

During the conference Xerxes sent a man on horseback to ascertain the strength of the Greek force and to observe what the troops were doing. He had heard before he left Thessaly that a small force was concentrated here, led by the Lacedaemonians under Leonidas of the house of Heracles. The Persian rider approached the camp and took a thorough survey of all he could see—which was not, however, the whole Greek army; for the men on the further side of the wall which, after its reconstruction, was now guarded, were out of sight. He did, non the less, carefully observe the troops who were stationed on the outside of the wall. At that moment these happened to be the Spartans, and some of them were stripped for exercise, while others were combing their hair. The Persian spy watched them in astonishment; nevertheless he made sure of their numbers, and of everything else he needed to know, as accurately as he could, and then rode quietly off. No one attempted to catch him, or took the least notice of him;.

Back in his own camp he told Xerxes what he had seen. Xerxes was bewildered; the truth, namely that the Spartans were preparing themselves to kill and to be killed according to their strength, was beyond his comprehension, and what they were doing seemed to him merely absurd. Accordingly he sent for Demaratus, the son of Ariston, who had come with the army, and questioned him about the spy's report, in the hope of finding out what the unaccountable behaviour of the Spartans might mean. "Once before," Demaratus said, "when we began our march against Greece, you heard me speak of these men. I told you then how I saw this enterprise would turn out, and you laughed at me. I strive for nothing, my lord, more earnestly than to observe the truth in your presence; so hear me once more. These men have come to fight us for possession of the pass, and for that struggle they are preparing. It is the common practice of the Spartans to pay careful attention to their hair when they are about to risk their lives. But I assure you that if you can defeat these men and the rest of the Spartans who are still at home, there is no other people in the world who will dare to stand firm or lift a hand against you. You have now to deal with the finest kingdom in Greece, and with the bravest men."

Xerxes, unable to believe what Demaratus said, asked further how it was possible that so small a force could fight with his army. "My lord," Demaratus replied, "treat me as a liar, if what I have foretold does not take place." But still Xerxes was unconvinced.

For four days Xerxes waited, in constant expectation that the Greeks would make good their escape; then, on the fifth, when still they had made no move and their continued presence seemed mere impudent and reckless folly, he was seized with rage and sent forward the Medes and Cissians with orders to take them alive and bring them into his presence. The Medes charged, and in the struggle which ensued many fell; but others took their places, and in spite of terrible losses refused to be beaten off. They made it plain enough to anyone, and not least to the king himself, that he had in his army many men, indeed, but few soldiers. All day the battle continued; the Medes, after their rough handling, were at length withdrawn and their place was taken by Hydarnes and his picked Persian troops—the King's Immortals—who advanced to the attack in full confidence of bringing the business to a quick and easy end. But, once engaged, they were no more successful than the Medes had been; all went as before, the two armies fighting in a confined space, the Persians using shorter spears than the Greeks and having no advantage from their numbers.

On the Spartan side it was a memorable fight; they were men who understood war pitted against an inexperienced enemy, and amongst the feints they employed was to turn their backs in a body and pretend to be retreating in confusion, whereupon the enemy would come on with a great clatter and roar, supposing the battle won; but the Spartans, just as the Persians were on them, would wheel and face them and inflict in the new struggle innumerable casualties. The Spartans had their losses too, but not many. At last the Persians, finding that their assaults upon the pass, whether by divisions or by any other way they could think of, were all useless, broke off the engagement and withdrew. Xerxes was watching the battle from where he sat; and it is said that in the course of the attacks three times, in terror for his army, he leapt to his feet.

Next day the fighting began again, but with no better success for the Persians, who renewed their onslaught in the hope that the Greeks, being so few in number, might be badly enough disabled by wounds to prevent further resistance. But the Greeks never slackened; their troops were ordered in divisions corresponding to the states from which they came, and each division took its turn in the line except the Phocian, which had been posted to guard the track over the mountains. So when the Persians found that things were no better for them than on the previous day, they once more withdrew.

How to deal with the situation Xerxes had no idea; but while he was still wondering what his next move should be, a man from Malis got himself admitted to his presence. This was Ephialtes, the son of Eurydemus, and he had come, in hope of a rich reward, to tell the king about the track which led over the hills to Thermopylae—-and the information he gave was to prove the death of the Greeks who held the pass.

Later on, Ephialtes, in fear of the Spartans, fled to Thessaly, and during his exile there a price was put upon his head at an assembly of the Amphictyons at Pylae. Some time afterwards he returned to Anticyra, where he was killed by Athenades of Trachis. In point of fact, Athenades killed him not for his treachery but for another reason, which I will explain further on; but the Spartans honoured him none the less on that account. According to another story, which I do not at all believe, it was Onetes, the son of Phanagoras, a native of Carystus, and Corydallus of Anticyra who spoke to Xerxes and showed the Persians the way round by the mountain track; but one may judge which account is the true one, first by the fact that the Amphictyons, who must surely have known everything about it, set a price not upon Onetes and Corydallus but upon Ephialtes of Trachis, and, secondly, by the fact that there is no doubt that the accusation of treachery was the reason for Ephialtes' flight. Certainly Onetes, even though he was not a native of Malis, might have known about the track, if he had spent much time in the neighbourhood—but it was Ephialtes, and no one else, who showed the Persians the way, and I leave his name on record as the guilty one.

Xerxes found Ephialtes' offer most satisfactory. He was delighted with it, and promptly gave orders to Hydarnes to carry out the movement with the troops under his command. They left camp about the time the lamps are lit.

The track was originally discovered by the Malians of the neighbourhood; they afterwards used it to help the Thessalians, taking them over it to attack Phocis at the time when the Phocians were protected from invasion by the wall which they had built across the pass. That was a long time ago, and no good ever came of it since. The track begins at the Asopus, the stream which flows through the narrow gorge, and, running along the ridge of the mountain—which, like the track itself, is called Anopaea—ends at Alpenus, the first Locrian settlement as one comes from Malis, near the track known as Black-Buttocks' Stone and the seats of the Cercopes. Just here is the narrowest part of the pass.

This then, was the mountain track which the Persians took, after crossing the Asopus. They marched throughout the night, with the mountains of Oeta on their right hand and those of Trachis on their left. By early dawn they were at the summit of the ridge, near the spot where the Phocians, as I mentioned before, stood on guard with a thousand men, to watch the track and protect their country. The Phocians were ready enough to undertake this service,

and had, indeed, volunteered for it to Leonidas, knowing that the pass at Thermopylae was held as I have already described.

The ascent of the Persians had been concealed by the oak-woods which cover this part of the mountain range, and it was only when they reached the top that the Phocians became aware of their approach; for there was not a breath of wind, and the marching feet made a loud swishing and rustling in the fallen leaves. Leaping to their feet, the Phocians were in the act of arming themselves when the enemy was upon them. The Persians were surprised at the sight of troops preparing to resist; they had not expected any opposition—yet here was a body of men barring their way. Hydarnes asked Ephialtes who they were, for his first uncomfortable thought was that they might be Spartans; but on learning the truth he prepared to engage them. The Persian arrows flew thick and fast, and the Phocians, supposing themselves to be the main object of the attack, hurriedly withdrew to the highest point of the mountain, where they made ready to face destruction. The Persians, however, with Ephialtes and Hydarnes paid no further attention to them, but passed on along the descending track with all possible speed.

The Greeks at Thermopylae had their first warning of the death that was coming with the dawn from the seer Megistias, who read their doom in the victims of sacrifice; deserters, too, had begun to come in during the night with news of the Persian movement to take them in the rear, and, just as day was breaking, the look-out men had come running from the hills. At once a conference was held, and opinion was divided, some urging that they must on no account abandon their post, others taking the opposite view. The result was that the army split; some dispersed, the men returning to their various homes, and others made ready to stand by Leonidas.

There is another account which says that Leonidas himself dismissed a part of his force, to spare their lives, but thought it unbecoming for the Spartans under his command to desert the post which they had originally come to guard. I myself am inclined to think that he dismissed them when he realized that they had no heart for the fight and were unwilling to take their share of the danger; at the same time honour forbade that he himself should go. And indeed by remaining at his post he left a great name behind him, and Sparta did not lose her prosperity, as might otherwise have happened; for right at the outset of the war the Spartans had been told by the oracle, when they asked for advice, that either their city must be laid waste by the foreigner or one of their kings be killed. The prophecy was in hexameter verse and ran as follows:

Hear your fate, O dwellers in Sparta of the wide spaces:
Either your famed, great town must be sacked by Perseus' sons.
Or, if that be not, the whole land of Lacedaemon
Shall mourn the death of a king of the house of Heracles,
For not the strength of lions or of bulls shall hold him,
Strength against strength: for he has the power of Zeus,
And will not be checked till one of these two he has consumed.

I believe it was the thought of this oracle, combined with his wish to lay up for the Spartans a treasure of fame in which no other city should share, that made Leonidas dismiss those troops; I do not think that they deserted, or went off without orders, because of a difference of opinion. Moreover, I am strongly supported in this view by the case of Megistias, the seer from Acarnania who foretold the coming doom by his inspection of the sacrificial victims: this man—he was said to be descended from Melampus—was with the army, and quite plainly received orders from Leonidas to quit Thermopylae, to save him from sharing the army's fate. But he refused to go, sending away instead an only son of his, who was serving with the forces.

Thus it was that the confederate troops, by Leonidas' orders, abandoned their posts and left the pass, all except the Thespians and the Thebans who remained with the Spartans. The Thebans were detained by Leonidas as hostages very much against their will—unlike the loyal Thespians, who refused to desert Leonidas and his men, but stayed, and died with them. They were under the command of Demophilus the son of Diadromes.

In the morning Xerxes poured a libation to the rising sun, and then waited till about the time of the filling of the market-place, when he began to move forward. This was according to Ephialtes' instructions, for the way down from the ridge is much shorter and more direct than the long and circuitous ascent. As the Persian army advanced to the assault, the Greeks under Leonidas, knowing that the fight would be their last, pressed forward into the wider part of the pass much further than they had done before; in the previous days' fighting they had been holding the wall and making sorties from behind it into the narrow neck, but now they left the confined space and battle was joined on more open ground. Many of the invaders fell; behind them the company commanders plied their whips, driving the men remorselessly on. Many fell into the sea and were drowned, and still more were trampled to death by their friends. No one could count the number of the dead. The Greeks, who knew that the enemy were on their way round by the mountain track and that death was inevitable, fought with reckless desperation, exerting every ounce of strength that was in them against the invader. By this time most of their spears were broken, and they were killing Persians with their swords.

In the course of that fight Leonidas fell, having fought like a man indeed. Many distinguished Spartans were killed at his side—their names, like the names of all the three hundred, I have made myself acquainted with, because they deserve to be remembered. Amongst the Persian dead, too, were many men of high distinction—for instance, two brothers of Xerxes, Habrocomes and Hyperanthes, both of them sons of Darius by Artanes' daughter Phratagune.

There was a bitter struggle over the body of Leonidas; four times the Greeks drove the enemy off, and at last by their valour succeeded in dragging it away. So it went on, until the fresh troops with Ephialtes were close at hand; and then, when the Greeks knew that they had come, the character of the fighting changed. They withdrew again into the narrow neck of the pass, behind the walls, and took up a position in a single compact body—all except the Thebans—on the little hill at the entrance to the pass, where the stone lion in memory of Leonidas stands today. Here they resisted to the last, with their swords, if they had them, and,

if not, with their hands and teeth, until the Persians, coming on from the front over the ruins of the wall and closing in from behind, finally overwhelmed them.

Of all the Spartans and Thespians who fought so valiantly on that day, the most signal proof of courage was given by the Spartan Dieneces. It is said that before the battle he was told by a native of Trachis that, when the Persians shot their arrows, there were so many of them that they hid the sun. Dieneces, however, quite unmoved by the thought of the terrible strength of the Persian army, merely remarked: "This is pleasant news that the stranger from Trachis brings us: for if the Persians hide the sun, we shall have our battle in the shade." He is said to have left on record other sayings, too, of a similar kind, by which he will be remembered. After Dieneces the greatest distinction was won by the two Spartan brothers, Alpheus and Maron, the sons of Orsiphantus; and of the Thespians the man to gain the highest glory was a certain Dithyrambus, the son of Harmatides.

The dead were buried where they fell, and with them the men who had been killed before those dismissed by Leonidas left the pass. Over them is this inscription, in honour of the whole force:

Four thousand here from Pelops' land
Against three million once did stand.

The Spartans have a special epitaph; it runs:

Go tell the Spartans, you who read
We took their orders, and are dead.

For the seer Megistias there is the following:

I was Megistias once, who died
When the Mede passed Spercheius' tide.
I knew death near, yet would not save
Myself, but share the Spartans' grave.

← THUCYDIDES

from the *History of the Peloponnesian War*

With Herodotus, Thucydides (ca. 460–400 B.C.) is recognized as the greatest of ancient Greek historians. Exiled by Athens for failing as a military commander while defending a Macedonian town, Thucydides traveled widely and wrote his History of the Peloponnesian War, *during which Athens suffered defeat in 404 B.C. at the hands of the Peloponnesians. Like Herodotus, Thucydides makes war his central subject. Thucydides disagrees with Herodotus, however, in claiming that the Peloponnesian War rather than the Persian War was the greatest and most important conflict of all time. For him, the war signalled the breakdown of the city-state structure that had prevailed for centuries and which reached its culmination during the Classical period, which ended with Athens' defeat.*

In the following passage, Thucydides presents the famous funeral oration given by Pericles over the bodies of the Greek heroes who died defending Athens. He clearly admires Perikles' integrity and ideals. Yet the historian is aware of the suffering Periclean Athens created.

In the same winter the Athenians, in accordance with their traditional institution, held a public funeral of those who had been the first to die in the war. The practice is this. Two days before the funeral they set up a tent and lay out in it the bones of the deceased, for each man to bring what offerings he wishes to his own kin. On the day of the procession, cypress-wood coffins are carried on wagons, one for each tribe, with each man's bones in his own tribe's coffin. In addition there is one empty bier carried, laid out for the missing, that is, for those whose bodies could not be found and recovered. Every man who wishes joins the procession, whether citizen or foreigner, and the women of the families are present to lament at the grave. In this way the dead are placed in the public tomb, which is situated in the most beautiful suburb of the city. Those who die in war are always buried there, apart from those who fell at Marathon, whose virtue was judged outstanding and who were given a tomb on the spot.

When they have been covered with earth, appropriate words of praise are spoken over them by a man chosen by the state for the intelligence of his mind and his outstanding reputation, and after that the people depart. That is how the funeral is conducted: this institution was followed throughout the war when occasion arose. Over these first casualties, then, Perikles son of Xanthippus was chosen to make the speech. When the time arrived, he came forward from the grave on to a high platform which had been erected so that he should be as clearly audible as possible to the crowd; and he spoke these lines.

"The majority of those who have spoken here before have praised the man who included this speech in our institution, and have claimed that it is good that they should make a speech over those who are buried in consequence of war. However, I should have thought that when men have been good in action it is sufficient for our honors of them to be made evident in action, as you see we have done in providing for this public funeral, and that the virtues of many ought not to be put at risk by being entrusted to one man, who speak well or ill. It is hard to speak appropriately in circumstances where even the appearance of truth can only with difficulty be confirmed. The listener who knows what has happened and is favorably disposed can easily think that the account given falls short of his wishes and knowledge, while the man lacking in experience may through jealousy think some claims exaggerated if he hears of things beyond his own capacity. Praise spoken of others is bearable up t the point where each man believes himself capable of doing the things he hears of: anything which goes beyond that arouses envy and so disbelief. Nevertheless, since in the past this has been approved as a good practice, I too must comply with our institution, and try as far as I can to coincide with the wishes and opinions of each of you.

"I shall begin first of all with our ancestors. It is right, and on an occasion like this it is appropriate, that this honor should be paid to their memory, for the same race of men has always occupied this land, as one generation has succeeded another, and by their valor they have handed it on as a free land until the present day. They are worthy of praise; and particularly worthy are our own fathers, who by their efforts gained the great empire which we now possess, in addition to what they had received, and left this too to us of the present generation. We ourselves, who are still alive and have reached the settled stage of life, have enlarged most parts of this empire, and we have made our city's resources

most ample in all respects both for war and for peace. The deeds in war by which each acquisition was won, the enthusiastic responses of ourselves or our fathers to the attacks of the barbarians or our Greek enemies, I do not wish to recount at length to those who already know of them, so I shall pass them over. What I shall expound first, before I proceed to praise these men, is the way of life which has enabled us to pursue these objectives, and the form of government and the habits which made our great achievements possible. I think in the present circumstances it is not unfitting for these things to be mentioned, and it is advantageous for this whole assemblage of citizens and foreigners to hear of them.

"We have a constitution which does not seek to copy the laws of our neighbors: we are an example to others rather than imitators of them. The name given to this constitution is democracy, because it is based not on a few but on a larger number. For the settlement of private disputes all are on an equal footing in accordance with the laws, while in public life men gain preferment because of their deserts, when anybody has a good reputation for anything: what matters is not rotation but merit. As for poverty, if a man is able to confer some benefit on the city, he is not prevented by the obscurity of his position. With regard to public life, we live as free men; and, as for the suspicion of one another which can arise from daily habits, if our neighbor behaves with a view to his own pleasure, we do not react with anger or put on those expressions of disgust which, though not actually harmful, are nevertheless distressing. In our private dealings with one another we avoid offense, and in the public realm what particularly restrains us from wrongdoing is fear; we are obedient to the officials currently in office, and to the laws, especially those which have been enacted for the protection of people who are wronged, and those which have not been written down but which bring acknowledged disgrace on those who break them.

"Moreover, we have provided the greatest number of relaxations from toil for the spirit, by holding contests and sacrifices throughout the year, and by tasteful private provisions, whose daily delight drives away sorrow. Because of the size of our city, everything can be imported from all over the earth, with the result that we have no more special enjoyment of our native goods than of the goods of the rest of mankind.

"In military practices we differ from our enemy in this way. We maintain an open city, and do not from time to time stage expulsions of foreigners to prevent them from learning or seeing things, when the sight of what we have not troubled to conceal might benefit an enemy, since we trust not so much in our preparations and deceit as in our own inborn spirit for action. In education, they start right from their youth to pursue manliness by arduous training, while we live a relaxed life but nonetheless go to confront the dangers to which we are equal. Here is a sign of it. Even the Spartans do not invade our territory on their own, but with all their allies; and we attack our neighbors' territory, and for the most part have no difficulty in winning battles on their land against men defending their own property. No enemy has yet encountered our whole force together, because we simultaneously maintain our fleet and send out detachments of our men in many directions by land. If they come into conflict with a part of our forces, either they boast that they have repelled all of us when they have defeated only some, or if beaten they claim that it was all of us who defeated them. Yet if we are prepared to face danger, though we live relaxed lives rather than making a practice of toil, and rely on courageous habits rather than legal compulsion, we have the advantage of not suffering in advance for future pain, and when we come to meet it we are shown to be no less daring than those committed to perpetual endurance. In this respect as well as in others our city can be seen to be worthy of admiration.

"We are lovers of beauty without extravagance, and of wisdom without softness. We treat wealth as an opportunity for action rather than a matter for boastful words, and poverty as a thing which it is not shameful for anyone to admit to, but rather is shameful not to act to escape from. The same men accept responsibility both for their own affairs and for the state's, and although different men are active in different fields they are not lacking in understanding of the state's concerns: we alone regard the man who refuses to take part in these not as noninterfering but as useless.

"We have the ability to judge or plan rightly in our affairs, since we think it is not speech which is an obstacle to action but failure to expound policy in speech before action has to be taken. We are different also in that we particularly combine boldness with reasoning about the business we are to take in hand, whereas for other people it is ignorance that produces courage and reasoning produces hesitation. When people have the clearest understanding of what is fearful and what is pleasant, and on that basis do not flinch from danger, they would rightly be judged to have the best spirit.

"With regard to displays of goodness, we are the opposite of most people, since we acquire our friends not by receiving good from them but by doing good to them. If you do good, you are in a better position to keep the other party's favor, as something owed in gratitude by the recipient: if you owe a return, you are less alert, knowing that when you do good it will not be as a favor but as the payment of a debt. We alone are fearless in helping others, not calculating the advantage so much as confident in our freedom.

"To sum up, I maintain that our city as a whole is an education to Greece; and I reckon that each individual man among us can keep his person ready to profit from the greatest variety in life and the maximum of graceful adaptability. That this is not just a momentary verbal boast but actual truth is demonstrated by the very strength of our city, which we have built up as a result of these habits. Athens alone when brought to the test proves greater than its current reputation; Athens alone does not give an enemy attacker the right to be indignant at the kind of people at whose hands he suffers, or a subject the right to complain that his rulers are unworthy of their position. Our power does not lack witnesses, but we provide mighty proof of it, to earn the admiration both of our contemporaries and of posterity. We do not need the praise of a Homer, or of anyone whose poetry gives immediate pleasure but whose impression of the facts is undermined by the truth. We have compelled the whole of sea and land to make itself accessi-

ble to our daring, and have joined in setting up everywhere undying memorials both of our failures and of our successes. Such is our city. These men fought and died, nobly judging that it would be wrong to be deprived of it; and it is right that every single one of those who are left should be willing to struggle for it."

✦ SOPHOCLES
Oedipus the King

Oedipus the King *begins at the point when Thebes is undergoing a series of catastrophes, most important of which is a devastating plague. Prior to this series of events, Oedipus had saved Thebes from the Sphinx, a winged creature with the body of a lion and the head of a woman. In return for slaying the creature, Oedipus is given the kingship of Thebes and the hand of its recently widowed queen, Jocasta (Iocastê). Unknown to Oedipus, but known to the Athenian audience, was the fact that Jocasta was his mother and that her recently slain husband, Laius, had been killed by Oedipus himself. All this and more Oedipus soon discovers.*

Aristotle chose Oedipus the King *to illustrate the elements of tragedy in his* Poetics. *In that first work of Western literary criticism, Aristotle described the perfect tragedy as having a plot that focused on a single conflict centered in a character who possesses a "tragic flaw" that precipitates the tragic action.*

Oedipus the King *raises questions about fate and human responsibility, particularly the extent to which Oedipus is responsible for his own tragic destiny. Sophocles portrays his tragic protagonists heroically, Oedipus the greatest among them. They suffer the consequences of their actions nobly and with grandeur, serving as models not only of fatal attitudes but also of courage and determination.*

CHARACTERS

OEDIPUS
A PRIEST
CREON
TEIRESIAS
IOCASTÊ
MESSENGER
SHEPHERD OF LAÏOS
SECOND MESSENGER
CHORUS OF THEBAN ELDERS

Scene. Before the palace of Oedipus, King of Thebes. A central door and two lateral doors open onto a platform which runs the length of the façade. On the platform, right and left, are altars; and three steps lead down into the "orchestra," or chorus-ground. At the beginning of the action these steps are crowded by Suppliants who have brought branches and chaplets of olive leaves and who lie in various attitudes of despair. Oedipus enters.

PROLOGUE

OEDIPUS My children, generations of the living
In the line of Kadmos,° nursed at his ancient hearth:

° *Kadmos:* legendary founder of Thebes.

Why have you strewn yourselves before these altars
In supplication, with your boughs and garlands?
The breath of incense rises from the city   5
With a sound of prayer and lamentation.
                                        Children,
I would not have you speak through messengers,
And therefore I have come myself to hear you—
I, Oedipus, who bear the famous name.
(*To a Priest.*) You, there, since you are eldest in the
company,   10
Speak for them all, tell me what preys upon you,
Whether you come in dread, or crave some blessing:
Tell me, and never doubt that I will help you
In every way I can; I should be heartless
Were I not moved to find you suppliant here.   15
PRIEST   Great Oedipus, O powerful King of Thebes!
You see how all the ages of our people
Cling to your altar steps: here are boys
Who can barely stand alone, and here are priests
By weight of age, as I am a priest of God,   20
And young men chosen from those yet unmarried;
As for the others, all that multitude,
They wait with olive chaplets in the squares,
At the two shrines of Pallas,° and where Apollo°
Speaks in the glowing embers.
                               Your own eyes   25
Must tell you: Thebes is in her extremity
And cannot lift her head from the surge of death.
A rust consumes the buds and fruits of the earth;
The herds are sick; children die unborn,
And labor is vain. The god of plague and pyre   30
Raids like detestable lightning through the city,
And all the house of Kadmos is laid waste,
All emptied, and all darkened: Death alone
Battens upon the misery of Thebes.
You are not one of the immortal gods, we know;   35
Yet we have come to you to make our prayer
As to the man of all men best in adversity
And wisest in the ways of God. You saved us
From the Sphinx,° that flinty singer, and the tribute
We paid to her so long; yet you were never   40
Better informed than we, nor could we teach you:
It was some god breathed in you to set us free.

Therefore, O mighty King, we turn to you:
Find us our safety, find us a remedy,
Whether by counsel of the gods or the men.   45
A king of wisdom tested in the past
Can act in a time of troubles, and act well.
Noblest of men, restore
Life to your city! Think how all men call you
Liberator for your triumph long ago;   50
Ah, when your years of kingship are remembered,
Let them not say *We rose, but later fell*—
Keep the State from going down in the storm!
Once, years ago, with happy augury,

You brought us fortune; be the same again!   55
No man questions your power to rule the land:
But rule over men, not over a dead city!
Ships are only hulls, citadels are nothing,
When no life moves in the empty passageways.
OEDIPUS   Poor children! You may be sure I know   60
All that you longed for in your coming here.
I know that you are deathly sick; and yet,
Sick as you are, not one is as sick as I.
Each of you suffers in himself alone
His anguish, not another's; but my spirit   65
Groans for the city, for myself, for you.

I was not sleeping, you are not waking me.
No, I have been in tears for a long while
And in my restless thought walked many ways.
In all my search, I found one helpful course,   70
And that I have taken: I have sent Creon,
Son of Menoikeus, brother of the Queen,
To Delphi, Apollo's place of revelation,
To learn there, if he can,
What act or pledge of mine may save the city.   75
I have counted the days, and now, this very day,
I am troubled, for he has overstayed his time.
What is he doing? He has been gone too long.
Yet whenever he comes back, I should do ill
To scant whatever hint the god may give.   80
PRIEST   It is a timely promise. At this instant
They tell me Creon is here.
OEDIPUS   O Lord Apollo!
May his news be fair as his face is radiant!
PRIEST   It could not be otherwise: he is crowned with bay,
The chaplet is thick with berries.
OEDIPUS   We shall soon know;   85
He is near enough to hear us now.

Enter Creon.

                                    O Prince:
Brother: son of Menoikeus:
What answer do you bring us from the god?
CREON   It is favorable. I can tell you, great afflictions
Will turn out well, if they are taken well.   90
OEDIPUS   What was the oracle? These vague words
Leave me still hanging between hope and fear.
CREON   Is it your pleasure to hear me with all these
Gathered around us? I am prepared to speak,
But should we not go in?
OEDIPUS   Let them all hear it.   95
It is for them I suffer, more than myself.
CREON   Then I will tell you what I heard at Delphi.

In plain words
The god commands us to expel from the land of
   Thebes
An old defilement that it seems we shelter.   100
It is a deathly thing, beyond expiation.
We must not let it feed upon us longer.
OEDIPUS   What defilement? How shall we rid ourselves of
   it?
CREON   By exile or death, blood for blood. It was

---

²⁴*Pallas:* Athena, goddess of wisdom.
²⁴*Apollo:* god of poetry and prophecy.
¹⁹*The Sphinx:* a monster with a lion's body, birds' wings, and woman's face.

Murder that brought the plague-wind on the city. *105*

OEDIPUS   Murder of whom? Surely the god has named
            him?

CREON   My lord: long ago Laïos was our king,
            Before you came to govern us.

OEDIPUS   I know;
            I learned of him from others; I never saw him.

CREON   He was murdered; and Apollo commands us now
            To take revenge upon whoever killed him.   *111*

OEDIPUS   Upon whom? Where are they? Where shall we
            find a clue
            To solve that crime, after so many years?

CREON   Here in this land, he said.
                                If we make enquiry,
            We may touch things that otherwise escape us.   *115*

OEDIPUS   Tell me: Was Laïos murdered in his house,
            Or in the fields, or in some foreign country?

CREON   He said he planned to make a pilgrimage.
            He did not come home again.

OEDIPUS.   And was there no one,
            No witness, no companion, to tell what happened?

CREON   They were all killed but one, and he got
            away   *121*
            So frightened that he could remember one thing
            only.

OEDIPUS   What was that one thing? One may be the key
            To everything, if we resolve to use it.

CREON   He said that a band of highwaymen attacked
            them,   *125*
            Outnumbered them, and overwhelmed the King.

OEDIPUS   Strange, that a highwayman should be so
            daring—
            Unless some faction here bribed him to do it.

CREON   We thought of that. But after Laïos' death
            New troubles arose and we had no avenger.   *130*

OEDIPUS   What troubles could prevent your hunting
            down the killers?

CREON   The riddling Sphinx's song
            Made us deaf to all mysteries but her own.

OEDIPUS   Then once more I must bring what is dark to
            light.
            It is most fitting that Apollo shows,   *135*
            As you do, this compunction for the dead.
            You shall see how I stand by you, as I should,
            To avenge the city and the city's god,
            And not as though it were for some distant friend,
            But for my own sake, to be rid of evil.   *140*
            Whoever killed King Laïos might—who knows?—
            Decide at any moment to kill me as well.
            By avenging the murdered king I protect myself.
            Come, then, my children: leave the altar steps,
            Lift up your olive boughs!
                                One of you go   *145*
            And summon the people of Kadmos to gather here.
            I will do all that I can; you may tell them that.

(Exit a Page.)

            So, with the help of God,
            We shall be saved—or else indeed we are lost.

PRIEST   Let us rise, children. It was for this we came,   *150*

And now the King has promised it himself.
Phoibos° has sent us an oracle; may he descend
Himself to save us and drive out the plague.

*Exeunt Oedipus and Creon into the palace by the central door.
The Priest and the Suppliants disperse right and left. After a
short pause the Chorus enters the orchestra.*

PÁRODOS°

Strophe 1

CHORUS   What is God singing in his profound
            Delphi of gold and shadow?
            What oracle for Thebes, the sunwhipped city?
            Fear unjoints me, the roots of my heart tremble.
            Now I remember, O Healer, your power, and
            wonder;   *5*
            Will you send doom like a sudden cloud, or weave it
            Like nightfall of the past?
            Speak, speak to us, issue of holy sound:
            Dearest to our expectancy: be tender!

Antistrophe 1

            Let me pray to Athenê, the immortal daughter of
            Zeus,   *10*
            And to Artemis her sister
            Who keeps her famous throne in the market ring,
            And to Apollo, bowman at the far butts of heaven—

            O gods, descend! Like three streams leap against
            The fires of our grief, the fires of darkness;   *15*
            Be swift to bring us rest!

            As in the old time from the brilliant house
            Of air you stepped to save us, come again!

Strophe 2

            Now our afflictions have no end,
            Now all our stricken host lies down   *20*
            And no man fights off death with his mind;

            The noble plowland bears no grain,
            And groaning mothers cannot bear—

            See, how our lives like birds take wing.
            Like sparks that fly when a fire soars,   *25*
            To the shore of the god of evening.

Antistrophe 2

            The plague burns on, it is pitiless,
            Though pallid children laden with death
            Lie unwept in the stony ways,

---

¹⁵² *Phoibos:* Phoebus Apollo, the sun god.
° *Párodos:* sung as the chorus enters the stage area. Presumably
they sang the *strophe* while dancing from right to left and the
antistrophe as they reversed direction.

And old gray women by every path   *30*
Flock to the strand about the altars

There to strike their breasts and cry
Worship of Phoibos in wailing prayers:
Be kind, God's golden child!

Strophe 3

There are no swords in this attack by fire,   *35*
No shields, but we are ringed with cries.
Send the besieger plunging from our homes
Into the vast sea-room of the Atlantic
Or into the waves that foam eastward of Thrace—
For the day ravages what the night spares—   *40*
Destroy our enemy, lord of the thunder!
Let him be riven by lightning from heaven!

Antistrophe 3

Phoibos Apollo, stretch the sun's bowstring,
That golden cord, until it sing for us,
Flashing arrows in heaven!

                 Artemis,° Huntress,   *45*
Race with flaring lights upon our mountains!
O scarlet god, O golden-banded brow,
O Theban Bacchos° in a storm of Maenads,°

         Enter Oedipus, center.

Whirl upon Death, that all the Undying hate!
Come with blinding cressets, come in joy!   *50*

SCENE I

OEDIPUS Is this your prayer? It may be answered. Come,
    Listen to me, act as the crisis demands,
    And you shall have relief from all these evils.

       Until now I was a stranger to this tale,
    As I had been a stranger to the crime.   *5*
    Could I track down the murderer without a clue?
    Bur now, friends,
    As one who became a citizen after the murder,
    I make this proclamation to all Thebans:
    If any man knows by whose hand Laïos, son of
       Labdakos,   *10*
    Met his death, I direct that man to tell me
      everything,
    No matter what he fears for having so long withheld
      it.
    Let it stand as promised that no further trouble
    Will come to him, but he may leave the land in
      safety.

    Moreover: If anyone knows the murderer to be

°*Artemis:* goddess of hunting and chastity.
°*Bacchos … Maenads:* god of wine and revelry with his attendants.

    foreign,   *15*
Let him not keep silent: he shall have his reward
    from me.
However, if he does conceal it; if any man
Fearing for his friend or for himself disobeys this
    edict,
Hear what I propose to do:

I solemnly forbid the people of this country,   *20*
Where power and throne are mine, ever to receive
    that man
Or speak to him, no matter who he is, or let him
Join in sacrifice, lustration, or in prayer.
I decree that he be driven from every house,

Being, as he is, corruption itself to us: the Delphic *25*
Voice of Zeus has pronounced this revelation.
Thus I associate myself with the oracle
and take the side of the murdered king.

As for the criminal, I pray to God—
Whether it be a lurking thief, or one of a number—
I pray that that man's life be consumed in evil and
    wretchedness.   *31*
And as for me, this curse applies no less
If it should turn out that the culprit is my guest here,
Sharing my hearth.
            You have heard the penalty.
I lay it on you now to attend to this   *35*
For my sake, for Apollo's, for the sick
Sterile city that heaven has abandoned.
Suppose the oracle had given you no command:
Should this defilement go uncleansed for ever?
You should have found the murderer: your king,   *40*
A noble king, had been destroyed!
               Now I,
Having the power that he held before me,
Having his bed, begetting children there
Upon his wife, as he would have, had he lived—
Their son would have been my children's brother,   *45*
If Laïos had had luck in fatherhood!
(But surely ill luck rushed upon his reign)—
I say I take the son's part, just as though
I were his son, to press the fight for him
And see it won! I'll find the hand that brought   *50*
Death to Labdakos' and Polydoros' child,
Heir of Kadmos' and Agenor's line.
And as for those who fail me,
May the gods deny them the fruit of the earth,
Fruit of the womb, and may they rot utterly!   *55*
Let them be wretched as we are wretched, and
    worse!

For you, for loyal Thebans, and for all
Who find my actions right, I pray the favor
Of justice, and of all the immortal gods.

CHORAGOS Since I am under oath, my lord, I swear   *60*
    I did not do the murder, I cannot name
    The murderer. Might not the oracle
    That has ordained the search tell where to find him?

OEDIPUS An honest question. But no man in the world

Can make the gods do more than the gods will. 65
CHORAGOS There is one last expedient—
OEDIPUS   Tell me what it is.
    Though it seem slight, you must not hold it back.
CHORAGOS A lord clairvoyant to the lord Apollo,
    As we all know, is the skilled Teiresias.
    One might learn much about this from him,
        Oedipus. 70
OEDIPUS I am not wasting time:
    Creon spoke of this, and I have sent for him—
    Twice, in fact; it is strange that he is not here.
CHORAGOS The other matter—that old report—seems
        useless.
OEDIPUS Tell me. I am interested in all reports. 75
CHORAGOS The King was said to have been killed by
        highwaymen.
OEDIPUS I know. But we have no witnesses to that.
CHORAGOS If the killer can feel a particle of dread,
    Your curse will bring him out of hiding!
OEDIPUS   No.
    The man who dared that act will fear no curse. 80

Enter the blind seer Teiresias, led by a Page

CHORAGOS But there is one man who may detect the
        criminal.
    This is Teiresias, this is the holy prophet
    In whom, alone of all men, truth was born.
OEDIPUS Teiresias: seer: student of mysteries,
    Of all that's taught and all that no man tells, 85
    Secrets of Heaven and secrets of the earth:
    Blind though you are, you know the city lies
    Sick with plague; and from this plague, my lord,
    We find that you alone can guard or save us.

    Possibly you did not hear the messengers? 90
    Apollo, when we sent to him,
    Sent us back word that this great pestilence
    Would lift, but only if we established clearly
    The identity of those who murdered Laïos.
    They must be killed or exiled.
                        Can you use 95
    Birdflight or any art of divination
    To purify yourself, and Thebes, and me
    From this contagion? We are in your hands.
    There is no fairer duty
    Than that of helping others in distress. 100
TEIRESIAS How dreadful knowledge of the truth can be
    When there's no help in truth! I knew this well,
    But did not act on it: else I should not have come.
OEDIPUS What is troubling you? Why are your eyes so
        cold?
TEIRESIAS Let me go home. Bear your own fate, and I'll
    Bear mine. It is better so: trust what I say. 106
OEDIPUS What you say is ungracious and unhelpful
    To your native country. Do not refuse to speak.
TEIRESIAS When it comes to speech, your own is neither
        temperate
        Nor opportune. I wish to be more prudent. 110
OEDIPUS In God's name, we all beg you—
TEIRESIAS.   You are all ignorant.

No; I will never tell you what I know.
    Now it is my misery; then, it would be yours.
OEDIPUS What! You do know something, and will not tell
        us?
    You would betray us all and wreck the State? 115
TEIRESIAS I do not intend to torture myself, or you.
    Why persist in asking? You will not persuade me.
OEDIPUS What a wicked old man you are! You'd try a
        stone's
    Patience! Out with it! Have you no feeling at all?
TEIRESIAS You call me unfeeling. If you could only see
    The nature of your own feelings … 121
OEDIPUS   Why,
    Who would not feel as I do? Who could endure
    Your arrogance toward the city?
TEIRESIAS   What does it matter!
    Whether I speak or not, it is bound to come.
OEDIPUS Then, if "it" is bound to come, you are bound
        to tell me. 125
TEIRESIAS No, I will not go on. Rage as you please.
OEDIPUS Rage? Why not!
                        And I'll tell you what I think:
    You planned it, you had it done, you all but
    Killed him with your own hands: if you had eyes,
    I'd say the crime was yours, and yours alone. 130
TEIRESIAS So? I charge you, then,
    Abide by the proclamation you have made:
    From this day forth
    Never speak again to these men or to me;
    You yourself are the pollution of this country. 135
OEDIPUS You dare say that! Can you possibly think you
        have
    Some way of going free, after such insolence?
TEIRESIAS I have gone free. It is the truth sustains me.
OEDIPUS Who taught you shamelessness? It was not your
        craft.
TEIRESIAS You did. You made me speak. I did not want
        to. 140
OEDIPUS Speak what? Let me hear it again more clearly.
TEIRESIAS Was it not clear before? Are you tempting me?
OEDIPUS I did not understand it. Say it again.
TEIRESIAS I say that you are the murderer whom you
        seek.
OEDIPUS Now twice you have spat out infamy. You'll pay
        for it! 145
TEIRESIAS Would you care for more? do you wish to be
        really angry?
OEDIPUS Say what you will. Whatever you say is
        worthless.
TEIRESIAS I say you live in hideous shame with those
    Most dear to you. You cannot see the evil.
OEDIPUS It seems you can go on mouthing like this for
        ever. 150
TEIRESIAS I can, if there is power in truth.
OEDIPUS   There is:
    But not for you, not for you,
    You sightless, witless, senseless, mad old man!
TEIRESIAS You are the madman. There is no one here
    Who will not curse you soon, as you curse me. 155
OEDIPUS You child of endless night! You cannot hurt me
    Or any other man who sees the sun.

TEIRESIAS   True: it is not from me your fate will come.
         That lies within Apollo's competence,
         As it is his concern.
OEDIPUS   Tell me: 160
         Are you speaking for Creon, or for yourself?
TEIRESIAS   Creon is no threat. You weave your own doom.
OEDIPUS   Wealth, power, craft of statesmanship!
         Kingly position, everywhere admired!
         What savage envy is stored up against these,   165
         If Creon, whom I trusted, Creon my friend,
         For this great office which the city once
         Put in my hands unsought—if for this power
         Creon desires in secret to destroy me!

         He has brought this decrepit fortune-teller, this   170
         Collector of dirty pennies, this prophet fraud—
         Why, he is no more clairvoyant than I am!
                                          Tell us:
         Has your mystic mummery ever approached the
              truth?
         When that hellcat the Sphinx was performing here,
         What help were you to these people?   175
         Her magic was not for the first man who came
              along:
         It demanded a real exorcist. Your birds—
         What good were they? or the gods, for the matter of
              that?
         But I came by,
         Oedipus, the simple man, who knows nothing—   180
         I thought it out for myself, no birds helped me!
         And this is the man you think you can destroy,
         That you may be close to Creon when he's king!
         Well, you and your friend Creon, it seems to me,
         Will suffer most. If you were not an old man,   185
         You would have paid already for your plot.
CHORAGOS   We cannot see that his words or yours
         Have been spoken except in anger, Oedipus,
         And of anger we have no need. How can God's
              will
         Be accomplished best? That is what most concerns
              us.   190
TEIRESIAS   You are a king. But where argument's
              concerned
         I am your man, as much a king as you.
         I am not your servant, but Apollo's.
         I have no need of Creon to speak for me.

         Listen to me. You mock my blindness, do you?   195
         But I say that you, with both your eyes, are blind:
         You cannot see the wretchedness of your life,
         Nor in whose house you live, no, nor with whom.
         Who are your father and mother? Can you tell
              me?
         You do not even know the blind wrongs   200
         That you have done them, on earth and in the
              world below.
         But the double lash of your parents' curse will whip
              you
         Out of this land some day, with only night
         Upon your precious eyes.
         Your cries then—where will they not be heard?   205

What fastness of Kithairon will not echo them?
And that bridal-descant of yours—you'll know it
     then,
The song they sang when you came here to
     Thebes
And found your misguided berthing.
All this, and more, that you cannot guess at now,   210
Will bring you to yourself among your children.
Be angry, then. Curse Creon. Curse my words.
I tell you, no man that walks upon the earth
Shall be rooted out more horribly than you.
OEDIPUS   Am I to bear this from him?—Damnation   215
         Take you! Out of this place! Out of my sight!
TEIRESIAS   I would not have come at all if you had not
              asked me.
OEDIPUS   Could I have told that you'd talk nonsense, that
         You'd come here to make a fool of yourself, and of
              me?
TEIRESIAS   A fool? Your parents thought me sane enough.
OEDIPUS   My parents again!—Wait: who were my
              parents?   221
TEIRESIAS   This day will give you a father, and break your
              heart.
OEDIPUS   Your infantile riddles! Your damned
              abracadabra!
TEIRESIAS   You were a great man once at solving riddles.
OEDIPUS   Mock me with that if you like; you will find it
              true.   225
TEIRESIAS   It was true enough. It brought about your
              ruin.
OEDIPUS   But if it saved this town?
TEIRESIAS   (to the Page). Boy, give me your hand.
OEDIPUS   Yes, boy; lead him away.
                              —While you are here
         We can do nothing. Go; leave us in peace.
TEIRESIAS   I will go when I have said what I have to
              say.   230
         How can you hurt me? And I tell you again:
         The man you have been looking for all this time,
         The damned man, the murderer of Laïos,
         That man is in Thebes. To your mind he is
              foreignborn,
         But it will soon be shown that he is a Theban,   235
         A revelation that will fail to please.
                                      A blind man,
         Who has his eyes now; a penniless man, who is rich
              now;
         And he will go tapping the strange earth with his
              staff;
         To the children with whom he lives now he will be
         Brother and father—the very same; to her   240
         Who bore him, son and husband—the very same
         Who came to his father's bed, wet with his father's
              blood.

         Enough. Go think that over.
         If later you find error in what I have said,
         You may say that I have no skill in prophecy.   245

         *Exit Teiresias, led by his Page, Oedipus goes into
                        the palace.*

ODE I°

Strophe 1

CHORUS   The Delphic stone of prophecies
    Remembers ancient regicide
    And a still bloody hand.
    That killer's hour of flight has come.
    He must be stronger than riderless   5
    Coursers of untiring wind,
    For the son of Zeus° armed with his father's thunder
    Leaps in lightning after him;
    And the Furies° follow him, the sad Furies.

Antistrophe 1

    Holy Parnossos' peak of snow   10
    Flashes and blinds that secret man,
    That all shall hunt him down:
    Though he may roam the forest shade
    Like a bull gone wild from pasture
    To rage through glooms of stone.   15
    Doom comes down on him; flight will not avail him;
    For the world's heart calls him desolate,
    And the immortal Furies follow, for ever follow.

Strophe 2

    But now a wilder thing is heard
    From the old man skilled at hearing Fate in the
      wingbeat of a bird.   20
    Bewildered as a blown bird, my soul hovers and
      cannot find
    Foothold in this debate, or any reason or rest of
      mind.
    But no man ever brought—none can bring
    Proof of strife between Thebes' royal house,
    Labdakos' line,° and the son of Polybos;°   25
    And never until now has any man brought word
    Of Laïos' dark death staining Oedipus the King.

Antistrophe 2

    Divine Zeus and Apollo hold
    Perfect intelligence alone of all tales ever told;
    And well though this diviner works, he works in his
      own night;   30
    No man can judge that rough unknown or trust in
      second sight,
    For wisdom changes hands among the wise.
    Shall I believe my great lord criminal
    At a raging word that a blind old man let fall?
    I saw him, when the carrion woman faced him of
      old,   35
    Prove his heroic mind! These evil words are lies.

° *Ode:* a poetic song sung by the chorus.
⁷ *son of Zeus:* Apollo.
⁹ *the Furies:* three women spirits who punished evildoers.
²⁵ *Labdakos' line:* his descendants.
²⁵ *Polybos:* King of Corinth who adopted Oedipus as an infant.

SCENE II

CREON   Men of Thebes:
    I am told that heavy accusations
    Have been brought against me by King Oedipus.
    I am not the kind of man to bear this tamely.

    If in these present difficulties   5
    He holds me accountable for any harm to him
    Through anything I have said or done—why, then,
    I do not value life in this dishonor.
    It is not as though this rumor touched upon
    Some private indiscretion. The matter is grave.   10
    The fact is that I am being called disloyal
    To the State, to my fellow citizens, to my friends.
CHORAGOS   He may have spoken in anger, not from his
    mind.
CREON   But did you not hear him say I was the one
    Who seduced the old prophet into lying?   15
CHORAGOS   The thing was said; I do not know how
    seriously.
CREON   But you were watching him! Were his eyes
    steady?
    Did he look like a man in his right mind?
CHORAGOS   I do not know.
    I cannot judge the behavior of great men.
    But here is the King himself.

Enter Oedipus

OEDIPUS   So you dared come back. 20
    Why? How brazen of you to come to my house,
    You murderer!
               Do you think I do not know
    That you plotted to kill me, plotted to steal my
      throne?
    Tell me, in God's name: am I coward, a fool,
    That you should dream you could accomplish this? 25
    A fool who could not see your slippery game?
    A coward, not to fight back when I saw it?
    You are the fool, Creon, are you not? hoping
    Without support or friends to get a throne?
    Thrones may be won or bought: you could do
      neither.   30
CREON   Now listen to me. You have talked; let me talk,
    too.
    You cannot judge unless you know the facts.
OEDIPUS   You speak well: there is one fact; but I find it
    hard
    To learn from the deadliest enemy I have.
CREON   That above all I must dispute with you.   35
OEDIPUS   That above all I will not hear you deny.
CREON   If you think there is anything good in being
    stubborn
    Against all reason, then I say you are wrong.
OEDIPUS   If you think a man can sin against his own
    kind
    And not be punished for it, I say you are mad.   40
CREON   I agree. But tell me: what have I done to you?
OEDIPUS   You advised me to send for that wizard, did you
    not?

CREON   I did. I should do it again.

OEDIPUS   Very well. Now tell me:
    How long has it been since Laïos—

CREON   What of Laïos?

OEDIPUS   Since he vanished in that onset by the road?   *45*

CREON   It was long ago, a long time.

OEDIPUS   And this prophet,
    Was he practicing here then?

CREON   He was; and with honor,
        as now.

OEDIPUS   Did he speak of me at that time?

CREON   He never did;
    At least, not when I was present.

OEDIPUS   But … the enquiry?
    I suppose you held one?

CREON   We did, but we learned
        nothing.   *50*

OEDIPUS   Why did the prophet not speak against me
        then?

CREON   I do not know; and I am the kind of man
    Who holds his tongue when he has no facts to go
        on.

OEDIPUS   There's one fact that you know, and you could
        tell it.

CREON   What fact is that? If I know it, you shall have it.   *55*

OEDIPUS   If he were not involved with you, he could not
        say
    That it was I who murdered Laïos.

CREON   If he says that, you are the one that knows it!—
    But now it is my turn to question you.

OEDIPUS   Put your questions. I am no murderer.   *60*

CREON   First, then: You married my sister?

OEDIPUS   I married your sister.

CREON   And you rule the kingdom equally with her?

OEDIPUS   Everything that she wants she has from me.

CREON   And I am the third, equal to both of you?

OEDIPUS   That is why I call you a bad friend.   *65*

CREON   No. Reason it out, as I have done.
        Think of this first. Would any sane man prefer
        Power, with all a king's anxieties,
        To that same power and the grace of sleep?
        Certainly not I.   *70*
        I have never longed for the king's power—only his
            rights.
        Would any wise man differ from me in this?
        As matters stand, I have my way in everything
        With your consent, and no responsibilities.
        If I were king, I should be a slave to policy.   *75*
        How could I desire a scepter more
        Than what is now mine—untroubled influence?
        No, I have not gone mad; I need no honors,
        Except those with the perquisites I have now.
        I am welcome everywhere; every man salutes me,   *80*
        And those who want your favor seek my ear,
        Since I know how to manage what they ask.
        Should I exchange this ease for that anxiety?
        Besides, no sober mind is treasonable.
        I hate anarchy   *85*
        And never would deal with any man who likes it.

        Test what I have said. Go to the priestess

At Delphi, ask if I quoted her correctly.
        And as for this other thing: if I am found
        Guilty of treason with Teiresias,   *90*
        Then sentence me to death! You have my word
        It is a sentence I should cast my vote for—
        But not without evidence!
                         You do wrong
        When you take good men for bad, bad men for
            good.
        A true friend thrown aside—why, life itself   *95*
        Is not more precious!
            In time you will know this well:
        For time, and time alone, will show the just man,
        Though scoundrels are discovered in a day.

CHORAGOS   This is well said, and a prudent man would
        ponder it.
    Judgments too quickly formed are dangerous.   *100*

OEDIPUS   But is he not quick in his duplicity?
    And shall I not be quick to parry him?
    Would you have me stand still, hold my peace, and
        let
    This man win everything, through my inaction?

CREON   And you want—what is it, then? To banish
        me?   *105*

OEDIPUS   No, not exile. It is your death I want,
    So that all the world may see what treason means.

CREON   You will persist, then? You will not believe me?

OEDIPUS   How can I believe you?

CREON   Then you are a fool.

OEDIPUS   To save myself?

CREON   In justice, think of me.   *110*

OEDIPUS   You are evil incarnate.

CREON   But suppose that you are wrong?

OEDIPUS   Still I must rule.

CREON   But not if you rule badly.

OEDIPUS   O city, city!

CREON   It is my city, too!

CHORAGOS   Now, my lords, be still. I see the Queen,
    Iocastê, coming from her palace chambers;   *115*
    And it is time she came, for the sake of you both.
    This dreadful quarrel can be resolved through her.

Enter Iocastê

IOCASTÊ   Poor foolish men, what wicked din is this?
    With Thebes sick to death, is it not shameful
    That you should rake some private quarrel up?   *120*

(To Oedipus)

Come into the house.
                         —And you, Creon, go now:
    Let us have no more of this tumult over nothing.

CREON   Nothing? No, sister: what your husband plans for
        me
    Is one of two great evils: exile or death.

OEDIPUS   He is right.
                         Why, woman, I have caught him
        squarely   *125*
    Plotting against my life.

CREON   No! Let me die

Accurst if ever I have wished you harm!
IOCASTÊ Ah, believe it, Oedipus!
    In the name of the gods, respect this oath of his
    For my sake, for the sake of these people here!   *130*

Strophe 1

CHORAGOS Open your mind to her, my lord. Be ruled by
        her, I beg you!
OEDIPUS What would you have me do?
CHORAGOS Respect Creon's word. He has never spoken
        like a fool,
    And now he has sworn an oath.
OEDIPUS You know what you ask?
CHORAGOS   I do.
OEDIPUS   Speak on, then.
CHORAGOS A friend so sworn should not be baited so, *135*
    In blind malice, and without final proof.
OEDIPUS You are aware, I hope, that what you say
    Means death for me, or exile at the least.

Strophe 2

CHORAGOS No, I swear by Helios, first in Heaven!
    May I die friendless and accurst,   *140*
        The worst of deaths, if ever I meant that!
            It is the withering fields
                That hurt my sick heart:
            Must we bear all these ills,
                And now your bad blood as well?   *145*
OEDIPUS Then let him go. And let me die, if I must,
    Or be driven by him in shame from the land of
        Thebes.
    It is your unhappiness, and not his talk,
    That touches me.
                As for him—
    Wherever he is, I will hate him as long as I live. *150*
CREON Ugly in yielding, as you were ugly in rage!
    Natures like yours chiefly torment themselves.
OEDIPUS Can you not go? Can you not leave me?
CREON   I can.
    You do not know me; but the city knows me,
    And in its eyes I am just, if not in yours.   *155*

                (Exit Creon)

Antistrophe 1

CHORAGOS Lady Iocastê, did you not ask the King to go
        to his chambers?
IOCASTÊ First tell me what has happened.
CHORAGOS There was suspicion without evidence; yet it
        rankled
    As even false charges will.
IOCASTÊ   On both sides?
CHORAGOS   On both.
IOCASTÊ But what was said?
CHORAGOS Oh let it rest, let it be done with!   *160*
    Have we not suffered enough?
OEDIPUS You see to what your decency has brought you:
    You have made difficulties where my heart saw none.

Antistrophe 2

CHORAGOS Oedipus, it is not once only I have told you—
    You must know I should count myself unwise   *165*
    To the point of madness, should I now forsake you—
    You, under whose hand,
        In the storm of another time,
        Our dear land sailed out free.
            But now stand fast at the helm!   *170*
IOCASTÊ In God's name, Oedipus, inform your wife as
        well:
    Why are you so set in this hard anger?
OEDIPUS I will tell you, for none of these men deserves
    My confidence as you do. It is Creon's work,
    His treachery, his plotting against me.   *175*
IOCASTÊ Go on, if you can make this clear to me.
OEDIPUS He charges me with the murder of Laïos.
IOCASTÊ Has he some knowledge? Or does he speak from
        hearsay?
OEDIPUS He would not commit himself to such a charge,
    But he has brought in that damnable soothsayer *180*
    To tell his story.
IOCASTÊ   Set your mind at rest.
    If it is a question of soothsayers, I tell you
    That you will find no man whose craft gives
        knowledge
    Of the unknowable.
                Here is my proof:
    An oracle was reported to Laïos once   *185*
    (I will not say from Phoibos himself, but from
    His appointed ministers, at any rate)
    That his doom would be death at the hands of his
        own son—
    His son, born of his flesh and of mine!

    Now, you remember the story: Laïos was killed *190*
    By marauding strangers where three highways meet;
    But his child had not been three days in this world
    Before the King had pierced the baby's ankles
    And left him to die on a lonely mountainside.

    Thus, Apollo never caused that child   *195*
    To kill his father, and it was not Laïos' fate
    To die at the hands of his son, as he had feared.
    This is what prophets and prophecies are worth!
    Have no dread of them.
                It is God himself
    Who can show us what he wills, in his own way. *200*
OEDIPUS How strange a shadowy memory crossed my
        mind,
    Just now while you were speaking; it chilled my
        heart.
IOCASTÊ What do you mean? What memory do you
        speak of?
OEDIPUS If I understand you, Laïos was killed
    At a place where three roads meet.
IOCASTÊ   So it was said; *205*
    We have no later story.
OEDIPUS   Where did it happen?
IOCASTÊ Phokis, it is called: at a place where the Theban
        Way

Divides into the roads towards Delphi and Daulia.
OEDIPUS   When?
IOCASTÊ   We had the news not long before you came
          And proved the right to your succession here.   *210*
OEDIPUS   Ah, what net has God been weaving for me?
IOCASTÊ   Oedipus! Why does this trouble you?
OEDIPUS   Do not ask me yet.
          First, tell me how Laïos looked, and tell me
          How old he was.
IOCASTÊ   He was tall, his hair just touched
          With white; his form was not unlike your own.   *215*
OEDIPUS   I think that I myself may be accurst
          By my own ignorant edict.
IOCASTÊ   You speak strangely.
          It makes me tremble to look at you, my King.
OEDIPUS   I am not sure that the blind man cannot see.
          But I should know better if you were to tell me— *220*
IOCASTÊ   Anything—though I dread to hear you ask it.
OEDIPUS   Was the King lightly escorted, or did he ride
          With a large company, as a ruler should?
IOCASTÊ   There were five men with him in all: one was a
              herald;
          And a single chariot, which he was driving.   *225*
OEDIPUS   Alas, that makes it plain enough!
                                          But who—
Who told you how it happened?
IOCASTÊ   A household servant,
          The only one to escape.
OEDIPUS   And is he still
          A servant of ours?
IOCASTÊ   No; for when he came back at last
          And found you enthroned in the place of the dead
              king,   *230*
          He came to me, touched my hand with his, and
              begged
          That I would send him away to the frontier district
          Where only the shepherds go—
          As far away from the city as I could send him.
          I granted his prayer; for although the man was a
              slave,   *235*
          He had earned more than his favor at my hands.
OEDIPUS   Can he be called back quickly?
IOCASTÊ   Easily.
          But why?
OEDIPUS   I have taken too much upon myself
          Without enquiry; therefore I wish to consult him.
IOCASTÊ   Then he shall come.
                              But am I not one also   *240*
          To whom you might confide these fears of yours!
OEDIPUS   That is your right; it will not be denied you,
          Now least of all; for I have reached a pitch
          Of wild foreboding. Is there anyone
          To whom I should sooner speak?   *245*
          Polybos of Corinth is my father.
          My mother is a Dorian: Meropê.
          I grew up chief among the men of Corinth
          Until a strange thing happened—
          Not worth my passion, it may be, but strange.   *250*

          At a feast, a drunken man maundering in his cups
          Cries out that I am not my father's son!

I contained myself that night, though I felt anger
And a sinking heart. The next day I visited
My father and mother, and questioned them. They
    stormed,   *255*
Calling it all the slanderous rant of a fool;
And this relieved me. Yet the suspicion
Remained always aching in my mind;
I knew there was talk; I could not rest;
And finally, saying nothing to my parents,   *260*
I went to the shrine at Delphi.
The god dismissed my question without reply;
He spoke of other things.
                          Some were clear,
Full of wretchedness, dreadful, unbearable:
As, that I should lie with my own mother, breed   *265*
Children from whom all men would turn their eyes;
And that I should be my father's murderer.
I heard all this, and fled. And from that day
Corinth to me was only in the stars
Descending in that quarter of the sky,   *270*
As I wandered farther and farther on my way
To a land where I should never see the evil
Sung by the oracle. And I came to this country
Where, so you say, King Laïos was killed.
I will tell you all that happened there, my lady.   *275*
There were three highways
Coming together at a place I passed;
And there a herald came towards me, and a chariot
Drawn by horses, with a man such as you describe
Seated in it. The groom leading the horses   *280*
Forced me off the road at his lord's command;
But as this charioteer lurched over towards me
I struck him in my rage. The old man saw me
And brought his double goad down upon my head
As I came abreast.
                    He was paid back, and more!   *285*
Swinging my club in this right hand I knocked him
Out of his car, and he rolled on the ground.
    I killed him.

I killed them all.
Now if that stranger and Laïos were—kin,
Where is a man more miserable than I?   *290*
More hated by the gods? Citizen and alien alike
Must never shelter me or speak to me—
I must be shunned by all.
                          And I myself
Pronounced this malediction upon myself!

Think of it: I have touched you with these hands, *295*
These hands that killed your husband. What
    defilement!

Am I all evil, then? It must be so,
Since I must flee from Thebes, yet never again
See my own countrymen, my own country,
For fear of joining my mother in marriage   *300*
And killing Polybos, my father.
                                Ah,
If I was created so, born to this fate,
Who could deny the savagery of God?

O holy majesty of heavenly powers!
May I never see that day! Never!   *305*
Rather let me vanish from the race of men
Than know the abomination destined me!
CHORAGOS We too, my lord, have felt dismay at this.
    But there is hope: you have yet to hear the shepherd.
OEDIPUS Indeed, I fear no other hope is left me.   *310*
IOCASTÊ What do you hope from him when he comes?
OEDIPUS   This much:
    If his account of the murder tallies with yours,
    Then I am cleared.
IOCASTÊ   What was it that I said
    Of such importance?
OEDIPUS   Why, "marauders," you said,
    Killed the King, according to this man's story.   *315*
    If he maintains that still, if there were several,
    Clearly the guilt is not mine: I was alone.
    But if he says one man, singlehanded, did it,
    Then the evidence all points to me.
IOCASTÊ You may be sure that he said there were
        several;   *320*
    And can he call back that story now? He cannot.
    The whole city heard it as plainly as I.
    But suppose he alters some detail of it:
    He cannot ever show that Laïos' death
    Fulfilled the oracle: for Apollo said   *325*
    My child was doomed to kill him; and my child—
    Poor baby!—it was my child that died first.

    No. From now on, where oracles are concerned,
    I would not waste a second thought on any.
OEDIPUS You may be right.
                        But come: let someone go   *330*
    For the shepherd at once. This matter must be
        settled.
IOCASTÊ I will send for him.
    I would not wish to cross you in anything,
    And surely not in this.—Let us go in.

Exeunt into the palace.

ODE II

Strophe 1

CHORUS Let me be reverent in the ways of right,
    Lowly the paths I journey on;
    Let all my words and actions keep
    The laws of the pure universe
    From highest Heaven handed down.   *5*
    For Heaven is their bright nurse,
    Those generations of the realms of light;
    Ah, never of mortal kind were they begot,
    Nor are they slaves of memory, lost in sleep:
    Their Father is greater than Time, and ages not.   *10*

Antistrophe 1

    The tyrant is a child of Pride
    Who drinks from his great sickening cup
    Recklessness and vanity,
    Until from his high crest headlong
    He plummets to the dust of hope.   *15*
    That strong man is not strong.
    But let no fair ambition be denied;
    May God protect the wrestler for the State
    In government, in comely policy,
    Who will fear God, and on His ordinance wait.   *20*

Strophe 2

    Haughtiness and the high hand of disdain
    Tempt and outrage God's holy law;
    And any mortal who dares hold
    No immortal Power in awe
    Will be caught up in a net of pain: *25*
    The price for which his levity is sold.
    Let each man take due earnings, then,
    And keep his hands from holy things,
    And from blasphemy stand apart—
    Else the crackling blast of heaven   *30*
    Blows on his head, and on his desperate heart;
    Though fools will honor impious men,
    In their cities no tragic poet sings.

Antistrophe 2

    Shall we lose faith in Delphi's obscurities,
    We who have heard the world's core   *35*
    Discredited, and the sacred wood
    Of Zeus at Elis praised no more?
    The deeds and the strange prophecies
    Must make a pattern yet to be understood.
    Zeus, if indeed you are lord of all,   *40*
    Throned in light over night and day,
    Mirror this in your endless mind:
    Our masters call the oracle
    Words on the wind, and the Delphic vision blind!
    Their hearts no longer know Apollo,   *45*
    And reverence for the gods has died away.

SCENE III

Enter Iocastê

IOCASTÊ Princes of Thebes, it has occurred to me
    To visit the altars of the gods, bearing
    These branches as a suppliant, and this incense.
    Our King is not himself: his noble soul
    Is overwrought with fantasies of dread,   *5*
    Else he would consider
    The new prophecies in the light of the old.
    He will listen to any voice that speaks disaster,
    And my advice goes for nothing.

She approaches the altar, right.

                        To you, then, Apollo,
    Lycean lord, since you are nearest, I turn in prayer.   *10*
    Receive these offerings, and grant us deliverance
    From defilement. Our hearts are heavy with fear
    When we see our leader distracted, as helpless sailors

Are terrified by the confusion of their helmsman.

Enter Messenger

MESSENGER Friends, no doubt you can direct me: 15
    Where shall I find the house of Oedipus,
    Or, better still, where is the King himself?
CHORAGOS It is this very place, stranger; he is inside.
    This is his wife and mother of his children.
MESSENGER I wish her happiness in a happy house,   20
    Blest in all the fulfillment of her marriage.
IOCASTÊ I wish as much for you: your courtesy
    Deserves a like good fortune. But now, tell me:
    Why have you come? What have you to say to us?
MESSENGER Good news, my lady, for your house and
    your husband.   25
IOCASTÊ What news? Who sent you here?
MESSENGER   I am from Corinth.
    The news I bring ought to mean joy for you,
    Though it may be you will find some grief in it.
IOCASTÊ What is it? How can it touch us in both ways?
MESSENGER The people of Corinth, they say,   30
    Intend to call Oedipus to be their king.
IOCASTÊ But old Polybos—is he not reigning still?
MESSENGER No. Death holds him in his sepulchre.
IOCASTÊ What are you saying? Polybos is dead?
MESSENGER If I am not telling the truth, may I die
    myself.   35
IOCASTÊ *(to a Maidservant)*. Go in, go quickly; tell this to
    your master.

    O riddlers of God's will, where are you now!
    This was the man whom Oedipus, long ago,
    Feared so, fled so, in dread of destroying him—
    But it was another fate by which he died.   40

Enter Oedipus, center

OEDIPUS Dearest Iocastê, why have you sent for me?
IOCASTÊ Listen to what this man says, and then tell me
    What has become of the solemn prophecies.
OEDIPUS Who is this man? What is his news for me?
IOCASTÊ He has come from Corinth to announce your
    father's death!   45
OEDIPUS Is it true, stranger? Tell me in your own words.
MESSENGER I cannot say it more clearly: the King is
    dead.
OEDIPUS Was it by treason? Or by an attack of illness?
MESSENGER. A little thing brings old men to their rest.
OEDIPUS It was sickness, then?
MESSENGER   Yes, and his many years. 50
OEDIPUS Ah!
    Why should a man respect the Pythian hearth,° or
    Give heed to the birds that jangle above his head?
    They prophesied that I should kill Polybos,
    Kill my own father; but he is dead and buried,   55

_____
°52 *Pythian hearth:* Delphi, also called Pytho because a large dragon, the Python, had guarded the chasm at Delphi until Apollo killed it and established his oracle on the site.

And I am here—I never touched him, never,
Unless he died in grief for my departure,
And thus, in a sense, through me. No. Polybos
Has packed the oracles off with him underground.
They are empty words.
IOCASTÊ   Had I not told you so?   60
OEDIPUS You had; it was my faint heart that betrayed me.
IOCASTÊ From now on never think of those things again.
OEDIPUS And yet—must I not fear my mother's bed?
IOCASTÊ Why should anyone in this world be afraid,
    Since Fate rules us and nothing can be foreseen?   65
    A man should live only for the present day.
    Have no more fear of sleeping with your mother:
    How many men, in dreams, have lain with their
    mothers!
    No reasonable man is troubled by such things.
OEDIPUS That is true; only—   70
    If only my mother were not still alive!
    But she is alive. I cannot help my dread.
IOCASTÊ Yet this news of your father's death is wonderful.
OEDIPUS Wonderful. But I fear the living woman.
MESSENGER Tell me, who is this woman that you fear? 75
OEDIPUS It is Meropê, man; the wife of King Polybos.
MESSENGER Meropê? Why should you be afraid of her?
OEDIPUS An oracle of the gods, a dreadful saying.
MESSENGER Can you tell me about it or are you sworn to
    silence?
OEDIPUS I can tell you, and I will.   80
    Apollo said through his prophet that I was the man
    Who should marry his own mother, shed his father's
    blood
    With his own hands. And so, for all these years
    I have kept clear of Corinth, and no harm has
    come—
    Though it would have been sweet to see my parents
    again.   85
MESSENGER And is this the fear that drove you out of
    Corinth?
OEDIPUS Would you have me kill my father?
MESSENGER   As for that
    You must be reassured by the news I gave you.
OEDIPUS If you could reassure me, I would reward you.
MESSENGER I had that in mind, I will confess: I
    thought   90
    I could count on you when you returned to Corinth.
OEDIPUS No: I will never go near my parents again.
MESSENGER Ah, son, you still do not know what you are
    doing—
OEDIPUS What do you mean? In the name of God tell
    me!
MESSENGER —If these are your reasons for not going
    home.   95
OEDIPUS I tell you, I fear the oracle may come true.
MESSENGER And guilt may come upon you through your
    parents?
OEDIPUS That is the dread that is always in my heart.
MESSENGER Can you not see that all your fears are
    groundless?
OEDIPUS How can you say that? They are my parents,
    surely?   100
MESSENGER Polybos was not your father.

OEDIPUS   Not my father?
MESSENGER   No more your father than the man speaking
          to you.
OEDIPUS   But you are nothing to me!
MESSENGER   Neither was he.
OEDIPUS   Then why did he call me son?
MESSENGER   I will tell you:
          Long ago he had you from my hands, as a gift.   105
OEDIPUS   Then how could he love me so, if I was not his?
MESSENGER   He had no children, and his heart turned to
          you.
OEDIPUS   What of you? Did you buy me? Did you find
          me by chance?
MESSENGER   I came upon you in the crooked pass of
          Kithairon.
OEDIPUS   And what were you doing there?
MESSENGER   Tending my flocks.110
OEDIPUS   A wandering shepherd?
MESSENGER   But your savior, son, that day.
OEDIPUS   From what did you save me?
MESSENGER   Your ankles should tell you that.
OEDIPUS   Ah, stranger, why do you speak of that
          childhood pain?
MESSENGER   I cut the bonds that tied your ankles
          together.
OEDIPUS   I have had the mark as long as I can
          remember.   115
MESSENGER   That was why you were given the name you
          bear.°
OEDIPUS   God! Was it my father or my mother who did
          it?
          Tell me!
MESSENGER   I do not know. The man who gave you to me
          Can tell you better than I.   120
OEDIPUS   It was not you that found me, but another?
MESSENGER   It was another shepherd gave you to me.
OEDIPUS   Who was he? Can you tell me who he was?
MESSENGER   I think he was said to be one of Laïos'
          people.
OEDIPUS   You mean the Laïos who was king here years
          ago?   125
MESSENGER   Yes; King Laïos; and the man was one of his
          herdsmen.
OEDIPUS   Is he still alive? Can I see him?
MESSENGER   These men here
          Know best about such things.
OEDIPUS   Does anyone here
          Know this shepherd that he is talking about?
          Have you seen him in the fields, or in the town?   130
          If you have, tell me. It is time things were made
          plain.
CHORAGOS   I think the man he means is that same
          shepherd
          You have already asked to see. Iocastê perhaps
          Could tell you something.
OEDIPUS   Do you know anything
          About him, Lady? Is he the man we have
          summoned?   135

---

116 *name you bear:* "Oedipus" means "swollen-foot."

Is that the man this shepherd means?
IOCASTÊ   Why think of him?
          Forget this herdsman. Forget it all.
          This talk is a waste of time.
OEDIPUS   How can you say that,
          When the clues to my true birth are in my hands?
IOCASTÊ   For God's love, let us have no more
          questioning!   140
          Is your life nothing to you?
          My own is pain enough for me to bear.
OEDIPUS   You need not worry. Suppose my mother a
          slave,
          And born of slaves: no baseness can touch you.
IOCASTÊ   Listen to me, I beg you: do not do this thing!145
OEDIPUS   I will not listen; the truth must be made known.
IOCASTÊ   Everything that I say is for your own good!
OEDIPUS   My own good
          Snaps my patience, then: I want none of it.
IOCASTÊ   You are fatally wrong! May you never learn who
          you are!
OEDIPUS   Go, one of you, and bring the shepherd here. 150
          Let us leave this woman to brag of her royal name.
IOCASTÊ   Ah, miserable!
          That is the only word I have for you now.
          That is the only word I can ever have.

Exit into the palace.

CHORAGOS   Why has she left us, Oedipus? Why has she
          gone   155
          In such a passion of sorrow? I fear this silence:
          Something dreadful may come of it.
OEDIPUS   Let it come!
          However base my birth, I must know about it.
          The Queen, like a woman, is perhaps ashamed
          To think of my low origin. But I   160
          Am a child of luck; I cannot be dishonored.
          Luck is my mother; the passing months, my
          brothers,
          Have seen me rich and poor.
                                If this is so,
          How could I wish that I were someone else?
          How could I not be glad to know my birth?   165

ODE III

Strophe

CHORUS   If ever the coming time were known
          To my heart's pondering,
          Kithairon, now by Heaven I see the torches
          At the festival of the next full moon,
          And see the dance, and hear the choir sing   5
          A grace to your gentle shade:
          Mountain where Oedipus was found,
          O mountain guard of a noble race!
          May the god who heals us lend his aid,
          And let that glory come to pass   10
          For our king's cradling-ground.

Antistrophe

Of the nymphs that flower beyond the years,
Who bore you, royal child,
To Pan of the hills or the timberline Apollo,
Cold in delight where the upland clears, *15*
Or Hermês for whom Kyllenê's heights° are piled?
Or flushed as evening cloud,
Great Dionysos, roamer of mountains,
He—was it he who found you there,
And caught you up in his own proud *20*
Arms from the sweet god-ravisher
Who laughed by the Muses' fountains?

SCENE IV

OEDIPUS   Sirs: though I do not know the man,
I think I see him coming, this shepherd we want:
He is old, like our friend here, and the men
Bringing him seem to be servants of my house.
But you can tell, if you have ever seen him. *5*

Enter Shepherd escorted by servants.

CHORAGOS   I know him, he was Laïos' man. You can trust
him.
OEDIPUS   Tell me first, you from Corinth: is this the
shepherd
We were discussing?
MESSENGER   This is the very man.
OEDIPUS   *(to* SHEPHERD*)*. Come here. No, look at me. You
must answer
Everything I ask.—You belonged to Laïos? *10*
SHEPHERD   Yes: born his slave, brought up in his house.
OEDIPUS   Tell me: what kind of work did you do for him?
SHEPHERD   I was a shepherd of his, most of my life.
OEDIPUS   Where mainly did you go for pasturage?
SHEPHERD   Sometimes Kithairon, sometimes the hills
near-by. *15*
OEDIPUS   Do you remember ever seeing this man out
there?
SHEPHERD   What would he be doing there? This man?
OEDIPUS   This man standing here. Have you ever seen
him before?
SHEPHERD   No. At least, not to my recollection.
MESSENGER   And that is not strange, my lord. But I'll
refresh *20*
His memory: he must remember when we two
Spent three whole seasons together, March to
September,
On Kithairon or thereabouts. He had two flocks;
I had one. Each autumn I'd drive mine home
And he would go back with his to Laïos'
sheepfold.— *25*
Is this not true, just as I have described it?
SHEPHERD   True, yes; but it was all so long ago.
MESSENGER   Well, then: do you remember, back in those
days

That you gave me a baby boy to bring up as my
own?
SHEPHERD   What if I did? What are you trying to say? *30*
MESSENGER   King Oedipus was once that little child.
SHEPHERD   Damn you, hold your tongue!
OEDIPUS   No more of that!
It is your tongue needs watching, not this man's.
SHEPHERD   My King, my Master, what is it I have done
wrong?
OEDIPUS   You have not answered his question about the
boy. *35*
SHEPHERD   He does not know … He is only making
trouble …
OEDIPUS   Come, speak plainly, or it will go hard with you.
SHEPHERD   In God's name, do not torture an old man!
OEDIPUS   Come here, one of you; bind his arms behind
him.
SHEPHERD   Unhappy king! What more do you wish to
learn? *40*
OEDIPUS   Did you give this man the child he speaks of?
SHEPHERD   I did.
And I would to God I had died that very day.
OEDIPUS   You will die now unless you speak the truth.
SHEPHERD   Yet if I speak the truth, I am worse than dead.
OEDIPUS   Very well; since you insist upon delaying— *45*
SHEPHERD   No! I have told you already that I gave him
the boy.
OEDIPUS   Where did you get him? From your house?
From somewhere else?
SHEPHERD   Not from mine, no. A man gave him to me.
OEDIPUS   Is that man here? Do you know whose slave he
was?
SHEPHERD   For God's love, my King, do not ask me any
more! *50*
OEDIPUS   You are a dead man if I have to ask you again.
SHEPHERD   Then … Then the child was from the palace
of Laïos.
OEDIPUS   A slave child? or a child of his own line?
SHEPHERD   Ah, I am on the brink of dreadful speech!
OEDIPUS   And I of dreadful hearing. Yet I must hear. *55*
SHEPHERD   If you must be told, then …
                                They said it was Laïos' child,
But it is your wife who can tell you about that.
OEDIPUS   My wife!—Did she give it to you?
SHEPHERD   My lord, she did.
OEDIPUS   Do you know why?
SHEPHERD   I was told to get rid of it.
OEDIPUS   An unspeakable mother!
SHEPHERD   There had been prophecies … *60*
OEDIPUS   Tell me.
SHEPHERD   It was said that the boy would kill his own
father.
OEDIPUS   Then why did you give him over to this old
man?
SHEPHERD   I pitied the baby, my King.
And I thought that this man would take him far away
To his own country.
                        He saved him—but for what a fate! *65*
For if you are what this man says you are,
No man living is more wretched than Oedipus.
OEDIPUS   Ah God!

It was true!
>All the prophecies!
>>—Now,
O Light, may I look on you for the last time! 70
I, Oedipus,
Oedipus, damned in his birth, in his marriage
>damned,
Damned in the blood he shed with his own hand!

He rushes into the palace.

ODE IV

Strophe 1

CHORUS   Alas for the seed of men.
>What measure shall I give these generations
>That breathe on the void and are void
>And exist and do not exist?

>Who bears more weight of joy 5
>Than mass of sunlight shifting in images,
>Or who shall make his thought stay on
>That down time drifts away?

>Your spendor is all fallen.

>O naked brow of wrath and tears, 10
>O change of Oedipus!
>I who saw your days call no man blest—
>Your great days like ghósts góne.

Antistrophe 1

>That mind was a strong bow.
>Deep, how deep you drew it then, hard archer, 15
>At a dim fearful range,
>And brought dear glory down!

>You overcame the stranger—
>The virgin with her hooking lion claws—
>And though death sang, stood like a tower 20
>To make pale Thebes take heart.

>Fortress against our sorrow!

>Divine king, giver of laws,
>Majestic Oedipus!
>No prince in Thebes had ever such renown, 25
>No prince won such grace of power.

Strophe 2

>And now of all men ever known
>Most pitiful is this man's story:
>His fortunes are most changed, his state
>Fallen to a low slave's 30
>Ground under bitter fate.

>O Oedipus, most royal one!
>The great door that expelled you to the light

>Gave at night—ah, gave night to your glory:
>As to the father, to the fathering son. 35

>All understood too late.

>How could that queen whom Laïos won,
>The garden that he harrowed at his height,
>Be silent when that act was done?

Antistrophe 2

>But all eyes fail before time's eye, 40
>All actions come to justice there.
>Though never willed, though far down the deep
>>past,
>Your bed, your dread sirings,
>Are brought to book at last.
>Child by Laïos doomed to die, 45
>Then doomed to lose that fortunate little death,
>Would God you never took breath in this air
>That with my wailing lips I take to cry:

>For I weep the world's outcast.

>I was blind, and now I can tell why: 50
>Asleep, for you had given ease of breath
>To Thebes, while the false years went by.

EXODUS

Enter, from the palace, Second Messenger.

SECOND MESSENGER   Elders of Thebes, most honored in
>this land,
>What horrors are yours to see and hear, what weight
>Of sorrow to be endured, if, true to your birth,
>You venerate the line of Labdakos!
>I think neither Istros nor Phasis, those great rivers, 5
>Could purify this place of the corruption
>It shelters now, or soon must bring to light—
>Evil not done unconsciously, but willed.

>The greatest griefs are those we cause ourselves.
CHORAGOS   Surely, friend, we have grief enough
>already; 10
>What new sorrow do you mean?
SECOND MESSENGER   The Queen is dead.
CHORAGOS   Iocastê? Dead? But at whose hand?
SECOND MESSENGER   Her own.
>The full horror of what happened you cannot know,
>For you did not see it; but I, who did, will tell you
>As clearly as I can how she met her death. 15

>When she had left us,
>In passionate silence, passing through the court,
>She ran to her apartment in the house,
>Her hair clutched by the fingers of both hands.
>She closed the doors behind her; then, by that bed 20
>Where long ago the fatal son was conceived—
>That son who should bring about his father's
>>death—

We heard her call upon Laïos, dead so many years,
And heard her wail for the double fruit of her
    marriage,
A husband by her husband, children by her child.   25

Exactly how she died I do not know:
For Oedipus burst in moaning and would not let us
Keep vigil to the end; it was by him
As he stormed about the room that our eyes were
    caught.
From one to another of us he went, begging a
    sword,   30
Cursing the wife who was not his wife, the mother
Whose womb had carried his own children and
    himself.
I do not know: it was none of us aided him,
But surely one of the gods was in control!
For with a dreadful cry   35
He hurled his weight, as though wrenched out of
    himself,
At the twin doors: the bolts gave, and he rushed in.
And there we saw her hanging, her body swaying
From the cruel cord she had noosed about her neck.
A great sob broke from him heartbreaking to hear, 40
As he loosed the rope and lowered her to the
    ground.

I would blot out from my mind what happened next!
For the King ripped from her gown the golden
    brooches
That were her ornament, and raised them, and
    plunged them down
Straight into his own eyeballs, crying, "No more,   45
No more shall you look on the misery about me,
The horrors of my own doing! Too long you have
    known
The faces of those whom I should never have seen,
Too long been blind to those for whom I was
    searching!
From this hour, go in darkness!" And as he spoke, 50
He struck at his eyes—not once, but many times;
And the blood spattered his beard,
Bursting from his ruined sockets like red hail.

So from the unhappiness of two this evil has sprung,
A curse on the man and woman alike. The old   55
Happiness of the house of Labdakos
Was happiness enough: where is it today?
It is all wailing and ruin, disgrace, death—all
The misery of mankind that has a name—
And it is wholly and for ever theirs.   60

CHORAGOS Is he in agony still? Is there no rest for him?
SECOND MESSENGER He is calling for someone to lead
    him to the gates
So that all the children of Kadmos may look upon
His father's murderer, his mother's—no,
I cannot say it!
                And then he will leave Thebes,   65
Self-exiled, in order that the curse
Which he himself pronounced may depart from the
    house.

He is weak, and there is none to lead him,
So terrible is his suffering.
                    But you will see:
Look, the doors are opening; in a moment   70
You will see a thing that would crush a heart of
    stone.

The central door is opened; Oedipus, blinded, is led in.

CHORAGOS Dreadful indeed for men to see.
    Never have my own eyes
    Looked on a sight so full of fear.

    Oedipus!   75
    What madness came upon you, what daemon
    Leaped on your life with heavier
    Punishment than a mortal man can bear?
    No: I cannot even
    Look at you, poor ruined one.   80
    And I would speak, question, ponder,
    If I were able. No.
    You make me shudder.

OEDIPUS God. God.
    Is there a sorrow greater?   85
    Where shall I find harbor in this world?
    My voice is hurled far on a dark wind.
    What has God done to me?

CHORAGOS Too terrible to think of, or to see.

Strophe 1

OEDIPUS O cloud of night,   90
    Never to be turned away: night coming on,
    I cannot tell how: night like a shroud!
    My fair winds brought me here.
        Oh God. Again
    The pain of the spikes where I had sight,
    The flooding pain   95
    Of memory, never to be gouged out.

CHORAGOS This is not strange.
    You suffer it all twice over, remorse in pain,
    Pain in remorse.

Antistrophe 1

OEDIPUS Ah dear friend   100
    Are you faithful even yet, you alone?
    Are you still standing near me, will you stay here,
    Patient, to care for the blind?
                        The blind man!
    Yet even blind I know who it is attends me,
    By the voice's tone—   105
    Though my new darkness hide the comforter.

CHORAGOS Oh fearful act!
    What god was it drove you to rake black
    Night across your eyes?

Strophe 2

OEDIPUS Apollo. Apollo. Dear   110
    Children, the god was Apollo.

He brought my sick, sick fate upon me.
But the blinding hand was my own!
How could I bear to see
When all my sight was horror everywhere?   115
CHORAGOS Everywhere; that is true.
OEDIPUS And now what is left?
          Images? Love? A greeting even,
          Sweet to the senses? Is there anything?
          Ah, no, friends: lead me away.   120
          Lead me away from Thebes.
                              Lead the great wreck
          And hell of Oedipus, whom the gods hate.
CHORAGOS Your fate is clear, you are not blind to that.
          Would God you had never found it out!

Antistrophe 2

OEDIPUS Death take the man who unbound   125
          My feet on that hillside
          And delivered me from death to life! What life?
          If only I had died,
          This weight of monstrous doom
          Could not have dragged me and my darlings
              down.   130
CHORAGOS I would have wished the same.
OEDIPUS Oh never to have come here
          With my father's blood upon me! Never
          To have been the man they call his mother's
              husband!
          Oh accurst! Oh child of evil,   135
          To have entered that wretched bed—
              the selfsame one!
          More primal than sin itself, this fell to me.
CHORAGOS I do not know how I can answer you.
          You were better dead than alive and blind.
OEDIPUS Do not counsel me any more. This
              punishment   140
          That I have laid upon myself is just.
          If I had eyes,
          I do not know how I could bear the sight
          Of my father, when I came to the house of Death,
          Or my mother: for I have sinned against them
              both   145
          So vilely that I could not make my peace
          By strangling my own life.
                        Or do you think my children,
          Born as they were born, would be sweet to my eyes?
          Ah never, never! Nor this town with its high walls,
          Nor the holy images of the gods.
                              For I,   150
          Thrice miserable—Oedipus, noblest of all the line
          Of Kadmos, have condemned myself to enjoy
          These things no more, by my own malediction
          Expelling that man whom the gods declared
          To be a defilement in the house of Laïos.   155
          After exposing the rankness of my own guilt,
          How could I look men frankly in the eyes?
          No, I swear it,
          If I could have stifled my hearing at its source,
          I would have done it and made all this body   160
          A tight cell of misery, blank to light and sound:

So I should have been safe in a dark agony
Beyond all recollection.
                    Ah Kithairon!
Why did you shelter me? When I was cast upon you,
Why did I not die? Then I should never   165
Have shown the world my execrable birth.

Ah Polybos! Corinth, city that I believed
The ancient seat of my ancestors: how fair
I seemed, your child! And all the while this evil
Was cancerous within me!
                    For I am sick   170
In my daily life, sick in my origin.

O three roads, dark ravine, woodland and way
Where three roads met you, drinking my father's
    blood,
My own blood, spilled by my own hand: can you
    remember
The unspeakable things I did there, and the
    things   175
I went on from there to do?
                    O marriage, marriage!
The act that engendered me, and again the act
Performed by the son in the same bed—
                              Ah, the net
Of incest, mingling fathers, brothers, sons,
With brides, wives, mothers: the last evil   180
That can be known by men: no tongue can say
How evil!
          No. For the love of God, conceal me
Somewhere far from Thebes; or kill me; or hurl me
Into the sea, away from men's eyes for ever.
Come, lead me. You need not fear to touch me.   185
Of all men, I alone can bear this guilt.

Enter Creon.

CHORAGOS We are not the ones to decide; but Creon
    here
          May fitly judge of what you ask. He only
          Is left to protect the city in your place.
OEDIPUS Alas, how can I speak to him? What right
          have I   190
          To beg his courtesy whom I have deeply wronged?
CREON I have not come to mock you, Oedipus,
          Or to reproach you, either.
              (To Attendants)—You, standing there:
          If you have lost all respect for man's dignity,
          At least respect the flame of Lord Helios: 195
          Do not allow this pollution to show itself
          Openly here, an affront to the earth
          And Heaven's rain and the light of day. No, take him
          Into the house as quickly as you can.
          For it is proper.   200
          That only the close kindred see his grief.
OEDIPUS I pray you in God's name, since your courtesy
          Ignores my dark expectation, visiting
          With mercy this man of all men most execrable:
          Give me what I ask—for your good, not for mine.
CREON And what is it that you would have me do?   206

Oedipus Drive me out of this country as quickly as may
        be
      To a place where no human voice can ever greet me.
Creon I should have done that before now—only,
      God's will had not been wholly revealed to me.   210
Oedipus But his command is plain: the parricide
      Must be destroyed. I am that evil man.
Creon That is the sense of it, yes: but as things are,
      We had best discover clearly what is to be done.
Oedipus You would learn more about a man like me? 215
Creon You are ready now to listen to the god.
Oedipus I will listen. But it is to you
      That I must turn for help. I beg you, hear me.

      The woman in there—
      Give her whatever funeral you think proper: 220
      She is your sister.
                  —But let me go, Creon!
      Let me purge my father's Thebes of the pollution
      Of my living here, and go out to the wild hills,
      To Kithairon, that has won such fame with me,
      The tomb my mother and father appointed for
        me,   225
      And let me die there, as they willed I should.
      And yet I know
      Death will not ever come to me through sickness
      Or in any natural way: I have been preserved
      For some unthinkable fate. But let that be.   230
      As for my sons, you need not care for them.
      They are men, they will find some way to live.
      But my poor daughters, who have shared my table,
      Who never before have been parted from their
        father—
      Take care of them, Creon; do this for me.   235
      And will you let me touch them with my hands
      A last time, and let us weep together?
      Be kind, my lord,
      Great prince, be kind!
                  Could I but touch them,
      They would be mine again, as when I had my
        eyes.   240

Enter Antigonê and Ismenê, attended.

      Ah, God!
      Is it my dearest children I hear weeping?
      Has Creon pitied me and sent my daughters?
Creon Yes, Oedipus: I knew that they were dear to you
      In the old days, and know you must love them
        still.   245
Oedipus May God bless you for this—and be a friendlier
      Guardian to you than he has been to me!

      Children, where are you?
      Come quickly to my hands: they are your brother's—
      Hands that have brought your father's once clear
        eyes   250
      To this way of seeing—
                  Ah dearest ones,
      I had neither sight not knowledge then, your father
      By the woman who was the source of his own life!

      And I weep for you—having no strength to see
        you—,
      I weep for you when I think of the bitterness   255
      That men will visit upon you all your lives.
      What homes, what festivals can you attend
      Without being forced to depart again in tears?
      And when you come to marriageable age,
      Where is the man, my daughters, who would dare 260
      Risk the bane that lies on all my children?
      Is there any evil wanting? Your father killed
      His father; sowed the womb of her who bore him;
      Engendered you at the fount of his own existence!
      That is what they will say of you.
                  Then, whom   265
      Can you ever marry? There are no bridegrooms for
        you,
      And your lives must wither away in sterile dreaming.
      O Creon, son of Menoikeus!
      You are the only father my daughters have,
      Since we, their parents, are both of us gone for
        ever.   270
      They are your own blood: you will not let them
      Fall into beggary and loneliness;
      You will keep them from the miseries that are mine!
      Take pity on them; see, they are only children,
      Friendless except for you. Promise me this,   275
      Great Prince, and give me your hand in token of it.

Creon clasps his right hand.

      Children:
      I could say much, if you could understand me,
      But as it is, I have only this prayer for you:
      Live where you can, be as happy as you can—   280
      Happier, please God, than God has made your
        father!
Creon Enough. You have wept enough. Now go within.
Oedipus I must; but it is hard.
Creon   Time eases all things.
Oedipus But you must promise—
Creon   Say what you desire.
Oedipus Send me from Thebes!
Creon   God grant that I may! 285
Oedipus But since God hates me …
Creon   No, he will grant your wish.
Oedipus You promise?
Creon   I cannot speak beyond my knowledge.
Oedipus Then lead me in.
Creon   Come now, and leave your children.
Oedipus No! Do not take them from me!
Creon   Think no longer
      That you are in command here, but rather think   290
      How, when you were, you served your own
        destruction.

*Exeunt into the house all but the Chorus; the Choragos chants
directly to the audience.*

Choragos Men of Thebes: look upon Oedipus.
      This is the king who solved the famous riddle
      And towered up, most powerful of men

No mortal eyes but looked on him with envy.   *295*
Yet in the end ruin swept over him.
Let every man in mankind's frailty
Consider his last day; and let none
Presume on his good fortune until he find
Life, at his death, a memory without pain.   *300*

✦ PLATO

from *The Phaedo*

In his Phaedo *Plato describes the final hours of Socrates, who was condemned to death by the Athenian authorities. Before taking the dose of hemlock that would kill him, Socrates discoursed with his friends on his favorite topics: the value of the spiritual and the immortality of the soul. Plato developed Socratic thinking about these interrelated issues in other works. Here, in* The Phaedo, *they have a special poignancy and power, as Socrates' actions and attitude reflect his profound belief in spiritual reality.*

… A man of sense ought not to say, nor will I be very confident, that the description which I have given of the soul and her mansions is exactly true. but I do say that, inasmuch as the soul is shown to be immortal, he may venture to think, not improperly or unworthily, that something of the kind is true. The venture is a glorious one, and he ought to comfort himself with words like these, which is the reason why I lengthen out the tale. Wherefore, I say, let a man be of good cheer about his soul, who having cast away the pleasures and ornaments of the body as alien to him and working harm rather than good, has sought after the pleasures of knowledge; and has arrayed the soul, not in some foreign attire, but in her own proper jewels, temperance, and justice, and courage, and nobility, and truth—in these adorned she is ready to go on her journey to the world below, when her hour comes. You, Simmias and Cebes, and all other men, will depart at some time or other. Me already, as a tragic poet would say, the voice of fate calls. Soon I must drink the poison; and I think that I had better repair to the bath first, in order that the women may not have the trouble of washing my body after I am dead.

When he had done speaking, Crito said: And have you any commands for us, Socrates—anything to say about your children, or any other matter in which we can serve you?

Nothing particular, Crito, he replied: only, as I have always told you, take care of yourselves; that is a service which you may be ever rendering to me and mine and to all of us, whether you promise to do so or not. But if you have no thought for yourselves, and care not to walk according to the rule which I have prescribed for you, not now for the first time, however much you may profess or promise at the moment, it will be of no avail.

We will do our best, said Crito: And in what way shall we bury you?

In any way that you like; but you must get hold of me, and take care that I do not run away from you. Then he turned to us, and added with a smile:—I cannot make Crito believe that I am the same Socrates who has been talking and conducting the argument; he fancies that I am the other Socrates whom he will soon see, a dead body—and he asks, How shall he bury me? And though I have spoken many words in the endeavour to show that when I have drunk the poison I shall leave you and go to the joys of the blessed,—these words of mine, with which I was comforting you and myself, have had, as I perceive, no effect upon Crito. And therefore I want you to be surety for me to him now, as at the trial he was surety for me to the judges: but let the promise be of another sort; for he was surety for me to the judges that I would remain, and you must be my surety to him that I shall not remain, but go away and depart; and then he will suffer less at my death, and not be grieved when he sees my body being burned or buried. I would not have him sorrow at my hard lot, or say at the burial, Thus we lay out Socrates, or, Thus we follow him to the grave or bury him; for false words are not only evil in themselves, but they infect the soul with evil. Be of good cheer then, my dear Crito, and say that you are burying my body only, and do with that whatever is usual, and what you think best.

When he had spoken these words, he arose and went into a chamber to bathe; Crito followed him and told us to wait. So we remained behind, talking and thinking of the subject of discourse, and also of the greatness of our sorrow; he was like a father of whom we were being bereaved, and we were about to pass the rest of our lives as orphans. When he had taken the bath his children were brought to him—(he had two young sons and an elder one); and the women of his family also came, and he talked to them and gave them a few directions in the presence of Crito; then he dismissed them and returned to us.

Now the hour of sunset was near, for a good deal of time had passed while he was within. When he came out, he sat down with us again after his bath, but not much was said. Soon the jailer, who was the servant of the Eleven, entered and stood by him, saying:—To you, Socrates, whom I know to be the noblest and gentlest and best of all who ever came to this place, I will not impute the angry feelings of other men, who rage and swear at me, when, in obedience to the authorities, I bid them drink the poison—indeed, I am sure that you will not be angry with me; for others, as you are aware, and not I, are to blame. And so fare you well, and try to bear lightly what must needs be—you know my errand. Then bursting into tears he turned away and went out.

Socrates looked at him and said: I return your good wishes, and will do as you bid. Then turning to us, he said, How charming the man is: since I have been in prison he has always been coming to see me, and at times he would talk to me, and was as good to me as could be, and now see how generously he sorrows on my account. We must do as he says, Crito; and therefore let the cup be brought, if the poison is prepared: if not, let the attendant prepare some.

Yet, said Crito, the sun is still upon the hilltops, and I know that many a one has taken the draught late, and after the announcement has been made to him, he has eaten and drunk, and enjoyed the society of his beloved; do not hurry—there is time enough.

Socrates said: Yes, Crito, and they of whom you speak are right in so acting, for they think that they will be gainers by the delay; but I am right in not following their example, for I do not think that I should gain anything by drinking the poison a little later; I should only be ridiculous in my own eyes for sparing and saving a life which is already forfeit. Please then to do as I say, and not to refuse me.

Crito made a sign to the servant, who was standing by; and he went out, and having been absent for some time, returned with the jailer carrying the cup of poison. Socrates said: You, my good friend, who are experienced in these matters, shall give me directions how I am to proceed. The man answered: You have only to walk about until your legs are heavy, and then to lie down, and the poison will act. At the same time he handed the cup to Socrates, who in the easiest and gentlest manner, without the least fear or change of colour or feature, looking at the man with all his eyes, Echecrates, as his manner was, took the cup and said: What do you say about making a libation out of this cup to any god? May I, or not? The man answered: We only prepare, Socrates, just so much as we deem enough. I understand, he said: but I may and must ask the gods to prosper my journey from this to the other world—even so—and so be it according to my prayer. Then raising the cup to his lips, quite readily and cheerfully he drank off the poison. And hitherto most of us had been able to control our sorrow; but now when we saw him drinking, and saw too that he had finished the draught, we could no longer forbear, and in spite of myself my own tears were flowing fast; so that I covered my face and wept, not for him, but at the thought of my own calamity in having to part from such a friend. Nor was I the first; for Crito, when he found himself unable to restrain his tears, had got up, and I followed; and at that moment, Apollodorus, who had been weeping all the time, broke out in a loud and passionate cry which made cowards of us all. Socrates alone retained his calmness: What is this strange outcry? he said. I sent away the women mainly in order that they might not misbehave in this way, for I have been told that a man should die in peace. Be quiet then, and have patience. When we heard his words we were ashamed, and refrained our tears; and he walked about until, as he said, his legs began to fail, and then he lay on his back, according to the directions, and the man who gave him the poison now and then looked at his feet and legs; and after a while he pressed his foot hard, and asked him if he could feel; and he said, No; and then his leg, and so upwards and upwards, and showed us that he was cold and stiff. And he felt them himself, and said: When the poison reaches the heart, that will be the end. He was beginning to grow cold about the groin, when he uncovered his face, for he had covered himself up, and said—they were his last words—he said: Crito, I owe a cock to Asclepius; will you remember to pay the debt? The debt shall be paid, said Crito; is there anything else? There was no answer to this question; but in a minute or two a movement was heard, and the attendants uncovered him; his eyes were set, and Crito closed his eyes and mouth.

Such was the end, Echecrates, of our friend; concerning whom I may truly say, that of all the men of his time whom I have known, he was the wisest and justest and best.

❧ PLATO

from *The Republic*

The Republic is Plato's longest and most complex book. In presenting his version of the ideal society, Plato explains the importance of true knowledge, which he distinguishes from false knowledge, really a form of ignorance. To convey the difference between true and false knowledge, Plato introduces an extended metaphor, the Allegory of the Cave. People chained to the floor of an underground cave imagine that the shadows cast on the cave's walls by the light of a fire behind them are real. The cave's inhabitants know only such shadows, which for them become the only reality they know. Their ignorance can only be dispelled by someone not limited to the shadowy notions of reality believed by the cave dwellers. Only the philosopher, who knows the true, the good, and the beautiful as they really exist in their pure ideal forms, can free humankind from its limited knowledge of material reality. Here Socrates is speaking to Glaucon.

And now, I said, let me show in a figure how far our nature is enlightened or unenlightened:—Behold! human beings living in an underground den, which has a mouth open towards the light and reaching all along the den; here they have been from their childhood, and have their legs and necks chained so that they cannot move, and can only see before them, being prevented by the chains from turning round their heads. Above and behind them a fire is blazing at a distance, and between the fire and the prisoners there is a raised way; and you will see, if you look, a low wall built along the way, like the screen which marionette players have in front of them, over which they show the puppets.

I see.

And do you see, I said, men passing along the wall carrying all sorts of vessels, and statues and figures of animals made of wood and stone and various materials, which appear over the wall? Some of them are talking, others silent.

You have shown me a strange image, and they are strange prisoners.

Like ourselves, I replied; and they see only their own shadows, or the shadows of one another, which the fire throws on the opposite wall of the cave?

True, he said; how could they see anything but the shadows if they were never allowed to move their heads?

And of the objects which are being carried in like manner they would only see the shadows?

Yes, he said.

And if they were able to converse with one another, would they not suppose that they were naming what was actually before them?

Very true.

And suppose further that the prison had an echo which came from the other side, would they not be sure to fancy when one of the passers-by spoke that the voice which they heard came from the passing shadow?

No question, he replied.

To them, I said, the truth would be literally nothing but the shadows of the images.

That is certain.

And now look again, and see what will naturally follow if the prisoners are released and disabused of their error. At first, when any of them is liberated and compelled suddenly to stand up and turn his neck round and walk and look towards the light, he will suffer sharp pains; the glare will distress him, and he will be unable to see the realities of which in his former state he had seen the shadows; and then conceive someone saying to him, that what he saw before was an illusion, but that now, when he is approaching nearer to being and his eye is turned towards more real existence, he has a clearer vision—what will be his reply? And you may further imagine that his instructor is pointing to the objects as they pass and requiring him to name them—will he not be perplexed? Will he not fancy that the shadows which he formerly saw are truer than the objects which are now shown to him?

Far truer.

And if he is compelled to look straight at the light, will he not have a pain in his eyes which will make him turn away to take refuge in the objects of vision which he can see, and which he will conceive to be in reality clearer than the things which are now being shown to him?

True, he said.

And suppose once more, that he is reluctantly dragged up a steep and rugged ascent, and held fast until he is forced into the presence of the sun himself, is he not likely to be pained and irritated? When he approaches the light his eyes will be dazzled, and he will not be able to see anything at all of what are now called realities.

Not all in a moment, he said.

He will require to grow accustomed to the sight of the upper world. And first he will see the shadows best, next the reflections of men and other objects in the water, and then the objects themselves; then he will gaze upon the light of the moon and the stars and the spangled heaven; and he will see the sky and the stars by night better than the sun or the light of the sun by day?

Certainly.

Last of all he will be able to see the sun, and not mere reflections of him in the water, but he will see him in his own proper place, and not in another; and he will contemplate him as he is.

Certainly.

He will then proceed to argue that this is he who gives the season and the years, and is the guardian of all that is in the visible world, and in a certain way the cause of all things which he and his fellows have been accustomed to behold?

Clearly, he said, he would first see the sun and then reason about him.

And when he remembered his old habitation, and the wisdom of the den and his fellow-prisoners, do you not suppose that he would felicitate himself on the change, and pity them?

Certainly, he would.

And if they were in the habit of conferring honours among themselves on those who were quickest to observe the passing shadows and to remark which of them went before, and which followed after, and which were together; and who were therefore best able to draw conclusions as to the future, do you think that he would care for such honours and glories, or envy the possessors of them? Would he not say with Homer,

Better to be the poor servant of a poor master,

and to endure anything, rather than think as they do and live after their manner?

Yes, he said, I think that he would rather suffer anything than entertain these false notions and live in this miserable manner.

Imagine once more, I said, such an one coming suddenly out of the sun to be replaced in his old situation; would he not be certain to have his eyes full of darkness?

To be sure, he said.

And if there were a contest, and he had to compete in measuring the shadows with the prisoners who had never moved out of the den, while his sight was still weak, and before his eyes had become steady (and the time which would be needed to acquire this new habit of sight might be very considerable), would he not be ridiculous? Men would say of him that up he went and down he came without his eyes; and that it was better not even to think of ascending; and if any one tried to loose another and lead him up to the light, let them only catch the offender, and they would put him to death.

No question, he said.

This entire allegory, I said, you may now append, dear Glaucon, to the previous argument; the prison-house is the world of sight, the light of the fire is the sun, and you will not misapprehend me if you interpret the journey upwards to be the ascent of the soul into the intellectual world according to my poor belief, which, at your desire, I have expressed—whether rightly or wrongly God knows. But, whether true or false, my opinion is that in the world of knowledge the idea of good appears last of all, and is seen only with an effort; and, when seen, is also inferred to be the universal author of all things beautiful and right, parent of light and of the lord of light in this visible world, and the immediate source of reason and truth in the intellectual; and that this is the power upon which he who would act rationally either in public or private life must have his eye fixed.

I agree, he said, as far as I am able to understand you.

Moreover, I said, you must not wonder that those who attain to this beatific vision are unwilling to descend to human affairs; for their souls are ever hastening into the upper world where they desire to dwell; which desire of theirs is very natural, if our allegory may be trusted.

Yes, very natural.

And is there anything surprising in one who passes from divine contemplations to the evil state of man, misbehaving himself in a ridiculous manner; if, while his eyes are blinking and before he has become accustomed to the surrounding darkness, he is compelled to fight in courts of law, or in other places, about the images or the shadows of images of justice, and is endeavouring to meet the conceptions of those who have never yet seen absolute justice?

Anything but surprising, he replied.

Any one who has common sense will remember that the bewilderments of the eyes are of two kinds, and arise from two causes, either from coming out of the light or from going into the light, which is true of the mind's eye, quite as much as of the bodily eye; and he who remembers this when he sees any one whose vision is perplexed and weak, will not be too ready to laugh; he will first ask whether that soul of man has come out of the brighter life, and is unable to see because unaccustomed to the dark, or having turned from darkness to the day is dazzled by excess of light. And he will count the one happy in his condition and state of being, and he will pity the other; or, if he have a mind to laugh at the soul which comes from below into the light, there will be more reason in this than in the laugh which greets him who returns from above out of the light into the den.

That, he said, is a very just distinction.

But then, if I am right, certain professors of education

must be wrong when they say that they can put a knowledge into the soul which was not there before, like sight into blind eyes.

They undoubtedly say this, he replied.

Whereas, our argument shows that the power and capacity of learning exists in the soul already; and that just as the eye was unable to turn from darkness to light without the whole body, so too the instrument of knowledge can only by the movement of the whole soul be turned from the world of becoming into that of being, and learn by degrees to endure the sight of being, and of the brightest and best of being, or in other words, of the good.

Very true.

And must there not be some art which will effect conversion in the easiest and quickest manner; not implanting the faculty of sight, for that exists already, but has been turned in the wrong direction, and is looking away from the truth?

Yes, he said, such an art may be presumed.

And whereas the other so-called virtues of the soul seem to be akin to bodily qualities, for even when they are not originally innate they can be implanted later by habit and exercise, the virtue of wisdom more than anything else contains a divine element which always remains, and by this conversion is rendered useful and profitable; or, on the other hand, hurtful and useless. Did you never observe the narrow intelligence flashing from the keen eye of a clever rogue—how eager he is, how clearly his paltry soul sees the way to his end; he is the reverse of blind, but his keen eyesight is forced into the service of evil, and he is mischievous in proportion to his cleverness?

Very true, he said.

But what if there had been a circumcision of such natures in the days of their youth; and they had been severed from those sensual pleasures, such as eating and drinking, which, like leaden weights, were attached to them at their birth, and which drag them down and turn the vision of their souls upon the things that are below—if, I say, they had been released from these impediments and turned in the opposite direction, the very same faculty in them would have seen the truth as keenly as they see what their eyes are turned to now.

Very likely.

Yes, I said; and there is another thing which is likely, or rather a necessary inference from what has preceded, that neither the uneducated and uninformed of the truth, or yet those who never make an end of their education, will be able ministers of State; not the former, because they have no single aim of duty which is the role of all their actions, private as well as public, nor the latter, because they will not act at all except upon compulsion, fancying that they are already dwelling apart in the islands of the blest.

Very true, he replied.

Then, I said, the business of us who are the founders of the State will be to compel the best minds to attain that knowledge which we have already shown to be the greatest of all—they must continue to ascend until they arrive at the good; but when they have ascended and seen enough we must not allow them to do as they do now.

What do you mean?

I mean that they remain in the upper world: but this must not be allowed; they must be made to descend again among the prisoners in the den, and partake of their labours and honours, whether they are worth having or not.

But is not this unjust? he said; ought we to give them a worse life, when they might have a better?

You have again forgotten, my friend, I said, the intention of the legislator, who did not aim at making any one class in the State happy above the rest; the happiness was to be in the whole State, and he held the citizens together by persuasion and necessity, making them benefactors of the State, and therefore benefactors of one another; to this end he created them, not to please themselves, but to be his instruments in binding up the State.

True, he said, I had forgotten.

Observe, Glaucon, that there will be no injustice in compelling our philosophers to have a care and providence of others; we shall explain to them that in other States, men of their class are not obliged to share in the toils of politics: and this is reasonable, for they grow up at their own sweet will, and the government would rather not have them. Being self-taught, they cannot be expected to show any gratitude for a culture which they have never received. But we have brought you into the world to be rulers of the hive, kings of yourselves and of the other citizens, and have educated you far better and more perfectly than they have been educated, and you are better able to share in the double duty. Wherefore each of you, when his turn comes, must go down to the general underground abode, and get the habit of seeing in the dark. When you have acquired the habit, you will see ten thousand times better than the inhabitants of the den, and you will know what the several images are, and what they represent, because you have seen the beautiful and just and good in their truth. And thus our State which is also yours will be a reality, and not a dream only, and will be administered in a spirit unlike that of other States, in which men fight with one another about shadows only and are distracted in the struggle for power, which in their eyes is a great good. Whereas the truth is that the State in which the rulers are most reluctant to govern is always the best and most quietly governed, and the State in which they are most eager, the worst.

Quite true, he replied.

And will our pupils, when they hear this, refuse to take their turn at the toils of State, when they are allowed to spend the greater part of their time with one another in the heavenly light?

Impossible, he answered; for they are just men, and the commands which we impose upon them are just; there can be no doubt that every one of them will take office as a stern necessity, and not after the fashion of our present rulers of State.

Yes, my friend, I said; and there lies the point. You must contrive for your future rulers another and a better life than that of a ruler, and then you may have a well-ordered State; for only in the State which offers this, will they rule who are truly rich, not in silver and gold, but in virtue and wisdom, which are the true blessings of life. Whereas if they go to the administration of public affairs, poor and hungering after their own private advantage, thinking that hence they are to snatch the chief good, order there can never be; for they will be fighting about office, and the civil and domestic broils which thus arise will be the ruin of the rulers themselves and of the whole State.

Most true, he replied.

And the only life which looks down upon the life of political ambition is that of true philosophy. Do you know of any other?

Indeed, I do not, he said.

✦ ARISTOTLE

from *The Nicomachean Ethics*

In the following passage from his Nicomachean Ethics, *Aristotle describes his principle of the mean between extremes. Although Aristotle emphasizes the acquisition of moral virtue, he also refers to how the doctrine of the mean applies to works of art. Moderation is a critical element in Aristotle's doctrine of the mean, as is the notion that the ideal mean of any feeling, impulse, or attitude is relative, varying from one person to another. In this section, also, Aristotle explains why achieving the balance of the mean is difficult.*

Virtue defined: the differentia

It is not sufficient, however, merely to define virtue in general terms as a characteristic: we must also specify what kind of characteristic it is. It must, then, be remarked that every virtue or excellence (1) renders good the thing itself of which it is the excellence, and (2) causes it to perform its function well. For example, the excellence of the eye makes both the eye and its function good, for good sight is due to the excellence of the eye. Likewise, the excellence of a horse makes it both good as a horse and good at running, at carrying its rider, and at facing the enemy. Now, if this is true of all things, the virtue or excellence of man, too, will be a characteristic which makes him a good man, and which causes him to perform his own function well. To some extent we have already stated how this will be true; the rest will become clear if we study what the nature of virtue is.

Of every continuous entity that is divisible into parts it is possible to take the larger, the smaller, or an equal part, and these parts may be larger, smaller, or equal either in relation to the entity itself, or in relation to us. The "equal" part is something median between excess and deficiency. By the median of an entity I understand a point equidistant from both extremes, and this point is one and the same for everybody. To take an example: if ten is many and two is few, six is taken as the median in relation to the entity, for it exceeds and is exceeded by the same amount, and is thus the median in terms of arithmetical proportion. But the median relative to us cannot be determined in this manner: if ten pounds of food is much for a man to eat and two pounds little, it does not follow that the trainer will prescribe six pounds, for this may in turn be much or little for him to eat; it may be little for Milo [the wrestler] and much for someone who has just begun to take up athletics. The same applies to running and wrestling. Thus we see that an expert in any field avoids excess and deficiency, but seeks the median and chooses it—not the median of the object but the median relative to us.

If this, then, is the way in which every science perfects its work, by looking to the median and by bringing its work up to that point—and this is the reason why it is usually said of a successful piece of work that it is impossible to detract from it or to add to it, the implication being that excess and deficiency destroy success while the mean safeguards it (good craftsmen, we say, look toward this standard in the performance of their work)—and if virtue, like nature, is more precise and better than any art, we must conclude that virtue aims at the median. I am referring to moral virtue: for it is moral virtue that is concerned with emotions and actions, and it is in emotions and actions that excess, deficiency, and median are found. Thus we can experience fear, confidence, desire, anger, pity, and generally any kind of pleasure and pain either too much or too little, and in either case not properly. But to experience all this at the right time, toward the right objects, toward the right people, for the right reason, and in the right manner—that is the median and the best course, the course that is a mark of virtue.

Similarly, excess, deficiency, and the median can also be found in actions. Now virtue is concerned with emotions and actions; and in emotions and actions excess and deficiency miss the mark, whereas the median is praised and constitutes success. But both praise and success are signs of virtue or excellence. Consequently, virtue is a mean in the sense that it aims at the median. This is corroborated by the fact that there are many ways of going wrong, but only one way which is right—for evil belongs to the indeterminate, as the Pythagoreans imagined, but good to the determinate. This, by the way, is also the reason why the one is easy and the other hard: it is easy to miss the target but hard to hit it. Here, then, is an additional proof that excess and deficiency characterize vice, while the mean characterizes virtue: for "bad men have many ways, good men but one."

We may thus conclude that virtue or excellence is a characteristic involving choice, and that it consists in observing the mean relative to us, a mean which is defined by a rational principle, such as a man of practical wisdom would use to determine it. It is the mean by reference to two vices: the one of excess and the other of deficiency. It is, moreover, a mean because some vices exceed and others fall short of what is required in emotion and in action, whereas virtue finds and chooses the median. Hence, in respect of its essence and the definition of its essential nature virtue is a mean, but in regard to goodness and excellence it is an extreme.

Not every action nor every emotion admits of a mean. There are some actions and emotions whose very names connote baseness, e.g., spite, shamelessness, envy; and among actions, adultery, theft, and murder. These and similar emotions and actions imply by their very names that they are bad; it is not their excess nor their deficiency which is called bad. It is, therefore, impossible ever to do right in performing them: to perform them is always to do wrong. In cases of this sort, let us say adultery, rightness and wrongness do not depend on committing it with the right woman at the right time and in the right manner, but the mere fact of committing such an action at all is to do wrong. It would be just as absurd to suppose that there is a mean, an excess, and a deficiency in an unjust or a cowardly or a self-indulgent act. For if there were, we would have a mean of excess and a mean of deficiency, and an excess of excess and a deficiency of deficiency. Just as there cannot be an excess and a deficiency of self-control and courage—because the intermediate is, in a sense, an extreme—so there cannot be a mean, excess, and deficiency in their respective opposites: their opposites are wrong regardless of how they are performed; for, in general, there is no such thing as the mean of an excess of a deficiency, or the excess and deficiency of a mean.

How to attain the mean

Our discussion has sufficiently established (1) that moral virtue is a mean and in what sense it is a mean; (2) that it is a mean between two vices, one of which is marked by excess and the other by deficiency; and (3) that it is a mean in the sense that it aims at the median in the emotions and in actions. That is why it is a hard task to be good; in every case it is a task to find the median: for instance, not everyone can find the middle of a circle, but only a man who has the proper knowledge. Similarly, anyone can get angry—that is easy—or can give away money or spend it; but to do all this to the right person, to the right extent, at the right time, for the right reason, and in the right way is no longer something easy that anyone can do. It is for this reason that good conduct is rare, praiseworthy, and noble.

The first concern of a man who aims at the median should, therefore, be to avoid the extreme which is more opposed to it, as Calypso advises: "Keep clear your ship of yonder spray and surf." For one of the two extremes is more in error than the other, and since it is extremely difficult to hit the mean, we must, as the saying has it, sail in the second best way and take the lesser evil; and we can best do that in the manner we have described.

Moreover we must watch the errors which have the greatest attraction for us personally. For the natural inclination of one man differs from that of another, and we each come to recognize our own by observing the pleasure and pain produced in us [by the different extremes]. We must then draw ourselves away in the opposite direction, for by pulling away from error we shall reach the middle, as men do when they straighten warped timber. In every case we must be especially on our guard against pleasure and what is pleasant, for when it comes to pleasure we cannot act as unbiased judges. Our attitude toward pleasure should be the same as that of the Trojan elders was toward Helen, and we should repeat on every occasion the words they addressed to her. For if we dismiss pleasure as they dismissed her, we shall make fewer mistakes.

✦ ARISTOTLE
from *The Poetics*

In the following passage from The Poetics, *Aristotle defines tragedy and identifies its elements or parts. The section focuses on plot, which, for Aristotle, is intimately and intricately related to character. Aristotle's comments about these two elements of drama have powerfully influenced literary criticism for nearly twenty-five hundred years.*

Thus, Tragedy is an imitation of an action that is serious, complete, and possessing magnitude; in embellished language, each kind of which is used separately in the different parts; in the mode of action and not narrated; and effecting through pity and fear the *catharsis* of such emotions. By "embellished language" I mean language having rhythm and melody, and by "separately in different parts" I mean that some parts of a play are carried on solely in metrical speech while others again are sung.

The constituent parts of tragedy

Since the imitation is carried out in the dramatic mode by the personages themselves, it necessarily follows, first, that the arrangement of Spectacle will be a part of tragedy, and next, that Melody and Language will be parts, since these are the media in which they effect the imitation. By "language" I mean precisely the composition of the verses, by "melody" only that which is perfectly obvious. And since tragedy is the imitation of an action and is enacted by men in action, these persons must necessarily possess certain qualities of Character and Thought, since these are the basis for our ascribing qualities to the actions themselves—character and thought are two natural causes of actions—and it is in their actions that men universally meet with success or failure. The imitation of the action is the Plot. By plot I here mean the combination of the events; Character is that in virtue of which we say that the personages are of such and such a quality; and Thought is present in everything in their utterances that aims to prove a point or that expresses an opinion. Necessarily, therefore, there are in tragedy as a whole, considered as a special form, six constituent elements, viz. Plot, Characters, Language, Thought, Spectacle, and Melody. Of these elements, two are the *media* in which they effect the imitation, one is the *manner*, and three are the *objects* they imitate; and besides these there are no other parts. So then they employ these six forms, not just some of them, so to speak; for every drama has spectacle, character, plot, language, melody, and thought in the same sense, but the most important of them is the organization of the events [the plot].

Plot and character

For tragedy is not an imitation of men but of actions and of life. It is in action that happiness and unhappiness are found, and the end we aim at is a kind of activity, not a quality; in accordance with their characters men are of such and such a quality, in accordance with their actions they are fortunate or the reverse. Consequently, it is not for the purpose of presenting their characters that the agents engage in action, but rather it is for the sake of their actions that they take on the characters they have. Thus, what happens—that is, the plot—is the end for which a tragedy exists, and the end of purpose is the most important thing of all. What is more, without action there could not be a tragedy, but there could be without characterization.

Now that the parts are established, let us next discuss what qualities the plot should have, since plot is the primary and most important part of tragedy. I have posited that tragedy is an imitation of an action that is a whole and complete in itself and of a certain magnitude—for a thing may be a whole, and yet have no magnitude to speak of. Now a thing is a whole if it has a beginning, a middle, and an end. A beginning is that which does not come necessarily after something else, either as its necessary sequel or as its usual sequel, but itself has nothing after it. A middle is that which both comes after something else and has another thing following it. A well-constructed plot, therefore, will neither begin at some chance point nor end at some chance point, but will observe the principles here stated.

Contrary to what some people think, a plot is not ipso facto a unity if it revolves about one man. Many things, indeed an endless number of things, happened to any one man some of which do not go together to form a unity, and similarly among the action one man performs there are many that do not go together to produce a single unified action. Those poets seem all to have erred, therefore, who have composed a *Heracleid*, a *Theseid*, and other such poems, it being their idea evidently that since Heracles was one man, their plot was bound to be unified.

From what has already been said, it will be evident that the poet's function is not to report things that have happened, but rather to tell of such things as might happen, things that are possibilities by virtue of being in themselves inevitable or probable. Thus the difference between the historian and the poet is not that the historian employs prose and poet verse—the work of Herodotus could be put into verse, and it be no less a history with verses than without them; rather the difference is that the one tells of things that have been and the other such things as might be. Poetry, therefore, is a more philosophical and a higher thing than history, in that poetry tends rather to express the universal, history rather the particular fact. A universal is: The sort of thing that (in the circumstances) a certain kind of person will say or do either probably or necessarily, which in fact is the universal that poetry aims for (with the addition of names for the persons); a particular, on the other hand, is: What Alcibiades did or had done to him.

Among plots and actions of the simple type, the episodic form is the worst. I call episodic a plot in which the episodes follow one another in no probable or inevitable sequence. Plots of this kind are constructed by bad poets on their own account, and by good poets on account of the actors; since they are composing entries for a competitive exhibition, they stretch the plot beyond what it can bear and are often compelled, therefore, to dislocate the natural order.

Some plots are simple, others complex; indeed the actions of which the plots are imitation are at once so differentiated to begin with. Assuming the action to be continuous and unified, as already defined, I call that action simple in which the change of fortune takes place without a reversal or recognition, and that action complex in which the change of fortune involves a recognition or a reversal or both. These events ought to be so rooted in the very structure of the plot that they follow from the preceding events as their inevitable or probably outcome; for there is a vast difference between following from and merely following after.

Reversal (Peripety) is, as aforesaid, a change from one state of affairs to its exact opposite, and this, too, as I say, should be in conformance with probability or necessity. For example, in *Oedipus*, the messenger comes to cheer Oedipus by relieving him of fear with regard to his mother, but by revealing his true identity, does just the opposite of this.

Recognition, as the word itself indicates, is a change from ignorance to knowledge, leading either to friendship or hostility on the part of those persons who are marked for good fortune or bad. The best form of recognition is that which is accompanied by a reversal, as in the example from *Oedipus*.

Next in order after the points I have just dealt with, it would seem necessary to specify what one should aim at and what avoid in the construction of plots, and what it is that will produce the effect proper to tragedy.

Now since in the finest kind of tragedy the structure should be complex and not simple, and since it should also be a representation of terrible and piteous events (that being the special mark of this type of imitation), in the first place, it is evident that good men ought not to be shown passing from prosperity to misfortune, for this does not inspire either pity or fear, but only revulsion; nor evil men rising from ill fortune to prosperity, for this is the most untragic plot of all—it lacks every requirement, in that it neither elicits human sympathy nor stirs pity or fear. And again, neither should an extremely wicked man be seen falling from prosperity into misfortune, for a plot so constructed might indeed call forth human sympathy, but would not excite pity or fear, since the first is felt for a person whose misfortune is undeserved and the second for someone like ourselves— pity for the man suffering undeservedly, fear for the man like ourselves—and hence neither pity nor fear would be aroused in this case. We are left with the man whose place is between these extremes. Such is the man who on the one hand does not fall into misfortune through vice or depravity, but falls because of some mistake; one among the number of the highly renowned and prosperous, such as Oedipus and Thyestes and other famous men from families like theirs.

It follows that the plot which achieves excellence will necessarily be single in outcome and not, as some contend, double, and will consist in a change of fortune, not from misfortune to prosperity, but the opposite from prosperity to misfortune, occasioned not by depravity, but by some great mistake on the part of one who is either such as I have described or better than this rather than worse. (What actually has taken place confirms this; for though at first the poets accepted whatever myths came to hand, today the finest tragedies are founded upon the stories of only a few houses, being concerned, for example, with Alcmeon, Oedipus, Orestes, Meleager, Thyestes, Telephus, and such others as have chanced to suffer terrible things or to do them.) So, then, tragedy having this construction is the finest kind of tragedy from an artistic point of view. And consequently, those persons fall into the same error who bring it as a charge against Euripides that this is what he does in his tragedies and that most of his plays have unhappy endings. For this is in fact the right procedure, as I have said; and the best proof is that on the stage and in the dramatic contests, plays of this kind seem the most tragic, provided they are successfully worked out, and Euripides, even if in everything else his management is faulty, seems at any rate the most tragic of the poets.

In the characters and the plot construction alike, one must strive for that which is either necessary or probable, so that whatever a character of any kind says or does may be the sort of thing such a character will inevitably or probably say or do and the events of the plot may follow one after another either inevitably or with probability.

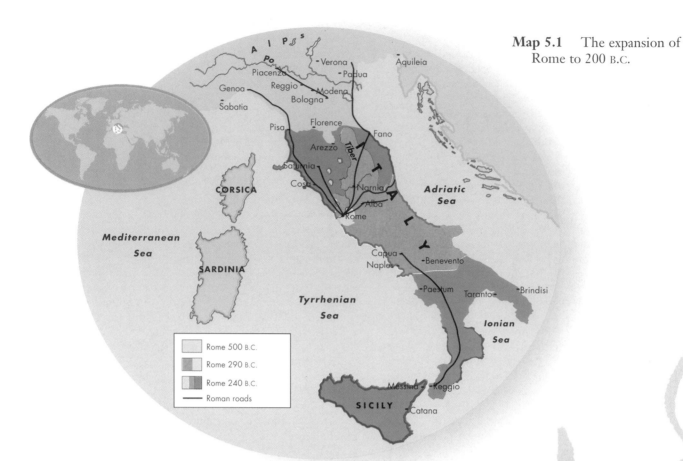

Map 5.1 The expansion of Rome to 200 B.C.

THE
ROMAN
WORLD

CHAPTER 5

↞ *Etruscan Civilization*

↞ *Republican Rome*

↞ *The Empire*

Pont du Gard, Nîmes, France, late first century B.C.–early first century A.D.

THE GREEK LEGACY AND THE ROMAN IDEAL

In many ways, Rome inherited its culture—its art, its literature, its philosophical and religious life—from Greece. The Italian peninsula was occupied by the Greeks by the seventh century B.C., which ensured the influence of Greek ways upon the developing Italian culture. However, it was the later Roman determination to control and rule the entire Western world that consolidated the Hellenization of the West and much of the Eastern world. Even more effectively than Alexander the Great, the Romans spread Greek art and literature as far as Britain in the north, Africa in the south, India in the east, and Spain in the west. Apart from disseminating Greek culture, Roman civilization produced remarkable achievements of its own, in the fields of politics, law, and engineering.

If the Romans held Greek art and literature in the highest esteem, they were not so impressed with the Greeks themselves. They found in the Greek love of music and poetry, their fascination with the human body, and their love of drama (as opposed to "real life") signs of weakness. The Roman satirist Juvenal, writing at the end of the first century A.D., expressed a low opinion of the Greek character: "These people are extremely clever at flattery; they praise the conversational skills of the biggest dimwit and physical beauty of an ugly friend … Greece is a nation of actors. Laugh, and they will laugh with you. Cry, and they cry too, although they feel no grief." Insincerity was, indeed, an entirely unRoman trait.

The Romans feared that the fate of Athens might be their own. Accordingly, they studied Greek history intently so that they might learn from it and avoid a similar decline. What they recognized in Greek culture was its lack of practical know-how. It is therefore no accident that it is for their genius for organization and problem-solving that the Western world is most indebted to the Romans. The Romans were superb engineers. The road system that they put in place across Europe is, in part, still in use today. The Romans built bridges and aqueducts that crossed rivers and valleys and carried fresh water to houses and public baths. Roman town architecture was eminently practical too. Great amphitheaters like the Colosseum in Rome were designed to accommodate vast crowds and to let them enter and exit more quickly and efficiently than today's sports fans can at similarly sized stadiums.

Romans' love of the efficient and practical is also seen in their political structure. The Romans invented the field of civil law—the branch of law that deals with property rights—which became the foundation for legal systems in many Western countries. The Romans were also responsible for the idea of "natural law," which emerged from the philosophy of Stoicism. Natural law, which postulated a set of rights beyond those described in civil (or property) law, became the basis for the inherently "inalienable rights" promised to all people by the framers of the American Declaration of Independence many centuries later (see Chapter 17). The Romans believed in the possibility of a society composed of "ideal" citizens, who respected others and possessed a deep sense of equity and fairness. This idea of civility in social behavior and civilized conduct and discourse in public life is perhaps Rome's greatest legacy (although it should be remembered that Rome had slaves and women had few rights); except perhaps for its language, Latin. Many major European languages—Italian, Spanish, French—in some degree descend from Latin. Though Germanic in root, English contains many Latin loan-words. All of these languages consequently bear within them the influence of Roman culture and ideals and all, of course, use the Roman alphabet.

ETRUSCAN CIVILIZATION
✦

While the Greeks were settling in southern Italy and Sicily, another people—the Etruscans—inhabited the central Italian mainland. Relatively little is known about the Etruscans. Their alphabet is derived from Greek, but their language seems unique, insofar as can be judged from the small amount of undeciphered literature and the few inscriptions on works of art that survive. Herodotus, the fifth-century B.C. Greek historian, said that the Etruscans came to Italy from Lydia (Turkey) in Asia Minor around 800 B.C. Etruscan civilization proper dates from about 700 B.C. and was at its peak in the seventh and sixth centuries B.C.—the same time as the Archaic period in Greece.

While Etruscan civilization was at its height, the future imperial capital of Rome remained little more than a cluster of mud huts inhabited by shepherds and farmers known as Latins. Why Rome would eventually be transformed into the most powerful city in the world is difficult to say, except that, positioned on the south bank of the Tiber River in central Italy, it was midway between the Etruscan settlements to the north and the Greek colonies in the south of the peninsula. Rome thus lay on the trade route between the two civilizations. The Etruscans were influenced by the Greeks and came to know them literally "through" Rome. They sent skillfully manufactured bronze household utensils down the Tiber through Rome and on to the Greeks in the south in return for Greek vases, many of which have been found in Etruscan tombs. Greek heroes and deities were incorporated into the Etruscan pantheon, and their temples reflected Greek influence. In turn, the Etruscans exerted an important civilizing influence over the Latins in Rome.

Figure 5.1 Reconstruction of an Etruscan temple according to Vitruvius, Istituto di Etruscologia e Antichità Italiche, University of Rome. To a great extent, the Etruscan temple form was a modification of the Greek. Different from the Greek, however, are the high flight of stairs on one side only, deeper porch, and wider cella.

TEMPLES

Only the stone foundations of Etruscan temples have survived. Fortunately, the ancient Roman author and architect VITRUVIUS [vi-TROO-vee-us] (fl. first century A.D.) provided a description of an Etruscan temple, on the basis of which it has been possible to create a reconstruction (fig. 5.1).

The Etruscan temple was similar to the Greek temple in its rectangular plan, raised podium, and peaked roof. Some temples were built with columns of the **Tuscan order**, which is the Doric order modified by the addition of a base. Nonetheless, the Etruscan temple differs from the Greek temple (see fig. 4.6) in several significant ways. For instance, the Etruscan temple has steps on only the south side, whereas the Greek temple has steps on all four sides. The Etruscan temple has a deep front porch, occupying much more of the platform than is occupied by the porch of a Greek temple. And the cella (enclosed part) of the Etruscan temple is divided into three rooms, further differing from the Greek temple plan.

TOMBS

Although Etruscan temples have disappeared, a significant number of tombs remain. Etruscan tombs were rich with weapons, gold work, and vases. As a result, like their Egyptian and Mycenaean counterparts, they were the targets of grave robbers. Scientific excavation of Etruscan tombs began only in the mid-nineteenth century.

The tombs are of two types: corbeled domes covered with mounds of earth, and rock-cut chambers with rectangular rooms. The most famous and most impressive of the rock-cut tombs at the ancient site of Cerveteri is the so-called Tomb of the Reliefs (fig. 5.2), of the third century B.C. The tomb is made of **tufa**, a type of stone

Figure 5.2 Tomb of the Reliefs, Cerveteri, third century B.C., interior. This exceptional tomb is believed to duplicate an actual Etruscan home in stone, even including pillows and pets. An entire family was buried here.

Figure 5.3   Tomb of Hunting and Fishing, Tarquinia, wall painting, ca. 520 B.C. This and other tomb paintings record the good life when Etruria prospered in the sixth century B.C. Later, as the economic situation declined, the outlook on the afterlife was less optimistic.

Figure 5.4   *Wife and Husband Sarcophagus*, from Cerveteri, ca. 520 B.C., terra cotta, length 6′7″ (2.01 m), Museo Nazionale di Villa Giulia, Rome. The deceased couple is shown as if alive, healthy, and enjoying themselves. The rounded forms are readily achieved in malleable terra cotta, unlike hard stone.

that is soft when cut, but hardens when exposed to the air, and tends to remain quite white. Such tombs were used for entire families. This one has places for over forty bodies. The interior of the Tomb of the Reliefs was designed to look like a home and provides a wonderful document of Etruscan life. The beds even have stone pillows! Roof beams are carved, and on the walls are depictions of weapons, armor, household items, and busts of the dead. The column capitals are similar to an early Ionic type that was brought to Greece from Asia Minor, which supports Herodotus's theory that the Etruscans originated in Lydia.

Other tombs were painted with scenes from everyday life. Particularly fine examples have been found at Tarquinia, where the subjects include scenes of hunting and fishing, banquets, musicians, dancers, athletic competitions, and religious ceremonies. The paintings in the Tomb of Hunting and Fishing (fig. 5.3), of ca. 520 B.C., in which fish jump out of the water in front of a man who attempts to catch them, and birds fly around a man who attempts to shoot one with a sling shot, convey a sense of energy and even humor.

This wall painting is presumably a view of the afterlife. Its optimism is also seen in Etruscan sculpture.

An early example is offered by a wife and husband sarcophagus, from Cerveteri (fig. 5.4), ca. 520 B.C. The sarcophagus, modeled in clay and once brightly painted, is shaped like a couch, with the deceased couple shown to recline on top; women and men were social equals. Like contemporary Greek statues, the pair have Archaic smiles (see Chapter 3). They are shown as if alive, comfortable, healthy, and happy, though they do not seem to be individualized portraits.

BRONZE WORK

The Etruscans were celebrated in antiquity for their ability to work in metal. Their homeland of Tuscany (which is named for the Etruscans) is rich in copper and iron and provided ample raw materials. From 600 B.C. onward, the Etruscans produced many bronze statuettes and utensils, some of which they exported. The most famous Etruscan bronze sculpture is the so-called *Capitoline She-Wolf* (fig. 5.5), of ca. 500 B.C. The two suckling babes were added only in the Renaissance. However, the she-wolf is authentic and has the energy and vitality characteristic of Etruscan art. A beautiful decorative surface is achieved by contrasting the crisp, curving patterns of the neck fur with the wolf's sleek, smooth body.

Although the work of an Etruscan artist, the statue has become the symbol of Rome. Its name, the *Capitoline She-Wolf*, derives from its long association with Rome's Capitoline Hill. Either this statue or another sculpture of a she-wolf was dedicated on the Capitoline Hill in 296 B.C., becoming in effect Rome's political mascot. The subject of the statue is connected with one of the myths

Figure 5.5 *Capitoline She-Wolf*, ca. 500 B.C., bronze, height $33\frac{1}{2}''$ (85.1 cm), Museo Capitolino, Rome. The Etruscans were famed in antiquity for their fine metalwork. With the twin infants, added in the Renaissance, this Etruscan bronze has become the symbol of Rome.

about the foundation of Rome. According to legend, the twin founders of the city, Romulus and Remus, were abandoned as children in the Tiber by a wicked uncle. By good fortune, they were washed up on the river bank, where they were discovered by a she-wolf, who suckled them. Subsequently raised by a shepherd, Romulus and Remus decided, in 753 B.C., to build a city on the Palatine Hill, above the spot along the river bank where the wolf rescued them. The auspicious founding of the city was marred by Romulus's murder of his brother during a quarrel, but Romulus went on to become Rome's first king, ruling for forty years.

Timeline 5.1 Control of Rome.

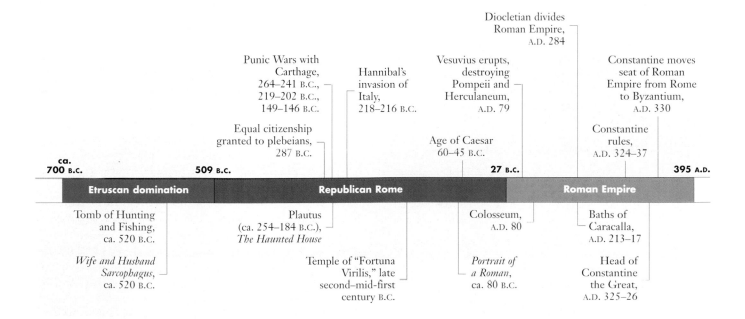

REPUBLICAN ROME

Beginning with Romulus, Rome was ruled first by a succession of kings and then, in 509 B.C., constituted itself a republic, which lasted until 27 B.C. Romulus himself is said to have established the traditional Roman distinction between the **patricians**, the land-owning aristocrats who served as priests and magistrates, lawyers and judges, and the **plebeians**, the poorer class who tilled the land, herded livestock, and worked for wages as craftspeople, tradespeople, and laborers.

At first, the plebeians depended upon the patricians for support. According to one ancient historian, each plebeian in Romulus's Rome could choose for himself any patrician as a patron, initiating the system known as **patronage**. "It was the duty of the patricians to explain the laws to their clients, to bring suits on their behalf if they were wronged or injured, and to defend them against prosecutors."

The essentially paternalistic relationship of patrician to plebeian reflects the family's central role in Roman society. At the head of the family was the *pater*, the father, and it was his duty to protect not only his wife and children, but also his clients, those who had submitted to his patronage. In return for the *pater*'s protection, his family and his clients were obligated to give him their total obedience and to defer to him in all things—an attitude the Romans referred to as *pietas*. The patrician males led the state as they led the family, contributing to the state's well-being in return for the people's gratitude and veneration. So fundamental was this attitude that by imperial times, the Roman emperor was referred to as the *pater patriae*, "the father of the fatherland."

THE REPUBLIC

Actual historical records documenting the development of Rome do not begin until 509 B.C., with the dedication of the Temple of Jupiter on the Capitoline Hill, but in the two centuries following Romulus's rule, the fundamentals of Rome's political, religious, and military customs were put in place. In truth, the development of Rome seems to have owed much to the Etruscans, who occupied it between 616 and 509 B.C. Prior to 616 B.C., Rome appears to have been very modest indeed. It was under the Etruscan kings that the boundaries of the city were gradually expanded from the Palatine to include all seven hills of Rome. The forum—the central political and social meeting place in the city—was established in the valley between the Palatine and Capitoline Hills, and a canal was dug to drain it. But apparently chafing at Etruscan rule, in 509 B.C. the Romans expelled King Tarquinius Superbus ("the Proud"), and decided to rule themselves without a king.

From 509 until 27 B.C., Rome was a republic based on the patrician/plebeian model in which every male citizen enjoyed the privilege of voting on matters of legislation as well as in elections of government officials. But from the outset, the republic was plagued by conflict between the patricians and the plebeians. There was obvious political inequality. The Senate, the political assembly responsible for formulating new law, was almost exclusively patrician. Thus, the plebeians formed their own legislative assembly, the Consilium Plebis, electing their own officers, called tribunes, to protect them from the patrician magistrates. Initially, patricians were not subject to legislation passed by the plebeian assembly—the plebiscite. Finally, in 287 B.C., however, the plebiscite became binding legislation on all citizens, whether plebeian or patrician, and something resembling equal citizenship was established for all.

At about the same time, Rome began a series of military campaigns that would, eventually, result in its control of the largest and most powerful empire ever created. By the middle of the third century B.C., Rome had established dominion over the Italian peninsula by creating municipalities and colonies in every region, offering land to plebeians willing to move. Beginning in 264 B.C., the city inaugurated a series of campaigns against Carthage, a Phoenician state in North Africa that controlled the wealthy island of Sicily, as well as the islands of Sardinia and Corsica. The Punic Wars ensued (from the Latin *poeni*, meaning "Phoenician"). When they ended, in 146 B.C., Carthage had been razed, and Rome had established an overseas empire, with control over the islands of Sicily, Corsica, and Sardinia.

As Rome moved in on the Hellenistic world, beginning in 146 B.C. with the invasion of Macedonia and Greece, both the dangers and rewards of military expansionism became increasingly apparent. The Carthaginian general Hannibal, who in 218 B.C. invaded Italy from the north, marching with his elephants over the Alps and laying the Italian farm country to waste as he burned everything in his path, had already revealed the real human cost of military conflict. But there were also vast monetary gains to be made from conquest—commercial opportunities in trading, shipping, business, banking, and agriculture that many Romans could not ignore. The Roman army had to adapt to meet the new challenge. It had traditionally been made up of citizen property owners, one of whose obligations was to defend the state. But citizens absent for long periods on military campaigns often returned to find their property taken over by others. Thus, in about 107 B.C., a general named Gaius Marius began to enroll men in the army who did not meet the property or citizenship qualification. These men saw military service as a career, and a professional army was soon in place. Each soldier served for twenty years and, when not involved in combat, was occupied by the construction of roads, bridges, and aqueducts. At the end of their service, they were given land in the province where they had served, as well as Roman citizenship.

The financial opportunities afforded by imperial conquest stimulated the growth of a new "class" of Roman citizen. Born into families that could pursue senatorial status, these men instead chose careers in business and finance. They called themselves *equites* ("equestrians"), probably because they served in the cavalry in the military—only the wealthy could afford horses—and they embraced a commercial world that their patrician brothers (sometimes quite literally their brothers) found crass and demeaning. By the first century B.C., these *equites* were openly in conflict with the Senate, pressing for greater and greater rights for both themselves and the plebeians. In an effort to quell rebellion, the Senate granted citizenship and equal status to all free men living on the Italian peninsula.

However, civil war between the senators and the *equites* erupted anyway. The general Lucius Cornelius SULLA [SOO-lah] ruled as dictator from 82 to 79 B.C., murdering thousands of his opponents and introducing a new constitution, which placed power firmly in the hands of the Senate. But all he finally succeeded in doing was exacerbating the situation. When the general Gnaeus Pompeius Magnus—Pompey the Great—returned to Rome in 62 B.C. after successful campaigns in the east, the Senate refused to ratify his settlements with the eastern provinces and, worse perhaps, refused to provide land allotments for his veterans. Pompey was outraged. In 60 B.C. he joined forces with both Marcus Licinius CRASSUS [CRASS-us], with whom he had suppressed the slave revolt of Spartacus in 71 B.C., and Gaius JULIUS CAESAR [SEE-zar] (fig. 5.6) to form the so-called First Triumvirate, an official alliance that used vast sums of money and the threat of civil war to dominate the Roman state. To cement the agreement, Pompey married Caesar's daughter, Julia, a year later.

But it was a tumultuous alliance. Realizing that military prowess was an absolute necessity if he were to continue in power, Caesar set off for Gaul (present-day France), which he quickly subdued. It was perhaps inevitable that Caesar could not long remain in happy alliance with Pompey and Crassus. When his daughter

Figure 5.6 Portrait bust of Julius Caesar, first century B.C., marble, height 38″ (96.5 cm), Museo Archeologico Nazionale, Naples. Like all Roman portrait sculpture of the time, the bust is stunningly realistic. Every anomaly of the facial terrain has been observed and recorded.

Julia died in 54 B.C., Caesar broke with Pompey, who in turn allied himself with the Senate. In 49 B.C., with Gaul under his control, Caesar decided to return home, it was feared with the intention of assuming absolute power for himself—in effect, becoming emperor. The Senate reminded him of a longstanding tradition that he should leave his army behind, but on January 10 Caesar led his army across the Rubicon River into Italy, and civil war began again. Pompey fled to Greece, where Caesar defeated him a year later. Pompey escaped

Timeline 5.2 Conquests of the Roman republic.

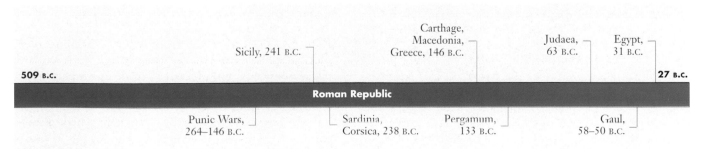

Cross Currents

THE ROMAN PANTHEON

The major gods of the Romans were essentially the same as those of the Greeks. In adopting the Greek gods, the Romans demonstrated in yet another way how the great military conquerors were themselves conquered by Greek culture. The accompanying chart identifies the deities of Rome with their Greek counterparts and their corresponding roles and responsibilities:

GREEK	ROMAN	ROLE/FUNCTION
Zeus	Jupiter/Jove	chief god/sky
Hera	Juno	wife of Zeus/Jove
Eros	Cupid	god of love
Dionysos	Bacchus	god of wine/revelry

Demeter	Ceres	earth goddess/grain
Persephone	Proserpina	queen of the underworld
Aphrodite	Venus	goddess of love and beauty
Ares	Mars	god of war
Apollo	Apollo	god of sun, music, and the arts
Artemis	Diana	goddess of the hunt
Hermes	Mercury	messenger of the gods
Poseidon	Neptune	god of the sea
Hades	Pluto	god of the underworld
Athena	Minerva	goddess of wisdom
Hephaistos	Vulcan	god of metalwork

There were, nonetheless, some important differences in the way the Romans viewed their gods. The Roman pantheon reflected the culture's political rather than spiritual values, and Roman gods tended to be less embodiments of various human virtues and foibles and more personifications of abstract ideas —love, war, and fortune, for instance.

The Romans also had a vast array of other, local gods. Every place, tree, stream, meadow, and wood had its own spirit. Unlike the gods of Greek origin, anthropomorphic, or human, characteristics were rarely attributed to these spirits. However, it was essential for, say, a farmer to keep on good terms with the spirit of his fields. Since so much depended upon annual water flow, the sources of rivers were especially venerated spots and were often decorated with numerous shrines.

once more, this time to Egypt, where he was murdered, and Caesar became dictator, not only of Rome, but of an empire that included Italy, Spain, Greece, Syria, Egypt, and North Africa. In 45 B.C., on the Ides of March—March 15—Caesar was stabbed twenty-three times by a group of some sixty senators on the floor of the Roman Senate at the base of a statue honoring the memory of Pompey. The people were outraged, the aristocracy disgraced, and Caesar martyred.

Caesar had been aware of the plot against him, and he had provided well for his adopted grand-nephew and heir, OCTAVIAN, not only monetarily—Caesar's military exploits had left him with a massive fortune— but politically. Octavian was only eighteen years of age, but he responded to his great-uncle's tutelage by acting quickly in the quagmire of the Roman political arena. He defeated his rival MARK ANTONY, Caesar's former supporter, in two successive encounters, and then adroitly formed a Second Triumvirate with Antony and LEPIDUS, an alliance so powerful that it quelled all dissent. Together Octavian and Antony went to war in the east, defeating Cassius and Brutus, two of Caesar's murderers, at the battle of Philippi in Macedonia.

The Triumvirate divided up the Roman world between them. Lepidus controlled Africa, Antony the eastern provinces, and Octavian the western provinces, including Rome itself. However, perhaps because Octavian kept Rome for himself, the other two rulers

soon plotted against him. When Lepidus challenged the young Octavian for power, Octavian managed to convince Lepidus's troops to desert their leader and join him instead. Lepidus retired, and Octavian doubled the size of his army. Meanwhile Mark Antony had pursued other republicans to Egypt and, after defeating them, formed an alliance with Cleopatra, Queen of Egypt, with whom he plotted Octavian's overthrow. When Octavian defeated Antony's army at Actium in 31 B.C., Antony and Cleopatra committed suicide. Octavian was now the sole power in Rome, the *pater patriae*, "father of the fatherland," and renamed himself Augustus, "the revered one." The constitutional government of the republic, which Julius Caesar had himself effectively ended when he took complete control after his return from Gaul, was finally and definitively overturned. And Octavian, now Caesar Augustus, was effectively emperor of the entire Roman world.

THE ART OF REPUBLICAN ROME

Roman troops conquered vast territories, bringing many different peoples under their domination. In turn, these peoples exerted an influence on Roman culture. In particular, Roman art was influenced by Greek art. The Romans conquered the Greeks militarily and politically, but the Greeks conquered the Romans artistically and culturally. As the first-century B.C. poet Horace put it, "*Graecia capta ferum victorem cepit*" ("Captive Greece conquered her wild conqueror"). Roman writers rarely make reference to Roman artists. Instead, they write about the Greek masters—Polykleitos, Phidias, Praxiteles, Lysippos. Roman authors refer to the Greeks as the "ancients"; Greek art already had the authority of antiquity for the Romans. The Romans not only imported Greek vases, marbles, and bronzes, but Greek artists as well, many of whom they then put to work copying Greek originals.

Yet Roman art is not solely a continuation, perpetuation, or amplification of Greek art. The Romans were very different from the Greeks, and their art is accordingly different in emphasis and focus. The Romans were impressed with great size—the size of their empire, of their buildings, of their sculptures. Above all, the Romans were a practical people. Their architecture shows them to have been superb engineers. Their sculpture and painting is realistic, with an emphasis on particulars—specific people, places, and times—a trend that continued until the second century A.D., when Christianity began to foster a more abstract and mystical direction.

Architecture. The Romans adopted the Greek orders—the Doric, Ionic, and Corinthian—but made modifications. Directly influenced by the Tuscan order of Etruscan architecture, the Romans made Doric columns taller and slimmer and gave them a base. The acanthus leaves of the Corinthian order were combined with the volutes of the Ionic order to create the **composite order**. The Romans used the orders with greater freedom than the Greeks, often taking elements from each for use on a single building. The Romans used the Corinthian order most, the Doric least—the opposite of the Greeks. Unlike Greek architects, Roman architects often used **engaged columns** (columns that are attached to the wall) on the inside and outside of buildings.

Much Roman building, like Greek building, was done with ashlar masonry, using carefully cut stone blocks laid in horizontal courses. But the Romans introduced new building materials and methods that were to have a lasting influence. In the late second century B.C. they developed a type of wall made by setting small broken stones in cement. Walls thus constructed were very strong and could be faced with different types of patterned stonework. This new construction method, as opposed to ashlar masonry, opened new directions in architecture, including construction using concrete, which consists of cement mixed with small pieces of stone. Concrete is strong, can be cast into any shape, and is far less costly than stone construction. The Romans did not invent concrete, but they did develop its potentials.

Roman rectangular temples have the same basic elements as Greek temples: cella, columns, the orders,

Figure 5.7 Temple of "Fortuna Virilis," Rome, late second to mid-first century B.C. The rectangular Roman temple form is essentially a combination of the Greek and Etruscan temple forms—compare to the Greek Parthenon (see fig. 4.5) and the Etruscan temple (see fig. 5.1).

entablature. This is seen in the Ionic Temple of "Fortuna Virilis," located in the Forum Boarium in Rome (fig. 5.7). This was built between the end of the second century and the middle of the first century B.C. and was probably dedicated to Portunus, the Roman god of harbors and rivers. Italo-Etruscan elements include the raised platform or podium, the entry on one end only by ascending a flight of stairs, a front porch that takes up about one-third of the whole podium area, and a cella as wide as the podium. As a result of the increased width of the cella, unlike the Greek temple, the Roman temple does not have a true peristyle and therefore cannot be described as **peripteral**—that is, it is not surrounded by a row of *freestanding* columns. Instead, it is **pseudoperipteral**, since the columns are engaged to the walls of the cella.

The Romans, unlike the Greeks, favored circular temples. A representative example is the Temple of Vesta in Rome (fig. 5.8), built ca. 80 B.C. Vesta was the goddess of the hearth and of fire. The temple is simple

Figure 5.8 Temple of Vesta, ca. 80 B.C., Rome. In addition to perpetuating the Greek and Etruscan rectangular temple, the Romans made significant use of the circular temple. Among the orders, Greeks used the simple Doric most, whereas the Romans preferred the ornate Corinthian order, seen here.

in plan and small in scale. Circular Roman temples were made of concrete and faced with brick or stone. The Corinthian columns here are tall and slender. The entablature is much reduced and the roof rests almost directly on the columns.

Aqueducts. A dramatic demonstration of Roman engineering is provided by the network of aqueducts the Romans constructed throughout their territories. An aqueduct is a "water tube," a device that uses gravity to move water from mountain springs to cities in the valleys below. Some of the aqueducts built by the Romans were many miles long, crossing valleys, spanning rivers, going over mountains and even passing underground. In Rome itself, beginning in 144 B.C., a system of aqueducts was built to bring water to all seven of the city's hills, paid for by spoils from the victory in Carthage.

The most famous and best-preserved of the ancient Roman aqueducts is known as the Pont du Gard (bridge over the Gard River) at Nîmes, in southern France (fig. 5.9), built between the first century B.C. and the first century A.D. The Pont du Gard is based on a series of arches, each arch being buttressed by the arches on either side of it. The water channel is at the very top and is lined with cement. Flat stone slabs were placed over the top to keep out leaves and debris.

Sculpture. The ancient Romans made extensive use of sculpture—on both the inside and outside of public and private buildings, on columns, arches, tombs, and elsewhere.

The Romans imported and copied Greek statues, and modeled their own sculpture on that of the Greeks. Roman sculpture reflects the earlier traditions so strongly that it has even been questioned if there was a truly Roman style. But the Romans did introduce something new—naturalistic portraiture. While the Greeks made statues of deities and idealized heroes, Roman sculpture focused on real people, particularly political figures.

The Roman custom of erecting commemorative portrait statues in public places dates back to the end of the period of kings and was very popular through the republican and early imperial periods. Eventually, there were so many that in the second century A.D. the Roman Senate tried to limit the number being put up.

The inclination of artists in the republican era to represent the figure without idealizing it is embodied in the *Portrait of a Roman* (fig. 5.10). The high level of realism evident here may have been assisted by the custom of making deathmasks, called *imagines* by the Romans. Shortly after death, a wax mask would be modeled on the

Figure 5.9 Pont du Gard, Nîmes, France, late first century B.C.–early first century A.D., height 180′ (54.9 m), current length approx. 900′ (275 m). Between 8,000 and 12,000 gallons of water were delivered to Nîmes per day through this aqueduct, which extended for thirty-one miles.

Figure 5.10 *Portrait of a Roman*, from the Palazzo Torlonia, Rome, ca. 80 B.C., marble, lifesize, Metropolitan Museum of Art, New York. This bust, remarkably realistic with its sunken cheeks and furrowed brow, documents every detail of personal appearance.

face of the deceased and was then sometimes transferred to stone. This greatly helped sculptors in portraying people as they actually looked. Republican-period portraits are brutally realistic. Every nook, cranny, and crevice is revealed, each irregularity, asymmetry, and anomaly recorded.

Republican-period portraiture seems to reflect the virtues lauded in the literature of this time: seriousness, honesty, and a straightforward approach to life. The character type most admired seems to have been stern and of unbending will and rigid moral virtue.

A Roman Patrician with Busts of His Ancestors (fig. 5.11), from the late first century B.C., also makes clear the great emphasis placed upon lineage by the ancient Romans. Masks of the ancestors of the deceased were carried or worn in funeral processions, and portrait busts and *imagines* of ancestors were generally displayed in homes. This man wears the toga, a garment fashionable in the republican era and documented in sculpture. The Etruscan and the republican Roman toga were made with less material than the later imperial-style toga. This earlier type was cut flat in a semi-circular shape, with no seams. Another garment of the republican era is the pallium, a rectangular piece of fabric. Statues can be dated based upon the type of toga or pallium worn and the way in which it is wrapped around the body.

Figure 5.11 *A Roman Patrician with Busts of His Ancestors*, late first century B.C., marble, lifesize, Museo Capitolino, Rome. The great importance attached to family and lineage by the ancient Romans, exemplified here in this austere sculpture, is one of the motivating forces in the development of highly realistic portraiture during the republican era.

LITERATURE

Like their counterparts in the visual arts, Roman writers owe an immense debt to their Greek predecessors. Although the efforts of Roman writers cannot be dismissed as mere slavish copies of Greek models, it is true that Roman writers never really matched the achievements of their illustrious forebears. For the most part, Roman poets used Greek genres, although satire appears to have been an authentic Roman invention. Roman playwrights sometimes adapted Greek plays, with varying degrees of ingenuity.

Lucretius. The greatest work of the Latin poet LUCRETIUS [loo-KREE-shus] (ca. 99–ca. 55 B.C.), the long didactic poem, *De Rerum Natura (Of the Nature of Things)*, is indebted to two Greek philosophers, Democritus and Epicurus. From Democritus, Lucretius borrowed the philosophy of atomism, which explains the universe as being composed entirely of tiny particles, or atoms. From Epicurus, Lucretius took the idea that the goal of life is to avoid pain and increase pleasure. Lucretius's poem attempts to clear the mind of superstition and ready it for reasoned discussion of the nature of things.

Catullus. Like the Greek lyric poet Sappho, CATULLUS [ka-TUL-us] (84–54 B.C.) wrote passionate love poems, one of which is, in fact, a translation into Latin of one of Sappho's most celebrated lyrics, "Seizure."

Reflecting daily life in first-century B.C. Rome, many of Catullus's poems are written in a racy colloquial style. Catullus also wrote twenty-five poems about his love affair with Lesbia. These demonstrate his range and show him at his passionate best. Catullus can also be moving in expressing grief, as his lament for the death of his brother demonstrates.

Roman Drama: Plautus and Terence. While Greek theater excelled in the grandeur of tragedy, the theatrical glory of Rome is its comedy. The two most important Roman comic dramatists are PLAUTUS [PLOW-tus] (ca. 254–184 B.C.) and TERENCE (195–159 B.C.). Terence's plays were aimed at an aristocratic audience, by whom he was subsidized, while Plautus wrote for the common people. Not surprisingly, Plautus is the more robust and ribald of the two. Although the plays of both dramatists are funny, Terence's wit is more cerebral than Plautus's, which more often elicits a belly laugh. Despite these differences, the works of both playwrights are adaptations of Greek originals.

Terence offers subtlety of plot for Plautus's farce; he provides character development and interplay for Plautus's stock figures; and he presents economical dialogue in place of Plautus's colorful word-play. Terence more obviously exhibits tolerance for his characters and appreciation for their mixed motives and muddled but often good intentions. He is more sympathetic toward the elderly, particularly the old fathers that Plautus ridicules. Terence is also more interested in women than Plautus, generally making them more complex and interesting characters.

Plautus's chief characters, those who run the dramatic engine of his plots, are typically slaves and parasites who turn the tables on their masters. With a notable lack of respect for authority, Plautus's characters flout social regulations, especially by undermining figures of authority. These include masters, fathers, and husbands. In Plautine comedy, slaves outwit their masters, sons fool their fathers, wives dupe their husbands.

The subversive dimension of Plautus's drama can be seen in the way filial loyalty is treated in *The Haunted House (Mostellaria)*. In the absence of his wealthy merchant father, Philolocles holds wild parties in the family home, and spends money profligately, egged on by the family slave Tranio. When the father returns unexpectedly, Tranio masterminds a series of outlandish schemes to avoid punishment for his actions. These include telling the returning father that his house is haunted and that he therefore should not enter. Tranio keeps up the deceit by involving the actors in ever more desperate ploys of quick-thinking outrageousness. In *The Haunted House* Plautus presents the opposite of the ideal relations that Romans believed should obtain between servant and master, and between father and son. The slave's shenanigans and the son's disobedient behavior disrupt the normative ideals of the culture, occasioning hilarity in the process.

But Plautus's subversion of Roman cultural values goes even further. It also includes blaspheming the Roman gods, which results in a questioning of the moral foundation of Roman society. Yet this irreverence and disrespect, the consistent undermining of moral values and religious principles, occurs only on stage. When the play is over, the Roman audience go back to being who they were in real life—noble, civil, obedient, law-abiding citizens of a restrictive Roman society.

THE EMPIRE
←

When Octavian, CAESAR AUGUSTUS (63 B.C.–14 A.D.), as he was soon known, assumed power in 27 B.C., he claimed to have restored the republic. In reality, however, he had complete authority over not only the Senate but over all of Roman life. By A.D. 12 he had been given the title *Pontifex Maximus*, or "High Priest," and when he died, two years later, the Senate ordered that he be venerated henceforth as a god. He was an emperor in all but name. Together with his wife Livia, who was herself an administrator of great skill, he created the conditions for a period of peace and stability in the empire that lasted for two hundred years. Known as the *Pax Romana*, the "Roman Peace," it was made possible in large part by

Augustus's sensitivity to the people that Rome had conquered. Augustus dispatched governors to all the provinces with armies to maintain law and order. But these armies, freed of the need to conduct wars, turned instead to building great public works—aqueducts, theaters, libraries, marketplaces, and roads. Trade was greatly facilitated, and economic prosperity spread throughout the empire. Rome, however, remained at the heart of this trade network. Addressing his words to the great capital in the second century A.D., Aelius Aristides, a Greek rhetorician, put it this way:

> Large continents lie all around the Mediterranean, and from them, to you, Rome, flow constant supplies of goods. Everything is shipped to you, from every land and from every sea—the products of each season, of each country, of each river and lake. If anyone wants to see all these items, he must either travel the whole world to behold them, or live in this city.

After nearly a century of political turmoil, Augustus's rule ushered in a new Golden Age. The art and literature of the Augustan period are regarded as the pinnacle of Roman cultural accomplishment.

The empire was so strong by the end of Augustus's reign that even a series of debauched and decadent emperors, such as CALIGULA [cal-IG-you-lah] (A.D. 12–41), who ruled for only four years before he was assassinated and who was probably insane, and NERO [NEAR-oh] (37–68 A.D.), whose fourteen-year reign ended when the Senate displaced him, could not destroy it. When fire devastated Rome in A.D. 64, burning the monumental center of the city, Nero blamed the Christians for the blaze, probably to divert public opinion from laying blame on his administration. Nonetheless, he seized the opportunity to rebuild the city on the grandest of scales, including erecting the Colossus, a giant statue of himself as the sun-god.

There were also some very able emperors. After the fall of Nero, the FLAVIAN [FLAY-vee-an] dynasty, consisting of three emperors, restored imperial finances. More successful still were the so-called "Five Good Emperors"—NERVA [NER-vah] (A.D. 96–98), TRAJAN [TRA-jan] (A.D. 98–117), HADRIAN [HAY-dree-an] (A.D. 117–138), ANTONINUS PIUS [PIE-us] (A.D. 138–161), and MARCUS AURELIUS [OW-REE-lee-us] (A.D. 161–180). Between them, these five ruled for eighty-four consecutive years, during which Rome flourished as never before. By A.D. 180 the Roman empire had grown to enormous proportions, extending from Spain in the west to the Persian Gulf in the Middle East, and from Britain and the Rhine River in the north to Egypt

Map 5.2 The Roman Empire at its greatest extent, ca. A.D. 180.

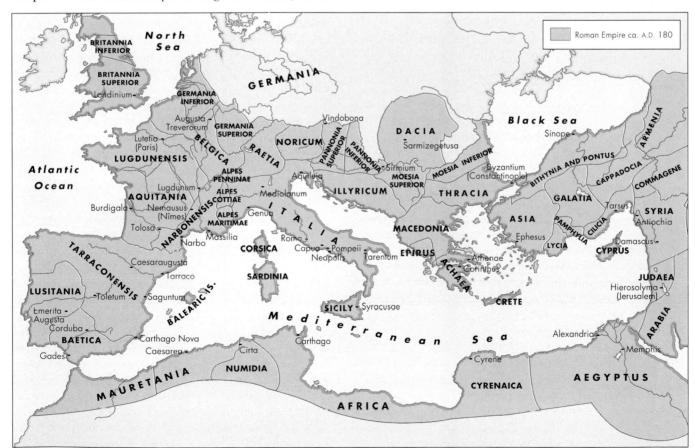

Timeline 5.3   The *Pax Romana*.

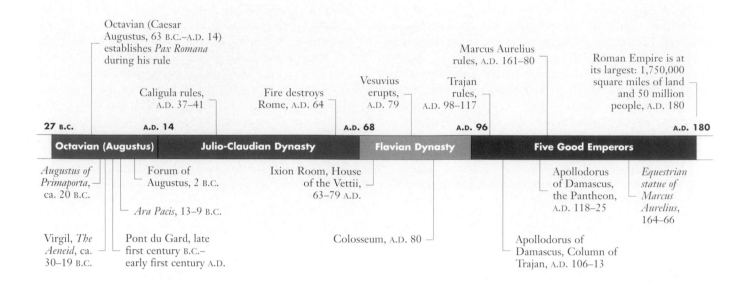

and the Sahara Desert in the south. It encompassed some 1,750,000 square miles and about fifty million people. Rather than chafing at Roman rule, the peoples of the empire longed to become citizens themselves. To satisfy this desire, citizenship was extended in A.D. 212 to all free people within the empire's vast borders.

However, beginning with the rule of Marcus Aurelius's son COMMODUS [coh-MODE-us] (r. A.D. 180–192), the empire started to flounder. Commodus was a tyrant whose murder inaugurated a series of civil wars. Of the twenty-six emperors to rule between A.D. 235 and 284, twenty-five were murdered. The Senate was powerless. The army acted only when it was bribed. Plague ravaged Rome—between A.D. 251 and 266 many thousands of Romans died from it. And, perhaps most ominously, the empire's borders began to be seriously threatened by barbarian hordes.

In A.D. 284, DIOCLETIAN [DI-oh-CLEE-shun] briefly restored order by dividing the empire into four portions—the **tetrarchy**—and assumed personal control of Asia Minor, Syria, and Egypt. His counterpart in the West was MAXIMIAN [mac-SIM-ee-an]. Each was designated "Augustus," and each appointed an heir, who held the title of Caesar and ruled lesser territories in order to gain experience. Diocletian's Caesar governed the Balkans, while Maximian's ruled Gaul, Spain, and Britain. At his headquarters in Nicomedia, Diocletian assumed the status of an Eastern king. He wore robes of blue and gold, symbolizing the sky and the sun. To affect an aura of heavenly inspiration, he sprinkled his hair with gold dust, and he sheathed himself in jewels. At all public appearances, he carried a giant golden staff, topped by a golden orb upon which

a golden Roman eagle perched with a sapphire in its beak. All present sank to the floor in obeisance until he was seated in his throne.

After the abdication of Diocletian and Maximian in A.D. 305, the tetrarchy briefly continued until CONSTANTINE [CON-stan-tine] seized control of the entire empire in A.D. 324, ruling until his death in A.D. 337. In A.D. 330, Constantine moved the seat of government from Rome to the port city of Byzantium, which he renamed Constantinople after himself—humility was not part of the job description of the Roman emperor (today the city is known as Istanbul and is in Turkey). Rome's long ascendancy as the cultural center of the Western world was at an end (see Chapter 7).

One invaluable source for our knowledge of the Roman empire was provided by a natural disaster. In A.D. 79, the volcano Vesuvius, located about 150 miles south of Rome near the bay of Naples, erupted, engulfing a number of small Roman towns, including the fashionable suburban residences of Herculaneum and Pompeii. Most inhabitants escaped—but with only their lives. Everything else was left in place, food literally still on the tables. Vesuvius buried Herculaneum in hot mud and lava that hardened like stone thirty-five to eighty feet deep. Pompeii was covered in twenty to thirty feet of pumice stone and ash. Excavation was begun at both sites in the mid-eighteenth century—a process that has been far easier at Pompeii, but which today is still not complete at either site and which has provided a great deal of information on first-century A.D. life in the Roman empire. Our knowledge of Roman painting, for instance, would be immeasurably poorer without the evidence of these towns.

DAILY LIFE IN IMPERIAL ROME

At the time Augustus assumed power, the city of Rome had about one million residents, making it the largest city of antiquity. Of these inhabitants, approximately ninety percent were of foreign extraction. Indeed, people from all Rome's colonies came to the city seeking Roman citizenship, which many were granted. Others were brought to Rome as slaves. Slaves in Rome performed not only the menial and back-breaking labor, but also served as bookkeepers, secretaries, and clerks. Many lived far more comfortably than those who were technically free.

Ancient Rome was notable for the extent and ingenuity of its water system. Eight giant aqueducts brought water streaming into the heart of the city, filling its hundreds of public fountains and supplying water for the kitchens, bathrooms, and private fountains of the wealthy. Water was not privately available to all, however. The financially less well-off, who lived in crowded and poorly constructed apartment blocks called *insulae*, fetched their water from public fountains in buckets. Inhabitants of these apartments also suffered from inadequate sewer facilities. Occupants of the upper floors of the apartment buildings typically dumped the contents of their chamber pots from the windows of the upper stories rather than carrying them down many flights of stairs for disposal in a pit or cesspool. Commenting on the Romans' habit of dumping all sorts of things from their residences, the satirist JUVENAL [JOO-ven-all] (ca. A.D. 60–140) wrote "You can suffer as many deaths as there are open windows to pass under. So offer up a prayer that people will be content with just emptying out their slop bowls."

Even with these inconveniences, Roman efficiency ensured that the streets were kept clean. An underground drainage system carried away waste and rain water; municipal street crews kept city streets clean and in good repair. In the best public toilets, which were cleaned regularly and flushed with rapidly flowing water, there were even marble seats, which were warmed in winter.

Following the devastating fire in A.D. 64, much of Rome had to be rebuilt. Streets, however, remained narrow, as they were before the fire. Many of them were also twisting, irregular, and illogically organized, which to this day makes driving in Rome dangerous and finding an address there an adventure. Juvenal also had some unflattering things to say about Rome's overcrowded and narrow streets, in which citizens could find themselves "hit by poles and elbows, buffeted by beams and barrels, and their toes trodden on by a soldier's hobnailed boot." It was also a city, in Juvenal's phrase in his Third Satire, where "the curses of drivers caught in traffic jams will rob even a deaf man of sleep."

The rich were not subject to such conditions. As Juvenal says, "Sleep comes only to the wealthy." Roman senators and their families would rise early in their peaceful villas, surrounded by walls painted with architectural and landscape views, as well as still-life images of animals and flowers, and walk upon marble and mosaic floors. Ornaments decorated shelves and window-sills, including images of Greek art and statues and busts of important ancestors.

The family took its main meal at home in the evening in the *triclinium*, a name derived from the three couches or benches upon which the diners reclined. Supporting themselves on their left elbows, they ate with their right hands, either spooning or fingering food to their mouths. Meals could last as long as three hours, sometimes even longer. Between the seven or more courses, wealthier citizens entertained their guests with acrobats, storytellers, musicians, and dancers. The food served might include oysters, snails, lobsters, capons, suckling pigs, veal, pheasant, asparagus, mushrooms, fruit, and cake. Wine flowed copiously.

Following dinner the guests might sit down to talk, drink more wine, and play games, or they might go out to one of Rome's many public baths, where they could congregate and gossip, wrestle, and play games. In addition to hot and cold pools, the baths had reading rooms, libraries, exhibition rooms, and promenades, even occasionally beauty parlors.

For entertainment there was also the Circus, the largest of which in Rome was the Circus Maximus. Here chariot races were held, with as many as a dozen chariots competing, drawn by anywhere from two to ten horses. The Circus Maximus was also a venue for daredevil riders and performers of other stunts and feats of skill. It could accommodate up to 15,000 spectators.

Great crowds would also fill the Roman Colosseum. Unlike in the Circus, here women were not permitted to sit next to men. Instead, they were exiled to the top story of the great amphitheater, where they shared an enclosed gallery with the poor. In the story beneath sat slaves and foreigners, with the bottom two of the four stories reserved for male citizens, who sat in marble seats. The main attraction for the crowds at the Colosseum was gladiatorial combat. These often fatal battles were punctuated with comic interludes of clownish displays. Other entertainment was provided by the slaying of thousands of animals and, during the reigns of Nero (A.D. 54–68) and Diocletian (A.D. 284–305), the slaughtering of Christians, who might be fed to lions, burned alive, or killed with arrows or swords.

The civilization of ancient Rome, then, was marked by different characteristics. On the one hand, there was the splendor of its marble buildings and its astonishing feats of organization and engineering; on the other, there were the crude entertainments of its Circuses and the cruelty of its Colosseum displays.

Figure 5.12   Roman Forum, Rome. A forum, a public area with markets, meeting places, and temples, was roughly the Roman equivalent of the Greek agora. The area of the Forum in Rome was expanded over many years.

THE ARCHITECTURE OF THE EMPIRE

Before Augustus took power, Sulla, Pompey, and Caesar had all inaugurated impressive building plans designed to celebrate their military exploits and victories. On the Capitoline Hill, Sulla had erected a giant temple of Jupiter Maximus in 83 B.C., importing its marble columns from the unfinished Temple of Zeus in Athens. Pompey completed Rome's first permanent stone theater in 55 B.C. Between it and the nearby temples, he created a vast enclosed green space of trees, fountains, and statues—the first public park. Caesar went even further, developing a new plan for the entire city, which included a large Forum Iulium, with colonnades, shops, and arcades, a new Senate House, and a basilica.

Augustus perpetuated this tradition. An active builder, he once claimed to have restored eighty-two temples in a single year. Suetonius's *Lives of the Caesars* says that Augustus boasted, "I found Rome a city of brick, and left it a city of marble," though he did so largely by putting a marble veneer over the brick.

The Roman Forum. One of Augustus's most ambitious projects was his forum, dedicated in 2 B.C. Augustus, a skilled manipulator of public opinion, gave political significance to this forum by dedicating its temple to Mars the Avenger. It was intended to serve as a reminder of the revenge he had taken on the murderers of his uncle, Julius Caesar, and the temple, with eight columns across its front, was one of the largest in the city, rivaling the Athenian Parthenon in size. The Forum of Augustus is actually one of many fora that are traditionally referred to collectively in the singular as "the Forum." The Roman Forum consists of nineteen fora—those of Julius Caesar, Augustus, Trajan, Nerva, a forum of peace, and so on—all abutting one another (fig. 5.12). The original use of the Forum was similar to that of the Greek agora. The Forum was the center of city life, serving as a public area where assemblies were held, justice was administered, and markets were located, with shops an important part of the Roman Forum. There were also a number of temples, such as two dedicated to Vesta, the Temple of

Saturn, the Temple of Castor and Pollux, and the Temple of Antoninus Pius and Faustina. Symmetry and order reigned within each forum, but the different fora combined were chaotic. The Romans, more cosmopolitan and materialistic than the ancient Greeks, built on a larger scale, using a greater variety of building materials, and paid less attention to minute details. The Roman predilection was for combining diverse elements in order to achieve a grand overall effect.

The Colosseum. Another form of public architecture was the theater. The celebrated Flavian Colosseum in Rome (fig. 5.13), so called because of its association with a colossal statue of the emperor Nero, was dedicated in A.D. 80, having taken up to ten years to build. The Colosseum is an **amphitheater**, a type of building developed by the Romans. The word "theater" refers to the semi-circular form. The prefix "amphi" means "both"; an amphitheater is a theater at both ends, and is therefore circular or oval in plan. The seating area of the Colosseum accommodated over fifty thousand people, each of whom had a clear view of the arena. To protect the audience from the brilliant Roman sunshine, an awning could be stretched over part of the Colosseum.

The supporting structure of the Colosseum is made of concrete, but the exterior was covered with a stone facing of **travertine** (a form of limestone) and tufa. Holes can now be seen in the stone where people have dug to get at the bronze clamps that held the facing in place. These stones hide the supporting structure. This is fundamentally different from the Greek approach to architecture, where the structure was not hidden but, rather, emphasized.

The exterior of the Colosseum is given definition by the entablatures that separate the stories and by the engaged columns that separate the arches. The three architectural orders are combined. The lowest level features the Tuscan variation on the Doric order; the second level is Ionic; and the third level is Corinthian. These columns are engaged (attached to the wall) and have no structural function. Anti-Greek in their use of the Greek orders, the Colosseum's columns cease to function as structural members. On the Colosseum, their only purpose is as surface decoration.

The practical Roman designers combined concrete structure with one of the other great architectural developments of the period—the arch principle. Arches are rare in Greek architecture; the Romans seem to have got the idea from the Etruscans. The visitor to the Colosseum can enter or exit through any of eighty arches around the Colosseum at street level. Each of these arches is buttressed by its neighbors and buttresses its neighbors in turn, as on the Pont du Gard. The interior is constructed with vaulted corridors and many staircases to permit free movement to a large number of people.

Figure 5.13 Colosseum, Rome, dedicated A.D. 80. The freestanding amphitheater, developed by the Romans, was made possible by the use of concrete and the arch principle. Compare this to the Greek theater of Epidauros where support for the seats is provided by the hillside (see fig. 4.18).

Figure 5.14 Apollodorus of Damascus, Pantheon, Rome, A.D. 118–25, exterior. A superb display of Roman engineering skill, the Pantheon includes a variety of ingenious devices to deal with the lateral thrust exerted by the dome. The paradigm of circular temples, the Pantheon would prove to be the model for many buildings in the following centuries.

A tremendous number of amphitheaters were built throughout the empire because it was official policy that the state should provide "entertainment" for the public. This entertainment fell into several categories of bloody combat: human versus human; human versus animal; animal versus animal; and naval battles—the Colosseum could be flooded to accommodate warships. The quality of this "entertainment" soon turned into a political issue, but the displays nonetheless became progressively more extravagant.

The Pantheon. Built between A.D. 118 and 125 in the reign of Emperor Hadrian and designed by the architect Apollodorus of Damascus, the magnificent Roman Pantheon (fig. 5.14) is a large circular temple dedicated to "all the gods" (the literal meaning of the word *pantheon*). Originally, steps led up to the entrance, but over the centuries the level of the street has been raised. Once there was also more to the porch; otherwise the Pantheon is very well preserved. In contrast to the Greek emphasis on the exterior of temples, the most important part of the Pantheon is the interior. One might almost fail to notice the enormous dome that crowns this building from the outside. Inside, however, the dome becomes the focus of attention and, because no columns are needed to support it, creates a feeling of vast spaciousness (fig. 5.15). The Pantheon was considered the most harmonious interior of antiquity.

Figure 5.15 Apollodorus of Damascus, Pantheon, Rome, A.D. 118–25, interior. A domed ceiling offers the advantage of an open interior space, uninterrupted by the supports required in the post and lintel system. The sole source of light inside the Pantheon is the circular oculus in the center of the ceiling.

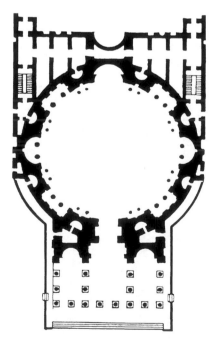

Figure 5.16 Apollodorus of Damascus, Pantheon, Rome, A.D. 118–25, plan. The enormous weight of the concrete dome is supported on a circular base with eight massive piers.

The dome is another of the great innovations of Roman architecture. A series of arches forms a **vault**. An arch rotated 180 degrees forms a **dome**.

The Pantheon's dome is raised on a high base, making the height and diameter of the dome the same—144 feet. The Pantheon was the largest dome until the twentieth century. The dome is made of concrete, the weight of which is concentrated on eight pillars distributed around its circumference (fig. 5.16). The **oculus**, the "eye" or opening in the center of the ceiling, is thirty feet across and is the sole source of light in the building. The squarish indentations in the dome, called **coffers**, were once plated with gold and each had a bronze rosette fastened in the center. The effect, with the brilliant sunlight of Rome coming from the central oculus above, must have been dazzling.

Baths.   The Baths of Caracalla in Rome (fig. 5.17), built A.D. 213–17), were once a massive structure, but are now largely ruined. The emperor Caracalla [ca-RA-cal-ah] (r. A.D. 211–217) based his baths on those built by his predecessors Titus and Trajan, but made his bigger than either of theirs. In general, it may be said that, just as emperors competed for the admiration of the people by financing ever more extravagant entertainments at the Colosseum, Roman buildings kept getting bigger as successive emperors tried to outdo the projects of their predecessors. Set in a walled park, the Baths of Caracalla form a large complex measuring over three hundred yards square. The entire plan is symmetrical, and includes three bathing halls with baths at different temperatures: the *frigidarium*—the cold bath; the *tepidarium*—the tepid bath; and the *caldarium*—the hot bath. A central heating system, a *hypocaust*, heated the floors and walls. The floors were supported by stone posts, and a fire was built beneath the floor. There were also many smaller side rooms, dressing rooms, exercise rooms, a *palaestra*—an open area for wrestling and games—lounges, and even a library. The baths were, in many ways, the center of Roman social life. A large portion of one's day could be spent here; business, reputable and otherwise. was conducted at the baths.

SCULPTURE

With Augustus's rise to power in 27 B.C., sculpture changed its style. Depictions of realistically rendered aging Republicans were jettisoned in favor of more idealized versions of youth, and an increased taste for things Greek. This change in taste was in part the result of Augustus's efforts to import Greek craftspeople and artists. In the new Augustan style, Greek idealism was combined with Roman realism.

Augustus of Primaporta.   The statue the *Augustus of Primaporta* (fig. 5.18), of ca. 20 B.C., is a slightly over-

Figure 5.17   Baths of Caracalla, Rome, A.D. 213–17, aerial overview. The bath was an important part of the ancient Roman way of life. The baths of Emperor Caracalla, enormous in scale, had all possible conveniences for the mind and body, including a library and exercise areas.

Figure 5.18 *Augustus of Primaporta*, ca. 20 B.C., marble, height 6′8″ (2.03 m), Braccio Nuovo, Musei Vaticani, Rome. Although this statue does record the appearance of Emperor Augustus, under his reign harsh Roman republican realism was somewhat softened by Greek idealism.

lifesize marble figure that was intended to glorify the Emperor and Roman peace under his rule. The statue is on the whole very well preserved, and many traces of pigment remain—the statue was originally painted. The face of the statue is recognizably that of Augustus; the same features are seen on other portraits of the Emperor, although here they are somewhat idealized. Augustus is shown to be heroic, aloof, self-contained. The prototype for this portrait is the *Doryphoros* (*Spear-Bearer*) of Polykleitos (see fig. 4.14); indeed, Augustus probably

held a spear in his left hand originally, but it has since been restored as a scepter. There is perhaps even a concession to traditional Greek nudity in showing the Emperor barefoot. The grand gesture with one arm extended—as if addressing his troops—was a common pose. The cupid riding on a dolphin beside Augustus's right leg is an allusion to Aeneas's mother, Venus, in Virgil's heroic poem, *The Aeneid* (see. p. 188), and suggests Augustus's own divine heritage. The relief on Augustus's cuirass (breastplate) is symbolic and refers to the *Pax Romana*, the peace and harmony that prevailed under his reign.

The Ara Pacis. At times the distinction between architecture and sculpture is blurred in buildings that are totally covered with relief sculpture, as in the *Ara Pacis* (*Altar of Peace*), built 13–9 B.C. by Augustus. Whether it is sculpture or architecture, however, it is undoubtedly the greatest artistic work of the Augustan age. Augustus billed himself as the "Prince of Peace" and this altar is a beautiful example of political propaganda.

The *Ara Pacis* is a small rectangular building. Among the extensive reliefs that adorn its sides is an imperial procession including Augustus and Livia (fig. 5.19). In their wake follow the imperial household, including children, priests with caps, and dignitaries. These figures move along both of the long walls of the altar, converging toward the entrance. The degree of realism achieved in this marble relief is striking. The depictions of people are varied—some stand still, others talk with their neighbors, or form groups, or look off in different directions; figures are seen from the front, from the side, and in three-quarter views. Drapery is skilfully rendered so that fabric falls realistically, yet also forms a pleasing rhythmic pattern of loops and curves across the whole relief.

Figure 5.19 *Ara Pacis*, relief of procession of figures, 13–9 B.C., height ca. 5′3″ (1.6 m). Augustus, now older, is depicted with his wife, Livia. Unlike the timeless, generalized, idealized Greek relief from the Parthenon (see fig. 4.9), the Roman relief shows specific people at a specific event.

An illusion of spatial recession has been created in stone relief. Figures in the front are a little larger than figures in the back, and are carved in higher relief. The different levels of relief create an illusion of space, so that any area left blank no longer looks like a solid wall but rather reads as actual space into and from which figures

Figure 5.21 Apollodorus of Damascus, Column of Trajan, Rome, A.D. 106–13, relief, detail of fig. 5.20. The long band of reliefs records Trajan's victories over the Dacians with documentary accuracy. Details of setting, armor, weapons, and even military tactics are included.

Figure 5.20 Apollodorus of Damascus, Column of Trajan, Rome, A.D. 106–13, marble, height with base 125′ (38.1 m). In spite of the obvious difficulty the viewer encounters in following a story told in a relief that spirals around a column rising high above, this was not the only such commemorative column erected by the Romans.

recede and emerge. A particularly clever illusionistic touch is the positioning of toes so that they protrude over the ledge on which the figures stand. It is as if the figures are genuinely three-dimensional and capable of stepping out of their space and into ours, adding to the immediacy of the work and to the illusion of reality that it creates.

The Column of Trajan. Columns, usually erected to celebrate a military victory, are another distinctively Roman architectural form. The emperor Trajan (r. A.D. 98–117) used art to show himself as an ideal leader, as the embodiment of valor and virtue. To this end, in A.D. 106–113 he erected the Column of Trajan (fig. 5.20) in the Forum of Trajan in Rome. The creator of the Pantheon, the Greek architect Apollodorus of Damascus, designed the column; the carving, however, was done by Romans. Upon his death, Trajan's sarcophagus was placed in the base, although barbarian invaders later took the sarcophagus for its gold and scattered the Emperor's ashes.

On top of the column there was originally an eagle. When Trajan died, his successor, Hadrian, replaced the eagle with a statue of Trajan. In 1587, Pope Sixtus removed the statue, melted it down, and recast the bronze into a statue of St. Peter, which now tops the column. The base is made of huge blocks with a square stairway inside, while a circular stairway consisting of 182 steps winds around the interior of the actual column. The surface of the column is covered with a continuous band of relief 656 feet long that makes twenty-three turns as it spirals upward like a twisting tapestry. As the column becomes narrower toward the top, the height of the relief band increases, presumably to make the upper relief easier to see from the ground. The relief consists of about 150 scenes and 2,500 figures.

The reliefs (fig. 5.21), reading from the bottom to the top, document an actual event—the military campaign of

Connections

THE ARA PACIS AND THE POLITICS OF FAMILY LIFE

Three generations of Augustus's family appear in the section of the *Ara Pacis* illustrated in figure 5.19. On the left, his head covered by his robe, is Marcus Agrippa. At the time of the carving he was married to Augustus's daughter Julia and was next in line to be emperor after Augustus, but he died in A.D. 12, two years before Augustus himself. Next to him in the relief is his eldest son, Gaius Caesar, who clings to Agrippa's robe. Augustus was particularly fond of Gaius and his younger brother Lucius. The two boys often traveled with the Emperor, and he took on important aspects of their education, teaching them to swim, to read, and to imitate his own handwriting. The proud grandmother, Augustus's wife Livia, stands beside Marcus Agrippa and Gaius Caesar. Behind her is her own son Tiberius, who would in

fact succeed Augustus as emperor. Behind Tiberius is Antonia, Augustus's niece and the wife of Tiberius's brother Drusus, at whom she is looking. Antonia holds the hand of her and Drusus's son, Germanicus. Drusus's nephew Gnaeus clings to his uncle's robe.

In the period before the *Ara Pacis*, there are very few examples of depictions of children in Roman public sculpture, a fact that raises an important question: What moved Augustus to include children so conspicuously in this monument? By the time Augustus took control of Rome, slaves and freed slaves threatened to outnumber Roman citizens in Rome itself, and they clearly outnumbered the Roman nobility. Augustus took this seriously and saw it as the result of a crisis in Roman family life. Adultery and divorce had become commonplace. Furthermore, the cost of maintaining a family was increasing. Consequently Roman families were becoming smaller and smaller.

Augustus introduced a series of measures to combat this decline in the traditional Roman family. He criminalized adultery and passed a number of laws designed to promote marriage as an institution and encourage larger families. Men between the ages of twenty-five and sixty and women between the ages of twenty and fifty were required to marry. A divorced woman was required to remarry within six months, a widow within a year. A childless woman, married or not, was required to pay large taxes on her property. A childless man was denied any inheritance. And the nobility were granted political advantages in line with the size of their families.

The *Ara Pacis* can be seen as part of Augustus's general program to revitalize the institution of marriage in Roman life. His own family, so prominently displayed in the frieze, was intended to serve as a model for all Roman families.

A.D. 101–03 to subdue the forces of Decebalus, prince of Dacia, present-day Romania. This was the first of Rome's wars against the Dacians. In the second, in A.D. 105–07, Trajan completely destroyed his enemy.

The story begins with a bridge of boats—a pontoon—and the crossing of the Danube River. A giant river-god looks on in approval. Just above, the Romans construct their military headquarters in Dacia. Higher on the column, the relief celebrates Trajan's ruthlessness in war. The Emperor ordered that no prisoners be taken, and the relief shows the beheading of several Dacians. At times horrifyingly frank, the Column of Trajan is a monument to realism and an invaluable document of ancient Roman politics, military tactics, and military life. As a reminder of the empire's might in war, it is also a great work of Roman propaganda.

The Equestrian Statue of Marcus Aurelius. The over-lifesize equestrian statue of Emperor Marcus Aurelius (fig. 5.22), of A.D. 164–66, became a favorite type of commemorative sculpture. This statue has survived to the present only because it was long mistaken for a portrait of Constantine, the first Christian emperor, and was thus spared the fate of being melted down as so many other "pagan" Roman bronzes were (for instance, the statue of Trajan on top of his column—see above). A philosopher-emperor, gentle and wise, who held Stoic

Figure 5.22 *Equestrian Statue of Marcus Aurelius,* A.D. 164–66, gilded bronze, height 11′6″ (3.51 m), Piazza del Campidoglio, Rome. This image became a model for future representations of military leaders.

is that Caracalla was so intent on power and authority that he had murdered his brother Geta to gain the emperorship.

Many copies of the bust survive—Caracalla must have approved of this image himself. It is as if brutality has become the very sign of power and authority. And the portrait set a style for the third century which emphasizes such animated and broken silhouettes. Although the carving is beautiful, with the vivid contrast between flesh and hair, it is no longer decorative.

Head of Constantine. The eyes of this head of Constantine the Great (fig. 5.24), the first Christian emperor, who ruled 306–37, gaze out into the distance like Caracalla's, but Constantine no longer seems to focus on anything in particular. Instead, in keeping with

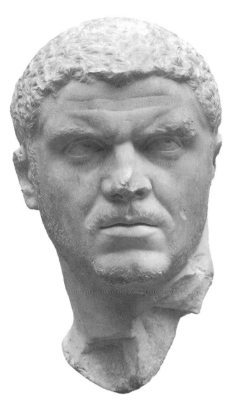

Figure 5.23 *Caracalla*, ca. A.D. 215, marble, lifesize, Metropolitan Museum of Art, New York. This bust records Emperor Caracalla's physical appearance, but goes beyond the superficial representation of the subject's facial terrain to reveal his personality—which was described as often angry.

Figure 5.24 *Constantine the Great*, head from a huge statue, A.D. 325–26, marble, height 8′5″ (2.58 m), Palazzo dei Conservatori, Rome. This image of Constantine, the first Christian emperor, impresses through enormous scale rather than photographic realism. With the spread of Christianity came a turn away from the factual and toward the spiritual.

beliefs, Marcus Aurelius is garbed in the traditional robes of the republican philosophers. He subdues his enemies without weapons or armor—originally, a barbarian lay beneath the horse's upraised hoof—and in victory brings with him the promise of peace.

Portrait Bust of Caracalla. A time of political revolution and social change, the third century in Rome was marked by continual strife at home and abroad and by a rapid turnover of rulers. The violence of the era is embodied in the portrait bust of Caracalla (fig. 5.23). The Emperor's real name was Antoninus, but he was nicknamed Caracalla after the *caracallus*, a floor-length coat, because he gave clothing to the people. In fact, his *Constitutio Antoniniana* gave everyone living in the Roman empire something that proved more lasting— civil rights.

But however generous he may have been, in the sculpture Caracalla seems to have been portrayed as the most brutal of despots. How has the sculptor accomplished this? Emphasis is on the eyes: The pupils are carved out and the irises are engraved. Caracalla gazes into the distance, but he seems to focus on a definite point. His forehead is furrowed, his brow contracted, as if in anxiety. The truth behind the portrait the spirituality of the times, he appears to be in a kind of trance. The head itself is over eight feet high, and was originally part of an enormous thirty-foot-high seated sculpture of the emperor, of which only a few marble fragments survive, among them a giant hand that points heavenward. Placed behind the altar of the Basilica Nova in Rome, it dominated the interior space. Constantine is both mystical and majestic. He is shown to be calm, capable, and composed by an image that is self-glorifying and self-exalting.

The Arch of Constantine. Constantine had come to power after defeating the emperor Maxentius at the Milvian Bridge, an entrance to Rome. The night before the battle, legend has it, Constantine saw a flaming cross in the sky, and heard these words, "*In hoc signo, vinces*" ("In this sign you will conquer"). The next day, he had painted on the shields and armor of all his men the Greek *chi* and *rho*, the first two letters of Jesus Christ's name (*chi* and *rho* were also a Roman abbreviation for "auspicious"). Constantine was victorious and became emperor,

and in A.D. 313 issued the Edict of Milan, granting freedom to all Christians and all other groups to practice their religions.

To celebrate Constantine's victory over Maxentius, the Senate erected a giant triple arch next to the Colosseum in Rome (fig. 5.25). Such triumphal arches, like columns, were characteristically Roman and were erected to commemorate military successes. Much of the decoration was taken from second-century A.D. monuments, and the figures changed to look like Constantine (fig. 5.26). The medallions decorating the arch were carved A.D. 128–38 during the time of Hadrian. In the medallion showing Emperor Hadrian hunting a boar, a variety of levels of relief create a sense of depth. Horses move on diagonals. Figures twist, turn, and bend in space. By way of contrast, the frieze below, carved in the early fourth century, had Constantine in the center, but he was later replaced by a figure of Jesus, and now the head is gone. A complete decay of the Classical tradition is evident here. No attempt is made to create space— there are no diagonals, there is no foreshortening, all the

Figure 5.25   Arch of Constantine, A.D. 312–15, Rome. The simple type of ancient Roman triumphal arch has a single opening; the more complex type like the Arch of Constantine has three openings. Typically Roman is the non-structural use of columns as surface decoration.

Figure 5.26 Arch of Constantine, north side, medallions carved A.D. 128–38, frieze carved early fourth century A.D., Rome. The contrast between the naturalism of the medallions and the simplified distortions and absence of interest in spatial illusionism in the frieze reveals major changes in Roman art.

carving is done to the same depth. The figures are not united in a common action. Instead, each figure is isolated. Rather than being depicted in the *contrapposto* pose, each figure has the weight equally distributed on both feet. Figures are indicated as being behind others by rows of heads above. The proportions of the figures are stocky and doll-like, very different from Classical Greek proportions.

PAINTING

Only a fraction of the paintings produced by ancient Roman artists remain. The small-scale portable paintings on ivory, stone, and wood are now almost entirely gone, though it is known that such paintings sold for high prices. Roman painting is generally assumed to derive largely from Greek painting, much as Roman architecture and sculpture were largely dependent on Greek models. Unfortunately, the extent of this dependence in painting cannot be very precisely determined. This is because, with a few minor exceptions, the only Greek painting to survive is on vases, while almost the only Roman painting to survive is found on walls in the form of **murals**.

The walls of private homes were usually painted. These paintings are almost exclusively decorative in intent. The best extant examples of ancient Roman wall painting were preserved in Herculaneum and Pompeii by the eruption of the volcano Vesuvius. A few examples that date from after A.D. 79 have survived in Rome, Ostia, and the provinces.

Ancient Roman wall painting was classified into four styles by the German historian August Mau in 1882. Although Mau's system continues to be used today, not all art historians are in agreement as to the dates at which one style ends and the next begins.

First Style. The First Style may be said to start in the second century B.C. and continue until 80 B.C. It is referred to as the "incrustation" or "masonry" style, since the paintings of this period are attempts to imitate the appearance of colored marble slabs. The wall surface in this example from the Casa di Sallustio at Pompeii (fig. 5.27), of the mid-second century B.C., is divided into

Figure 5.27 Casa di Sallustio, Pompeii, second century B.C. The first of the four styles of ancient Roman wall painting (a system of classification developed not by the ancient Romans but by a nineteenth-century historian) is readily recognizable. Also known as the "incrustation" style, the First Style consists of painted imitations of marble slabs.

squares and rectangles, which are painted to look like costly marble wall-facing. There are no figures and no attempt to give the illusion of three-dimensional space—the only illusion is that of costly building materials.

Second Style. The Second Style begins about 80 B.C. and lasts until 30 or 20 B.C. and is often referred to as the "architectonic," the "architectural," or the "illusionistic" style. In this period actual architectural structures, which were themselves colored, were copied in paint. An example of the Second Style is in the Villa of the Mysteries, outside Pompeii (fig. 5.28), which dates to the mid-first century B.C. One room here is especially famous, partly for the puzzle it presents. Many theories have been suggested to explain the activities depicted on the four walls of this room. The subject may have to do with a bridal initiation into the mystery cult of Dionysos.

The figures are solid and substantial, and almost all female. They move in a shallow space with green floors and red walls, which are divided up into sections. A novel feature in this room is that the figures act and react across the corners of the room, animating and activating the space of the room.

A more characteristic example of the Second Style is the *cubiculum* (fig. 5.29) from the Villa at Boscoreale, a mile north of Pompeii, built shortly after the mid-first century B.C. The bedroom of a wealthy Roman by the name of Publius Fannius Synistor, this room was at the northwest corner of a colonnaded court of the house. It

was buried by the eruption of Mount Vesuvius in A.D. 79 and was only redisovered in the late nineteenth century.

The walls of the room are painted with illusionistic architecture that creates a free prospect into space. The painter has extended the space of the room. The solid wall is obliterated. It has been suggested that this was inspired by stage painting—there are theater masks at the top. Vitruvius refers to the use of stage scenery as house decoration. Or perhaps this reflects actual contemporary architecture. Might this be a portrayal of an ideal villa? Could this be a visual retreat—the idea of escaping from daily cares into this fantastic architectural realm?

The wall is treated as if it were a window to an imaginary outdoor vista. Perspective is used, but it is not scientific or consistent. It is not possible to make a logical groundplan of this cityscape. What do the buildings stand on? Yet the light falls as if from the actual window in the back wall. The use of highlights and shadows is determined on the basis of the way the light would actually fall from this window and cast shadows.

Both the First and Second Styles evidence the Roman delight in fooling the viewer's eyes. Such realism was admired in antiquity. In his *Natural History*, Pliny says a certain painted decoration was praised "because some crows, deceived by a painted representation of roof-tiles, tried to alight on them." With different textures, with

Figure 5.28 Scenes of Dionysiac mystery cult, Villa of the Mysteries, outside Pompeii, ca. 50 B.C. Although the exact subject depicted in this room remains unclear, it seems to be connected with the cult of Dionysos, god of wine. Clever use is made of space, for the figures interact with one another on adjoining walls across the corners of the room.

marble columns that appear round, with painted colonnades on a projecting base, a fairly convincing illusion of three dimensions is created on a two-dimensional surface. The Boscoreale *cubiculum* is intended to trick the eye on a grand scale. The murals may be indicative of the villa owner's desire to amuse, to entertain, and, especially, to impress his guests.

Third Style. The Third Style dates from the late first century B.C. to the mid-first century A.D. The Third Style is variously known as the "ornamental/ornamented" style, the "capricious" style, the "ornate" style, the "candelabra" style, or the "classic" style. There

is a new concern with decorative detail here. The abrupt shift evident in the Third Style coincides with the reign of Augustus. It is a revolutionary style, reacting against the preceding one, rather than building upon it.

The Third Style places an emphasis on the wall surface rather than on illusions of depth (fig. 5.30). Walls are now often almost monochromatic, the range of colors restricted to red, black, or white. These large areas of monochrome seem to acknowledge the wall's two-dimensionality. Landscapes are no longer spread over the wall to create spatial illusions. Instead, landscapes are treated as framed pictures on the wall, as vignettes, like mirages, not located in depth behind the wall surface

Figure 5.29 Villa at Boscoreale, *cubiculum*, overview, first century B.C., Metropolitan Museum of Art, New York. In this example of the Second Style, also known as the "architectonic" style, an entire bedroom is painted with illusionistic architecture and distant cityscapes.

Figure 5.30   House of M. Lucretius Fronto, Pompeii, mid-first century A.D. In the Third Style, also known as the "ornamental" style, there is a return to a flatter effect with large areas of solid color and landscapes treated as framed pictures hanging on the wall.

but floating on the surface. These landscapes serve as settings for mythological stories. The surrounding flat fields of colors are painted with elaborate details of architecture, plant forms, and figures, delicate and decorative. The massive columns and architectural framework of the Second Style have given way to spindly non-structural columns.

Fourth Style.   The Fourth, and final, Style largely dates from the mid-first century A.D. or from the earthquake in A.D. 62 until the eruption of the volcano Vesuvius in A.D. 79, although there are extant examples that postdate the eruption of Vesuvius, in Rome, Ostia, and the provinces. The Fourth Style is the most elaborate of all and is known as the "composite," "fantasy," or "intricate" style. The technique is freer, sketchier, more impressionistic than the First, Second, or Third Styles. There is greater use of still life and landscape.

The Ixion Room of the House of the Vettii in Pompeii (fig. 5.31), painted A.D. 63–79, is typical of the Fourth Style. Within the Fourth Style are returns to "false" earlier styles. This example combines the simulated marble inlay of the First Style on the lower wall, the illusionistic architecture of the Second Style on the upper wall, and the framed vignette floating on a flat area of solid color of the Third Style. A completely painted fantasy is achieved. Figures and architecture are combined. What more could possibly be added to this playful and decorative ornament?

PHILOSOPHY

Stoicism.   Like so much else in the artistic and philosophical traditions of Greece, Stoicism migrated to Rome (see Chapter 4). From the second century B.C. through the period of the Roman empire, Stoicism was

Then & Now

GRAFFITI

The urge to write on walls is apparently as old as civilization itself. Before the invention of writing, for instance, prehistoric people outlined their hands on cave walls, as if to say, "I was here." In contemporary society, our national parks and monuments are plagued by this apparently basic human need to announce our presence, as generation after generation have inscribed their names and dates of visit on canyon walls and giant redwoods. One of the earliest records of the Spanish conquest of the American Southwest is preserved on Inscription Rock at El Morro National Monument in New Mexico. It reads, "Passed by here the Adelantado Don Juan de Oñate, from the discovery of the Sea of the South, the 16th April of 1605." It is the first of a long legacy of such inscriptions, culminating in the graffiti that today "decorates" so much of the local landscape—the so-called "tags," or names, of graffiti "writers" that vie for prominence on almost every wall of urban America.

The Romans, it seems, were themselves great practitioners of the "art" of graffiti. In Pompeii alone over 3,500 graffiti have been found. Among them is the normal fare: "Successus was here"; "Publius Comicius Restitutus stood here with his brother"; and "We are here, two dear friends, comrades forever. If you want to know our names, they are Gaius and Aulus." But the Romans were also adept at the kind of graffiti we normally associate today with "bathroom humor": "Gaius Julius Primigenius was here. Why are you late?" One wit apparently paraphrases Julius Caesar's famous boast "I came, I saw, I conquered," transforming it into "I came here, I screwed, I returned home." There are as well many graffiti of the kind "Marcus loves Spendusa" and "Serena hates Isidore" variety. But one writer sums up the feelings of future generations of graffiti readers: "I am amazed, O wall, that you have not collapsed and fallen, since you must bear the tedious stupidities of so many scrawlers."

Figure 5.31 Ixion Room, House of the Vettii, Pompeii, A.D. 63–79. The Fourth Style, also known as the "composite" style, combines aspects of the earlier styles: imitation marble incrustation; illusionistic architecture; and areas of flat color with small framed scenes.

the dominant Roman philosophy. The great Roman orator Marcus Tullius CICERO [SIS-ur-oh] (106–43 B.C.) and the dramatist and statesman Lucius Annaeus SENECA [SEN-uh-cuh] (ca. 4 B.C.–A.D. 65) commented on it, but Stoicism's two best-known adherents and practitioners were EPICTETUS [eh-pic-TEE-tus] (ca. A.D. 60–110), a Greek slave and secretary in the imperial administration, and Epictetus's student MARCUS AURELIUS, who reigned as emperor some years after Nero.

Like the Greek philosophers who came after Aristotle, Epictetus was a practical philosopher. His interest lay less in elaborating a metaphysical system than in providing guidance for living a life of virtue and equanimity. Epictetus exemplified the Stoic ideal in his own life, living simply and avoiding the temptations and distractions of the world as much as possible. He urged his followers in his *Discourses* to control what elements of their lives they could and to avoid worrying about those they could not. Epictetus accepted, for example, that he could not change the fact that he was a slave. What he could control, however, was his attitude toward his situation. It was this attitude, according to Epictetus, that determined one's moral worth, not one's external circumstances.

Unlike Epictetus, Marcus Aurelius was born into a wealthy Roman family. He succeeded his uncle, Antoninus Pius, to the imperial throne in A.D. 161. This was a time of great difficulty for Rome, which had suffered a devastating plague as well as incursions into its territories by barbarians. As emperor, Marcus Aurelius spent nearly half his life on military campaigns. It was during his military duties that he composed his *Meditations*, a series of reflections on the proper conduct of life.

The *Meditations* are more attentive to religious questions than Epictetus's *Discourses*. Like his Greek Stoic predecessors, Marcus Aurelius described the divine less in terms of a personal god in the Judaeo-Christian tradition and more as an indwelling spirit of rationality. Marcus Aurelius considered the entire universe to be governed by reason, and accepted the world as being fundamentally good. It is the ethical dimension of *The Meditations*, however, that has determined their popularity and influence. In preaching a doctrine of acceptance, Marcus Aurelius recommended that a person not return evil for evil, but rather ignore the evil that others did to one, since what happened to an individual's person and possessions was insignificant. According to Marcus Aurelius, only the soul, the inner self, counted.

LITERATURE

Poetry in the Roman empire flourished as never before under the rule of Augustus. Augustus himself appears to have been a significant patron of the literary arts and he encouraged writers to glorify the themes of his reign—peace and the imperial destiny of Rome.

Virgil. Latin poets celebrated Roman culture while emulating the cultural achievements of their Greek predecessors. The poet who best harmonized these two cultural and literary strains was Publius Vergilius Maro, known simply as VIRGIL [VER-jil] (70–19 B.C.), whose poem *The Aeneid* [ee-NEE-id] rivals the Homeric epics in literary splendor and cultural significance.

Virgil was almost certainly commissioned by the Emperor himself to write his great epic. There is much in the poem that is Augustan in theme.

The Aeneid is a heroic account of the events that led to the founding of the city of Rome and the Roman empire, especially the misfortunes and deprivations that accompany heroic deeds. The poem concerns the Trojan prince Aeneas [ee-NEE-as] as he flees his home as it is being destroyed at the end of the Trojan War and sails away to found a new city in Italy—the successor to the great Trojan civilization. Clearly Aeneas's new city is the forerunner of Rome, and the person of Aeneas in the poem is obviously in some degree intended to honor Augustus himself—the links between Augustus and Aeneas were alluded to by other artists (see p. 178).

It is probable that Augustus felt that his great empire should have a literary work to rival Homer. Like Homer's *Iliad*, Virgil's epic depicts the horrors and the glories of war. Like Homer's *Odyssey*, Virgil's poem describes its hero's adventures, both dangerous and amorous. In spite of Virgil's debt to Greek epic, however, *The Aeneid* is a thoroughly Roman poem. It is saturated in Roman traditions and marked at every turn by its respect for family and country. This can perhaps best be characterized by the term *pietas*, or piety. *Pietas* involves a devotion to duty, especially love and honor of one's family and country in the context of devotion to the gods. As he sails from Troy to Italy, Aeneas is shipwrecked in North Africa at Carthage, where he falls in love with Queen Dido. However, Aeneas is forced to leave the Queen when a messenger from the gods appears to remind him of his duty and destiny.

Horace. Among the other poetic genres important in Roman literature were the ode and the satire. The most important writer of **odes**—lyric poems on particular subjects made up of lines of varying lengths—was Quintus Horatius Flaccus, known simply as HORACE (65–8 B.C.). Of humble origins, Horace was freed from economic worry when he was befriended by Virgil, who helped him secure the support of Maecenas, a wealthy patron of the arts. Like Virgil, Horace was also encouraged to write poetry by Augustus. Horace's odes espouse a philosophy of moderation, which derives from earlier Greek culture. Horace's influence on English poetry was perhaps greatest from the sixteenth to eighteenth centuries, with one of his most famous poems, "Ars Poetica" ("The Art of Poetry"), being especially valued as a guide to poetic practice during the Renaissance and the eighteenth century.

Ovid. Augustan Rome's successor to Catullus, OVID [O-vid] (43–17 B.C.), wrote witty and ironic poems. The titles of Ovid's books reveal his persistent interest in the erotic—the *Amores (Loves)* and the *Ars Amatoria (The Art of Love)*. His most famous work, the *Metamorphoses* [meh-tah-MOR-foh-sees], is based on a series of stories about transformation, many derived from Greek mythology. These are often related with an erotic twist. Ovid's poetry combines skillful narrative with elegance and grace. In addition, Ovid is generally recognized as a subtle analyst of the human heart. Though ironic, Ovid's poetry is not cruel or sarcastic; rather, Ovid seems almost compassionate toward the characters whose experiences he describes.

Petronius. First-century A.D. Rome was a place saturated in material rather than spiritual values. The Roman emperor Nero set the tone with elaborate banquets, orgiastic feastings, and bloody entertainments. During Nero's reign, the satirist PETRONIUS [peh-TROHN-ee-us] provided a sharply realistic picture of the manners, luxuries, and vices of the age. **Satire** aims to bring about moral reform through making contemporary vices or habits appear ridiculous. The *Satyricon* [sah-TIR-ih-con], which is usually attributed to Petronius, depicts the pragmatic materialism of first-century A.D. Rome. Although only fragments of the work survive, the *Satyricon* nonetheless vividly conveys early Rome's veneration of material wealth and infatuation with physical pleasure.

In the longest extant section of the work, "Dinner with Trimalchio," an aristocratic narrator describes a meal he and his friends share with the slave-turned-millionaire, Trimalchio. The dinner conversation reflects the temper of early Roman civilization in the characters' selfishness, their anti-intellectualism, and their obsession with cheating one another. The satire is enhanced by means of numerous echoes of the Greek heroic traditions with references to Homer's *Iliad* and *Odyssey*. The ironic references reflect the Roman characters' distance from the heroic ideal as they live only for themselves and only for the moment. Already the idealism of Augustan Rome seems very distant.

READINGS
→

← VIRGIL

from *The Aeneid*

The first excerpt printed below represents the very first lines of Virgil's epic poem in which the destiny of his hero Aeneas is described: "so hard and huge / A task it was to found the Roman people." In the passage that follows from Book II, Aeneas has escaped from Troy after it has been devastated by the Greeks and has landed in Carthage, where he has met the queen, Dido. Here he relates to Dido the story of the fall of Troy, how the Greeks entered the city walls inside the infamous Trojan horse. There are Homeric references to Agamemnon's slaying of Iphigenia and to the fate of Priam, father of the slain Trojan hero Hector. The conclusion of Book II shows Aeneas separated from his wife Creusa, leading his father and son out of Troy.

from BOOK I

I sing of warfare and a man at war.°
From the sea-coast of Troy in early days
He came to Italy by destiny.
To our Lavinian° western shore,
A fugitive, this captain, buffeted   5
Cruelly on land as on the sea
By blows from powers of the air—behind them
Baleful Juno° in her sleepless rage.
And cruel losses were his lot in war.
Till he could found a city and bring home   10
His gods to Latium, land of the Latin race.
The Alban° lords, and the high walls of Rome.

---

[1] *a man at war:* Aeneas, a Trojan champion in the fight for Troy, son of Venus and Anchises, and a member of the royal house of Troy.   [4] *Lavinian:* Near Rome, named after the city of Lavinium. After the fall of Troy, Aeneas went in search of a new home, eventually settling here.   [8] *Juno:* Wife of the ruler of the gods (Hera in Greek). As in the *Iliad*, she is a bitter enemy of the Trojans.   [12] *Alban:* The city of Alba Longa was founded by Aeneas's son Ascanius. Romulus and Remus, the builders of Rome, were also from Alba. Latium is the coastal plain on which Rome is situated.

Tell me the causes now. O Muse, how galled
In her divine pride, and how sore at heart
From her old wound, the queen of gods compelled
   him—   15
A man apart, devoted to his mission—
To undergo so many perilous days
And enter on so many trials. Can anger
Black as this prey on the minds of heaven?
Tyrian° settlers in that ancient time   20
Held Carthage,° on the far shore of the sea.
Set against Italy and Tiber's° mouth,
A rich new town, warlike and trained for war.
And Juno, we are told, cared more for Carthage
Than for any walled city of the earth,   25
More than for Samos,° even. There her armor
And chariot were kept, and, fate permitting,
Carthage would be the ruler of the world.
So she intended, and so nursed that power.
But she had heard long since   30
That generations born of Trojan blood
Would one day overthrow her Tyrian walls,
And from that blood a race would come in time
With ample kingdoms, arrogant in war,
For Libya's ruin: so the Parcae° spun.   35
In fear of this, and holding in memory
The old war she had carried on at Troy
For Argos'° sake (the origins of that anger,
That suffering, still rankled: deep within her,
Hidden away, the judgment Paris° gave,   40
Snubbing her loveliness: the race she hated;
The honors given ravished Ganymede).
Saturnian Juno,° burning for it all,
Buffeted on the waste of sea those Trojans
Left by the Greeks and pitiless Achilles,   45
Keeping them far from Latium. For years
They wandered as their destiny drove them on
From one sea to the next: so hard and huge
A task it was to found the Roman people.

BOOK II

The room fell silent, and all eyes were on him,
As Father Aeneas from his high couch began:
"Sorrow too deep to tell, your majesty,

---

[20] *Tyrian:* From Tyre, on the coast of Palestine, the principal city of the Phoenicians, a seafaring people.   [21] *Carthage:* On the coast of North Africa, opposite Sicily. Originally a Tyrian colony, it became a rich commercial center, controlling traffic in the western Mediterranean.   [22] *Tiber's:* The river that flows through Rome.   [26] *Samos:* A large island off the coast of Asia Minor, famous for its cult of Hera (Juno).   [35] *Parcae:* The Fates, who were imagined as female divinities who spun human destinies. Rome captured and destroyed Carthage in 146 B.C. Libya is used as an inclusive name for the North African coast.   [38] *Argos':* Home city of the Achaean (Greek) kings Agamemnon and Menelaus. Juno was on their side when they went to Troy to retrieve Helen, Menelaus' wife.   [40] *Paris:* Son of King Priam of Troy. He was asked to judge which goddess—Venus, Juno, or Minerva (Athena)—was most beautiful. All three offered bribes, but Venus's promise (of Helen's love) prevailed, and Paris awarded her the prize.   [43] *Saturnian Juno:* Her father was Saturn, a Titan. Ganymede was a Trojan boy of extreme beauty who was taken up into heaven by Jupiter (Zeus), ruler of the gods.

You order me to feel and tell once more:
How the Danaans° leveled in the dust   5
The splendor of our mourned-forever kingdom—
Heartbreaking things I saw with my own eyes
And was myself a part of. Who could tell them,
Even a Myrmidon or Dolopian
Or ruffian of Ulysses,° without tears?   10
Now, too, the night is well along, with dewfall
Out of heaven, and setting stars weigh down
Our heads toward sleep. But if so great desire
Moves you to hear the tale of our disasters,
Briefly recalled, the final throes of Troy,   15
However I may shudder at the memory
And shrink again in grief, let me begin.

Knowing their strength broken in warfare, turned
Back by the fates, and years—so many years—
Already slipped away, the Danaan captains   20
By the divine handicraft of Pallas built
A horse of timber, tall as a hill,
And sheathed its ribs with planking of cut pine.
This they gave out to be an offering
For a safe return by sea, and the word went round.   25
But on the sly they shut inside a company
Chosen from their picked soldiery by lot,
Crowding the vaulted caverns in the dark—
The horse's belly—with men fully armed.

Offshore there's a long island, Tenedos,   30
Famous and rich while Priam's kingdom lasted,
A treacherous anchorage now, and nothing more.
They crossed to this and hid their ships behind it
On the bare shore beyond. We thought they'd gone,
Sailing home to Mycenae before the wind,   35
So Teucer's town is freed of her long anguish,
Gates thrown wide! And out we go in joy
To see the Dorian° campsites, all deserted,
The beach they left behind. Here the Dolopians
Pitched their tents, here cruel Achilles lodged,   40
There lay the ships, and there, formed up in ranks,
They came inland to fight us. Of our men
One group stood marveling, gaping up to see
The dire gift of the cold unbedded goddess,°
The sheer mass of the horse.
                    Thymoetes shouts   45
It should be hauled inside the walls and moored
High on the citadel—whether by treason
Or just because Troy's fate went that way now.
Capys opposed him; so did the wiser heads:
'Into the sea with it,' they said, 'or burn it,   50
Build up a bonfire under it,
This trick of the Greeks, a gift no one can trust,
Or cut it open, search the hollow belly!'

Contrary notions pulled the crowd apart.
Next thing we knew, in front of everyone,   55
Laocoön with a great company

Came furiously running from the Height,°
And still far off cried out: 'O my poor people,
Men of Troy, what madness has come over you?
Can you believe the enemy truly gone?   60
A gift from the Danaans, and no ruse?
Is that Ulysses' way, as you have known him?
Achaeans must be hiding in this timber,
Or it was built to butt against our walls,
Peer over them into our houses, pelt   65
The city from the sky. Some crookedness
Is in this thing. Have no faith in the horse!
Whatever it is, even when Greeks bring gifts
I fear them, gifts and all.'
                    He broke off then
And rifled his big spear with all his might   70
Against the horse's flank, the curve of belly.
It stuck there trembling, and the rounded hull
Reverberated groaning at the blow.
If the gods' will had not been sinister,
If our own minds had not been crazed,   75
He would have made us foul that Argive den
With bloody steel, and Troy would stand today—
O citadel of Priam, towering still!

But now look: hillmen, shepherds of Dardania,
Raising a shout, dragged in before the king   80
An unknown fellow with hands tied behind—
This all as he himself had planned,
Volunteering, letting them come across him,
So he could open Troy to the Achaeans.
Sure of himself this man was, braced for it   85
Either way, to work his trick or die.
From every quarter Trojans run to see him,
Ring the prisoner round, and make a game
Of jeering at him. Be instructed now
In Greek deceptive arts: one barefaced deed   90
Can tell you of them all.
As the man stood there, shaken and defenceless,
Looking around at ranks of Phrygians,
'Oh god,' he said, 'what land on earth, what seas
Can take me in? What's left me in the end,   95
Outcast that I am from the Danaans,
Now the Dardanians will have my blood?'

The whimpering speech brought us up short; we felt
A twinge for him. Let him speak up, we said,
Tell us where he was born, what news he brought,   100
What he could hope for as a prisoner.
Taking his time, slow to discard his fright,
He said:
            'I'll tell you the whole truth, my lord,
No matter what may come of it. Argive
I am by birth, and will not say I'm not.   105
That first of all: Fortune has made a derelict
Of Sinon, but the bitch
Won't make an empty liar of him, too.
Report of Palamedes° may have reached you,

---

⁵ Danaans: Greeks ¹⁰ Ulysses: Odysseus in Greek. Myrmidons and Dolopians were Achilles' soldiers. ³⁸ Dorian: Greek. ⁴⁴ unbedded goddess: Athena.

⁵⁷ the Height: the citadel ¹⁰⁹ Palamedes: A Greek warrior who advised Agamemnon to abandon the war against Troy; his downfall was engineered by Ulysses.

Scion of Belus' line, a famous man   110
Who gave commands against the war. For this,
On a trumped-up charge, on perjured testimony,
The Greeks put him to death—but now they mourn
        him,
Now he has lost the light. Being kin to him,
In my first years I joined him as companion,   115
Sent by my poor old father on this campaign,
And while he held high rank and influence
In royal councils, we did well, with honor.
Then by the guile and envy of Ulysses—
Nothing unheard of there!—he left this world,   120
And I lived on, but under a cloud, in sorrow,
Raging for my blameless friend's downfall.
Demented, too, I could not hold my peace
But said if I had luck, if I won through
Again to Argos, I'd avenge him there.   125
And I roused hatred with my talk; I fell
Afoul now of that man. From that time on,
Day in, day out, Ulysses
Found new ways to bait and terrify me,
Putting out shady rumors among the troops,   130
Looking for weapons he could use against me.
He could not rest till Calchas° served his turn—
But why go on? The tale's unwelcome, useless,
If Achaeans are all one,
And it's enough I'm called Achaean, then   135
Exact the punishment, long overdue;
The Ithacan° desires it; the Atridae
Would pay well for it.'
                Burning with curiosity,
We questioned him, called on him to explain—
Unable to conceive such a performance,   140
The art of the Pelasgian. He went on,
Atremble, as though he feared us:
                          'Many times
The Danaans wished to organize retreat,
To leave Troy and the long war, tired out.
If only they had done it! Heavy weather   145
At sea closed down on them, or a fresh gale
From the Southwest would keep them from embarking,
Most of all after this figure here,
This horse they put together with maple beams,
Reached its full height. Then wind and
        thunderstorms   150
Rumbled in heaven. So in our quandary
We sent Eurypylus to Phoebus'° oracle,
And he brought back this grim reply:

'Blood and a virgin slain°
You gave to appease the winds, for your first voyage 155
Troyward, O Danaans. Blood again
And Argive blood, one life, wins your return.'

When this got round among the soldiers, gloom
Came over them, and a cold chill that ran
To the very marrow. Who had death in store?   160

Whom did Apollo call for? Now the man
Of Ithaca haled Calchas out among us
In tumult, calling on the seer to tell
The true will of the gods. Ah, there were many
Able to divine the crookedness   165
And cruelty afoot for me, but they
Looked on in silence. For ten days the seer
Kept still, kept under cover, would not speak
Of anyone, or name a man for death,
Till driven to it at last by Ulysses' cries—   170
By prearrangement—he broke silence, barely
Enough to designate me for the altar.°
Every last man agreed. The torments each
Had feared for himself, now shifted to another,
All could endure. And the infamous day came,   175
The ritual, the salted meal, the fillets° …
I broke free, I confess it, broke my chains,
Hid myself all night in a muddy marsh,
Concealed by reeds, waiting for them to sail
If they were going to.
                Now no hope is left me   180
Of seeing my home country ever again,
My sweet children, my father, missed for years.
Perhaps the army will demand they pay
For my escape, my crime here, and their death,
Poor things, will be my punishment. Ah, sir,   185
I beg you by the gods above, the powers
In whom truth lives, and by what faith remains
Uncontaminated to men, take pity
On pain so great and so unmerited!'

For tears we gave him life, and pity, too.   190
Priam himself ordered the gyves removed
And the tight chain between. In kindness then
He said to him:
                'Whoever you may be,
The Greeks are gone; forget them from now on;
You shall be ours. And answer me these questions: 195
Who put this huge thing up, this horse?
Who designed it? What do they want with it?
Is it religious or a means of war?'

These were his questions. Then the captive, trained
In trickery, in the stagecraft of Achaea,   200
Lifted his hands unfettered to the stars.
'Eternal fires of heaven,' he began,
'Powers inviolable, I swear by thee,
As by the altars and blaspheming swords
I got away from, and the gods' white bands°   205
I wore as one chosen for sacrifice,
This is justice, I am justified
In dropping all allegiance to the Greeks—
As I had cause to hate them; I may bring
Into the open what they would keep dark.   210
No laws of my own country bind me now.
Only be sure you keep your promises
And keep faith, Troy, as you are kept from harm

---

132 *Calchas:* the prophet of the Greek army.   137 *The Ithacan:* Ulysses.   152 *Phoebus':* Apollo. Eurypylus was a minor Greek chieftain.   154 *a virgin slain:* Iphigenia, Agamemnon's daughter.

172 *the altar:* of sacrifice.   176 *fillets:* Tufts of wool attached to the victim.   205 *bands:* The fillets.

If what I say proves true, if what I give
Is great and valuable.
      The whole hope   *215*
Of the Danaans, and their confidence
In the war they started, rested all along
In help from Pallas. Then the night came
When Diomedes and that criminal,
Ulysses, dared to raid her holy shrine.   *220*
They killed the guards on the high citadel
And ripped away the statue, the Palladium,°
Desecrating with bloody hands the virginal
Chaplets of the goddess. After that,
Danaan hopes waned and were undermined,   *225*
Ebbing away, their strength in battle broken,
The goddess now against them. This she made
Evident to them all with signs and portents.
Just as they set her statue up in camp,
The eyes, cast upward, glowed with crackling flames,
And salty sweat ran down the body. Then—   *231*
I say it in awe—three times, up from the ground,
The apparition of the goddess rose
In a lightning flash, with shield and spear atremble.
Calchas divined at once that the sea crossing   *235*
Must be attempted in retreat—that Pergamum
Cannot be torn apart by Argive swords
Unless at Argos first they beg new omens,
Carrying homeward the divine power
Brought overseas in ships. Now they are gone   *240*
Before the wind to the fatherland, Mycenae,
Gone to enlist new troops and gods. They'll cross
The water again and be here, unforeseen.
So Calchas read the portents. Warned by him,
They set this figure up in reparation   *245*
For the Palladium stolen, to appease
The offended power and expiate the crime.
Enormous, though, he made them build the thing
With timber braces, towering to the sky,
Too big for the gates, not to be hauled inside   *250*
And give the people back their ancient guardian.
If any hand here violates this gift
To great Minerva,° then extinction waits,
Not for one only—would god it were so—
But for the realm of Priam and all Phrygians.   *255*
If this proud offering, drawn by your hands,
Should mount into your city, then so far
As the walls of Pelops' town° the tide of Asia
Surges in war: that doom awaits our children.'

This fraud of Sinon, his accomplished lying,   *260*
Won us over; a tall tale and fake tears
Had captured us, whom neither Diomedes
Nor Larisaean° Achilles overpowered,
Nor ten long years, nor all their thousand ships.

And now another sign, more fearful still,   *265*
Broke on our blind miserable people,
Filling us all with dread. Laocoön,

Acting as Neptune's priest that day by lot,
Was on the point of putting to the knife
A massive bull before the appointed altar,   *270*
When ah—look there!
From Tenedos, on the calm sea, twin snakes—
I shiver to recall it—endlessly
Coiling, uncoiling, swam abreast for shore,
Their underbellies showing as their crests   *275*
Reared red as blood above the swell; behind
They glided with great undulating backs.
Now came the sound of thrashed seawater foaming;
Now they were on dry land, and we could see
Their burning eyes, fiery and suffused with blood,   *280*
Their tongues a-flicker out of hissing maws.
We scattered, pale with fright. But straight ahead
They slid until they reached Laocoön.
Each snake enveloped one of his two boys,
Twining about and feeding on the body.   *285*
Next they ensnared the man as he ran up
With weapons: coils like cables looped and bound him
Twice round the middle; twice about his throat
They whipped their back-scales, and their heads
   towered,
While with both hands he fought to break the knots,   *290*
Drenched in slime, his head-bands black with venom,
Sending to heaven his appalling cries
Like a slashed bull escaping from an altar,
The fumbled axe shrugged off. The pair of snakes
Now flowed away and made for the highest shrines,   *295*
The citadel of pitiless Minerva,
Where coiling they took cover at her feet
Under the rondure of her shield. New terrors
Ran in the shaken crowd; the word went round
Laocoön had paid, and rightfully,   *300*
For profanation of the sacred hulk
With his offending spear hurled at its flank.

'The offering must be hauled to its true home,'
They clamored. 'Votive prayers to the goddess
Must be said there!'
      So we breached the walls   *305*
And laid the city open. Everyone
Pitched in to get the figure underpinned
With rollers, hempen lines around the neck.
Deadly, pregnant with enemies, the horse
Crawled upward to the breach. And boys and girls   *310*
Sang hymns around the towrope as for joy
They touched it. Rolling on, it cast a shadow
Over the city's heart. O Fatherland,
O Ilium, home of gods! Defensive wall
Renowned in war for Dardanus's people!   *315*
There on the very threshold of the breach
It jarred to a halt four times, four times the arms
In the belly thrown together made a sound—
Yet on we strove unmindful, deaf and blind,
To place the monster on our blessed height.   · *320*
Then, even then, Cassandra's° lips unsealed

---

²²² *the Palladium:* the statue of Pallas Athena.   ²⁵³ *Minerva:*
Athena.   ²⁵⁸ *Pelops' town:* Argos. Pelops was Atreus' father.
²⁶³ *Larisaean:* After Larissa, a town in Achilles' homeland.

³²¹ *Cassandra:* Daughter of King Priam of Troy. She was able to
foretell the future correctly, but because of a curse, no one
believed her.

The doom to come: lips by a god's command
Never believed or heeded by the Trojans.
So pitiably we, for whom that day
Would be the last, made all our temples green   325
With leafy festal boughs throughout the city.

As heaven turned, Night from the Ocean stream
Came on, profound in gloom on earth and sky
And Myrmidons in hiding. In their homes
The Teucrians lay silent, wearied out,   330
And sleep enfolded them. The Argive fleet,
Drawn up in line abreast, left Tenedos
Through the aloof moon's friendly stillnesses
and made for the familiar shore. Flame signals
Shone from the command ship. Sinon, favored   335
By what the gods unjustly had decreed,
Stole out to tap the pine walls and set free
The Danaans in the belly. Opened wide,
The horse emitted men; gladly they dropped
Out of the cavern, captains first, Thessandrus,   340
Sthenelus and the man of iron, Ulysses;
Hand over hand upon the rope, Acamas, Thoas,
Neoptolemus° and Prince Machaon,
Menelaus and then the master builder,
Epeos, who designed the horse decoy.   345
Into the darkened city, buried deep
In sleep and wine, they made their way,
Cut the few sentries down,
Let in their fellow soldiers at the gate,
And joined their combat companies as planned.   350

That time of night it was when the first sleep,
Gift of the gods, begins for all mankind,
Arriving gradually, delicious rest.
In sleep, in dream, Hector appeared to me,
Gaunt with sorrow, streaming tears, all torn—   355
As by the violent car on his death day—
And black with bloody dust,
His puffed-out feet cut by the rawhide thongs.
Ah god, the look of him! How changed
From that proud Hector who returned to Troy   360
Wearing Achilles' armor,° or that one
Who pitched the torches on Danaan ships;
His beard all filth, his hair matted with blood,
Showing the wounds, the many wounds, received
Outside his father's city walls. I seemed   365
Myself to weep and call upon the man
In grieving speech, brought from the depth of me:

'Light of Dardania, best hope of Troy,
What kept you from us for so long, and where?
From what far place, O Hector, have you come,   370
Long, long awaited? After so many deaths
Of friends and brothers, after a world of pain
For all our folk and all our town, at last,
Boneweary, we behold you! What has happened
To ravage your serene face? Why these wounds?'   375

He wasted no reply on my poor questions
But heaved a great sigh from his chest and said:
'Ai! Give up and go, child of the goddess,
Save yourself, out of these flames. The enemy
Holds the city walls, and from her height   380
Troy falls in ruin. Fatherland and Priam
Have their due; if by one hand our towers
Could be defended, by this hand, my own,
They would have been. Her holy things, her gods
Of hearth and household° Troy commends to you.   385
Accept them as companions of your days;
Go find for them the great walls that one day
You'll dedicate, when you have roamed the sea.'
As he said this, he brought out from the sanctuary
Chaplets and Vesta,° Lady of the Hearth,   390
With her eternal fire.

                   While I dreamed,
The turmoil rose, with anguish, in the city.
More and more, although Anchises' house
Lay in seclusion, muffled among trees,
The din at the grim onset grew; and now   395
I shook off sleep, I climbed to the roof top
To cup my ears and listen. And the sound
Was like the sound a grassfire makes in grain,
Whipped by a Southwind, or a torrent foaming
Out of a mountainside to strew in ruin   400
Fields, happy crops, the yield of plowing teams,
Or woodlands borne off in the flood; in wonder
The shepherd listens on a rocky peak.
I knew then what our trust had won for us,
Knew the Danaan fraud: Deïphobus'°   405
Great house in flames, already caving in
Under the overpowering god of fire;
Ucalegon's already caught nearby;
The glare lighting the straits beyond Sigeum;°
The cries of men, the wild calls of the trumpets.   410

To arm was my first maddened impulse—not
That anyone had a fighting chance in arms;
Only I burned to gather up some force
For combat, and to man some high redoubt.
So fury drove me, and it came to me   415
That meeting death was beautiful in arms.
Then here, eluding the Achaean spears,
Came Panthus, Orthrys' son, priest of Apollo,
Carrying holy things, our conquered gods,
and pulling a small grandchild along: he ran   420
Despairing to my doorway.
                      'Where's the crux,
Panthus,' I said. 'What strongpoint shall we hold?'

Before I could say more, he groaned and answered:
'The last day for Dardania has come,
The hour not to be fought off any longer.   425
Trojans we have been; Ilium has been;

---

343 *Neoptolemus:* Son of Achilles. 361 *Achilles's armor:* Hector stripped it from the corpse of Patroclus, whom Hector killed in battle. Achilles avenged Patroclus by killing Hector.

385 *Of hearth and household:* The Romans kept images of household gods, the Penatës, in a shrine in their homes; the custom is here transferred, unhistorically, to Troy. 390 *Vesta:* the goddess of the hearth and fire. 405 *Deïphobus':* A son of Priam. 409 *Sigeum:* A promontory overlooking the strait that connects the Ægean with the Black Sea.

The glory of the Teucrians is no more;
Black Jupiter has passed it on to Argos.
Greeks are the masters in our burning city.
Tall as a cliff, set in the heart of town,   *430*
Their horse pours out armed men. The conqueror,
Gloating Sinon, brews new conflagrations.
Troops hold the gates—as many thousand men
As ever came from great Mycenae; others
Block the lanes with crossed spears; glittering   *435*
In a combat line, swordblades are drawn for slaughter.
Even the first guards at the gates can barely
Offer battle, or blindly make a stand.'

Impelled by these words, by the powers of heaven,
Into the flames I go, into the fight,   *440*
Where the harsh Fury, and the din and shouting,
Skyward rising, calls. Crossing my path
In moonlight, five fell in with me, companions:
Ripheus, and Epytus, a great soldier,
Hypanis, Dymas, cleaving to my side   *445*
With young Coroebus, Mygdon's son. It happened
That in those very days this man had come
To Troy, aflame with passion for Cassandra,
Bringing to Priam and the Phrygians
A son-in-law's right hand. Unlucky one,   *450*
To have been deaf to what his bride foretold!
Now when I saw them grouped, on edge for battle,
I took it all in and said briefly,
                              'Soldiers,
Brave as you are to no end, if you crave
To face the last fight with me, and no doubt of it,   *455*
How matters stand for us each one can see.
The gods by whom this kingdom stood are gone,
Gone from the shrines and altars. You defend
A city lost in flames. Come, let us die,
We'll make a rush into the thick of it.   *460*
The conquered have one safety: hope for none.'

The desperate odds doubled their fighting spirit:
From that time on, like predatory wolves
In fog and darkness, when a savage hunger
Drives them blindly on, and cubs in lairs   *465*
Lie waiting with dry famished jaws—just so
Through arrow flights and enemies we ran
Toward our sure death, straight for the city's heart,
Cavernous black night over and around us.
Who can describe the havoc of that night   *470*
Or tell the deaths, or tally wounds with tears?
The ancient city falls, after dominion
Many long years. In windows, on the streets,
In homes, on solemn porches of the gods,
Dead bodies lie. And not alone the Trojans   *475*
Pay the price with their heart's blood; at times
Manhood returns to fire even the conquered
And Danaan conquerors fall. Grief everywhere,
Everywhere terror, and all shapes of death.

Androgeos was the first to cross our path   *480*
Leading a crowd of Greeks; he took for granted
That we were friends, and hailed us cheerfully:

'Men, get a move on! Are you made of lead
To be so late and slow? The rest are busy
Carrying plunder from the fires and towers.   *485*
Are you just landed from the ships?'
                              His words
Were barely out, and no reply forthcoming
Credible to him, when he knew himself
Fallen among enemies. Thunderstruck,
He halted, foot and voice, and then recoiled   *490*
Like one who steps down on a lurking snake
In a briar patch and jerks back, terrified,
As the angry thing rears up, all puffed and blue.
So backward went Androgeos in panic.
We were all over them in a moment, cut   *495*
And thrust, and as they fought on unknown ground,
Startled, unnerved, we killed them everywhere.
So Fortune filled our sails at first. Coroebus,
Elated at our feat and his own courage,
Said:
          'Friends, come follow Fortune. She has shown   *500*
The way to safety, shown she's on our side.
We'll take their shields and put on their insignia!
Trickery, bravery: who asks, in war?
The enemy will arm us.'
                              He put on
The plumed helm of Androgeos, took the shield   *505*
With blazon and the Greek sword to his side.
Ripheus, Dymas—all were pleased to do it,
Making the still fresh trophies our equipment.
Then we went on, passing among the Greeks,
Protected by our own gods now no longer;   *510*
Many a combat, hand to hand, we fought
In the black night, and many a Greek we sent
To Orcus.° There were some who turned and ran
Back to the ships and shore; some shamefully
Clambered again into the horse, to hide   *515*
In the familiar paunch.
                              When gods are contrary
They stand by no one. Here before us came
Cassandra, Priam's virgin daughter, dragged
By her long hair out of Minerva's shrine,
Lifting her brilliant eyes in vain to heaven—   *520*
Her eyes alone, as her white hands were bound.
Coroebus, infuriated, could not bear it,
But plunged into the midst to find his death.
We all went after him, our swords at play,
But here, here first, from the temple gable's height,   *525*
We met a hail of missiles from our friends,
Pitiful execution, by their error,
Who thought us Greek from our Greek plumes and
    shields.
Then with a groan of anger, seeing the virgin
Wrested from them, Danaans from all sides   *530*
Rallied and attacked us: fiery Ajax,°
Atreus' sons, Dolopians in a mass—

---

513 *Orcus:* The abode of the dead.   531 *Ajax:* The lesser Ajax, son
of Oileus, who raped Cassandra after dragging her away from
the shrine; as punishment, he was drowned on his way back to
Greece. This is not the great Greek warrior Ajax; he had
committed suicide before Troy fell.

As, when a cyclone breaks, conflicting winds
Will come together, Westwind, Southwind, Eastwind
Riding high out of the Dawnland; forests   535
Bend and roar, and raging all in spume
Nereus° with his trident churns the deep.
Then some whom we had taken by surprise
Under cover of night throughout the city
And driven off, came back again: they knew   540
Our shields and arms for liars now, our speech
Alien to their own. They overwhelmed us.
Coroebus fell at the warrior goddess' altar,
Killed by Peneleus; and Ripheus fell,
A man uniquely just among the Trojans,   545
The soul of equity; but the gods would have it
Differently. Hypanis, Dymas died,
Shot down by friends; nor did your piety,
Panthus, nor Apollo's fillets shield you
As you went down.
                        Ashes of Ilium!   550
Flames that consumed my people! Here I swear
That in your downfall I did not avoid
One weapon, one exchange with the Danaans,
And if it had been fated, my own hand
Had earned my death. But we were torn away   555
From that place—Iphitus and Pelias too,
One slow with age, one wounded by Ulysses,
Called by a clamor at the hall of Priam.
Truly we found here a prodigious fight,
As though there were none elsewhere, not a death   560
In the whole city: Mars° gone berserk, Danaans
In a rush to scale the roof; the gate besieged
By a tortoise shell of overlapping shields.°
Ladders clung to the wall, and men strove upward
Before the very doorposts, on the rungs,   565
Left hand putting the shield up, and the right
Reaching for the cornice. The defenders
Wrenched out upperworks and rooftiles: these
For missiles, as they saw the end, preparing
To fight back even on the edge of death.   570
And gilded beams, ancestral ornaments,
They rolled down on the heads below. In hall
Others with swords drawn held the entrance way,
Packed there, waiting. Now we plucked up heart
To help the royal house, to give our men   575
A respite, and to add our strength to theirs,
Though all were beaten. And we had for entrance
A rear door, secret, giving on a passage
Between the palace halls; in other days
Andromachë, poor lady, often used it,   580
Going alone to see her husband's parents
Or taking Astyanax° to his grandfather.
I climbed high on the roof, where hopeless men
Were picking up and throwing futile missiles.
Here was a tower like a promontory   585

Rising toward the stars above the roof:
All Troy, the Danaan ships, the Achaean camp,
Were visible from this. Now close beside it
With crowbars, where the flooring made loose joints,
We pried it from its bed and pushed it over.   590
Down with a rending crash in sudden ruin
Wide over the Danaan lines it fell;
But fresh troops moved up, and the rain of stones
With every kind of missile never ceased.

Just at the outer doors of the vestibule   595
Sprang Pyrrhus,° all in bronze and glittering,
As a serpent, hidden swollen underground
By a cold winter, writhes into the light,
On vile grass fed, his old skin cast away,
Renewed and glossy, rolling slippery coils,   600
With lifted underbelly rearing sunward
And triple tongue a-flicker. Close beside him
Giant Periphas and Automedon,
His armor-bearer, once Achilles' driver,
Besieged the place with all the young of Scyros,°   605
Hurling their torches at the palace roof.
Pyrrhus shouldering forward with an axe
Broke down the stony threshold, forced apart
Hinges and brazen door-jambs, and chopped through
One panel of the door, splitting the oak,   610
To make a window, a great breach. And there
Before their eyes the inner halls lay open,
The courts of Priam and the ancient kings,
With men-at-arms ranked in the vestibule.
From the interior came sounds of weeping,   615
Pitiful commotion, wails of women
High-pitched, rising in the formal chambers
To ring against the silent golden stars;
And, through the palace, mothers wild with fright
Ran to and fro or clung to doors and kissed them.   620
Pyrrhus with his father's brawn stormed on,
No bolts or bars or men availed to stop him:
Under his battering the double doors
Were torn out of their sockets and fell inward.
Sheer force cleared the way: the Greeks broke
        through   625
Into the vestibule, cut down the guards,
And made the wide hall seethe with men-at-arms—
A tumult greater than when dykes are burst
And a foaming river, swirling out in flood,
Whelms every parapet and races on   630
Through fields and over all the lowland plains,
Bearing off pens and cattle. I myself
Saw Neoptolemus furious with blood
In the entrance way, and saw the two Atridae;
Hecuba° I saw, and her hundred daughters,   635
Priam before the altars, with his blood
Drenching the fires that he himself had blessed.
Those fifty bridal chambers, hope of a line
So flourishing; those doorways high and proud,
Adorned with takings of barbaric gold,   640

---

⁵³⁷ *Nereus:* An old sea god and the father of the Nereids, the sea nymphs.   ⁵⁶¹ *Mars:* The war god (Ares in Greek). ⁵⁶³ *overlapping shields:* When attacking a walled position, Roman soldiers protected themselves from overhead missiles by holding their shields above their heads, forming a "roof," which looked like the plates of a tortoiseshell.   ⁵⁸² *Astyanax:* Son of Andromachë and Hector.

⁵⁹⁶ *Pyrrhus:* Neoptolemus.   ⁶⁰⁵ *Scyros:* The island in the north Aegean where Neoptolemus grew up.   ⁶³⁵ *Hecuba:* Mother of Hector.

Were all brought low: fire had them, or the Greeks.

What was the fate of Priam, you may ask.
Seeing his city captive, seeing his own
Royal portals rent apart, his enemies
In the inner rooms, the old man uselessly   645
Put on his shoulders, shaking with old age,
Armor unused for years, belted a sword on,
And made for the massed enemy to die.
Under the open sky in a central court
Stood a big altar; near it, a laurel tree   650
Of great age, leaning over, in deep shade
Embowered the Penatës. At this altar
Hecuba and her daughters, like white doves
Blown down in a black storm, clung together,
Enfolding holy images in their arms.   655
Now, seeing Priam in a young man's gear,
She called out:
            'My poor husband, what mad thought
Drove you to buckle on these weapons?
Where are you trying to go? The time is past
For help like this, for this kind of defending,   660
Even if my own Hector could be here.
Come to me now: the altar will protect us,
Or else you'll die with us.'
                        She drew him close,
Heavy with years, and made a place for him
To rest on the consecrated stone.
                        Now see   665
Politës, one of Priam's sons, escaped
From Pyrrhus' butchery and on the run
Through enemies and spears, down colonnades,
Through empty courtyards, wounded. Close behind
Comes Pyrrhus burning for the death-stroke: has
        him,   670
Catches him now, and lunges with the spear.
The boy has reached his parents, and before them
Goes down, pouring out his life with blood.
Now Priam, in the very midst of death,
Would neither hold his peace nor spare his anger.   675
'For what you've done, for what you've dared,' he said,
'If there is care in heaven for atrocity,
May the gods render fitting thanks, reward you
As you deserve. You forced me to look on
At the destruction of my son: defiled   680
A father's eyes with death. That great Achilles
You claim to be the son of—and you lie—
Was not like you to Priam, his enemy;
To me who threw myself upon his mercy
He showed compunction, gave me back for burial   685
The bloodless corpse of Hector, and returned me
To my own realm.'
                        The old man threw his spear
With feeble impact; blocked by the ringing bronze,
It hung there harmless from the jutting boss.
Then Pyrrhus answered:
                        'You'll report the news   690
To Pelidës,° my father; don't forget

My sad behavior, the degeneracy
Of Neoptolemus. Now die.'
                        With this,
To the altar step itself he dragged him trembling,
Slipping in the pooled blood of his son,   695
And took him by the hair with his left hand.
The sword flashed in his right; up to the hilt
He thrust it in his body.
                        That was the end
Of Priam's age, the doom that took him off,
With Troy in flames before his eyes, his towers   700
Headlong fallen—he that in other days
Had ruled in pride so many lands and peoples,
The power of Asia.
                        On the distant shore
The vast trunk headless lies without a name.

For the first time that night, inhuman shuddering   705
Took me, head to foot. I stood unmanned,
And my dear father's image came to mind
As our king, just his age, mortally wounded,
Gasped his life away before my eyes.
Creusa° came to mind, too, left alone;   710
The house plundered; danger to little Iulus.
I looked around to take stock of my men,
But all had left me, utterly played out,
Giving their beaten bodies to the fire
Or plunging from the roof.
                        It came to this,   715
That I stood there alone. And then I saw
Lurking beyond the doorsill of the Vesta,
In hiding, silent, in that place reserved,
The daughter of Tyndareus.° Glare of fires
Lighted my steps this way and that, my eyes   720
Glancing over the whole scene, everywhere.
That woman, terrified of the Trojans' hate
For the city overthrown, terrified too
Of Danaan vengeance, her abandoned husband's
Anger after years—Helen, that Fury   725
Both to her own homeland and Troy, had gone
To earth, a hated thing, before the altars.
Now fires blazed up in my own spirit—
A passion to avenge my fallen town
And punish Helen's whorishness.
                        'Shall this one   730
Look untouched on Sparta and Mycenae
After her triumph, going like a queen,
And see her home and husband, kin and children,
With Trojan girls for escort, Phrygian slaves?
Must Priam perish by the sword for this?   735
Troy burn, for this? Dardania's littoral
Be soaked in blood, so many times, for this?
Not by my leave. I know
No glory comes of punishing a woman,
The feat can bring no honor. Still, I'll be   740
Approved for snuffing out a monstrous life,
For a just sentence carried out. My heart
Will teem with joy in this avenging fire,

---

690 *Pelidës:* Achilles, son of Peleus.

710 *Creusa:* Aeneas's wife.   719 *daughter of Tyndareus:* Helen.

And the ashes of my kin will be appeased.'

So ran my thoughts, I turned wildly upon her,   745
But at that moment, clear, before my eyes—
Never before so clear—in a pure light
Stepping before me, radiant through the night,
My loving mother came: immortal, tall,   750
And lovely as the lords of heaven know her.
Catching me by the hand, she held me back,
Then with her rose-red mouth reproved me:
                               'Son,
Why let such suffering goad you on to fury
Past control? Where is your thoughtfulness
For me, for us? Will you not first revisit   755
The place you left your father, worn and old,
Or find out if your wife, Creusa, lives,
And the young boy, Ascanius—all these
Cut off by Greek troops foraging everywhere?
Had I not cared for them, fire would by now   760
Have taken them, their blood glutted the sword.
You must not hold the woman of Laconia,°
That hated face, the cause of this, nor Paris.
The harsh will of the gods it is, the gods,
That overthrows the splendor of this place   765
And brings Troy from her height into the dust.
Look over there: I'll tear away the cloud
That curtains you, and films your mortal sight,
The fog around you.—Have no fear of doing
Your mother's will, or balk at obeying her.—   770
Look: where you see high masonry thrown down,
Stone torn from stone, with billowing smoke and dust,
Neptune is shaking from their beds the walls
That his great trident pried up, undermining,
Toppling the whole city down. And look: 775
Juno in all her savagery holds
The Scaean Gates,° and raging in steel armor
Calls her allied army from the ships.
Up on the citadel—turn, look—Pallas Tritonia
Couched in a stormcloud, lightening, with her
      Gorgon!°   780
The Father himself empowers the Danaans,
Urges assaulting gods on the defenders.
Away, child; put an end to toiling so.
I shall be near, to see you safely home.'

She hid herself in the deep gloom of night,   785
And now the dire forms appeared to me
Of great immortals, enemies of Troy.
I knew the end then: Ilium was going down
In fire, the Troy of Neptune° going down,
As in high mountains when the countrymen   790
Have notched an ancient ash, then make their axes
Ring with might and main, chopping away
To fell the tree—ever on the point of falling,
Shaken through all its foliage, and the treetop
Nodding; bit by bit the strokes prevail   795

Until it gives a final groan at last
And crashes down in ruin from the height.

Now I descended where the goddess guided,
Clear of the flames, and clear of enemies,
For both retired; so gained my father's door,   800
My ancient home. I looked for him at once,
My first wish being to help him to the mountains;
But with Troy gone he set his face against it,
Not to prolong his life, or suffer exile.

'The rest of you, all in your prime,' he said,   805
'Make your escape; you are still hale and strong.
If heaven's lords had wished me a longer span
They would have saved this home for me. I call it
More than enough that once before I saw
My city taken and wrecked,° and went on living.   810
Here is my death bed, here. Take leave of me.
Depart now. I'll find death with my sword arm.
The enemy will oblige; they'll come for spoils.
Burial can be dispensed with. All these years
I've lingered in my impotence, at odds   815
With heaven, since the Father of gods and men
Breathed high winds of thunderbolt upon me
And touched me with his fire.'°   He spoke on
In the same vein, inflexible. The rest of us,
Creusa and Ascanius and the servants,   820
Begged him in tears not to pull down with him
Our lives as well, adding his own dead weight
To the fates' pressure. But he would not budge,
He held to his resolve and to his chair.
I felt swept off again to fight, in misery   825
Longing for death. What choices now were open,
What chance had I?
             'Did you suppose, my father,
That I could tear myself away and leave you?
Unthinkable; how could a father say it?
Now if it please the powers above that nothing   830
Stand of this great city; if your heart
Is set on adding your own death and ours
To that of Troy, the door's wide open for it:
Pyrrhus will be here, splashed with Priam's blood;
He kills the son before his father's eyes,   835
The father at the altars.
              My dear mother,
Was it for this, through spears and fire, you brought
    me,
To see the enemy deep in my house,
To see my son, Ascanius, my father,
And near them both, Creusa,   840
Butchered in one another's blood? My gear,
Men, bring my gear. The last night calls the conquered.
Give me back to the Greeks. Let me take up
The combat once again. We shall not all
Die this day unavenged.'
              I buckled on   845

---

762 *woman of Laconia:* Helen. 777 *Scaean Gates:* One of the principal entrances to Troy. 780 *Gorgon:* Monster whose appearance turned people to stone; Athena had a Gorgon face on her shield. 789 Neptune was hostile to Troy.

810 *My city taken and wrecked:* By the hero Heracles. 818 Anchisës was struck by a thunderbolt and crippled as punishment by Jupiter.

Swordbelt and blade and slid my left forearm
Into the shield-strap, turning to go out,
But at the door Creusa hugged my knees,
Then held up little Iulus to his father.

'If you are going out to die, take us   850
To face the whole thing with you. If experience
Leads you to put some hope in weaponry
Such as you now take, guard your own house here.
When you have gone, to whom is Iulus left?
Your father. Wife?—one called that long ago.'   855

She went on, and her wailing filled the house,
But then a sudden portent came, a marvel:
Amid his parents' hands and their sad faces
A point on Iulus' head seemed to cast light,
A tongue of flame that touched but did not burn
        him,   860
Licking his fine hair, playing round his temples.
We, in panic, beat at the flaming hair
And put the sacred fire out with water;
Father Anchises lifted his eyes to heaven
And lifted up his hands, his voice, in joy: 865

'Omnipotent Jupiter, if prayers affect you,
Look down upon us, that is all I ask,
If by devotion to the gods we earn it,
Grant us a new sign, and confirm this portent!'
The old man barely finished when it thundered   870
A loud crack on the left. Out of the sky
Through depths of night a star fell trailing flame
And glided on, turning the night to day.
We watched it pass above the roof and go
To hide its glare, its trace, in Ida's° wood;   875
But still, behind, the luminous furrow shone
And wide zones fumed with sulphur.
                          Now indeed
My father, overcome, addressed the gods,
And rose in worship of the blessed star.

'Now, now, no more delay. I'll follow you.   880
Where you conduct me, there I'll be.
                          Gods of my fathers,
Preserve this house, preserve my grandson. Yours
This portent was. Troy's life is in your power.
I yield. I go as your companion, son.'
Then he was still. We heard the blazing town   885
Crackle more loudly, felt the scorching heat.

'Then come, dear father. Arms around my neck:
I'll take you on my shoulders, no great weight.
Whatever happens, both will face one danger,
Find one safety. Iulus will come with me,   890
My wife at a good interval behind.
Servants, give your attention to what I say.
At the gate inland there's a funeral mound
And an old shrine of Ceres the Bereft;°
Near it an ancient cypress, kept alive   895

For many years by our fathers' piety.
By various routes we'll come to that one place.
Father, carry our hearthgods, our Penatës.
It would be wrong for me to handle them—
Just come from such hard fighting, bloody work—   900
Until I wash myself in running water.'

When I had said this, over my breadth of shoulder
And bent neck, I spread out a lion skin
For tawny cloak and stooped to take his weight.
Then little Iulus put his hand in mine   905
And came with shorter steps beside his father.
My wife fell in behind. Through shadowed places
On we went, and I, lately unmoved
By any spears thrown, any squads of Greeks,
Felt terror now at every eddy of wind,   910
Alarm at every sound, alert and worried
Alike for my companion and my burden.
I had got near the gate, and now I thought
We had made it all the way, when suddenly
A noise of running feet came near at hand,   915
And peering through the gloom ahead, my father
Cried out:
              'Run, boy: here they come; I see
Flame light on shields, bronze shining.'
                                    I took fright,
And some unfriendly power, I know not what,
Stole all my addled wits—for as I turned   920
Aside from the known way, entering a maze
Of pathless places on the run—
                          Alas,
Creusa, taken from us by grim fate, did she
Linger, or stray, or sink in weariness?
There is no telling. Never would she be   925
Restored to us. Never did I look back
Or think to look for her, lost as she was,
Until we reached the funeral mound and shrine
Of venerable Ceres. Here at last
All came together, but she was not there;   930
She alone failed° her friends, her child, her husband.
Out of my mind, whom did I not accuse,
What man or god? What crueller loss had I
Beheld, that night the city fell? Ascanius,
My father, and the Teucrian Penatës,   935
I left in my friends' charge, and hid them well
In a hollow valley.
                  I turned back alone
Into the city, cinching my bright harness.
Nothing for it but to run the risks
Again, go back again, comb all of Troy,   940
And put my life in danger as before:
First by the town wall, then the gate, all gloom,
Through which I had come out—and so on backward,
Tracing my own footsteps through the night;
And everywhere my heart misgave me: even   945
Stillness had its terror. Then to our house,
Thinking she might, just might, have wandered there.

---

875 *Ida:* The mountain range near Troy.

894 *Ceres the Bereft:* So-called because she mourns the loss of her daughter.   931 *failed:* The original Latin does not imply fault and is better read "was not to be found."

Danaans had got in and filled the place,
And at that instant fire they had set,
Consuming it, went roofward in a blast; 950
Flames leaped and seethed in heat to the night sky.
I pressed on, to see Priam's hall and tower.
In the bare colonnades of Juno's shrine
Two chosen guards, Phoenix and hard Ulysses,
Kept watch over the plunder. Piled up here 955
Were treasures of old Troy from every quarter,
Torn out of burning temples: altar tables,
Robes, and golden bowls. Drawn up around them,
Boys and frightened mothers stood in line.
I even dared to call out in the night; 960
I filled the streets with calling; in my grief
Time after time I groaned and called Creusa,
Frantic, in endless quest from door to door.
Then to my vision her sad wraith appeared—
Creusa's ghost, larger than life, before me. 965
Chilled to the marrow, I could feel the hair
On my head rise, the voice clot in my throat;
But she spoke out to ease me of my fear:

'What's to be gained by giving way to grief
So madly, my sweet husband? Nothing here 970
Has come to pass except as heaven willed.
You may not take Creusa with you now;
It was not so ordained, nor does the lord
Of high Olympus give you leave. For you
Long exile waits, and long sea miles to plough. 975
You shall make landfall on Hesperia
Where Lydian Tiber flows, with gentle pace,
Between rich farmlands, and the years will bear
Glad peace, a kingdom, and a queen for you.
Dismiss these tears for your beloved Creusa. 980
I shall not see the proud homelands of Myrmidons
Or of Dolopians, or go to serve
Greek ladies, Dardan lady that I am
And daughter-in-law of Venus the divine.
No: the great mother of the gods detains me 985
Here on these shores. Farewell now; cherish still
Your son and mine.'
                    With this she left me weeping,
Wishing that I could say so many things,
And faded on the tenuous air. Three times
I tried to put my arms around her neck, 990
Three times enfolded nothing, as the wraith
Slipped through my fingers, bodiless as wind,
Or like a flitting dream.
                    So in the end
As night waned I rejoined my company.
And there to my astonishment I found 995
New refugees in a great crowd: men and women
Gathered for exile, young—pitiful people
Coming from every quarter, minds made up,
With their belongings, for whatever lands
I'd lead them to by sea.
                    The morning star 1000
Now rose on Ida's ridges, bringing day.
Greeks had secured the city gates. No help
Or hope of help existed.
So I resigned myself, picked up my father,

And turned my face toward the mountain range."

↜ CATULLUS
Selected Poems

Catullus is the author of one of the best-known series of love poems ever written, which has provided a model for many poets since in their own amorous writings. Catullus addressed twenty-five pieces of verse to a mistress, Lesbia, in which he demonstrates a magnificent range of moods . Three examples are printed below, beginning with "We should live, my Lesbia, and love," which was translated and reworked by , among others, the English poets Ben Jonson and Andrew Marvell in the seventeenth century.

We Should Live, My Lesbia, and Love

We should live, my Lesbia, and love
And value all the talk of stricter
Old men at a single penny.
Suns can set and rise again,
For us, once our brief light has set, 5
There's one unending night for sleeping.
Give me a thousand kisses, then a hundred,
Then another thousand, then a second hundred;
Then still another thousand, then a hundred;
Then, when we've made many thousands, 10
We'll muddle them so as not to know
Or lest some villain overlook us
Knowing the total of our kisses.

That Man Is Seen by Me as a God's Equal

That man is seen by me as a God's equal
Or (if it may be said) the God's superior,
Who sitting opposite again and again
Watches and hears *you*

Sweetly laughing—which dispossesses poor me 5
Of all my senses, for no sooner, Lesbia,
Do I look at you than there's no power left me
(Of speech in my mouth,)

But my tongue's paralysed, invisible flame
Courses down through my limbs, with din
  of their own 10
My ears are ringing and twin darkness covers
The light of my eyes.

Leisure, Catullus, does not agree with you.
At leisure you're restless, too excitable.
Leisure in the past has ruined rulers and 15
Prosperous cities.

I Hate and Love

I hate and love. Perhaps you're asking why I do that?
I don't know, but I feel it happening, and am racked.

✦ HORACE
Ah God How They Race

Horace wrote poems in many different forms, including satire and the ode, the genre for which he is best known. In the following poem, Horace treats a common theme—the inevitability of death ending the lives of everyone—in an unusual way. While addressing the lines directly to his friend, Postumus, Horace widens their application to all of us—the "we" mentioned in the poem's final stanzas.

> Ah god how they race, Postumus, Postumus,
> how the years run out, and doing what is right
> will not delay wrinkles and age's
> onslaught and death who cannot be beaten;
>
> no, dear friend, not even if every day   *5*
> you tried with three hundred bulls to please Pluto,
> who has no tears, who holds in prison
> three-bodied Geryon and Tityos
>
> by the sorrowful river whose crossing is
> certain for those who live by the gifts of the earth,   *10*
> a must for all, the high and mighty
> and the poverty-stricken small farmers.
>
> It will do no good to escape bloody Mars
> and breaking waves on the rough Adriatic,
> it will do no good to spend autumn   *15*
> in terror of sirocco and sickness:
>
> we must see the dark waters of Cocytos
> winding slowly, and the infamous daughters
> of Danaus, and Sisyphus, son of
> Aeolus, condemned to endless labor.   *20*
>
> We must leave behind us earth and home and dear
> wife, and of all the trees that you care for now,
> not one will follow you, so briefly
> its master, only the loathsome cypress.
>
> An heir who deserves it will drink Caecuban   *25*
> you kept safe with a hundred keys, and he will
> soak the floor with magnificent wine,
> finer than the priests drink at their festivals.

✦ MARCUS AURELIUS
from *The Meditations*

The Meditations *of the Roman emperor Marcus Aurelius reflects the philosophical idea of Stoicism. Marcus Aurelius jotted his meditations in odd moments between his imperial duties at court and his many months and years in the field with his Roman troops defending the city against enemy incursions. Book II is characteristic of the emperor's method, which is to record his reflections on a variety of topics in no special order. What holds* The Meditations *together in Book II and overall is the tone of unswerving endurance in the face of pain and suffering and the recognition that the human spirit can withstand any difficulty life puts in its path.*

1. Say to yourself in the morning: I shall meet people who are interfering, ungracious, insolent, full of guile, deceitful and antisocial; they have all become like that because they have no understanding of good and evil. But I who have contemplated the essential beauty of good and the essential ugliness of evil, who know that the nature of the wrongdoer is of one kin with mine—not indeed of the same blood or seed but sharing the same mind, the same portion of the divine—I cannot be harmed by any one of them, and no one can involve me in shame. I cannot feel anger against him who is of my kin, nor hate him. We were born to labor together, like the feet, the hands, the eyes, and the rows of upper and lower teeth. To work against one another is therefore contrary to nature, and to be angry against a man or turn one's back on him is to work against him.

2. Whatever it is which I am, it is flesh, breath of life, and directing mind. The flesh you should despise: blood, bones and a network woven of nerves, veins and arteries. Consider too the nature of the life-breath: wind, never the same, but disgorged and then again gulped in, continually. The third part is the directing mind. Throw away your books, be no longer anxious: that was not your given role. Rather reflect thus as if death were now before you: "You are an old man, let this third part be enslaved no longer, nor be a mere puppet on the strings of selfish desire; no longer let it be vexed by your past or present lot, or peer suspiciously into the future."

3. The works of the gods are full of Providence. The works of Chance are not divorced from Nature or from the spinning and weaving together of those things which are governed by Providence. Thence everything flows. There is also Necessity and what is beneficial to the whole ordered universe of which you are a part. That which is brought by the nature of the Whole, and preserves it, is good for every part. As do changes in the elements, so changes in their compounds preserve the ordered universe. That should be enough for you, these should ever be your beliefs. Cast out the thirst for books that you may not die growling, but with true graciousness, and grateful to the gods from the heart.

4. Remember how long you have delayed, how often the gods have appointed the day of your redemption and you have let it pass. Now, if ever, you must realize of what kind of ordered universe you are a part, of what kind of governor of that universe you are an emanation, that a time limit has now been set for you and that if you do not use it to come out into the light, it will be lost, and you will be lost, and there will be no further opportunity.

5. Firmly, as a Roman and a man should, think at all times how you can perform the task at hand with precise and genuine dignity, sympathy, independence, and justice, making yourself free from all other preoccupations. This you will achieve if you perform every action as if it was the last of your life, if you rid yourself of all aimless thoughts, of all emotional opposition to the dictates of reason, of all pretence, selfishness and displeasure with your lot. You see how few are the things a man must overcome to enable him to live a smoothly flowing and godly life; for even the gods will require nothing further from the man who keeps to these beliefs.

6. You shame yourself, my soul, you shame yourself, and you will have no further opportunity to respect yourself; the

life of every man is short and yours is almost finished while you do not respect yourself but allow your happiness to depend upon the souls of others.

7. Do external circumstances to some extent distract you? Give yourself leisure to acquire some further good knowledge and cease to wander aimlessly. Then one must guard against another kind of wandering, for those who are exhausted by life, and have no aim at which to direct every impulse and generally every impression, are foolish in their deeds as well as in their words.

8. A man is not easily found to be unhappy because he takes no thought for what happens in the soul of another; it is those who do not attend to the disturbances of their own soul who are inevitably in a state of unhappiness.

9. Always keep this thought in mind: what is the essential nature of the universe and what is my own essential nature? How is the one related to the other, being so small a part of so great a Whole? And remember that no one can prevent your deeds and your words being in accord with nature.

10. Theophrastus speaks as a philosopher when, in comparing sins as a man commonly might, he states that offences due to desire are worse than those due to anger, for the angry man appears to be in the grip of pain and hidden pangs when he discards Reason, whereas he who sins through desire, being overcome by pleasure, seems more licentious and more effeminate in his wrongdoing. So Theophrastus is right, and speaks in a manner worthy of philosophy, when he says that one who sins through pleasure deserves more blame than one who sins through pain. The latter is more like a man who was wronged first and compelled by pain to anger; the former starts on the path to sin of his own accord, driven to action by desire.

11. It is possible to depart from life at this moment. Have this thought in mind whenever you act, speak, or think. There is nothing terrible in leaving the company of men, if the gods exist, for they would not involve you in evil. If, on the other hand, they do not exist or do not concern themselves with human affairs, then what is life to me in a universe devoid of gods or of Providence? But they do exist and do care for humanity, and have put it altogether within a man's power not to fall into real evils. And if anything else were evil they would have seen to it that it be in every man's power not to fall into it. As for that which does not make man worse, how could it make the life of man worse?

Neither through ignorance nor with knowledge could the nature of the Whole have neglected to guard against this or correct it; nor through lack of power or skill could it have committed so great a wrong, namely that good and evil should come to the good and the evil alike, and at random. True, death and life, good and ill repute, toil and pleasure, wealth and poverty, being neither good nor bad, come to the good and the bad equally. They are therefore neither blessings nor evils.

12. How swiftly all things vanish; in the universe the bodies themselves, and in time the memories of them. Of what kind are all the objects of sense, especially those which entice us by means of pleasure, frighten us by means of pain, or are shouted about in vainglory; how cheap they are, how contemptible, sordid, corruptible and dead—upon this our intellectual faculty should fix its attention. Who are these men whose voice and judgment make or break reputations?

What is the nature of death? When a man examines it in itself, and with his share of intelligence dissolves the imaginings which cling to it, he conceives it to be no other than a function of nature, and to fear a natural function is to be only a child. Death is not only a function of nature but beneficial to it.

How does man reach god, with what part of himself, and in what condition must that part be?

13. Nothing is more wretched than the man who runs around in circles busying himself with all kinds of things—investigating things below the earth, as the saying goes—always looking for signs of what his neighbors are feeling and thinking. He does not realize that it is enough to be concerned with the spirit within oneself and genuinely to serve it. This service consists in keeping it free from passions, aimlessness, and discontent with its fate at the hands of gods and men. What comes from the gods must be revered because of their goodness; what comes from men must be welcomed because of our kinship, although sometimes these things are also pitiful in a sense, because of men's ignorance of good and evil, which is no less a disability than to be unable to distinguish between black and white.

14. Even if you were to live three thousand years or three times ten thousand, remember nevertheless that no one can shed another life than this which he is living, nor live another life than this which he is shedding, so that the longest and the shortest life come to the same thing. The present is equal for all, and that which is being lost is equal, and that which is being shed is thus shown to be but a moment. No one can shed that which is past, nor what is still to come; for how could he be deprived of what he does not possess?

Therefore remember these two things always: first, that all things as they come round again have been the same from eternity, and it makes no difference whether you see the same things for a hundred years, or for two hundred years, or for an infinite time; second, that the longest-lived or the shortest-lived sheds the same thing at death, for it is the present moment only of which he will be deprived, if indeed only the present moment is his, and no man can discard what he does not have.

15. "All is but thinking so." The retort to the saying of Monimus the Cynic is obvious, but the usefulness of the saying is also obvious, if one accepts the essential meaning of it insofar as it is true.

16. The human soul violates itself most of all when it becomes, as far as it can, a separate tumor or growth upon the universe; for to be discontented with anything that happens is to rebel against that Nature which embraces, in some part of itself, all other natures. The soul violates itself also whenever it turns away from a man and opposes him to do him harm, as do the souls of angry men; thirdly, whenever it is overcome by pleasure or pain; fourthly, whenever it acts a part and does or says anything falsely and hypocritically; fifthly, when it fails to direct any action or impulse to a goal, but acts at random, without purpose, whereas even the most trifling actions must be directed toward the end; and this end, for reasonable creatures, is to follow the reason and the law of the most honored commonwealth and constitution.

17. In human life time is but a point, reality a flux, perception indistinct, the composition of the body subject to easy corruption, the soul a spinning top, fortune hard to make out, fame confused. To put it briefly: physical things are but a flowing stream, things of the soul dreams and vanity; life is but a struggle and the visit to a strange land, posthumous fame but a forgetting.

What then can help us on our way? One thing only: philosophy. This consists in guarding our inner spirit inviolate and unharmed, stronger than pleasures and pains, never acting aimlessly, falsely or hypocritically, independent of the actions or inaction of others, accepting all that happens or is given as coming from hence one came oneself, and at all times awaiting death with contented mind as being only the release of the elements of which every creature is composed. It is nothing fearful for the elements themselves that one should continually change into another. Why should anyone look with suspicion upon the change and dissolution of all things? For this is in accord with nature and nothing evil is in accord with nature.

PETRONIUS

from the *Satyricon*

First-century A.D. Rome was a place saturated in material rather than spiritual values. During Nero's reign the satirist Petronius provided a sharply realistic picture of the manners, luxuries, and vices of the age. In the longest section of the Satyricon *extant, "Dinner with Trimalchio," Petronius depicts an aristocratic narrator and his friends as they share a meal with the slave turned millionaire, Trimalchio. Petronius emphasizes the characters' selfishness, their anti-intellectualism, and their obsession with cheating one another. The satire is enhanced by means of numerous echoes of the Greek heroic tradition with references to Homer's* Iliad *and* Odyssey. *The ironic references reflect the Roman characters' distance from the heroic ideal as they live only for themselves and only for the moment.*

Dinner with Trimalchio

The next day but one finally arrived. But we were so knocked about that we wanted to run rather than rest. We were mournfully discussing how to avoid the approaching storm, when one of Agamemnon's slaves broke in on our frantic debate.

"Here," said he, "don't you know who's your host today? It's Trimalchio—he's terribly elegant … He has a clock in the dining-room and a trumpeter all dressed up to tell him how much longer he's got to live."

This made us forget all our troubles. We dressed carefully and told Giton, who was very kindly acting as our servant, to attend us at the baths.

We did not take our clothes off but began wandering around, or rather exchanging jokes while circulating among the little groups. Suddenly we saw a bald old man in a reddish shirt, playing ball with some long-haired boys. It was not so much the boys that made us watch, although they alone were worth the trouble, but the old gentleman himself. He was taking his exercise in slippers and throwing a green ball around. But he didn't pick it up if it touched the ground; instead there was a slave holding a bagful, and he

supplied them to the players. We noticed other novelties. Two eunuchs stood around at different points: one of them carried a silver chamber pot, the other counted the balls, not those flying from hand to hand according to the rules, but those that fell to the ground. We were still admiring these elegant arrangements when Menelaus hurried up to us.

"This is the man you'll be dining with," he said. "In fact, you are now watching the beginning of the dinner."

No sooner had Menelaus spoken than Trimalchio snapped his fingers. At the signal the eunuch brought up the chamber pot for him, while he went on playing. With the weight off his bladder, he demanded water for his hands, splashed a few drops on his fingers and wiped them on a boy's head.

It would take too long to pick out isolated incidents. Anyway, we entered the baths where we began sweating at once and we went immediately into the cold water. Trimalchio had been smothered in perfume and was already being rubbed down, not with linen towels, but with bathrobes of the finest wool. As this was going on, three masseurs sat drinking Falernian in front of him. Through quarreling they spilled most of it and Trimalchio said they were drinking his health. Wrapped in thick scarlet felt he was put into a litter. Four couriers with lots of medals went in front, as well as a go-cart in which his favourite boy was riding—a wizened, bleary-eyed youngster, uglier than his master. As he was carried off, a musician with a tiny set of pipes took his place by Trimalchio's head and whispered a tune in his ear the whole way.

We followed on, choking with amazement by now, and arrived at the door with Agamemnon at our side. On the doorpost a notice was fastened which read:

ANY SLAVE LEAVING THE HOUSE WITHOUT HIS MASTER'S PERMISSION WILL RECEIVE ONE HUNDRED LASHES

Just at the entrance stood the hall-porter, dressed in a green uniform with a belt of cherry red. He was shelling peas into a silver basin. Over the doorway hung—of all things—a golden cage from which a spotted magpie greeted visitors.

As I was gaping at all this, I almost fell over backwards and broke a leg. There on the left as one entered, not far from the porter's cubbyhole, was a huge dog with a chain around its neck. It was painted on the wall and over it, in big capitals, was written:

BEWARE OF THE DOG

My colleagues laughed at me, but when I got my breath back I went to examine the whole wall. There was a mural of a slave market, price tags and all. Then Trimalchio himself, holding a wand of Mercury and being led into Rome by Minerva. After this a picture of how he learned accounting and, finally how he became a steward. The painstaking artist had drawn it all in great detail with descriptions underneath. Just where the colonnade ended Mercury hauled him up by the chin and rushed him to a high platform. …

I began asking the porter what were the pictures they had in the middle.

"The *Iliad*, and *Odyssey*, and the gladiatorial show given by Laenas," he told me.

Time did not allow us to look at many things there ... by now we had reached the dining-room ...

Finally we took our places. Boys from Alexandria poured iced water over our hands. Others followed them and attended to our feet, removing any hangnails with great skill. But they were not quiet even during this troublesome operation: they sang away at their work. I wanted to find out if the whole staff were singers, so I asked for a drink. In a flash a boy was there, singing in a shrill voice while he attended to me—and anyone else who was asked to bring something did the same. It was more like a musical comedy than a respectable dinner party.

Some extremely elegant hors d'oeuvre were served at this point—by now everyone had taken his place with the exception of Trimalchio, for whom, strangely enough, the place at the top was reserved. The dishes for the first course included an ass of Corinthian bronze with two panniers, white olives on one side and black on the other. Over the ass were two pieces of plate, with Trimalchio's name and the weight of the silver inscribed on the rims. There were some small iron frames shaped like bridges supporting dormice sprinkled with honey and poppy seed. There were steaming hot sausages too, on a silver gridiron with damsons and pomegranate seeds underneath.

We were in the middle of these elegant dishes when Trimalchio himself was carried in to the sound of music and set down on a pile of tightly stuffed cushions. The sight of him drew an astonished laugh from the guests. His cropped head stuck out from a scarlet coat; his neck was well muffled up and he had put round it a napkin with a broad purple stripe and tassels dangling here and there. On the little finger of his left hand he wore a heavy gilt ring and a smaller one on the last joint of the next finger. This I thought was solid gold, but actually it was studded with little iron stars. And to show off even more of his jewellery, he had his right arm bare and set off by a gold armlet and an ivory circlet fastened with a gleaming metal plate.

After picking his teeth with a silver toothpick, he began: "My friends, I wasn't keen to come into the dining room yet. But if I stayed away any more, I would have kept you back, so I've deprived myself of all my little pleasures for you. However, you'll allow me to finish my game."

A boy was at his heels with a board of terebinth wood with glass squares, and I noticed the very last word in luxury—instead of white and black pieces he had gold and silver coins. While he was swearing away like a trooper over his game and we were still on the hors d'oeuvre, a tray was brought in with a basket on it. There sat a wooden hen, its wings spread round it the way hens are when they are broody. Two slaves hurried up and as the orchestra played a tune they began searching through the straw and dug out peahens' eggs, which they distributed to the guests.

Trimalchio turned to look at this little scene and said: "My friends, I gave orders for that bird to sit on some peahens' eggs. I hope to goodness they are not starting to hatch. However, let's try them and see if they are still soft."

We took up our spoons (weighing at least half a pound each) and cracked the eggs, which were made of rich pastry. To tell the truth, I nearly threw away my share, as the chicken seemed already formed. But I heard a guest who was an

old hand say: "There should be something good here." So I searched the shell with my fingers and found the plumpest little figpecker, all covered with yolk and seasoned with pepper.

At this point Trimalchio became tired of his game and demanded that all the previous dishes be brought to him. He gave permission in a loud voice for any of us to have another glass of mead if we wanted it. Suddenly there was a crash from the orchestra and a troop of waiters—still singing— snatched away the hors d'oeuvre. However in the confusion one of the side-dishes happened to fall and a slave picked it up from the floor. Trimalchio noticed this, had the boy's ears boxed and told him to throw it down again. A cleaner came in with a broom and began to sweep up the silver plate along with the rest of the rubbish. Two long-haired Ethiopians followed him, carrying small skin bottles like those they use for scattering sand in the circus, and they poured wine over our hands—no one ever offered us water.

Our host was complimented on these elegant arrangements. "You've got to fight fair," he replied. "That is why I gave orders for each guest to have his own table. At the same time these smelly slaves won't crowd so."

Carefully sealed wine bottles were immediately brought, their necks labelled:

FALERNIAN
CONSUL OPIMIUS
ONE HUNDRED YEARS OLD

While we were examining the labels, Trimalchio clapped his hands and said with a sigh:

"Wine has a longer life than us poor folks. So let's wet our whistles. Wine is life. I'm giving you real Opimian. I didn't put out such good stuff yesterday, though the company was much better class."

Naturally we drank and missed no opportunity of admiring his elegant hospitality. In the middle of this a slave brought in a silver skeleton, put together in such a way that its joints and backbone could be pulled out and twisted in all directions. After he had flung it about on the table once or twice, its flexible joints falling into various postures, Trimalchio recited:

> "Man's life alas! is but a span,
> So let us live it while we can,
> We'll be like this when dead." ...

"Nobody believes in heaven, see, nobody fasts, nobody gives a damn for the Almighty. No, people only bow their heads to count their money. In the old days high-class ladies used to climb up the hill barefoot, their hair loose and their hearts pure, and ask God for rain. And he'd send it down in bucketfuls right away—it was then or never—and everyone went home like drowned rats. Since we've given up religion the gods nowadays keep their feet well wrapped up. The fields just lie ..."

"Please, please," broke in Echion the rag merchant, "be a bit more cheerful. 'First it's one thing, then another,' as the yokel said when he lost his spotted pig. What we haven't got today, we'll have tomorrow. That's the way life goes. Believe me, you couldn't name a better country, if it had the people.

As things are, I admit, it's having a hard time, but it isn't the only place. We mustn't be soft. The sky don't get no nearer wherever you are. If you were somewhere else, you'd be talking about the pigs walking round ready roasted back here.

"And another thing, we'll be having a holiday with a three-day show that's the best ever—and not just a hack troupe of gladiators but freedmen for the most part. My old friend Titus has a big heart and a hot head. Maybe this, maybe that, but something at all events. I'm a close friend of his and he does nothing by halves. He'll give us cold steel, no quarter and the slaughterhouse right in the middle where all the stands can see it. And he's got the wherewithal—he was left thirty million when his poor father died. Even if he spent four hundred thousand, his pocket won't feel it and he'll go down in history. He's got some big brutes already, and a woman who fights in a chariot and Glyco's steward, who was caught having fun with his mistress. You'll see quite a quarrel in the crowd between jealous husbands and romantic lovers. But that half-pint Glyco threw his steward to the lions, which is just giving himself away. How is it the servant's fault when he's forced into it? It's that old pisspot who really deserves to be tossed by a bull. But if you can't beat the ass you beat the saddle. But how did Glyco imagine the poisonous daughter of Hermogenes would ever turn out well? The old man could cut the claws off a flying kite, and a snake don't hatch old rope. Glyco—well, Glyco's got his. He's branded for as long as he lives and only the grave will get rid of it. But everyone pays for their mistakes …"

This was the sort of conversation flying round when Trimalchio came in, dabbed his forehead and washed his hands in perfume. There was a short pause, then he said:

"Excuse me, dear people, my inside has not been answering the call for several days now. The doctors are puzzled. But some pomegranate rind and resin in vinegar has done me good. But I hope now it will be back on its good behaviour. Otherwise my stomach rumbles like a bull. So if any of you wants to go out, there's no need for him to be embarrassed. None of us was born solid. I think there's nothing so tormenting as holding yourself in. This is the one thing even God Almighty can't object to. Yes, laugh, Fortunata [Trimalchio's wife], but you generally keep me up all night with this sort of thing.

"Anyway, I don't object to people doing what suits them even in the middle of dinner—and the doctors forbid you to hold yourself in. Even if it's a longer business, everything is there just outside—water, bowls, and all the other little comforts. Believe me, if the wind goes to your brain it starts flooding your whole body too. I've known a lot of people die from this because they wouldn't be honest with themselves."

We thanked him for being so generous and considerate and promptly proceeded to bury our amusement in our glasses. Up to this point we'd not realized we were only in mid-stream, as you might say.

The orchestra played, the tables were cleared, and then three white pigs were brought into the dining-room, all decked out in muzzles and bells. The first, the master of ceremonies announced, was two years old, the second three, and the third six. I was under the impression that some acrobats were on their way in and the pigs were going to do some tricks, the way they do in street shows. But Trimalchio dispelled this impression by asking:

"Which of these would you like for the next course? Any clodhopper can do you a barnyard cock or a stew and trifles like that, but my cooks are used to boiling whole calves."

He immediately sent for the chef and without waiting for us to choose he told him to kill the oldest pig.

He then said to the man in a loud voice:

"Which division are you from?"

When he replied he was from number forty, Trimalchio asked:

"Were you bought or were you born here?"

"Neither," said the chef, "I was left to you in Pansa's will."

"Well, then," said Trimalchio, "see you serve it up carefully—otherwise I'll have you thrown into the messenger's division."

So the chef, duly reminded of his master's magnificence, went back to his kitchen, the next course leading the way.

Trimalchio looked around at us with a gentle smile: "If you don't like the wine, I'll have it changed. It is up to you to do it justice. I don't buy it, thank heaven. In fact, whatever wine really tickles your palate this evening, it comes from an estate of mine which as yet I haven't seen. It's said to join my estates at Tarracina and Tarentum. What I'd like to do now is add Sicily to my little bit of land, so that when I want to go to Africa, I could sail there without leaving my own property.

"But tell me, Agamemnon, what was your debate about today? Even though I don't go in for the law, still I've picked up enough education for home consumption. And don't you think I turn my nose up at studying, because I have two libraries, one Greek, one Latin. So tell us, just as a favour, what was the topic of your debate?"

Agamemnon was just beginning, "A poor man and a rich man were enemies …" when Trimalchio said: "What's a poor man?" "Oh, witty!" said Agamemnon, and then told us about some fictitious case or other. Like lightning Trimalchio said: "If this happened, it's not a fictitious case— if it didn't happen, then it's nothing at all."

We greeted this witticism and several more like it with the greatest enthusiasm.

"Tell me, my dear Agamemnon," continued Trimalchio, "do you remember the twelve labours of Hercules and the story of Ulysses—how the Cyclops tore out his thumb with a pair of pincers. I used to read about them in Homer, when I was a boy. In fact, I actually saw the Sibyl at Cumae with my own eyes dangling in a bottle, and when the children asked her in Greek: 'What do you want, Sybil?' she used to answer: 'I want to die.'" …

Up came another squad and as the first set called out: "Good night, Gaius!" the new arrivals shouted: "Good evening, Gaius!"

This led to the first incident that damped the general high spirits. Not a bad-looking boy entered with the newcomers and Trimalchio jumped at him and began kissing him at some length. Fortunata, asserting her just and legal rights, began hurling insults at Trimalchio, calling him a low scum and a disgrace, who couldn't control his beastly desires. "You dirty dog!" she finally added.

Trimalchio took offence at this abuse and flung his glass into Fortunata's face. She screamed as though she'd lost an eye and put her trembling hands across her face. Scintilla was terrified too and hugged the quaking woman to her breast. An obliging slave pressed a little jug of cold water to her cheek, while Fortunata rested her head on it and began weeping. Trimalchio just said:

"Well, well, forgotten her chorus days, has she? She doesn't remember, but she was bought and sold, and I took her away from it all and made her as good as the next. Yet she puffs herself up like a frog and doesn't even spit for luck. Just a great hunk, not a woman. But those as are born over a shop don't dream of a house. May I never have a day's good luck again, if I don't teach that Cassandra in clogs some manners!

"There was I, not worth twopence, and I could have had ten million. And you know I'm not lying about it ... But to come back to earth—I want you to enjoy yourselves, my dear people. After all, I was once like you are, but being the right sort, I got where I am. It's the old headpiece that makes a man, the rest is all rubbish. 'Buy right—sell right!'—that's me! Different people will give you a different line. I'm just on top of the world, I'm that lucky ... However, as I'd started to say, it was my shrewd way with money that got me to my present position. I came from Asia as big as this candlestick. In fact, every day I used to measure myself against it, and to get some whiskers round my beak quicker, I used to oil my lips from the lamp. Still, for fourteen years I was the old boy's fancy. And there's nothing wrong if the boss wants it. But I did all right by the old girl too. You know what I mean—I don't say anything because I'm not the boasting sort.

"Well, as heaven will have it, I became boss in the house, and the old boy, you see, couldn't think of anything but me. That's about it—he made me co-heir with the Emperor and I got a senator's fortune. But nobody gets enough, never. I wanted to go into business. Not to make a long story of it, I built five ships, I loaded them with wine—it was absolute gold at the time—and I sent them to Rome. You'd have thought I ordered it—every single ship was wrecked. That's fact, not fable! In one single day Neptune swallowed up thirty million. Do you think I gave up? This loss honestly wasn't more than a flea-bite to me—it was as if nothing had happened. I built more boats, bigger and better and luckier, so nobody could say I wasn't a man of courage. You know, the greater the ship, the greater the confidence. I loaded them again—with wine, bacon, beans, perfumes and slaves. At this point Fortunata did the decent thing, because she sold off all her gold trinkets, all her clothes, and put ten thousand in gold pieces in my hand. This was the yeast my fortune needed to rise. What heaven wants, soon happens. In one voyage I carved out a round ten million. I immedi-

ately bought back all my old master's estates. I built a house, I invested in slaves, and I bought up the horse trade. Whatever I touched grew like a honeycomb. Once I had more than the whole country, then down tools! I retired from business and began advancing loans through freedmen ...

"Meantime, under the protection of Mercury, I built this house. As you know, it was still a shack, now it's a shrine. It has four dining-rooms, twenty bedrooms, two marble colonnades, a row of boxrooms up above, a bedroom where I sleep myself, a nest for this viper, and a really good lodge for the porter. The guest apartment takes a hundred guests. In fact, when Scaurus came here, he didn't want to stay anywhere else, even though he's got his father's guest house down by the sea. And there are a lot of other things I'll show you in a second.

"Believe me: have a penny, and you're worth a penny. You got something, you'll be thought something. Like your old friend—first a frog, now a king.

"Meantime, Stichus, bring out the shroud and the things I want to be buried in. Bring some cosmetic cream too, and a sample from that jar of wine I want my bones washed in."

Stichus did not delay over it, but brought his white shroud and his formal dress into the dining-room ... Trimalchio told us to examine them and see if they were made of good wool. Then he said with a smile:

"Now you, Stichus, see no mice or moths get at those—otherwise I'll burn you alive. I want to be buried in style, so the whole town will pray for my rest."

He opened a bottle of nard on the spot, rubbed some on all of us and said:

"I hope this'll be as nice when I'm dead as when I'm alive." The wine he had poured into a big decanter and he said:

"I want you to think you've been invited to my wake."

The thing was becoming absolutely sickening, when Trimalchio, showing the effects of his disgusting drunkenness, had a fresh entertainment brought into the dining-room, some cornet players. Propped up on a lot of cushions, he stretched out along the edge of the couch and said: "Pretend I'm dead and say something nice."

The cornet players struck up a dead march. One man in particular, the slave of his undertaker (who was the most respectable person present) blew so loudly that he roused the neighbourhood. As a result the fire brigade, thinking Trimalchio's house was on fire, suddenly broke down the front door and began kicking up their own sort of din with their water and axes.

Seizing this perfect chance, we gave Agamemnon the slip and escaped as rapidly as if there really were a fire.

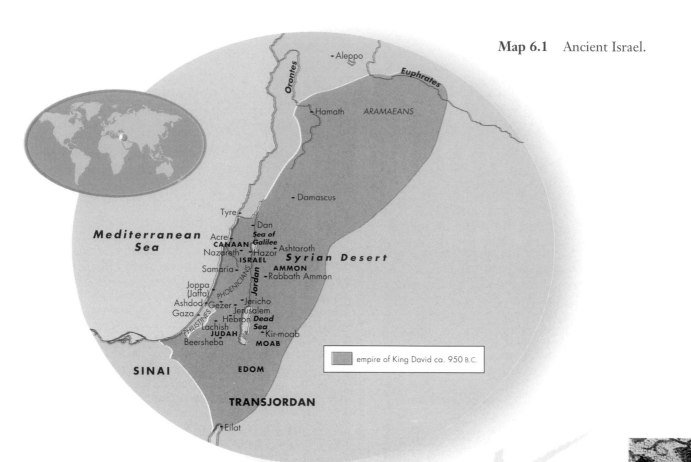

Map 6.1 Ancient Israel.

- Aleppo

Euphrates

Orontes

- Hamath   *ARAMAEANS*

- Damascus

Tyre -

Mediterranean Sea

- Dan

Acre -   *Sea of Galilee*

CANAAN   - Hazor   - Ashtaroth

Nazareth -   **ISRAEL**   *Syrian Desert*

Samaria -   **AMMON**

- Rabbath Ammon

Joppa (Jaffa) -

PHOENICIANS

Jordan

Ashdod -   Gezer -   - Jericho

Gaza -   - Jerusalem

Lachish -   - Hebron   *Dead Sea*

PHILISTINES   **JUDAH**   - Kir-moab

Beersheba -   **MOAB**

empire of King David ca. 950 B.C.

SINAI   **EDOM**

TRANSJORDAN

- Eilat

JUDAISM AND THE RISE OF CHRISTIANITY

206

Wine-Making Scene, ca. A.D. 350, Santa Costanza, Rome.

JUDAISM

➔

The Greeks and the Romans had dominated the ancient world politically and socially, but there was a different tradition that, while not as significant artistically or politically, came to be one of the two main influences on Western civilization. The founders of this tradition were a tribe who called themselves the "Children of Israel," the Israelites, or Hebrews (from *Habiru*, meaning "nomad" or "outcast"). Later they became known as Jews, a name derived from their place of habitation, the area around Jerusalem known as Judaea.

While the Greco-Roman tradition was bound up with the rational and the practical, and was dedicated to the arts, the Hebrew tradition was associated more with the spiritual and the mystical and was founded on faith. The Jews produced a "religion of the book" which evolved into the Old Testament portion of the Bible, providing not only the spiritual, but also the moral foundation of Western culture. Judaism itself was a religion that sought no converts—the Hebrew scriptures represented God's will and words to his "Chosen People." It emphasized a special national destiny, privilege, and responsibility. Christianity, which grew out of Judaism, did seek converts, and was from its earliest days in the first century A.D. a missionary religion, seeking to attract as many followers as possible. It spread the word of God through **evangelists**, from the Greek *euangelos*, meaning "bearer of good news"—*eu* means "good" and *angelos* "messenger." It was because of this missionary zeal on the part of the Early Christians that the Greco-Roman and biblical traditions were finally united. In A.D. 313 the Roman emperor Constantine granted toleration to Christians, then on his deathbed in 337 he received Christian baptism and Christianity became the official state religion.

The nomadic Hebrew people were forced out of their home in the Mesopotamian basin about 2000 B.C. by the warlike Akkadians and the threat posed by the ascendancy of the Babylonians. Led by the patriarch Abraham, the Hebrews settled in Canaan, the hilly country between the Jordan River and the eastern Mediterranean coast. Canaan became their homeland and was, the Hebrews believed, promised to them by their god. **Monotheistic** (meaning the belief in only one God), as opposed to the polytheistic religions of Greece, Rome, and other Near Eastern peoples, the Hebrew religion had but one God—Yahweh, a name so sacred that even today the pious never speak or write it.

In contrast, other Near Eastern tribes worshiped the various powers of nature as independent and multiple divine beings. The Babylonians, for instance, paid homage to, among others, a storm-god and a rain-god. Where the gods of Egypt and Mesopotamia were considered immanent, or present in nature, the Hebrew god was believed to be transcendent, apart from nature, which he also controlled. Thus, the sun, which the Egyptians worshiped as a god, was for the Hebrews subject to the power of their God, who had created it. Moreover, they considered the divine figures of other religions subordinate to the God of Israel.

Unlike the gods of the Greeks and Romans, Yahweh did not engage in amorous play with other gods or with human beings. He would only punish mortals with just cause and for a reason that ultimately benefited the human race. He was represented as a righteous God, whose justice was tempered with mercy, and who wished his Chosen People to live righteous and honorable lives in accordance with his commandments. As the biblical story of Noah and the Ark demonstrates, the Hebrew God had the power to destroy humankind, yet he also had the capacity for mercy.

HISTORY AND RELIGION

The history and religion of the Hebrews are essentially one and the same, and that history and religion are recorded in the Bible. The Hebrew Bible, which consists only of that part of the Christian Bible known as the Old Testament, can be read as the history of the Hebrews' relationship with their God. For the Israelites, God's power was made manifest in particular historical events, such as the very creation of the world and its destruction in the great flood.

Creation.   The Hebrews believed that God created the world in a perfect state. The Bible describes both the world and the human beings that originally populated it as "good." The reason why it is no longer the paradise originally created, however, results directly from humankind's disobedience, as illustrated in Genesis by the story of Adam and Eve in the Garden of Eden and their eating of the forbidden fruit. Adam and Eve's act inaugurates a pattern of exile from divinity that is repeated in other biblical stories, and which foretells the wanderings of the patriarchs.

Patriarchs.   The early patriarchs of ancient Israel were unusual men who believed they were favored by God and consequently led lives that honored God. The first of the patriarchs was Abraham, whose name has come to signify the ancient Judaic faith in God. When God called Abraham out of the land of Ur in ancient Sumeria to Canaan, Abraham's response was an immediate and total acceptance of God's will.

To Abraham and his descendants God made the solemn promise of the **covenant**. An agreement between God and his people, it was passed down to the patriarchs who followed Abraham—to his son Isaac and his grandson Jacob, or Israel. In the covenant, God agrees to be the Hebrew deity if the Hebrews agree, in turn, to be his people and to follow his will. With each of the Hebrew patriarchs, God renews the following covenant originally made with Noah after the flood:

> I am God Almighty; be fruitful and multiply; a nation and a company of nations shall come from you, and kings shall spring from you. The land which I gave to Abraham and Isaac I will give to you, and I will give the land to your descendants after you. (Gen. 35:11–12)

This covenant is referred to many times in the first five books of the Bible, which are called the Law, or the *Torah* (Hebrew for "instruction" or "teaching").

Perhaps the most important renewal of the covenant took place seven hundred years after the time of Abraham, in about 1250 B.C., when the Hebrews had been living in Egypt for many years. Why they had left Canaan for Egypt in about 1600 B.C. we do not know, but they prospered there until the Egyptians enslaved them. In outright defiance of the pharaoh, the patriarch Moses led his people out of Egypt (the exodus) and into the Sinai desert, which lies on the peninsula between Egypt and Canaan. There, on the top of a mountain, God is said to have given Moses the Ten Commandments, also known as the Decalogue.

1. You shall have no other gods before me.
2. You shall not make for yourself a graven image, or any likeness of any thing that is in heaven above, or that is on the earth beneath, or that is in the water under the earth.
3. You shall not take the name of the Lord your God in vain.
4. Observe the sabbath day, to keep it holy, as the Lord your God commanded you.
5. Honor your father and your mother.
6. You shall not kill.
7. Neither shall you commit adultery.
8. Neither shall you steal.
9. Neither shall you bear false witness against your neighbor.
10. Neither shall you covet your neighbor's wife, or anything that is your neighbor's.

The Hebrews carried the Ten Commandments with them, carved into stone tablets kept in a sacred chest called the Ark of the Covenant (fig. 6.1). Other sacred objects were also kept in the Ark such as the menorahs (seven-branched candelabra), which had been described by God to Moses, and which originally lit the Ark in its portable tabernacle. The Ten Commandments are the essence of the religious law of the ancient Judaeo-Christian world. As a set of guiding principles, they are the first word in moral rectitude, not the last. They require repeated interpretation, elaboration, and evaluation. Their influence has been enormous. Beginning with the six hundred and more laws recorded in the book of Leviticus, and continuing with the exploration of morality in the time of Jesus, the Commandments have long provided a basis for moral reflection and analysis.

Figure 6.1 *Menorahs and Ark of the Covenant,* wall painting in a Jewish catacomb, third century A.D., 3′11″ × 5′9″ (1.19 × 1.8 m), Villa Torlonia, Rome. The form of the menorah probably derives from the Tree of Life, an ancient Mesopotamian symbol.

For the ancient Hebrews, divine acts like the conferring of the Ten Commandments were acknowledgements of their status as God's Chosen People. After Moses's death, however, the Hebrews wandered for forty years "in the wilderness" of the Sinai, until they were delivered to the Promised Land, the land of "milk and honey," by the patriarch Joshua, who led them across the Jordan River and into Canaan once again. Over the next two hundred years, they gradually gained control of the entire region, calling themselves Israelites, after the patriarch Jacob, who had named himself Israel.

Prophets. Despite the imperative of God's covenant, the ancient Hebrews believed that human beings were ultimately responsible for their own actions and for doing whatever was necessary to improve their lot. When something was wrong in the social order, the onus was on believers to correct it. This would become the central message of the biblical prophets from the eighth through the sixth century B.C.

The Israelite prophets spoke for God. They were not "prophetic" in the sense that they foretold the future. Instead they functioned as mouthpieces, preaching what they had been instructed by God in visions or through ecstasy. They taught people the importance of living according to the Ten Commandments. In many cases, the prophets operated as voices of conscience, confronting the Israelite kings with their wrongdoings. The best known and most important of the biblical prophets were Isaiah, Jeremiah, and Ezekiel, although there were another twelve whose books are still included in the Old Testament.

Isaiah called for social justice and for an end to war. It is a mark of the enduring influence of the language and moral code of the Israelites that a verse from the biblical book of Isaiah adorns the United Nations building in New York City: "And they shall beat their swords into ploughshares, and their spears into pruning hooks; nation shall not lift up sword against nation, neither shall they learn war any more" (Isa. 2:4).

Kings. The process by which the descendants of the twelve sons of Jacob (Israel) became the twelve tribes of Israel winds through a long and bloody series of military campaigns, as described in the books of Joshua, Judges, and Samuel. By 1000 B.C., the kingdom of Israel was at last established, with SAUL (r. ca. 1040-1000 B.C.) as its first king. The first book of Samuel describes Saul's kingship and the arrival of David, who saves the Israelites from their enemy, the Philistines, by slaying the giant Goliath with a stone from a slingshot.

DAVID (r. ca. 1000–961 B.C.) was Israel's greatest king. His reign lasted about forty years and was a time of military success, a period that included the capture of Jerusalem, which David made the capital of his kingdom. David's rule did not prevent him from composing poetry and music, including some of the biblical Psalms.

Perhaps the most interesting aspect of David, however, is his imperfection, for the Bible depicts him as a person who was both a sinner and a penitent. His transgressions include having one of his soldiers, Uriah, dispatched to the front line where he would undoubtedly be killed, so that David could marry his widow, Bathsheba. Yet, David was also to suffer the death of his son Absalom, who mounted a military rebellion against him. These episodes are among the most powerful in all of ancient literature, and, one might argue, among the most realistic. The books of Samuel reveal political intrigues and complex familial dynamics with great subtlety and literary artistry.

The last important Israelite king was David's son, SOLOMON [SOL-oh-mun] (r. ca. 961–922 B.C.). Famous for his wisdom, Solomon is also associated with the Temple he had built in Jerusalem, where the Ark of the Covenant was kept, signifying God's presence. Like his father, Solomon was a poet. He is the reputed author of the biblical Song of Songs, a sensual love poem that has been read by later critics as a metaphor for the love between God and his people.

Following the death of Solomon, the kingdom of Israel was split in two. The Northern Kingdom retained the name Israel while the Southern Kingdom was called Judah. The Northern Kingdom fell to the Assyrians in 722 B.C.; the Southern Kingdom was overrun in 587 B.C. by the Babylonians under the command of Nebuchadnezzar [ne-BYUK-ad-NEZ-ah], who destroyed Solomon's magnificent temple. The Southern Kingdom Hebrews were carried off into exile, which inaugurated a period known as the Babylonian Captivity.

Return from Exile. The Hebrews remained in exile for over sixty years. On their return to their homeland around 539 B.C., they rebuilt their Temple, which was destroyed again by the Romans in A.D. 70. The intervening period was one of almost continuous foreign occupation. However, the Roman destruction of the Temple and of Jerusalem in A.D. 70 marked the end of Jewish power in the region until the middle of the twentieth century.

THE BIBLE AS LITERATURE

The Hebrew Bible (from the Greek name for the city of Byblos, the major exporter of papyrus, the material used for making books in the ancient world) consists of the canon of books accepted and officially sanctioned by Judaism. These include three major groupings: the Law, the Prophets, and the Writings. The Law comprises the first five books: Genesis, Exodus, Leviticus, Numbers, and Deuteronomy. (Authorship of these books is ascribed to Moses.) The Prophets include those mentioned above and, in addition, the books of Joel, Obadiah, Jonah, Micah, Nahum, Habakkuk, Zephaniah, Haggai, Zechariah, and Malachi, as well as six historical books: Joshua, Judges, Samuel (two books), and Kings (two books). The remaining books are categorized as the Writings, and include the narrative books of Ruth, Esther, and Daniel; the poetic books of Psalms and the Song of Songs; and the wisdom books of Proverbs, Job, and Ecclesiastes. Also part of the Writings are Chronicles, Lamentations, Ezra, and Nehemiah.

A number of biblical books can be cited for their outstanding literary accomplishment. The stories of David in the book of Samuel, and those of Daniel and of Jonah, the poetry of the Song of Songs and the Psalms, the wisdom of Ecclesiastes—all warrant claims as significant literary achievements, regardless of their status as holy scripture. Two books of the Hebrew Bible, however, tower above the rest: Genesis and Job—Genesis for its fascinating narratives, and Job for its sublime philosophical poetry. Both Genesis and Job, moreover, reflect the important cultural ideals of ancient Israel.

History and Fiction. The narratives in the book of Genesis can be read in different ways. They may be treated as being literally true. However, if they are looked at from a more literary perspective, they may be divided into two broad categories: prehistoric myths and historicized fiction. The stories of the Creation and the Fall, of the Great Flood and the Tower of Babel, are mythic narratives designed to explain such things as the origin of the universe and its creatures, the reason human beings suffer pain and death, and the emergence of the world's languages. These **etiological stories**, or stories

about the origins and causes of things, occupy the first eleven chapters of Genesis. Among them is an explanation of why rainbows appear in the sky (they function as a sign of Yahweh's covenant), and why snakes crawl on their bellies (the reptilian curse for tempting Adam and Eve to eat the forbidden fruit).

The second category of narrative—historicized fiction—includes the stories of the patriarchs Abraham, Isaac, and Jacob. Certain elements of these stories are ancient, having been passed down through oral tradition, and having only achieved written form around the twelfth to the tenth centuries B.C. The patriarchal stories as written have the character of history, to the extent that they are presented as detailed accounts of deeds performed by particular individuals. However, they differ from later biblical narratives, such as the books of Samuel. The later, more historical writing of the period of the kings has been termed "fictionalized history" to distinguish it from the historicized fiction of the Genesis patriarchal narratives.

The stories about David in the book of Samuel use fictional literary techniques and take imaginative liberties with the historical facts upon which they are based. The earlier patriarchal stories describe perhaps fictitious characters and situations in their enterprise to convey important theological ideas and to account for historical realities, such as how the Hebrews found themselves in Egypt (which is explained in the stories about Joseph and his brothers [Gen. 37–50]).

Timeline 6.1   Early Jewish history.

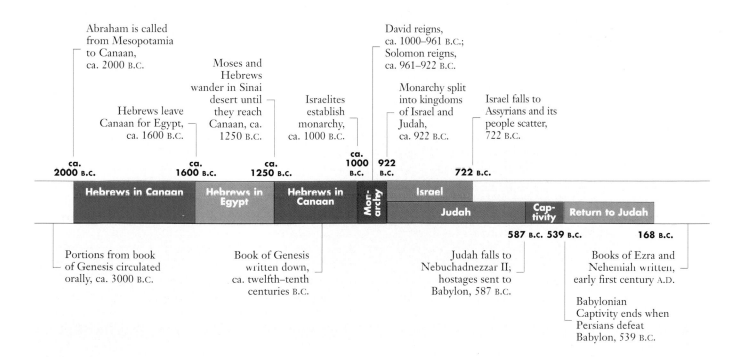

Then & Now

THE BIBLE

The books of the Hebrew Bible were composed over a period of nearly three thousand years, from approximately 3000 B.C., when the earliest Genesis materials appear orally, until near the beginning of the first century A.D., when the books of Ezra and Nehemiah were written. The original manuscripts of the biblical books have not survived. The earliest extant passages are those found in caves in Qumran—the "Dead Sea Scrolls"—which include parchment scrolls of the prophetic book of Isaiah (fig. 6.2).

Originally written in Hebrew, with brief sections in Aramaic, a Near Eastern Semitic language, the present-day Bible in English has been influenced by a series of different translations: Greek (the Septuagint); Latin (the Vulgate—translated by St. Jerome); and Renaissance English, initially translated by John Wycliffe and William Tyndale. The most important early English translation, however, was that undertaken by a committee established by King James I. Known as the "King James translation" or the "Authorized Version" or "AV," this rendering has exerted a profound influence on English and American literature for nearly four hundred years.

During the 1940s and 1950s, the King James translation was updated and corrected, taking account of archaeological discoveries made in the late nineteenth and early twentieth centuries, and reflecting developments in historical and linguistic scholarship. The resulting Revised Standard Version (RSV) was revised once more and published as the New Revised Standard Version (NSRV) in the 1990s.

Figure 6.2 The Dead Sea Isaiah Scroll (detail), first century B.C.–first century A.D. The Scrolls are copies of the Hebrew Bible made by a radical Jewish sect that disavowed the leadership of Jerusalem. The Scroll contains all sixty-six chapters of the Bible's longest book.

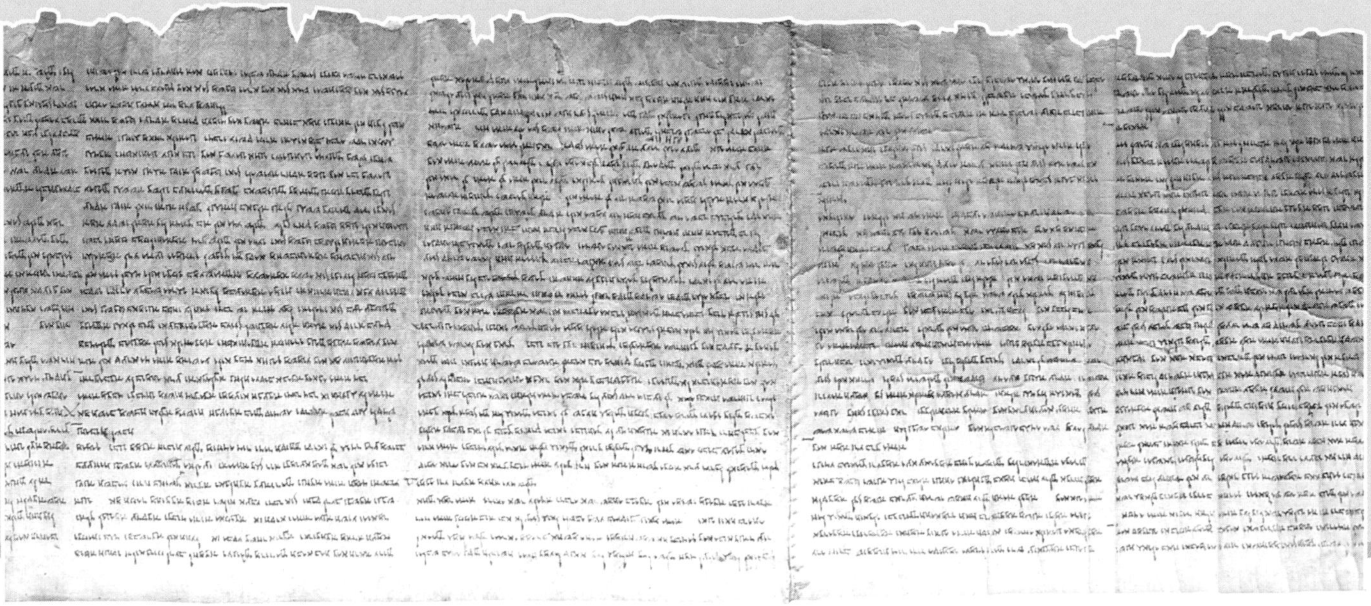

Biblical Poetry.   The biblical poetic tradition goes back more than three thousand years. As with other ancient civilizations, such as those in Greece, Hebraic poetry was bound up with the religious, social, and military life of the Hebrews. War victories were celebrated in verse, as were various other achievements, such as the liberation of the Hebrew slaves from their Egyptian masters. Indeed, the two oldest recorded Hebrew poems are celebrations of great accomplishments. The Bible's oldest poem, the Song of Deborah (Judges 5:1–31) describes how its heroine, Jael, saves the Hebrew people by killing the Canaanite military leader Sisera. Better known is the "Song of the Sea," which celebrates the destruction of the Egyptian pharaoh's army, along with his chariots and horsemen, in the Red Sea.

The most consistent important concern of ancient Hebrew poetry, however, is religious faith. This can be clearly identified in the poetry of the Psalms, the prophecies of Isaiah, and the wisdom of Job. Complementing these morally oriented and religiously grounded poetic works are other biblical poems in a more secular and less ostensibly religious vein (although they, too, have been interpreted allegorically as being religious). The most beautiful and famous of these are the Song of Songs, (also known as the Song of Solomon) and the book of Ecclesiastes.

EARLY CHRISTIANITY

With its belief that a Messiah would come into the world to save humankind, thereby fulfilling God's promises, Judaism was crucial in the emergence of Christianity and to the formulation of many of the new religion's central tenets. Many apocalyptic Hebrew writings, including chapters 7–10 of the book of Daniel, predicted the coming of such a Savior. John the Baptist further prepared the way for Jesus's ministry by preaching that a Messiah was at hand. Those who believed Jesus when he preached that the Kingdom of God was imminent, and who saw that Kingdom as represented in Jesus, became the first Christians.

Just as Jews believe that they are God's Chosen People and Muslims that their holy book, the Quran, is the word of God, Christians believe that Jesus is God and Savior. Moreover, they maintain that by accepting Jesus as their Savior, they will share eternal life with him in heaven when they die. One of the most important elements of their faith is the belief that Jesus rose from the dead after being crucified by the Romans. Their faith gave rise to a revisionary interpretation of the Messianic prophecy, which converted a prior hope for an earthly king into a belief in a divine and spiritual king, whose coming to earth signaled new hope in human redemption. Jesus's kingdom would be a kingdom of the next world, the afterlife, to which the redeemed Christian soul would be taken after death.

JESUS AND HIS MESSAGE

It is important to remember that Jesus was Jewish. His followers, who identified him as the Christ—which means "Messiah" or "Anointed One"—were the first Christians. Jesus was born in Judaea, a land under the political control of the Romans, during the reign of the emperor Augustus.

The public ministry of Jesus began when he was thirty years old, with the performance of his first miracle, the changing of water into wine, at the marriage feast of Cana, a small village north of Nazareth, where Jesus was born. This first miracle is recorded in the New Testament Gospel of John, where it is presented less as an astounding feat than as a sign identifying the presence of God in Jesus. Other miracles followed, including healing the blind and the lame, curing paralytics, and even raising the dead. This aspect of Jesus's mission is the one that draws most attention, as the miracles are typically read as manifestations of his divine power. However, emphasis is placed not only on Jesus's healing miracles, but also on his natural miracles, such as his calming of a storm on the sea of Galilee, his walking on water, and his feeding of thousands of people with only a few fishes and loaves of bread.

Yet, it is Jesus's teaching, rather than his miracles, that is central to Christian beliefs and values. Jesus preached the promise of hope and salvation. He preached that those who believed in him, and in the heavenly Father who had sent him into the world, would have eternal life. He delivered his message in simple and direct language that common people could understand: Believe in him

Map 6.2   The spread of Christianity by A.D. 600.

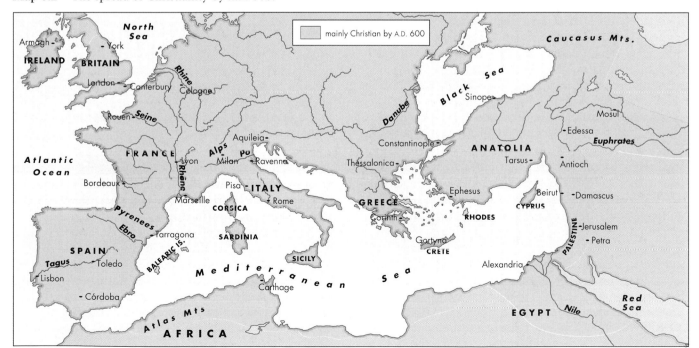

Timeline 6.2   Early Christian history.

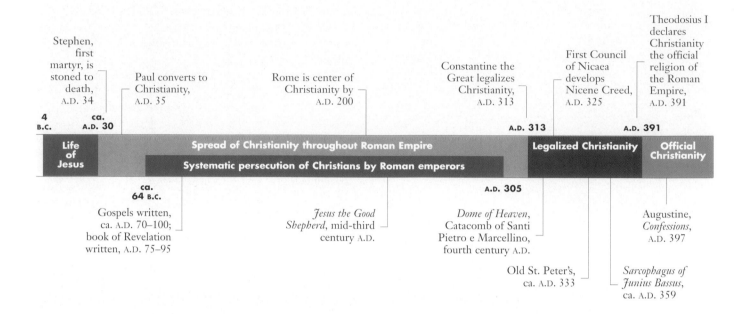

and be saved; beware of false prophets; don't get lost in the intricacies of religious ritual observance; stick to the essentials of faith in God, love of humanity, and hope for the future. He explained this relatively straightforward doctrine through stories, or **parables**, such as that of the Good Samaritan. Parables illustrate an essential Christian principle: in the case of the Good Samaritan, that believing Christians should love their "neighbors"—and that their neighbors included all human beings.

Jesus's increasing popularity, which derived both from the power of his preaching and from the fame of his miracles, angered the Jewish religious authorities of the time. It was the Roman authorities, however, who held the real power in Jesus's day in Galilee, where Jesus did most of his preaching, and it was Pontius Pilate, the procurator of Judaea, who was ultimately responsible for Jesus's crucifixion and death.

Although Jesus did not himself claim to be the son of God, others claimed that exalted status for him. This, in fact, was the crime against the state that led to Jesus's execution, because only the emperor was considered divine. Any mortal suspected of harboring such august notions of self was in violation of the law, the punishment for which was death.

Jesus preached not only the hope of life after death and the need to love one's neighbor as oneself, but also the need to love God with all one's mind, heart, and soul. His preaching was meant to encourage, yet also challenge. He challenged the rich to give up their material possessions; he challenged the poor to be content with their lot; he challenged believers to come and follow him,

to live their lives in simplicity while going about spreading his message and performing good deeds.

Jesus's teaching can be reduced to two essential commandments: to love God above all, and to love others as one loves oneself. In addition to preaching faith and love, Jesus also articulated ethical ideals and proposed standards of moral behavior. Most of them are summed up in the Sermon on the Mount, the fullest version of which is contained in the Gospel of Matthew.

EARLY CHRISTIAN HISTORY

After the death of Jesus, Christianity spread throughout the Mediterranean due to the efforts of martyrs such as Stephen and Sebastian and missionaries such as Paul. Stephen, the first Christian martyr, was stoned to death in A.D. 34 for preaching blasphemy against the Jewish God, while Sebastian was tied to a tree and shot full of arrows for refusing to acknowledge the Roman gods. According to one legend, he survived this only to be beaten to death. Paul was perhaps the most important of the first-century Christians in spreading the new religion. Born Saul, he was at first strongly opposed to Christianity until he underwent conversion near Damascus in A.D. 35 (the so-called "Damascene conversion"). From then until his execution ca. A.D. 62, he proselytized tirelessly for Christianity, formulating doctrine, writing to other Christian communities, and traveling at least as far west as Rome.

The next centuries were a period of slow growth for Christianity and of continual persecution at the hands of the Romans. For instance, in A.D. 64 Nero blamed the Christians for a fire that burned down the imperial capital, though it seems likely that he himself was responsible for it. Two hundred years later, the emperor Decius expelled the Christians from Rome. Such persecution was unusual in the Roman Empire, where other sects and religions were usually tolerated. The problem for the Roman authorities appears to have been the Christians' refusal to worship the Roman gods alongside their own God. The first great turning point came in A.D. 313, when the emperor Constantine issued the Edict of Milan, which granted Christianity toleration as a religion. Constantine convened the first of a series of councils concerned with various matters of faith, such as the trinitarian nature of the godhead. The First Council of Nicaea developed the Nicene Creed, the conventional statement of Christian belief. After Constantine's death, Julian briefly attempted to restore paganism, but in A.D. 391 Theodosius I officially declared Christianity the Roman state religion, banning all pagan cults.

EARLY CHRISTIAN ART

There is no such thing as a coherent or consistent "Early Christian style" of art. In fact, Christianity was at first averse to art because art served the worship of idols. However, Christians recognized that art could be appropriated to help many illiterate followers with visual representations of the Bible's teachings—when, that is, art itself was no longer the object of worship but a *means* to worship, it became an important instrument of theology.

Figure 6.3   Old St. Peter's, Rome, begun ca. A.D. 333, reconstruction drawing. Based on the Roman basilica, which would house, in the apse, a statue of the emperor, the new Christian church placed a *cathedra* or "throne of the bishop" in the emperor's place—hence the origin of the word "cathedral."

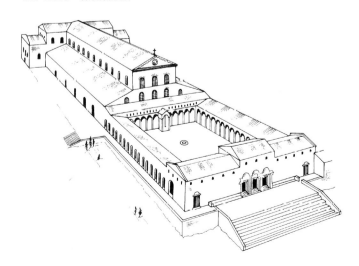

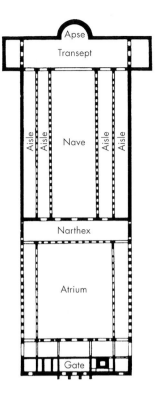

Figure 6.4   Old St. Peter's, Rome, begun ca. A.D. 333, plan. The type of church established here, known as the Early Christian basilica, would be the basis for all churches built with a longitudinal axis—the Latin-cross plan.

Architecture.   When Christianity became an official state religion, the need for churches arose. The type of church built is known as the Early Christian basilica and, by the fourth century, was well established. Old St. Peter's in Rome (fig. 6.3), the quintessential example, located over the tomb of St. Peter, was erected by Constantine. It was destroyed in the fifteenth century to make way for the present St. Peter's (see Chapter 13).

When entering an Early Christian basilica like Old St. Peter's (fig. 6.4), the visitor first came into the **atrium**, a rectangular forecourt, open in the center to the sky, surrounded on all four sides by columnar arcades. The atrium was the area for people not yet baptized. Next, the visitor passed through the **narthex**, an entrance hall or vestibule. Having now reached the actual church, the visitor entered the **nave**, a large rectangular space needed for the masses of people, and flanked on either side by one or two **aisles**, separated from the nave by colonnades. At the end of the nave was the **transept**. Finally, the building ended with the **apse**, a semi-circular space at the back of the church. The altar was in front of the apse, so that the visitor had to walk from one end of the church to the other to reach it.

The reconstruction drawing of the exterior (see fig. 6.3) shows the nave with **clerestory** windows, that is, a

Figure 6.5 Santa Maria Maggiore, Rome, ca. A.D. 430, later modified, view of nave looking toward altar. An advantage of the longitudinal axis of the Early Christian basilica is that, upon entering, the visitor's eyes are automatically directed toward the altar. But a disadvantage of its post and lintel construction is the limited open space, and fire was a constant threat to a building in which candles burned below a wooden ceiling.

row of windows on a section of wall that rises above the part of the roof over the side aisle. Because the nave roof was of lightweight wood, it was easy to support, windows could be made in the walls, and a light interior achieved. The disadvantage of wood was the danger of fire.

A surviving example of an Early Christian basilica, but one that has now been expanded and modified, is Santa Maria Maggiore in Rome (fig. 6.5), originally built ca. A.D. 430. Early Christian basilicas had drab exteriors—the outside of the building was not the part intended to be admired. But the interiors, as demonstrated by Santa Maria Maggiore, were very elaborate, with patterned marble floors, marble columns, and mosaics of colored stone, glass, and gold on the walls and ceilings.

In addition to the basilica plan with its longitudinal axis, as used in Old St. Peter's and Santa Maria Maggiore, round or polygonal buildings with domed roofs were also built in the Early Christian era. The finest example is Santa Costanza in Rome (figs. 6.6 and fig. 6.7), built

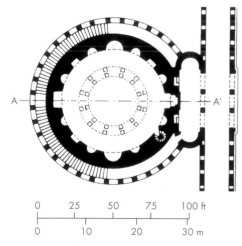

Figure 6.6 Santa Costanza, Rome, ca. A.D. 350, plan. A central plan (circular or polygonal) building, when roofed with a dome, as here, offers an uninterrupted interior space.

Figure 6.7 Santa Costanza, Rome, ca. A.D. 350, interior. The basic scheme of Santa Costanza would later be used by Byzantine architects, and would also serve as the model for the baptisteries that were connected to Christian churches.

Figure 6.8 *Wine-Making Scene*, ca. A.D. 350, mosaic, ambulatory vault of Santa Costanza, Rome. Demonstrating the Christian adaptation of pagan subjects, the vine here represents the words of Jesus, "I am the true vine." The grapes came to symbolize the eucharistic wine and, therefore, the blood of Jesus.

ca. A.D. 350. This was a mausoleum constructed for the emperor Constantine's daughter Constantia, and was once part of a larger church.

The exterior, made of unadorned brick, is plain and simple, but the interior is ornate, with rich materials, textures, colors, and designs. Light comes in through the clerestory windows. The surrounding circular aisle or **ambulatory** is covered with a barrel vault, which is ornamented with mosaics (fig. 6.8).

These mosaics consist of a vine pattern with small scenes along the sides. Laborers are shown picking grapes and putting them into carts, transporting the grapes to a press, where three men crush them underfoot. This subject, common on tavern floor mosaics, may seem out of place here. But because wine plays an important part in the Christian liturgy, it was possible to adopt and adapt a pagan subject to Christian needs.

Sculpture. In the Early Christian era, due to Christianity's disdain for idol worship, sculpture was always secondary to painting and mosaic. One of the rare examples of Early Christian figure sculpture is the statue of *Jesus the Good Shepherd* (fig. 6.9), which dates from the mid-third century A.D., and depicts Jesus carrying a sheep across his shoulders. The subject was common in catacomb painting (see fig. 6.12). There are several versions of this statue, this being one of the earliest and the best. Jesus is portrayed in the Classical tradition. The pose is free, natural, and relaxed, with the weight on one foot

Figure 6.9 *Jesus the Good Shepherd*, mid-third century A.D., marble, height 39″ (99 cm), Vatican Museums, Rome. Large-scale sculptures such as this are extremely rare in Early Christian art. The lamb represents Jesus's followers, whom he guards and guides.

and the head turned to the side, the *contrapposto* stance similar to that of the ancient Greek *Spear-Bearer* (see fig. 4.14). The idealized head has the youthful Jesus gazing into the distance.

For the most part, sculptors turned to small-scale relief work on stone **sarcophagi** (coffins) and ivory panels. Marble sarcophagi, the fronts and occasionally the lids of which were carved with small figures in high relief, are among the earliest works of Christian sculptors, with examples dating from the early third century A.D. onward. The *Sarcophagus of Junius Bassus*, a prefect of Rome (a high position similar to that of a governor or administrator), is among the most notable of these (fig. 6.10). Bassus converted to Christianity shortly before his death in 359. The front of his sarcophagus is divided by

two tiers of columns into ten neat and orderly areas. The subjects depicted in these panels are drawn from the Old and New Testaments of the Bible. The upper row, left to right, shows the sacrifice of Isaac; St. Peter taken prisoner; Jesus enthroned with Saints Peter and Paul; and, in two separate sections, Jesus before Pontius Pilate. The lower row, left to right, shows the misery of Job; Adam and Eve after eating from the Tree of Knowledge; Jesus entering Jerusalem; Daniel in the lions' den; and St. Paul being led to his death. The proportions of the figures are far from Classical and reflect the late Roman change in relief style, as also seen in the fourth-century reliefs on the Arch of Constantine in Rome (see fig. 5.26). Large heads are supported on boneless doll-like bodies with muscleless arms and legs. Background setting is almost

Figure 6.10 *Sarcophagus of Junius Bassus*, ca. A.D. 359, marble, 3′10½″ × 8′ (1.18 × 2.44 m), Museo Petriano, St. Peter's, Rome. Early Christian sculpture consists primarily of reliefs carved on sarcophagi and small ivory plaques. Greater importance was attached to the recognition of the subjects than to realistic representation of the human body.

Figure 6.11 *Archangel Michael*, leaf of a diptych, early sixth century A.D., ivory relief, 17 × 5½″ (43.2 × 14 cm), British Museum, London. Although the carving is technically exquisite, there is little evidence of interest in a realistic spatial relation between figure and setting. Michael's precarious position suggests that he will soon need to make use of his wings to keep his balance.

entirely eliminated in these crowded scenes, action or drama kept to a minimum, and the figures, even when the story suggests they should be animated, are passive and calm. However, these little vignettes are not intended to provide the viewer with a highly detailed narrative. They are only required to bring to mind a story that the viewer is expected to know already.

A representative example of an Early Christian ivory is that of the Archangel Michael (fig. 6.11), made in the early sixth century, one leaf of a **diptych**—a pair of hinged panels. Here pagan Greek forms have been appropriated for Christian purposes. Michael derives from the winged victory figures of Classical art (see fig. 4.27) and his drapery is rendered in the "wet" style of fifth-century B.C. Greek sculpture. The figure, if seen in isolation, would be convincing. However, the treatment of space around it is not. In spite of the architectural setting, there is no sense of depth. Michael's feet dangle over three steps. His hands are shown to be in front of the columns, yet the column bases are in front of the stairs, which implies that Michael is placed at a precarious angle. Without understanding the basic spatial concept of Greek art, the Christian artist has carefully copied the superficial forms.

Painting. The earliest Christian art was found in the **catacombs**—the underground cemeteries of the Christians in and around Rome. The catacombs were practically underground towns of sepulchers and funeral chapels, miles of subterranean passageways cut into the rock.

A painted ceiling in the Catacomb of Santi Pietro e Marcellino in Rome (fig. 6.12), from the fourth century, is an especially well-preserved example. The walls of catacombs were decorated with **frescoes**, paintings made quickly on wet lime plaster. The subjects depicted were generally related to the soul's future life. Especially common was the subject of *Jesus the Good Shepherd*, seen also in sculpture (see fig. 6.9). Filling the center of the ceiling, the painting embodies the idea that the Christian people make up Jesus's flock and, as the Good Shepherd, Jesus watches over and cares for them. The arrangement painted here represents the dome of heaven, with the decoration positioned to form a cross. The story of Jonah is shown in the surrounding semi-circles. Jonah is thrown overboard into the mouth of the waiting whale (the curly serpent-dog makes clear that whales were not known from first-hand experience in fourth-century Rome). Jonah emerges from the whale and then relaxes in safety under the vines. The figures that stand between the semi-circles have assumed a common early prayer pose—the *orans* (from the Latin word for "praying"), with hands raised to heaven.

Popular Old Testament subjects for catacomb paintings were Noah and the Ark, Moses, Jonah and the whale, Daniel in the lions' den, and the story of Susanna.

Figure 6.12 *Dome of Heaven*, painted ceiling in the catacomb of Santi Pietro e Marcellino, Rome, fourth century A.D. Catacombs, the underground burial areas of the Early Christians, were painted with symbolic subjects. Jesus was repeatedly shown as the Good Shepherd with his flock of followers.

Popular New Testament themes were taken from the life of Jesus, especially the miracles, such as the healing of the paralytic and the resurrection of Lazarus. The subjects selected from the scriptures illustrate how God is merciful and will intervene to save the faithful. The rewards of constant prayer are emphasized. Depictions of Jesus's passion (his suffering at the end of his life) are entirely omitted; the earliest known representations of the passion are fifth-century carvings. The catacomb paintings do not treat the subject of Jesus's death and resurrection, which was a popular subject in the Renaissance (see Chapters 13 and 14).

THE NEW TESTAMENT AS LITERATURE

The New Testament is for Christianity what the Hebrew scriptures are for Judaism and the Quran is for Islam: the repository of revealed religious truth. The New Testament, which was written in Greek, records and interprets the acts and words of the Christian Savior,

Cross Currents

CHRISTIANITY AND THE EASTERN CULTS

To the Romans, who had tolerated Judaism, Christianity appeared at first to be another cult from the East, of the kind that had long been attracting converts in the republic. A Bacchus cult, for instance, had acquired a popular following by the second century B.C. God of wine, Bacchus promised his followers salvation and immortality, in the manner of the grapevine itself, which appears to die each autumn, only to be reborn in the spring. His followers engaged in Bacchanalia, high-spirited rites which soon gained the reputation of being little more than drunken orgies, and although the Senate restricted its activities in a law of 186 B.C., the cult of Bacchus persisted for many centuries.

By the time of Christianity's arrival, two other cults had enjoyed success similar to that of Bacchus—the cult of Isis and the cult of Mithras. The worship of Isis originated in Egypt. Each year, when she saw Egypt's arid and barren landscape, she would cry in compassion for the Egyptian people, her tears causing the Nile to flood, thus bringing life back to the earth. As in the Bacchus cult, this rebirth of the land promised human immortality. The cult of Mithras was of particular appeal to the military. Mithras was sent to earth to kill a divine bull, and from the bull's blood all living things sprang. The cult had seven stages of initiation, one of which was a baptism, but because it was a mystery cult, open only to people initiated into its rites, we know very little about it. Mithras, we do know, was a god of truth and light, associated with

the sun, and his birthday was celebrated on December 25, just after the winter solstice, when the sun is "reborn" for another year.

Elements from all of these cult religions survive in Christianity—in its ritual use of wine, in its emphasis on an Isis-like compassion, and in its celebration of Jesus's birth on December 25. It is possible, moreover, that Christianity borrowed some of their traits to attract converts. All of these so-called cults, Christianity chief among them, promised redemption and salvation. While the Bacchus cult had no explicit moral dimension, both the Isis and Mithras cults, like Christianity, had ethical codes that guided the individual's behavior. Such guidance was absent in the state religion, the chief deity of which, Jove/Zeus, was monstrously immoral.

Jesus Christ. The New Testament contains four distinct types of writing: the gospels, or accounts of Jesus's life and ministry, the epistles, or letters to the early Christian churches; the Acts of the Apostles, a history of the spread of Christianity during the thirty years after Jesus's death and resurrection; and Revelation, or the Apocalypse, the last biblical book, which is concerned with the end of the world.

Gospels. Written from about forty to two hundred years after the death of Jesus, the New Testament is far closer in time of composition to the events it describes than is the Old Testament to the events it describes. Three of the four gospels contain much common material, and present a similar overview of Jesus's life and ministry. These three "synoptic" gospels (or gospels to be "viewed together") are those of Matthew, Mark, and Luke. The fourth and final gospel, ascribed to John, provides more analysis and interpretation of Jesus's life than the other three. John's, one might argue, is the most metaphorical of the gospels, and the one least concerned with Jesus's miracles and his attempts to reform first-century Judaism.

The gospels were, apart from Paul's letters, the earliest books of the New Testament. None, however, is an actual eyewitness account of Jesus's life and work. An early source may have been composed during Jesus's lifetime. This source is referred to by scholars as "Q" (for the German word *Quelle*, which means source). This Q

gospel was written, perhaps, by one of the twelve apostles, and may have been drawn upon by the later gospel writers.

Of the surviving gospels, the Gospel of Mark is the earliest, composed around A.D. 70. It portrays Jesus as a miracle worker as well as a dynamic and vibrant social reformer. The Gospel of Mark is action-centered, moving quickly from one event to the next, describing Jesus's life, ministry, passion, and death.

The Gospel of Matthew, written ten to twenty years after that of Mark, which probably along with Q provided its source, emphasizes Jesus as the Messiah referred to in Old Testament prophecies, the one who would complete the Jewish community's destiny. Matthew cites the Hebrew scriptures more than fifty times to show how Jesus could be seen as the fulfillment of the Old Testament prophecies,

Luke is the most literary and artistic of the gospel writers. His gospel displays an unusual stylistic elegance that distinguishes it from the immediacy of Mark and the allusiveness of Matthew. Luke's gospel is the only one that describes Jesus's birth in a manger in Bethlehem. Luke's gospel also focuses more on women—from Mary the mother of Jesus, to Mary Magdalene, the sinner Jesus forgives, to the adulterous woman with whom Jesus converses as he disbands a mob about to stone her to death.

The Gospel of John differs radically from the three synoptic gospels, even as those three gospels differ from one another in focus, emphasis, and degree of literary sophistication. John's is the most theological of the gospels, the one most attuned to the religious and philosophical implications of Jesus's work and words. John's gospel begins, for example, with an idea inherited from Greek thought. Jesus is the *Logos*, the divine word that came into the world as a light into darkness. He is represented not only as one who speaks words of salvation to those ignorant of spiritual realities, but also as a physical embodiment of the meaning of his message. He is an emblem of the living light that dispels the darkness of ignorance, fear, superstition, and disbelief.

Another image that pervades John's gospel is that of water. John describes Jesus as the living water who quenches the spiritual thirst of those unable to find satisfaction in their lives. This image is closely tied to Jesus's emphasis on being reborn into the kingdom of heaven through the agency of baptism in water and a spiritual and metaphorical baptism of the spirit.

Epistles. The New Testament contains twenty-one epistles addressed to Early Christian communities. Fourteen of these are traditionally ascribed to the apostle Paul. The titles of the Pauline epistles are derived from their recipients: Romans, Corinthians, Ephesians, and so on. They were written as a means of explaining points of doctrine, clarifying misunderstandings, and as a way of exhorting Christians in various communities to remain committed to their faith in Jesus. The importance of Paul to the spread of Christianity in the first century A.D. and his influence in formulating Christian doctrine can hardly be exaggerated. Along with his travels to preach Jesus's message, Paul's epistles served as part of his missionary vocation, giving impetus to the spread of Christianity throughout the Greco-Roman world.

Paul preached and wrote on a wide range of subjects relating to the lives of the Early Christians. He urged them to believe in the risen Jesus as the Savior who redeemed them from sin and death. He also exhorted them to live holy and chaste lives, ignoring the demands of the flesh, so that they could join Jesus at the final resurrection, when the bodies of all those believers who had died would be joined with their souls and taken up into heaven.

Two of the most important and influential Christian doctrines expounded in Paul's epistles are the Incarnation and the Atonement, or Redemption. The Incarnation refers to the birth of God in human form as Jesus. As the second person of the Holy Trinity (the union of the Father, Son, and the Holy Ghost in a single godhead) and equal to the Father and the Holy Spirit, Jesus is a divine being. In taking on human form, becoming a man in the flesh and living and dying like any mortal, Jesus revealed his love for humankind.

Paul argued that Jesus became human so that he could suffer and die for the sins of humankind. The theological explanation of this, referred to as the Atonement, involves a number of Christian concepts, including sin and salvation. Essentially, Jesus's sacrifice of himself on the cross atones or compensates for human beings' sins against God, because as a human, he can act as substitute for the actual sinners, and as a divine being, his sacrifice is acceptable to God the Father. Only a human could perform the sacrifice, since it is humans who have sinned; only a divine being could provide acceptable compensation, since divinity was sinned against.

The theological analysis contained in the Pauline epistles is intricate and complex. In developing theories to explain various Christian beliefs, such as the resurrection of the body and the immortality of the soul, Paul relies both on Greek philosophical ideas and on the Old Testament, which he interprets in light of the new teaching. Paul's ideas have influenced Christian teaching for nearly two thousand years, and are reflected in many works of Western literature, including Chaucer's *Canterbury Tales*, Dante's *Divine Comedy*, Shakespeare's plays, and Milton's *Paradise Lost*.

Revelation. Also known as "The Apocalypse," the Greek word for "unveiling," Revelation presents a visionary account of the Last Judgment and the end of the world. Written sometime near the end of the first century A.D., ca. 75–95, this final book of the Bible presents a symbolic vision of the future. The symbols used include the seven seals, the seven lamps, the Great Beast, the seven bowls, and the woman, child, and dragon. The actual meaning of this symbolism is complex and controversial, and has spawned numerous conflicting interpretations through the centuries.

EARLY CHRISTIAN MUSIC

The music of the Early Christian Church had its roots in Jewish worship. Jewish religious rites were accompanied by chanting of sacred texts, with an instrumental accompaniment on the harp or lyre. Essentially, two different kinds of singing developed in Christian services: **responsorial** and **antiphonal**. In Christian services, the congregation sang simple responses to trained cantors and choirs, which sang the more complex parts. In singing a psalm, for example, the cantor or choir would sing the verses and the congregation the standard response of "Amen" or "Alleluia."

This responsorial type of chanting was complemented by antiphonal singing, in which either a cantor and the congregation or different parts of the congregation alternated in singing verses of the psalm. In some cases the congregation would be divided into parts, usually positioned on opposite sides of the church, to enhance the effectiveness of this alternation of the chant.

Early Christianity, unlike Judaism, prohibited instrumental accompaniment of any kind, which was

Connections

GNOSTICISM AND CHRISTIANITY

Alternative, suppressed forms of quasi-Christian belief existed alongside orthodox Christianity in the Early Church. One influential form of Early Christianity was Gnosticism, central to which was a belief that redemption could be achieved through possessing special secret knowledge. Gnostics believed that they had access to secret wisdom (*gnosis* is the Greek word for "knowledge"). This special knowledge was restricted to small groups of Gnostic adherents who pursued lives of asceticism and who observed strict dietary practices, refraining from sensual indulgence and removing themselves from temptation.

Gnosticism was a dualist philosophy which, like Zoroastrianism and Manicheism, divided the world into good and evil. The evil part, which was material rather than spiritual, was created by a demonic spirit. It was this demonic spirit that was said to be responsible for the fall of humanity. Second-century A.D. Gnostics believed that humankind predates the fall and that, before that event, all human beings contained a spark of divinity within them.

Gnosticism shocked the followers of early orthodox Christianity, who were dismayed by Gnostic beliefs in reincarnation and equality for women. Gnosticism nonetheless managed to establish itself as an alternative form of Christianity. Suppressed Gnostic texts co-existed with the canonical Christian scriptures, the Gospel of Thomas, dating from the second century A.D., being perhaps the best known and most widely disseminated.

---

considered pagan. Up until the fourth century, Early Christian **liturgical music** (music used in religious ritual) was based exclusively on sacred texts. Starting in the fifth century, some nonscriptural hymns supplemented these scripture-based chants.

Musical practice differed somewhat in churches that followed the Byzantine liturgy rather than that of St. Ambrose. The Western liturgy of Ambrose made accommodations for active musical participation by the congregation. This required that the music be kept relatively simple, with a single note sung to each syllable. In contrast, Byzantine liturgical music was more complex, with many notes sung to a syllable in a more florid style. These sixth-century Byzantine liturgical musical practices were modified, however, by the seventh-century reforms toward less complex chant melodies.

PHILOSOPHY: AUGUSTINE AND THE NEOPLATONIC INHERITANCE

The spread of Christianity during the early centuries was accompanied by a need to explain and systematize Christian thought. The single most important expounder of Christian doctrine was AUGUSTINE (A.D. 354–430) from Hippo (near present-day Algeria), in northern Africa. Augustine's early life was influenced by Manicheism, a dualistic faith that divides the universe into forces of light and darkness, good and evil. However, it was only when Augustine discovered the philosophy of Plotinus, a third-century Greek Neoplatonist, that he really became aware of Christianity.

Augustine achieved a synthesis of the Platonic philosophical tradition and the Judaeo-Christian emphasis on divine revelation. For Augustine, human beings can only know true ideas when they are illuminated in the soul by God. Augustine dismissed knowledge derived from sense experience as unreliable. Such empirical knowledge was considered suspect due to humanity's fall from grace. To Plato's emphasis on pure ideas—now spiritualized by God's inner light—Augustine added a source of equal importance: divinely revealed truth as recorded in sacred scripture and interpreted by Church tradition.

In his early adulthood, Augustine had lived a life of self-indulgence and debauchery. His *Confessions* describe his dissatisfaction with this way of life, his search for spiritual fulfillment, and, finally, his conversion to Christianity. It functions both as an autobiography and as an allegory of the journey of a soul toward salvation. In recounting his life, Augustine proposes a process of scriptural interpretation that was to become influential for hundreds of years. According to Augustine's theory, the Old Testament prefigures or anticipates the New Testament, with Old Testament characters and events serving as "types" or prefigurations of those in the New Testament. Jesus, for example, is the second Adam. Adam's sin is redeemed by Jesus. New Testament redemption in Jesus from the bondage of sin is prefigured in the deliverance of the Israelites from their captivity in Egypt. Mary is the second Eve, the spiritual mother of humankind, as Eve was its biological mother. Augustine himself serves as a type for the lost soul who finds salvation in an acceptance of Christian revelation.

As the first Western autobiography, Augustine's *Confessions* was enormously influential. Throughout the Middle Ages the book was read, copied, and imitated. The book's image of the spiritual journey influenced medieval poems of pilgrimage, such as William Langland's *Piers Ploughman* and Dante's *Divine Comedy*. As well as providing a framework for these and other forms of spiritual autobiography, the *Confessions* paved the way for the Renaissance rediscovery of the self.

In addition to his *Confessions*, Augustine wrote *On Christian Doctrine*, which analyzes and explains the central tenets of Christian teaching, and the *City of God*, in which he explores the relationship between faith and reason, and the cause of history as a movement toward the clash of two opposite visions of life, represented by two contrasting cities, the city of God and the city of the Devil.

One of Augustine's central philosophical ideas is that evil does not possess reality in the same sense that good does. According to Augustine, evil is a deficiency in good rather than something that exists in its own right. God did not create evil; rather, evil entered the world through incorrect choices made by human beings, as when Adam chose to disobey God's injunction not to eat the forbidden fruit (Genesis 1). Regardless of the source of sin, however, Augustine follows St. Paul in explaining how Christ redeemed humanity, and how life is a spiritual pilgrimage toward God, in whom human beings find their salvation and their eternal rest.

Like Paul, whose epistles he echoes frequently, Augustine distrusted the fleshly body, which he held accountable for humankind's fall from grace. Augustine, in fact, described the original sin as "concupiscence," or lust, to which he had himself succumbed during his early adulthood. This distrust of the physical body and his subordination of it to the faculties of the spiritual soul were to affect Church teaching for many centuries.

Another influential Augustinian idea was that of humankind's inability to obtain salvation on its own. Augustine argued that only God could freely grant this grace. A thousand years later, Martin Luther would argue that people's good works were valueless, and that faith alone could fulfill Christians. Moreover, Augustine argued that since God was omniscient, existing beyond time in the realm of eternity, he comprehends everything in an eternal present. He thus knows who will be saved and who will be damned. This idea of God's foreknowledge would develop later into Calvin's theory of predestination (see Chapter 14).

According to Augustine, since human beings were unable to save themselves, their only hope for salvation lay in accepting God's truth as revealed in sacred scripture, including the New Testament. Furthermore, since human beings were prone to error, misunderstanding, and sin due to the corruption they inherited from Adam and Eve's original sin, they were not in a position to understand the complexities of divine revelation on their own. For that, they needed the authoritative teaching of the Church.

Augustine wrote voluminously in support of Church authority and unity in matters of doctrine. He made vigorous attacks on the doctrines that circulated around the Church in the early centuries. He also defended Christianity against charges that the new religion was responsible for the decline of Roman civilization.

Instead, Augustine saw the fall of Rome as part of God's providential plan for the progressive development of human history toward its fulfillment in the Parousia—the return of Jesus to earth at the end of the world.

Readings

Genesis
The Creation to the Tower of Babel

In the following selections from the book of Genesis, the biblical writers describe the creation of the world and the first human beings, as well as the story of their temptation and fall. The origin of human evil, including the first murder, is described as well as Yahweh's anger at humankind and his punishment by sending a great flood, his preservation of a remnant in the family of Noah, and the later attempt to build a tower that reached heaven. Among the world's best known stories, these oldest of biblical narratives continue to engage readers of diverse backgrounds and faiths. Only recently, for example, a series of ten television shows on Genesis was shown on public television and made available for purchase and rental on videocassette.

The Creation

1 In the beginning God created the heaven and the earth.

2 And the earth was without form, and void; and darkness was upon the face of the deep. And the Spirit of God moved upon the face of the waters.

3 And God said, Let there be light: and there was light.

4 And God saw the light, that it was good: and God divided the light from the darkness.

5 And God called the light Day, and the darkness he called Night. And the evening and the morning were the first day.

6 And God said, Let there be a firmament in the midst of the waters, and let it divide the waters from the waters.

7 And God made the firmament, and divided the waters which were under the firmament from the waters which were above the firmament: and it was so.

8 And God called the firmament Heaven. And the evening and the morning were the second day.

9 And God said, Let the waters under the heaven be gathered together unto one place, and let the dry land appear: and it was so.

10 And God called the dry land earth; and the gathering together of the waters called he Seas: and God saw that it was good.

11 And God said, Let the earth bring forth grass, the herb yielding seed, and the fruit tree yielding fruit after his kind, whose seed is in itself, upon the earth: and it was so.

12 And the earth brought forth grass, and herb yielding seed after his kind, and the tree yielding fruit, whose seed was in itself, after his kind: and God saw that it was good.

13 And the evening and the morning were the third day.

14 And God said, Let there be lights in the firmament of the heaven to divide the day from the night; and let them be for signs, and for seasons, and for days, and years:

15 And let them be for lights in the firmament of the heaven to give light upon the earth: and it was so.

16 And God made two great lights; the greater light to rule the day, and the lesser light to rule the night: he made the stars also.

17 And God set them in the firmament of the heaven to give light upon the earth,

18 And to rule over the day and over the night, and to divide the light from the darkness: and God saw that it was good.

19 And the evening and the morning were the fourth day.

20 And God said, Let the waters bring forth abundantly the moving creature that hath life, and fowl that may fly above the earth in the open firmament of heaven.

21 And God created great whales, and every living creature that moveth, which the waters brought forth abundantly, after their kind, and every winged fowl after his kind: and God saw that it was good.

22 And God blessed them, saying, Be fruitful, and multiply, and fill the waters in the seas, and let fowl multiply in the earth.

23 And the evening and the morning were the fifth day.

24 And God said, Let the earth bring forth the living creature after his kind, cattle, and creeping thing, and beast of the earth after his kind: and it was so.

25 And God made the beast of the earth after his kind, and cattle after their kind, and every thing that creepeth upon the earth after his kind: and God saw that it was good.

26 And God said, Let us make man in our image, after our likeness: and let them have dominion over the fish of the sea, and over the fowl of the air, and over the cattle, and over all the earth, and over every creeping thing that creepeth upon the earth.

27 So God created man in his own image, in the image of God created he him; male and female created he them.

28 And God blessed them, and God said unto them, Be fruitful, and multiply, and replenish the earth, and subdue it: and have dominion over the fish of the sea, and over the fowl of the air, and over every living thing that moveth upon the earth.

29 And God said, Behold, I have given you every herb bearing seed, which is upon the face of all the earth, and every tree, in the which is the fruit of a tree yielding seed; to you it shall be for meat.

30 And to every beast of the earth, and to every fowl of the air, and to every thing that creepeth upon the earth, wherein there is life, I have given every green herb for meat: and it was so.

31 And God saw every thing that he had made, and, behold, it was very good. And the evening and the morning were the sixth day.

2 Thus the heavens and the earth were finished, and all the host of them.

2 And on the seventh day God ended his work which he had made; and he rested on the seventh day from all his work which he had made.

3 And God blessed the seventh day, and sanctified it: because that in it he had rested from all his work which God created and made.

4 These are the generations of the heavens and of the earth when they were created, in the day that the LORD God made the earth and the heavens,

5 And every plant of the field before it was in the earth, and every herb of the field before it grew: for the LORD God had not caused it to rain upon the earth, and there was not a man to till the ground.

6 But there went up a mist from the earth, and watered the whole face of the ground.

7 And the LORD God formed man of the dust of the ground, and breathed into his nostrils the breath of life; and man became a living soul.

8 And the LORD God planted a garden eastward in Eden; and there he put the man whom he had formed.

9 And out of the ground made the LORD God to grow every tree that is pleasant to the sight, and good for food; the tree of life also in the midst of the garden, and the tree of knowledge of good and evil.

10 And a river went out of Eden to water the garden; and from thence it was parted, and became into four heads.

11 The name of the first is Pison: that is it which compasseth the whole land of Havilah, where there is gold;

12 And the gold of that land is good: there is bdellium and the onyx stone.

13 And the name of the second river is Gihon: the same is it that compasseth the whole land of Ethiopia.

14 And the name of the third river is Hiddekel: that is it which goeth toward the east of Assyria. And the fourth river is Euphrates.

15 And the LORD God took the man, and put him into the garden of Eden to dress it and to keep it.

16 And the LORD God commanded the man, saying, Of every tree of the garden thou mayest freely eat:

17 But of the tree of the knowledge of good and evil, thou shalt not eat of it: for in the day that thou eatest thereof thou shalt surely die.

18 And the LORD God said, It is not good that the man should be alone; I will make him an help meet for him.

19 And out of the ground the LORD God formed every beast of the field, and every fowl of the air; and brought them unto Adam to see what he would call them: and whatsoever Adam called every living creature, that was the name thereof.

20 And Adam gave names to all cattle, and to the fowl of the air, and to every beast of the field; but for Adam there was not found an help meet for him.

21 And the LORD God caused a deep sleep to fall upon Adam, and he slept: and he took one of his ribs, and closed up the flesh instead thereof;

22 And the rib, which the LORD God had taken from man, made he a woman, and brought her unto the man.

23 And Adam said, This is now bone of my bones, and flesh of my flesh: she shall be called Woman, because she was taken out of Man.

24 Therefore shall a man leave his father and his mother, and shall cleave unto his wife: and they shall be one flesh.

25 And they were both naked, the man and his wife, and were not ashamed.

3 Now the serpent was more subtil than any beast of the field which the LORD God had made. And he said unto the woman, Yea, hath God said, Ye shall not eat of every tree of the garden?

2   And the woman said unto the serpent, We may eat of the fruit of the trees of the garden:

3   But of the fruit of the tree which is in the midst of the garden, God hath said, Ye shall not eat of it, neither shall ye touch it, lest ye die.

4   And the serpent said unto the woman, Ye shall not surely die:

5   For God doth know that in the day ye eat thereof, then your eyes shall be opened, and ye shall be as gods, knowing good and evil.

6   And when the woman saw that the tree was good for food, and that it was pleasant to the eyes, and a tree to be desired to make one wise, she took of the fruit thereof, and did eat, and gave also unto her husband with her; and he did eat.

7   And the eyes of them both were opened, and they knew that they were naked; and they sewed fig leaves together, and made themselves aprons.

8   And they heard the voice of the LORD God walking in the garden in the cool of the day: and Adam and his wife hid themselves from the presence of the LORD God amongst the trees of the garden.

9   And the LORD God called unto Adam, and said unto him, Where art thou?

10   And he said, I heard thy voice in the garden, and I was afraid, because I was naked; and I hid myself.

11   And he said, Who told thee that thou wast naked? Hast thou eaten of the tree, whereof I commanded thee that thou shouldest not eat?

12   And the man said, The woman whom thou gavest to be with me, she gave me of the tree, and I did eat.

13   And the LORD God said unto the woman, What is this that thou hast done? And the woman said, The serpent beguiled me, and I did eat.

14   And the LORD God said unto the serpent, Because thou hast done this, thou art cursed above all cattle, and above every beast of the field; upon thy belly shalt thou go, and dust shalt thou eat all the days of thy life:

15   And I will put enmity between thee and the woman, and between thy seed and her seed; it shall bruise thy head, and thou shalt bruise his heel.

16   Unto the woman he said, I will greatly multiply thy sorrow and thy conception; in sorrow thou shalt bring forth children; and thy desire shall be to thy husband, and he shall rule over thee.

17   And unto Adam he said, Because thou hast hearkened unto the voice of thy wife, and hast eaten of the tree, of which I commanded thee, saying, Thou shalt not eat of it; cursed is the ground for thy sake; in sorrow shalt thou eat of it all the days of thy life;

18   Thorns also and thistles shall it bring forth to thee; and thou shalt eat the herb of the field;

19   In the sweat of thy face shalt thou eat bread, till thou return unto the ground; for out of it wast thou taken: for dust thou art, and unto dust shalt thou return.

20   And Adam called his wife's name Eve; because she was the mother of all living.

21   Unto Adam also and to his wife did the LORD God make coats of skins, and clothed them.

22   And the LORD God said, Behold, the man is become as one of us, to know good and evil: and now, lest he put forth his hand, and take also of the tree of life, and eat, and live for ever:

23   Therefore the LORD God sent him forth from the garden of Eden, to till the ground from whence he was taken.

24   So he drove out the man; and he placed at the east of the garden of Eden Cherubims, and a flaming sword which turned every way, to keep the way of the tree of life.

4 And Adam knew Eve his wife; and she conceived, and bare Cain, and said, I have gotten a man from the LORD.

2   And she again bare his brother Abel. And Abel was a keeper of sheep, but Cain was a tiller of the ground.

3   And in process of time it came to pass, that Cain brought of the fruit of the ground an offering unto the LORD.

4   And Abel, he also brought of the firstlings of his flock and of the fat thereof. And the LORD had respect unto Abel and to his offering:

5   But unto Cain and to his offering he had not respect. and Cain was very wroth, and his countenance fell.

6   And the LORD said unto Cain, Why art thou wroth? and why is thy countenance fallen?

7   If thou doest well, shalt thou not be accepted? and if thou doest not well, sin lieth at the door. And unto thee shall be his desire, and thou shalt rule over him.

8   And Cain talked with Abel his brother: and it came to pass, when they were in the field, that Cain rose up against Abel his brother, and slew him.

9   And the LORD said unto Cain, Where is Abel thy brother? And he said, I know not: Am I my brother's keeper?

10   And he said, What hast thou done? the voice of thy brother's blood crieth unto me from the ground.

11   And now art thou cursed from the earth, which hath opened her mouth to receive thy brother's blood from thy hand;

12   When thou tillest the ground, it shall not henceforth yield unto thee her strength; a fugitive and a vagabond shalt thou be in the earth.

13   And Cain said unto the LORD, My punishment is greater than I can bear.

14   Behold, thou hast driven me out this day from the face of the earth; and from thy face shall I be hid; and I shall be a fugitive and a vagabond in the earth; and it shall come to pass, that every one that findeth me shall slay me.

15   And the LORD said unto him, Therefore whosoever slayeth Cain, vengeance shall be taken on him sevenfold. And the LORD set a mark upon Cain, lest any finding him should kill him.

16   And Cain went out from the presence of the LORD, and dwelt in the land of Nod, on the east of Eden.

…

Noah and the Ark

6 AND it came to pass, when men began to multiply on the face of the earth, and daughters were born unto them,

2   That the sons of God saw the daughters of men that

they were fair; and they took them wives of all which they chose.

3   And the LORD said, My spirit shall not always strive with man, for that he also is flesh: yet his days shall be an hundred and twenty years.

4   There were giants in the earth in those days; and also after that, when the sons of God came in unto the daughters of men, and they bare children to them, the same became mighty men which were of old, men of renown.

5   And God saw that the wickedness of man was great in the earth, and that every imagination of the thoughts of his heart was only evil continually.

6   And it repented the LORD that he had made man on the earth, and it grieved him at his heart.

7   And the LORD said, I will destroy man whom I have created from the face of the earth; both man, and beast, and the creeping thing, and the fowls of the air; for it repenteth me that I have made them.

8   But Noah found grace in the eyes of the LORD.

9   These are the generations of Noah: Noah was a just man and perfect in his generations, and Noah walked with God.

10   And Noah begat three sons, Shem, Ham, and Japheth.

11   The earth also was corrupt before God, and the earth was filled with violence.

12   And God looked upon the earth, and, behold, it was corrupt; for all flesh had corrupted his way upon the earth.

13   And God said unto Noah, The end of all flesh is come before me; for the earth is filled with violence through them: and, behold, I will destroy them with the earth.

14   Make thee an ark of gopher wood; rooms shalt thou make in the ark, and shalt pitch it within and without with pitch.

15   And this is the fashion which thou shalt make it of: The length of the ark shall be three hundred cubits, the breadth of it fifty cubits, and the height of it thirty cubits.

16   A window shalt thou make to the ark, and in a cubit shalt thou finish it above; and the door of the ark shalt thou set in the side thereof; with lower, second, and third stories shalt thou make it.

17   And, behold, I, even I, do bring a flood of waters upon the earth, to destroy all flesh, wherein is the breath of life, from under heaven; and every thing that is in the earth shall die.

18   But with thee will I establish my covenant; and thou shalt come into the ark, thou, and thy sons, and thy wife, and thy sons' wives with thee.

19   And of every living thing of all flesh, two of every sort shalt thou bring into the ark, to keep them alive with thee; they shall be male and female.

20   Of fowls after their kind, and of cattle after their kind, of every creeping thing of the earth after his kind, two of every sort shall come unto thee, to keep them alive.

21   And take thou unto thee of all food that is eaten, and thou shalt gather it to thee; and it shall be for food for thee, and for them.

22   Thus did Noah; according to all that God commanded him, so did he.

7   AND the LORD said unto Noah, Come thou and all thy house into the ark; for thee have I seen righteous before me in this generation.

2   Of every clean beast thou shalt take to thee by sevens, the male and his female: and of the beasts that are not clean by two, the male and his female.

3   Of fowls also of the air by sevens, the male and the female; to keep seed alive upon the face of all the earth.

4   For yet seven days, and I will cause it to rain upon the earth forty days and forty nights; and every living substance that I have made will I destroy from off the face of the earth.

5   And Noah did according unto all that the LORD commanded him.

6   And Noah was six hundred years old when the flood of waters was upon the earth.

7   And Noah went in, and his sons, and his wife, and his sons' wives with him, into the ark, because of the waters of the flood.

8   Of clean beasts, and of beasts that are not clean, and of fowls, and of every thing that creepeth upon the earth,

9   There went in two and two unto Noah into the ark, the male and the female, as God had commanded Noah.

10   And it came to pass after seven days, that the waters of the flood were upon the earth.

11   In the six hundreth year of Noah's life, in the second month, the seventeenth day of the month, the same day were all the fountains of the great deep broken up, and the windows of heaven were opened.

12   And the rain was upon the earth forty days and forty nights.

13   In the selfsame day entered Noah, and Shem, and Ham, and Japheth, the sons of Noah, and Noah's wife, and the three wives of his sons with them, into the ark:

14   They, and every beast after his kind, and all the cattle after their kind, and every creeping thing that creepeth upon the earth after his kind, and every fowl after his kind, every bird of every sort.

15   And they went in unto Noah into the ark two and two of all flesh, wherein is the breath of life.

16   And they that went in, went in male and female of all flesh, as God had commanded him: and the LORD shut him in.

17   And the flood was forty days upon the earth; and the waters increased, and bare up the ark, and it was lift up above the earth.

18   And the waters prevailed, and were increased greatly upon the earth; and the ark went upon the face of the waters.

19   And the waters prevailed exceedingly upon the earth; and all the high hills, that were under the whole heaven, were covered.

20   Fifteen cubits upward did the waters prevail; and the mountains were covered.

21   And all flesh died that moved upon the earth, both of fowl, and of cattle, and of beast, and of every creeping thing that creepeth upon the earth, and every man:

22   All in whose nostrils was the breath of life, of all that was in the dry land, died.

23   And every living substance was destroyed which was upon the face of the ground, both man, and cattle, and the creeping things, and the fowl of the heaven; and they were destroyed from the earth; and Noah only remained alive, and they that were with him in the ark.

24 And the waters prevailed upon the earth an hundred and fifty days.

The Tower of Babel

11 And the whole earth was of one language, and of one speech.

2 And it came to pass, as they journeyed from the east, that they found a plain in the land of Shinar; and they dwelt there.

3 And they said one to another, Go to, let us make brick, and burn them throughly. And they had brick for stone, and slime had they for morter.

4 And they said, Go to, let us build us a city and a tower, whose top may reach unto heaven; and let us make us a name, lest we be scattered abroad upon the face of the whole earth.

5 And the LORD came down to see the city and the tower, which the children of men builded.

6 And the LORD said, Behold, the people is one, and they have all one language; and this they begin to do: and now nothing will be restrained from them, which they have imagined to do.

7 Go to, let us go down, and there confound their language, that they may not understand one another's speech.

8 So the LORD scattered them abroad from thence upon the face of all the earth: and they left off to build the city.

9 Therefore is the name of it called Babel; because the LORD did there confound the language of all the earth: and from thence did the LORD scatter them abroad upon the face of all the earth.

✦ THE BOOK OF JOB
Chapters 1–3, 38–42

The poetry contained in the Book of Job is among the most sublime in the Bible. The Book of Job includes a frame story, a narrative legend that describes a wager between God and Satan that God's faithful servant Job would curse God if Job were made to suffer. When God grants Satan power to kill Job's flocks, servants, and children, Job responds by praising God rather than cursing him. However, before God restores Job's fortune, Job raises important theological and philosophical questions, such as why the good suffer and the wicked prosper. Job challenges his friends and then God to provide answers to some of his questions.

1 THERE was a man in the land of Uz, whose name was Job; and that man was perfect and upright, and one that feared God, and eschewed evil.

2 And there were born unto him seven sons and three daughters.

3 His substance also was seven thousand sheep, and three thousand camels, and five hundred yoke of oxen, and five hundred she asses, and a very great household; so that this man was the greatest of all the men of the east.

4 And his sons went and feasted in their houses, every one his day; and sent and called for their three sisters to eat and to drink with them.

5 And it was so, when the days of their feasting were gone about, that Job sent and sanctified them, and rose up early in the morning, and offered burnt offerings according to the number of them all: for Job said, It may be that my sons have sinned, and cursed God in their hearts. Thus did Job continually.

6 Now there was a day when the sons of God came to present themselves before the LORD, and Satan came also among them.

7 And the LORD said unto Satan, Whence comest thou? Then Satan answered the LORD, and said, From going to and fro in the earth, and from walking up and down in it.

8 And the LORD said unto Satan, Hast thou considered my servant Job, that there is none like him in the earth, a perfect and an upright man, one that feareth God, and escheweth evil?

9 Then Satan answered the LORD, and said, Doth Job fear God for nought?

10 Hast not thou made an hedge about him, and about his house, and about all that he hath on every side? thou hast blessed the work of his hands, and his substance is increased in the land.

11 But put forth thine hand now, and touch all that he hath, and he will curse thee to thy face.

12 And the LORD said unto Satan, Behold, all that he hath is in thy power; only upon himself put not forth thine hand. So Satan went forth from the presence of the LORD.

13 And there was a day when his sons and his daughters were eating and drinking wine in their eldest brother's house:

14 And there came a messenger unto Job, and said, The oxen were plowing, and the asses feeding beside them:

15 And the Sabeans fell upon them, and took them away; yea, they have slain the servants with the edge of the sword; and I only am escaped alone to tell thee.

16 While he was yet speaking, there came also another, and said, The fire of God is fallen from heaven, and hath burned up the sheep, and the servants, and consumed them; and I only am escaped alone to tell thee.

17 While he was yet speaking, there came also another, and said, The Chaldeans made out three bands, and fell upon the camels, and have carried them away, yea, and slain the servants with the edge of the sword; and I only am escaped alone to tell thee.

18 While he was yet speaking, there came also another, and said, Thy sons and thy daughters were eating and drinking wine in their eldest brother's house:

19 And, behold, there came a great wind from the wilderness, and smote the four corners of the house, and it fell upon the young men, and they are dead; and I only am escaped alone to tell thee.

20 Then Job arose, and rent his mantle, and shaved his head, and fell down upon the ground, and worshipped,

21 And said, Naked came I out of my mother's womb, and naked shall I return thither: the LORD gave, and the LORD hath taken away; blessed be the name of the LORD.

22 In all this Job sinned not, nor charged God foolishly.

2 AGAIN there was a day when the sons of God came to present themselves before the LORD, and Satan came also among them to present himself before the LORD.

2 And the LORD said unto Satan, From whence comest thou? And Satan answered the LORD, and said, From going to and fro in the earth, and from walking up and down in it.

3   And the LORD said unto Satan, Hast thou considered my servant Job, that there is none like him in the earth, a perfect and an upright man, one that feareth God, and escheweth evil? and still he holdeth fast his integrity, although thou movedst me against him, to destroy him without cause.

4   And Satan answered the LORD, and said, Skin for skin, yea, all that a man hath will he give for his life.

5   But put forth thine hand now, and touch his bone and his flesh, and he will curse thee to thy face.

6   And the LORD said unto Satan, Behold, he is in thine hand; but save his life.

7   So went Satan forth from the presence of the LORD, and smote Job with sore boils from the sole of his foot unto his crown.

8   And he took him a potsherd to scrape himself withal; and he sat down among the ashes.

9   Then said his wife unto him, Dost thou still retain thine integrity? curse God, and die.

10   But he said unto her, Thou speakest as one of the foolish women speaketh. What? shall we receive good at the hand of God, and shall we not receive evil? In all this did not Job sin with his lips.

11   Now when Job's three friends heard of all this evil that was come upon him, they came every one from his own place; Eliphaz the Temanite, and Bildad the Shuhite, and Zophar the Naamathite: for they had made an appointment together to come to mourn with him and to comfort him.

12   And when they lifed up their eyes afar off, and knew him not, they lifted up their voice, and wept; and they rent every one his mantle, and sprinkled dust upon their heads toward heaven.

13   So they sat down with him upon the ground seven days and seven nights, and none spake a word unto him: for they saw that his grief was very great.

3 AFTER this opened Job his mouth, and cursed his day.

2   And Job spake, and said,

3   Let the day perish wherein I was born, and the night in which it was said, There is a man child conceived.

4   Let that day be darkness; let not God regard it from above, neither let the light shine upon it.

5   Let darkness and the shadow of death stain it; let a cloud dwell upon it; let the blackness of the day terrify it.

6   As for that night, let darkness seize upon it; let it not be joined unto the days of the year, let it not come into the number of the months.

7   Lo, let that night be solitary; let no joyful voice come therein.

8   Let them curse it that curse the day, who are ready to raise up their mourning.

9   Let the stars of the twilight thereof be dark; let it look for light, but have none; neither let it see the dawning of the day:

10   Because it shut not up the doors of my mother's womb, nor hid sorrow from mine eyes.

11   Why died I not from the womb? why did I not give up the ghost when I came out of the belly?

12   Why did the knees prevent me? or why the breasts that I should suck?

13   For now should I have lain still and been quiet, I should have slept: then had I been at rest,

14   With kings and counsellors of the earth, which built desolate places for themselves;

15   Or with princes that had gold, who filled their houses with silver:

16   Or as an hidden untimely birth I had not been; as infants which never saw light.

17   There the wicked cease from troubling; and there the weary be at rest.

18   There the prisoners rest together; they hear not the voice of the oppressor.

19   The small and great are there; and the servant is free from his master.

20   Wherefore is light given to him that is in misery, and life unto the bitter in soul;

21   Which long for death, but it cometh not; and dig for it more than for hid treasures;

22   Which rejoice exceedingly, and are glad, when they can find the grave?

23   Why is light given to a man whose way is hid, and whom God hath hedged in?

24   For my sighing cometh before I eat, and my roarings are poured out like the waters.

25   For the thing which I greatly feared is come upon me, and that which I was afraid of is come unto me.

26   I was not in safety, neither had I rest, neither was I quiet; yet trouble came.

. . . .

38 THEN the LORD answered Job out of the whirlwind, and said,

2   Who is this that darkeneth counsel by words without knowledge?

3   Gird up now thy loins like a man; for I will demand of thee, and answer thou me.

4   Where wast thou when I laid the foundations of the earth? declare, if thou hast understanding.

5   Who hath laid the measures thereof, if thou knowest? or who hath stretched the line upon it?

6   Whereupon are the foundations thereof fastened? or who laid the corner stone thereof;

7   When the morning stars sang together, and all the sons of God shouted for joy?

8   Or who shut up the sea with doors, when it brake forth, as if it had issued out of the womb?

9   When I made the cloud the garment thereof, and thick darkness a swaddlingband for it,

10   And brake up for it my decreed place, and set bars and doors,

11   And said, Hitherto shalt thou come, but no further: and here thy proud waves be stayed?

12   Hast thou commanded the morning since thy days; and caused the dayspring to know his place;

13   That it might take hold of the ends of the earth, that the wicked might be shaken out of it?

14   It is turned as clay to the seal; and they stand as a garment.

15   And from the wicked their light is withholden, and the high arm shall be broken.

16   Hast thou entered into the springs of the sea? or hast

thou walked in the search of the depth?

17   Have the gates of death been opened unto thee? or hast thou seen the doors of the shadow of death?

18   Hast thou perceived the breadth of the earth? declare if thou knowest it all.

19   Where is the way where light dwelleth? and as for darkness, where is the place thereof,

20   That thou shouldest take it to the bound thereof, and that thou shouldest know the paths to the house thereof?

21   Knowest thou it, because thou wast then born? or because the number of thy days is great?

22   Hast thou entered into the treasures of the snow? or hast thou seen the treasures of the hail,

23   Which I have reserved against the time of trouble, against the day of battle and war?

24   By what way is the light parted, which scattereth the east wind upon the earth?

25   Who hath divided a watercourse for the overflowing of waters, or a way for the lightning of thunder;

26   To cause it to rain on the earth, where no man is; on the wilderness, wherein there is no man;

27   To satisfy the desolate and waste ground; and to cause the bud of the tender herb to spring forth?

28   Hath the rain a father? or who hath begotten the drops of dew?

29   Out of whose womb came the ice? and the hoary frost of heaven, who hath gendered it?

30   The waters are hid as with a stone, and the face of the deep is frozen.

31   Canst thou bind the sweet influences of Pleiades, or loose the bands of Orion?

32   Canst thou bring forth Mazzaroth in his season? or canst thou guide Arcturus with his sons?

33   Knowest thou the ordinances of heaven? canst thou set the dominion thereof in the earth?

34   Canst thou lift up thy voice to the clouds, that abundance of waters may cover thee?

35   Canst thou send lightnings, that they may go, and say unto thee, Here we are?

36   Who hath put wisdom in the inward parts? or who hath given understanding to the heart?

37   Who can number the clouds in wisdom? or who can stay the bottles of heaven,

38   When the dust groweth into hardness, and the clods cleave fast together?

39   Wilt thou hunt the prey for the lion? or fill the appetite of the young lions,

40   When they couch in their dens, and abide in the covert to lie in wait?

41   Who provideth for the raven his food? when his young ones cry unto God, they wander for lack of meat.

39   KNOWEST thou the time when the wild goats of the rock bring forth? or canst thou mark when the hinds do calve?

2   Canst thou number the months that they fulfil? or knowest thou the time when they bring forth?

3   They bow themselves, they bring forth their young ones, they cast out their sorrows.

4   Their young ones are in good liking, they grow up with corn; they go forth, and return not unto them.

5   Who hath sent out the wild ass free? or who hath loosed the bands of the wild ass?

6   Whose house I have made the wilderness, and the barren land his dwellings.

7   He scorneth the multitude of the city, neither regardeth he the crying of the driver.

8   The range of the mountains is his pasture, and he searcheth after every green thing.

9   Will the unicorn be willing to serve thee, or abide by thy crib?

10   Canst thou bind the unicorn with his band in the furrow? or will he harrow the valleys after thee?

11   Wilt thou trust him, because his strength is great? or wilt thou leave thy labour to him?

12   Wilt thou believe him, that he will bring home thy seed, and gather it into thy barn?

13   Gavest thou the goodly wings unto the peacocks? or wings and feathers unto the ostrich?

14   Which leaveth her eggs in the earth, and warmeth them in the dust,

15   And forgetteth that the foot may crush them, or that the wild beast may break them.

16   She is hardened against her young ones, as though they were not her's: her labour is in vain without fear;

17   Because God hath deprived her of wisdom, neither hath he imparted to her understanding.

18   What time she lifteth up herself on high, she scorneth the horse and his rider.

19   Hath thou given the horse strength? hast thou clothed his neck with thunder?

20   Canst thou make him afraid as a grasshopper? the glory of his nostrils is terrible.

21   He paweth in the valley, and rejoiceth in his strength: he goeth on to meet the armed men.

22   He mocketh at fear, and is not affrighted; neither turneth he back from the sword.

23   The quiver rattleth against him, the glittering spear and the shield.

24   He swalloweth the ground with fierceness and rage: neither believeth he that it is the sound of the trumpet.

25   He saith among the trumpets, Ha, ha; and he smelleth the battle afar off, the thunder of the captains, and the shouting.

26   Doth the hawk fly by thy wisdom, and stretch her wings toward the south?

27   Doth the eagle mount up at thy command, and make her nest on high?

28   She dwelleth and abideth on the rock, upon the crag of the rock, and the strong place.

29   From thence she seeketh the prey, and her eyes behold afar off.

30   Her young ones also suck up blood: and where the slain are, there is she.

40   MOREOVER the LORD answered Job, and said,

2   Shall he that contendeth with the Almighty instruct him? he that reproveth God, let him answer it.

3   Then Job answered the LORD, and said,

4   Behold, I am vile; what shall I answer thee? I will lay mine hand upon my mouth.

5   Once have I spoken; but I will not answer: yea, twice; but I will proceed no further.

6   Then answered the LORD unto Job out of the whirlwind, and said,

7   Gird up thy loins now like a man: I will demand of thee, and declare thou unto me.

8   Wilt thou also disannul my judgment? wilt thou condemn me, that thou mayest be righteous?

9   Hast thou an arm like God? or canst thou thunder with a voice like him?

10   Deck thyself now with majesty and excellency; and array thyself with glory and beauty.

11   Cast abroad the rage of thy wrath: and behold every one that is proud, and abase him.

12   Look on every one that is proud, and bring him low; and tread down the wicked in their place.

13   Hide them in the dust together; and bind their faces in secret.

14   Then will I also confess unto thee that thine own right hand can save thee.

15   Behold now behemoth, which I made with thee; he eateth grass as an ox.

16   Lo now, his strength is in his loins, and his force is in the navel of his belly.

17   He moveth his tail like a cedar: the sinews of his stones are wrapped together.

18   His bones are as strong pieces of brass; his bones are like bars of iron.

19   He is the chief of the ways of God: he that made him can make his sword to approach unto him.

20   Surely the mountains bring him forth food, where all the beasts of the field play.

21   He lieth under the shady trees, in the covert of the reed, and fens.

22   The shady trees cover him with their shadow; the willows of the brook compass him about.

23   Behold, he drinketh up a river, and hasteth not: he trusteth that he can draw up Jordan into his mouth.

24   He taketh it with his eyes: his nose pierceth through snares.

41   CANST thou draw out leviathan with an hook? or his tongue with a cord which thou lettest down?

2   Canst thou put an hook into his nose? or bore his jaw through with a thorn?

3   Will he make many supplications unto thee? will he speak soft words unto thee?

4   Will he make a covenant with thee? wilt thou take him for a servant for ever?

5   Wilt thou play with him as with a bird? or wilt thou bind him for thy maidens?

6   Shall the companions make a banquet of him? shall they part him among the merchants?

7   Canst thou fill his skin with barbed irons? or his head with fish spears?

8   Lay thine hand upon him, remember the battle, do no more.

9   Behold, the hope of him is in vain: shall not one be cast down even at the sight of him?

10   None is so fierce that dare stir him up: who then is able to stand before me?

11   Who hath prevented me, that I should repay him? whatsoever is under the whole heaven is mine.

12   I will not conceal his parts, nor his power, nor his comely proportion.

13   Who can discover the face of his garment? or who can come to him with his double bridle?

14   Who can open the doors of his face? his teeth are terrible round about.

15   His scales are his pride, shut up together as with a close seal.

16   One is so near to another, that no air can come between them.

17   They are joined one to another, they stick together, that they cannot be sundered.

18   By his neesings a light doth shine, and his eyes are like the eyelids of the morning.

19   Out of his mouth go burning lamps, and sparks of fire leap out.

20   Out of his nostrils goeth smoke, as out of a seething pot or caldron.

21   His breath kindleth coals, and a flame goeth out of his mouth.

22   In his neck remaineth strength, and sorrow is turned into joy before him.

23   The flakes of his flesh are joined together: they are firm in themselves; they cannot be moved.

24   His heart is as firm as a stone; yea, as hard as a piece of the nether millstone.

25   When he raiseth up himself, the mighty are afraid: by reason of breakings they purify themselves.

26   The sword of him that layeth at him cannot hold: the spear, the dart, nor the habergeon.

27   He esteemeth iron as straw, and brass as rotten wood.

28   The arrow cannot make him flee: slingstones are turned with him into stubble.

29   Darts are counted as stubble: he laugheth at the shaking of a spear.

30   Sharp stones are under him: he spreadeth sharp pointed things upon the mire.

31   He maketh the deep to boil like a pot: he maketh the sea like a pot of ointment.

32   He maketh a path to shine after him; one would think the deep to be hoary.

33   Upon earth there is not his like, who is made without fear.

34   He beholdeth all high things: he is a king over all the children of pride.

42   THEN Job answered the LORD, and said,

I know that thou canst do every thing, and that no thought can be withholden from thee.

3   Who is he that hideth counsel without knowledge? therefore have I uttered that I understood not; things too wonderful for me, which I knew not.

4   Hear, I beseech thee, and I will speak: I will demand of thee, and declare thou unto me.

5   I have heard of thee by the hearing of the ear: but now mine eye seeth thee.

6   Wherefore I abhor myself, and repent in dust and ashes.

7   And it was so, that after the LORD had spoken these

words unto Job, the LORD said to Eliphaz the Temanite, My wrath is kindled against thee, and against thy two friends: for ye have not spoken of me the thing that is right, as my servant Job hath.

8 Therefore take unto you now seven bullocks and seven rams, and go to my servant Job, and offer up for yourselves a burnt offering; and my servant Job shall pray for you: for him will I accept: lest I deal with you after your folly, in that ye have not spoken of me the thing which is right, like my servant Job.

9 So Eliphaz the Temanite and Bildad the Shuhite and Zophar the Naamathite went, and did according as the LORD commanded them: the LORD also accepted Job.

10 And the LORD turned the captivity of Job, when he prayed for his friends: also the LORD gave Job twice as much as he had before.

11 Then came there unto him all his brethren, and all his sisters, and all they that had been of his acquaintance before, and did eat bread with him in his house: and they bemoaned him, and comforted him over all the evil that the LORD had brought upon him: every man also gave him a piece of money, and every one an earring of gold.

12 So the LORD blessed the latter end of Job more than his beginning: for he had fourteen thousand sheep, and six thousand camels, and a thousand yoke of oxen, and a thousand she asses.

13 He had also seven sons and three daughters.

14 And he called the name of the first, Jemima; and the name of the second, Kezia; and the name of the third, Kerenhappuch.

15 And in the land were no women found so fair as the daughters of Job: and their father gave them inheritance among their brethren.

16 After this lived Job an hundred and forty years, and saw his sons, and his sons' sons, even four generations.

17 So Job died, being old and full of days.

✦ GOSPEL OF MATTHEW

Chapters 5–7

So much of Early Christian teaching is concentrated in the Sermon on the Mount that some scholars have suggested it is less a single sermon than a collection of Jesus's sayings from many different occasions. Whatever the historical circumstances of their utterance, the arrangement of the sermon in its present form conveys its message powerfully. One of Jesus's most pervasive and powerful rhetorical techniques is his use of contrast, which takes a variety of forms in the Sermon on the Mount, such as "You have heard it said, but I say to you" and "Don't do that, do this." In addition, Jesus enriches his carefully balanced utterances with metaphors, such as the wide gate and path that lead to destruction and the narrow gate and road that lead to salvation, which identify the moral and spiritual ideals he encouraged his listeners to embrace.

The Sermon on the Mount

5 AND seeing the multitudes, he went up into a mountain: and when he was set, his disciples came unto him:

2 And he opened his mouth, and taught them, saying,

3 Blessed are the poor in spirit: for their's is the kingdom of heaven.

4 Blessed are they that mourn: for they shall be comforted.

5 Blessed are the meek: for they shall inherit the earth.

6 Blessed are they which do hunger and thirst after righteousness: for they shall be filled.

7 Blessed are the merciful: for they shall obtain mercy.

8 Blessed are the pure in heart: for they shall see God.

9 Blessed are the peacemakers: for they shall be called the children of God.

10 Blessed are they which are persecuted for righteousness' sake: for their's is the kingdom of heaven.

11 Blessed are ye, when men shall revile you, and persecute you, and shall say all manner of evil against you falsely, for my sake.

12 Rejoice, and be exceeding glad: for great is your reward in heaven: for so persecuted they the prophets which were before you.

13 Ye are the salt of the earth: but if the salt have lost his savour, wherewith shall it be salted? it is thenceforth good for nothing, but to be cast out, and to be trodden under foot of men.

14 Ye are the light of the world. A city that is set on an hill cannot be hid.

15 Neither do men light a candle, and put it under a bushel, but on a candlestick; and it giveth light unto all that are in the house.

16 Let your light so shine before men, that they may see your good works, and glorify your Father which is in heaven.

17 Think not that I am come to destroy the law, or the prophets: I am not come to destroy, but to fulfil.

18 For verily I say unto you, Till heaven and earth pass, one jot or one tittle shall in no wise pass from the law, till all be fulfilled.

19 Whosoever therefore shall break one of these least commandments, and shall teach men so, he shall be called the least in the kingdom of heaven: but whosoever shall do and teach them, the same shall be called great in the kingdom of heaven.

20 For I say unto you, That except your righteousness shall exceed the righteousness of the scribes and Pharisees, ye shall in no case enter the kingdom of heaven.

21 Ye have heard that it was said by them of old time, Thou shalt not kill; and whosoever shall kill shall be in danger of the judgment:

22 But I say unto you, That whosoever is angry with his brother without a cause shall be in danger of the judgment: and whosoever shall say to his brother, Raca, shall be in danger of the council: but whosoever shall say, Thou fool, shall be in danger of hell fire.

23 Therefore if thou bring thy gift to the altar, and there rememberest that thy brother hath ought against thee;

24 Leave there thy gift before the altar, and go thy way; first be reconciled to thy brother, and then come and offer thy gift.

25 Agree with thine adversary quickly, whiles thou art in the way with him; lest at any time the adversary deliver thee to the judge, and the judge deliver thee to the officer, and thou be cast into prison.

26 Verily I say unto thee, Thou shalt by no means come out thence, till thou hast paid the uttermost farthing.

27 Ye have heard that it was said by them of old time, THOU SHALT NOT COMMIT ADULTERY:

28 But I say unto you, That whosoever looketh on a woman to lust after her hath committed adultery with her already in his heart.

29 And if thy right eye offend thee, pluck it out, and cast it from thee: for it is profitable for thee that one of thy members should perish, and not that thy whole body should be cast into hell.

30 And if thy right hand offend thee, cut it off, and cast it from thee: for it is profitable for thee that one of thy members should perish, and not that thy whole body should be cast into hell.

31 It hath been said, WHOSOEVER SHALL PUT AWAY HIS WIFE, LET HIM GIVE HER A WRITING OF DIVORCEMENT:

32 But I say unto you, That whosoever shall put away his wife, saving for the cause of fornication, causeth her to commit adultery: and whosoever shall marry her that is divorced committeth adultery.

33 Again, ye have heard that it hath been said by them of old time, Thou shalt not forswear thyself, but shalt perform unto the Lord thine oaths:

34 But I say unto you, Swear not at all; neither by heaven; for it is God's throne:

35 Nor by the earth; for it is his footstool: neither by Jerusalem; for it is the city of the great King.

36 Neither shalt thou swear by thy head, because thou canst not make one hair white or black.

37 But let your communication be, Yea, yea; Nay, nay: for whatsoever is more than these cometh of evil.

38 Ye have heard that it hath been said, AN EYE FOR AN EYE, AND A TOOTH FOR A TOOTH:

39 But I say unto you, That ye resist not evil: but whosoever shall smite thee on thy right cheek, turn to him the other also.

40 And if any man will sue thee at the law, and take away thy coat, let him have thy cloke also.

41 And whosoever shall compel thee to go a mile, go with him twain.

42 Give to him that asketh thee, and from him that would borrow of thee turn not thou away.

43 Ye have heard that it hath been said, THOU SHALT LOVE THY NEIGHBOUR, AND HATE THINE ENEMY.

44 But I say unto you, Love your enemies, bless them that curse you, do good to them that hate you, and pray for them which despitefully use you, and persecute you;

45 That ye may be the children of your Father which is in heaven: for he maketh his sun to rise on the evil and on the good, and sendeth rain on the just and on the unjust.

46 For if ye love them which love you, what reward have ye? do not even the publicans the same?

47 And if ye salute your brethren only, what do ye more than others? do not even the publicans so?

48 Be ye therefore perfect, even as your Father which is in heaven is perfect.

6 TAKE heed that ye do not your alms before men, to be seen of them: otherwise ye have no reward of your Father which is in heaven.

2 Therefore when thou doest thine alms, do not sound a trumpet before thee, as the hypocrites do in the synagogues and in the streets, that they may have glory of men. Verily I say unto you, They have their reward.

3 But when thou doest alms, let not thy left hand know what thy right hand doeth:

4 That thine alms may be in secret: and thy Father which seeth in secret himself shall reward thee openly.

5 And when thou prayest, thou shalt not be as the hypocrites are: for they love to pray standing in the synagogues and in the corners of the streets, that they may be seen of men. Verily I say unto you, They have their reward.

6 But thou, when thou prayest, enter into thy closet, and when thou hast shut thy door, pray to thy Father which is in secret; and thy Father which seeth in secret shall reward thee openly.

7 But when ye pray, use not vain repetitions, as the heathen do: for they think that they shall be heard for their much speaking.

8 Be not ye therefore like unto them: for your Father knoweth what things ye have need of, before ye ask him.

9 After this manner therefore pray ye: Our Father which art in heaven, Hallowed be thy name.

10 Thy kingdom come. Thy will be done in earth, as it is in heaven.

11 Give us this day our daily bread.

12 And forgive us our debts, as we forgive our debtors.

13 And lead us not into temptation, but deliver us from evil: For thine is the kingdom, and the power, and the glory, for ever. Amen.

14 For if ye forgive men their trespasses, your heavenly Father will also forgive you:

15 But if ye forgive not men their trespasses, neither will your Father forgive your trespasses.

16 Moreover when ye fast, be not, as the hypocrites, of a sad countenance: for they disfigure their faces, that they may appear unto men to fast. Verily I say unto you, They have their reward.

17 But thou, when thou fastest, anoint thine head, and wash thy face;

18 That thou appear not unto men to fast, but unto my Father which is in secret: and thy Father, which seeth in secret, shall reward thee openly.

19 Lay not up for yourselves treasures upon earth, where moth and rust doth corrupt, and where thieves break through and steal:

20 But lay up for yourselves treasures in heaven, where neither moth nor rust doth corrupt, and where thieves do not break through nor steal:

21 For where your treasure is, there will your heart be also.

22 The light of the body is the eye: if therefore thine eye be single, thy whole body shall be full of light.

23 But if thine eye be evil, thy whole body shall be full of darkness. If therefore the light that is in thee be darkness, how great is that darkness!

24 No man can serve two masters: for either he will hate the one, and love the other; or else he will hold to the one, and despise the other. Ye cannot serve God and mammon.

25 Therefore I say unto you, Take no thought for your life, what ye shall eat, or what ye shall drink; nor yet for your

body, what ye shall put on. Is not the life more than meat, and the body than raiment?

26 Behold the fowls of the air: for they sow not, neither do they reap, nor gather into barns; yet your heavenly Father feedeth them. Are ye not much better than they?

27 Which of you by taking thought can add one cubit unto his stature?

28 And why take ye thought for raiment? Consider the lilies of the field, how they grow; they toil not, neither do they spin:

29 And yet I say unto you, That even Solomon in all his glory was not arrayed like one of these.

30 Wherefore, if God so clothe the grass of the field, which to day is, and to morrow is cast into the oven, shall he not much more clothe you, O ye of little faith?

31 Therefore take no thought, saying, What shall we eat? or, What shall we drink? or, Wherewithal shall we be clothed?

32 (For after all these things do the Gentiles seek:) for your heavenly Father knoweth that ye have need of all these things.

33 But seek ye first the kingdom of God, and his righteousness; and all these things shall be added unto you.

34 Take therefore no thought for the morrow: for the morrow shall take thought for the things of itself. Sufficient unto the day is the evil thereof.

7 JUDGE not, that ye be not judged.
2 For with what judgment ye judge, ye shall be judged: and with what measure ye mete, it shall be measured to you again.

3 And why beholdest thou the mote that is in thy brother's eye, but considerest not the beam that is in thine own eye?

4 Or how wilt thou say to thy brother, Let me pull out the mote out of thine eye; and, behold, a beam is in thine own eye?

5 Thou hypocrite, first cast out the beam out of thine own eye; and then shalt thou see clearly to cast out the mote out of thy brother's eye.

6 Give not that which is holy unto the dogs, neither cast ye your pearls before swine, lest they trample them under their feet, and turn again and rend you.

7 Ask, and it shall be given you; seek, and ye shall find; knock, and it shall be opened unto you:

8 For every one that asketh receiveth; and he that seeketh findeth; and to him that knocketh it shall be opened.

9 Or what man is there of you, whom if his son ask bread, will he give him a stone?

10 Or if he ask a fish, will he give him a serpent?

11 If ye then, being evil, know how to give good gifts unto your children, how much more shall your Father which is in heaven give good things to them that ask him?

12 Therefore all things whatsoever ye would that men should do to you, do ye even so to them: for this is the law and the prophets.

13 Enter ye in at the strait gate: for wide is the gate, and broad is the way, that leadeth to destruction, and many there be which go in thereat:

14 Because strait is the gate, and narrow is the way, which leadeth unto life, and few there be that find it.

15 Beware of false prophets, which come to you in sheep's clothing, but inwardly they are ravening wolves.

16 Ye shall know them by their fruits. Do men gather grapes of thorns, or figs of thistles?

17 Even so every good tree bringeth forth good fruit; but a corrupt tree bringeth forth evil fruit.

18 A good tree cannot bring forth evil fruit, neither can a corrupt tree bring forth good fruit.

19 Every tree that bringeth not forth good fruit is hewn down, and cast into the fire.

20 Wherefore by their fruits ye shall know them.

21 Not every one that saith unto me, Lord, Lord, shall enter into the kingdom of heaven; but he that doeth the will of my Father which is in heaven.

22 Many will say to me in that day, Lord, Lord, have we not prophesied in thy name? and in thy name have cast out devils? and in thy name done many wonderful works?

23 And then will I profess unto them, I never knew you: depart from me, ye that work iniquity.

24 Therefore whosoever heareth these sayings of mine, and doeth them, I will liken him unto a wise man, which built his house upon a rock:

25 And the rain descended, and the floods came, and the winds blew, and beat upon that house; and it fell not: for it was founded upon a rock.

26 And every one that heareth these sayings of mine, and doeth them not, shall be likened unto a foolish man, which built his house upon the sand:

27 And the rain descended, and the floods came, and the winds blew, and beat upon that house; and it fell: and great was the fall of it.

28 And it came to pass, when Jesus had ended these sayings, the people were astonished at his doctrine:

29 For he taught them as one having authority, and not as the scribes.

← **GOSPEL OF LUKE**

Chapter 15

One of the most eloquent and elegant features of Luke's writing is the way he presents Jesus's teaching through parables. Chapter 15 of Luke's gospel contains three related parables, the most famous of these being the parable of the prodigal son, which has inspired numerous artists throughout the ages.

Three Parables

15 THEN drew near unto him all the publicans and sinners for to hear him.
2 And the Pharisees and scribes murmured, saying, This man receiveth sinners, and eateth with them.
3 And he spake this parable unto them, saying,
4 What man of you, having an hundred sheep, if he lose one of them, doth not leave the ninety and nine in the wilderness, and go after that which is lost, until he find it?
5 And when he hath found it, he layeth it on his shoulders, rejoicing.
6 And when he cometh home, he calleth together his friends and neighbours, saying unto them, Rejoice with me; for I have found my sheep which was lost.
7 I say unto you, that likewise joy shall be in heaven over

one sinner that repenteth, more than over ninety and nine just persons, which need no repentance.

8   Either what woman having ten pieces of silver, if she lose one piece, doth not light a candle, and sweep the house, and seek diligently till she find it?

9   And when she hath found it, she calleth her friends and her neighbours together, saying, Rejoice with me; for I have found the piece which I had lost.

10   Likewise, I say unto you, there is joy in the presence of the angels of God over one sinner that repenteth.

11   And he said, A certain man had two sons:

12   And the younger of them said to his father, Father, give me the portion of goods that falleth to me. And he divided unto them his living.

13   And not many days after the younger son gathered all together, and took his journey into a far country, and there wasted his substance with riotous living.

14   And when he had spent all, there arose a mighty famine in that land; and he began to be in want.

15   And he went and joined himself to a citizen of that country; and he sent him into his fields to feed swine.

16   And he would fain have filled his belly with the husks that the swine did eat: and no man gave unto him.

17   And when he came to himself, he said, How many hired servants of my father's have bread enough and to spare, and I perish with hunger!

18   I will arise and go to my father, and will say unto him, Father, I have sinned against heaven, and before thee,

19   And am no more worthy to be called thy son: make me as one of thy hired servants.

20   And he arose, and came to his father. But when he was yet a great way off, his father saw him, and had compassion, and ran, and fell on his neck, and kissed him.

21   And the son said unto him, Father, I have sinned against heaven, and in thy sight, and am no more worthy to be called thy son.

22   But the father said to his servants, Bring forth the best robe, and put it on him; and put a ring on his hand, and shoes on his feet:

23   And bring hither the fatted calf, and kill it; and let us eat, and be merry:

24   For this my son was dead, and is alive again; he was lost, and is found. And they began to be merry.

25   Now his elder son was in the field: and as he came and drew nigh to the house, he heard musick and dancing.

26   And he called one of the servants, and asked what these things meant.

27   And he said unto him, Thy brother is come; and thy father hath killed the fatted calf, because he hath received him safe and sound.

28   And he was angry, and would not go in: therefore came his father out, and intreated him.

29   And he answering said to his father, Lo, these many years do I serve thee, neither transgressed I at any time thy commandment: and yet thou never gavest me a kid, that I might make merry with my friends:

30   But as soon as this thy son was come, which hath devoured thy living with harlots, thou hast killed for him the fatted calf.

31   And he said unto him, Son, thou art ever with me, and all that I have is thine.

32   It was meet that we should make merry, and be glad: for this thy brother was dead, and is alive again; and was lost, and is found.

↵ ST. PAUL
Epistles

Paul preached and wrote on a wide range of topics directly relevant to the lives of the early Christians. He urged them to believe in the risen Christ as the Savior who redeemed them from sin and death. He exhorted them to live holy and chaste lives so that they could join Christ at the final resurrection, when the bodies of all those believers who have died would be joined with their souls and taken up into Heaven. Notable among Paul's advice and teaching were his views on marriage and sexuality, which he expounded in his first epistle to the Corinthians and in his letter to the church at Ephesus. Here are Paul's views.

Corinthians

7   Now concerning the matters about which you wrote. It is well for a man not to touch a woman.

2   But because of the temptation to immorality, each man should have his own wife and each woman her own husband.

3   The husband should give to his wife her conjugal rights, and likewise the wife to her husband.

4   For the wife does not rule over her own body, but the husband does; likewise the husband does not rule over his own body, but the wife does.

5   Do not refuse one another except perhaps by agreement for a season, that you may devote yourselves to prayer; but then come together again, lest Satan tempt you through lack of self-control.

6   I say this by way of concession, not of command.

7   I wish that all were as I myself am. But each has his own special gift from God, one of one kind and one of another.

8   To the unmarried and the widows I say that it is well for them to remain single as I do.

9   But if they cannot exercise self-control, they should marry. For it is better to marry than to be aflame with passion.

10   To the married I give charge, not I but the Lord, that the wife should not separate from her husband

11   (but if she does, let her remain single or else be reconciled to her husband)—and that the husband should not divorce his wife.

12   To the rest I say, not the Lord, that if any brother has a wife who is an unbeliever, and she consents to live with him, he should not divorce her.

13   If any woman has a husband who is an unbeliever, and he consents to live with her, she should not divorce him.

14   For the unbelieving husband is consecrated through his wife, and the unbelieving wife is consecrated through her husband. Otherwise, your children would be unclean, but as it is they are holy.

15   But if the unbelieving partner desires to separate, let it be so; in such a case the brother or sister is not bound. For God has called us to peace.

16   Wife, how do you know whether you will save your

husband? Husband, how do you know whether you will save your wife?

17 Only, let every one lead the life which the Lord has assigned to him, and in which God has called him. This is my rule in all the churches.

18 Was any one at the time of his call already circumcised? Let him not seek to remove the marks of circumcision. Was any one at the time of his call uncircumcised? Let him not seek circumcision.

19 For neither circumcision counts for anything nor uncircumcision, but keeping the commandments of God.

20 Every one should remain in the state in which he was called.

21 Were you a slave when called? Never mind. But if you can gain your freedom, avail yourself of the opportunity.

22 For he who was called in the Lord as a slave is a freedman of the Lord. Likewise he who was free when called is a slave of Christ.

23 You were bought with a price; do not become slaves of men.

24 So, brethren, in whatever state each was called, there let him remain with God.

25 Now concerning the unmarried, I have no command of the Lord, but I give my opinion as one who by the Lord's mercy is trustworthy.

26 I think that in view of the present distress it is well for a person to remain as he is.

27 Are you bound to a wife? Do not seek to be free. Are you free from a wife? Do not seek marriage.

28 But if you marry, you do not sin, and if a girl marries she does not sin. Yet those who marry will have worldly troubles, and I would spare you that.

29 I mean, brethren, the appointed time has grown very short; from now on, let those who have wives live as though they had none,

30 and those who mourn as though they were not mourning, and those who rejoice as though they were not rejoicing, and those who buy as though they had no goods,

31 and those who deal with the world as though they had no dealings with it. For the form of this world is passing away.

32 I want you to be free from anxieties. The unmarried man is anxious about the affairs of the Lord, how to please the Lord;

33 but the married man is anxious about worldly affairs, how to please his wife,

34 and his interests are divided. And the unmarried woman or girl is anxious about the affairs of the Lord, how to be holy in body and spirit; but the married woman is anxious about worldly affairs, how to please her husband.

35 I say this for your own benefit, not to lay any restraint upon you, but to promote good order and to secure your undivided devotion to the Lord.

36 If any one thinks that he is not behaving properly toward his betrothed, if his passions are strong, and it has t o be, let him do as he wishes: let them marry—it is no sin.

37 But whoever is firmly established in his heart, being under no necessity but having his desire under control, and has determined this in his heart, to keep her as his betrothed, he will do well.

38 So that he who marries his betrothed does well; and he who refrains from marriage will do better.

39 A wife is bound to her husband as long as he lives. If the husband dies, she is free to be married to whom she wishes, only in the Lord.

40 But in my judgment she is happier if she remains as she is. And I think that I have the Spirit of God.

Ephesians

5 Be subject to one another out of reverence for Christ. Wives, be subject to your husbands, as to the Lord.

23 For the husband is the head of the wife as Christ is the head of the church, his body, and is himself its Saviour.

24 As the church is subject to Christ, so let wives also be subject in everything to their husbands.

25 Husbands, love your wives, as Christ loved the church and gave himself up for her,

26 that he might sanctify her, having cleansed her by the washing of water with the word,

27 that he might present the church to himself in splendour, without spot or wrinkle or any such thing, that she might be holy and without blemish.

28 Even so husbands should love their wives as their own bodies. He who loves his wife loves himself.

29 For no man ever hates his own flesh, but nourishes and cherishes it, as Christ does the church,

30 because we are members of his body.

31 "For this reason a man shall leave his father and mother and be joined to his wife, and the two shall become one flesh."

32 This mystery is a profound one, and I am saying that it refers to Christ and the church;

33 however, let each one of you love his wife as himself, and let the wife see that she respects her husband.

← GNOSTIC GOSPEL OF THOMAS
Sayings of Jesus

The following passage from the Gnostic Gospel of Thomas includes a series of Jesus's sayings. The sayings, which are described as "secret," include paradoxes and parables, as do the canonical or officially accepted gospels. They are also rich in comparisons and images, and are presented with Jesus's canonical concreteness and directness. Their gnosticism is evident in their emphasis on enlightenment.

Prologue These are the secret sayings that the living Jesus spoke and Judas Thomas the Twin recorded.

Saying 1 He said, "Whoever finds the interpretation of these sayings will not taste death."

Saying 2 Jesus said, "Let one who seeks not stop seeking until one finds.

When one finds, one will be disturbed.

When one is disturbed, one will be amazed, and will reign over all."

Saying 3 Jesus said, "If your leaders say to you, 'Behold, the kingdom is in the sky,' then the birds in the sky will get there before you. If they say to you, 'It is in the sea,' then the fish will get there before you.

"Rather, the kingdom is inside you and outside you.

When you know yourselves, then you will be known, and will understand that you are children of the living Father. But if you do not know yourselves, then you live in poverty, and embody poverty."

Saying 4   Jesus said, "The older person many days old will not hesitate to ask a little child seven days old about the realm of life, and this person will live. For many of the first will be last, and will become a single one."

Saying 5   Jesus said, "Know what is within your sight, and what is hidden from you will become clear to you. For there is nothing hidden that will not be revealed."

Saying 6   His disciples asked him and said,

Do you want us to fast?
How shall we pray?
Shall we give to charity?
What food may we eat?

Jesus said, "Do not lie or do what you dislike, since all things are clear before heaven. For there is nothing hidden that will not be revealed, and nothing covered that will not be uncovered."

Saying 7   Jesus said,

"Blessed is the lion that the human eats,
    so that the lion becomes human.
Cursed is the human that the lion eats,
    so that the lion becomes human."

Saying 8   He said, "A person is like a wise fisher who cast a net into the sea, and drew it up from the sea full of little fish. Among them the wise fisher discovered a fine big fish. So the fisher threw all the little fish back into the sea, and with no hesitation kept the big fish. Whoever has ears to hear ought to listen."

Saying 9   Jesus said, "Behold, the sower went out, took a handful of seeds, and scattered them. Some fell on the road, and the birds came and ate them. Others fell on rock, and they did not take root in the soil or produce any heads of grain. Others fell among thorns, and the thorns choked the seeds and worms consumed them. Still others fell on good soil, and brought forth a good crop: it yielded sixty per measure and one hundred twenty per measure."

Saying 10   Jesus said, "I have thrown fire on the world and, behold, I am guarding it until it is ablaze."

Saying 11   Jesus said,

"This heaven will pass away,
    and the heaven above it will pass away.
The dead are not alive,
    and the living will not die.
During the days when you ate what is dead,
    you made it alive.
When you become enlightened,
    what will you do?
On the day when you were one,
    you became two.
But when you become two,
    what will you do?"

Saying 12   The disciples said to Jesus, "We know you will leave us. Who is going to be our leader then?"

Jesus said to them, "No matter where you reside, you are to go to James the Just, for whose sake heaven and earth came into being."

Saying 13   Jesus said to his disciples, "Compare me with someone, and tell me whom I am like."

Simon Peter said to him, "You are like a just angel."

Matthew said to him, "You are like a wise philosopher."

Thomas said to him, "Teacher, my mouth is utterly unable to say whom you are like."

Jesus said, "I am not your teacher. You have become intoxicated because you have drunk from the bubbling spring that I have tended." And he took Thomas and withdrew, and told him three things.

When Thomas came back to his friends, they asked him, "What did Jesus tell you?"

Thomas said to them, "If I tell you even one of the things he told me, you will pick up rocks and stone me. Then fire will come forth from the rocks and devour you."

Saying 14   Jesus said to them,

"If you fast, you will bring sin upon yourselves.
If you pray, you will be condemned.
If you give to charity, you will harm your spirits.

"When you go into any country and wander from place to place, and the people receive you, eat what they serve you and heal their sick. For what goes into your mouth will not contaminate you; rather, what comes out of your mouth will contaminate you."

Saying 15   Jesus said, "When you see one who was not born of a woman, bow down and worship. That is your Father."

Saying 16   Jesus said, "Perhaps people think that I have come to bring peace to the world. They do not know that I have come to bring conflict to the earth: fire, sword, war. For five people will be in a house:

It will be three against two
and two against three,
father against son
and son against father,
and they will stand alone."

Saying 17   Jesus said, "I shall give you

what no eye has seen
what no ear has heard
what no hand has touched,
and what has never arisen
in a human mind."

Saying 18   The disciples said to Jesus, "Tell us about the end."

Jesus said, "Have you already discovered the beginning, that now you can seek after the end? For where the beginning is, the end will be.

Blessed is one who stands at the beginning:
    that one will know the end, and will not taste death."

Saying 19   Jesus said,

"Blessed is one who came to life before coming to life.

"If you become my disciples and hearken to my sayings, these stones will serve you.

"For there are five trees in Paradise for you. They do not change, summer or winter, and their leaves do not drop. Whoever knows about them will not taste death."

Saying 20   The disciples said to Jesus, "Tell us what the kingdom of heaven is like."

He said to them, "It is like a mustard seed, the tiniest of all seeds. But when it falls on prepared soil, it grows into a large plant and shelters the birds of the sky."

Saying 21   Mary said to Jesus, "Whom are your disciples like?"

He said, "They are like little children living in a field that is not theirs. When the owners of the field come, they will say, 'Give our field back to us.' The children will take off their clothes in the presence of the owners, and thus give the field back and return it to them.

"For this reason I say: if the owner of a house knows that a thief is coming, the owner will be on guard before the thief arrives, and will not let the thief break into the house of the estate and steal the possessions.

"As for you, then, be on guard against the world. Gird yourselves and prepare for action, so that the robbers will find no way to prevail against you, for the trouble you expect will come.

"Let there be among you a person who understands. When the crop ripened, a reaper came quickly with sickle in hand and harvested it. Whoever has ears to hear ought to listen."

Saying 22   Jesus saw some babies nursing. He said to his disciples, "These nursing babies are like those who enter the kingdom."

They said to him "Then shall we enter the kingdom as babies?"

Jesus said to them,
"When you make the two into one,
when you make the inner like the outer
 and the outer like the inner,
 and the upper like the lower,
when you make male and female into a single one,
 so that the male will not be male
 and the female will not be female,
when you make eyes replacing an eye,
 a hand replacing a hand,
 a foot replacing a foot,
 and an image replacing an image,
then you will enter the kingdom."

Saying 23   Jesus said, "I shall choose you,
 one from a thousand
 and two from ten thousand,
and these will stand as a single one."

Saying 24   His disciples said, "Show us the place where you are, for we must seek it."

He said to them, "Whoever has ears ought to listen. There is a light within an enlightened person, and it shines on the whole world. If the light does not shine, it is dark."

✦ AUGUSTINE
from *The Confessions*

Augustine's Confessions *is both an autobiography and an allegory of the journey of a soul toward salvation. In the course of describing his life, Augustine illustrates and explains a process of scriptural interpretation that was to become influential for hundreds of years. According to Augustine's typological interpretation, the Old Testament prefigures or anticipates the New Testament, with Old Testament characters and events serving as types or prefigurations of those in the New Testament. Christ for example, is the second Adam. Augustine himself serves as a type for the lost soul who finds salvation in an acceptance of Christian revelation.*

As the first Western autobiography, Augustine's Confessions *was enormously influential. Besides providing an influence and framework for other spiritual autobiographies, the* Confessions *paved the way for the Renaissance rediscovery of the self. In the following excerpt*

from this spiritual autobiography Augustine describes his early wickedness and his conversion.

Childhood

What have I to say to Thee, God, save that I know not where I came from, when I came into this life-in-death—or should I call it death-in-life? I do not know. I only know that the gifts Your mercy had provided sustained me from the first moment: not that I remember it but so I have heard from the parents of my flesh, the father from whom, and the mother in whom, You fashioned me in time.

Thus for my sustenance and my delight I had woman's milk: yet it was not my mother or my nurses who stored their breasts for me: it was Yourself, using them to give me the food of my infancy, according to Your ordinance and the riches set by You at every level of creation. It was by Your gift that I desired what You gave and no more, by Your gift that those who suckled me willed to give me what You had given them: for it was by the love implanted in them by You that they gave so willingly that milk which by Your gift flowed in the breasts. It was a good for them that I received good from them, though I received it not from them but only through them: since all good things are from You, O God, and from God is all my health.[1] But this I have learnt since: You have made it abundantly clear by all that I have seen You give, within me and about me. For at that time I knew how to suck, to lie quiet when I was content, to cry when I was in pain: and that was all I knew.

Later I added smiling to the things I could do, first in sleep, then awake. This again I have on the word of others, for naturally I do not remember; in any event, I believe it, for I have seen other infants do the same. And gradually I began to notice where I was, and the will grew in me to make my wants known to those who might satisfy them; but I could not, for my wants were within me and those others were outside: nor had they any faculty enabling them to enter into my mind. So I would fling my arms and legs about and utter sounds, making the few gestures in my power—these being as apt to express my wishes as I could make them: but they were not very apt. And when I did not get what I wanted, either because my wishes were not clear or the things not good for me, I was in a rage—with my parents as though I had a right to their submission, with free human beings as though they had been bound to serve me; and I took my revenge in screams. That infants are like this, I have learnt from watching other infants; and that I was like it myself I have learnt more clearly from these other infants, who did not know me, than from my nurses who did. … From infancy I came to boyhood, or rather it came to me, taking the place of infancy. Yet infancy did not go: for where was it to go to? Simply it was no longer there. For now I was not an infant, without speech, but a boy, speaking. This I remember; and I have since discovered by observation how I learned to speak. I did not learn by elders teaching me words in any systematic way, as I was soon after taught to read and write. But of my own motion, using the mind which You, my God, gave me, I strove with cries and vari-

---

[1] Throughout the *Confessions* Augustine quotes liberally from the Bible; the quotations are set off in italics.

ous sounds and much moving of my limbs to utter the feelings of my heart—all this in order to get my own way. Now I did not always manage to express the right meanings to the right people. So I began to reflect [I observed that] my elders would make some particular sound, and as they made it would point at or move towards some particular thing: and from this I came to realize that the thing was called by the sound they made when they wished to draw my attention to it. That they intended this was clear from the motions of their body, by a kind of natural language common to all races which consists in facial expressions, glances of the eye, gestures, and the tones by which the voice expresses the mind's state—for example whether things are to be sought, kept, thrown away, or avoided. So, as I heard the same words again and again properly used in different phrases, I came gradually to grasp what things they signified; and forcing my mouth to the same sounds, I began to use them to express my own wishes. Thus I learnt to convey what I meant to those about me; and so took another long step along the stormy way of human life in society, while I was still subject to the authority of my parents and at the beck and call of my elders.

O God, my God, what emptiness and mockeries did I now experience: for it was impressed upon me as right and proper in a boy to obey those who taught me, that I might get on in the world and excel in the handling of words to gain honor among men and deceitful riches. I, poor wretch, could not see the use of the things I was sent to school to learn; but if I proved idle in learning, I was soundly beaten. For this procedure seemed wise to our ancestors: and many, passing the same way in days past, had built a sorrowful road by which we too must go, with multiplication of grief and toil upon the sons of Adam.

Yet, Lord, I observed men praying to You: and I learnt to do likewise, thinking of You (to the best of my understanding) as some great being who, though unseen, could hear and help me. As a boy I fell into the way of calling upon You, my Help and my Refuge; and in those prayers I broke the strings of my tongue—praying to You, small as I was but with no small energy, that I might not be beaten at school. And when You did not hear me (not as giving me over to folly), my elders and even my parents, who certainly wished me no harm, treated my stripes as a huge joke, which they were very far from being to me. Surely, Lord, there is no one so steeled in mind or cleaving to You so close—or even so insensitive, for that might have the same effect—as to make light of the racks and hooks and other torture instruments (from which in all lands men pray so fervently to be saved) while truly loving those who are in such bitter fear of them. Yet my parents seemed to be amused at the torments inflicted upon me as a boy by my masters, though I was no less afraid of my punishments or zealous in my prayers to You for deliverance. But in spite of my terrors I still did wrong, by writing or reading or studying less than my set tasks. It was not, Lord, that I lacked mind or memory, for You had given me as much of these as my age required; but the one thing I revelled in was play; and for this I was punished by men who after all were doing exactly the same things themselves. But the idling of men is called business; the idling of boys, though exactly like, is punished by those same men: and no one pities either boys or men. Perhaps an

unbiased observer would hold that I was rightly punished as a boy for playing with a ball: because this hindered my progress in studies—studies which would give me the opportunity as a man to play at things more degraded. And what difference was there between me and the master who flogged me? For if on some trifling point he had the worst of the argument with some fellow-master, he was more torn with angry vanity than I when I was beaten in a game of ball …

But to continue with my boyhood, which was in less peril of sin than my adolescence. I disliked learning and hated to be forced to it. But I was forced to it, so that good was done to me though it was not my doing. Short of being driven to it, I certainly would not have learned. But no one does well against his will, even if the thing he does is a good thing to do. Nor did those who forced me do well: it was by You, O God, that well was done. Those others had no deeper vision of the use to which I might put all they forced me to learn, but to sate the insatiable desire of man for wealth that is but penury and glory that is but shame. But You, Lord, by Whom the very hairs of our head are numbered, used for my good the error of those who urged me to study; but my own error, in that I had no will to learn, you used for my punishment—a punishment richly deserved by one so small a boy and so great a sinner. Thus, You brought good for me out of those who did ill, and justly punished me for the ill I did myself. So You have ordained and so it is: that every disorder of the soul is its own punishment.

To this day I do not quite see why I so hated the Greek tongue that I was made to learn as a small boy. For I really liked Latin—not the rudiments that we got from our first teachers but the literature that we came to be taught later. For the rudiments—reading and writing and figuring—I found as hard and hateful as Greek. Yet this too could come only from sin and the vanity of life, because I was flesh, and a wind that goes away and returns not. For those first lessons were the surer. I acquired the power I still have to read what I find written and to write what I want to express; whereas in the studies that came later I was forced to memorize the wanderings of Aeneas—whoever he was—while forgetting my own wanderings; and to weep for the death of Dido who killed herself for love, while bearing dry-eyed my own pitiful state, in that among these studies I was becoming dead to You, O God, my life.

Nothing could be more pitiful than a pitiable creature who does not see to pity himself, and weeps for the death that Dido suffered through love of Aeneas and not for the death he suffers himself through not loving You, O God, Light of my heart, Bread of my soul, Power wedded to my mind and the depths of my thought. I did not love You and I went away from You in fornication: and all around me in my fornication echoed applauding cries "Well done! Well done!" For the friendship of this world is fornication against Thee: and the world cries "Well done" so loudly that one is ashamed of unmanliness not to do it. And for this I did not grieve; but I grieved for Dido, slain as she sought by the sword an end to her woe, while I too followed after the lowest of Your creatures, forsaking You, earth going unto earth. And if I were kept from reading, I grieved at not reading the tales that caused me such grief. This sort of folly is held nobler and richer than the studies by which we learn to read and write!

But now let my God cry aloud in my soul, and let Your truth assure me that it is not so: the earlier study is the better. I would more willingly forget the wanderings of Aeneas and all such things than how to write and read. Over the entrance of these grammar schools hangs a curtain: but this should be seen not as lending honor to the mysteries, but as a cloak to the errors taught within. Let not those masters—who have now lost their terrors for me—cry out against me, because I confess to You, my God, the desire of my soul, and find soul's rest in blaming my evil ways that I may love Your holy ways. Let not the buyers or sellers of book-learning cry out against me. If I ask them whether it is true, as the poet says, that Aeneas ever went to Carthage, the more ignorant will have to answer that they do not know, the more scholarly that he certainly did not. But if I ask with what letters the name Aeneas is spelt, all whose schooling has gone so far will answer correctly, according to the convention men have agreed upon for the use of letters. Or again, were I to ask which loss would be more damaging to human life—the loss from men's memory of reading and writing or the loss of these poetic imaginings—there can be no question what anyone would answer who had not lost his own memory. Therefore as a boy I did wrong in liking the empty studies more than the useful—or rather in loving the empty and hating the useful. For one and one make two, two and two make four, I found a loathsome refrain; but such empty unrealities as the Wooden Horse with its armed men, and Troy on fire, and Creusa's Ghost, were sheer delight.

Give me leave, O my God, to speak of my mind, Your gift, and of the follies in which I wasted it. It chanced that a task was set me, a task which I did not like but had to do. There was the promise of glory if I won, the fear of ignominy, and a flogging as well, if I lost. It was to declaim the words uttered by Juno in her rage and grief when she could not keep the Trojan prince from coming to Italy. I had learnt that Juno had never said these words, but we were compelled to err in the footsteps of the poet who had invented them: and it was our duty to paraphrase in prose what he had said in verse. In this exercise that boy won most applause in whom the passions of grief and rage were expressed most powerfully and in the language most adequate to the majesty of the personage represented.

What could all this mean to me, O My true Life, My God? Why was there more applause for the performance I gave than for so many classmates of my own age? Was not the whole business so much smoke and wind? Surely some other matter could have been found to exercise mind and tongue. Thy praises, Lord, might have upheld the fresh young shoot of my heart, so that it might not have been whirled away by empty trifles, defiled, a prey to the spirits of the air. For there is more than one way of sacrificing to the fallen angels …

The Pear Tree

I propose now to set down my past wickedness and the carnal corruptions of my soul, not for love of them but that I may love Thee, O my God. I do it for love of Thy love, passing again in the bitterness of remembrance over my most evil ways that Thou mayest thereby grow ever lovelier to me, O Loveliness that dost not deceive, Loveliness happy and abiding: and I collect my self out of that broken state in which my very being was torn asunder because I was turned away from Thee, the One, and wasted myself upon the many.

Arrived now at adolescence I burned for all the satisfactions of hell, and I sank to the animal in a succession of dark lusts: my beauty consumed away, and I stank in Thine eyes, yet was pleasing in my own and anxious to please the eyes of men.

My one delight was to love and to be loved. But in this I did not keep the measure of mind to mind, which is the luminous line of friendship; but from the muddy concupiscence of the flesh and the hot imagination of puberty mists steamed up to becloud and darken my heart so that I could not distinguish the white light of love from the fog of lust. Both love and lust boiled within me, and swept my youthful immaturity over the precipice of evil desires to leave me half drowned in a whirlpool of abominable sins. Your wrath had grown mighty against me and I knew it not. I had grown deaf from the clanking of the chain of my mortality, the punishment for the pride of my soul: and I departed further from You, and You left me to myself: and I was tossed about and wasted and poured out and boiling over in my fornications: and You were silent, O my late-won Joy. You were silent, and I, arrogant and depressed, weary and restless, wandered further and further from You into more and more sins which could bear no fruit save sorrows …

Where then was I, and how far from the delights of Your house, in that sixteenth year of my life in this world, when the madness of lust—needing no licence from human shamelessness, receiving no licence from Your laws—took complete control of me, and I surrendered wholly to it? My family took no care to save me from this moral destruction by marriage: their only concern was that I should learn to make as fine and persuasive speeches as possible …

Your law, O Lord, punishes theft; and this law is so written in the hearts of men that not even the breaking of it blots it out: for no thief bears calmly being stolen from—not even if he is rich and the other steals through want. Yet I chose to steal, and not because want drove me to it—unless a want of justice and contempt for it and an excess for iniquity. For I stole things which I already had in plenty and of better quality. Nor had I any desire to enjoy the things I stole, but only the stealing of them and the sin. There was a pear tree near our vineyard, heavy with fruit, but fruit that was not particularly tempting either to look at or to taste. A group of young blackguards, and I among them, went out to knock down the pears and carry them off late one night, for it was our bad habit to carry on our games in the streets till very late. We carried off an immense load of pears, not to eat—for we barely tasted them before throwing them to the hogs. Our only pleasure in doing it was that it was forbidden. Such was my heart, O God, such was my heart: yet in the depth of the abyss You had pity on it. Let that heart now tell You what it sought when I was thus evil for no object, having no cause for wrongdoing save my wrongness. The malice of the act was base and I loved it—that is to say I loved my own undoing, I loved the evil in me—not the thing for which I did the evil, simply the evil: my soul was depraved, and hurled itself down from security in You into utter destruction, seeking no profit from wickedness but only to be wicked …

Student at Carthage

I came to Carthage where a cauldron of illicit loves leapt and boiled about me. I was not yet in love, but I was in love with love, and from the very depth of my need hated myself for not more keenly feeling the need. I sought some object to love, since I was thus in love with loving; and I hated security and a life with no snares for my feet. For within I was hungry, all for the want of that spiritual food which is Thyself, my God; yet [though I was hungry for want of it] I did not hunger for it: I had no desire whatever for incorruptible food, not because I had it in abundance but the emptier I was, the more I hated the thought of it. Because of all this my soul was sick, and broke out in sores, whose itch I agonized to scratch with the rub of carnal things—carnal, yet if there were no soul in them, they would not be objects of love. My longing then was to love and to be loved, but most when I obtained the enjoyment of the body of the person who loved me.

Thus I polluted the stream of friendship with the filth of unclean desire and sullied its limpidity with the hell of lust. And vile and unclean as I was, so great was my vanity that I was bent upon passing for clean and courtly. And I did fall in love, simply from wanting to. O my God, my Mercy, with how much bitterness didst Thou in Thy goodness sprinkle the delights of that time! I was loved, and our love came to the bond of consummation: I wore my chains with bliss but with torment too, for I was scourged with the red hot rods of jealousy, with suspicions and fears and tempers and quarrels.

I developed a passion for stage plays, with the mirror they held up to my own miseries and the fuel they poured on my flame. How is it that a man wants to be made sad by the sight of tragic sufferings that he could not bear in his own person? Yet the spectator does want to feel sorrow, and it is actually his feeling of sorrow that he enjoys. Surely this is the most wretched lunacy? For the more a man feels such sufferings in himself, the more he is moved by the sight of them on the stage. Now when a man suffers himself, it is called misery; when he suffers in the suffering of another, it is called pity. But how can the unreal sufferings of the stage possibly move pity? The spectator is not moved to aid the sufferer but merely to be sorry for him; and the more the author of these fictions makes the audience grieve, the better they like him. If the tragic sorrows of the characters—whether historical or entirely fictitious—be so poorly represented that the spectator is not moved to tears, he leaves the theatre unsatisfied and full of complaints; if he is moved to tears, he stays to the end, fascinated and revelling in it …

Those of my occupations at that time which were held as reputable were directed towards the study of the law, in which I meant to excel—and the less honest I was, the more famous I should be. The very limit of human blindness is to glory in being blind. By this time I was a leader in the School of Rhetoric and I enjoyed this high station and was arrogant and swollen with importance: though You know, O Lord, that I was far quieter in my behavior and had no share in the riotousness of the eversores—the Overturners—for this blackguardly diabolical name they wore as the very badge of sophistication. Yet I was much in their company and much ashamed of the sense of shame that kept me from

being like them. I was with them and I did for the most part enjoy their companionship, though I abominated the acts that were their specialty—as when they made a butt of some hapless newcomer, assailing him with really cruel mockery for no reason whatever, save the malicious pleasure they got from it. There was something very like the action of devils in their behavior. They were rightly called Overturners, since they had themselves been first overturned and perverted, tricked by those same devils who were secretly mocking them in the very acts by which they amused themselves in mocking and making fools of others.

With these men as companions of my immaturity, I was studying the books of eloquence; for in eloquence it was my ambition to shine, all from a damnable vaingloriousness and for the satisfaction of human vanity. Following the normal order of study I had come to a book of one Cicero, whose tongue practically everyone admires, though not his heart. That particular book is called *Hortensius* and contains an exhortation to philosophy. Quite definitely it changed the direction of my mind, altered my prayers to You, O Lord, and gave me a new purpose and ambition. Suddenly all the vanity I had hoped in I saw as worthless, and with an incredible intensity of desire I longed after immortal wisdom. I had begun that journey upwards by which I was to return to You. My father was now dead two years; I was eighteen and was receiving money from my mother for the continuance of my study of eloquence. But I used that book not for the sharpening of my tongue; what won me in it was what it said, not the excellence of its phrasing …

So I resolved to make some study of the Sacred Scriptures and find what kind of books they were. But what I came upon was something not grasped by the proud, not revealed either to children, something utterly humble in the hearing but sublime in the doing, and shrouded deep in mystery. And I was not of the nature to enter into it or bend my neck to follow it. When I first read those Scriptures, I did not feel in the least what I have just said; they seemed to me unworthy to be compared with the majesty of Cicero. My conceit was repelled by their simplicity, and I had not the mind to penetrate into their depths. They were indeed of a nature to grow in Your little ones. But I could not bear to be a little one; I was only swollen with pride, but to myself I seemed a very big man …

Worldly Ambitions

By this time my mother had come to me, following me over sea and land with the courage of piety and relying upon You in all perils. For they were in danger from a storm, and she reassured even the sailors—by whom travelers newly ventured upon the deep are ordinarily reassured—promising them safe arrival because thus You had promised her in a vision. She found me in a perilous state through my deep despair of ever discovering the truth. But even when I told her that if I was not yet a Catholic Christian, I was no longer a Manichean, she was not greatly exultant as at some unlooked-for good news, because she had already received assurance upon that part of my misery; she bewailed me as one dead certainly, but certainly to be raised again by You, offering me in her mind as one stretched out dead, that You might say to the widow's son: *"Young man, I say to thee arise"*: and he should sit up and begin to speak and You should give him to his mother …

Nor did I then groan in prayer for Your help. My mind was intent upon inquiry and unquiet for argumentation. I regarded Ambrose as a lucky man by worldly standards to be held in honor by such important people: only his celibacy seemed to me a heavy burden. I had no means of guessing, and no experience of my own to learn from, what hope he bore within him, what struggles he might have against the temptations that went with his high place, what was his consolation in adversity, and on what joys of Your bread the hidden mouth of his heart fed. Nor did he know how I was inflamed nor the depth of my peril. I could not ask of him what I wished as I wished, for I was kept from any face to face conversation with him by the throng of men with their own troubles, whose infirmities he served. The very little time he was not with these he was refreshing either his body with necessary food or his mind with reading. When he read, his eyes traveled across the page and his heart sought into the sense, but voice and tongue were silent. No one was forbidden to approach him nor was it his custom to require that visitors should be announced; but when we came into him we often saw him reading and always to himself; and after we had sat long in silence, unwilling to interrupt a work on which he was so intent, we would depart again. We guessed that in the small time he could find for the refreshment of his mind, he would wish to be free from the distraction of other men's affairs and not called away from what he was doing. Perhaps he was on his guard lest [if he read loud] someone listening should be troubled and want an explanation if the author he was reading expressed some idea over-obscurely, and it might be necessary to expound or discuss some of the more difficult questions. And if he had to spend time on this, he would get through less reading than he wished. Or it may be that his real reason for reading to himself was to preserve his voice, which did in fact readily grow tired. But whatever his reason for doing it, that man certainly had a good reason …

I was all hot for honors, money, marriage: and You made mock of my hotness. In my pursuit of these, I suffered most bitter disappointments, but in this You were good to me since I was thus prevented from taking delight in anything not Yourself. Look now into my heart, Lord, by whose will I remember all this and confess it to You. Let my soul cleave to You now that You have freed it from the tenacious hold of death. At that time my soul was in misery, and You pricked the soreness of its wound, that leaving all things it might turn to You, who are over all and without whom all would return to nothing, that it might turn to You and be healed. I was in utter misery and there was one day especially on which You acted to bring home to me the realization of my misery. I was preparing an oration in praise of the Emperor in which I was to utter any number of lies to win the applause of people who knew they were lies. My heart was much wrought upon by the shame of this and inflamed with the fever of the thoughts that consumed it. I was passing along a certain street in Milan when I noticed a beggar. He was jesting and laughing and I imagine more than a little drunk. I fell into gloom and spoke to the friends who were with me about the endless sorrows that our own insan-

ity brings us: for here was I striving away, dragging the load of my unhappiness under the spurring of my desires, and making it worse by dragging it: and with all our striving, our one aim was to arrive at some sort of happiness without care: the beggar had reached the same goal before us, and we might quite well never reach it at all. The very thing that he had attained by means of a few pennies begged from passers-by—namely the pleasure of a temporary happiness—I was plotting for with so many a weary twist and turn.

Certainly his joy was no true joy; but the joy I sought in my ambition was emptier still. In any event he was cheerful and I worried, he had no cares and I nothing but cares. Now if anyone had asked me whether I would rather be cheerful or fearful, I would answer: "Cheerful"; but if he had gone on to ask whether I would rather be like that beggar or as I actually was, I would certainly have chosen my own state though so troubled and anxious. Now this was surely absurd. It could not be for any true reason. I ought not to have preferred my own state rather than his merely because I was the more learned, since I got no joy from my learning, but sought only to please men by it—not even to teach them, only to please them. Therefore did You break my bones with the rod of Your discipline. …

Great effort was made to get me married. I proposed, the girl was promised me. My mother played a great part in the matter for she wanted to have me married and then cleansed with the saving waters of baptism, rejoicing to see me grow every day more fitted for baptism and feeling that her prayers and Your promises were to be fulfilled in my faith. By my request and her own desire she begged You daily with the uttermost intensity of her heart to show her in a vision something of my future marriage, but You would never do it. She did indeed see certain vain fantasies, under the pressure of her mind's preoccupation with the matter; and she told them to me, not, however, with the confidence she always had when You had shown things to her, but as if she set small store by them; for she said that there was a certain unanalyzable savor, not to be expressed in words, by which she could distinguish between what You revealed and the dreams of her own spirit. Still she pushed on with the matter of my marriage, and the girl was asked for. She was still two years short of the age for marriage but I liked her and agreed to wait.

There was a group of us friends who had much serious discussion together, concerning the cares and troubles of human life which we found so hard to ensure. We had almost decided to seek a life of peace, away from the throng of men. This peace we hoped to attain by putting together whatever we could manage to get, and making one common household for all of us: so that in the clear trust of friendship, things should not belong to this or that individual, but one thing should be made of all our possessions, and belong wholly to each one of us, and everybody own everything. It seemed that there might be perhaps ten men in this fellowship. Among us there were some very rich men, especially Romanianus, our fellow townsman, who had been a close friend of mine from childhood and had been brought to the court in Milan by the press of some very urgent business. He was strongest of all for the idea and he had considerable influence in persuasion because his wealth was much greater than anyone else's. We agreed that two officers should be chosen every year to handle the details of our life together, leaving the rest undisturbed. But then we began to wonder whether our wives would agree, for some of us already had wives and I meant to have one. So the whole plan, which we had built up so neatly, fell to pieces in our hands and was simply dropped. We returned to our old sighing and groaning and treading of this world's broad and beaten ways: for many thoughts were in our hearts, but *Thy counsel standeth forever*. And out of Thy counsel didst Thou deride ours and didst prepare Thine own things for us, meaning to *give us meat in due season and to open Thy hands and fill our souls with Thy blessing.*

Meanwhile my sins were multiplied. She with whom I had lived so long was torn from my side as a hindrance to my forthcoming marriage. My heart which had held her very dear was broken and wounded and shed blood. She went back to Africa, swearing that she would never know another man, and left with me the natural son I had had of her. But I in my unhappiness could not, for all my manhood, imitate her resolve. I was unable to bear the delay of two years which must pass before I was to get the girl I had asked for in marriage. In fact it was not really marriage that I wanted. I was simply a slave to lust. So I took another woman, not of course as a wife; and thus my soul's disease was nourished and kept alive as vigorously as ever, indeed worse than ever, that it might reach the realm of matrimony in the company of its ancient habit. Nor was the wound healed that had been made by the cutting off of my former mistress. For there was first burning and bitter grief; and after that it festered, and as the pain grew duller it only grew more hopeless …

Conversion

Thus I was sick at heart and in torment, accusing myself with a new intensity of bitterness, twisting and turning in my chain in the hope that it might be utterly broken, for what held me was so small a thing! But it still held me. And You stood in the secret places of my soul, O Lord, in the harshness of Your mercy redoubling the scourges of fear and shame lest I should give way again and that small slight tie which remained should not be broken but should grow again to full strength and bind me closer even than before. For I kept saying within myself: "Let it be now, let it be now," and by the mere words I had begun to move toward the resolution. I almost made it, yet I did not quite make it. But I did not fall back into my original state, but as it were stood near to get my breath. And I tried again and I was almost there, and now I could all but touch it and hold it: yet I was not quite there, I did not touch it or hold it. I still shrank from dying unto death and living unto life. The lower condition which had grown habitual was more powerful than the better condition which I had not tried. The nearer the point of time came in which I was to become different, the more it struck me with horror; but it did not force me utterly back nor turn me utterly away, but held me there between the two.

Those trifles of all trifles, and vanities of vanities, my one-time mistresses, held me back, plucking at my garment of flesh and murmuring softly: "Are you sending us away?"

And "From this moment shall we not be with you, now or forever?" And "From this moment shall this or that not be allowed you, now or forever?" What were they suggesting to me in the phrase I have written "this or that," what were they suggesting to me, O my God? Do you in your mercy keep from the soul of Your servant the vileness and uncleanness they were suggesting. And now I began to hear them not half so loud; they no longer stood against me face to face, but they were there as I tried to depart, plucking stealthily at me to make me look behind. Yet even that was enough, so hesitating was I, to keep me from snatching myself free, from shaking them off and leaping upwards on the way I was called: for the strong force of habit said to me: "Do you think you can live without them?"

But by this time its voice was growing fainter. In the direction toward which I had turned my face and was quivering in fear of going, I could see the austere beauty of Continence, serene and indeed joyous but not evilly, honorably soliciting me to come to her and not linger, stretching forth loving hands to receive and embrace me, hands full of multitudes of good examples. With her I saw such hosts of young men and maidens, a multitude of youth and of every age, gray widows and women grown old in virginity, and in them all Continence herself, not barren but the fruitful mother of children, her joys, by You, Lord, her Spouse. And she smiled upon me and her smile gave courage as if she were saying: "Can you not do what these men have done, what these women have done? Or could men or women have done such in themselves, and not in the Lord their God? The Lord their God gave me to them. Why do you stand upon yourself and so not stand at all? Cast yourself upon Him and be not afraid; He will not draw away and let you fall. Cast yourself without fear, He will receive you and heal you."

Yet I was still ashamed, for I could still hear the murmuring of those vanities, and I still hung hesitant. And again it was as if she said: "Stop your ears against your unclean members, that they may be mortified. They tell you of delights, but not of such delights as the law of the Lord your God tells." This was the controversy raging in my heart, a controversy about myself against myself. And Alypius stayed by my side and awaited in silence the issue of such agitation as he had never seen in me.

When my most searching scrutiny had drawn up all my vileness from the secret depths of my soul and heaped it in my heart's sight, a mighty storm arose in me, bringing a mighty rain of tears. That I might give way to my tears and lamentations, I rose from Alypius: for it struck me that solitude was more suited to the business of weeping. I went far enough from him to prevent his presence from being an embarrassment to me. So I felt, and he realized it. I suppose I had said something and the sound of my voice was heavy with tears. I arose, but he remained where we had been sitting, still in utter amazement. I flung myself down somehow under a certain fig tree and no longer tried to check my tears, which poured forth from my eyes in a flood, *an acceptable sacrifice to Thee*. And much I said not in these words but to this effect: *"And Thou, O Lord, how long? How long, Lord; wilt Thou be angry forever? Remember not our former iniquities."* For I felt that I was still bound by them. And I continued my miserable complaining: "How long, how long shall

I go on saying tomorrow and again tomorrow? Why not now, why not have an end to my uncleanness this very hour?"

Such things I said, weeping in the most bitter sorrow of my heart. And suddenly I heard a voice from some nearby house, a boy's voice or a girl's voice, I do not know: but it was a sort of singsong, repeated again and again. "Take and read, take and read." I ceased weeping and immediately began to search my mind most carefully as to whether children were accustomed to chant these words in any kind of game, and I could not remember that I had ever heard any such thing. Damming back the flood of my tears I arose, interpreting the incident as quite certainly a divine command to open my book of Scripture and read the passage at which I should open. For it was part of what I had been told about Anthony, that from the Gospel which he happened to be reading he had felt that he was being admonished as though what he read was spoken directly to himself: *Go, sell what thou hast and give to the poor and thou shalt have treasure in heaven; and come follow Me.* By this experience he had been in that instant converted to You. So I was moved to return to the place where Alypius was sitting, for I had put down the Apostle's book there when I arose. I snatched it up, opened it and in silence read the passage upon which my eyes first fell: *Not in rioting and drunkenness, not in chambering and impurities, not in contention and envy, but put ye on the Lord Jesus Christ and make not provision for the flesh in its concupiscences.* [Romans 13.13.] I had no wish to read further,

and no need. For in that instant, with the very ending of the sentence, it was as though a light of utter confidence shone in all my heart, and all the darkness of uncertainty vanished away. Then leaving my finger in the place or marking it by some other sign, I closed the book and in complete calm told the whole thing to Alypius and he similarly told me what had been going on in himself, of which I knew nothing. He asked to see what I had read. I showed him, and he looked further than I had read. I had not known what followed. And this is what followed: *"Now him that is weak in faith, take unto you."* He applied this to himself and told me so. And he was confirmed by this message, and with no troubled wavering gave himself to God's goodwill and purpose—a purpose indeed most suited to his character, for in these matters he had been immeasurably better than I.

Then we went in to my mother and told her, to her great joy. We related how it had come about: she was filled with triumphant exultation, and praised You who are mighty beyond what we ask or conceive: for she saw that You had given her more than with all her pitiful weeping she had ever asked. For You converted me to Yourself so that I no longer sought a wife nor any of this world's promises, but stood upon that same rule of faith in which You had shown me to her so many years before. Thus You changed her mourning into joy, a joy far richer than he had thought to wish, a joy much dearer and purer than she had thought to find in grandchildren of my flesh.

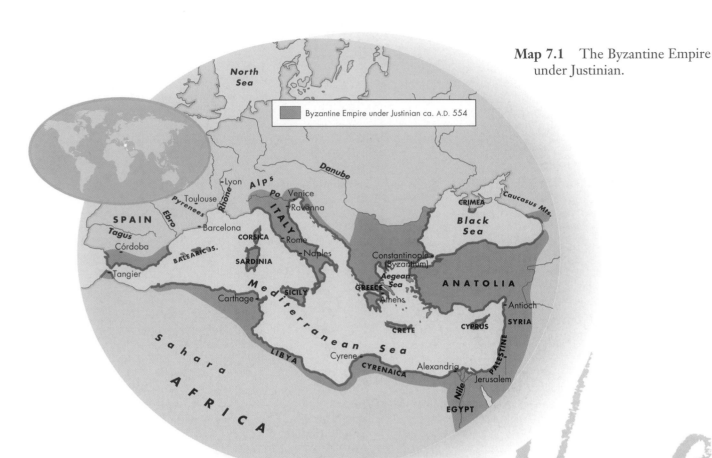

Map 7.1 The Byzantine Empire under Justinian.

BYZANTINE AND ISLAMIC CIVILIZATIONS

Court of the Lions, Alhambra Palace, Granada, Spain, 1354–91.

BYZANTINE CIVILIZATION

In A.D. 330, with the Roman Empire in severe economic and political decline, the emperor Constantine established the trading city of Byzantium as his new Eastern capital, renaming it Constantinople in the process.

From this time on, power and influence increasingly deserted Rome, which became a favorite target for invading barbarian hordes from the north. Rome suffered a further indignity when, in A.D. 402, the emperor Honorius moved the capital of the Western empire to Ravenna, a seaport south of Venice on the Adriatic coast of Italy. Then, in 410, a barbarian tribe from Germany, the Visigoths, laid siege to the former capital and, when the Senate refused to pay the invaders tribute, Rome was sacked for the first time in eight hundred years. Another group, the Vandals, sacked the city again in 455.

Meanwhile, the Western empire was crumbling. Successive waves of Saxons, Angles, and Jutes attacked and occupied Britain, while Burgundians wrested large parts of France from the Romans, and the Vandals came to control North Africa and Spain. The last Western emperor died in Rome in 476 when the Goths seized the city and established their own king, ODOACER [oh-doh-AH-sur], there. By the end of the fifth century, Roman power in the West had disintegrated, and the empire had been replaced by a patchwork of barbarian kingdoms.

In the east, however, imperial life flourished in the capital of Constantinople. There, a new and influential Christian civilization took root, usually known as BYZANTIUM [bi-ZAN-tee-um] after Constantinople's original name. (The city has changed name again in the twentieth century and is now called Istanbul.) Christian Byzantium continued to thrive for hundreds of years, although after the seventh century it had to compete increasingly with the rising civilization of Islam for control of the Mediterranean basin. Finally, in the fifteenth century, Constantinople itself was occupied by Muslim forces.

Of the early Byzantine emperors, JUSTINIAN [jus-TIN-ee-an] (r. 527–565) exerted the greatest cultural and political influence. His armies defeated Germanic tribes in Italy, Spain, and North Africa, reuniting the Mediterranean in a semblance of the original empire. Perhaps most important, however, was his undertaking of a massive rebuilding program in Constantinople itself, necessitated by the rebellion of 532, which had virtually destroyed the city. It was Justinian's wife and empress, THEODORA [THEE-oh-DOOR-ah], who in a famous speech to her husband persuaded him not to abandon Constantinople: "If you wish to save yourself, O Emperor, that is easy. For we have much money, there is the sea, here are the boats. But think whether after you have been saved you may not come to feel that you would have preferred to die." Theodora became one of the most powerful people of her day, controlling public policy, and was the first of three women to rule alone in the course of Byzantine history. Together, Justinian and Theodora sought to restore the grandeur of the empire and of their capital, Constantinople.

THE GOLDEN AGE OF CONSTANTINOPLE

Constantinople lies on the straits of Bosphorus, at the confluence of the Black Sea and the Sea of Marmara. The city has one of the finest harbors in the world, controlling the land route from Europe to Asia and the waterways that lead to the ports on the Black Sea, the Aegean, and the Mediterranean. Fortified by great walls on three sides and the straits on the other, it withstood attacks for more than a thousand years, until the Turks captured it in 1453, after which it became a Muslim city.

Life in Constantinople at the time of the emperor Justinian was rich in pleasures. The well-to-do enjoyed a high standard of living with a level of hygiene and health unknown in Europe at the time. Entertainments included chariot races at the amphitheater and theatrical productions that were notorious for their indecency. The empress Theodora had been an actress before marrying Justinian and had gained a somewhat unsavory reputation as a result. This, however, was only one aspect of the city. Constantinople was also a place of elegance and splendor, with one of the most magnificent religious buildings ever constructed, the Church of the Holy Wisdom, or Hagia Sophia, built by Justinian and Theodora after the revolt in 532. The great domed structure stands as testimony to their ambitions (fig. 7.1).

Well into the ninth and tenth centuries Constantinople remained the largest, richest, and most sophisticated city in the world. The immense city walls with their 37 gates and 486 towers—not to mention Constantinople's hundreds of churches and chapels and the monumental Hagia Sophia, which was used as a lighthouse by ships twenty miles out at sea—gave the impression of indomitable power.

The wealth of Constantinople was legendary. The city produced manuscripts and jewelry of every description, as well as rich fabrics in cotton, linen, and silk, embroidered with gold. Valuable metals, ivory, and precious stones were abundant, as were spices, including ginger and cloves, pepper, and saffron. So too were medicinal drugs and ingredients for dyeing fabric.

As the world's richest and largest market, Constantinople was tightly controlled; its customs duties were high and restrictive. Demand for its goods was maintained by limiting their supply and by keeping prices high. Although commerce with cities throughout Western Europe developed, only Venice was given privileged trading status.

Figure 7.1 Anthemius of Tralles and Isidorus of Miletus, Hagia Sophia, Istanbul, 532–37. The towers surrounding Hagia Sophia are a later, Muslim addition. They are, in fact, minarets, from which the Muslim faithful are called to worship.

By virtue of its easy access to land and sea trade routes, Constantinople was well situated to transport goods between East and West. Yet despite this abundant mercantile exchange, there was still a certain mutual mistrust, bred of a lack of understanding and of important differences between Constantinople and the West.

Most important of all, there were deep-rooted differences between the Christian Churches of the West and East, which, because of the splitting of the Roman empire in the fourth century, developed distinct traditions. Latin was the language of the Roman Church, Greek that of the Byzantine Church. In Rome, the Church was ruled by local bishops, who, in the absence of an imperial ruler, elected a pope as their head. In Constantinople, the Church was controlled by a patriarch who was often appointed, and even more often disposed of, by the emperor. In the West, priests were encouraged to be celibate and in 1139 celibacy became compulsory; in the East, priests could and often did marry. These differences were exacerbated when the Eastern patriarch refused to submit to the authority of the Roman pope in 1054, precipitating a final and permanent **schism,** or split, between the Eastern and Western Churches.

These differences are seen in miniature in the Western Church's response to the iconoclastic controversy in the Byzantine empire. The word **iconoclasm** derives from the Greek for "image-breaking," and twice, in the years 726–87 and 813–42, zealots who believed that the Bible forbade the worship of "graven images" systematically destroyed **icons** (sacred images) throughout the Byzantine empire. By way of contrast, the leaders of the Western Churches, the popes, had a far more tolerant view of images, believing that they served a valuable educational function.

Constantinople finally fell to the Turks in 1453, and Hagia Sophia was converted into an Islamic mosque. But the city's power had been diminishing since the end of the twelfth century. With the ascendancy of Turkish rule, Greek Byzantine scholars were dispersed throughout Europe, many taking refuge in Italy, where they contributed to the resurgence of interest in the preservation of ancient Greek culture throughout Western Europe— a development that was fundamental in bringing about the Renaissance (see Chapter 13).

BYZANTINE ART

So generously did Justinian patronize the arts that his reign is referred to as the First Golden Age of Byzantine art, with Constantinople as its artistic capital. However, because of the iconoclastic practices of later ages, much of the art created during this First Golden Age survives only outside Constantinople, in particular in the city of

Ravenna and in the monastery of St. Catherine built by Justinian at Mount Sinai.

Moreover, the influence of Byzantine artistic practices was particularly long-lasting, as the examples that follow attest. This continuing influence was the result of two factors. First, until the fifteenth century, Constantinople remained the cultural heart of the Eastern Christian world. Second, Eastern Christianity proved very conservative, and so there was little pressure for artistic change once conventions for, say, mosaic scenes and icon painting had been established.

San Vitale, Ravenna. The architecture and mosaics of the church of San Vitale in Ravenna (fig. 7.2), dated 526–47, are especially important accomplishments of the First Golden Age. Though begun by Bishop Maximian in 526, San Vitale bears the imprint of the influence of Constantinople and Justinian. It is octagonal in plan, a shape favored in Constantinople. Light is admitted to the interior by windows on the lower levels. However, this light is filtered through the aisles, which are two stories high, before reaching the nave. The only direct light, and therefore the strongest and most dramatic, enters the nave from the the third-story clerestory above.

Like the circular church of Santa Costanza in Rome (see fig. 6.6) the polygonal San Vitale has no longitudinal axis and is therefore referred to as having a central plan. Unlike the Early Christian churches of the basilica type that have a longitudinal axis (see figs. 6.3–6.5), such structures have no need of rows of columns to hold up

Timeline 7.1 The Byzantine empire.

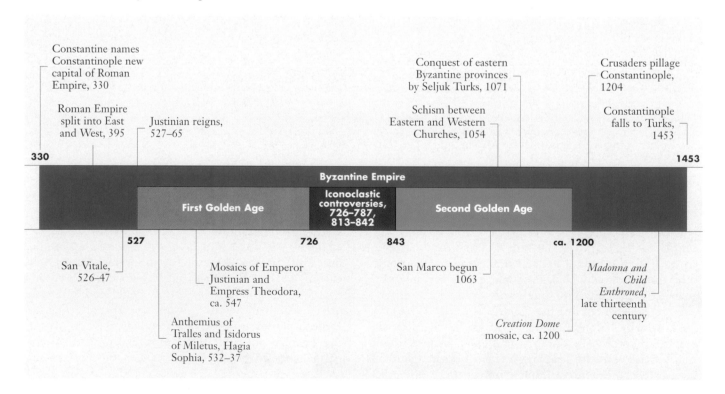

Cross Currents

THE SILK TRADE

As early as the first century B.C., silk from China began to reach Rome, where it was received with astonishment and admiration. Here was the lightest and most beautiful cloth ever seen, but the secrets of its production remained closely guarded by the Chinese.

The trade route that linked China to the West, and most importantly to Rome, was called the "Silk Road." Less a direct land route than a shifting network of caravan trails between remote kingdoms and trading posts, the Silk Road traversed China from the Han capital of Xian north and west across the Taklamakan Desert and on to the oasis city of Kashgar. From there, caravans carrying Chinese silk proceeded across the mountain passes of northern India, and on into the ancient Persian cities of Samarkand and Bukhara. Eventually the land route would come to an end at Constantinople, or at the Mediterranean ports of Antioch or Tyre, after which ships would complete the journey to Rome.

Although silk was the primary commodity traded with the West, eastern merchants also loaded camels with ceramics, fur, and lacquered goods. In exchange, they received gold, wool, ivory, amber, and glass from the West. It was Chinese silk, however, that captured the imagination of Rome, so much so that the Romans, who had learned about the Chinese from the Greeks, called the material *serica*, from the Greek word for the Chinese, *Seres*. For the Romans, China was synonymous with silk.

Until the sixth century A.D., silk was regularly supplied to the Romans by the Persians, who monopolized the silk trade and charged high prices. It was the Byzantine emperor Justinian who eventually broke this monopoly in the sixth century. According to the historian Procopius (died A.D. 562), "certain monks from India, knowing with what zeal the emperor Justinian endeavored to prevent the Romans from buying silk from the Persians (who were his enemy), came to visit the emperor and promised him that they would undertake the manufacture of silk." These monks explained to Justinian that silk was made by silkworms fed on mulberry leaves; Justinian promised them "great favors" if they would smuggle the requisite worms and mulberry trees back to Constantinople and begin to cultivate them there for him. This they did, and Justinian initiated a flourishing silk trade that was to become one of the chief sources of his vast wealth.

Figure 7.2 San Vitale, Ravenna, 526–47. A central-planned building is either circular, like Santa Costanza (see fig. 6.6), or polygonal, like San Vitale. An advantage of the central dome is the large space covered, while a potential disadvantage is that the visitor's eyes tend to be attracted up into the dome rather than toward the altar.

Figure 7.3 San Vitale, Ravenna, 526–47, interior. This view only begins to indicate the complexity of San Vitale's interior space. As the worshiper moves through it, the play of light on the mosaics changes continually.

their roofs and are capped with domes, which are supported by the walls instead. The result is that the interior feels light and spacious. However, two focal points compete for the visitor's attention. Whereas in a church with a longitudinal axis, on entering the worshiper is naturally directed toward the altar, the center of the ritual, this is less obviously the case at San Vitale, where the worshiper's eyes are also drawn up to the dome.

In striking contrast to its drab exterior, the interior of San Vitale (fig. 7.3) is opulent in its ornament, made colorful by mosaics that cover all the upper portions (the angels on clouds are later additions), by thin slabs of marble veneer, and by marble columns with carved and painted capitals (fig. 7.4). Seemingly immaterial, the lacy delicacy of the surface decoration belies the underlying strength of the structure.

Flanking the altar at San Vitale and drawing the worshiper's gaze down from the dome are the celebrated mosaics of the emperor Justinian and the empress Theodora (fig. 7.5) of ca. 547. Justinian and Theodora, each accompanied by attendants, are shown as good Christian rulers to be ever in attendance at the religious service. The figures are not necessarily intended to be recognizable portraits of specific individuals. Instead, everyone looks much alike, with big dark eyes, curved eyebrows, long noses, and small mouths—the characteristic Byzantine facial type. Their drapery gives no

Figure 7.4 San Vitale, Ravenna, 526–47, capital. The surfaces of the capital and impost block above are carved to appear lace-like, which belies the strength of the underlying structure.

Figure 7.5 *Theodora and Her Attendants*, ca. 547, mosaic, San Vitale, Ravenna. The typical Byzantine face is shown to have large eyes, a long nose, and a tiny mouth. The body is characteristically slender and weightless—or so one might hope, since the figures appear to step on one another's feet.

suggestion of a body beneath; the only indication that these people have legs is the appearance of feet below the hem of their garments. Their elongated bodies seem insubstantial, ethereal and immaterial, motionless, their gestures frozen.

The flat frontal figures form a rhythmic pattern across the surface of the mosaic. Three-quarter views, which suggest a degree of movement and dimension, are avoided. The Byzantine lack of concern for realistic or even consistent representation of space is illustrated by the doorway on the left, the top and bottom of which are seen from two different vantage points. The ancient Roman interest in specific details is gone. Yet, whatever this architectural decoration may lose in realism, it gains in splendor. Realism is not the goal here. Glittering mosaic is an ideal medium with which to enhance the image of divine power promoted by the Byzantine emperor and empress, while simultaneously increasing the splendor of San Vitale.

Hagia Sophia. Hagia Sophia, the Church of the Holy Wisdom in Constantinople (see fig. 7.1), was built for Justinian and Theodora between 532 and 537 by the architects Anthemius of Tralles and Isidorus of Miletus. There is little exterior decoration (the four minarets, or towers, are later Turkish additions). Seen from the outside, Hagia Sophia appears to be a very solid structure, building up by waves to the huge central dome.

The plan (fig. 7.7) shows the arrangement around the central dome, with half-domes on opposite sides, which are in turn flanked by smaller half-domes. Thus, Hagia Sophia, although domed, is not a pure central-plan church like San Vitale, because a longitudinal axis is created by the oval nave. Hagia Sophia's ingenious plan has a single focus of attention as well as a great open space, combining the advantages of the longitudinal basilica plan with those of the domed central plan.

Unlike the dome of the Roman Pantheon (see fig. 5.14), which rests on a circular base, the dome of Hagia

Figure 7.6 Anthemius of Tralles and Isidorus of Miletus, Hagia Sophia, Istanbul, 532–37, interior. Triangular pendentives provide the transition between the circular dome and the square base on which it rests. The closely spaced windows at the base of the dome create a ring of light that makes the dome appear to float.

Figure 7.7 Anthemius of Tralles and Isidorus of Miletus, Hagia Sophia, Istanbul, 532–37, plan. Hagia Sophia demonstrates that the advantages of the longitudinal axis of the basilica plan can be combined with those of the dome of the central plan. Here the central dome is buttressed by half-domes, which are buttressed in turn by smaller half-domes.

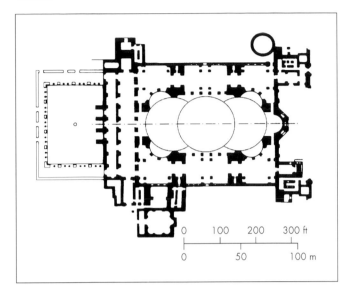

Sophia is supported by a square base formed by four huge piers. Transition from circle to square is achieved by the architects through their use of four **pendentives**, pieces of triangular supporting masonry. In effect, the dome rests on a larger dome from which segments have been removed. Hagia Sophia is one of the earliest examples of a dome on pendentives.

The interior (fig. 7.6) is an extremely lofty, light-filled, unobstructed space. From the inside, the dome seems to billow or to float—as if it were suspended from above rather than supported from below. Because the dome is made of lightweight tiles, it was possible for the architects to puncture the base of the dome with a band of forty windows. The light that streams through these windows is used as an artistic element, for it is reflected in the mosaics and the marbles. A richly polychrome scheme is created by the red and green porphyry columns, the polished marble slabs on the lower walls, and the mosaics on the upper walls. Like San Vitale, the elaborate surface decoration conceals the strength of the underlying structure.

St. Mark's, Venice. The First Golden Age of Byzantine art ended with the "iconoclastic controversy." Yet when in 843 the **iconophiles**—the lovers of artistic

Figure 7.8 St. Mark's, Venice, begun 1063. A dramatic silhouette is created by the five domes. St. Mark's Greek-cross plan, with four equal arms, differs from the Latin-cross plan with one dominant axis, represented by Old St. Peter's (see fig. 6.4).

images—triumphed over the iconoclasts, a Second Golden Age of Byzantine art began, lasting until the beginning of the thirteenth century. The biggest and most elaborate church of the Second Golden Age is St. Mark's in Venice, begun in 1063. Its location on one side of a large **piazza** (open public area) is particularly impressive. The original facade has since been modified.

The plan is a **Greek cross**—that is, a cross with four arms of equal length. There is a dome over the center, plus a dome over each arm (fig. 7.8). All five domes are covered with wood and gilt copper, making them very striking and giving St. Mark's a distinctive silhouette.

The interior of St. Mark's (fig. 7.10) offers the visitor an experience in ultimate splendor. The vast space is quite dark, originally illuminated only by windows in the bases of the domes and the flickering light of countless candles. Yet all the surfaces glitter, for they are covered with mosaics, many of which are made with gold tesserae.

Among the celebrated mosaics of St. Mark's, the most famous is the Creation Dome in the narthex, made about 1200. The story of Genesis is told in a series of scenes arranged in three concentric circles. The narrative begins in the innermost circle with the creation of heaven and earth. The story of Adam and Eve occupies part of the second circle and the outermost circle (fig. 7.9). In the scene shown here, God is pictured creating Eve from Adam's rib. Among the other memorable scenes is that in which God is shown giving Adam his soul, usually represented by a tiny winged figure entering Adam's mouth.

These mosaic figures hardly appear to have been taken from live models. Instead, the figures—doll-like

Figure 7.9 *God Creates Eve*, detail of the Creation Dome, ca. 1200, mosaic, narthex of St. Mark's, Venice. Engaging narrative is more important than realism in these mosaics. The intended audience was assumed to be familiar with the biblical stories told here, which, therefore, could be depicted in summary rather than in detail.

her bodily proportions elongated. Jesus's proportions are those of a tiny adult. Moreover, he acts as an adult, holding the scroll of law in one hand and blessing with the other.

Mary is traditionally shown wearing garments of red and blue   both primary colors. Jesus wears orange and green, two secondary colors. Byzantine drapery is

Figure 7.10   St. Mark's, Venice, begun 1063. Glittering gold mosaics covering the walls and vaults successfully transport the visitor from the crowded streets of the island-city of Venice to an extraordinary otherworldly environment.

Figure 7.11   *Madonna and Child Enthroned*, egg tempera on panel, $32\frac{1}{8}'' \times 19\frac{3}{8}''$ (81.6×49.2 cm), late thirteenth century, National Gallery of Art, Washington, D.C. An icon such as this is meant to bring certain religious concepts to the viewer's mind. Because the image must be readily recognizable to be effective, it is quite standardized— artistic innovation was not the goal.

and stocky with big heads—are intended to express the superhuman nature of the subject portrayed. The setting is symbolic only and represented in the simplest manner possible to convey the ideas. To elucidate the narrative, aids, such as bands of lettering and symbols, are employed. Emphasis is on design, decoration, and on the didactic message.

Madonna and Child Enthroned.   Characteristic of this Byzantine style is the *Madonna and Child Enthroned* (fig. 7.11), a late thirteenth-century egg tempera painting on a wooden panel. Egg tempera (pigment mixed with egg yolk) was the standard medium used to paint on wood throughout the Middle Ages.

Madonna and Child Enthroned represents a type repeated over and over according to strict rules. It is an **icon**, a painted image of a religious figure or religious scene used in worship. The figures typically face out directly to the front, encouraging the viewer's spiritual engagement. In this *Madonna and Child Enthroned*, Mary's typically Byzantine face has a somewhat wistful or melancholy expression. She is gentle and graceful,

Then & Now

JERUSALEM

The possession of the city of Jerusalem has historically been contested by three major world faiths: Judaism, Christianity, and Islam. The city's history is one of warring religious factions, all claiming its holy ground for themselves. Today, within a space of five hundred yards, sometimes in peaceful coexistence, sometimes not, lie the western wall of ancient Israel's Temple of Solomon, the rock marking the place of Jesus's tomb, and the Muslim shrine designating the site where Muhammad is believed to have ascended to heaven.

Archaeological evidence indicates that Jerusalem began in the Bronze Age as a mere nine-acre settlement at the edge of the Judaean desert. The Hebrew king David made Jerusalem the capital of the unified country of ancient Israel during the early tenth century B.C. He extended the city limits, building towers and battlements throughout. The city's most glorious years, however, occurred during the reign of King Solomon, David's successor. Solomon built a magnificent temple to house the holy Ark of the Covenant. To this temple he attached an equally magnificent palace, while also extending the city walls and further enlarging its defenses.

Numerous times in its history, Jerusalem has been captured or destroyed. Alexander the Great took the city without resistance in 332 B.C. In 250 B.C. Ptolemy the Great destroyed the city walls. In 168 B.C. the Syrian king Antiochus Epiphanes enslaved Jerusalem's inhabitants. The Roman leader Pompey captured the city in the first century B.C., and the Roman general Titus crushed a rebellion a century later, leveling the city in the process. A thousand years later, the Crusaders conquered the city, taking it from the Muslims, and leaving it little more than a military outpost, dispersing those citizens who were spared from death.

During the era of the Jewish king Herod in the first century A.D., the rebuilding of Solomon's Temple, which had been destroyed by the Babylonians under King Nebuchadnezzar in 587 B.C., took place amidst the most unusual circumstances. To preserve the sanctity of the temple grounds, the king trained a thousand priests as carpenters and stonemasons, whose work did not interrupt religious worship. Herod also constructed temples to Greek and Roman gods and personally presided over the Olympic Games.

Muslims, Jews, and Christians all lay claim to the Temple Mount, the site of Solomon's Temple. For Muslims, the Temple Mount and the magnificent mosque constructed upon it, the Dome of the Rock (fig. 7.12), are second only to Mecca and Medina as holy sites. For Jews and Christians, this was the site of the patriarch Abraham's aborted sacrifice of his son Isaac. For members of all three faiths, Solomon's Temple was the site of Jesus's debate with the rabbis and a place where he preached.

The city of Jerusalem is constructed out of the history and cultures of many peoples. Roman vaults are coupled with Christian convents; an Arab arch cannot be separated from a Jewish wall. This complex mix of religions and cultures makes Jerusalem a truly multicultural city, whose bedrock is a faith in God, albeit a God called by various names, and conceived under a variety of identities.

Figure 7.12   Dome of the Rock, Jerusalem, late 680s–692.

characterized by elaborate and unrealistic folds, seemingly having a life of their own, independent of the body beneath. The hard ornamental highlights contrast with the soft skin of the figures.

These figures, barely of our species, do not inhabit our earthly realm. Compression of space is emphasized by the flat decorative designs. The throne, which has been compared to the Colosseum in Rome, is drawn in such a way that the interior and exterior do not correspond. Similarly, the footstool does not obey the rules of **linear perspective**, which require objects to diminish in scale as they recede into space.

Floating in this golden realm are two half-angels. Each carries a staff, a symbol of Jesus's passion, and an orb or globe with a cross, which signifies Jesus's domination over the world. These are examples of **iconography**, the language of symbols, which was especially useful in an era when few people were literate. It was intended that the audience would be able to recognize the subject immediately. Consistency in the use of symbols, therefore, was important. The quest for innovation, for the novel, for things unique, has no place in Byzantine religious art.

ISLAMIC CIVILIZATION

Islam is the youngest of the world's major religions. It was first proclaimed by MUHAMMAD (ca. 570–632) in the town of Mecca, in Arabia, in about the year 610. The followers of Islam, Muslims, consider their faith to be the third and final revelation of God's truth—the first and second manifestations being Judaism and Christianity. Muslims view their religion as a continuation and fulfillment of Judaism and Christianity, and thus accept the sanctity of significant portions of Hebrew and Christian scripture. All three religions believe in a single God and are, thus, monotheistic. In Islam, God is called "Allah."

The rapid expansion of Islam throughout the Mediterranean was the result of three factors—the human appeal of the religion, the overpopulation of the Arabian peninsula where it originated, and a fundamental unwillingness on the part of the nomadic population of Arabia to submit to the authority of the caliphs, the religious leaders who assumed the mantle of Muhammad's representatives on earth after his death. These last two factors led, by 750, to the spread of Islam eastward to the Indus River and the frontiers of China, and westward across North Africa into Spain. In 725, Muslim forces had pushed as far north as Tours in France, from where, seven years later, French troops forced them back into Spain. Muslim rulers remained in Spain until the end of the fifteenth century. They left behind, in France and Europe as a whole, not so much their religion but magnificent architecture, particularly in Spain, and another of their cultural inventions—the institution of courtly love, including both its poetry and the instruments the poet used to sing to his mistress, such as the lute, tambourine, and guitar (all Arabic words) (see Chapter 11).

In the East, the spread of Islam underwent no such reversal. In 1453 the great Byzantine capital of Constantinople fell to the Muslim Ottomans from Turkey and Justinian's great Christian church, Hagia Sophia, was converted into a mosque.

RELIGION

Muhammad. Muhammad is revered as a prophet. Muslims consider him the "seal," or final culmination, of the prophetic tradition that extends from the biblical patriarch Abraham through Moses and on to Jesus, whom Muslims also revere as a prophet but do not consider a divinity. The word *Muslim* literally means "one who surrenders"; *Islam* means "submission to God." In the first place, Muslims surrender themselves to the prophet Muhammad and through him to Allah, by obeying Muhammad's instructions for living.

A merchant by profession, Muhammad received, at about the age of forty, what he described as a call to become God's messenger and prophet. According to Islamic tradition, Muhammad heard a voice enjoining him to "recite," to which he responded, "What shall I recite?" The answer came to him in the form of a series of revelations from Allah that lasted more than twenty years, beginning at Mecca and continuing in Medina, a city north of Mecca, to which Muhammad fled in 622 because of hostility to his religious message and where he died ten years later. Muhammad's flight to Medina is known as the *Hijrah* or *Hegira*, and marks the beginning of the Muslim calendar (A.D. 622 = 1 for Muslims).

Upon Muhammad's death, a succession of caliphs took his place, which led to a division among the Islamic faithful. In 656, those who favored choosing only a member of Muhammad's family as caliph, rallied around ALI [AH-lee], Muhammad's cousin. They called themselves Shi'ites [SHE-ites]. But when Ali was chosen caliph, civil war broke out, Ali was murdered, and the UMAYYAD [OO-MY-ad] dynasty, who bore no family relation with Muhammad, took control. The ninety-year Umayyad rule was marked by prosperity, but Shi'ite resentment remained. In 750, led by the great-grandson of a cousin of Muhammad, Abu-l Abbas, the Shi'ites overthrew the Umayyad caliphs, and the capital of Islam was moved east to Baghdad, where the ABASSID [a-BAA-sid] dynasty ruled until 1258.

The Quran. Despite this political strife, Islam remained strong. At the center of the religion is the Quran (or Koran), the scripture of Islam. The word *Quran* means "recitation" and reflects the Muslim belief that the book is a recitation of God's words to Muhammad. Muhammad, who was illiterate, memorized the messages he received and dictated them to various scribes. Unlike the Hebrew scriptures, which were composed over a period of more than twelve hundred years and which for a long time remained in many different versions, the text of the Quran was definitively established after Muhammad's death by the third caliph, Uthman, around 650.

Slightly shorter than the New Testament, the Quran is divided into 114 **Surahs** or chapters, which become shorter as the Quran progresses. The first Surah contains 287 **ayas**, or verses, while the last contains only three. Each Surah begins with the words, "In the name of Allah, the Beneficent, the Merciful."

The words of the Quran are the first Muslims hear when they are born and the last many hear before death. The Quran forms the core of Muslim education and serves as a textbook for the study of Arabic. Moreover, verses from it are inscribed on the walls of Muslim homes as decoration and as a reminder of their faith.

An additional important source of Islamic teaching, the **hadith** ("narrative" or "report"), consists of the sayings of Muhammad and anecdotes about him, which were initially passed on orally, but in the ninth century were collected and written down by scholars. Six canonical collections of hadith are used to determine points of Islamic theology and doctrine.

Basic Tenets and the Five Pillars of Islam. The basic tenets of Islam concern the nature of God, creation, humankind, and the afterlife. According to Islam, God is one, immaterial, invisible, and omnipotent. This single God dominates the entire universe with his power and his mercy. He is also the creator of the universe, which, because it is his creation, is also beautiful and good. For the Muslims, the natural world reflects God's presence and is a way of being at one with Him.

The supreme creation of Allah, however, is humankind. As in the Judaeo-Christian scriptures, human beings, made in the image of God, are viewed as the culmination of creation. Women and men possess distinct, individual souls, which are immortal, and can live eternally with God—provided individuals live their earthly lives according to Islamic teaching.

To achieve heaven, Muslims must accept belief in Allah as the supreme being and the only God. They must also practice their religion by fulfilling the obligations characterized as the "five pillars" of Islam. These are:

Map 7.2   The expansion of Islam to ca. A.D. 850.

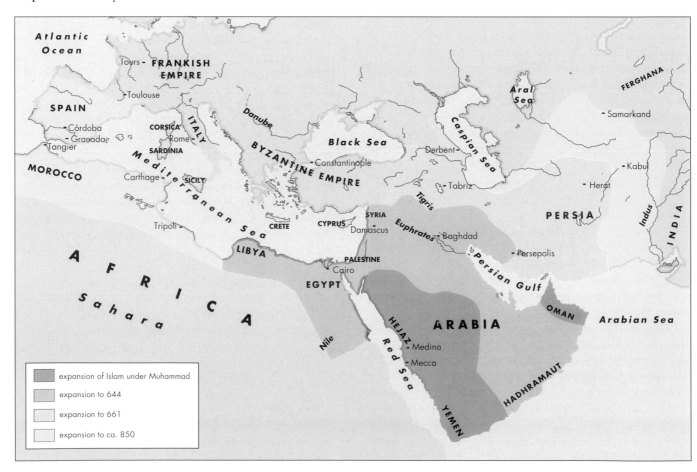

Timeline 7.2 Islamic civilization.

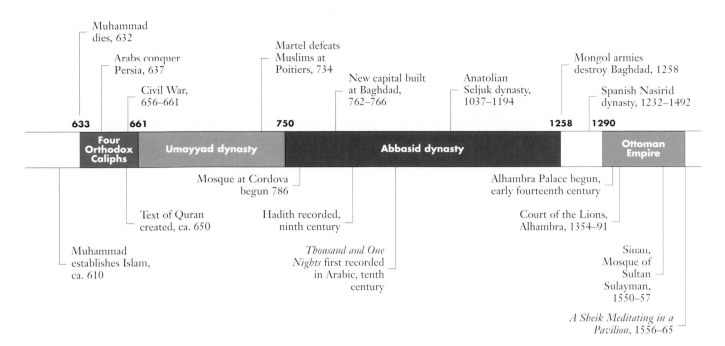

repetition of the creed, daily prayer, almsgiving, fasting during Ramadan, and pilgrimage to Mecca.

The Islamic creed (*shahadah*) consists of a single sentence: *La ilaha illa Allah; Muhammad rasul Allah* ("There is no God but Allah; Muhammad is the messenger of Allah"). All Muslims must say this creed slowly, thoughtfully, and with conviction at least once during their lives, though many practicing Muslims recite it several times each day.

Daily prayer (*salat*) is recited five times: at dawn, midday, mid-afternoon, sunset, and nightfall. In Muslim communities, *muezzins* call the faithful to prayer from mosque towers. Whether the people pray where they are or go to the mosque, they must cleanse themselves of impurities before praying. During prayer, Muslims face Mecca and perform a series of ritual gestures that includes bowing and prostration.

Charity or almsgiving (*zakat*) is the third pillar of Islam. In addition to *ad hoc* giving to the poor, Islam instructs its followers to contribute one-fortieth of their income and assets to the needy. Originally a form of tax, today the *zakat* is a respected form of holy offering.

The fourth pillar is the fast (*sawm*) during the holy month of Ramadan, the ninth month of the Muslim lunar calendar. Depending on the moon's cycles, Ramadan may last twenty-nine or thirty days, and shifts from year to year, spanning all the seasons over a thirty-three-year period. The fast includes abstaining from food, drink, medicine, tobacco, and sexual intercourse from sunrise to sundown. Moreover, during the month of fasting, Muslims are expected to recite the entire

Quran at least once. Ramadan is considered the Islamic holy month because it was during Ramadan that Muhammad received his initial call as a prophet and during Ramadan that he made his historic flight from Mecca to Medina ten years later.

The final pillar of Islam is the pilgrimage (*hajj*) to Mecca, which all healthy adult Muslims are expected to complete at least once. The goal of pilgrimage is to heighten devotion through veneration of Islam's sacred shrines, the most notable being the *Kaaba* ("Cube"), the sacred black stone enshrined at the place where Abraham and his son Ishmael, the ancestors of all Muslims, were directed by God to build a sanctuary.

Islamic Mysticism: The Sufis. Like all other major religions, Islam has its mystics. Because it developed in Byzantium, where there was a strong Jewish and Christian mystical tradition, and also in India, which had its own ascetic tradition, Islam was influenced to find its own mystical path. This path was followed most powerfully by the Sufis. The word *sufi* means "woolen" and refers to the coarse woolen clothing the Sufis wear as a sign of their rejection of worldly comforts.

Although the Sufis trace their lineage back to the seventh century, it is more likely that the movement began in earnest in the ninth century, when there was an increase in materialism; the Sufis' choice of austerity was a direct response to this. During the twelfth century, the Sufis organized themselves into monastic orders, much like the monks of medieval Christendom. A convert to a Sufi order was called a *fakir* ("poor man") or *dervish* ("beggar"), terms intended to indicate the monk's experience of poverty and begging. Although the monastic practices of the Sufis varied, they generally included strict discipline along with abstinence, poverty, and sometimes celibacy.

The legacy of the Sufis also includes their attention to the spirit rather than the letter of Islamic religious law. Their goal was to get to the spiritual heart of every aspect of Islamic religious life, from the simplest prayers to the most elaborate ritual.

One of the more notable features of Sufism in early Islam is that it recognized women as fully equal to men. A woman, for example, could become a Sufi leader or *shaykh* (feminine *shaykha*). Among the most prominent of *shaykhas* was RABIA AL-ADAWIYYA [RAA-be-ah] (d. 801), who preached an intensely devotional love of God with a corresponding withdrawal from the ordinary world. Her emphasis on worshiping God out of pure love, rather than for either temporal or eternal reward, served as both inspiration and a model for other Sufis.

Prominent among Sufi ideas is the soul's yearning and perpetual search for God, since God is the ultimate source of all life. This notion is expressed in the poetry of the thirteenth-century Persian mystic JALALODDIN RUMI [ROO-me] (1207–1273), whose poems often feature a lover seeking his beloved as a metaphor for the soul's seeking of God.

PHILOSOPHY

Avicenna and Averroes. If the Quran expresses Islamic theology and the Sufis the mystical element of Islamic thought, Islam's philosophical bent is best figured by AVICENNA [ah-vee-SEN-ah] (980–1037) and AVERROES [a-VER-o-ease] (1126–1198).

Better known as a doctor than as a philosopher, Avicenna articulated the beliefs of Islam in terms drawn from Aristotle and Plato, wedding two divergent Greek philosophical traditions as well as linking Greek philosophy with Islamic beliefs. Following Aristotle, Avicenna argued that God was the creator, or Prime Cause, of all that exists, a necessary being whose existence and essence were one and the same.

The second major voice of Islamic philosophy was raised not in Arabia but in Spain by Averroes, another physician-philosopher. Like Avicenna, Averroes attempted to build a bridge between the philosophy of Aristotle and the more Neoplatonically based theology of Islamic thinkers.

By following Aristotle's lead in paying renewed attention to the natural world, Averroes paved the way for Thomas Aquinas (see Chapter 12) to develop his scholastic philosophical system, which was also indebted to Aristotle and which, like the philosophy of Averroes, privileged reason above faith. Both Aquinas and Averroes, for example, argue that the existence of God can be proved by reason without the aid of revelation.

Averroes and Avicenna helped preserve the Western intellectual tradition through their reverence for education, books, and philosophy. The libraries acquired by Islamic rulers and philosophers continued the philosophic tradition that began in the West with the Greeks and found renewed expression in the religious thought of the Middle Ages and scientific spirit of later centuries.

Figure 7.13 Mosque, Cordova, begun 786, exterior. This mosque, a masterpiece of Islamic architecture, was started by Abd-al Rahman I. It is an example of the work of the Umayyad dynasty in Spain.

Figure 7.14 Mosque, Cordova, begun 786, plan. Although the original structure was enlarged four times, the traditional plan continued to be organized and precise, as if laid out on a grid. The mosque includes a court, prayer hall, and arcades.

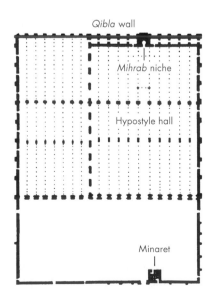

Figure 7.15   Mosque, Cordova, begun 786, interior. Decoration in plaster and marble creates an effect of delicacy and lightness, of the material made immaterial. Walls have not one plane but many, and the layers of space overlap, becoming mesh-like.

ISLAMIC ART AND ARCHITECTURE

Islamic art is not the art of one particular group of people, nor that of one country. Rather, it is the art associated with the life of one person, Muhammad, and the teachings of one book, the Quran. It is, therefore, a fusion of many different cultures, the most influential of which are Turkish, Persian, and, particularly and originally, Arabic.

The Mosque.   There is little evidence of art in Arabia before Islam, and, at first, Islam did not encourage art. Islam opposes idol worship—Muhammad had all pagan idols destroyed. Furthermore, a Muslim could pray anywhere without the need of religious architecture. Nonetheless, in the late seventh century, Muslim rulers started to build palaces and **mosques**—the buildings in which Muslims assemble for religious purposes. In an attempt to compete with Byzantium, the caliphs built with materials and on a scale to rival Christian churches. Typically, a mosque is rectangular in plan, with an open court, and a fountain in the center used for

purification. Covered walkways, with flat roofs supported on columns and arches, lead to the side, on which is located the **mihrab**, a small niche indicating the side facing Mecca. All mosques are oriented toward Mecca, Muhammad's place of birth, and it is the direction in which Muslims turn when praying. **Minarets** are towers beside mosques from which the faithful are called to prayer by the **muezzin**, the person who ascends a spiral staircase to a platform at the top.

Construction of the mosque at Cordova in Spain (fig. 7.13) was started in 786. The plan (fig. 7.14) is simple, making it easy to enlarge the mosque by adding more aisles, as happened on several occasions. The interior (fig. 7.15) contains hundreds of columns. A visitor must follow the aisles through this forest to reach the mihrab side. There are two tiers of arches, which create a light and airy interior, an impression enhanced by the contrasting stripes of the **voussoirs**—the wedge-shaped stones that make up the arches. The individual arches are the characteristically Muslim horseshoe shape. The result is a fluid, almost mystical space.

Figure 7.16 Sinan, Mosque of Sultan Sulayman, Istanbul, 1550–57, exterior. Like Hagia Sophia, built in the same city by the Christian Byzantines a millennium earlier, this Islamic mosque consists of a large central dome with abutting half-domes and smaller semi-domes.

The Mosque of Sultan Sulayman (Suleiman) (fig. 7.16), built 1550–57, is the main mosque of Constantinople, an enormous complex including tombs, hospitals, and facilities for traveling merchants and which symbolizes the city's importance as the center of Western Islamic civilization. The architect of the mosque was SINAN [SIGH-nan], the greatest master of his day. The mosque appears to build up in waves, as does Hagia Sophia which was built a thousand years earlier in the same city: the Muslims were clearly attempting to rival the Byzantines. The very tall minarets give emphasis to the vertical; those at Hagia Sophia are later Muslim additions. The similarity between the buildings continues with the domes: like Hagia Sophia, the mosque has a large dome, two big half-domes, and several smaller ones. The surface decoration of the facade is so light and lacy that it makes the building appear delicate and fragile. The courtyard is constructed with columns and arches but, rather than a flat roof, there is a series of domes—the same roofing system employed in the mosque itself, creating a sense of unity between inside and out.

Figure 7.17 Sinan, Mosque of Sultan Sulayman, Istanbul, 1550–57, interior. The interior of this Islamic mosque, with a ring of windows at the base of the dome, is worthy of comparison with the interiors of the Byzantine churches of Hagia Sophia and St. Mark's.

with several courts and a number of towers added by successive rulers.

Here, architectural function is obscured. Walls become lace-like webs. Surfaces are decorated with intricate patterns that disguise and seem to dissolve material substance. The solidity of stone is eclipsed as domes filled with designs seem to become floating lace canopies. The dissolution of matter is a fundamental principle of Islamic art. This ephemeral style is unlike any other in the history of art.

Decoration is made of tile and stucco, which is either modeled in low relief or is built up in layers which are then cut away to create the effect of stalactites. Surfaces are covered with a seemingly infinite variety of complex geometric patterns. Decoration is exquisite, achieving the height of sophistication, refinement, and richness. Ornament is profuse, yet the whole is controlled by a predilection for symmetry and repeated rhythms. Much use is made of calligraphic designs, including decorative Cufic writing, floral patterns, and purely abstract linear elements. Arabic **calligraphy**—fine handwriting—pervades Islamic art, appearing not only in manuscripts, but also on buildings, textiles, pottery, and elsewhere. The popularity of calligraphy is in part a result of traditional Muslim iconoclasm. Because the figurative arts were discouraged, artists elaborated the abstract beauty of handwriting.

Figure 7.18 Court of the Lions, Alhambra Palace, Granada, 1354–91. Rather than stressing the supporting structure, emphasis is on the decorative surfaces, the slender columns, and the extreme sophistication with which all surfaces are ornamented.

The interior of the mosque (fig. 7.17) has a ring of windows at the base of the dome, which makes the dome appear weightless and floating, and a large number of windows in the walls, turning them into airy screens. The shimmering tile decoration has the effect of separating the surface from its underlying structural function. Ornamental patterns and inscriptions can be found everywhere. The tiles are often floral and polychromatic; the ceramic artist and architect worked together to create an effect whereby visitors feel surrounded by gardens of luxurious flowers.

The Alhambra Palace. The Alhambra Palace in Granada, Spain, is one of the finest examples of Islamic architecture. A palace fortress, the Alhambra is the most remarkable legacy of the Nasirid dynasty, which ruled southern Spain from 1232 until the united armies of Catholic Spain under the leadership of Ferdinand and Isabella chased the last Muslim rulers out of the country in 1492.

The Alhambra is built on top of a hill overlooking the city of Granada, providing spectacular views and a cool respite from the heat of southern Spain. Surrounded by gardens built in terraces, the palace is irregular in plan,

The Court of the Lions (fig. 7.18), built 1354–91 by Mohammed V, is probably the most famous part of the Alhambra. It is named for the stone lions that form the base of a fountain in the middle of the court; such free-standing figurative sculpture is extremely rare in Islamic art. The Court of the Lions is considered the quintessence of the Moorish style. Slender columns surround the courtyard, arranged singly or in pairs, and support a series of arches of fantastic shapes.

Ceramics and Miniature Painting. Islamic pictorial arts were curtailed by Muhammad's opposition to idolatry. The Quran's view that statues are the work of the devil largely eliminated sculpture. The lions in the Court of the Lions at the Alhambra Palace are rare examples, and, moreover, they serve a functional purpose, acting as supports for the water basin of the fountain. Although the Quran does not mention painting or any other medium, the argument against the portrayal of human figures or animals—or, indeed, anything living—is that only God can create life and the artist must not try to imitate God. Thus, mosques contain no figurative representations. Nonetheless, Islamic art does include some images of living things, but they are not large-scale, nor made for display. Instead, such images are usually restricted to small-scale or functional objects, such as textiles and vessels (fig. 7.19). Otherwise, geometric and plant designs were preferred.

Figure 7.20 *A Sheik Meditating in a Pavilion*, illustrating the poem *Haft Aurang (The Seven Thrones)*, by Jami, 1556–65, $13\frac{1}{2} \times 9\frac{1}{8}''$ (34.3 × 23.9 cm), Freer Gallery of Art, Smithsonian Institution, Washington, D.C.

Figure 7.19 Bowl, from Iran, twelfth or thirteenth century, ceramic, diameter $8\frac{1}{2}''$ (21.7 cm), Khalili Collection, London. The figurative design showing a couple in a garden was popular in the period. The decorative bands of script that are around the rim of the plate repeat two words, "Glory" and "Piety."

Despite this ban on figurative images, a rich tradition of figurative miniature painting extends from the thirteenth to the late seventeenth century, depicting the hadith, or traditional legends appended to the Quran, as well as the poetry of religious mystics. For example, *A Sheik Meditating in a Pavilion* (fig. 7.20) illustrates a scene from the poem *Haft Aurang (The Seven Thrones)*, written by the Persian poet JAMI [JAR-me] (1414–1492).

LITERATURE

Arabic and Persian Poetry. Like English poetry, Arabic poetry began appearing in written form around 700. Arab lexicographers and philologists began collecting and recording poems that had survived orally in various Arab tribal traditions. These poems had long been chanted by *rawi*, professional reciters, who kept the verse alive.

One of the oldest forms of Arabic poetry is the *qasidah*, a highly formalized ode. The *qasidah* has three parts: (1) a visit to an abandoned encampment to find the beloved, whose departure the poet laments; (2) the poet's journey to find her, replete with descriptions of flowers and animals, especially his camel, which he eulogizes; and (3) a eulogy on a neighbor or tribe that often includes a tribute to the poet's own ancestry. The *qasidah* ranges from 30 to 120 lines in length, each line ending with the same rhyme. Central to any *qasidah* is the image, or rather a series of juxtaposed images, that vividly expresses what the poet has observed.

When Arabs invaded and conquered Persia in A.D. 637, they brought with them Islam and their Arabic script, which the Persians adopted in place of their complicated ideograms. Many Arabic words passed into Persian and some literary forms underwent modification. With the adoption of the Arabic script came an explosion of Persian poetry, including work by the early Persian poet FIRDAWSI [fear-DOW-See] (late tenth–early eleventh century). Like other Persian poets of his time and later, Firdawsi wrote in both Arabic and Persian, translating poems readily from one language to the other. The first major Persian poet and one of the greatest, Firdawsi wrote the epic *Shah-namah* (*Book of Kings*), a work of sixty thousand couplets (fig. 7.21).

One consequence of translating Persian poems into Arabic was the introduction into Arabic poetry of the quatrain (*ruba'i*, plural *ruba'iyat*), a Persian form of four lines with rhyming pattern of AABA. The *ruba'i* is familiar to readers of English through Edward Fitzgerald's translation of *The Ruba'iyat of Omar Khayyam*. The influence of the two poetic traditions, however, was reciprocal, and the Arabic *qasidah* was taken into Persian. The exchange of forms also includes the *ghazal*, a short Arabic love lyric of five to fifteen couplets believed to be of Persian origin.

Persian poetry is almost always lyrical, and its most frequent subject is love. Common features include the distraught lover, who, anguished over imagined slights, is completely at the mercy of a haughty and indifferent beloved. Some scholars have suggested that the relationship of sorrowful lover to paramour is a metaphor for the relationship between the believer and God. In fact, there is a school of Persian poetry, influenced by the mystical ideas of Sufism, that uses many of the same images as love poetry. The ambiguity of subject found in some Persian love poetry can also be found in the biblical Song of Songs. In addition, the technique of using the language of physical love to describe the love of divinity is analogous to that of certain Western poets, such as John Donne and Emily Dickinson. Persian writers, moreover, have a long history of using mysticism and symbolism to veil meaning in politically perilous times.

A further characteristic of Persian poetry is its celebration of spring, a time of renewal and hope. Seasonal

Figure 7.21 Page from a copy of the *Shah-namah* (*Book of Kings*), by Firdawsi, 1562–83, watercolor and gold on paper, 18½ × 13″ (43.0 × 33.0 cm), Museum of Fine Arts, Boston. Until recent times, every Muslim text began with the phrase "In the name of Allah." Called the *bismillah*, the phrase opens the Quran. Here it is at the top right hand corner (Arabic texts read right to left). To write the *bismillah* as beautifully as possible is the highest form of Islamic art.

celebration has a prominence in Persian poetry for a number of reasons. One reason has to do with the climate and topography of Persia, an area that is largely desert, in which the blossoming of flowers in the spring is an especially welcome sight. Another is that, since Persians celebrate their solar New Year on March 21, the first day of spring, the season is associated with gift-giving and a renewal of hope. In addition, Persian poets often celebrate the transience of the flowers of spring as emblems of the transience of earthly joy.

Poetry of Islamic Spain. One of the legacies of the invasion of Spain by the Umayyad Muslims in 711 is a splendid profusion of Arabic Andalusian poems. Many of the most distinctive of the Andalusian poems (Arabic

Connections

SUFISM, DANCING, AND MUSIC

Sufism attempted to achieve direct contact with God through mystical trance. One method of achieving trance and thus connection with the divine was through dance, especially the spinning circular form of dance that became associated with the "whirling dervishes." Dance provided the Sufi with an outlet for emotion and an opportunity to achieve ecstasy through psychic illumination in trance.

The music that accompanied such dancing would probably have been primarily percussive, for example, a drum beat, that pounded out a steady rhythm, or would perhaps have included wooden flutes, tambourines, or even a stringed instrument, such as an *ud*, or Arabic lute.

The beautiful painting reproduced here (fig. 7.22) appears in a Turkish manuscript dating from the sixteenth century. The dancers in the center raise their hands in ecstatic celebration, while the figures in the foreground may have succumbed to dizziness. Music and dancing were disapproved of by some Muslims, but they were nonetheless practiced by many Sufi orders, for whom the dance may be seen as representing the soul's movement toward God.

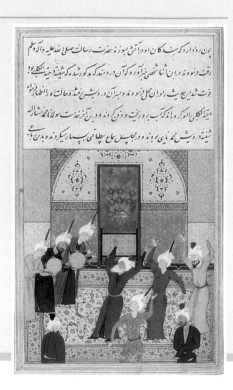

Figure 7.22 Turkish miniature of dervishes dancing, from a copy of the *Sessions of the Lovers*, sixteenth century, illuminated manuscript, ca. 9 × 6″ (25.0 × 15.0 cm), Bodleian Library, Oxford.

poetry written in Spain) date from the eleventh century, when Andalusian poetry acquired a distinctiveness that set it apart from its Middle Eastern Arabic counterpart. Arabic Andalusian poetry tends toward lyric simplicity and directness, emphasizing the beauty of nature. Many of the poems are highly metaphoric. The most distinctive form, the *muwashshah*, includes Spanish colloquialisms mixed in with Arabic verse, and can be read as an analogy of the way in which the two cultures became interwoven.

Andalusian poems are Spanish versions of Arabic poems that were collected in the 1243 codex (manuscript volume) of Ibn Sa'id. A Spanish scholar of Arabic acquired the codex in Cairo in 1928, and proceeded to translate and publish a selection of the poems as *Poemas Arabigoandaluces* two years later. So great has been its popularity that many modern Spanish-speaking poets have acknowledged its influence on their work. The translator Cola Franzen suggests that in the manner of "wooing a woman, the Arabs courted, cosseted, adored, and adorned Spain with orchards, gardens, fountains and pools, cities and palaces, and century after century sang her praises in unforgettable verse … The courtship lasted almost eight hundred years; the suitor was rejected in the end, and we are left with the love letters."

Arabic Prose: The Thousand and One Nights. One of the most famous of all Arabic works of literature is *The Thousand and One Nights*, better known in the West as *The Arabian Nights*. Of Indo-Persian origin, the stories recounted in *The Thousand and One Nights* were introduced into written Arabic some time during the tenth century, and were subsequently embellished, polished, and expanded. Different as their ethnic origins may be—Persian, Indian, Arabic—the stories of *The Thousand and One Nights* became assimilated to reflect the cultural and artistic history of the Arabic Islamic tradition.

The stories cast a romantic glow of Eastern enchantment, and, while they do not chronicle the adventures of a single hero as do medieval narratives such as the *Song of Roland* or the *Divine Comedy*, they are linked by the device of a single narrator, Shahrazad, the wife of the Persian king Shahrayar, who is entertained night after night by her storytelling, which prolongs her life and cures his hatred of women. The stories are remarkable for their blending of the marvelous with the everyday.

With their exotic settings and rich aura of fantasy, the tales of *The Thousand and One Nights* captured the imagination of European readers. Although they did not reach the West until after Chaucer and Boccaccio had written their comic masterpieces, Chaucer's "Squire's Tale" from *The Canterbury Tales* and some of the tales from Boccaccio's *Decameron* were of Arabian origin.

MUSIC

During the period of the four orthodox caliphs, or representatives of Muhammad, who reigned from the prophet's death in 632 until 661, music was classed as one of the *malahi*, or forbidden pleasures. Associated with frivolity, sensuality, and luxury, it was deemed to be at odds with the religious values of Islam. With the advent of the Umayyad dynasty (661–750), however, music began to find a favorable audience throughout the Islamic world. The Umayyads held a lively court in Damascus, one that encouraged the development of the arts and sciences.

Persian music had an influence on Arabic music, and vice versa. Moreover, in the same way that Islam influenced poetry in southern Spain, so the Cordovan Islamic community supported the development of a new and distinctive musical style in Andalusian Spain. Music, especially Arabic music, flourished most, however, during the Abbasid dynasty (750–1258), the period immediately following the reign of the Umayyads. During the reign of the Abbasids, music became an obligatory accomplishment for every educated person, much as it did later at the courts of Renaissance Europe. Yet with the collapse of the Abbasid dynasty and the destruction of Baghdad by the Mongol armies in 1258, music declined during a period of general intellectual and cultural stagnation.

Medieval Arabic music was influenced to a significant degree by ancient Greek musical theory, which reached Near Eastern scholars in the ninth century when the works of Ptolemy, Pythagoras, and other Greek theorists were translated into Arabic. One Arabic theorist in particular who was influenced by Greek musical theory was AL-KINDI [al-KIN-dee] (790-874), who, like his Greek precursors, was interested in the effects of music on people's feelings and behavior.

Although much Islamic music was court music, which served either as vocal entertainment or as an accompaniment for dancing by professional dancers in palaces and private residences, religion also made use of music. Music was, and still is, used in calling Muslims to prayer, in chanting verses of the Quran, in hymns for special occasions and holy days, and in the *dhikr*, in which music accompanies the solemn repetition of the name of God.

READINGS

✦ THE QURAN
Selected Passages

The following passages, excerpted from the Quran, describe the contrasting positions of women and men in ancient (and modern) Islamic society. Women's subservience to men is strongly accentuated in the first passage. The second emphasizes man's responsibilities to God, while revealing the material and spiritual rewards he will reap due to the beneficence of the Almighty.

Women

In the Name of God, the Compassionate, the Merciful

Men, have fear of your Lord, who created you from a single soul. From that soul He created its mate, and through them He bestrewed the earth with countless men and women.

Fear God, in whose name you plead with one another, and honour the mothers who bore you. God is ever watching over you.

Give orphans the property which belongs to them. Do not exchange their valuables for worthless things or cheat them of their possessions: for this would surely be a great sin. If you fear that you cannot treat orphans with fairness, then you may marry other women who seem good to you: two, three, or four of them. But if you fear that you cannot maintain equality among them, marry one only or any slave-girls you may own. This will make it easier for you to avoid injustice.

Give women their dowry as a free gift; but if they choose to make over to you a part of it, you may regard it as lawfully yours.

Do not give the feeble-minded the property with which God has entrusted you for their support; but maintain and clothe them with its proceeds, and give them good advice.

Put orphans to the test until they reach a marriageable age. If you find them capable of sound judgement, hand over to them their property, and do not deprive them of it by squandering it before they come of age.

Let not the rich guardian touch the property of his orphan ward; and let him who is poor use no more than a fair proportion of it for his own advantage.

When you hand over to them their property, call in some witnesses; sufficient is God's accounting of your actions.

Men shall have a share in what their parents and kinsmen leave; and women shall have a share in what their parents and kinsmen leave: whether it be little or much, they shall be legally entitled to their share.

If relatives, orphans, or needy men are present at the division of an inheritance, give them, too, a share of it, and speak to them kind words.

Let those who are solicitous about the welfare of their young children after their own death take care not to wrong orphans. Let them fear God and speak for justice.

Those that devour the property of orphans unjustly, swallow fire into their bellies; they shall burn in a mighty conflagration.

God has thus enjoined you concerning your children:

A male shall inherit twice as much as a female. If there be more than two girls, they shall have two-thirds of the inheritance; but if there be one only, she shall inherit the half. Parents shall inherit a sixth each, if the deceased have a child; but if he leave no child and his parents be his heirs, his mother shall have a third. If he have brothers, his mother shall have a sixth after payment of any legacy he may have bequeathed or any debt he may have owed.

You may wonder whether your parents or your children are more beneficial to you. But this is the law of God; God is all-knowing and wise.

You shall inherit the half of your wives' estate if they die childless. If they leave children, a quarter of their estate shall be yours after payment of any legacies they may have bequeathed or any debt they may have owed.

Your wives shall inherit one quarter of your estate if you die childless. If you leave children, they shall inherit one-eighth, after payment of any legacies you may have bequeathed or any debts you may have owed.

If a man or a woman leave neither children nor parents and have a brother or sister, they shall each inherit one-sixth. If there be more they shall equally share the third of the estate, after payment of any legacy that he may have bequeathed or any debt he may have owed, without prejudice to the rights of the heirs. That is a commandment from God. God is all-knowing and gracious.

Such are the bounds set by God. He that obeys God and His apostle shall dwell for ever in gardens watered by running streams. That is the supreme triumph. But he that defies God and His apostle and transgresses His bounds, shall be cast into a fire wherein he will abide for ever. A shameful punishment awaits him.

If any of your women commit fornication, call in four witnesses from among yourselves against them; if they testify to their guilt confine them to their houses till death overtakes them on till God finds another way for them.

If two men among you commit indecency punish them both. If they repent and mend their ways, let them be. God is forgiving and merciful.

God forgives those who commit evil in ignorance and then quickly turn to Him in repentance. God will pardon them. God is wise and all-knowing. But He will not forgive those who do evil and, when death comes to them, say: 'Now we repent!' Nor those who die unbelievers: for them We have prepared a woeful scourge.

Believers, it is unlawful for you to inherit the women of your deceased kinsmen against their will, or to bar them from re-marrying, in order that you may force them to give up a part of what you have given them, unless they be guilty of a proven crime. Treat them with kindness; for even if you dislike them, it may well be that you may dislike a thing which God has meant for your own abundant good.

If you wish to (replace a wife with) another, do not take from her the dowry you have given her even if it be a talent of gold. That would be improper and grossly unjust; for how can you take it back when you have lain with each other and entered into a firm contract?

You shall not marry the women whom your fathers married. That was an evil practice, indecent and abominable.

Forbidden to you are your mothers, your daughters, your sisters, your paternal and maternal aunts, the daughters of your brothers and sisters, your foster-mothers, your foster sisters, the mothers of your wives, your step-daughters who are in your charge, born of the wives with whom you have lain (it is no offence for you to marry your step-daughters if you have not consummated your marriage with their mothers), and the wives of your own begotten sons. You are also forbidden to take in marriage two sisters at one and the same time: all previous such marriages excepted. God is forgiving and merciful.

Also married women, except those whom you own as slaves. Such is the decree of God. All women other than these are lawful to you, provided you seek them with your wealth in modest conduct, not in fornication. Give them their dowry for the enjoyment you have had of them as a duty; but it shall be no offence for you to make any other agreement among yourselves after you have fulfilled your duty. God is all-knowing and wise.

If any one of you cannot afford to marry a free believing woman, let him marry a slave-girl who is a believer (God best knows your faith: you are born one of another). Marry them with the permission of their masters and give them their dowry in all justice, provided they are honourable and chaste and have not entertained other men. If after marriage they commit adultery, they shall suffer half the penalty inflicted upon free adulteresses. Such is the law for those of you who fear to commit sin: but if you abstain, it will be better for you. God is forgiving and merciful.

God desires to make this known to you and to guide you along the paths of those who have gone before you, and to turn to you in mercy. God is all-knowing and wise.

God wishes to forgive you, but those who follow their own appetites wish to see you far astray. God wishes to lighten your burdens, for man was created weak.

Believers, do not consume your wealth among yourselves in vanity, but rather trade with it by mutual consent.

Do not destroy yourselves. God is merciful to you, but he that does that through wickedness and injustice shall be burned in fire. That is easy enough for God.

If you avoid the enormities you are forbidden, We shall pardon your misdeeds and usher you in with all honour. Do not covet the favours by which God has exalted some of you above others. Men shall be rewarded according to their deeds, and women shall be rewarded according to their deeds. Rather implore God to bestow on you His gifts. God has knowledge of all things.

To every parent and kinsman We have appointed heirs who will inherit from him. As for those with whom you have entered into agreements, let them, too, have their due. God bears witness to all things.

Men have authority over women because God has made the one superior to the other, and because they spend their wealth to maintain them. Good women are obedient. They guard their unseen parts because God has guarded them. As for those from whom you fear disobedience, admonish them and send them to beds apart and beat them. Then if they obey you, take no further action against them. God is high, supreme.

If you fear a breach between a man and his wife, appoint an arbiter from his people and another from hers. If they wish to be reconciled God will bring them together again. God is all-knowing and wise.

Serve God and associate none with Him. Show kindness to your parents and your kindred, to orphans and to the helpless, to near and distant neighbours, to those that keep company with you, to the traveller in need, and to the slaves whom you own. God does not love arrogant and boastful men, who are themselves niggardly and enjoin others to be niggardly; who conceal the riches which God of His bounty has bestowed upon them (We have prepared a shameful punishment for the unbelievers); and who spend their wealth for the sake of ostentation, believing neither in God nor in the Last Day. He that chooses Satan for his friend, an evil friend has he.

Man

In the Name of God, the Compassionate, the Merciful

Does there not pass over man a space of time when his life is a blank?

We have created man from the union of the two sexes so that We may put him to the proof. We have endowed him with hearing and sight and, be he thankful or oblivious of Our favours, We have shown him the right path.

For the unbelievers We have prepared fetters and chains, and a blazing Fire. But the righteous shall drink of a cup tempered at the Camphor Fountain, a gushing spring at which the servants of God will refresh themselves: they who keep their vows and dread the far-spread terrors of Judgement-day; who, though they hold it dear, give sustenance to the poor man, the orphan, and the captive, saying: "We feed you for God's sake only; we seek of you neither recompense nor thanks: for we fear from God a day of anguish and of woe."

God will deliver them from the evil of that day and make their faces shine with joy. He will reward them for their steadfastness with robes of silk and the delights of Paradise. Reclining there upon soft couches, they shall feel neither the scorching heat nor the biting cold. Trees will spread their shade around them, and fruits will hang in clusters over them.

They shall be served with silver dishes, and beakers as large as goblets; silver goblets which they themselves shall measure: and cups brim-full with ginger-flavoured water from the Fount of Salsabil. They shall be attended by boys graced with eternal youth, who to the beholder's eyes will seem like sprinkled pearls. When you gaze upon that scene you will behold a kingdom blissful and glorious.

They shall be arrayed in garments of fine green silk and rich brocade, and adorned with bracelets of silver. Their Lord will give them pure nectar to drink.

Thus you shall be rewarded; your high endeavours are gratifying to God.

We have made known to you the Koran by gradual revelation; therefore wait with patience the judgement of your Lord and do not yield to the wicked and the unbelieving. Remember the name of your Lord morning and evening; in the nighttime worship Him: praise Him all night long.

The unbelievers love this fleeting life too well, and thus prepare for themselves a heavy day of doom. *We* created them, and endowed their limbs and joints with strength; but if We please We can replace them by other men.

This is indeed an admonition. Let him that will, take the right path to his Lord. Yet you cannot will, except by the will of God. God is wise and all-knowing.

He is merciful to whom He will: but for the wrongdoers He has prepared a woeful punishment.

⬦ ## THE THOUSAND AND ONE NIGHTS

The Tale of the Merchant

The following selection from The Thousand and One Nights *(also known as* The Arabian Nights*) is taken from near the beginning of the series of linked stories. These are the first stories told by Shahrazad to her royal husband. Their high level of narrative interest coupled with the narrator's postponed revelation of the outcome, ensures both the reader's interest and her survival to tell a tale another day.*

The First Night

It is said, O wise and happy King, that once there was a prosperous merchant who had abundant wealth and investments and commitments in every country. He had many women and children and kept many servants and slaves. One day, having resolved to visit another country, he took provisions, filling his saddlebag with loaves of bread and with dates, mounted his horse, and set out on his journey. For many days and nights, he journeyed under God's care until he reached his destination. When he finished his business, he turned back to his home and family. He journeyed for three days, and on the fourth day, chancing to come to an orchard, went in to avoid the heat and shade himself from the sun of the open country. He came to a spring under a walnut tree and, tying his horse, sat by the spring, pulled out from the saddlebag some loaves of bread and a handful of dates, and began to eat, throwing the date pits right and left until he had had enough. Then he got up, performed his ablutions, and performed his prayers.

But hardly had he finished when he saw an old demon, with sword in hand, standing with his feet on the ground and his head in the clouds. The demon approached until he stood before him and screamed, saying, "Get up, so that I may kill you with this sword, just as you have killed my son." When the merchant saw and heard the demon, he was terrified and awestricken. He asked, "Master, for what crime do you wish to kill me?" The demon replied, "I wish to kill you because you have killed my son." The merchant asked, "Who has killed your son?" The demon replied, "You have killed my son." The merchant said, "By God, I did not kill your son. When and how could that have been?" The demon said, "Didn't you sit down, take out some dates from your saddlebag, and eat, throwing the pits right and left?" The merchant replied, "Yes, I did." The demon said, "You killed my son, for as you were throwing the stones right and left, my son happened to be walking by and was struck and killed by one of them, and I must now kill you." The merchant said, "O my lord, please don't kill me." The demon replied, "I must kill you as you killed him—blood for blood." The merchant said, "To God we belong and to God we turn. There is no power or strength, save in God the Almighty, the Magnificent. If I killed him, I did it by mistake. Please forgive me." The demon replied, "By God, I must kill you, as you killed my son." Then he seized him and, throwing him to the ground, raised the sword to strike him. The merchant began to weep and mourn his family and his wife and children. Again, the demon raised his sword to strike, while the merchant cried until he was drenched with tears, saying, "There is no power or strength, save in God the Almighty, the Magnificent." Then he began to recite the following verses:

> "Life has two days: one peace, one wariness,
> And has two sides: worry and happiness.
> Ask him who taunts us with adversity,
> "Does fate, save those worthy of note, oppress?

Don't you see that the blowing, raging storms
Only the tallest of the trees beset,
And of earth's many green and barren lots,
Only the ones with fruits with stones are hit,
And of the countless stars in heaven's vault
None is eclipsed except the moon and sun?
You thought well of the days, when they were good,
Oblivious to the ills destined for one.
You were deluded by the peaceful nights,
Yet in the peace of night does sorrow stun."

When the merchant finished and stopped weeping, the demon said, "By God, I must kill you, as you killed my son, even if you weep blood." The merchant asked, "Must you?" The demon replied, "I must," and raised his sword to strike.

But morning overtook Shahrazad, and she lapsed into silence, leaving King Shahrayar burning with curiosity to hear the rest of the story. Then Dinarzad said to her sister Shahrazad, "What a strange and lovely story!" Shahrazad replied, "What is this compared with what I shall tell you tomorrow night if the king spares me and lets me live? It will be even be better and more entertaining." The king thought to himself, "I will spare her until I hear the rest of the story; then I will have her put to death the next day." When morning broke, the day dawned, and the sun rose; the king left to attend to the affairs of the kingdom, and the vizier, Shahrazad's father, was amazed and delighted. King Shahrayar governed all day and returned home at night to his quarters and got into bed with Shahrazad. Then Dinarzad said to her sister Shahrazad, "Please, sister, if you are not sleepy, tell us one of your lovely little tales to while away the night." The king added, "Let it be the conclusion of the story of the demon and the merchant, for I would like to hear it." Shahrazad replied: "With the greatest pleasure, dear, happy King":

The Second Night

It is related, O wise and happy King, that when the demon raised his sword, the merchant asked the demon again, "Must you kill me?" and the demon replied, "Yes." Then the merchant said, "Please give me time to say good-bye to my family and my wife and children, divide my property among them, and appoint guardians. Then I shall come back, so that you may kill me." The demon replied, "I am afraid that if I release you and grant you time, you will go and do what you wish, but will not come back." The merchant said, "I swear to keep my pledge to come back, as the God of heaven and earth is my witness." The demon asked, "How much time do you need?" The merchant replied, "One year, so that I may see enough of my children, and bid my wife good-bye, discharge my obligations to people, and come back on New Year's Day." The demon asked, "Do you swear to God that if I let you go, you will come back on New Year's Day?" The merchant replied, "Yes, I swear to God."

After the merchant swore, the demon released him, and he mounted his horse sadly and went on his way. He journeyed until he reached his home and came to his wife and children. When he saw them, he wept bitterly, and when his family saw his sorrow and grief, they began to reproach him for his behavior, and his wife said, "Husband, what is the matter with you? Why do you mourn, when we are happy, celebrating your return?" He replied, "Why not mourn when I have only one year to live?" Then told her of his encounter with the demon and informed her that he had sworn to return on New Year's Day, so that the demon might kill him.

When they heard what he said, everyone began to cry. His wife struck her face in lamentation and cut her hair, his daughters wailed, and his little children cried. It was a day of mourning, as all the children gathered around their father to weep and exchange goodbyes. The next day he wrote his will, dividing his property, discharged his obligations to people, left bequests and gifts, distributed alms, and engaged reciters to read portions of the Quran in his house. Then he summoned legal witnesses and in their presence freed his slaves and slave-girls, divided among his elder children their shares of the property, appointed guardians for his little ones, and gave his wife her share, according to her marriage contract.

He spent the rest of the time with his family, and when the year came to an end, save for the time needed for the journey, he performed his ablutions, performed his prayers, and, carrying his burial shroud, began to bid his family good-bye. His sons hung around his neck, his daughters wept, and his wife wailed. Their mourning scared him, and he began to weep, as he embraced and kissed his children good-bye. He said to them, "Children, this is God's will and decree, for man was created to die." Then he turned away and, mounting his horse, journeyed day and night until he reached the orchard on New Year's Day.

He sat at the place where he had eaten the dates, waiting for the demon, with a heavy heart and tearful eyes. As he waited, an old man, leading a deer on a leash, approached and greeted him, and he returned the greeting. The old man inquired, "Friend, why do you sit here in this place of demons and devils? For in this haunted orchard none come to good." The merchant replied by telling him what had happened to him and the demon, from beginning to end. The old man was amazed at the merchant's fidelity and said, "Yours is a magnificent pledge," adding, "By God, I shall not leave until I see what will happen to you with the demon." Then he sat down beside him and chatted with him. As they talked ...

But morning overtook Shahrazad, and she lapsed into silence. As the day dawned, and it was light, her sister Dinarzad said, "What a strange and wonderful story!" Shahrazad replied, "Tomorrow night I shall tell something even stranger and more wonderful than this."

The Third Night

When it was night and Shahrazad was in bed with the king, Dinarzad said to her sister Shahrazad, "Please, if you are not sleepy, tell us one of your lovely little tales to while away the night." The king added, "Let it be the conclusion of the merchant's story." Shahrazad replied, "As you wish":

I heard, O happy King, that as the merchant and the man with the deer sat talking, another old man approached, with two black hounds, and when he reached them, he greeted them, and they returned his greeting. Then he asked them about themselves, and the man with the deer told him the story of the merchant and the demon, how the merchant had sworn to return on New Year's Day, and how the demon was waiting to kill him. He added that when he himself heard the story, he swore never to leave until he saw what would happen between the merchant and the demon. When the man with the two dogs heard the story, he was amazed, and he too swore never to leave them until he saw what would happen between them. Then he questioned the merchant, and the merchant repeated to him what had happened to him with the demon.

While they were engaged in conversation, a third old man approached and greeted them, and they returned his greeting. He asked, "Why do I see the two of you sitting here, with this merchant between you, looking abject, sad, and dejected?" They told him the merchant's story and explained that they were sitting and waiting to see what would happen to him with the demon. When he heard the story, he sat down with them, saying, "By God, I too like you will not leave, until I see what happens to this man with the demon." As they sat, conversing with one another, they suddenly saw the dust rising from the open country, and when it cleared, they saw the demon approaching, with a drawn steel sword in his hand. He stood before them without greeting them, yanked the merchant with his left hand, and, holding him fast before him, said, "Get ready to die." The merchant and the three old men began to weep and wail.

But dawn broke and morning overtook Shahrazad, and she lapsed into silence. Then Dinarzad said, "Sister, what a lovely story!" Shahrazad replied, "What is this compared with what I shall tell you tomorrow night? It will be even better; it will be more wonderful, delightful, entertaining, and delectable if the king spares me and lets me live." The king was all curiosity to hear the rest of the story and said to himself, "By God, I will not have her put to death until I hear the rest of the story and find out what happened to the merchant with the demon. Then I will have her put to death the next morning, as I did with the others." Then he went out to attend to the affairs of his kingdom, and when he saw Shahrazad's father, he treated him kindly and showed him favors, and the vizier was amazed. When night came, the king went home, and when he was in bed with Shahrazad, Dinarzad said, "Sister, if you are not sleepy, tell us one of your lovely little tales to while away the night." Shahrazad replied, "With the greatest pleasure."

✦ JALALODDIN RUMI
The Question

Jalaloddin Rumi is the best known and the most influential of Persian poets. His deeply mystical works reflect the spirituality of the Sufis, emphasizing their withdrawal from the material world and their desire to achieve union with the divine. In the following poem two visions of the divine are described—a fire and a stream. Each is reflected by a voice that calls out to come and enter it. The contrasting images and voices of the fire and the water, however, are presented in a paradoxical relationship in which what appears to be one thing is its opposite.

One dervish to another, *What was your vision of God's presence?*
I haven't seen anything.
But for the sake of conversation, I'll tell you a story.

God's presence is there in front of me, a fire on the left,
a lovely stream on the right.   5
One group walks toward the fire, *into* the fire, another
toward the sweet flowing water.
No one knows which are blessed and which not.
Whoever walks into the fire appears suddenly in the stream.
A head goes under on the water surface, that head   10
pokes out of the fire.
Most people guard against going into the fire;
and so end up in it.
Those who love the water of pleasure and make it their
devotion
are cheated with this reversal.   15

The trickery goes further.
The voice of the fire tells the *truth*, saying *I am not fire.
I am fountainhead. Come to me and don't mind the sparks.*

If you are a friend of God, fire is your water.
You should wish to have a hundred thousand sets of
mothwings,   20
so you could burn them away, one set a night.
The moth sees light and goes into fire. You should see fire
and go toward light. Fire is what of God is world-
consuming.
Water, world-protecting.
Somehow each gives the appearance of the other. To these
eyes you have now   25
what looks like water burns. What looks like
fire is a great relief to be inside.
You've seen a magician make a bowl of rice
seem a dish full of tiny, live worms.
Before an assembly with one breath he made the floor
swarm   30
with scorpions that weren't there.
How much more amazing God's tricks.
Generation after generation lies down, defeated, they think,
but they're like a woman underneath a man, circling him,
One molecule-mote-second thinking of God's reversal of
comfort and pain   35
is better than any attending ritual. That splinter
of intelligence is substance.
The fire and water themselves:
Accidental, done with mirrors.

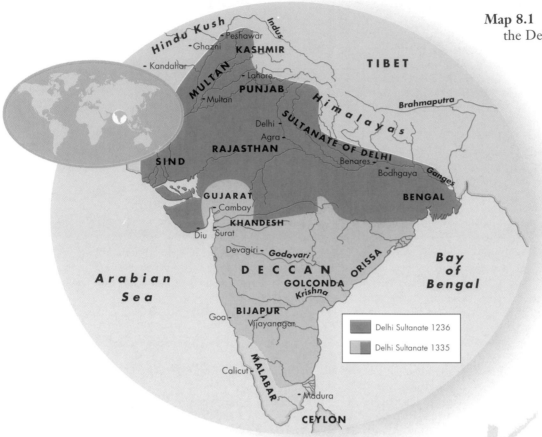

Map 8.1   Muslim India under the Delhi Sultanate.

Hindu Kush
• Peshawar
• Ghazni
KASHMIR
• Kandahar
MULTAN
Indus
• Lahore
PUNJAB
• Multan
TIBET
Himalayas
Brahmaputra
Delhi •
SULTANATE OF DELHI
Agra •
RAJASTHAN
Benares •
Ganges
SIND
Bodhgaya •
GUJARAT
BENGAL
• Cambay
KHANDESH
Diu • • Surat
Devagiri •
Godavari
Arabian
Sea
DECCAN
ORISSA
GOLCONDA
Bay
of
Bengal
Krishna
BIJAPUR
Goa •
Vijayanagar •
MALABAR
Calicut •
• Madura
CEYLON

	Delhi Sultanate 1236
	Delhi Sultanate 1335

INDIAN
← CIVILIZATION

CHAPTER 8

Great Stupa, Sanchi, third century B.C.–early first century A.D.

THE VEDIC PERIOD

India, as we know it today, is a distinct subcontinent bordered on the north by the Himalayan mountains, on the east by the Bay of Bengal, and on the west by the Arabian Sea. The only land routes into or out of the country are the northwestern passes through the Hindu Kush, the mountains separating India from Iran, and eastward past the mouth of the Ganges River, through Burma into China.

But despite its relative geographic isolation, India has long been the center of trade between East and West, on both land and sea. In his *Geography*, the ancient author Ptolemy records the visits of Western traders to stations on the Silk Road in the second century A.D. Between the fifth and ninth centuries A.D. the Chinese regularly traveled along Indian trade routes. In addition, maritime trade routes up and down the Indian coast connected China to the West long after Mongol hordes had laid waste the Silk Road itself in the thirteenth century.

The Vedic period, named after the oldest surviving sacred Indian writings, the *Vedas*, extends from about 1500 B.C. to just before 300 B.C. and represents a time of cultural assimilation that proved critical to India's subsequent development.

Sometime around 1500 B.C., Aryan tribes from the west settled in northern India. In many ways they were much less advanced—technologically and intellectually—than the native Indian population, the Dasas, or "slaves." The Aryans were nomadic, whereas the Dasas had built two great cities—Mohenjo-Daro and Harrapa—on the Indus River a thousand years before. However, the Aryans brought with them early forms of a language—Sanskrit—and of a religion—Hinduism—that would evolve to become very important to Indian cultural life.

It would take over a thousand years for the Aryans and Dasas to become fully integrated. During this period, in response to the growing complexity and social rigidity of Hinduism, various alternative religions emerged—most notably Buddhism and Jainism, both of which challenged the Hindu hereditary class structure.

HINDUISM

The origins of Hinduism are unknown, although they are believed to date to around the sixth century B.C., perhaps even as early as 1500 B.C. The word *Hindu* derives from the Sanskrit name for the Indus River, *Sindhu*. Like the Ganges, another important Indian river, the Indus was used for religious ceremonies, especially for rites of purification.

Figure 8.1 *Vishnu Narayana on the Cosmic Waters*, relief panel in the Vishnu Temple at Deogarh, Uttar Pradesh, India, ca. 530 B.C. In this scene, Vishnu lies on the waters of the cosmos at the very beginning of creation. He sleeps on the serpent of infinity. The goddess Lakshmi holds his foot as he dreams the universe into existence, by thinking "May I become Many."

Timeline 8.1 Early Indian civilization.

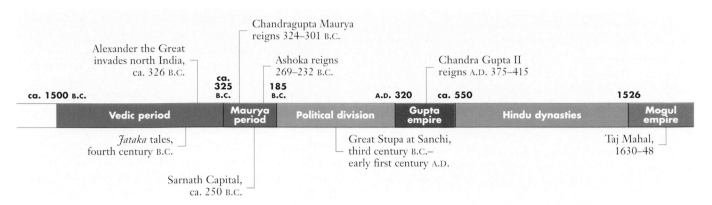

Hindu Gods. At the center of Hindu religious thought is the idea of BRAHMAN [BRAH-man], the indivisible essence of all spiritual reality, the divine source of all being. In ancient Hinduism (sometimes called Brahmanism), Brahman is a god who represents creation, preservation, and destruction. In later Hinduism, Brahman's three functions are divided among three gods: BRAHMA [BRAH-mah], the creator (as distinct from Brahman, the ubiquitous spirit of the universe); VISHNU [VISH-noo], the preserver (fig. 8.1); and SHIVA [SHE-vah], the destroyer.

The most popular of the three gods is Vishnu, the preserver. Vishnu is the god of benevolence, forgiveness, and love. He enjoys games and pranks. His consort, or companion, is LAKSHMI [LACK-shmee], with whom he is often depicted. Because of his great love for humankind, Vishnu is said to have appeared on earth many times in various forms, including that of a man. Among his avatars, or appearances in earthly form, is his incarnation as KRISHNA [KRISH-nah], a charioteer who advises the warrior Arjuna about his military responsibilities. Krishna is also believed by some Hindus to have been reincarnated as Gautama, or the Buddha.

Shiva, the destroyer, is the god of disease and death. He is also the god of dance. His most frequent consort is KALI [KAH-lee], a goddess of destruction, even more terrible than Shiva. Kali is often depicted with a necklace of human skulls. Since, for Hindus, death is a prelude to rebirth, Shiva and Kali are also gods of sexuality and reproduction. Devout Hindus profess their faith in one or more of these and other gods, and worship at temples built to honor them.

Karma. The idea of karma is central to Hindu thought. **Karma** (which means "action") involves a kind of moral cause-and-effect, in which people's actions affect their moral development. Each act individuals perform turns them more and more into a particular kind of being: for example, a sage, a warrior, or a thief. People's spirits are reincarnated and have many successive existences. The law of karma suggests that the present condition of a person's life has been determined by actions in previous existences.

Hindu Class Structure. The social structure of ancient Indian society derives from and reflects these religious concepts and beliefs, and is based on the division of society into four distinct classes or castes.

At the top of the social order, the Brahmins serve as Hindu society's priests, leaders, seers, and religious authorities. Next in rank are the Kshatriyas, who in ancient times were Hindu society's kings and aristocratic warriors, but more recently have been its administrators, politicians, and civil authorities. Beneath the Kshatriyas are the Vaishyas, the society's entrepreneurs, in ancient times merchants and traders, in more recent times its professionals, such as doctors, lawyers, and teachers. The Shudras are Hindu society's laborers, its servant class. Outcastes, who fall outside the four main castes, are considered "untouchable" and are therefore avoided by members of other castes. Outcastes are either non-Aryan by birth or were originally members of the other castes but violated caste laws, such as those regarding work or marriage.

This hierarchical model of society was later challenged by certain communities which were based on different religious ideals, such as the Jains and the Buddhists. The caste system, however, has continued to be the governing principle of Indian society for two thousand years.

LITERATURE: THE HINDU CLASSICS

The Vedas. The earliest Indian literature was composed by the Aryans, the nomads who migrated to India around 1500 B.C. Composed between 1500 and 1000 B.C. in Sanskrit, this consists of a set of hymns known as *The Vedas*, which praise the Hindu gods. All later works ultimately derive from these Vedic songs, and most are a commentary on them. Transmitted orally at first, *The Vedas* would be chanted during religious rituals, accompanied by various instruments.

The Upanishads. *The Upanishads*, an anthology of philosophical poems and discourses, were later added to *The Vedas*, the most ancient form of Hindu scripture. *The Upanishads*, though not as popular with ordinary people as the hymns and prayers of *The Vedas*, have been influential in Indian philosophy. They contain discussion and teachings that, while at odds with the polytheism of Vedic myth and legend, explain key Hindu ideas such as maya (illusion) and karma (action).

Based on the central tenet that there is one true spiritual reality in the universe (Brahman), *The Upanishads* explain how all existence is a tissue of false appearances— maya—that conceal this fundamental spiritual reality. According to *The Upanishads*, human beings do not realize that what appears real to the senses is entirely illusory, and that what counts eternally is the spiritual essence of life, of which they are a part.

The Upanishads typically illustrate the idea of maya and ignorance with a story about a tiger. The tiger had been orphaned as a cub and raised among goats. Believing itself to be a goat, the cub ate grass and made goat noises. One day, another tiger came upon it and took the confused tiger to a pool in which his tiger-image was reflected. It was then that the cub realized his true nature. In the same way, human beings need to realize their true nature, the divinity that resides within all.

The Ramayana. The oldest of Hindu epics, *The Ramayana* (*The Way of Rama*) by VALMIKI [val-MIH-kee] (sixth century B.C.), is also the most popular work of Indian literature, and arguably among the most influential literary works in the world. The story of Prince Rama and his queen, Sita, has its narrative origins in Indian folk traditions that go back to as early as the seventh century B.C. *The Ramayana* itself is dated approximately 550 B.C., when Valmiki, much like Homer in ancient Greece, gathered the various strands of the story into a cohesive work of literature organized in seven *kanda*, or books.

Blending historical sagas, myths, legends, and moral tales with religious and social teaching, *The Ramayana* has long been the single most important repository of Indian social, moral, and ethical values. Rama is believed by devout Hindus to be one of the two most important avatars or incarnations of the god Vishnu, who assumed human form to save humankind. Reading or witnessing a performance of episodes from *The Ramayana* is thus considered a religious exercise, as is repeating the name of Rama.

The Ramayana stands, moreover, as an enduring monument and a living guide to political, social, and family life in Vedic India. The behavior of its hero, Prince Rama, serves as a model for the behavior of the ideal son, brother, husband, warrior, and king. Rama's respect for his father and love for his wife, along with his regal bearing and self-control, represent the paradigm for Indian males to emulate. Rama's behavior is also closely linked to the religious values embodied in the epic. His wife Sita loves, honors, and serves her husband with absolute fidelity. In being governed by *dharma* (the "teachings") rather than self-interest, Rama and Sita stand as models for Hindu life.

The story of *The Ramayana* is complex and intricate. One of its central motifs concerns Rama's disinheritance, which is instigated by the jealous queen, Rama's stepmother Kaikeyi, who wants her own son, Bharatha, to become king instead of Rama. The king, Rama's father, reluctantly has his son exiled, but thereafter soon dies, desolate over Rama's departure. With his wife, Sita, and his brother, Lakshmana, Rama lives in the wilderness of central India. There they encounter the fierce king of the demons, Ravana, a god whom no one can harm except a mortal being. It was only in the form of Rama, therefore, that Vishnu could destroy Ravana. He accomplishes his goal with the help of Rama's family and friends, many of whom are gods living in the form of monkeys. In the process, however, Sita dies. Like Rama, who goes on to rule as a wise and compassionate king, Sita is portrayed in the epic as the embodiment of ideal conduct.

The Mahabharata. The second great Indian epic is *The Mahabharata*, which was composed over a period of more than eight hundred years, between 400 B.C. to A.D. 400. Unlike *The Ramayana*, which focuses on the adventures of one central hero, *The Mahabharata* chronicles the story of a pair of rival warring families, the Pandavas and the Kauravas. The warlike world of *The Mahabharata* is more akin to that of *The Iliad*, while the adventure-filled quest of *The Ramayana* has more of the character of Homer's other great epic, *The Odyssey*. With its hundred thousand verses, *The Mahabharata* is four times the length of *The Ramayana*, and more than eight times that of *The Iliad* and *The Odyssey* combined. What *The Mahabharata* lacks in unity and focus, however, it makes up for in multi-plicity of incident, breadth of social panorama, and philosophical discursiveness.

Forming part of the sixth book of *The Mahabharata* is the *Bhagavad Gita*, the section most familiar to Western readers. It is also the epic's most important source of spiritual teaching. Written early in the first century B.C., the *Bhagavad Gita* centers on the moral conflict experienced by Arjuna, a warrior who struggles with his duty to kill his kinsmen during the war between the Pandavas and Kauravas, a great battle that ends in the destruction of both armies.

When Arjuna sees his relatives ready to do battle against one another, he puts down his weapons and refuses to fight. His charioteer, Krishna, an avatar of the god Vishnu, explains that it is Arjuna's duty to fight: even

Connections

THE LOGIC OF JAINISM

Jainism, which arose at the same time as Buddhism, was also a reaction to Hinduism, particularly the caste system and the claims of the Brahmins to social superiority. Its founder was MAHAVI-RA [ma-ha-VEE-rah] (599–527 B.C.), which means "Great Man." His early life resembles that of Sakyamuni, the founder of Buddhism. Born a prince, who, as legend has it, was attended by five nurses, "a wet-nurse, a nurse to bathe him, one to dress him, one to play with him, and one to carry him," Mahavira was raised in the lap of luxury. But as he grew older, he tired of this life, and at the age of thirty joined a band

of monks who practiced an ascetic existence. But even the monks had too indulgent a lifestyle for his taste, and so Mahavira set out on his own, wandering the Indian countryside entirely naked, maintaining that salvation is possible only through severe deprivation of the pleasures of life and the practice of ahimsa, not causing harm to any living thing.

Jainism has gained a wide following in India, and today the Jains number about two million, with an especially large community in Bombay, where MAHATMA GANDHI [GAHN-dee] (1869–1948), the great twentieth-century pacifist leader, was influenced by its tenets. Jainism stresses the

importance of asceticism, meditation, and ahimsa. But one of the most distinctive features of the Jain philosophy is a special sensitivity to the relativity of all things. A favorite Jain parable is the story of the six blind men, each of whom puts his hands on a different part of an elephant and describes what he feels in totally different terms—it is like a fan, a wall, a snake, a rope, and so on. In Jainist thought, each description is satisfactory given each person's limited knowledge of the whole of the elephant. In one sense, an elephant is like a snake, but only in a very limited way. By extension, all knowledge is, from one point of view, true, and, from another, false.

though the Hindu religion generally prohibits killing, the sanction is lifted for members of Arjuna's warrior class, the Kshatriyas. He also tells Arjuna that fighting can break the karmic cycle of **samsara**, the endless cycle of birth, death, and reincarnation to which mortal beings are subject, and move him toward spiritual liberation. Arjuna learns that the spirit in which an act is performed counts more than the act itself. Since Arjuna is not fighting to achieve any particular goal but only to fulfill his duty, his behavior is irreproachable.

THE MAURYA PERIOD

In ancient India, each region was politically autonomous. These regions were governed by small dynasties which remained relatively immune from outside influences and challenges. From time to time, however, the governments of individual regions would join together in loose federations to create empires. One of the earliest and most important of these was the empire of the Maurya, which emerged in response to a power vacuum created by Alexander the Great's conquest of northern India around 326 B.C.

CHANDRAGUPTA MAURYA [MOW-ya], effectively the first emperor of India, reigned 324–301 B.C. His empire extended from the Ganges River to the Indus and into the northern mountains. After Chandragupta's death, and following the reign of his son Bindusara, came the most important of Mauryan emperors, ASHOKA [a-SHOW-ka], who assumed the throne in 269 B.C. Lasting nearly forty years (269–232 B.C.), Ashoka's reign marked a critical turning point in Indian history—the emergence

of Buddhism as a political force in India. Regretting the terrible destruction his armies had wrought in a victorious battle with the armies of a neighboring region, Ashoka embraced Buddhism, which had begun to displace the more worldly Hinduism three centuries earlier.

The connection between political power and religious idealism continued throughout Ashoka's life and for half a century after his death. The emperor sent missionaries, including his daughter and son, throughout India to spread the Buddhist faith. He also had sites marked that were of religious and historical significance to Buddhists, and a shrine to house the possessions and remains of the Buddha.

BUDDHISM

Buddhism begins with a man, SIDDHARTHA GAUTAMA SAKYA (ca. 563–483 B.C.), also known as Sakyamuni, meaning "the sage or silent one of the Sakya." At his birth, it was prophesied that Sakyamuni would be either a king or a world redeemer. He was raised in a princely household, and so as a young man was sheltered from pain and suffering. Legend has it that he was suddenly transformed when, on a journey, he became acquainted with age by passing an old man, with disease by seeing a sick person, with death by seeing a corpse, and with want by encountering a group of monks with their begging bowls. Shaken by his discovery that life is subject to age and death, he determined to find a realm where human beings are immune from these facts of physical existence.

So he set off on a journey. He studied for six years with Hindu masters. He joined a band of ascetics and practiced austerity and self-discipline. When he realized that asceticism would not bring him enlightenment, he sat under a fig tree to meditate, determined not to rise until he experienced the wisdom of enlightenment.

After meditating for forty-nine days and nights, Sakyamuni experienced a mental epiphany, an awakening involving rapture, bliss, and enlightenment. While in this state, he was subjected to a number of temptations. Among these was the temptation to be satisfied that he had attained this state of rapture himself but to assume that no one else could understand his experience. But he resisted and set off to become a wandering preacher, whose goal was to help other people achieve the same state of enlightenment. After forty-five years of preaching and dedicating himself to others, the Buddha (a word derived from the name of the tree under which he first achieved enlightenment—the Bo tree, short for Bodhi, meaning "wisdom" or "enlightenment") died at the age of eighty.

Buddhism versus Hinduism.   Unlike Hinduism, which developed over many centuries, Buddhism seemed to arise overnight, even if it took many centuries for a political leader to adopt it. The Buddha challenged Hindu religious practice in a number of ways. He argued that the caste of Brahmins was granted too much power and given too many privileges. The forms of ritual had become, he believed, devoid of meaning, and were debased by being linked with commercial transactions. Hindu philosophical thought had become excessively intricate and arcane, and consequently increasingly disconnected from everyday spiritual life. Religious mystery had degenerated into mystification and magic.

Superstition and divination had replaced miracle and true mysticism. Perhaps worst of all, too many people, in the Buddha's view, had come to believe that their actions did not matter, that whatever they believed they would be caught up in samsara, the endless cycle of rebirth, from which escape was impossible.

The Buddha responded to this by providing an alternative religious practice in which each individual had to find her or his own way to enlightenment. So devoid of the notion of higher authority is Buddhism that it is a religion without a god. There is only enlightenment. Furthermore, ritual is an irrelevant diversion from the real work of achieving enlightenment. The Buddha argued that it need not take hundreds of lifetimes or thousands of reincarnations to break out of the round of existence. A determined individual could achieve enlightenment in a single lifetime and so attain **nirvana**, that is, liberation from the limitations of existence and rebirth in the cycle of samsara.

As a result of these new objectives, Buddhism developed few of the characteristics of traditional religions. As already stated, it was a religion without a god and without the concept of immortality. It posited no creation or last judgment. It presented no revelation from a god. Instead, it emphasized the here and now.

The Four Noble Truths and the Eight-Fold Path. The Eight-Fold Path can be seen as a course of spiritual treatment for the diseased human condition. Buddhist thought is based on an analysis of the human condition that is founded on four axioms or truths. These basic principles have come to be known as the Four Noble Truths:

Timeline 8.2   Culture and religion in India.

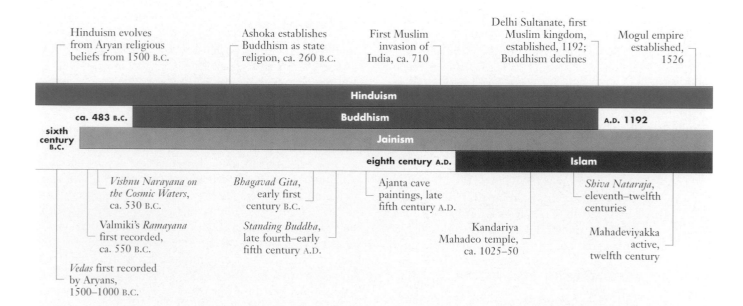

1. Life consists of suffering, impermanence, imperfection, incompleteness.
2. The cause of life's suffering is selfishness.
3. Suffering and selfishness can be brought to an end.
4. The answer to life's problems of suffering is the Eight-Fold Path.

The Eight-Fold Path itself consists of knowledge of these Four Noble Truths, the first step on the path, followed by seven other steps: right aspiration toward the goal of enlightenment; right speech that is honest and charitable; right conduct—no drinking, killing, lying, or lust; right living according to the goals of Buddhism; right effort; right thinking with an emphasis on self-awareness; and the right use of meditation to achieve enlightenment.

MAURYA ART

The earliest significant body of Indian art extant today dates from the Maurya period, chiefly from the reign of the emperor Ashoka. Much of this work was created to celebrate Ashoka's conversion to Buddhism. Ashoka ordered the construction of numerous **stupas**, or memorial buildings, that enshrined relics of the Buddha, marking sites sacred to his memory. Many of the eighty thousand or more stupas erected during Ashoka's reign were dedicated to the Buddha and his miracles. Later, stupas were used for burial of the remains of sacred monks.

The Sarnath Capital. Ashoka also had a large number of stone columns built to memorialize significant events in the Buddha's life. Carved into many of these, as well as into rocks and caves, were political edicts that promoted various aspects of the Buddhist creed. The stone pillars usually had capitals, often carved in the form of an animal, usually a lion. One of the most magnificent of these is a beautifully preserved lion capital (fig. 8.2) from a pillar at Sarnath that dates from about 250 B.C.

The Sarnath capital consists of three elements. On top of a fluted bell are four royal animals and four wheels carved in relief. Above these are four lions carved back to back all the way round the capital. The stylization of the lions' facial features and claws, along with the decorative handling of their manes and upper torsos, is similar to that of the lion sculptures at Persepolis, a city destroyed by Alexander the Great before his invasion of northern India. As was described in Chapter 4, Alexander's forces made an enduring cultural impression on the region. It is highly likely that either Persian sculptors or Persian-trained Greek sculptors created this capital, which marks a dramatic growth in the style, complexity, and beauty of Indian sculpture.

The seven-foot sculpture was originally surmounted by a large stone wheel on the lions' shoulders. This capital (now used as the emblem of the modern Republic of

Figure 8.2 Lion capital of a pillar erected by Ashoka at Sarnath, Mauryan, ca. 250 B.C., Chunar sandstone, height 7′ (2.15 m), Archaeological Museum, Sarnath. This lion capital reveres the lion as king of the animal world while honoring the Buddha as king or lion among religious teachers.

Figure 8.3 Great Stupa, Sanchi, from the east, third century B.C.–early first century A.D. For the increasing numbers of Buddhist faithful, the stupa became a central symbol of religious faith.

India) is highly symbolic. Hailing from a period during which Buddhist art avoided representing the Buddha directly, the Sarnath lion capital suggests his presence in other ways. Most importantly, since Sarnath is recognized as the site where the Buddha first preached about *dharma*, the wheel signifies the wheel of the law of *dharma*. The lion itself was perceived as the most powerful and magnificent of animals, and thus suggests that the Buddha is a lion among religious leaders. The four animals sculpted on the plinth—the elephant, horse, bull, and lion—represent the four parts of the world to which the Buddha's law of *dharma* was to extend.

The Great Stupa at Sanchi. Many of the stupas erected by Ashoka were enlarged by subsequent dynasties in the second and first centuries B.C. For instance, at Sanchi in central India, Ashoka had built a stupa sixty feet in diameter and twenty-five feet high. The Andhras, who ruled in the region toward the end of the first century B.C., doubled its size (fig. 8.3). They replaced Ashoka's wooden railings with new stone ones nine feet high. A sixteen-foot-high passage encircling the stupa was also added. At the very top of the stupa three umbrellas represent the three "jewels" of Buddhism: the Buddha, the law, and the community of monks.

Surrounding these umbrellas is a square railing that reflects the ancient tradition of putting a fence around a sacred tree.

However, the architectural glories of the Sanchi stupa are four carved stone gates, each of which is more than thirty feet high (fig. 8.4). Begun during the first century B.C., but only completed during the first century A.D., the gates are adorned with symbols associated with the Buddha, including the wheel of the law, folktales from his life, and his animal incarnations. Additional figures include elephants, peacocks, and *yakshis*, or protective female earth spirits.

The Sanchi stupa symbolizes the world, its four gates representing the four corners of the universe. Its umbrella points toward the sky, linking heaven with earth and a life of bliss with that of pain and suffering below. Entering the eastern gate of the stupa, a visitor would move clockwise in a circle around it on a path especially constructed for that purpose. Even though the stupa, one might argue, is more a work of sculpture than of architecture, like Hindu temples it invites worshipers to enter into a spiritual state of mind.

Figure 8.4 Gate of the Great Stupa, Sanchi, inner facade of the north gate, stone, height 34′ (10.35 m), third century B.C.–early first century A.D. Depicted on the columns and cross beams of this large stone gate are events in the life of the Buddha and stories from the *Jataka* tales.

THE GUPTA ERA

At the beginning of the Christian era in Europe, events were also occurring in India that would have a tremendous influence on the country's cultural and religious future. Buddhism was undergoing important changes; in the new form of the religion, the goal was no longer to reach nirvana for oneself, but instead the attainment of buddhahood for everyone in the universe. As a result, a category of princely beings known as **bodhisattvas**, "those whose essence is wisdom," developed. These are great beings, who will achieve buddhahood, but who have stayed behind in the world to help others attain the same state. Popular mainly in northern India, this new Mahayana form of Buddhism spread rapidly to China, Japan, and Korea, along the trade routes that ran through India's mountain passes.

Of the ancient Indian empires that developed in this period, the most important was that of the Gupta, which lasted from the fourth to the sixth century A.D. During the reign of the Guptas, India flourished culturally and commercially. Significant scientific discoveries were made; important developments occurred in literature, music, sculpture, and painting. It was during the reign of CHANDRA GUPTA II (A.D. 375–415), for example, that the cave paintings at Ajanta were undertaken. In terms of Indian cultural achievements the Gupta era is comparable to Periklean Athens, Han China, and Augustan Rome.

The Gupta empire eventually collapsed under repeated onslaughts by the Huns, who had previously invaded and conquered the Roman world. Regional autonomy was reestablished as the empire became increasingly fractured. From early in the eighth century Islamic influences began to appear in India, culminating five hundred years later, when northern India and the Ganges area fell directly under Turkish Islamic control. Buddhism was eclipsed to a large extent, and as Hinduism gradually reasserted itself, it became mixed with Muslim influences.

GUPTA ART

Gupta art has become associated with the deeply spiritual figure of the Buddha, standing with equanimity, eyes seemingly closed in concentration. Whether standing or seated, Buddhas sculpted in the Gupta Buddhist style appear calm, their worldly cares replaced by an inner tranquillity that suggests other-worldliness. Their hands are placed in prescribed positions, called **mudras**, that arc highly symbolic. The *Standing Buddha* (fig. 8.5) reaches forward with his right hand (now missing) in the *abhaya* mudra, a sign of reassurance, blessing, and protection. His left hand drops to his side in the *varada*

Figure 8.5 *Standing Buddha*, from Mathura, Gupta, late fourth–early fifth century A.D., red sandstone, height 7'⅜" (2.17 m), National Museum, New Delhi. The elegance of this standing figure, especially its calm serenity, characterizes the Gupta Buddhist style of sculpture.

mudra, signifying charity and the fulfillment of all wishes. The *Seated Buddha*'s hands form the *dharmachakra* mudra (fig. 8.6), a sign of teaching in which the hands make a circle with the thumb and forefinger, a reference to the wheel of *dharma*. The mudra most familiar to Westerners is the *dhyana* mudra, in which the hands rest on the buddha's lap, palms facing upward. A gesture of meditation and harmony, it symbolizes the path to enlightenment.

Something of this serenity appears in the cave paint-

Figure 8.7 *Bodhisattva Padmapani*, wall painting, Ajanta caves, Gupta, late fifth century A.D. Oblivious to the figures that surround him, this bodhisattva is encircled in an otherworldly light, created by the burnishing of the painting's outer coating with a smooth stone.

Figure 8.6 *Seated Buddha*, Sarnath, Gupta, fifth century A.D., sandstone, height 5'3" (1.60 m), Archaeological Museum, Sarnath. Seated on a throne in the meditation posture, this Buddha's hands are positioned in the sign of the *dharmachakra* mudra, a teaching gesture that sets the wheel of the Buddhist law in motion.

ings from Ajanta. The paintings describe the various lives and incarnations of the Buddha as narrated in the *Jataka* tales. One depicting the Bodhisattva Padmapani shows him holding a blue lotus and standing in the classic *tribhanga* sculptural pose (fig. 8.7), in which the figure leans precariously to the side, with his weight on one leg. The scene shows the serene bodhisattva oblivious to the activity around him.

THE *JATAKA* AND THE *PANCATANTRA*

Ancient Indian literature contains many folktales and animal stories. One of the most important collections of early stories is the *Jataka*, which means "the story of a birth," consisting of 547 tales that describe the lives the Buddha passed through before achieving enlightenment. The *Pancatantra* is a group of didactic stories, designed with the practical aim of providing advice about getting on in the world.

One of the most famous tales of the fourth-century B.C. *Jataka* describes a hare who sacrifices itself to feed a hungry brahmin. The tale's action reveals the hare to be a bodhisattva in the form of an animal. Like another *Jataka* hero, a monkey who gives up his life for others, the hare displays the perfection of spiritual being in a completely selfless act.

This is quite different from the spirit and flavor of the *Pancatantra*, in which the behavior of its animal heroes is more self-serving and pragmatic. The title, *Pancatantra*, which means "the five strategies," suggests the book's pragmatic inclination. Composed during the second or third century A.D., the stories are linked so that one story is joined to another in a continuous chain. This is similar to the connected stories of *The Thousand and One Nights* (see Chapter 7), which may have been influenced by the *Pancatantra*. The authors of the *Jataka* and the *Pancatantra* provide fast-moving action, witty dialogue, and memorable counsel in stories that entertain as they instruct, be that in Buddhist spirituality or in more worldly wisdom.

THE HINDU DYNASTIES

Although Buddhism flourished during the Gupta era, the Gupta monarchs themselves were increasingly attracted to Hinduism. Temples and sculptures of Hindu gods began to appear, and they continued to proliferate well into the fifteenth and sixteenth centuries, when Muslim kings from Persia took control of most of the subcontinent. Particularly in the south, where the warring Hindu dynasties of the Pallavas and the Cholas vied for power, a long period of great artistic production was set in motion, marked both by decorated temples, rich in stone sculpture, and by the rise of bronze as a favored medium for sculpture.

THE HINDU TEMPLE

The structure and design of the Hindu temple were established in the series of ancient texts called **shastras**. The shastras function as guides to many different activities, not just temple-building, and include advice on cooking, warfare, lovemaking, poetry, and music. The guides to architecture, especially those concerning temple architecture, do not always concur in every detail with actual temple construction.

Temples in the south are better preserved than northern temples, since the Muslim incursion into India was most destructive in the north. One of the most magnificent of medieval Hindu temples and one in an exceptional state of preservation is the Kandariya Mahadeo temple at Khajuraho, dating from the eleventh century (fig. 8.8). As with many temples of that period, it forms part of a cluster of temples in the area.

Figure 8.8 Kandariya Mahadeo temple, Khajuraho, Chandella, ca. 1025–50. This temple's tower soars more than a hundred feet into the air, its eighty-four subordinate towers providing a visual display of majestic grandeur.

Then & Now

MUSLIM INDIA

*I*slam arrived in India as early as the eighth century, but it was not until the twelfth century that it began to have a powerful impact on the subcontinent. In 1192, the Afghan king Muhammad of Ghur, invading from the north by land, defeated the Hindus. To celebrate his victory he erected the giant Quwwat ul-Islam ("Might of Islam") mosque on the site of Delhi's largest Hindu temple, incorporating columns pillaged from other local Hindu shrines. The resulting structure is a curious amalgamation of two cultures—an Islamic mosque with Hindu decoration.

After initial fighting, a spirit of peaceful coexistence lasted for several centuries. But no two religions could be more different than Hinduism and Islam. Hinduism is sufficiently loose in its religious structure to allow great divergences in spiritual beliefs and practices, while Islam controls almost every aspect of daily life. But where Hinduism is intellectually liberal and Islam conservative, the opposite is true socially. The social restrictions of Hinduism's caste system, in contrast to the possibilities of social mobility and equality offered by Islam, may have led many Indians to adopt the Islamic faith. Especially around Delhi and Agra, where the Muslim rulers held sway, Islam took firm hold and was respon-

sible for the creation of some of the greatest monuments of Indian culture.

Possibly the most famous building in India is the Taj Mahal (fig. 8.9), in Agra, built 1630–48 by the Muslim Shah Jahan as a mausoleum for his wife, Mumtaz Mahal. The Taj Mahal's white marble walls are deeply cut with arched recesses that catch shadows, creating a three-dimensional facade. The building appears to be weightless, the dome floating like a balloon. Decoration includes floral relief carving and gray stone inlay. The landscape setting continues the formal concern with symmetry, as the building is reflected in a long pool flanked by rows of small trees and shrubs. The Taj Mahal is celebrated for its exquisite refinement and enchanting elegance.

By the twentieth century, relations between India's Hindus and Muslims had reached crisis point, and in 1947, after a violent and bloody partition, the independent Muslim state of Pakistan was born, consisting of two separate areas: West Pakistan, with its capital at Islamabad near the Khyber Pass on the Indus River, and East Pakistan (which seceded from the union in 1971 to become Bangladesh), with its capital at Dacca. The fifty million Muslims who were left in India became an official minority with the right to be represented in the Indian parliament.

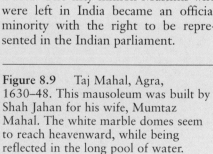

Figure 8.9 Taj Mahal, Agra, 1630–48. This mausoleum was built by Shah Jahan for his wife, Mumtaz Mahal. The white marble domes seem to reach heavenward, while being reflected in the long pool of water.

The Kandariya Mahadeo temple is situated on a high masonry platform with richly decorated walls. Intricate dome-like roofs rise like successive mountain peaks in a crescendo of grandeur. Equally compelling is the vibrancy and richness of their surface ornamentation. Niches and screens, pillars and openings, pavilions and courtyards enhance the splendor of the edifice. Adorning the temple is a wealth of sculpture that depicts historical and mythological subjects, such as the monarchs who reigned during the temple's construction; the *Surasun-*

daris, or divine nymphs, in amatory poses; figures of dancers and musicians; mothers with children, lovers, women adjusting their hair, and a vast array of other images.

BRONZE SCULPTURE

Bronze was the medium most favored by the southern Indian Chola dynasties from the tenth to the twelfth century. Chola sculptors employed the **cire perdue** or

Figure 8.10 *Shiva Nataraja (Lord of the Dance)*, Chola, eleventh–twelfth centuries, bronze, height $32\frac{1}{2}''$ (82 cm), Von der Heydt Collection, Museum Rietherg, Zurich. The most famous of Hindu icons, the dancing Shiva is both the creator and destroyer of the universe.

lost-wax process. In this technique, a model of the subject is first made in wax, which is easy to mold. The wax model is then encased in clay and heated; the wax melts but the clay does not. Holes are made in the clay surround before it is heated, however, to permit the wax to run out. The hollow clay case is then filled with molten bronze. When the bronze has cooled and hardened, the clay is broken away, leaving a finished bronze cast.

The *Shiva Nataraja (Lord of the Dance)* (fig. 8.10) is perhaps the most famous of Hindu icons. Numerous examples of this icon exist—strict rules governing its production have resulted in a remarkable consistency across individual instances—and it continues to be produced in southern India to this day. The icon depicts the dancing Shiva as creator and destroyer of the universe, symbolized by the ring around him. With his hair flying out in two directions, and his arms and legs seemingly in motion, the dancing Shiva crushes the dwarf of ignorance, promising relief from life's illusoriness, and also reassurance and blessing in the *abhaya* mudra of his front right hand. This dance is said to herald the last night of the world, when all the stars fall from the sky and the universe is reduced to ashes. But the dance promises the renewal of creation itself.

HINDU LYRIC POETRY

The poetry of the twelfth-century mystic MAHA-DEVIYAKKA [ma-ha-de-VEE-ha-ka], the foremost Indian woman poet before the modern era, represents the quintessential medieval genre of **bhakti** or devotional religious poetry. Bhakti poetry was part of a larger movement in which the poets were recognized as saints and celebrated as models of religious devotion. Their poems honored the chief Hindu gods Shiva and Vishnu, especially the latter's major avatars as Krishna and Rama.

Bhakti devotional poetry is rooted in deeply felt emotion. As with the mystical and devotional poetry of other cultures, it uses colloquial language and draws on imagery from everyday experience in an attempt to convey a sense of earthly longing for the divine. Like the poems of the English Renaissance poet John Donne (see Chapter 14), those of Mahadeviyakka employ images of physical love and experience to convey a sense of spiri-tuality. Mahadeviyakka's poetry also exhibits a carefree, daredevil attitude that is, perhaps surprisingly, not at odds with a deep longing for communion with the godhead.

MUSIC

Indian music is essentially melodic. Harmony is present only as a backdrop, in the form of the continuous sounding of a single tone, while the complex melody is elaborated over the top. Indian music is rarely written out formally as a score. This independence from notation offers performers great interpretive latitude, allowing them the opportunity to improvise creatively and develop the mood of the pieces they play. The music is typically performed by a soloist, who plays or sings the melody; a drummer, who supplies the rhythm; and a third player, who provides the drone chord, which is a single three-note chord that is sounded continuously throughout the piece, usually on the lute-like *tambura*.

Although also serving a purpose as entertainment, Indian music is rich in religious associations. Hindu deities, for example, are frequently evoked in classical dance and songs. Moreover, it is not uncommon for musicians to consider their performance as an act of religious devotion.

The most important instrument in the performance of Indian music is the human voice. With its great flexibility and expressiveness, the voice provides a model for other instruments. As in the Western classical tradition, singers of Indian music are trained to be able to perform an extensive range of vocal intricacies. These vocal acro-

Cross Currents

RAVI SHANKAR AND PHILIP GLASS

Born in Baltimore in 1937, American composer PHILIP GLASS was trained at the Julliard School of Music in New York. He was frustrated with the state of contemporary music until, in the 1960s, he was hired to work on the soundtrack for a now-forgotten "alternative" film entitled *Chappaqua*. His job was to take the improvised Indian ragas of Indian musician RAVI SHANKAR [SHAN-kah] (b. 1920) and transcribe them into Western musical notation, so that Western musicians could perform them on the soundtrack. Glass was particularly impressed with the background drone chord of the raga. He thought it was made up of units of two and three notes that formed long chains of modular rhythmic patterns. He was in fact entirely wrong in terms of musicology, but it led him, as misreadings so often can, to invent his own distinct musical style. He traveled to India many times and gradually developed an almost hypnotic rhythmic style of his own. The music he began to compose consisted of the rhythmic units he had heard in Shankar's work, with simple and apparently arbitrarily chosen notes or pitches strung together in cyclical groups. The repetitiveness of the musical form suggests the drone chord of the raga.

The culmination of the Indian connection in Glass's music was his opera *Satyagraha*, first performed in Rotterdam, Holland, in 1980. The work consists of several stories from the life of the young Mahatma Gandhi, the great pacificist and political and spiritual leader who led the campaign to free India from British rule. The work's title, *Satyagraha*, means "holding fast to the truth" and refers to Gandhi's nonviolent method of non-cooperation and civil disobedience. Slow and meditative in its rhythm, the music evokes the image of Gandhi sitting in protest, as he fasted and meditated, in full confidence that India would eventually triumph.

---

batics include modulations of pitch involving many more tones than those of standard Western musical scales.

The **sitar** is a lute-shaped instrument with an extended neck (fig. 8.11). Its movable frets enable performers to produce an enormous number of tones. The standard sitar has five melody strings, two drone strings, and a dozen or more "sympathetic" strings beneath them. These lower strings are not struck with the fingers or a plectrum as are the others. Instead, they vibrate in "sympathy" with those actually played, lending the music an enriched shimmering sound.

The sitar is the chief instrument used in playing **ragas,** musical compositions based on one of the eight primary **rasas**—moods or flavors—of Indian aesthetics: love, courage, hatred, anger, mirth, terror, pity, and surprise. A raga, then, is a piece of music that conveys a distinct impression (the word *raga* means "passion" or "feeling"). Because of their highly specific character, ragas are typically associated with a particular Hindu deity, a particular time of day or season of the year, or a particular religious festival.

A standard raga form will include an improvised prelude or introductory section called an **alap**, played in a free tempo. The purpose of the alap is to introduce the spirit and mood of the raga. The alap is followed by a formally composed musical section for a solo instrument with a percussion accom-paniment. The final section is an improvisation on the composed music with many returns of the theme, in a form loosely comparable to the **rondo** (or returning theme) of Western music. Toward the end of a raga performance, the emphasis shifts from melodic elaboration to a display of the performer's own virtuosity.

Figure 8.11 Ravi Shankar playing the sitar, *Life* magazine, 1958. The sitar is a lute-shaped instrument with an extended neck and movable frets that enable performers to produce a wide range of scale tones.

READINGS

↦ **BHAGAVAD GITA**

Krishna and Arjuna

In the following passage from the Bhagavad Gita, *Lord Krishna advises the warrior Arjuna about more than his military responsibilities. Krishna explains that the goal of life is to overcome desire, to cease wishing for any particular consequence of action. The goal and aim of life is to learn detachment from the fruits of action while fulfilling one's duties responsibly.*

LORD KRISHNA:
Look to your own duty;
do not tremble before it;
nothing is better for a warrior
than a battle of sacred duty.

The doors of heaven open   5
for warriors who rejoice
to have a battle like this
thrust on them by chance.

If you fail to wage this war
of sacred duty,   10
you will abandon your own duty
and fame only to gain evil.

People will tell
of your undying shame,
and for a man of honor   15
shame is worse than death …

Be intent on action,
not on the fruits of action;
avoid attraction to the fruits
and attachment to inaction!   20

Perform actions, firm in discipline,
relinquishing attachment;
be impartial to failure and success—
this equanimity is called discipline.

Arjuna, action is far inferior   25
to the discipline of understanding;
so seek refuge in understanding—pitiful
are men drawn by fruits of action.

Disciplined by understanding,
one abandons both good and evil deeds;   30
so arm yourself for discipline—
discipline is skill in actions.

Wise men disciplined by understanding
relinquish the fruit born of action;
freed from these bonds of rebirth,   35
they reach a place beyond decay.

When your understanding passes beyond
the swamp of delusion,
you will be indifferent to all
that is heard in sacred lore.   40

When your understanding turns
from sacred lore to stand fixed,
immovable in contemplation,
then you will reach discipline.

ARJUNA: 45
Krishna, what defines a man
deep in contemplation whose insight
and throught are sure? How would he speak?
How would he sit? How would he move?

LORD KRISHNA: 50
When he gives up desires in his mind,
is content with the self within himself,
then he is said to be a man
whose insight is sure, Arjuna.

When suffering does not disturb his mind,   55
when his craving for pleasures has vanished,
when attraction, fear, and anger are gone,
he is called a sage whose thought is sure.

When he shows no preference
in fortune or misfortune   60
and neither exults nor hates,
his insight is sure.

When, like a tortoise retracting
its limbs, he withdraws his senses
completely from sensuous objects,   65
his insight is sure.

↦ **VALMIKI**

from *The Ramayana*

The following excerpt is taken from near the end of the Ramayana, *when, after fourteen years in exile, the rightful king, Rama, returns to his kingdom and is reconciled with his step-mother, Kaikeyi, who had caused his disinheritance in the first place.*

Rama explained that he had to adopt this trial in order to demonstrate Sita's purity beyond a shadow of doubt to the whole world. This seemed a rather strange inconsistency on the part of one who had brought back to life and restored to her husband a person like Ahalya, who had avowedly committed a moral lapse; and then there was Sugreeva's wife, who had been forced to live with Vali, and whom Rama commended as worthy of being taken back by Sugreeva after Vali's death. In Sita's case Ravana, in spite of repeated and desperate attempts, could not approach her. She had remained inviolable. And the fiery quality of her essential being burnt out the god of fire himself, as he had admitted after Sita's ordeal. Under these circumstances, it was very strange that Rama should have spoken harshly as he had done at the first sight of Sita, and subjected her to a dreadful trial.

The gods, who had watched this in suspense, were now profoundly relieved but also had an uneasy feeling that Rama had, perhaps, lost sight of his own identity. Again and again this seemed to happen. Rama displayed the tribulations and the limitations of the human frame and it was necessary from time to time to remind him of his divinity. Now Brahma, the Creator, came forward to speak and addressed Rama thus: "Of the Trinity, I am the Creator. Shiva is the Destroyer and Vishnu is the Protector. All three of us derive our existence from the Supreme God and we are subject to dissolution and rebirth. But the Supreme God who creates us is without a beginning or an end. There is neither birth nor growth nor death for the Supreme God. He is the origin of everything and in him everything is assimilated at the end. That God is yourself, and Sita at your side now is a part of that Divinity. Please remember that this is your real identity and let not the fear and doubts that assail an ordinary mortal ever move you. You are beyond everything; and we are all blessed indeed to be in your presence."

In the high heavens, Shiva encouraged Dasaratha to go down to the earth and meet Rama. He said, "Rama needs your benediction after having carried out your commands, and having gone through so much privation for fourteen years in order to safeguard the integrity of your promises." Dasaratha descended in his true form into the midst of his family. Rama was overjoyed to see him again and prostrated himself at his feet.

Dasaratha said, "This moment is one of supreme joy for me. For the first time in all these years, my heart is lighter. The memory of the evil use that Kaikeyi had made of my promise to her had stuck in my heart like a splinter and had stayed there. Although I had shed my physical body, the pain had remained unmitigated—until this minute. It is now gone. You with Sita are the primordial being and I was indeed blessed to have begotten you as my son. This is a moment of fulfilment for me. I have nothing more to say and I will go back to my world and repose there in eternal peace. But before I go I want you to ask of me something, anything, any wish I could fulfil for you."

Rama said, "Your arrival here is the greatest boon for me, and I have nothing more to seek. All along, my only desire has been to see you again, and that is fulfilled." Dasaratha still insisted that Rama should state a wish that he could grant. Rama said, "If that is so, please find a place in your heart for both Kaikeyi and Bharatha, and take back your vow by which you cut off their blood connection with you. I cannot think of her except as a mother and Bharatha as a brother."

Dasaratha at once replied, "Bharatha is different. He has proved his greatness. Yes, I will accept him. But Kaikeyi— she ruined us all. She prevented your being crowned at the last moment. I can never forgive her."

Rama explained, "It was not her mistake. I committed an unforgivable blunder in straightway accepting the kingship when you offered it, without pausing to consider the consequences. I should have had more forethought. It was not her mistake." Rama continued his plea for Kaikeyi so earnestly that Dasaratha finally acceded to it. A burden was lifted from Rama's mind, and he felt completely at peace with the world again. Dasaratha offered him his blessings and a few words of guidance, and bade farewell to him. Then he took leave of Sita and Lakshmana separately, and returned to his place in heaven.

When this was over, the gods counselled Rama, "Tomorrow, the fifth day of the full moon, you will be completing the fourteenth year of your exile and it is imperative that you reappear in Ayodhya on completion of this term. Bharatha waits for you at Nandigram single-mindedly. If you do not appear there at the precise hour we dread to think what he may do to himself."

Rama realized the urgency and turning to Vibishana asked, "Is there any means by which you can help me return to Ayodhya within a day?"

Vibishana said, "I will give you the Pushpak Vimana. It was Kubera's at one time; later Ravana appropriated it for his own use. It will take you back to Ayodhya within any time you may wish." He immediately summoned the Vimana to be brought.

Rama ascended this vehicle, taking with him an entire army and all his supporters, such as Vibishana, Sugreeva, and others, who were unwilling to part from him, and started back in the direction of Ayodhya. As they flew along, he pointed out to Sita various landmarks that he had crossed during his campaign, and when they crossed the northern portals of Lanka he pointed out to her the spot far below where Ravana had finally fallen. They flew over mountains and forests; every inch of ground had a meaning for Rama. He made a brief descent at Kiskinda, where Sita had expressed a desire to gather a company of women to escort her when she re-entered Ayodhya. His next halt was at the ashram of Sage Bharadwaj, who had been hospitable to him once. At this point, Rama dispatched Hanuman to go forward in advance to Nandigram and inform Bharatha of his coming.

At Nandigram, Bharatha had been counting the hours and realized that the fourteenth year was nearly over. There was no sign of Rama yet; nor any news. It seemed as though all his austerities and penances of all these years were fruitless. He looked forlorn. He had kept Rama's sandals enthroned on a pedestal and was reigning as a regent. He summoned his brother Sathrugna and said, "My time is up. I cannot imagine where Rama is gone or what fate has overtaken him. I gave my word to wait for fourteen years and in a few moments I will have passed it. I have no right to live beyond that. Now I pass on my responsibilities to you. You will go back to Ayodhya and continue to rule as a regent." He made preparations to immolate himself in fire.

Sathrugna argued and tried to dissuade Bharatha in various ways, but Bharatha was adamant. Luckily, just at this moment, Hanuman arrived in the form of a brahmin youth, and the first thing he did was to put out the fire. Bharatha asked, "Who are you? What right have you to extinguish a fire I have raised?"

Hanuman explained, "I have brought you a message from Rama. He will be here presently."

Bharatha would not believe him, whereupon Hanuman assumed for a moment his gigantic form, explaining who he was, and then narrated to Bharatha all the incidents that had taken place these fourteen years. "Now make a public announcement of Rama's coming," he concluded, "and let all the streets and buildings be decorated to receive him."

This changed the whole atmosphere. Bharatha immediately dispatched messengers to the city and made preparations to receive Rama and lead him to his rightful place back in Ayodhya.

Shortly, Rama's Vimana arrived. Rama's mothers, including Kaikeyi, had assembled at Nandigram to receive him. The reunion was a happy one. The first thing that Rama did was to discard his austere garments. He groomed and clothed himself as befitting a King, and he advised Sita to do likewise. Vasishtha received the new King and Queen and fixed the hour for the coronation, interrupted fourteen years before.

↤ PANCATANTRA
Selected Tales

The Pancatantra *is a delightful, worldly collection of stories which offer a pragmatic perspective on life. The tales are linked together in a continuous chain—a structure that may have influenced the later* Thousand and One Nights *(see Chapter 7).*

The Monk Who Left His Body Behind

In the Koshala country is a city called Unassailable. In it ruled a king named Fine-Chariot, over whose footstool rippled rays of light from the diadems of uncounted vassal princes.

One day a forest ranger came with this report: "Master, all the forest kings have become turbulent, and in their midst is the forest chief named Vindhyaka. It is the king's affair to teach him modest manners." On hearing this report, the king summoned Counselor Strong, and despatched him with orders to chastise the forest chieftains.

Now in the absence of the counselor, a naked monk arrived in the city at the end of the hot season. He was master of the astronomical specialties, such as problems and etymologies, rising of the zodiacal signs, augury, ecliptic intersection, and the decanate; also stellar mansions divided into nine parts, twelve parts, thirty parts; the shadow of the gnomon, eclipses, and numerous other mysteries. With these the fellow in a few days won the entire population, as if he had bought and paid for them.

Finally, as the matter went from mouth to mouth, the king heard a report of its character, and had the curiosity to summon the monk to his palace. There he offered him a seat and asked: "Is it true, Professor, as they say, that you read the thoughts of others?" "That will be demonstrated in the sequel," replied the monk, and by discourses adapted to the occasion he brought the poor king to the extreme pitch of curiosity.

One day he failed to appear at the regular hour, but the following day, on entering the palace, he announced: "O King, I bring you the best of good tidings. At dawn today I flung this body aside within my cell, assumed a body fit for the world of the gods, and, inspired with the knowledge that all the immortals thought of me with longing, I went to heaven and have just returned. While there, I was request-ed by the gods to inquire in their name after the king's welfare."

When he heard this, the king said, his extreme curiosity begetting a feeling of amazement: "What, Professor! You go to heaven?" "O mighty King," replied the fellow, "I go to heaven every day." This the king believed—poor dullard!—so that he grew negligent of all royal business and all duties toward the ladies, concentrating his attention on the monk.

While matters were in this state, Strong entered the king's presence, after settling all disturbances in the forest domain. He found the master wholly indifferent to every one of his counselors, withdrawn in private conference with that naked monk, discussing what seemed to be some miraculous occurrence, his lotus-face ablossom. And on learning the facts, Strong bowed low and said: "Victory, O King! May the gods give you wit!"

Thereupon the king inquired concerning the counselor's health, and said: "Sir, do you know this professor?" To which the counselor replied: "How could there be ignorance of one who is lord and creator of a whole school of professors? Moreover, I have heard that this professor goes to heaven. Is it a fact?" "Everything that you have heard," answered the king, "is beyond the shadow of doubt."

Thereupon the monk said: "If this counselor feels any curiosity, he may see for himself." With this he entered his cell, barred the door from within, and waited there. After the lapse of a mere moment, the counselor spoke: "O King," he said, "how soon will he return?" And the king replied: "Why this impatience? You must know that he leaves his lifeless body within this cell, and returns with another, a heavenly body."

"If this is indeed the case," said Strong, "then bring a great quantity of firewood, so that I may set fire to this cell." "For what purpose?" asked the king. And the counselor continued: "So that, when this lifeless body has been burned, the gentleman may stand before the king in that other body which visits heaven. In this connection I will tell you the story of

The Girl Who Married a Snake

In Palace City lived a Brahman named Godly, whose childless wife wept bitterly when she saw the neighbors' youngsters. But one day the Brahman said: "Forget your sorrow, mother dear. See! When I was offering the sacrifice for birth of children, an invisible being said to me in the clearest words: 'Brahman, you shall have a son surpassing all mankind in beauty, character, and charm.'"

When she heard this, the wife felt her heart swell with supreme delight. "I only hope his promises come true," she said. Presently she conceived, and in course of time gave birth to a snake. When she saw him, she paid no attention to her companions, who all advised her to throw him away. Instead, she took him and bathed him, laid him with motherly tenderness in a large, clean box, and pampered him with milk, fresh butter, and other good things, so that before many days had passed, he grew to maturity.

But one day the Brahman's wife was watching the marriage festival of a neighbor's son, and the tears streamed down her face as she said to her husband: "I know that you despise me, because you do nothing about a marriage festival for my boy." "My good wife," answered he, "am I to go to the depths of the underworld and beseech Vasuki the serpent-king? Who else, you foolish woman, would give his own daughter to this snake?"

But when he had spoken, he was disturbed at seeing the utter woe in his wife's countenance. He therefore packed provisions for a long journey, and undertook foreign travel from love of his wife. In the course of some months he arrived at a spot called Kutkuta City in a distant land. There in the house of a kinsman whom he could visit with pleasure since each respected the other's character, he was hospitably received, was given a bath, food, and the like, and there he spent the night.

Now at dawn, when he paid his respects to his Brahman host and made ready to depart, the other asked him: "What was your purpose in coming hither? And where will your errand lead you?"

To this he replied: "I have come in search of a fit wife for my son." "In that case," said his host, "I have a very beautiful daughter, and my own person is yours to command. Pray take her for your son." So the Brahman took the girl with her attendants and returned to his own place.

But when the people of the country beheld her incomparable opulence of beauty, her supreme loveliness and superhuman graces, their eyes popped out with pleasure, and they said to her attendants: "How can right-thinking persons bestow such a pearl of a girl upon a snake?" On hearing this, all her elderly relatives without exception were troubled at heart, and they said: "Let her be taken from this imp-ridden creature." But the girl said: "No more of this mockery! Remember the text:

> Do once, once only, these three things:
> Once spoken, stands the word of kings;
> The speech of saints has no miscarriage;
> A maid is given once in marriage.

And again:

> All fated happenings, derived
> From any former state,
> Must changeless stand: the very gods
> Endured poor Blossom's fate."

Whereupon they all asked in chorus: "Who was this Blossom person?" And the girl told the story of

Poor Blossom

God Indra once had a parrot named Blossom. He enjoyed supreme beauty, loveliness, and various graces, while his intelligence was not blunted by his extensive scientific attainments.

One day he was resting on the palm of great Indra's hand, his body thrilling with delight at that contact, and was reciting a variety of authoritative formulas, when he caught sight of Yama, lord of death, who had come to pay his respects at the time appointed. Seeing the god, the parrot edged away. And all the thronging immortals asked him: "Why did you move away, sir, upon beholding that personage?" "But," said the parrot, "he brings harm to all living creatures. Why not move away from him?"

Upon hearing this, they all desired to calm his fears, so

said to Yama: "As a favor to us, you must please not kill this parrot." And Yama replied: "I do not know about that. It is Time who determines these matters."

They therefore took Blossom with them, paid a visit to Time, and made the same request. To which Time replied: "It is Death who is posted in these affairs. Pray speak to him."

But when they did so, the parrot died at the mere sight of Death. And they were all distressed at seeing the occurrence, so that they said to Yama: "What does this mean?" And Yama said: "It was simply fated that he should die at the mere sight of Death." With this reply they went back to heaven.

> "And that is why I say:
> All fated happenings, ...

and the rest of it. Furthermore, I do not want my father reproached for double dealing on the part of his daughter." When she had said this, she married the snake, with the permission of her companions, and at once began devoted attendance upon him by offering milk to drink and performing other services.

One night the serpent issued from the generous chest which had been set for him in her chamber, and entered her bed. "Who is this?" she cried. "He has the form of a man." And thinking him a strange man, she started up, trembling in every limb, unlocked the door, and was about to dart away when she heard him say: "Stay, my dear wife. I am your husband." Then, in order to convince her, he re-entered the body which he had left behind in the chest, issued from it again, and came to her.

When she beheld him flashing with lofty diadem, with earrings, bracelets, armbands, and rings, she fell at his feet, and then they sank into a glad embrace.

Now his father, the Brahman, rose betimes and discovered how matters stood. He therefore seized the serpent's skin that lay in the chest, and consumed it with fire, for he thought: "I do not want him to enter that again." And in the morning he and his wife, with the greatest possible joy, introduced to everybody as their own an extraordinarily handsome son, quite wrapped up in his love affair.

↢ MAHADEVIYAKKA

Selected Poems

Mahadeviyakka, who wrote in the twelfth century, was the foremost woman poet in India before the modern period. She writes in the most characteristic medieval genre of bhakti, *or devotional religious poetry. The poems are addressed to the Hindu gods, but the language is colloquial, and the speaker's carefree—though still devout—attitude gives the poems a very appealing flavor.*

What's to Come Tomorrow

> What's to come tomorrow
> let it come today.
> What's to come today
> let it come right now.
>
> Lord white as jasmine,
> don't give us your *nows* and *thens!*

5

You Can Confiscate

You can confiscate
money in hand;
can you confiscate
the body's glory?

Or peel away every strip   5
you wear,

But can you peel
the Nothing, the Nakedness
that covers and veils?

To the shameless girl   10
wearing the White Jasmine Lord's
light of morning,
you fool,
where's the need for cover and jewel?

I Love the Handsome One

I love the Handsome One:
he has no death
decay nor form
no place or side
no end nor birthmarks.   5
I love him O mother. Listen.

I love the Beautiful One
with no bond nor fear
no clan no land
no landmarks   10
for his beauty.

So my lord, white as jasmine, is my husband.

Take these husbands who die,
decay, and feed them
to your kitchen fires!

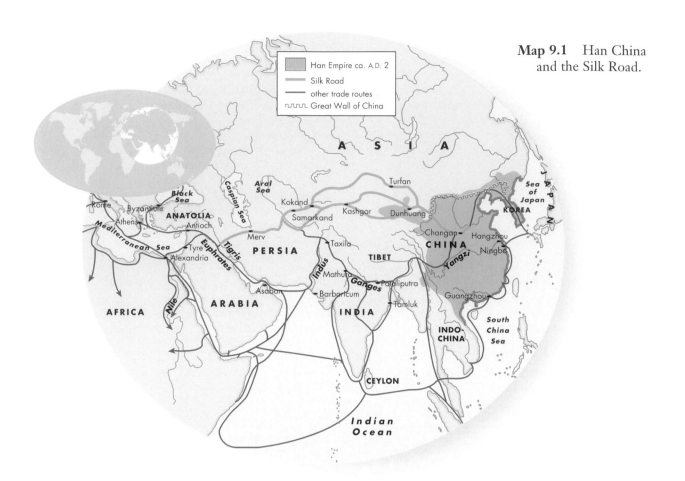

Map 9.1 Han China and the Silk Road.

EARLY CHINESE
AND JAPANESE
CIVILIZATIONS

CHAPTER 9

Zhu Jan, *Seeking the Tao in the Autumn Mountains*, ca. 970, Collection of National Palace Museum, Taipei, Taiwan.

CHINA BEFORE 1279

THE SHANG AND ZHOU DYNASTIES

China is the world's oldest civilization, tracing its roots back as far as the fifth millennium B.C., although the earliest of the Chinese eras for which archaeological evidence has been found is that of the Shang dynasty, dating from ca. 1760 B.C. The Shang dynasty itself was long believed to be only legend and myth, until its existence was verified through twentieth-century excavations. These excavations have yielded not only ancient artifacts but also the oldest examples of Chinese writing. This written language has remained virtually unchanged for centuries, uniting a country about the size of the USA where the spoken form of the language varies so much that it cannot be understood from region to region.

The ancient Shang people inhabited the central Yellow River Valley area of China and developed the most advanced technology of the Chinese Bronze Age. The ruler of the Shang state had a quasi-divine status, which was honored by the people in ritual ceremonies and through serving the ruler in war. The talents of Shang craftworkers were also deployed in honoring their god-king rulers.

Although the oldest Shang city at Cheng Chow dates from the sixteenth century B.C., it is the later city site of

Figure 9.1 *Fang ding*, Tomb 1004, Houjiazhang, Anyang, Henan, Shang dynasty, bronze, twelfth century B.C., British Museum, London. The ornate design on this square vessel was typical for Shang bronze artifacts. The emphasis on animal motifs suggests the importance of hunting.

Anyang (ca. 1384–1111 B.C.) that has yielded the majority of Shang artifacts. At Anyang, archaeologists have found rich burial sites, but no city walls or dwellings, leading them to believe that Anyang may have been a royal burial site for another city.

The Shang kings ruled until about 1100 B.C., when the Zhou people came from the northwest and conquered them. The Zhou dynasty (1100–221 B.C.) introduced organized agriculture, which replaced the Shang emphasis on hunting. The Zhou established a feudal society—in which land was granted to someone by the king or an overlord in return for support in war and loyalty—with the Zhou king ruling as a "Tian" or "Son of Heaven." The principles of societal relationships that the Zhou formulated were to influence later Chinese civilization, and they can be found in such Chinese classics as the *Book of Odes* and the *Book of Ritual*. Yet while the Zhou modified the social and religious practices of the Shang, they adopted other aspects of Shang culture, in particular the Shang use of bronze casting and their decorative techniques.

Shang and Zhou Bronzes. Although jade and glazed pottery artifacts dating from the Shang dynasty have been found, by far the most numerous and important Shang artifacts are made of bronze. The *fang ding* (fig. 9.1) was used for storing food and wine for social and religious ceremonial functions. The emphasis on animal motifs, which is typical of the intricate ornamental design found in Shang bronze artifacts, suggests the importance of hunting in Shang culture. Yet the strange creatures depicted here evoke a sense of mystery and fear associated with the supernatural, and thus may be of religious significance as well.

Such bronze objects remained of great importance throughout the Zhou period that followed. One indication of the great wealth of the Zhou rulers is the monumental carillon, consisting of sixty-five bronze bells, discovered in the tomb of Marquis Yi of Zheng (fig. 9.2). The bells, which are believed to have been used to communicate with the supernatural, produce two quite distinct tones when struck near the center and at the rim.

Confucianism. Toward the middle of the Zhou dynasty, the two great philosophical and religious traditions indigenous to China took hold—Confucianism and Taoism. Like Buddhism (see Chapter 8), which would later have its own impact on China, Confucianism is based on the teachings of one man. CONFUCIUS [con-FYOU-shus] (551–479 B.C.) was the son of aristocratic parents who had lost their wealth during the decline of feudalism in China. Confucius's father died before he was born, and he was raised by his mother in poverty. He received an education from the village tutor, studying poetry, history, music, hunting, fishing, and archery—the traditional educational disciplines of the time. After a

Figure 9.2 Bronze bells, Zhou dynasty, 433 B.C., frame height 9′ (2.74 m), length 25′ (7.62 m), Hubei Provincial Museum, Wuhan. These ancient ceremonial bells, which were believed to have been used to communicate with the supernatural, produce two distinct tones when struck near the center and at the rim.

brief stint as a government official, Confucius embarked on a career as a teacher. He wandered from place to place, offering his services as an advisor on human conduct and on government. After many years as a successful and famous teacher, Confucius spent the last part of his life quietly teaching at home.

After his death, Confucius's sayings, along with those of his followers, were collected together during the fifth century in a volume called *The Analects*. Drawing on cultural values anchored in ancient Chinese tradition, these eminently practical sayings focus on this world rather than the next. Although Confucius deeply respected the Chinese cultural heritage, valuing its best aspects, he adapted ancient traditions to the circumstances of his own time. Confucius lived in a period of political chaos and moral confusion; perhaps for that reason he emphasized the importance of the traditional values of self-control, propriety, and filial piety to a productive and good society. It was through such virtues that Confucius believed that anarchy could be overcome and social cohesion restored.

Confucius's point of departure was the individual rather than society. He believed that if each individual could be virtuous, then the family would live in harmony. Similarly, if each family lived according to certain moral principles, the village would be harmonious. Village harmony, in turn, would lead to a country focused on moral values, coupled with an aesthetic sensibility that would allow life to be lived to its fullest creative potential.

Four qualities in particular—*li*, *jen*, *te*, and *wen*—were valued in Confucian teaching. *Li* equates to propriety, ceremony, and civility, and requires the development of proper attitudes and a due respect for established forms of conduct. At its heart are the four basic social rules of human relationships: courtesy, politeness, good manners, and respect, especially a reverence for age. These are supplemented by a fifth rule or concept, that of *yi* or duty, a sense of the obligation one has to others. These five key rules strongly underpin the centrality of the family in Chinese life. Children's duty to their parents is the root from which moral and social virtues grow. In talking to an older person, for example, the younger person responds only after the elder has spoken. The younger person also listens with due deference, and does not interrupt or contradict.

Jen refers to the ideal relationship that should exist between people. Based on respect for oneself, *jen* extends this self-respect to others and manifests itself in acts of charity and courtesy. *Jen* and *li* together make for a superior human being according to the Confucian ideal.

Te refers to virtue. Originally it referred to the quality of greatness that enabled an individual to subdue enemies, inspire respect, and influence others. However, in Confucian teaching it came to signify a different kind of power—the power of moral example rather than that of physical strength or might. A strong leader who guides by example exhibits *te*. So do the forces of nature, as the following saying from *The Analects* illustrates:

Asked by the ruler whether the lawless should be executed, Confucius answered: "What need is there of the death penalty in government? If you showed a sincere desire to be good, your people would likewise be good. The virtue of the prince is like the wind; the virtue of the people is like grass. It is the nature of grass to bend when the wind blows upon it."

The final characteristic of Confucian tradition, *wen*, refers to the arts of peace, that is, to music, poetry, art, and other cultural activities. Confucius considered the arts a form of moral education. He saw music as especially conducive to order and harmony, and he believed that the greatest painting and poetry functioned in the same way as an excellent leader, insofar as they provided a model of excellence.

Ultimately, Confucius was an empiricist, justifying the value of his moral prescriptions by an appeal to experience. His teachings were designed to help his followers live a better life in the present rather than to achieve an eternal reward after death. Morality, moreover, depended on context. There was no inflexible "thou shalt not." Instead, any moral decision was guided by the circumstances of a particular problem.

Taoism.   Like Confucianism, Taoism [DOW-ism] is principally concerned with morality and ethical behavior insofar as they benefit people in the present world. Thus it is often considered a philosophy rather than a religion. Its founder was LAOZI [LOW-ZEE] (b. 604 B.C.), whose name means "the Old Boy" or "the Old Master." Little is known about Laozi, though a number of legends exist to explain how he came to write the *Taodejing* (*The Way and Its Power*), which summarizes Taoist teaching.

In the most popular of these legends, Laozi, having retired from court life, was journeying out of China when a guard at a mountain pass recognized him and insisted that he write down the sum of his wisdom before leaving the country.

The **Tao** (or Dao) is the ultimate reality behind existence, a transcendent and eternal spiritual essence. Mysterious and mystical, it is finally incomprehensible and ineffable. As the *Taodejing* states: "The Tao which can be conceived is not the real Tao ... Those who know don't say, and those who say don't know."

At the same time, however, the Tao is immanent—that is, it exists in nature, manifesting its ordering principle in the cycle of the seasons, in the flowing of rivers, in the singing of birds. In this second sense, the Tao is the governing order of life represented by the rhythm and force of nature.

Taoism is a way of ordering one's life. It is a set of principles by which to control one's life, so as to achieve peace and harmony with the rest of creation. Like Confucianism, Taoism values *te*, or power. In Taoism, however, the *te* of a thing is its power in the sense of its essential virtue, its identity, and integrity. So the characteristic nature of each thing is its *te*. The *te* of a person is her or his integrity or genuineness—one's authentic self at its best. One expresses *te* through meekness and humility. Instead of competition, *te* proposes cooperation; instead of insistent willfulness, patient attentiveness.

Along with *te*, Taoists encourage *wu-wei*, a kind of creative calm. *Wu-wei* involves relaxing the conscious mind. Like the Buddhist and Hindu ascetic ideals, *wu-wei* seeks the denial of the personal and the dissolution of the

Timeline 9.1   Early Chinese culture.

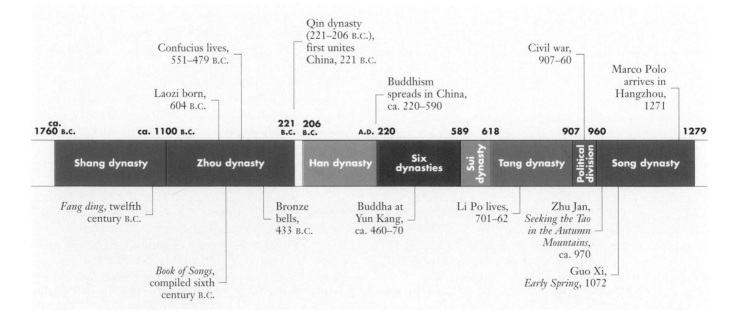

Figure 9.3 The yin/yang symbol. Yin and yang represent the complementary negative and positive principles of the universe.

conscious individual self. Taoism illustrates the concept of *wu-wei* with examples from nature, especially water. Supple yet strong, water adapts itself to its surroundings, flowing over or filling what it encounters.

The Taoist ideal of *p'u*, which literally means "unpainted wood," stresses simplicity. The Taoist prefers unvarnished wood, and thus Taoist architecture employs wood in its natural state, leaving gilt and lacquer to the Confucians, along with ceremonialism and the intricate forms and formulae of civilized life. Taoist painting uses only simple lines, suggesting much in little. Human figures in such paintings are kept small in relation to the vastness of nature.

Yin and Yang. One of the best known of all Chinese images is that of the yin and yang (fig. 9.3). **Yin and yang** represent contrasting but complementary principles that sum up life's basic opposing elements—pain and pleasure, good and evil, light and dark, male and female, and so on. Instead of seeing these contrasting elements as contradictory, the Chinese emphasize the way in which they complement one another.

Illustrating the philosophical ideal of harmonious integration, the two forms, yin and yang, coexist peacefully within a larger circle. Each form provides the border for its opposite, partly defining it. In the very center of each form, there is the defining aspect of the complementary form: the dark teardrop contains a spot of white; the white teardrop includes a small dark circle. The one cannot exist without the other.

Yin is the negative form, associated with earth, darkness, and passivity. Conversely, the yang form is positive and associated with heaven, light, and the constructive impulse. Yin and yang represent the perpetual interplay and mutual relation of all things.

Lyric Poetry. Unlike most national literatures, which typically have their origins in prose tales, epic poetry, or other narrative forms, the earliest known Chinese literature is lyric poetry. Lyrics are usually written to be set to music and are personal in nature. Educated Chinese were expected not only to understand and appreciate poetry, but also to compose it.

The Book of Songs, which contains material passed down orally from as far back as the tenth century B.C.,

was first written down in the sixth century B.C. in Confucius's time. It is one of the five ancient Confucian classics; some scholars have suggested that Confucius himself edited the collection. The poems are variously concerned with love and war, lamentation and celebration, and reflect the perspectives of all strata of ancient Zhou society, from peasants to kings.

As is suggested by its title, *The Book of Songs* contains poems that were meant to be accompanied by music. More than half of the 305 poems are classified as folk songs; the remainder were either written for performance at court or as part of a ritual. The individualism and occasional rebelliousness of the speakers in the poems sometimes make them seem at odds with the Confucian ideal. However, the depth of feeling they express and the richness of the experience they draw on have ensured that *The Book of Songs* remains not only popular but also essential reading for educated Chinese to the present day.

Music. During the time of Confucius and Laozi, music was categorized according to its social functions. Particular types of music played on certain instruments in specified tonalities were designated for use in accompanying the chanting of poetry, the worship of ancestors, as well as at court banquets, country feasts, archery contests, military parades, and the like. Confucius, like Plato, believed that music should be used to educate. Music was to display the qualities of moderation and harmony, mirroring the emphasis that Confucius placed on those virtues in social and political life. Certain dangerous aspects of music were to be avoided, such as its ability to induce excited states of emotion.

EMPIRE: THE QIN AND HAN DYNASTIES

Both Confucianism and Taoism developed in response to the political instability of the Zhou dynasty, which began to be undermined by invasions from the west in 771 B.C. Political fragmentation continued until the QIN [CHIN—the origin of the name China] dynasty (221–206 B.C.) unified the country for the first time.

Although the Qin dynasty's rule was brief, it introduced many measures to ensure that the empire could be ruled efficiently and would remain unified, which indeed it has down to the present day. The Qin rulers established a central bureaucracy, divided the country into administrative units, and standardized the writing system, as well as the currency, weights, and measures. All citizens were made subject to Qin laws, and everyone had to pay taxes to the Qin emperor.

The Qin initiated major building projects—networks of roads and canals that would link the different parts of the empire. It was also the Qin who created most of the fourteen-hundred-mile-long Great Wall as a defense for their empire against invaders. The Great Wall was made

Figure 9.4   Tomb figures, from the mausoleum of the first Qin emperor, Lintong, Shaanxi.
Qin dynasty, ca. 210 B.C., earthenware, lifesize. This army of terra cotta figures, found buried
in the mausoleum of the first Qin emperor, was meant to serve him in the afterlife.

by joining together the border walls of the formerly independent regions.

There was a downside to this great imperial ambition, however. In order to maintain control, the Qin suppressed free speech, persecuting scholars and destroying classical literary and philosophical texts, which were only preserved by the ingenuity of those who memorized and later reconstructed them. Confucianism was temporarily supplanted with a new philosophical system called Legalism created by Qin intellectuals. Reflecting a belief in the absolute power of the emperor, Qin rule proved so harsh that rebellions soon broke out and the dynasty was overthrown after only fifteen years in power.

Some idea of the aspirations of grandeur of the Qin dynasty can be gained from viewing the tomb of the first Qin emperor, SHINHUANGDI [SHIN-HU-AN-TI] (221–206 B.C.) (fig. 9.4). Excavators working in Shaanxi province inadvertently uncovered thousands of lifesize earthenware figures, which had been buried in the emperor's tomb to accompany and serve him in the afterlife. The emperor's burial ground was richly stocked with furniture, as well as with wooden chariots, and even contained a model of the Qin universe, with representations of rivers and constellations of stars and planets.

With the advent of the Han dynasty (206 B.C.–A.D. 220), Chinese culture found its most characteristic and defining forms. Han emperors restored Confucianism to favor, making it the state philosophy, established a national academy to train civil servants, and reinvigorated classical scholarship and learning by honoring scholars and employing them in the national bureaucracy.

It was under the Han dynasty that the Silk Road trade route was established. It was along the Silk Road that goods traveled from China to India, and on to Greece and finally Rome. It was also by this route that religious missionaries from the West brought Christianity to India and Persia, and Buddhism spread from India into China, where it soon flourished.

THE SIX DYNASTIES

Intrigue and rebellion led to political and social disunity during the period of the "Six Dynasties" (A.D. 220–589), which followed the Han dynasty. Warring factions fought for control of the country, with six successive dynasties gaining power for a brief time. From this period of political turmoil there survives a series of monumental stone sculptures cut into caves at Yun Kang (Yungang, Shaanxi). The most colossal of these is a forty-five-foot-high image of the Buddha (fig. 9.5), made around A.D. 460–470. The statue is carved directly into the rock cave, in the manner of Indian monumental sculpture, from which this Buddhist figure clearly derives (compare fig. 8.6). This earliest of Buddhist styles of sculpture in China has been termed "archaic," and, as in

ancient Greece (see fig. 3.26), the figures characteristically wear what has been called on an "archaic smile."

THE TANG DYNASTY

At the end of the Six Dynasties period, the Sui rulers (A.D. 589–618) reunited China. The Sui, the last of the six dynasties, were quickly overcome, however, by the Tang dynasty, who went on to reestablish China as a world power during nearly three hundred years of prosperity and cultural enrichment (A.D. 618–907).

The Tang emperors restored the Silk Road, which had fallen into disuse during the Six Dynasties period, forging trade and cultural links with other countries, especially Persia, India, and Japan. During the Tang dynastic period, literature and the other arts were held in high esteem, with civil servants and gentry required to master the Confucian classics and to compose poetry of their own.

Li Bai and Du Fu. Much early Chinese poetry was composed according to ancient folk-song models. These poems were called **shih**. Two of the great practitioners of shih were LI BAI [LEE PO] (701–762) and DU FU [DOO FOO] (712–770). Both poets have long been associated with Confucianism and Taoism. Du Fu is

Figure 9.5 Colossal Buddha, cave 20, Yungang, Shaanxi, A.D. 460–70, stone, height 45′ (13.72 m). Like the less monumental sculptures of ancient Greek civilization (see fig. 3.26), this archaic figure possesses a similar smiling expression.

Connections

THE SEVEN SAGES OF THE BAMBOO GROVE

*E*arly in the Six Dynasties period, seven Taoist poet-philosophers, seeking relief from the formalities of Confucianism, began to hold meetings in a bamboo grove. There, these "Seven Sages" gathered to consider the spiritual side of their life, write and discuss poetry, play musical instruments, play chess, contemplate nature, and, perhaps above all, drink wine. The latter, they felt, released the spirit from all constraint. As one famous saying of the Sages had it:

> *Brief indeed is a man's life!*
> *So, let's sing over our wine.*

Ruan Ji was said to have given up a high official post in order to live near a brewery. In one of his famous poems, entitled "Singing from My Heart," he remembers his seriousness as a youth and comments that now "I mock myself for my past gloom." Liu Ling, another Sage, wrote the "Hymn to the Virtue of Wine" and is notorious for having tricked his teetotalling wife by telling her that he too had decided to give up alcohol and having her prepare a feast for the gods, and then drinking all the wine intended for the gods himself.

The Seven Sages inaugurated a tradition that would last for many centuries in China and still finds an echo today in the West in a film such as *Dead Poets' Society*. During the Tang dynasty, the poet Li Bai took his followers on a similar retreat to a garden of peach and plum trees on a moonlit spring night. There, they too drank wine and, having liberated themselves from the constraints of their everyday lives, composed their poems. Both the gathering of the Seven Sages in the bamboo grove and Li Bai's conclave in the orchard would be a subject for painters for generations to come (fig 9.6).

Figure 9.6 Liang Kai, *The Poet Li Bai Walking and Chanting a Poem*, Southern Song dynasty, ca. 1200, hanging scroll, ink on paper, $31\frac{3}{4} \times 11\frac{7}{8}''$ (80.6 × 30.2 cm), Tokyo National Museum, Japan. This depiction of Li Bai juxtaposes the quick brushstrokes used to describe the robe with the precise and detailed work on his face, suggesting a tension between the freedom of the poet's spirit and the intensity of his intelligence.

---

often described as a Confucian poet. Du Fu's poems stress the importance of love of family and of harmonious social relationships. They also celebrate the Confucian ideals of self-discipline and serenity.

The poems of Li Bai (or Li Po, as he is sometimes known) are written in a more open style and take greater liberties with the formal poetic conventions of the time than the poems of Du Fu. Li Bai (fig. 9.6) has been described as a poetic individualist and a precursor of the Western Romantic poets (see Chapter 18). His verse has been profoundly influential in China and also in Japan, where he is known as Rihaku. Through the translations of Ezra Pound and the Sinologist Arthur Waley, he has also had a strong impact on modern American poetry.

THE SONG DYNASTY

When the Tang dynasty came to an end in 907, China was thrown into a half-century of civil war. The empire was reunified in 960 under the Song rulers, who inaugurated a period of great technological advancement. During the Song dynasty (960–1279), China saw within its borders the invention of the navigational compass, paper currency, gunpowder, and printing, well before Gutenberg's invention of movable type in fifteenth-century Germany. The rule of the Song emperors created two conditions necessary for artistic development: first, an abundance of leisure time, which allowed for intellectual pursuits, including a reformulation of Confucian ideals; second, the availability of patronage, which helped bring about a resurgence in the art of painting and, with it, elaborations of art theory.

Painting. The art of painting flourished during the Song period. *Seeking the Tao in the Autumn Mountains* (fig. 9.7), by ZHU JAN [JOO JAN] (fl. ca. 960–980), is, as its title suggests, representative of the Taoist artistic tradition. Huge mountains evoke a sense of the remote and the eternal. Rising dramatically and powerfully in the center of the painting, they suggest the modest position of humanity in the grand scale of the natural world.

Neo-Confucianism, which developed during the Song dynasty, unified Taoism and Buddhism into a single system of thought. *Early Spring* (fig. 9.8), by GUO XI

Figure 9.7 Zhu Jan, *Seeking the Tao in the Autumn Mountains*, ca. 970, ink on silk, 61½ × 30¾″ (156.2 × 78.1 cm), Collection of National Palace Museum, Taipei, Taiwan. Long sweeping brushstrokes complemented by carefully placed dots of dark ink accentuate the mountain's highlights as they guide the viewer's gaze upward.

[GOO-OH SEE] (after 1000–ca. 1090), embodies the Confucian ideal of *li*, which is at the heart of nature. As in Zhu Jan's painting, the human presence in this landscape passes almost unnoticed, so vast is the scale of the central mountain. Small figures can be identified in the lower foreground on both the left and right, and in the middle distance on the right a village is tucked between the hills. The mountain, representing Nature, is a powerful symbol of eternity that dwarfs human existence.

A court painter during the reign of Emperor Shenzong (r. 1068–85), Guo Xi was given the task of painting all the murals in the Forbidden City, the imperial compound in Beijing that foreigners were prohibited from entering. His ideas about painting were recorded by his son Guo Si in a book entitled *The Lofty Message of the Forests and Streams*. According to Guo Si, the central peak in *Early Spring* symbolizes the Emperor himself, its tall pines the gentlemanly ideals of the court. Here Guo Xi has painted the ideal Confucian and Buddhist world; the Emperor, like the Buddha surrounded by his bodhisattvas, gathers all around him, just as in *Early Spring* the mountain, the trees and hills suggest the proper order and rhythm of the universe.

Figure 9.8 Guo Xi, *Early Spring*, 1072, Northern Song dynasty, hanging scroll, ink and slight color on silk, length 5′ (1.52 m), National Palace Museum, Taipei, Taiwan. Everything has its appropriate place in the Chinese universe, and thus we gaze up at the central mountain here, which represents the Emperor, and down into a deep gorge, where at the bottom right a human figure rows a boat, underscoring the insignificance of the individual in the face of both nature and, symbolically, the emperor.

Cross Currents

MARCO POLO'S HANGZHOU

Little was known about China and the Far East in the West before the nineteenth century. One of the most important sources was the account written by the Venetian traveler MARCO POLO (ca. 1254–1324). His description of the Song capital, Hangzhou, is particularly vivid.

Hangzhou, formerly called Kinsai, or the "City of Heaven," might also have been known as the "City of Bridges," since twelve thousand wood and stone bridges cross its wide waterways. Described by Polo, who arrived in the city in 1271, as, "without doubt the finest and most splendid city in the world," the Hangzhou of the Song dynasty was an important commercial center as well as the imperial capital of China. Its population—of more than a million people—was then the largest in the world. Thirty-foot-high crenelated walls, studded with towers, protected the city against enemy attack. Guards stationed strategically at the bridges to repulse invaders also served as time-keepers, striking a gong and drum to mark the passing of the hours.

Polo's descriptions evoked life in Hangzhou for his Western audiences. On the city's streets, porters carried goods suspended from long poles in baskets and jars. On its canals, boats and ships of many sizes transported food and building materials. Its markets, open three days a week in the city's squares, were crammed with food and spices, books and flowers, cloth and gemstones, in addition to a huge variety of meats and game. Dress, as in the West, was a mark of social and financial status for both women and men. The rank of mandarins (government officials) was indicated by robes and head-gear. On special occasions, these mandarins wore silk robes embroidered with flowers, animals, and symbols. Their belt buckles were made of jade or rhinoceros horn, and their caps were adorned with buttons, again signaling the officials' importance.

Among the places people congregated, according to Polo, were parks and lakes, especially the great West Lake, which was often filled with boats, barges, and floating teahouses, from which passengers could view the numerous palaces, temples, pagodas, and pavilions that dotted the surrounding landscape. On land, the wealthy congregated in clubs and centers to read poems, see plays, sing, and dance, as well as practice calligraphy and painting. It was especially important for young men with the ambition to become scholar officials to become well versed in the Chinese classics in preparation for the civil service examinations. Young women were also expected to take lessons, with classes in music, dancing, spinning, embroidery, and social etiquette preparing them for the good marriages they hoped to contract.

JAPAN BEFORE THE FIFTEENTH CENTURY

→

Until some time during the first centuries A.D., Japan remained politically fragmented, split into more than a hundred independent warring states. Then some regions began to form tribal confederacies. These were typically ruled by an aristocratic warrior clan. Around A.D. 300 one of these clans, the YAMATO [ya-MAH-toh], emerged as a dominant force throughout the country.

Yamato rule, which begins the KOFUN period, was indebted in many respects to the Chinese model. Chinese political administration, Chinese religion and philosophy, and the Chinese system of writing soon became ingrained in Japan. At first, this influence came through Korea, with which both Japan and China maintained close relations. Then, from around A.D. 625 to A.D. 825, Japan had direct contact with China, largely through the Japanese students and political ambassadors who traveled between the two countries.

RELIGION

Buddhism and Shinto. Of the religious influences Japan inherited from China, the strongest was that of Buddhism, which China had itself imported from India. But whereas China stressed the philosophical elements of Buddhism, Japan stressed its religious aspects. This difference in cultural style is especially evident in the way Japan modified and adapted the Chinese form of Ch'an, later developing what became known as Zen (see p. 307).

Japan, however, already had its own religious practices, designated as **Shinto** to distinguish them from the imported forms of Buddhism. Shinto later developed from a kind of nature worship into a state religion of patriotic appreciation of the Japanese land. Shinto requires a commemoration of Japanese heroes and significant events from the nation's history. Shinto can also include aspects of animism, nature worship, and ancestor worship, and Shinto rituals may be carried out in private homes as well as in Shinto temples.

To some extent, the development of Shinto was a reaction against Chinese religious and cultural influence. In addition, in the seventh and eighth centuries, the Japanese collected their native myths in the *Kojiki,* "Chronicles of Ancient Events." In explaining the origin of Japanese culture, the *Kojiki* describe the creation of the Japanese islands by two *kami,* or gods, Izanagi and his consort Izanami. All other gods descend from these two, of whom the most important is Ameterasu, the sun goddess, said to be the ancestor of the Japanese emperors.

ASUKA AND NARA PERIODS

Art and Architecture. The earliest Japanese sculpture and architecture, that of the Asuka period, A.D. 552–646, is closely identified with Buddhism. One of the best-preserved and most important Japanese temples is Horyu-ji, the oldest wooden temple in the world (ca. 670) (fig. 9.9). Horyu-ji's architectural design reveals how Buddhist-inspired Chinese architecture influenced early Japanese temple-building.

Among the many treasures housed in the buildings of Horyu-ji is a sculpture known as the *Shaka Triad* (fig. 9.10). This is, as its title suggests, a triple image of the Buddha, whose Japanese name is Shakyamuni. The oversized figures, especially the Buddha sitting in the center, and the decorative motifs, reveal the sculptor TORI BUSSHYI's [BOOSH-yi] awareness of the Chinese sculptural tradition.

From the late seventh century on, Japanese rulers were true monarchs, no longer merely aristocratic warlords. Around the same time, Nara became Japan's first true capital. Although the rulers of ancient Japan are often referred to as emperors, these rulers are best thought of as sovereigns. The distinction is important as it signals a shift from the military authority of the earlier warlords to a genuine pursuit of political and cultural cohesion.

Figure 9.9 Horyu-ji compound, with pagoda and Golden Hall, Nara, Japan, ca. A.D. 670, aerial view. Visitors entering this temple compound move through the first building and then must take a turn to the right or the left rather than moving in a straight line from one building to the next. This favoring of lateral over linear movement is a characteristic of Japanese artistic style.

Figure 9.10 Tori Busshyi, *Shaka Triad*, Asuka period, A.D. 623, bronze, height 5'9" (1.76 m), Horyu-ji, Nara, Asuka period, A.D. 623. The Buddha, flanked by attendants, sits in regal stiffness on a simple throne against a decorative background medallion that testifies to his importance.

THE HEIAN PERIOD

In 794, the Japanese capital was moved to Heian, which in the process became one of the most densely populated cities in the world. The Heian period was a period of rich productivity and peace. At this time, the Japanese sovereign had the support of aristocratic families. Court culture during the Heian era became extremely refined and elegant, and the arts flourished. Among the great works produced was the world's first major work of prose fiction, *The Tale of Genji*.

The Tale of Genji. One of the most enduring and influential works of Japanese literature is *The Tale of Genji* (*Genji monogatari*, ca. 1021), a sprawling narrative of court life, spanning many generations and featuring a host of characters. Considered the first important novel in world literature, *The Tale of Genji*, was written by MURASAKI SHIKIBU [moo-rah-SAH-key] (ca. 976–ca. 1026), a member of the lower echelons of medieval Japanese aristocracy. Her work is highly regarded for its psychological subtlety and its rich portrayal of character.

The Heian era was a time of cultural sophistication, during which Japanese painters and poets broke away from the Chinese aesthetic influence of previous periods. To some extent, the novel romanticizes courtly life as the author experienced it, though without idealizing the characters so much that they lose their credibility. According to an eighteenth-century Japanese scholar, Matoori Noringa, the greatness of *The Tale of Genji* lies in the way it conveys the sorrow of human existence as reflected in the behavior of its hero, Genji. Though he violates the religious injunctions of Confucianism and Buddhism, Genji nonetheless "combines in himself all good things." Like the author who created him, Genji exhibits great sensitivity to the people who cross his path, especially the many women who share his love.

Heian Handscrolls.   The art of the Heian period sees a movement away from religious subjects to more secular concerns. The art also shows the development of a more distinctively indigenous Japanese style. Japanese landscape painting, for example, departed from Chinese depictions of majestic mountains, replacing them with representations of paddy fields and cherry blossoms. In general, Japanese landscapes of this period are more intricate than Chinese landscape paintings, evoking the sense of transience and poignant sadness frequently found in Japanese poetry.

One of the most distinctive of secular Japanese painting styles is exhibited in the painting of narrative handscrolls, or *emaki-mano*, associated with court life, and usually attributed to the artist TAKAYOSHI [ta-ka-YOH-shi]. Some of the most celebrated handscrolls are linked with *The Tale of Genji* (fig. 9.11). The oldest illustrations of this work date from ca. 1120, and survive only in fragments, along with short pieces of the handwritten text.

The highly decorative *Genji* illustrations emphasize the placement of figures, their costumes, and the use of color. The artist breaks up the composition by using screens, walls, and the kind of sliding panels found in the traditional Japanese home. Figures are shown at an angle, with the viewpoint from above. Women are depicted in broadly draped garments that hide their figures, leaving only their heads and hands visible. They are engaged in calm activity, one combing another's hair, while others read and look at picture scrolls. The overall effect is to convey a sense of court life quietly, with little dramatic action.

Map 9.2   Japan before the fifteenth century.

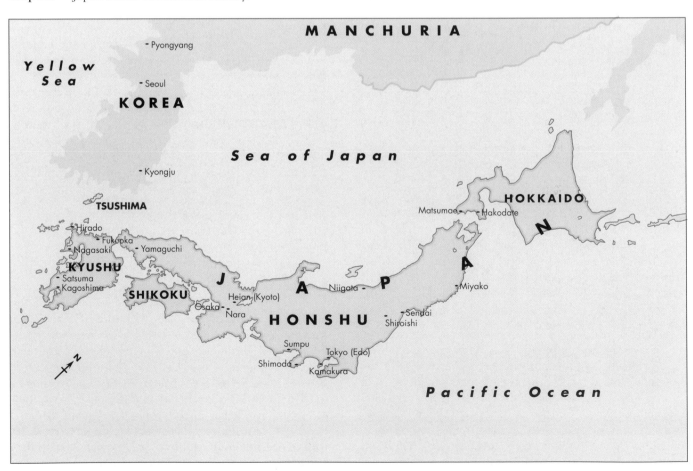

Figure 9.11 Attributed to Takayoshi, illustration to the Azumaya chapter of *The Tale of Genji*, late Heian period, twelfth century, handscroll, ink and color on paper, height $8\frac{1}{2}''$ (21.6 cm), Tokugawa Art Museum, Nagoya. This handscroll illustrates a scene from the world's oldest novel. Unlike Buddhist didactic illustrations, *Genji* illustrations were aimed at an aristocratic audience and reveal a nostalgia for the passing of an era of elegance, peace, and artistic prosperity.

THE KAMAKURA PERIOD

During the Heian era, rulers began to see their power diminish at the hands of the **samurai**, highly regarded and honored regional warriors in the service of the governing nobility. These warriors were at the disposal of warring families competing for the throne, and they were instrumental in the ascendancy of many rulers. The period is known as the Kamakura period because the capital was now moved to Kamakura. In a tradition inaugurated by MINAMOTO YORITOMO [MI-na-MO-to] (1147–1199), these warriors began to give themselves the title of **shogun** (general-in-chief) of the samurai. They continued to pay lip service to the official sovereign, but increasingly it was the shogun who exercised authority, a tradition that lasted in various forms until 1868 when imperial rule was properly restored. The shogun and his samurai prided themselves on their self-reliance, and they were particularly attracted to Zen, a form of Buddhism that promoted self-sufficiency.

Zen Buddhism. By the ninth century, Buddhism and Shinto had converged, to a certain extent, with the boundaries between the two religions becoming blurred. Shinto *kami* and Buddhist deities, for example, gradually became conflated. Buddhist priests used Shinto temples for meditation and worship; Shinto temples assumed elements of the Buddhist architectural style. Buddhism, however, began to assume prominence, temporarily

eclipsing Shintoism. Buddhism itself then underwent a transformation, as the Japanese converted the Chinese form of Buddhism they had inherited into their own uniquely Japanese form of Zen.

Nothing dominates Japanese cultural life after the rise of the shogunate more than Zen. Though it grew out of Indian and Chinese Buddhism, today Zen is often considered a distinctly Japanese religion, one that has influenced almost every aspect of Japanese cultural life, from civil ceremony and social etiquette, to flower arranging, the tea ceremony, painting, swordsmanship, haiku writing, and landscape architecture.

Zen has been defined as "the art of seeing into the nature of one's own being." It is less a religion or a philosophy than a way of life, an attitude, an active stance toward everyday experience. Like the Buddhism from which it sprang, Zen has no scripture, enforces no creed, requires no ritual ceremonies, has developed no theology. Nor is Zen concerned with the afterlife—with heaven or hell—or with the immortality of the soul. Its focus instead is on the world. When a Zen master was asked about life after death, he replied: "Leave that to Buddha, it is no business of ours."

When another Zen master was questioned as to how one could escape the reality of cold and heat, the pangs of hunger and the parching of thirst, he answered: "In winter you shiver, in summer you sweat. When you are hungry eat, and drink when you are thirsty." The point is

Then & Now

ZEN

Zen Buddhism was popularized in the United States through the writings of Teitaro Suzuki, especially his *Essays on Zen Buddhism*. These were first published in 1927 and then reprinted several times in the 1950s and 1960s as first the Beat generation and then the "hippies" discovered the philosophy. Suzuki was especially influential among artists, most notably the Abstract Expressionist painter Willem de Kooning and the composer John Cage, who studied with Suzuki in the 1940s (see Chapter 23).

So prominent and reverend a figure was Suzuki in the West that Christian Humphries, who was for many years president of the Buddhist Society in London, wrote in the preface to Suzuki's collected works, "To those unable to sit at the feet of the Master, his writings must be a substitute." But Suzuki was hardly a master. Raised a Zen Buddhist, he traveled to the USA in 1893 as interpreter for Soyen Shaku, a genuine Zen master, who was to introduce Zen to the World's Parliament of Religions in Chicago. A Chicago publisher soon enticed Suzuki to return to the United States to work as a translator. He became the first, and for many years remained probably the only, Zen Buddhist living in the USA.

Suzuki himself never claimed to be anything other than a lay authority on Zen, but he was taken by almost everyone to be a master. Whatever the case, Suzuki's version of Zen was very different from traditional Japanese Zen. Suzuki promised the possibility of "sudden" *satori*, or enlightenment. It should be said that of the three main Zen sects, only one is interested in *satori*—the one in which Suzuki was raised—and even for that sect it is only a starting point on the road to the negation of personality. But for Suzuki, *satori* was key. "Satori finds," he claimed, "a meaning hitherto hidden in our daily concrete particular experiences." This was an idea that American artists, well versed in the writings of Emerson and Thoreau, found compelling. The "Zen-man" was the consummate artist. As Suzuki himself put it in *Zen and Japanese Culture*, "While the artists have to resort to the canvas and brush or mechanical instruments to express themselves, Zen has no need of things external … The Zen-man is an artist [who] transforms his own life into a work of creation!" Suzuki's "Zen-man" is hardly the personality deprived of all sense of self, the product of Zen meditation. It is, rather, a distinctively American phenomenon.

---

that one does not try to escape physical reality. In Zen, one accepts it for what it is. Life is to be lived, not transcended, and Zen informs everything in one's life, from getting dressed and eating, to reading, working, and relaxing. Life is to be lived simply, directly, and attentively, even appreciatively. There is no mystery about it.

One aspect of Zen particularly attractive to Westerners is **satori**, the achievement of enlightenment. This is enlightenment of the kind taught by the Buddha, symbolized by a third eye, which opens not on a hidden world but on the world seen by the other two eyes. The third eye sees things as they really are, sees what is ever present but is yet to be discovered or noticed. Satori, then, is less an attainment of a special state of bliss or mystic ecstasy, than a realization or state of awareness. With enlightenment comes a transformation of the world from one that contains contradictions and oppositions to one that reflects unity, consistency, and harmony.

THE ASHIKAGA PERIOD

The Kamakura period ended in civil war in 1333, and insurrections of one kind or another continued to plague Japan almost continuously until 1573, when a central government was formed. During this era, known as the

---

Timeline 9.2 Early Japanese culture.

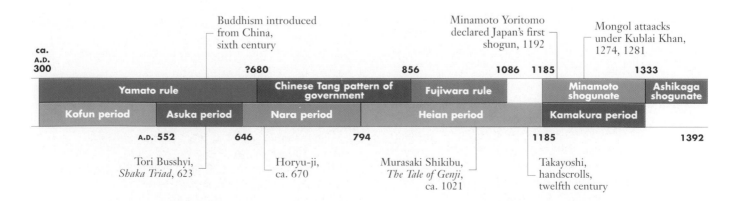

Figure 9.12 Shokintei (Pavilion of the Pine Lute), Katsura Palace gardens, near Kyoto, early 1660s. Named after the sound of wind in the pines that surround it, the pavilion is larger than many tea huts, but its setting is almost ideal.

Ashikaga period, Japan was ruled by shoguns and their samurai warriors, and as a result Zen practice dominated Japanese life.

Tea Ceremony. One of the major cultural institutions founded on Zen thinking is the *cha-no-yu*, or the "tea ceremony," which developed during the Ashikaga period and survives to this day. According to Rikyu, one of its founders, "The tea ceremony is nothing more than boiling water, making tea, and drinking it." But it is a much more elaborate ceremony than Rikyu lets on, one that the Portuguese Jesuit priest Joao Rodrigues (1562–1633) described after thirty years of life in Japan as a ritual designed "to produce courtesy, politeness, modesty, moderation, calmness, peace of body and soul, without pride or arrogance, fleeing from all ostentation, pomp, external grandeur and magnificence."

The tea ceremony began in the 1470s when the Ashikaga ruler Yoshimasa retreated from the conflicts that dominated urban life to collect Chinese paintings and ceramics at his villa on the island of Higashiyama. The monk Murata Juko suggested to him that by drinking tea in a small hut like that illustrated here, in the Katsura Palace gardens (fig. 9.12), with only a few companions, he could experience **wabi**, "lonely seclusion." Wabi is a heightened sense of awareness, in which the practitioner experiences, for instance, "the cold winter wind on his skin."

In the tea ceremony proper, the kettle, the simple pottery tea cups made in local Japanese kilns, even the

bamboo tea scoop were objects to be contemplated and appreciated for their humble practicality. The tea hut was decorated with a hanging scroll of painting or perhaps a flower arrangement appropriate for the time of year, and the hut itself was placed in a carefully designed garden. The self-conscious simplicity, even starkness, of the tea ceremony has continued to influence Japanese design and taste to this day.

READINGS

← THE BOOK OF SONGS
Selected Poems

The following lyrics from the ancient Chinese Book of Songs *reflect the importance of appropriate social behavior. They also reveal the way ancient Chinese poets used imagery, particularly images from nature to convey emotion.*

She Threw a Quince to Me

She threw a quince to me;
In requital I gave a bright girdle-gem.
No, not just as requital;
But meaning I would love her for ever.

She threw a tree-peach to me;
As requital I gave her a bright greenstone.

5

No, not just as requital;
But meaning I would love her for ever.

She threw a tree-plum to me;
In requital I gave her a bright jet-stone.   10
No, not just as requital,
But meaning I would love her for ever.

I Beg of You, Chung Tzu

I beg of you, Chung Tzu,
Do not climb into our homestead,
Do not break the willows we have planted.
Not that I mind about the willows,
But I am afraid of my father and mother.   5
Chung Tzu I dearly love;
But of what my father and mother say
Indeed I am afraid.

I beg of you, Chung Tzu,
Do not climb over our wall,   10
Do not break the mulberry-trees we have
    planted.
Not that I mind about the mulberry-trees,
But I am afraid of my brothers.
Chung Tzu I dearly love;
But of what my brothers say   15
Indeed I am afraid.

I beg of you, Chung Tzu,
Do not climb into our garden,
Do not break the hard-wood we have planted.
Not that I mind about the hard-wood,   20
But I am afraid of what people will say.
Chung Tzu I dearly love;
But of all that people will say
Indeed I am afraid.

If Along the Highroad

If along the highroad
I caught hold of your sleeve,
Do not hate me;
Old ways take time to overcome.

If along the highroad   5
I caught hold of your hand,
Do not be angry with me;
Friendship takes time to overcome.

By the Willows of the Eastern Gate

By the willows of the Eastern Gate,
Whose leaves are so thick,
At dusk we were to meet;
And now the morning star is bright.

By the willows of the Eastern Gate,   5
Whose leaves are so close,
At dusk we were to meet;
And now the morning star is pale.

✦ **CONFUCIUS**
from *The Analects*

Soon after Confucius's death, his sayings and those of his followers were gathered together in a collection called The Analects. *Not surprisingly, especially since Confucius lived in a period of great social unrest in China, these emphasize the duties and obligations of the individual and proper forms of human conduct. Confucius is referred to as the "Master."*

Book I

1. The Master said, "Is it not a pleasure, having learned something, to try it out at due intervals? Is it not a joy to have friends come from afar? Is it not gentlemanly not to take offence when others fail to appreciate your abilities?"
11. The Master said, "Observe what a man has in mind to do when his father is living, and then observe what he does when his father is dead. If, for three years, he makes no changes to his father's ways, he can be said to be a good son."

Book II

1. The Master said, "The rule of virtue can be compared to the Pole Star which commands the homage of the multitude of stars without leaving its place."
2. The Master said, "The *Odes* [*The Book of Songs*] are three hundred in number. They can be summed up in one phrase,

   Swerving not from the right path."

3. The Master said, "Guide them by edicts, keep them in line with punishments, and the common people will stay out of trouble but will have no sense of shame. Guide them by virtue, keep them in line with the rites, and they will, besides having a sense of shame, reform themselves."
4. The Master said, "At fifteen I set my heart on learning; at thirty I took my stand; at forty I came to be free from doubts; at fifty I understood the Decree of Heaven; at sixty my ear was atuned; at seventy I followed my heart's desire without overstepping the line."
19. Duke Ai asked, "What must I do before the common people will look up to me?"

   Confucius answered, "Raise the straight and set them over the crooked and the common people will look up to you. Raise the crooked and set them over the straight and the common people will not look up to you."
7. The Master said, "There is no contention between gentlemen. The nearest to it is, perhaps, archery. In archery they bow and make way for one another as they go up and on coming down they drink together. Even the way they contend is gentlemanly."
21. Duke Ai asked Tsai Wo about the altar to the god of earth. Tsai Wo replied, " The Hsia used the pine, the Yin used the cedar, and the men of Chou used the chestnut (*li*), saying that it made the common people tremble (*li*)."

   The Master, on hearing of this reply, commented, "One does not explain away what is already done, one does not argue against what is already accomplished, and one does not condemn what has already gone by."

✦ LI BAI

Selected Poems

Li Bai is often associated with the influences of Confucianism and Taoism. However, Li Bai has himself exerted a tremendous influence, first of all on Chinese and Japanese poets, but also in the West, where, through his ability to express profound feelings through his use of landscape, he is sometimes referred to as the "first Romantic" poet.

Yearning

Endless yearning
    Here in Ch'ang-an,
Where the cricket spinners cry autumn
    by the rail of the golden well,
Where flecks of frost blow chill,   *5*
    and the bedmat's color, cold.
No light from the lonely lantern,
    the longing almost broken—
Then roll up the curtain, gaze on the moon,
    heave the sigh that does no good.   *10*
A lady lovely like the flowers,
    beyond that wall of clouds,
And above, the blue dark of heavens high,
And below, the waves of pale waters
Endless the sky, far the journey,   *15*
    the fleet soul suffers in flight,
And in its dreams can't touch its goal
    through the fastness of barrier mountains—
        Then endless yearning
    Crushes a man's heart.   *20*

Dialogue in the Mountains

You ask me why I lodge in these emerald hills;
I laugh, don't answer—my heart is at peace.
Peach blossoms and flowing waters
    go off to mysterious dark,
And there is another world,   *5*
    not of mortal men.

✦ MURASAKI SHIKIBU

from *The Tale of Genji*

One modern critic has suggested that The Tale of Genji *is "a study of the distinctive features of love—its language, forms, and conventions" and that its author is "really interested in the dynamics of love at the emotional and psychological level." These qualities are well illustrated in the following excerpt.*

The Shell of the Locust

Genji lay sleepless.

"I am not used to such treatment. Tonight I have for the first time seen how a woman can treat a man. The shock and the shame are such that I do not know how I can go on living."

The boy was in tears, which made him even more charming. The slight form, the not too long hair—was it Genji's imagination that he was much like his sister? The resemblance was very affecting, even if imagined. It would be undignified to make an issue of the matter and seek the woman out, and so Genji passed the night in puzzled resentment. The boy found him less friendly than usual.

Genji left before daylight. Very sad, thought the boy, lonely without him.

The lady too passed a difficult night. There was no further word from Genji. It seemed that he had had enough of her. She would not be happy if he had in fact given her up, but with half her mind she dreaded another visit. It would be as well to have an end of the affair. Yet she went on grieving.

For Genji there was gnawing dissatisfaction. He could not forget her, and he feared he was making a fool of himself.

"I am in a sad state," he said to the boy. "I try to forget her, and I cannot. Do you suppose you might contrive another meeting?"

It would be difficult, but the boy was delighted even at this sort of attention. With childish eagerness he watched for an opportunity. Presently the governor of Kii had to go off to his province. The lady had nothing to do through the long twilight hours. Under cover of darkness, the boy took Genji to the governor's mansion in his own carriage. Genji had certain misgivings. His guide was after all a mere child. But this was no time for hesitation. Dressed inconspicuously, he urged the boy on, lest they arrive after the gates were barred. The carriage was brought in through a back gate and Genji dismounted.

So young a boy attracted little attention and indeed little deference from the guards. He left Genji at an east door to the main hall. He pounded on the south shutters and went inside.

"Shut it, shut it!" shrieked the women. "The whole world can see us."

"But why do you have them closed on such a warm evening?"

"The lady from the west wing has been here since noon. They have been at Go."

Hoping to see them at the Go board, Genji slipped from his hiding place and made his way through the door and the blinds. The shutter through which the boy had gone was still raised. Genji could see through to the west. One panel of a screen just inside had been folded back, and the curtains, which should have shielded off the space beyond, had been thrown over their frames, perhaps because of the heat. The view was unobstructed.

There was a lamp near the women. The one in silhouette with her back against a pillar—would she be the one on whom his heart was set? He looked first at her. She seemed to have on a purple singlet with a woven pattern, and over it a cloak of which the color and material were not easy to determine. She was a small, rather ordinary lady with delicate features. She evidently wanted to conceal her face even from the girl opposite, and she kept her thin little hands tucked in her sleeves Her opponent was facing east, and Genji had a full view of her face. Over a singlet of white gossamer she had thrown a purplish cloak, and both garments were somewhat carelessly open all the way to the band of the red trousers She was very handsome, tall and plump and of a fair complexion, and the lines of her head and forehead were strong and pleasing. It was a sunny face, with a beguiling cheerfulness about the eyes and mouth. Though not particularly long, the hair was rich and thick, and very beautiful where it fell about her shoulders. He could detect no marked flaws, and saw why her father, the governor of Iyo, so cherished her. It might help, to be sure, if she were just a little quieter. Yet she did not seem to be merely silly. She brimmed with good spirits as she placed a stone upon a dead spot to signal the end of the game.

"Just a minute, if you please," said the other very calmly. "It is not quite over. You will see that we have a *ko to get out of the way first.*"

"I've lost, I've lost. Let's just see what I have in the corners." She counted up on her fingers. "Ten, twenty, thirty, forty." She would have had no trouble, he thought, taking the full count of the baths of Iyo — though her manner might have been just a touch inelegant.

The other woman, a model of demureness, kept her face hidden. Gazing at her, Genji was able to make out the details of the profile. The eyelids seemed a trifle swollen, the lines of the nose were somewhat erratic, and there was a weariness, a want of luster, about the face. It was, one had to admit, a little on the plain side. Yet she clearly paid attention to her appearance, and there were details likely to draw the eye to a subtler sensibility than was evident in her lively companion. The latter, very engaging indeed, laughed ever more happily. There was no denying the bright gaiety, and in her way she was interesting enough. A shallow, superficial thing, no doubt, but to his less than pure heart she seemed a prize not to be flung away. All the ladies he knew were so prim and proper. This was the first time he had seen one so completely at her ease. He felt a little guilty, but not so guilty that he would have turned away had he not heard the boy coming back. He slipped outside.

Apologetic that his master should still be at the beginning, the boy said that the unexpected guest had interfered with his plans.

"You mean to send me off frustrated once more? It is really too much."

"No, sir. But I must ask you to wait until the other lady has gone. I'll arrange everything then, I promise you."

Things seemed to be arranging themselves. The boy was very young, but he was calmly self-possessed and had a good eye for the significant things.

The game of Go was apparently over. There was a stir inside, and a sound as of withdrawing.

"Where will that boy have gone?" Now there was a banging of shutters. "Let's get the place closed up."

"No one seems to be stirring." said Genji after a time. "Go and do your best."

The boy knew well enough that it was not his sister's nature to encourage frivolity. He must admit Genji when there was almost no one with her.

"Is the guest still here?" asked Genji. "I would like a glimpse of her."

"Quite impossible. There are curtains inside the shutters."

Genji was amused, but thought it would be bad manners to let the boy know that he had already seen the lady. "How slowly time does go by."

This time the boy knocked on the corner door and was admitted.

"I'll just make myself comfortable here," he said, spreading bedclothes where one or two of the sliding doors had been left open. "Come in, breezes."

Numbers of older women seemed to be sleeping out near the veranda The girl who had opened the door seemed to have joined them. The boy feigned sleep for a time. Then, spreading a screen to block the light, he motioned Genji inside.

Genji was suddenly shy, fearing he would be defeated once more. He followed the boy all the same. Raising a curtain, he slipped into the main room. It was very quiet, and his robes rustled alarmingly.

With one part of her mind the woman was pleased that he had not given up. But the nightmare of the earlier evening had not left her. Brooding days, sleepless nights — it was summer, and yet it was 'budless spring.'

Her companion at Go, meanwhile, was as cheerful as could be. "I shall stay with you tonight," she announced. It was not likely that she would have trouble sleeping.

The lady herself sensed that something was amiss. Detecting an unusual perfume, she raised her head. It was dark where the curtain had been thrown over the frame, but she could see a form creeping toward her. In a panic, she got up. Pulling a singlet of raw silk over her shoulders, she slipped from the room.

Genji was delighted to see that there was only one lady asleep behind the curtains. There seemed to be two people asleep out toward the veranda. As he pulled aside the bedclothes it seemed to him that the lady was somewhat larger than he would have expected. He became aware of one odd detail after another in the sleeping figure, and guessed what had happened. How very stupid! And how ridiculous he would seem if the sleeper were to awaken and see that she was the victim of a silly mistake. It would be equally silly to pursue the lady he had come for, now that she had made her feelings so clear. A new thought came to him: might this be the girl who had so interested him in the lamplight? If so, what had he to lose? It will be observed that a certain fickleness was at work.

The girl was now awake, and very surprised. Genji felt a little sorry for her. But though inexperienced in the ways of love, she was bright and modern, and she had not entirely lost her composure. He was at first reluctant to identify himself. She would presently guess, however, and what did it matter if she did? As for the unfriendly one who had fled him and who was so concerned about appearances—he did have to think of her reputation, and so he said to the girl that he had taken advantage of directional taboos to visit her. A more experienced lady would have had no trouble guessing the truth, but this one did not sense that his explanation was a little forced. He was not displeased with her, nor was he strongly drawn to her. His heart was resentfully on the other. No doubt she would be off in some hidden chamber gloating over her victory. She had shown a most extraordinary firmness of purpose. In a curious way, her hostility made her memorable. The girl beside him had a certain young charm of her own, and presently he was deep in vows of love.

"The ancients used to say that a secret love runs deeper than an open one." He was most persuasive. "Think well of me. I must worry about appearances, and it is not as if I could go where my desires take me. And you: there are people who would not at all approve. That is sad. But you must not forget me."

"I'm afraid." Clearly she was afraid. "I won't be able to write to you."

"You are right that we would not want people to know. But there is the little man I brought with me tonight. We can exchange notes through him. Meanwhile you must behave as if nothing has happened." He took as a keepsake a summer robe the other lady seemed to have thrown off.

The boy was sleeping nearby. The adventure was on his mind, however, and Genji had no trouble arousing him. As he opened the door an elderly serving woman called out in surprise.

"Who's there?"

"Just me," replied the boy in some confusion.

"Wherever are you going at this time of the night?" The woman came out, wishing to be helpful.

"Nowhere," said the boy gruffly. "Nowhere at all."

He pushed Genji through the door. Dawn was approaching. The woman caught sight of another figure in the moonlight.

"And who is with you? Oh, Mimbu, of course. Only Mimbu reaches such splendid heights." Mimbu was a lady who was the victim of much humor because of her unusual stature. So he was out walking with Mimbu, muttered the old woman. "One of these days you'll be as tall as Mimbu yourself." Chattering away, she followed after them. Genji was horrified, but could not very well shove her inside. He pulled back into the darkness of a gallery.

Still she followed. "You've been with our lady, have you? I've been having a bad time with my stomach these last few days and I've kept to my room. But she called me last night and said she wanted more people around. I'm still having a terrible time. Terrible," she muttered again, getting no answer. "Well, goodbye, then."

She moved on, and Genji made his escape. He saw more than ever how dangerous these adventures can be.

The boy went with him to Nijo. Genji recounted the happenings of the night. The boy had not done very well, he said, shrugging his shoulders in annoyance at the thought of the woman's coldness. The boy could find no answer.

"I am rejected, and there is nothing to be done for me. But why could she not have sent a pleasant answer? I'm no match for that husband of hers. That's where the trouble lies." But when he went to bed he had her cloak beneath his own. He kept the boy beside him, audience for his laments.

"It's not that you aren't a nice enough boy, and it's not that I'm not fond of you. But because of your family I must have doubts about the durability of our relationship."

A remark which plunged the boy into the darkest melancholy.

Genji was still unable to sleep. He said that he required an inkstone. On a fold of paper he jotted down a verse as if for practice:
'Beneath a tree, a locust's empty shell.
Sadly I muse upon the shell of a lady.'

He wondered what the other one, the stepdaughter, would be thinking of him; but though he felt rather sorry for her and though he turned the matter over in his mind, he sent no message. The lady's fragrance lingered in the robe he had taken. He kept it with him, gazing fondly at it.

The boy, when he went to his sister's house, was crushed by the scolding he received. "This is the sort of thing a person cannot be expected to put up with. I may try to explain what has happened, but can you imagine that people will not come to their own conclusions? Does it not occur to you that even your good master might wish to see an end to this childishness?"

Badgered from the left and badgered from the right, the poor boy did not know where to turn. He took out Genji's letter. In spite of herself his sister opened and read it. That reference to the shell of the locust: he had taken her robe, then. How very embarrassing. A sodden rag, like the one discarded by the fisherman of Ise.

The other lady, her stepdaughter, returned in some disorder to her own west wing. She had her sad thoughts all to herself, for no one knew what had happened. She watched the boy's comings and goings, thinking that there might be some word; but in the end there was none. She did not have the imagination to guess that she had been a victim of mistaken identity. She was a lighthearted and inattentive creature, but now she was lost in sad thoughts.

The lady in the main hall kept herself under tight control. She could see that his feelings were not to be described as shallow, and she longed for what would not return, her maiden days. Besides his poem she jotted down a poem by Lady Ise:

The dew upon the fragile locust wing
Is lost among the leaves. Lost are my tears.

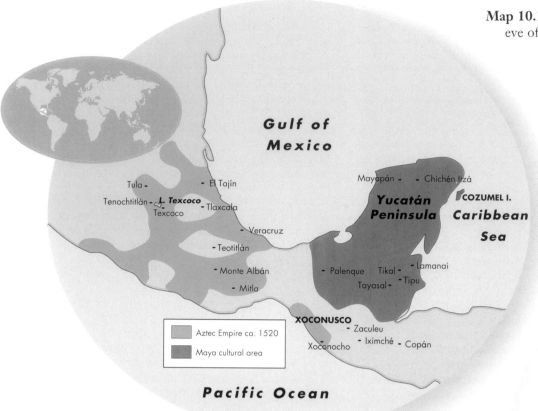

Map 10.1   Mesoamerica on the eve of the Spanish conquest.

Gulf of
Mexico

Tula -   - El Tajín

Tenochtitlán - **L. Texcoco**
                - Tlaxcala
        Texcoco

Mayapán -   - Chichén Itzá

**Yucatán
Peninsula**   **COZUMEL I.**
                **Caribbean
                Sea**

                - Veracruz

                - Teotitlán

                - Monte Albán   - Palenque   Tikal -   - Lamanai
                                                        - Tipu
                    - Mitla   Tayasal -

XOCONUSCO
                        - Zaculeu

                Xoconocho   - Iximché   - Copán

	Aztec Empire ca. 1520
	Maya cultural area

Pacific Ocean

THE
← CIVILIZATIONS
OF THE AMERICAS

314

CHAPTER 10

⤙ *Mesoamerica*

⤙ *The Cultures of Peru*

⤙ *North America*

Machu Picchu, Peru, ca. A.D. 1450.

Sometime between 30,000 and 12,000 years ago, at the height of the Ice Age, tribal hunters began to migrate from Asia into the Americas across a land bridge that extended for perhaps a thousand miles south of the present-day Bering Straits. This giant plain was rich in grass and animal life, and the tribes were naturally drawn on further across it, and then on southward, in pursuit of game. By 11,000 B.C., they had reached the tip of South America and the Atlantic coast of North America.

As the ice melted and the oceans rose at the close of the Ice Age, the tribes in the Americas were cut off from Asia and Europe. This isolation lasted until October 12, 1492, when Christopher Columbus landed on San Salvador in the Bahamas. Thinking he was on the east coast of Asia, near India, Columbus called the people who met him "Indios," Indians. While these Native Americans seemed simple and uncivilized to Columbus, they were in fact the descendants of ancient and often quite magnificent civilizations, some of which dated back to the first millennium B.C.

MESOAMERICA

Mesoamerica extends from central Mexico to Honduras, and includes Belize and Guatemala. The ancient Mesoamerican cultures include those of the Olmecs (1300–600 B.C.), the Maya (250 B.C.–A.D. 1000), the Zapotecs (400–800), and the Toltecs (900–1200), precursors of the Aztecs (1350–1521), along with the civilization of Teotihuacán (100–800). The Mesoamericans spoke many languages. Among these was the Nahua family of languages, which includes thes language of the Aztecs and the Maya, dialects of which survive to this day in southern Mexico and Guatemala. The diverse early Mesoamerican civilizations shared other cultural features, including hieroglyphic writing, an applied knowledge of astronomy, and a form of monarchical government intimately linked with religious ideas and practices.

THE OLMECS

The earliest Mesoamerican art dates from about 1300 B.C., when the Olmecs inhabited the southern coast of the Gulf of Mexico, especially the area between Veracruz and Tabasco. There is some question whether the Olmecs were a distinct people and culture or whether the term "Olmec," which derives from a word for rubber, refers to an artistic style that prevailed throughout ancient Central America.

Whoever they were, the Olmecs were outstanding stone carvers. The most remarkable carvings that have survived to the present day are a series of sixteen colossal stone heads up to twelve feet high (fig. 10.1). Eight of these heads were found in San Lorenzo, Veracruz, where they were placed facing outward on the circumference

Figure 10.1 Colossal Head, from La Venta, Mexico, Olmec culture, ca. 900–500 B.C., basalt, height 7′5″ (2.26 m), La Venta Park, Villahermosa, Tabasco, Mexico. This example of a giant carved stone head represents the height of sculptural achievement among the ancient Olmecs.

of a ceremonial area. They are carved of basalt. Since the nearest basalt quarry is fifty miles away in the Tuxtla Mountains, the enormous stones from which the heads were carved had, apparently, to be dragged down from the mountains, loaded onto rafts, floated down to the Gulf of Mexico, then up river to San Lorenzo, and finally dragged up and positioned on the ceremonial plateau.

Believed to be portraits of Olmec rulers, the heads share similar facial features, including flattened noses, thick lips, and puffy cheeks. They all are capped with headgear similar to old-style American football helmets. This is believed to have served as protection in war and in a type of ceremonial ball game played throughout Mesoamerica. Among other discoveries at San Lorenzo are stone figurines of ball players and a ball court.

TEOTIHUACÁN

Among the most splendid of all Mesoamerican sites must be the ancient city of Teotihuacán [te-oh-te-wu-KAN], which means "where one becomes a god." Teotihuacán (fig. 10.2) grew to dominance after 300 B.C. By the time it reached the height of its political and cultural influence, between ca. A.D. 350–650, its population numbered between 100,000 and 200,000, making it one of the largest cities on earth at the time.

The people of Teotihuacán were great pyramid-builders. The city is laid out in a grid pattern with a giant avenue (the Avenue of the Dead) at its center. This central artery links two great pyramids, the Pyramids of the Moon and of the Sun, which are the focal points of six hundred smaller pyramids, five hundred workshop areas, nearly two thousand apartment compounds, numerous plazas, and a giant market area. Built in about A.D. 150 over a natural cave (but only rediscovered in 1971), the Pyramid of the Sun is oriented to mark the passage of the sun from east to west and the rising of the stellar constellation the Pleiades on the days of the equinox. Thus it links the underworld to the heavens, the forces of life and death.

Along the Avenue of the Dead are a series of ziggurat-like structures with numerous steps leading to an elevated platform, which originally supported a temple.

After the Pyramids of the Sun and the Moon, the most important structure in Teotihuacán was the Temple of Quetzalcoatl, the god of priestly wisdom. This temple contains elaborate relief carvings, which include the heads of feathered serpents and fire serpents.

The overall design and layout of Teotihuacán suggests its role as an astronomical and ritualistic center. The relation of the Pyramid of the Sun to the others suggests the order of the universe, a cosmological order that influenced all aspects of life, including political organization, social behavior, and religious ritual. Even time was represented. Each of the two staircases of the Pyramid of the Sun, for example, contains 182 steps, which, when the platform at the apex is added, together total 365. This spatial representation of the solar calendar is echoed in the Temple of Quetzalcoatl, which has 364 serpent fangs.

By about 700, Teotihuacán's influence had waned, and the city was sacked and burned in about 750. We can only speculate about what finally led to its demise, but an ecological explanation is possible. The surrounding countryside had been pillaged to provide lime for the mortar used to build Teotihuacán. As the city's population grew, adequate provision of food became a problem.

Figure 10.2 Teotihuacán, Mexico, Teotihuacán culture, A.D. 350–650. The city of Teotihuacán covered an area of nine miles square and contained between 100,000 and 200,000 people, an enormous scale and population for a culture of its time.

Coupled with the effects of drought, the environmental catastrophe wreaked upon the countryside probably made it impossible to maintain a stable civilization.

MAYAN CULTURE

The ancient Maya inhabited the Yucatán peninsula, which extends into Belize and Guatemala, parts of the Mexican states of Chiapas and Tabasco, and the western part of Honduras and El Salvador. The culture appears to have lasted from about 250 B.C. to A.D. 1000. Although the Maya possessed their own form of hieroglyphic writing, they shared with other Mesoamerican peoples the use of books made of fig-bark paper or deerskin that unfolded into screens. The ancient Maya are set apart from their ancient Mesoamerican neighbors, however, in their arithmetical and astronomical knowledge, which rivaled that of the ancient Babylonians. The Maya possessed a profound understanding of the regularity and continuity of the heavenly bodies, which they saw as a metaphor for the ruler's consistent safeguarding of his people.

The Mayan Universe.   For the Maya, the universe consisted of three layers—the Upperworld of the heavens, the Middleworld of human civilization, and the Underworld below—linked by a great tree, the Wacah Chan, which grew from the center of the Middleworld and from which the cardinal directions flowed. Each direction possessed its own symbolic significance and was represented by its own color, bird, and gods. East was the principal direction, since the sun rose there, and its color was red. North was the direction of the dead, and its color was white. The king was the personification of the Wacah Chan. When he stood at the top of a pyramid in ritual activity, he was seen to link the three layers of the universe in his own person. During such rituals, the king would let his own blood in order to give sustenance to the spiritual world. While ritual bloodletting seems to many people to be a barbaric or at least an exotic practice, it should be remembered that Christians symbolically drink the blood of Jesus when they celebrate Holy Communion—the role of blood in Mayan ritual is similar.

To the Maya, time was not linear, as we conceive it, but cyclical. They used two calendars. The first was a 365-day farming calendar which consisted of eighteen "months" of twenty days each and one short month of just five days. The second was a sacred calendar of 260 days which probably relates to the average length of human gestation from the first missed menstrual flow to birth (which is actually 266 days). It is clear that this second calendar possesses a close connection to Mayan bloodletting rituals. The Mayans combined the two calendars to create a long cycle of fifty-two years, or 18,980 days (a particular day in one calendar will fall on the same day in the other calendar every fifty-two years), at the end of which time repeated itself.

Tikal.   Among the most important sites of classic Mayan culture is that of Tikal [te-KAL], in present-day Guatemala. There, one of the great "ancestors" of Mayan civilization, Yax Moch Xoc (r. A.D. 219–238), ruled over a city which contained in an area of just over six square miles six giant temple-pyramids used for the celebration of religious rituals of the kind described above.

The meticulously ordered layout of Teotihuacán is not characteristic of Mayan cities. Tikal and other Mayan urban centers seem instead to have grown by accretion, undergoing rebuilding and modification over centuries. Most striking among the remains of Tikal's buildings are

---

Timeline 10.1   Mesoamerican cultures.

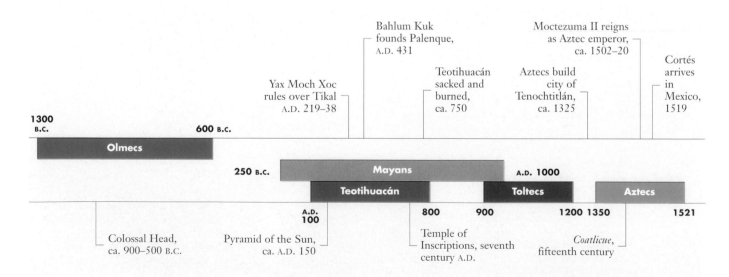

Figure 10.3 Tikal, Guatemala, Maya culture, ca. A.D. 700. Since Maya rituals were conducted in the open air, temple architecture atop pyramids emphasized external features.

six enormous temple-pyramids (fig. 10.3). Two of these are unusually steep, rising to a height of nearly 230 feet, and face each other across a large grassy square. Each is topped by an extension that resembles the comb of a rooster, called a "roof comb," and gives the impression of an elevated throne on an enormously high dais.

War dominated Tikal life. For two hundred years after A.D. 300, Tikal exercised power over the southeastern region of Mesoamerica. Its patron and protector was the Jaguar God, whose strength and hunting ability were likened to the power of the king himself and the warlike ferocity of the Tikal people. Like the king, the jaguar can adapt to every environment, hunting with equal facility on land, in water, and even in the Upperworld of the trees. That it hunts at night, with eyesight that penetrates the darkness, suggests its magical powers.

The Jaguar Kings of Palenque. The Jaguar God is common to all Mesoamerican cultures, from the Olmecs to the Aztecs. At Palenque, the Mayan kings called themselves Bahlum, "Jaguar," and their history is recorded on the Temple of Inscriptions (fig. 10.4). According to king-lists carved in the temple's corridors, the first king was Bahlum Kuk ("Jaguar Quetzal"), who founded the city on March 11, A.D. 431.

These king-lists, which record a dynasty of some twelve kings, were commissioned by two rulers, Pacal ("Shield") and his oldest son Chan Bahlum ("Snake Jaguar"). Pacal ruled for sixty-seven years, beginning in 615, and the Temple of Inscriptions was erected as his

tomb. In 1952, the Mexican archaeologist Alberto Ruz discovered a hidden staircase at the heart of the temple, and at its bottom Pacal's body, adorned with a jade collar and green headband, lying in a red-painted stone sarcophagus. The outside of the sarcophagus is decorated

Figure 10.4 Temple of Inscriptions, Palenque, Mexico, Maya culture, seventh century A.D. Rising in nine steps, like the temples at Tikal, the temple is inscribed with the history of the Palenque kings and rests over the grave of Pacal, one of its greatest leaders.

Then & Now

THE MAYA

Like Pacal himself, Palenque and the other Mayan states would eventually fall. Some time in the ninth century, the Maya abandoned their cities and returned to the countryside to farm, where their descendants work the fields to this day. Scattered across the southern Mexican state of Chiapas and throughout Guatemala, the contemporary Mayans speak twenty different dialects of their original language and engage in distinctly different cultural practices, sometimes in villages separated by no more than ten or twelve miles. In Chiapas, for instance, the Mayan inhabitants of the village of Zinacantán characteristically dress in bright red and purple and celebrate fiestas with loud bands and fireworks, while in nearby Chamula the men wear white or black wool serapes, carry large,

intimidating sticks, and practice a stern, mystical brand of Catholicism that blends Mayan interest in the spirit world of animals with a part-Christian, part-Mayan sense of self-sacrifice.

Many traditional Mayan practices survive in contemporary culture. Not only do the beautiful embroidery and weaving of the contemporary Mayans contain references to ancient Mayan hieroglyphics, but Mayan women still associate giving birth with the ancient 260-day calendar. In fact, children born on particular days are still esteemed by contemporary Mayans as "daykeepers," persons able to receive messages from the external world, both natural and supernatural, through their bodies. These daykeepers describe a sensation in their bodies as if air were rapidly moving over it in a flickering manner, similar to sheet lightning moving over a lake at night. The daykeepers learn to

interpret these tremblings and will eventually become the head "mother-fathers" or priest-shamans of their respective families.

Blood also continues to play a significant role in contemporary Mayan culture. Throughout Guatemala and Chiapas, blood is still considered to be an animate object, capable of speaking. Shamans can receive messages from a patient's blood by "pulsing," or touching a patient's body at various pressure points. An ancient poem, which continues to be recited among contemporary Mayan peoples who no longer practice the ritual, describes the dance of the bowman, who sharpens his arrows and dances around the victims in preparation for their sacrifice. The song recalls and memorializes the staging of the sacrificial action, and testifies to the importance of memory as an aspect of Mayan culture.

with a magnificent stone relief carving (fig. 10.5), which depicts Pacal's fall down the Wacah Chan, the great tree at the center of the world. Pacal lands at the bottom on an altarlike image that represents the setting sun.

THE TOLTECS AND AZTECS

Among the best known of the Mesoamerican civilizations is that of the Aztecs (or Mexica, as they referred to themselves). This civilization flourished relatively late, after approximately 1350, and continued until it was overcome by the Spaniards in 1521.

The greatest Aztec families claimed descent from the Toltecs, who were said to have invented the calendar and who were the mightiest of warriors. The Toltecs came to power in Tula in Hidalgo Province around A.D. 900 after Teotihuacán's power had diminished. In the twelfth century the militaristic Toltecs came to a violent end, when Tula was burned and its inhabitants scattered. Among the escaping tribes were the Mexica, who wandered into the Valley of Mexico around 1325 and built a village on the shores of Lake Texcoco. There they dug canals, draining high areas of the lake and converting

Figure 10.5 Sarcophagus lid, tomb of Pacal, Temple of Inscriptions, Palenque, Mexico, Maya culture, ca. A.D. 683, limestone, ca. 12′6″ × 7′ (3.80 × 2.14 m). The lid represents Pacal's fall in death from the sacred tree of the Maya, whose roots are in the earth and whose branches are in the heavens.

them into fertile fields, and also built the magnificent city of Tenochtitlán. By 1440, when MONTEZUMA ILHUICAMINA [mon-tay-ZOO-mah] (r. 1440–1486) assumed power, they considered themselves masters of the entire world.

Perhaps the most frequently cited aspect of Aztec culture is human sacrifice, which was linked with religious ritual. As in Mayan culture, the shedding of human blood was seen as necessary for the continuance of the earth's fertility. The sun, moon, earth, and vegetation gods required human blood for their sustenance and the continuance of human life. During the reign of Moctezuma Ilhuicamina's successor, AHUITZOTL (r. 1486–1501), no fewer than twenty thousand captives were sacrificed in the city.

The central activity of the Aztec state was war, with the primary goal being to secure enough captives for sacrifice. Young men were prepared for war from their birth. A newborn male was greeted with war cries by his midwife, who took him from the mother and dedicated him to the Sun and to battle. His umbilical cord was buried by a veteran warrior in a place of battle. Following soon upon birth was the naming ceremony, during which the baby boy's hand was closed around a tiny bow, arrows, and shield. Shortly after this ceremony, priests fitted the child with the decorative lip-plug worn by Aztec warriors.

At puberty most commoner (i.e. non-royal) boys, with the exception of those destined to become priests, were placed under the jurisdiction of the youth house, which was associated with a local warrior house. Although young boys were trained for war, they were also taught various horticultural, mercantile, hunting, and fishing skills. Nonetheless, the way a young man secured prestige and fame was in war rather than in the pursuit of a vocation, with success measured in the number of enemy captured alive for later ritual killing on ceremonial occasions.

For Aztec men, dying in battle was considered a great honor, as is made evident in the following Nahuatl song:

> There is nothing like death in war,
> nothing like the flowery death
> so precious to Him who gives life:
> far off I see it: my heart yearns for it!

Aztec art typically reflects the fierceness of the culture. A colossal statue of Coatlicue, the "Serpent Skirt," (fig. 10.6), goddess of the earth, shows a face with two serpent heads set on a thick powerful body. The serpents may represent blood jetting from the heads of ritually sacrificed women. Coatlicue's necklace is made up of human hearts and hands, with a human skull dangling at its base. Her skirt, which consists of writhing snakes, suggests sexual activity and its aftermath, birth.

Coatlicue is said to embody the Aztecs' belief in the creative principle, an attitude reflected in their love of

Figure 10.6 Coatlicue, Aztec, fifteenth century, stone, height 8′6″ (2.65 m), Museo Nacional de Antropologia, Mexico City. With her two rattlesnake heads and her skirt of serpents, along with large serpent fangs and necklace of human body parts, this Aztec deity induces awe in some, amazement in others who stand in her presence.

poetry. For the Aztecs, poetic speech, chanted or sung, was a creative force, one that not only conveyed their vision of the world but simultaneously enacted it. This power of the poetic spoken word was further displayed in the Aztec emphasis on systematic memorizing of poems and songs to preserve Aztec cultural traditions. Poetry was called "flower-song." In Aztec painted scrolls, poetry is represented as a flowered scroll emanating from an open mouth. This use of images—of flower and song together—was characteristic of Nahuatl metaphor, standing for poetry specifically, and more generally for the symbolic dimension of art.

THE CULTURES OF PERU
←

Peru is a land of dramatic geographical contrasts. Along the Pacific coast is one of the driest deserts in the world, where the rivers that descend out of the Andes mountains to the east form strips of oases. The Andes themselves are mammoth mountains, steep and high. Beyond them, to the east, lies the jungle, the tropical rainforest of the Amazon basin. These various terrains were home to a series of cultures, in particular the Moche and the Inca, before the arrival of Spanish colonists.

THE MOCHE

Among the early cultures to develop in Peru was that of the Moche, who controlled the area along the Peruvian north coast from A.D. 200 to 700. They lived around great **huacas**, pyramids made of sun-dried bricks, that rose high above the river floodplains. The largest was Huaca del Sol, the Pyramid of the Sun (fig. 10.7), which is 135 feet high—about two-thirds the height of the Pyramid of the Sun at Teotihuacán. Its truncated summit, however, is much vaster than Teotihuacán's. At least two-thirds of the pyramid was destroyed in the seventeenth century when Spanish colonists, searching for gold, diverted the Moche River into it and used the river's fast current to erode the mound. The colonists did indeed discover many gold artifacts buried with the dead in the sides of the structure. Unfortunately, they melted these artifacts down for bullion. What they left, however, is a record of the pyramid's construction. The sliced-away mound reveals at least eight stages of construction, and we can extrapolate to conclude that around 143 million bricks, made in rectangular molds from river silt, were used to build it.

The Moche were gifted metalsmiths, and they employed the same lost-wax technique used by the Romans. They adorned their copper sculptures with gold

Figure 10.8 *Moche Lord with a Feline*, Moche culture, Moche valley, Peru, ca. 100 B.C.–A.D. 500, painted ceramic, height 7½″ (19 cm), Art Institute of Chicago. Vessels such as this one were buried in large quantities with people of high rank.

by binding liquid gold to the copper surface at temperatures reaching as high as 1472°F (800°C). Further decorated with turquoise and shells, the results were often astonishingly beautiful. But the Moche were, above all, the most gifted ceramic artists in the Americas. In addition to working with potter's wheels, they also produced clay objects from molds, allowing them to reproduce the same objects again and again. Their most distinctive designs are found on bottles with stirrup-shaped spouts

Figure 10.7 Huaca del Sol (Pyramid of the Sun), Moche culture, Moche valley, Peru, ca. A.D. 500, height 135′ (41.1 m). Destroyed by Spanish colonizers seeking gold, this giant pyramid was built of more than 143 million sun-dried bricks.

that curve out from the body of the vessel. Bottles might be decorated with images of anything from the king or high official—as illustrated here (fig. 10.8), in ceremonial headdress and stroking a jaguar cub—to strange part-animal/part-human deities, and to everyday scenes such as a design for a typical Moche house. Warriors do battle on some of the vessels, prisoners are decapitated and dismembered on others, while on another famous example, a ruler in a giant feather headdress looks on as a line of naked prisoners passes before him.

Around 800, Moche society vanished. Evidence suggests that some time between 650 and 700 a great earthquake rattled the Andes, causing massive landslides, filling the rivers with debris, and blocking the normal channels to the ocean. As the sand washed ashore, huge dunes were formed, and the coastal plain was suddenly subject to vast, blinding sandstorms. It seems clear as well that El Niño, the warm current that slides up and down the Pacific coast of the Americas, changed the climate, destroying the fisheries and bringing torrential floods to the normally dry desert plain. It was all apparently too much, and the Moche disappeared.

THE INCA

Roughly contemporaneous with the rise of the Aztecs in Tenochtitlán was the emergence of the Inca civilization in Peru around 1300. The Incas inhabited the central Andes in what is today primarily Bolivia and Peru. They became a dominant military force around 1500, and appear also to have developed an organizational capacity to rival the engineering genius of the Romans. The Inca capital was at Cuzco, a city of 100,000 inhabitants at its height, built on a broad open valley between the Andes mountains north of Lake Titicaca. They called their empire *Tawantinsuyu*, "Land of Four Quarters," and, in fact, four highways emanated from Cuzco's central plaza, dividing the kingdom into quadrants. The 19,000 miles of roads and tracks that extended throughout their empire provide some indication of their engineering skill. The Incas understood the need for a functional communications system in a territory as large as theirs. Along these roadways, official runners could carry messages as far as 125–50 miles per day. And along them as well llamas carried goods and products for trade.

Map 10.2   The Inca empire, ca. 1525.

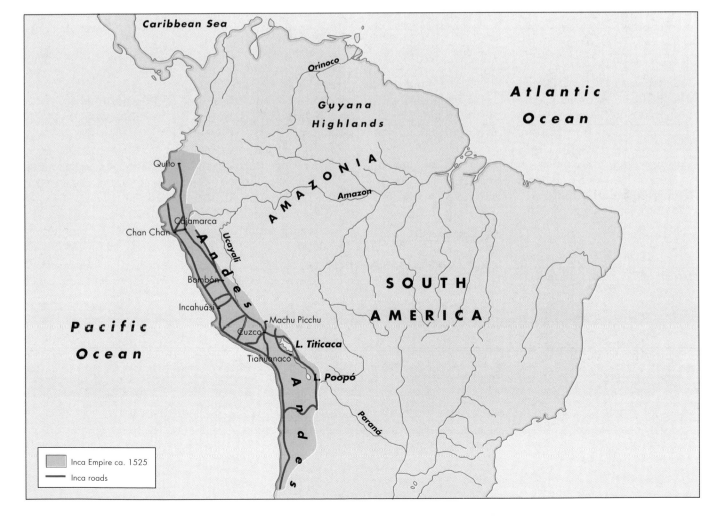

Figure 10.9   Machu Picchu, Inca culture, Peru, ca. 1450. This beautiful mountain habitation escaped destruction when the Spaniards overwhelmed the Inca civilization in 1532, partly because of its remote location high in the Andes mountains, and partly because it was not a large city like the Inca capital of Cuzco.

One of the most impressive of all Inca accomplishments is the fortified town of Machu Picchu (fig. 10.9), built around 1450. Located high in the Andes mountains, Machu Picchu was built perhaps as a refuge for Inca monarchs, perhaps as a place of religious retreat. Terraced fields adorn the slopes of the mountain that rises from the valley thousands of feet below. The stones for the walls and buildings were hoisted without benefit of carts or any wheeled contrivance, as the wheel was not used in either the Andes or Mesoamerica before the arrival of the Spaniards. Tools used for fitting the stones together snugly were primitive—mostly stone

hammers, since neither the Andean nor Mesoamerican civilizations had developed metal implements at this time.

Machu Picchu was abandoned shortly after the arrival of Francisco Pizarro and the Spanish Conquistadores. The Spaniards destroyed Inca civilization with technologically advanced weapons by enlisting the allied assistance of Inca enemies, and through the agency of contagious diseases, especially smallpox. Just a dozen years after Montezuma and the Aztecs had been defeated by the Spanish under Hernán Cortés, the Andean Inca civilization suffered an equally ignoble demise. Machu

Timeline 10.2   Peruvian cultures.

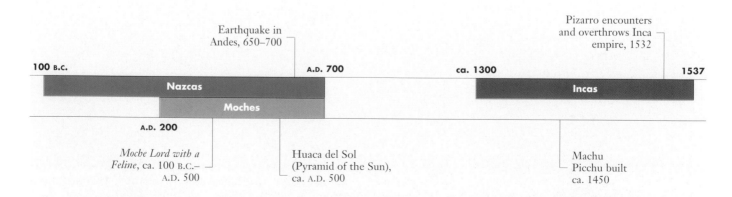

Connections

THE MYSTERY OF THE NAZCA LINES

*P*erhaps no phenomenon better underscores the intimate connection between art, archaeology, and science than the mystery of the famous Nazca lines. These are giant drawings made on the plains of the south Peruvian coast where the earth is covered by a topsoil of fine sand and pebbles that, when dug away, reveals white alluvium. A culture that traded with the Moche to the north and thrived from 100 B.C. to A.D. 700, the Nazca dug away this top soil to create a web of lines, some running straight for as long as five miles, others forming complex geometric designs in the shape, for instance, of a monkey with a coiled tail or, as illustrated here, a hummingbird (fig. 10.10).

Ever since the German-born mathematician and astronomer Maria Reiche became obsessed by the lines in 1932, they have been the center of controversy. Reiche singlehandedly surveyed all of the lines over the course of her career and concluded that the straight lines point to celestial activity on the horizon and that the animals represent ancient constellations. In 1963, Nazca was visited by Gerald Hawkins of Boston University, whose computer calculations of Stonehenge had helped reveal its astronomical relations, but he was unable to link many of the lines to the configuration of the heavens in the Nazca period. In the early 1970s, Erich von Däniken theorized that the lines were guidance patterns for alien spacecraft, a proposal that soon gained a wide and vocal following.

More recently, archaeologists have proposed that these **geogylphs**, as they are called, are actually depictions of giant gods whose job it is to guarantee both the availability of water and the fertility of the Nazca valleys. This theory is supported by the fact that in several sites, the straight lines point, not at aspects on the horizon, but directly at natural springs and water sources.

Figure 10.10 Earth drawing of a hummingbird, Nazca Plain, southwest Peru, Nazca culture, ca. 200 B.C.–A.D. 200, length ca. 450′ (138 m), wingspan ca. 200′ (60.5 m). Aerial photographs and satellite images have revealed not only figurative designs such as this one, but over eight hundred miles of straight lines.

Picchu was overlooked by the Spaniards, perhaps in part because it was a small village of five hundred inhabitants. To this day it remains one of the architectural wonders of the world.

NORTH AMERICA

The Native American populations in North America were far less densely concentrated than those in Meso- and South America. The peoples of the region lived primarily nomadic lives, hunting and fishing, until around 1200 B.C., when the production of maize spread from Mexico into the southwest region of the present-day United States, inaugurating agricultural production in the north thousands of years after its introduction in the south. The climate of North America was not, in fact, conducive to raising corn, and the practice was slow to take hold. As a result, the organized and complex civilizations that have usually accompanied agricultural development were also slow to form. Indeed, down to the time of the European colonization of the region at the end of the fifteenth century, many native peoples continued to live as they had since the time of the extinction of the vast herds of mammoth, mastodon, and other species that inhabited the continent at the end of the Ice Age, ca. 6000 B.C.

THE NORTHWEST COAST

One of the oldest cultures of the north developed along the northwest coast of the continent, in present-day Oregon, Washington State, British Columbia, and Alaska. Reaching back to approximately 3500 B.C., when the world's oceans had more or less stabilized at their current levels, rich fishing grounds developed in the region, with vast quantities of salmon and steelhead migrating inland up the rivers annually to spawn. One

Figure 10.11 Haida mortuary poles and house frontal poles at Skedans Village, British Columbia, 1878, National Archives, Canada. Totem poles were traditionally carved to honor the leader of a clan upon his death, and they also stood in front of homes, serving a spiritual function.

of the richest habitats on earth in natural resources, the northwest was home to over three hundred edible animal species.

Here the native peoples—among them the Tlingit, the Haida, and the Kwakiutl—gathered wild berries and nuts, fished the streams and inlets, and hunted game. In the winters, they came together in plank houses, made with wood from the abundant forests, and engaged in a rich ceremonial life. By 450 B.C., they had become expert woodworkers, not only building their winter homes out of timber and rough-sawn planks, but also carving out canoes and making elaborate decorative sculpture. The most famous form of this decorative sculpture is the so-called totem pole (fig. 10.11). These mortuary poles, erected to memorialize dead chiefs, consist of animal and spirit emblems or totems stacked one upon the other, for which the poles are named.

The kinship ties of the extended family tribe were celebrated at elaborate ceremonies called **potlatches**, hosted by the chief. Guests arrived in ceremonial dress, formal speeches of welcome followed, and gifts were distributed. Then dancing would follow long into the night. The potlatch was intended to confirm the chief's authority and insure the loyalty of his tribal group.

THE SOUTHWEST

The native populations of the desert southwest faced severe difficulties in adapting to conditions following the end of the Ice Age. Like the Moche in Peru who lived in similar desert conditions, tribes gathered around rivers, streams, and springs that brought precious water from the mountains. However, water in the North American

desert was far less abundant than in the South American river oases. Nonetheless, the inhabitants of the region, called the Anasazi (meaning "ancient ones"), slowly learned to recognize good moisture-bearing soil, to plant on north- and east-facing slopes protected from the direct sunlight of late day, and to take advantage of the natural irrigation of floodplains.

Small farming communities developed in the canyons and on the mesas of the region. In the thirty-two square miles of Chaco Canyon, in the northeastern region of present-day Arizona, thirteen separate towns, centered around circular underground ceremonial rooms called **kivas**, had begun to take shape by A.D. 700. In the kiva, the community celebrated its connection to the earth, from which all things were said to emanate and to which all things return—not just humans, but, importantly, water as well. Connected to other sites in the area by a network of wide straight roads, the largest of these towns was Pueblo Benito, which was constructed between 900 and 1250. Shaped like a massive letter "D," its outer perimeter was 1300 feet long. At the center of the "D" was a giant plaza, built on top of the two largest kivas (there are thirty other kivas at Pueblo Benito).

Perhaps the most famous Anasazi site is Mesa Verde (fig. 10.12) in southwestern Colorado, near the Four

Figure 10.12 Mesa Verde, Spruce Tree House, Anasazi culture, A.D. 1200–1300. Visible in front of the buildings to the right are three round kivas. Originally, these would have been roofed, and the roofs would have formed a common plaza in front of the buildings. The Anasazi farmed on the mesatop above.

Cross Currents

CONQUEST AND DISEASE

The end of the great buffalo herds was not the only devastation the conquering Europeans brought with them. In 1519, in Veracruz, Mexico, one of the invading Spanish soldiers came ashore with smallpox. The Native Americans had no natural immunity. Of the approximately eleven million people living in Mexico before the arrival of the Spaniards, only 6.4 million remained by 1540. By 1607, perhaps two million indigenous people remained. When the Spanish arrived in California in 1679, the population was approximately 310,000. By 1900, there were only 20,000 Native Americans in the region. Along the eastern seaboard of the United States, through the Ohio Valley and the Midwest, entire populations were exterminated by disease. In the matter of a month or two, an entire village might lose ninety percent of its people.

The destruction of Native American peoples, and with them their traditions and cultures, is movingly stated by the Wanapum prophet Smohalla, whose people died *en masse* not long after the 1844 arrival of Marcus Whitman to establish a mission in the Walla Walla Valley of Washington State:

The whites have caused us great suffering. Dr. Whitman many years ago made a journey to the east to get a bottle of poison for us. He was gone about a year, and after he came back, strong and terrible diseases broke out among us. The Indians killed Dr. Whitman, but it was too late. He had uncorked his bottle and all the air was poisoned. Before there was little sickness among us, but since then many of us have died. I have had children and grandchildren, but they are all dead ... We are now so few and weak that we can offer no resistance, and their preachers have persuaded them to let a few of us live, so as to claim credit with the Great Spirit for being generous and humane.

Corners where Colorado, Utah, Arizona, and New Mexico all meet. Discovered in 1888 by two cowboys, Richard Wetherill and Richard Morgan, searching for stray cattle, Mesa Verde consists of a series of cliff dwellings built into the cavelike overhangs of the small canyons and arroyos that descend from the mesa top. While as many as 30,000 people lived in the Montezuma Valley below, probably no more than 2,500 people ever lived on the mesa itself. On the mesa these inhabitants developed an elaborate irrigation system consisting of a series of small ditches which filled a mesatop reservoir capable of holding nearly half a million gallons of water.

In about 1150, severe drought struck the Four Corners region, and the Anasazi at both Chaco and Mesa Verde abandoned their communities. They migrated into the Rio Grande Valley of New Mexico, where they were absorbed into the later native societies of the southwest, particularly the Hopi and the Zuni.

THE MOUNDBUILDERS

Throughout the Mississippi and Ohio River basins, beginning in about 1000 B.C. with the arrival of maize from Mesoamerica, small farming villages began building monumental earthworks in which to bury their dead. By far the largest of these was at Cahokia, in present-day East St. Louis, Illinois, where as many as 30,000 people lived between A.D. 1050 and 1250. The so-called Monk's Mound, the biggest earthwork ever constructed in North America, rises in four stages to a height of nearly one hundred feet and extends over sixteen acres.

The moundbuilders had begun by burying their dead in low ridges overlooking river valleys. The sites were apparently sacred, and as more and more burials were added, the mounds became increasingly large, especially as large burial chambers started to be constructed, at about the time of Jesus, to contain important tribal leaders. Sheets of mica, copper ornaments, and carved stone pipes were buried with these chiefs and shamans, and the mounds became increasingly elaborate. One of the most famous is the Great Serpent Mound (fig. 10.13), built by the Adena culture between 600 B.C. and A.D. 200. Overlooking a small stream, it rises from its coiled tail as

Figure 10.13 Great Serpent Mound, Adams County, Ohio, Adena culture, 600 B.C.–A.D. 200, length ca. 1254′ (382.5 m). Though the Great Serpent Mound in Adams County is perhaps the most spectacular example, there are between three and five hundred such mounds in the Ohio Valley alone.

if to strike a giant oval form which its mouth has already encircled. What it symbolizes is as mysterious as the forms of the Nazca lines in Peru.

THE BUFFALO HUNTERS

It remains unclear what led to the extinction of the great game species at the end of the Ice Age—perhaps a combination of over-hunting and climatic change. But one large pre-extinction mammal continued to thrive—the bison, commonly known as the buffalo. The species survived because it learned to eat the grasses that soon spread across the Great Plains of North America, where it roamed. Hunting it became the chief occupation of the peoples who inhabited the region.

Archaeological evidence suggests that as much as 8500 years ago a group of Native Americans who lived southeast of Kit Carson, Colorado, stampeded an entire herd of buffalo off a cliff. The fall killed about 152 of the animals, and they were butchered where they lay for their hides and meat. The practice of stampeding continued, essentially unchanged, down to the time of the Spanish conquest, when horses were reintroduced to the Americas—the native variety had grown extinct by A.D. 600—and with the horse, the rifle.

But perhaps the most devastating change as far as the buffalo were concerned was the coming of the Europeans themselves. The great herds that roamed the continent quickly disappeared. Between 1830 and 1870, the buffalo population in the West dropped from around thirty million to an estimated eight million. Between 1872 and 1874, hunters killed an estimated 4,374,000 buffalo on the Great Plains. As the railroad builder Granville Dodge reported in the late summer of 1873: "The vast plain, which only a short twelvemonth before teemed with animal life, was a dead, solitary, putrid desert." The Crow warrior, Two Legs, put it this way: "Nothing happened after that. We just lived. There were no more war parties, no capturing horses from the Piegan and the Sioux, no buffalo to hunt. There is nothing more to tell."

READINGS

← SELECTED POEMS AND SONGS

The following three selections suggest the range of roles and functions of song and poetry in Mesoamerican civilizations. The first, "The Midwife Addresses the Newly Delivered Woman," is an Aztec poem which describes the valiant heroism of women, whose responsibility is to bear children. Women's endurance of the pains of childbirth is compared to the endurance of male warriors in battle. For the Aztec and for other Mesoamerican peoples, poetic speech was called "flower-song," which suggests both its beauty and its creative power. The importance of poetry in everyday life is conveyed in the second work,

"With flowers you write," a fifteenth-century Nahuatl song. The third selected is a Maya song that testifies to their emphasis on blood sacrifice to ensure fertility and the renewal of life. "Oh watcher, watcher from the trees" describes the dance of the bowman, who sharpens his arrows and dances around the victims in preparation for the sacrifice.

The Midwife Addresses the Newly Delivered Woman

> O my daughter, O valiant woman, you worked, you
>   toiled.
> You soared like an eagle, you sprang like a jaguar,
> you put all your strength behind the shield, behind the
>   buckler;
> you endured.
> You went forth into battle, you emulated Our Mother,
>   Cihuacoatl Quilaztli,   *5*
> and now our lord has seated you on the Eagle Mat, the
>   Jaguar Mat.°
> You have spent yourself, O my daughter, now be
>   tranquil.
> What does our lord Tloque Nahuaque° will?
> Shall he bestow his favors upon each of you separately, in
>   separate places?
> Perhaps you shall go off and leave behind the child that
>   has arrived.   *10*
> Perhaps, small as he is the Creator will summon him, will
>   call out to him,
> or perhaps he shall come to take you.
> Do not be boastful of [the child].
> Do not consider yourself worthy of it.
> Call out humbly to our lord, Tloque Nahuaque.   *15*

With Flowers You Write

> With flowers you write,
> Oh Giver of Life!
> With songs you give color,
> with songs you shade
> those who must live on the earth.   *5*
>
> Later you will destroy
> eagles and tigers;
> we live only in your painting
> here, on the earth.
>
> With black ink you will blot out   *10*
> all that was friendship,
> brotherhood, nobility.
>
> You give shading
> to those who must live on the earth.
>
> Later You will destroy   *15*
> eagles and tigers;
> we live only in your painting
> here, on the earth.

° *Jaguar Mat:* Warriors' seat of honor.
° *Tloque Nahuaque:* Ever Present, Ever Near, the supreme spirit.

Oh Watcher, Watcher from the Trees

Oh watcher, watcher from the trees,
with one, with two,
we go to hunt at the edge of the grove,
in a lively dance up to three.
Raise your head high,   5
do not mistake,
instruct well your eyes
to gather the prize.

Make sharp the tip of your arrow,
make taut the cord   10
of your bow; now you have good
resin of *catsim* on the feathers
at the end of the arrow's rod.
You have rubbed well
the fat of a male deer   15
on your biceps, on your muscles,
on your knees, on your twin muscles,
on your shoulders, on your chest.

Go nimbly three times round
about the painted stone column,   20
where stands that virile lad,
unstained, undefiled, a man.
Go once, on the second round
take up your bow, put in the arrow,
point it at his chest; you need not   25
use all your strength
so as to kill him,
or wound him deeply.
Let him suffer
little by little,   30
as He wishes it,
the magnificent Lord God.

The next time you go round
this stony blue column, the next time
you go round, shoot another arrow.   35
This you must do without
stopping your dance, because
thus it is done by well-bred
men, fighters, those who
are sought after, pleasing   40
in the eyes of the Lord God.

And as the Sun appears
over the forest to the east,
the song of the bowman begins.
These well-bred men, fighters,   45
do their utmost.

✦ **PABLO NERUDA**
from *The Heights of Machu Picchu*

In his poem The Heights of Machu Picchu, *the Nobel Prize-winning Chilean poet Pablo Neruda (1904–1973) memorialized the settlement as a place where garments for celebration and mourning were woven of the native vicuña's wool, where maize, the primary crop that sustained the Inca people, was harvested, where what endures is the achievement and the memory of the people who created the city and the civilization it represents.*

Then up the ladder of the earth I climbed
through the barbed jungle's thickets
until I reached you Machu Picchu.

Tall city of stepped stone,
home at long last of whatever earth   5
had never hidden in her sleeping clothes.
In you two lineages that had run parallel
met where the cradle both of man and light
rocked in a wind of thorns.

Mother of stone and sperm of condors.   10

High reef of the human dawn.

Spade buried in primordial sand.

This was the habitation, this is the site:
here the fat grains of maize grew high
to fall again like red hail.   15

The fleece of the vicuña was carded here
to clothe men's loves in gold, their tombs and mothers,
the king, the prayers, the warriors.

Up here men's feet found rest at night
near eagles' talons in the high   20
meat-stuffed eyries. And in the dawn
with thunder steps they trod the thinning mists,
touching the earth and stones that they might recognize
that touch come night, come death.

I gaze at clothes and hands,   25
traces of water in the booming cistern,
a wall burnished by the touch of a face,
that witnessed with my eyes the earth's carpet of tapers,
oiled with my hands the vanished wood:
for everything, apparel, skin, pots, words,   30
wine, loaves, has disappeared,
fallen to earth.

And the air came in with lemon blossom fingers
to touch those sleeping faces:
a thousand years of air, months, weeks of air,   35
blue wind and iron cordilleras—
these came with gentle footstep hurricanes
cleansing the lonely precinct of the stone.

Map 11.1 The Carolingian world, ca. A.D. 814.

Frankish control

temporary Frankish control

Muslim lands

THE EARLY MIDDLE AGES AND THE ROMANESQUE

Purse cover, from the burial ship found at Sutton Hoo, England, 625–33.

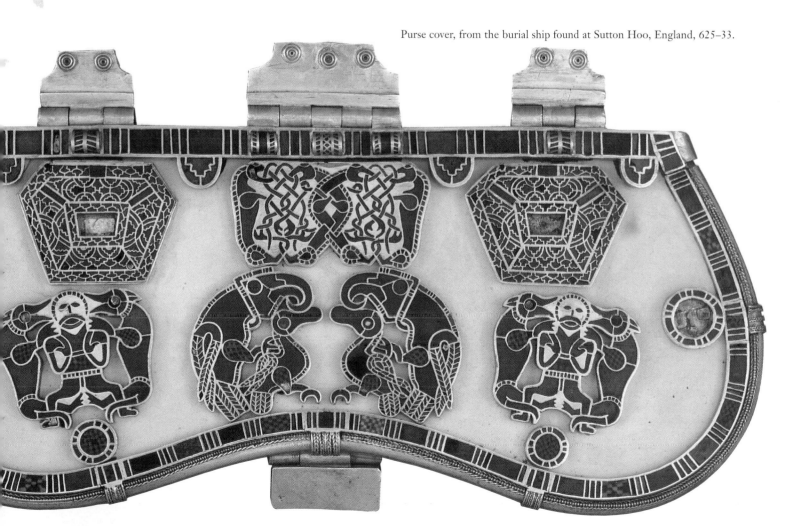

EARLY MEDIEVAL CULTURE

While Byzantine culture flourished in the Eastern Mediterranean, in the West, especially north of Italy, the fall of Rome led to a fragmentation in European political, social, and artistic culture. Spanning from Constantine's move from Rome to Constantinople in A.D. 330 and the emergence in the fifteenth century of the powerful Italian city-states such as Florence, Venice, and Milan, this medieval period has often been considered one of relative cultural poverty, culminating in the great catastrophe of the "Black Death," the epidemic of bubonic plague that spread across Europe after 1348.

This perspective is misleading. The period referred to as the "Dark Ages" stretched only from the sixth to the eighth century, and was followed by the rise of some remarkable cultures. The Early Middle Ages are recognized as a period of tremendous cultural accomplishment in their own right. Certainly, the fifteenth-century flowering of Western civilization that we call the Renaissance or "rebirth" was only possible because of what took place in the thousand years that preceded it. The beginning of this period was marked by the collision of two very different cultural forces—the Christian Church, which gradually spread northward from Rome, and the Germanic tribes and other barbarian groups, who controlled civic and social life in northern Europe. It was their mutual cultural assimilation that would come to shape early medieval life.

THE MERGING OF CHRISTIAN AND CELTO-GERMANIC TRADITIONS

In the first half of the fifth century A.D., Anglo-Saxons invaded Britain from northeastern Europe as part of the vast migration of Germanic tribes into the former territories of the Roman Empire. The Anglo-Saxons were actually three different tribes, the Angles, the Saxons, and the Jutes, who, though distinct, shared the same ancestors, traditions, and language. In Britain, they quickly suppressed the indigenous Christian inhabitants, the Celts. By 550, under the influence of the Anglo-Saxon invaders, Christianity had disappeared from all but the most remote corners of Britain, and the culture of the country had become distinctly Germanic. However, a reversal began in 597, when St. Augustine was sent to Britain as a missionary by Pope Gregory. At the same time missionaries from Ireland arrived in the northern part of the country and began to preach the Christian message there. King Ethelbert of Kent was converted to the Roman faith, and within seventy-five years Britain was once again predominantly Christian. Its language remained Anglo-Saxon—Old English, as it is called today—yet this language soon started to be increasingly "Latinized," especially after the Norman Conquest in

1066, to become the English we know today. In the same way, the culture itself started to blend the visual and literary ideals of Christianity and the heroic Germanic tradition. However, there is little trace of Christianity in some of the earliest artifacts from this period.

The Animal Style. Some of the finest examples of the art of these Germanic tribes are the exquisite objects discovered in the rich burial ship of an East Anglian king, dated between 625 and 633, at Sutton Hoo in Suffolk, England. As part of the king's funeral rite, the ship was lifted out of the water, dragged some distance inland, and then buried. Excavation of the site was carried out in 1939. Among the artifacts discovered was a purse cover (fig. 11.1) made of gold, garnet, and enamel (the background has been restored), with a clasp made of enamel on gold. This is decorated in what is called the "animal style." The ornamental patterns consist of distorted creatures, their bodies twisted and stretched. Some are made up of parts from different animals. Interlaced with these bestial forms are purely abstract patterns. But this is by no means wild, undisciplined design. On the contrary, the symmetrical compositions are meticulously compiled of smaller units that are, in themselves, symmetrical. The unifying aesthetic suggests a preference for vigorous, ornamental patterns. The swirling lines and animal interlace seen here are the two basic forms that later appear in Irish Anglo-Saxon manuscript illumination.

Evidence for this "animal style" is found outside Britain too. A burial ship uncovered at Oseberg, in southern Norway, dating from about 825, contained two wooden animal heads (fig. 11.2). The shapes of these heads are quite naturalistic, but the treatment of their surfaces is not. They are covered with organic and

Figure 11.1 Purse cover, from the burial ship found at Sutton Hoo, England, 625–33, gold, garnets, and enamel (background restored), length 8″ (20.3 cm), British Museum, London. This and other exquisite objects show how inappropriate it is to call the era during which they were created the "Dark Ages." Working with the highest technical skill, artists created symmetrical patterns from animal shapes.

Figure 11.2 Animal head, from the burial ship found at Oseberg, Norway, ca. 825, wood, height of head ca. 5″ (12.7 cm), University Museum of National Antiquities, Oslo. Intricate interlacing patterns cover the surface of this animal head. Attached to the prow of a ship, this and other similar animal heads that have survived may explain the origin of certain tales about sea monsters.

abstract shapes, which are combined in a style that is at once disciplined yet free. Animal heads such as these were used on the prows of ships, perhaps giving rise to the tales of "sea monsters," of which the Loch Ness monster is a modern survivor.

Christian Gospel Books. The animal-style artifacts from the Sutton Hoo and Oseberg finds are among the few examples of art to have survived from these early years. Evidence of other art forms has almost entirely vanished. Paintings were executed on the walls and ceilings of churches, but little now remains. In fact, the only paintings that survive in good condition from the early medieval era are in illuminated manuscripts produced in monasteries in northern England and Ireland after the mid-seventh century. **Illuminated manuscripts** are books written by hand on **parchment** (animal skin; the finest quality is called **vellum**) and elaborately decorated with paintings. Each separate page is referred to as a

folio. Early examples are usually copies of the four Christian gospels of Matthew, Mark, Luke, and John. In terms of decoration, these show the Christian assimilation of the Anglo-Saxon animal style.

A **cross page**, also referred to as a **carpet page**, in the *Lindisfarne Gospels*, ca. 700 (fig. 11.3), is entirely covered with a symmetrical geometric pattern filled with curvilinear shapes made up of "animal interlace"—birds and animals so elongated and intertwined that they look like ribbons. The page is decorated much as a piece of precious jewelry might be.

The *Book of Kells*, the finest gospel book of the Early Middle Ages still in existence, was written and decorated by Irish monks, probably around 800, but the exact date and place of origin are uncertain. The first known document mentioning the *Book of Kells* records its theft in 1006; the *Book of Kells* was already at that date referred to as "the chief relic of the Western world." Such a book was not intended for daily devotional use. Rather,

Figure 11.3 Cross page from the *Lindisfarne Gospels*, ca. 700, manuscript illumination, $13\frac{1}{2}'' \times 9\frac{1}{4}''$ (34.3 × 23.5 cm), British Library, London. This dense, intricate work is created by interlacing ribbon-like animals, organized by an underlying cross pattern. The care lavished on the decoration of a manuscript was intended to indicate the importance accorded the words of the text.

Figure 11.4 *St. John*, ornamental page from the *Book of Kells*, ca. 800 (?), manuscript illumination, 13 × 9½″ (33 × 24.1 cm), Trinity College Library, Dublin. The human body, treated as no more three-dimensional than the surface on which it is painted, becomes part of a flat design. The past Classical tradition of realism and pictorial illusionism is not identifiable here. Do not overlook the "footnotes" at the "foot of the page."

it was created as a work of art, presumably to be used only on very special occasions.

The *Book of Kells* contains the texts of the four gospels in Latin. As is clear from the ornamental page depicting St. John (fig. 11.4), in the illustration work perfection is sought on the smallest scale humanly possible. Curiously, the fine technical execution is accompanied by an extremely inaccurate representation of the human body. John is seen from the front yet appears flat, no more three-dimensional than the page on which he is painted. The human figure is treated as a pattern of lines. The curvilinear drapery falls in impossible folds, forming a two-dimensional decorative design that gives little hint of a solid body beneath. This Celtic style of manuscript illumination, like its Byzantine counterpart (see Chapter 7), takes us far from nature and the Classical tradition's allegiance to portraying the visible world.

The Beowulf Epic and the Christian Poem. Little secular literature survives from this earliest period of the Middle Ages. The greatest of the Anglo-Saxon Germanic epics is *Beowulf*. It was probably composed in the first half of the eighth century, though the only version of it that survives dates from the tenth century, and that version was itself badly damaged in 1731 in a London fire. Much of the poem has been lost, which only adds to the difficulty of deciphering the Old English text.

Beowulf is an almost completely Germanic tale. Set in Denmark, its action ideally exemplifies the values of a warrior society. As a good king Beowulf is referred to as "ring-giver," or "dispenser of treasure," and his duty is to take care of his loyal thanes or noblemen. Yet the act of giving has a spiritual side as well—out of generosity, unity and brotherhood emerge. This spiritual bonding, called *comitatus*, is balanced by the omnipresent threat of death. In fact, *Beowulf* is a poem permeated by a strong sense of doom, as its main narrative indicates. As a youth, Beowulf wins the admiration of his peers by killing the monster Grendel, which has been attacking the hall of the Danish king. Having killed Grendel, Beowulf must next avenge Grendel's mother's killing of a number of Beowulf's companions in revenge for her son's death. He tracks her down to a swamp, where he storms into her cave and kills her with a weapon forged by the giants of old. However, his victory over Grendel and his mother is tempered by the fact that his own men are dead, and, in the poem's final episode, after he has become king, Beowulf is himself slain when he goes to fight a mighty dragon that is terrorizing his people. However great a hero's courage, Fate (*wyrd*) can always intervene to destroy him, and sooner or later will.

There are hints of a Christian perspective in *Beowulf*, though these are very submerged. In the poem, *wyrd* can also be read as God's will, and Beowulf's heroic duty to rid the land of Grendel and his mother as ridding the world of the devil's influence. Indeed, Grendel is described as a descendant of Cain. But Jesus is never mentioned, and Beowulf's funeral, in a burial ship like that found at Sutton Hoo, is entirely pagan. The immortality that is his reward is the pagan form of immortality—the celebration of his memory in the poem itself.

In contrast to *Beowulf*, the short *Caedmon's Hymn*, the oldest extant Old English poem, composed between 658 and 680, employs the language of Anglo-Saxon heroic verse in an explicitly Christian context. Like a heroic king, God is referred to as the *Weard*, or Guardian, of his kingdom. The legend of the poem's composition is recounted by the historian-monk the VENERABLE BEDE [BEED] (ca. 673–735) in his *Ecclesiastical History of the English People*, completed in 731. An illiterate cowherd named Caedmon heard a voice in a dream that called out, "Caedmon, sing me something." "I don't know how to sing," he replied. "All the same," the voice insisted, "you must sing for me." "What must I sing?"

Caedmon asked. "Sing about the Creation," was the reply. And thus Caedmon sang. The first four lines of his hymn appear below in both Old and modern English:

Nu sculon herigan   heofronrices Weard
Now we must praise   heaven-kingdom's Guardian

Meotodes meahte   and his modgethanc
the Measurer's might   and his mind-plans,

worc Wuldor-Fæder   swa he wundra gehwæs
the work of the Glory-   when he of every wonder
Father

ece Drihten   or onstealde.
eternal Lord,   the beginning established.

After this visitation, Caedmon retired to the monastery of Whitby, ruled by the abbess HILDA (614–680), where he is said to have written other works.

CHARLEMAGNE AND THE CAROLINGIAN ERA

Perhaps the greatest example of the convergence of Christian and Germanic cultures is found in the rule of Charles the Great or CHARLEMAGNE [SHAR-lu-main] (742–814), king of the Franks. His rule is generally reckoned to have inaugurated a period of cultural reawakening in Western Europe. This period is known as the Carolingian era after his own Latin name, Carolus Magnus.

A vastly capable warrior, Charlemagne fought the Muslims in Spain and conquered the Saxons in a war that lasted some thirty years, seizing their home territory below Denmark and forcibly converting them to Christianity. By the end of his life he ruled all of present-day France, northern Spain as far south as Barcelona, most of northern Italy except for the Papal States, and,

to the east, Bohemia, much of Austria, and parts of Hungary and Croatia. As a reward for converting the peoples he conquered to Christianity, Charlemagne was crowned emperor of the West by Pope Leo III in Rome on Christmas Day of the year 800—the official beginning of a new "Holy" Roman Empire with a Christian emperor. Often credited with the major achievements of the so-called Carolingian Renaissance, Charlemagne saw himself very much as a successor to the great Roman emperors and therefore encouraged a revival of classical learning and arts. His court at Aachen was a focal point for these interests.

Feudal Society. Charlemagne's government was essentially an early version of **feudalism**, a legal and social system that developed in Western Europe in the eighth century. Under feudalism a lord would offer protection and land to his vassals, or servants, in return for an oath of fealty, or loyalty, and military support. Charlemagne's primary officials were his household staff—his chamberlain, his count of the stable (that is, his "constable"), and so on. Like Beowulf, Charlemagne depended upon the *comitatus* of those under his command. However, Charlemagne ruled an enormous empire, which he could not hope to control effectively without a wider network of support. He therefore divided his territory into approximately three hundred counties, each governed by a count who was given authority to rule over it. Such a land grant was called a *feudum*, a fief, from which the term "feudal" derives. A fiefdom was hereditary, that is, passed on at the death of the vassal to his heir.

Architecture. To match his imperial ambitions, Charlemagne had created for himself a new capital, at Aachen in Germany. Here he built a sumptuous palace and a magnificent royal chapel (fig. 11.5), designed by

Timeline 11.1 The Carolingian era.

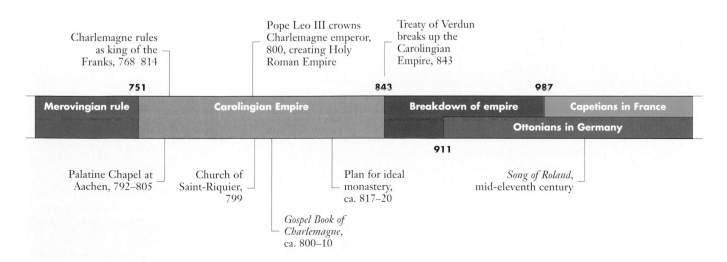

Figure 11.5 Odo of Metz, Palatine Chapel, Aachen, Germany, A.D. 792–805. Charlemagne was determined to make his chapel worthy of his piety, and so had materials brought from Rome and Ravenna to enrich it.

ODO OF METZ [OH-doh]. Apart from this chapel, little Carolingian architecture has survived. Nonetheless, it is clear that Carolingian builders developed ideas that influenced later medieval styles. An important example of this is provided by the church of Saint-Riquier in Abbeville, France (fig. 11.6), consecrated in 799, the greatest basilica church of its time. Although Saint-Riquier has been destroyed, its appearance is known from a 1612 engraving of an eleventh-century manuscript illumination. The Early Christian basilica plan was modified to accommodate the changing needs of the people and of the Church in the Carolingian era. Innovations found at Saint-Riquier that were to have future importance are: (1) a **westwork** (a monumental entryway) with two circular staircases; (2) a vaulted narthex that projects beyond the aisles, forming a second transept; (3) two towers, one over the crossing of the nave and west transept, one over the crossing of the nave and east transept; and (4) the addition of a square **choir** (where the monks sang the Divine Office) between the apse and nave. Its multiple towers formed what was to become the typical church silhouette of medieval Western Europe.

Literature: The Song of Roland. One of the most famous of all early medieval French literary works is the *Song of Roland*, a **chanson de geste**, or "song of deeds," which dates from the mid-eleventh century in Brittany. It consists of more than four thousand lines, which are given their regularity and shape by the use of **assonance**, or the repetition of vowel and consonantal sounds, rather than by pure rhyme. The poem tells the story of the Christian army of Charlemagne doing battle against the Muslim Saracens. The poem is based on a historical incident from the year 778, when Charlemagne, returning home from a war in northern Spain, was attacked as he crossed the Pyrenees. The poet transforms the factual details into a heroic poem in which near miraculous feats are performed by the Christian soldiers led by Charlemagne's nephew Roland, one of his twelve Paladins, or princes. Roland is made the focus of the poem's action, while Charlemagne remains a significant background figure.

Roland is betrayed by one of his military colleagues, Ganelon, who informs the Saracen enemy leader of Roland's route through Roncesvalles, where his army is consequently ambushed by 400,000 Saracens. The poem recounts the valorous deeds of Roland and his men. Roland's dying act is to sound his hunting horn to warn Charlemagne of the enemy's presence. Upon finding Roland and his army dead, and discovering Ganelon's treachery, Charlemagne has the traitor executed and goes on to defeat the Saracens.

The poem is noted for its clarity and for the elegance of its language, the simplicity of its narrative, and the masterful precision of its detail. Of considerable importance is the feudal code of honor that serves as a foundation for, and standard against which to measure, the actions of its major characters. Celebrating loyalty over treachery, courage over cowardice, good judgment over foolishness, the *Song of Roland* exemplifies the values of French feudal society. Like the heroes of the Greek and Roman epics whose actions reflect the ideals of their societies, Roland embodies the ideals of medieval chivalry. He is at once a valiant warrior, an obedient and faithful servant of his king, and a warm and affectionate friend, whose behavior is governed by a Christian sense of moral rectitude.

MONASTICISM

The Rule of St. Benedict and Cluniac Reform. Monasticism, a term derived from the Greek word *monos*, meaning "alone," had been an integral part of Christian life since the third century. During the Middle Ages, monasticism developed rapidly, resulting in an increasing number of monasteries and influential religious orders of monks and nuns. However, the observance of rules was anything but strict, and the lifestyle enjoyed in many monasteries was often quite relaxed. The earliest monastic guidelines were those provided by ST. BENEDICT (480–543), who established a monastery at Monte

Figure 11.6   Church of Saint-Riquier, Abbeville, consecrated 799, now destroyed, engraving made in 1612 from an eleventh-century manuscript illumination, Bibliothèque Nationale, Paris. Although this church no longer exists, certain features here became standard in church architecture: a massive entryway, two transepts, multiple towers with staircases, and a choir.

Connections

THE MYSTERY PLAYS AND THE GUILDS

*B*etween the years 1000 and 1300, the population of Europe nearly doubled (to roughly seventy million), and urban areas began to grow as people gathered together in the interest of trade and commerce. The populations of these newly developing towns, which tended to form around old Roman settlements, along trade routes, and near the castles of great landowners, were, at least to a degree, free of feudal control, a fact that made them also free of organized government.

One of the chief means of establishing order in the growing towns and cities was the guild system. **Guilds** were associations of artisans and craftspeople (and soon merchants and bankers too) that regulated the quality of work produced in their own trade and the prices that an individual shopkeeper or tradesperson could charge. The guilds also controlled the training of apprentices and craftspeople, set

wages, supervised contracts, and approved new businesses. They built guild halls around the central square of the town, usually in front of the church. They also provided insurance and burial services for their members.

The guilds actively participated in the presentation of the so-called **mystery plays**—an early English corruption of the Latin word *ministerium*, or "occupation," referring to the guilds—a form of liturgical drama that began to develop in the ninth century. The mystery plays were dramatizations of narratives in the Old and New Testaments, usually composed in cycles containing as many as forty-eight individual plays. Typically, they would begin with the Creation, then recount the Fall of Adam and Eve, the Flood and Noah's Ark, David and Goliath, and so on, through the Old Testament to the Nativity, the events of Jesus's life, the Crucifixion, and the Last Judgment.

Each guild was responsible for an individual play, which was sometimes connected with its own trade. The

shipwrights' guild might present the story of Noah's Ark, for instance, and the bankers the story of Jesus and the moneylenders. These dramas were performed in the open air at different places around the town. In some towns, each guild would have its own wagon that served as a stage, and the wagons would proceed from one location to another, with the actors performing at each stop, so that the audience could see the whole cycle without moving. In other towns, the plays were probably acted out on a single stage or platform in the main city square.

The mystery plays were performed every summer, either at Whitsuntide, the week following the seventh Sunday after Easter, or at Corpus Christi, a week later. They served as both entertainment and education for their largely illiterate audience. They also functioned as festive celebrations which brought together every aspect of medieval life—social, political, economic, and religious—for the entire community.

Cassino, south of Rome, and created the Benedictine order. Charlemagne believed deeply in the Benedictine guidelines, and brought the Benedictine monk ALCUIN of York [AL-coo-in] (ca. 735–804) to his kingdom in order to impose them on the Frankish monasteries. In fact, the earliest surviving copy of the Rule of St. Benedict is one Charlemagne himself had made in 814, which is kept at St. Gall in Switzerland. Dividing their day into organized periods of prayer, work, and study, the Benedictines had a life that was summed up in the motto: "Pray and work." Their lives were based on four vows: they were to possess nothing (poverty); live in one place their entire life (stability); follow the abbot's direction (obedience); and remain unmarried (chastity).

In addition to these vows, the monks at the monastery in Cluny, France, decided to undertake reforms. Bishops had, up until then, lived like local feudal lords, often buying and selling Church offices to the highest bidder. The Cluniacs removed themselves from the feudal structure, answering only to the pope in Rome. They soon spread beyond their original monastery to establish similar monastic houses throughout Europe. In addition, they influenced the founding and development of other religious orders such as the Cistercians, established by ST. BERNARD OF CLAIRVAUX [clare-VOH] (1090–

1153) in the twelfth century. The Cistercians were a far more ascetic order than the Benedictines. For example, they simplified their religious services, stripping them of elaborate ceremony and complex ritual, as well as removing much religious art from their surroundings. The Cistercians also fasted and prayed longer and more frequently than the Benedictines.

The Monastery. The original plan for an ideal Carolingian monastery that was never built (fig. 11.7) is kept in the library of the Benedictine monastery of St. Gall, Switzerland. The plan, with Latin inscriptions explaining the function of each part, is drawn in red ink on parchment. In 816–17 a council had met near Aachen and decided upon a basic monastery plan, which it sent off to the abbot of St. Gall. It was intended to serve as a model, though each monastery was to adapt it to its specific needs.

Although no monastery exactly like this was ever built, the plan gives a good idea of what a medieval monastery was like. The monastery was intended to be self-contained and self-sufficient. Everything necessary for living is provided within this plan. The largest building is the church. Suited to the needs of monks rather than to those of a congregation, there is an apse and an altar at infirmary, a short distance from the cemetery. The plan shows several kitchens, located throughout the monastery. Countering today's assumptions about the austerity of medieval monastic life, it is worth noting that the plan includes more than one building for servants. However, little if any heating was part of the plan, and winters must have been extremely difficult to endure.

Manuscript Illumination. Much of the work carried out by the monks consisted of revising, copying, and illustrating liturgical books. Alcuin of York, for instance, published both a **sacramentary**, a book of prayers and rites for the administration of the sacraments, and a book of Old and New Testament passages in Latin for reading during mass. Medieval manuscripts were more often than not lavishly bound—it was felt that the cover enclosing the words of God should be as splendid as possible. Among the most sumptuous of all book covers ever created is that of the *Lindau Gospels* (fig. 11.8), made in about 870, out of gold, pearls, and semi-precious stones. In the Middle Ages, gemstones were not cut in facets, as they are today. Instead, they were smoothed and rounded

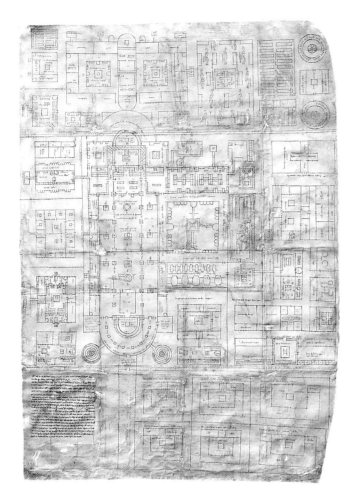

Figure 11.7 Plan for a monastery, ca. 817–820, red ink on parchment, 2′4″ × 3′8⅛″ (71.1 × 112.1 cm), Stiftsbibliothek, St. Gall, Switzerland. This plan for a prototype monastery was intended to be adopted and adapted to the specific needs of each monastic community—no monastery was ever built that precisely matched its layout. However, the drawing illustrates the basic ideal, which was that the monastery should be self-sufficient, providing for all the monks' needs.

Figure 11.8 Cover of the *Lindau Gospels,* gold, pearls, and semi-precious stones, ca. 870, 13¾ × 10⅜″ (34.9 × 26.4 cm), Pierpont Morgan Library, New York. This lavish and carefully handcrafted book cover can be contrasted with today's mass-produced paperback books. The stones are treated as cabochons—smoothed and polished rather than cut in facets as is now customary.

both ends, several entrances along the sides, and partitions dividing the nave. To the south of the church is the cloister, which is a standard part of the medieval monastery. The **cloister** is a square or rectangular space, open to the sky, usually with a source of water such as a fountain or well in the center, surrounded on all four sides by covered walkways. In the cloister garden, or **garth**, the monks might read, study, meditate, talk, and have contact with nature within the confines of the cloistered life. Also on the south side are the **refectory**, where meals were taken, the dormitory, baths, latrines, and various workshops. To the west are places where animals could be kept. To the north are the guest house, school (monasteries played an important part in the revival of learning, for it was here that education was available), and abbot's house. To the east are the physician's quarters (with bloodletting mentioned on the plan), and the into what are known as **cabochons**, like the ones on the *Lindau Gospels* cover. The cabochons are not set into the gold, but raised up on little feet, some by almost an inch, so that light can pass right through them, enhancing their brilliance. A rich variety of colors, shapes, and patterns is created by the cross, the heavily jeweled border, and the four jeweled medallions between the arms of the cross. Jesus is not depicted here as suffering. His body, rather than hanging from the cross, appears weightless. He simply appears to be standing. It seems as if he is speaking, in triumph over death. Between the arms of the cross, each of the eight tiny figures is in a different pose, according to the space available. They are all done in **repoussé** (hammered out from the back), against a plain background.

Due to the classical influences encouraged by Charlemagne, the human figure once again became important

Figure 11.10 *St. Luke*, from the *Gospel Book of Archbishop Ebbo*, 816–35, manuscript illumination, $10\frac{1}{4} \times 8\frac{3}{4}''$ (26 × 22.2 cm), Bibliothèque Municipale, Épernay. The style here is animated, if not agitated. Each of the four evangelists is identified by a symbol, Luke's being the winged ox. Iconography, the language of symbols, was especially useful in an era when most people were illiterate.

Figure 11.9 *St. John*, from the *Gospel Book of Charlemagne (Coronation Gospels)*, ca. 800–810, manuscript illumination, $12\frac{3}{4} \times 9\frac{7}{8}''$ (32.4 × 25.1 cm), Schatzkammer, Kunsthistorisches Museum, Vienna. Emperor Charlemagne encouraged a revival of the antique—in part for political purposes. The impact of the antique is evident in this depiction of St. John, which is more realistic than that in the *Book of Kells* (see fig. 11.4).

in the visual arts. This can be seen in the many manuscripts of the gospels and other sacred texts produced by Carolingian scribes and illuminators working in monastic and royal workshops. An image of St. John (fig. 11.9) is included in the *Gospel Book of Charlemagne*, also known as the *Coronation Gospels*, dated ca. 800–810. The manuscript is said to have been found in Charlemagne's tomb at his court in Aachen. St. John is portrayed in the Roman tradition—the style is similar to wall paintings found at Pompeii and Herculaneum (see figs. 5.27–5.30). A frame has been painted onto the vellum folio, creating the impression that the viewer is looking through a window to see John outside. The legs of John's footstool overlap the frame, as if the frame were genuinely three-dimensional. The proportions of John's body are accurate and he wears a garment much like a Roman toga.

The representation of St. Luke (fig. 11.10) in the *Gospel Book of Archbishop Ebbo*, dated 816–35, differs from its restrained classical prototypes in its suggestion of movement and emotion. The drapery swirls around the figure, as if blown by a very strong wind into flame-like, nervous ripples. Even the landscape is oddly animated, for the hills seem to sweep upward. Everything appears to be moving in this energetic and dynamic style. Luke is shown in the process of writing his gospel. He holds an ink horn and is writing with a quill pen, although his writing stand is strikingly unstable.

Music: Gregorian Chant.   Music, which in the Middle Ages was largely linked to religion, was a particular passion of Charlemagne's, who brought monks to his kingdom from Rome to standardize ecclesiastical music. In church services for the laity (non-clergy) and in worship in the monasteries, the predominant form of music was **plainchant**, in which Latin liturgical texts were sung to a single melody line (**monophony**) without instrumental accompaniment.

The monks from Rome brought with them a particular tradition of Church music. This was **Gregorian chant**, which took its name from Pope GREGORY THE GREAT (540–604), who by legend is connected with the development of this form of music. A distinctly Frankish chant remained popular in Charlemagne's time too. During the centuries that followed, many new types of chant were composed, some of which were elaborated with tropes or turns in which other texts or melodies were introduced. Chants became more complex as the development of **polyphony** took place, in which two or more voice lines are sung simultaneously.

The basic chants have a serene, otherworldly quality with their flexible rhythms and melodic lines that typically move in tandem within a narrow range of pitch. Part of this quality comes from the use of church modes rather than major-minor scales. It also derives from the lack of musical accompaniment, in part because of the large resonating space of the cathedrals or monastery churches in which chants are frequently sung. The free-floating rhythms of the chant, with a lack of a steady beat or pattern of rhythmic accents, contribute to its solemnity, so much so that chant is sometimes described as "prayer on pitch."

During the reign of Charlemagne, Gregorian chants, which had formerly been passed down orally, were codified and written down in a rudimentary form of musical notation that used small curved strokes called **neumes** to indicate the up and down movement of the chant melody. In the eleventh century, an Italian monk, GUIDO D'AREZZO [da-RET-zoh] (ca. 997–1050), created a musical graph, or set of lines, on which to mark the various chanted musical pitches. Guido's graph used colored lines to make the representation of the musical pitches easy to read. It took two more centuries for the musical staff to develop, and until the sixteenth and seventeenth centuries before notes were written in the rounded forms common today.

ROMANESQUE CULTURE
↙

After Charlemagne's death in 814, the personal bonds that held the Holy Roman Empire together soon dissolved. After two further centuries of political fragmentation, however, around the year 1000, a few powerful feudal families began to extend their influence, conquering weaker feudal rulers and cementing their gains by intermarriage. These families soon developed into full-fledged monarchies. Two in particular—in France and in England—rose to real and lasting prominence. In 800, Charlemagne had allowed himself to be crowned emperor by the pope, thereby in some degree acknowledging

Timeline 11.2   The Romanesque era.

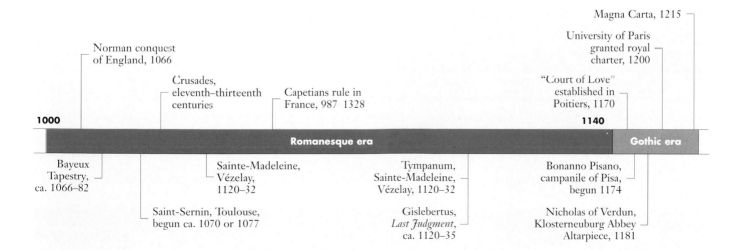

the Church's superior power. At first, neither of the emerging dynasties in England or France could contemplate open conflict with the authority of the papacy in Rome. However, as the secular power of these monarchs grew, the influence of the Church was increasingly threatened.

THE FEUDAL MONARCHS

The Capetians. When HUGH CAPET [CA-pay] (ca. 938–996) ascended to the French throne, he established a dynasty of kings that would rule for nearly 350 years. Hugh already controlled his own fiefdom, the Île de France (roughly the area between Paris on the Seine down to Orléans on the Loire); in part because of this personal power, he was accepted by all the feudal lords of France as their king in 987. Throughout the subsequent CAPETIAN [ca-PEA-shun] era, the dukes of Normandy, technically vassals of the Capetian throne but at least initially more powerful, quarreled with their king. Nevertheless, the Capetian monarchs gradually consolidated power around themselves, and Paris became the political and intellectual center of Europe.

The Norman Conquest. The dukes of Normandy, however, had other plans. Though servants to the Capetian kings in France, they claimed England for themselves and ruled as kings in their own right. The story of their conquest of England is recounted in the Bayeux Tapestry, dated ca. 1066–82. Probably made by English women soon after the Norman victory, it is actually a giant embroidery, measuring approximately 231 feet in length and $19\frac{1}{2}$ inches high, in which the design is sewn in wool threads onto a linen fabric background.

The story begins in 1064, when the heirless king of England, EDWARD THE CONFESSOR (r. 1042–1066), sent Harold of Wessex to tell WILLIAM, duke of Normandy (ca. 1027–1087), that he had been chosen as heir to the English throne (fig. 11.11). However, when Edward died, on January 6, 1066, Harold had himself crowned king of England, justifying his action by saying that Edward had changed his mind on his deathbed and made Harold his heir. Understandably, William was angered. On October 14, 1066, at Hastings in southern England, King Harold of England and Duke William of Normandy, who had crossed the English Channel with his army, engaged in battle. Harold's death, which the Bayeux Tapestry portrays as the result of an arrow penetrating his eye, permitted William to be crowned king of England, in Westminster Abbey, on Christmas Day, 1066. William became the first Norman king of England, and was known thereafter as William the Conqueror.

William divided England up into fiefs for his Norman barons, ruling as a feudal monarch. He also gave the

Figure 11.11 *King Edward Sends Harold of Wessex to Normandy*, detail of the Bayeux Tapestry, ca. 1066–82, wool embroidery on linen, height approx. $19\frac{1}{2}''$ (49.5 cm), total length ca. 231' (70.41 m), Centre Guillaume le Conquérant, Bayeux, France. The entire story of the invasion of England by William of Normandy, thereafter known as William the Conqueror, is told on this so-called tapestry. A wonderful document of military tactics and weaponry, the various parts of the work show the soldiers in battle, preparing for combat, traveling, and eating.

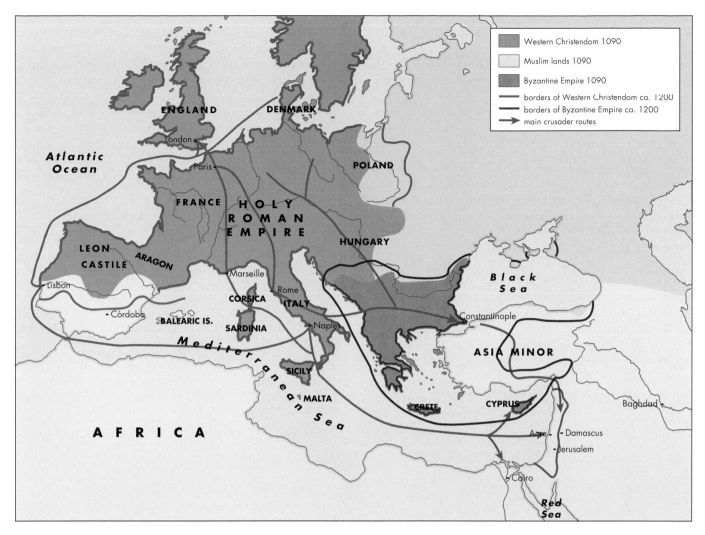

Map 11.2 The Crusades.

Church a quarter of the land, in an attempt to win its loyalty. Finally, he maintained Anglo-Saxon custom and law, thereby trying to gain the respect of the common people. Nonetheless, Norman culture proved very influential in England. For instance, the Latin-influenced French language spoken by the Norman invaders gradually began to mix with the native Anglo-Saxon, and the English language as we know it today started to emerge.

Magna Carta. Relations between the rulers of England and France remained difficult. King LOUIS VII of France (r. 1137–1180) had married ELEANOR OF AQUITAINE (ca. 1122–1204), Aquitaine being the great duchy that consists of most of southwestern France. But when she failed to provide a male heir, he annulled the marriage, and she promptly married HENRY II of England (r. 1154–1189), thus making the English king lord of more than half of France.

The Capetians balked at this, and Louis's successor, Philip II, or PHILIP AUGUSTUS (r. 1180–1223),

plotted with John, Henry II's younger son, to overthrow John's older brother, RICHARD "THE LION-HEARTED," who had assumed the English throne in 1189. Richard was often absent from England, either on crusade in the Holy Land or fighting with Philip Augustus. Both endeavors were financially crippling. Heavy taxes were consequently levied on the English barons, and many possessions were confiscated. Thus, when his brother John finally acceded to the English throne in 1199, the crown was bankrupt. Philip Augustus succeeded in expelling the English from France north of the Loire River, and, outraged at the expense of John's continued campaign against France, the English barons drew up a list of demands that John was forced to sign on June 15, 1215. Called the Magna Carta, or "Great Charter," it stated, among other things, that no taxation should be levied "except by the common consent of the realm." Similarly, it laid down that "No freeman shall be arrested or imprisoned, or dispossessed or outlawed or banished or in any way molested; nor will we set forth against him, nor send against him, unless by the lawful judgment of his peers and by the law of the land." These provisions for the first time set a limit on the power of the ruler. The Magna Carta is often seen as a crucial political document that paved the way for constitutional monarchy and the development of democracy in Western Europe.

The Crusades.   The **crusades** were a series of military expeditions organized in Western Europe with the principal aim of recovering the Holy Land in Palestine, especially Jerusalem, from its Muslim occupiers. The First Crusade was launched by Pope Urban in 1095. Two years later, a hundred thousand soldiers from all over Europe arrived in Constantinople. They came for all manner of reasons, both spiritual and mercenary.

Jerusalem fell to the first crusaders on July 15, 1099, but by the middle of the next century, Muslim authority had begun to reassert itself. In 1189, forces led by Richard the Lionhearted, the Holy Roman Emperor Frederick Barbarossa, and Philip Augustus of France reached the outskirts of Jerusalem, and probably would have won the city back had their mutual animosity not shattered their chances.

Politically and religiously, the crusades were a failure. However, for nearly a century, they succeeded in giving the feudal nobility something to do other than attack one another. As unstable as France and England were politically during this time, they benefited immeasurably from

the absence of so many warriors. More importantly, trade between Asia and Europe was greatly stimulated as a result of the conflicts, and with it intellectual commerce as well, as the ideals of ancient Greece became more current once again in the European imagination.

ROMANESQUE ARCHITECTURE

The Pilgrimage and the Church.   Part of the inspiration for the crusades to retake Jerusalem was provided by the medieval practice of pilgrimage. The chief purpose of a pilgrimage was to worship **relics** of the saints (objects connected with sacred figures), especially relics that were claimed to have miraculous powers. Pilgrimages were a social phenomenon of medieval life. They were obviously an important expression of religious faith, but they also represented a social opportunity: pilgrims could meet different kinds of people and were a kind of early tourist.

The medieval pilgrim's goal was likely to be the church of Santiago de Compostela (St. James of Compostela) in northwestern Spain, if not Rome or Jerusalem. Santiago de Compostela began to attract pilgrims in the ninth century, when it was claimed that it housed the tomb of St. James. A Romanesque cathedral was built on the site of the tomb in 1078–1211. For the many people who traveled great distances along the pilgrim routes, facilities were available at abbeys, priories, monasteries, and hospices. Some of these were built specifically for pilgrims, at intervals of twenty or so miles, not a difficult distance to cover in a day, even then. People slept in big open halls, and there were special chapels for religious services. Charities were set up to aid the sick and the destitute, and to take care of the dead.

Churches visited in this way by medieval pilgrims are referred to as "pilgrimage churches." There were originally five great pilgrimage churches. Two are now gone: Saint-Martin in Tours and Saint-Martial in Limoges. Three remain: Sainte-Foy in Conques, Saint-Sernin in Toulouse, and the ultimate goal of the pilgrim, Santiago de Compostela. All have the same basic plan and certain similarities of construction. Their style is called **Romanesque**, and indeed the architecture relies on the basic Roman elements of the basilica plan (see fig. 6.4), employing rounded arches, vaulted ceilings, columns for support, and thick, sturdy walls, although the style is not called Romanesque for this reason. All pilgrimage churches had large naves with flanking aisles, a transept, choir, ambulatory, and radiating chapels on the east end.

Saint-Sernin, Toulouse.   Among the most important buildings constructed in the eleventh century is Saint-Sernin in Toulouse (fig. 11.12), the best known of the great pilgrimage churches. Saint-Sernin was started ca. 1070 or 1077 but never finished. The west facade,

Figure 11.12   *Saint-Sernin, Toulouse, begun ca. 1070 or 1077, aerial view from the southwest. The exterior of the building reflects the interior. Each section of space is clearly defined and neatly separated, unlike the flowing spaces that will characterize Gothic architecture.*

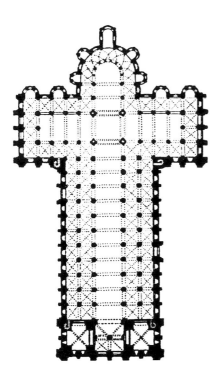

Figure 11.13 Saint-Sernin, Toulouse, begun ca. 1070 or 1077, plan. This Latin-cross plan with ambulatory and radiating chapels is typical of churches located along the pilgrimage route leading to Santiago de Compostela. In the many chapels, pilgrims venerated relics, especially if a relic was believed to be miracle-working.

which underwent restoration in 1855, has been generously described as an "awkward bulk." The builders' original intent (and the Romanesque norm) was to have two facade towers, but they were never completed. The apse end was completed by about 1098, with many different roof levels that reflect the interior plan. Each chapel is seen as a separate bulge from the outside; above the ambulatory, the apse protrudes; and the levels build up to the crossing tower. Each space is separate, as is typical of Romanesque architecture.

Saint-Sernin, like the other four great pilgrimage churches, has a Latin-cross plan (fig. 11.13)—a cruciform plan with one long arm—as opposed to the Greek-cross plan, which has four arms of equal length. The proportions of Saint-Sernin are mathematically determined: the aisles are composed of a series of square bays that serve as the basic unit. The nave and transept bays are twice as large. The crossing tower is four times the basic unit, as are the bases of the intended facade towers. Certain ancient Greek temples had similar numerical ratios between their different parts.

The nave of Saint-Sernin (fig. 11.14) is typically Romanesque, with thick walls, closely spaced piers, engaged columns on the walls, and a stone vault. The barrel vault covering the nave is a structural system which offers several advantages. Here, the acoustics are superb, with voices reverberating through the vaulted space. The threat of fire is reduced—a constant danger in the Middle Ages, especially to structures with wooden ceilings. The large interior is open, free of the intrusive posts necessary to the post and lintel system. Yet the barrel vault also has its disadvantages. An extension of the arch principle, it exerts a constant lateral thrust that must be buttressed. This is accomplished largely by the great thickness of the walls, which means that any opening in the supporting walls weakens the system.

Figure 11.14 Saint-Sernin, Toulouse, begun ca. 1070 or 1077, nave looking toward altar. Romanesque masons experimented with various vaulting methods, using most frequently the barrel (tunnel)vault based upon the semi-circular arch. Advantages of this stone vault, compared to the wooden ceiling of the Early Christian basilica, include superb acoustics and minimized risk of fire; disadvantages include lack of direct light into the nave.

Figure 11.15 Sainte-Madeleine, Vézelay, nave looking toward altar, 1120–32. A solution to the problem of obtaining direct light in the nave is found in the use of cross (groin) vaults, which provide a space for windows on the nave walls.

Consequently the windows in Romanesque churches are few and small, and the interiors often very dark.

Sainte-Madeleine, Vézelay. Another pilgrimage church, Sainte-Madeleine in Vézelay, occupies a spectacular site at the top of the crooked streets of this tiny town, the start of one of the roads leading to Santiago de Compostela. A Carolingian church was originally erected on this site and consecrated in 878. Vézelay's real rise began in the early eleventh century, however, when it was claimed that the town possessed the bones of Mary Magdalene. The Romanesque church of Sainte-Madeleine was built between 1096 and 1132. At its peak,

Vézelay had eight hundred monks and lay brothers living in its monastery. Unfortunately, most of the monastery was torn down during the French Revolution—only the church and part of the cloister remain.

The nave (fig. 11.15), built between 1120 and 1132, is very light for a Romanesque church. It is also very harmonious. Simple mathematics determines the proportions of the interior, which is two hundred feet long, sixty feet high, and forty feet wide. The alternating light and dark voussoirs (wedge-shaped blocks of stone that make up the arches) are inconsistent in size, resulting in irregular stripes. The supports are massive. Romanesque supports tend to vary: a simple pier or column may be elaborated by the addition of engaged columns. Sometimes the supports alternate—as is often the case in later Romanesque buildings. The nave elevation is two stories high, as at both Saint-Sernin and Santiago de Compostela. At Vézelay, however, the upper level is a clerestory with a row of windows. This is made possible because the nave bays are covered by **cross vaults** (also called **groin vaults**)—two tunnel (barrel) vaults intersecting at right angles, which automatically create a flat space on the wall where a window can be constructed. Vézelay's interior therefore offers a solution to the problem of obtaining direct light in the nave. However, despite the theoretical success of the structure, the

Figure 11.16 Cathedral group, Pisa: baptistery, begun 1153; cathedral, begun 1063; campanile, begun 1174. In addition to marble incrustation, the architecture of Romanesque Pisa is characterized by tiers of arcades. The "leaning tower of Pisa" owes its fame to foundations that were not made properly.

Cross Currents

THE PISA GRIFFIN

From 1100 until 1828, a three-and-a-half-foot-high Islamic bronze griffin (fig. 11.17) sat on top of the cathedral in Pisa. Half-eagle, half-lion, it may have originally been a fountain spout, but how it came to Pisa is unknown. Scholars have suggested that its provenance might be Persia, in the east, or perhaps Spain, in the west. But whatever its origins, placed on top of the cathedral which was itself built to celebrate Pisa's 1063 victory over Muslim forces in the western Mediterranean, it soon came to symbolize the city's place at the very center of Mediterranean trade.

The bronze griffin is decorated with incised feathers on its wings, and the carving of its back suggests silk drapery, linking it with Asia. A favorite symbol of both the Assyrians and Persians, the griffin was said to guard the gold of India, and the Greeks believed that these creatures watched over the gold of the Scythians. For Muslims, the eagle-like qualities of the beast signified vigilance, and its lion-like qualities courage. By the time it was placed on Pisa cathedral, Christians had appropriated the beast to their own iconological ends, where it came to signify the dual nature of Christ, his divinity (the eagle) and his humanity (the lion).

Figure 11.17 Griffin, from the Islamic Mediterranean, eleventh century, bronze, height $3'6\frac{1}{8}''$ (1.07 m), Museo dell'Opera del Duomo, Pisa. With the body of a lion, symbolizing courage, and the wings, head, and claws of an eagle, symbolizing vigilance, this griffin stood atop Pisa cathedral until it was moved to the cathedral museum in 1828.

reality is that it was neither well built nor adequately buttressed. Problems developed and the walls began to lean. Flying buttresses were added in the Gothic era and then rebuilt in the nineteenth century. The walls now lean outward by about twenty inches.

Pisa. Of all the Romanesque cathedrals constructed outside the pilgrimage routes, perhaps one of the most striking is that in Pisa, Italy. The "Cathedral Group" in Pisa (fig. 11.16) consists of the cathedral, begun in 1063; the baptistery, begun in 1153; and the **campanile** (the bell tower), of 1174, the famous "Leaning Tower of Pisa." All three buildings are covered in white marble, inlaid with dark green marble, a technique used by the ancient Romans.

The baptistery is circular and domed. The first two floors are Romanesque, with marble panels and arcades. The pointy gables are fourteenth-century Gothic. The architect of the cathedral was Buscheto, though the facade was designed by Rainaldo. The marble arcades are a Pisan hallmark. Blind arcades create a lacy effect, with colorful light and shade patterns. The five stories of arcades on the facade match the interior: the bottom corresponds to the nave arcade; the first open arcade reflects the galleries; the second open arcade the roof of the galleries; the third the clerestory; and the last the roof. Simple mathematical ratios determine the dimensions: the blind arcade is one-third the height of the facade, whereas each open arcade is one-sixth the height.

Pisa's most famous monument is undoubtedly the "Leaning Tower." The bell tower is usually a separate building in Italy; in other countries there are normally two bell towers on the facade of a Romanesque church. The designer of the campanile was Bonanno Pisano, who was also known as a sculptor, a fact reflected in the sculptural effect of the eight stories of arcades. The campanile leans because the foundations were poorly laid and offer uneven resistance. Most Italian towers of the Middle Ages leaned, but rarely to this degree. Pisa's campanile began to settle unevenly even while being built. The tower is 179 feet tall and is now approximately sixteen feet out of plumb. Any further tilting has been stopped by a modern foundation. Although said not to pose any threat to safety today, no "Keep off the Grass" sign is needed on the side of the tower's potential descent.

ARCHITECTURAL SCULPTURE

Romanesque sculpture offers an enormous quantity of information. As Victor Hugo put it, "In the Middle Ages human genius had no important thought which it did not engrave in stone." The vast majority of people living in Western Europe during the Middle Ages were illiterate—a portion of the clergy included. Sermons were therefore, literally, carved in stone, with sculptors creating the equivalent of picture books for those who could not read. This was accomplished in a very expressive non-naturalistic style. The lack of realism certainly does not signify a lack of skill.

Figure 11.18 *Mission of the Apostles*, tympanum, Sainte-Madeleine, Vézelay, 1120–32. This tympanum (the semi-circle above the entry) contains relief sculpture that is simultaneously decorative and didactic. The message is that Jesus's ideas, shown to travel from his fingertips to the heads of the apostles, are to be conveyed to all parts of the world at all times of the year, as represented symbolically around the tympanum.

Romanesque architectural sculpture is concentrated on church portals, especially on **tympana** (the **tympanum** is the semi-circular section above the doorway, with a horizontal lintel at the bottom, supported by a central **trumeau** or post), and column capitals. This kind of sculpture was once painted with bright colors.

The typical Romanesque tympanum has a figure of Jesus in the center, in majesty. He is surrounded by a **mandorla**, a glory of light in the shape of a pointed oval. Outside the mandorla, the subjects of different tympana vary. For example, in France at Conques and Autun it is the Last Judgment, and at Moissac it is the Apocalypse.

The Vézelay Tympanum.   An extraordinary tympanum can be found in the narthex of the church of Sainte-Madeleine in Vézelay (fig. 11.18), carved 1120–32. The subject depicted here is the *Mission of the Apostles*, presented as an allegory of the congregation's own mission to continually spread the Christian message to all the peoples of the earth. Yet how is the story told visually? Romanesque narration is simple and direct. To show

Jesus's thoughts passing into the minds of the apostles, rays emanate from Jesus's hands as he touches the head of each of them. To show that the message must be spread at all times, the second **archivolt** (or arch above the tympanum) depicts the signs of the zodiac and the labors of the months. The task of showing all the peoples of the earth was perhaps the most difficult for the sculptor. The innermost archivolt and lintel depict the various types of people believed to inhabit the distant regions of the earth. Shown there, as described in fanciful travelers' tales of the time, are people with dog-heads, who communicate by barking—the Cynocephali—and a pig-snouted tribe. Such figures continue on the lintel where the different races approach Peter and Paul. Last are the Panotii, whose ears are so large that they can be used to envelope the body like a blanket if it is cold, or to fly away if in danger. The diminutive stature of the pygmies is indi-cated by their use of ladders to mount their horses. Vézelay's tympanum provides the modern visitor with a revealing insight into the twelfth-century view of the world, which was based largely upon ancient literary sources, rather than upon contemporary accounts of actual travel and contact with other peoples.

The style in which this tympanum is carved seems to accept distortion as the norm, for even the central figures in the scene appear to be barely human. Jesus's elongated body becomes a flattened frame of bent pipes to hold drapery. The apostles vary in size according to the space available. They appear nervous, even frantic. The space in which they exist is not our space; their movements are not realistically portrayed. Much as in manuscript illumination, the drapery consists of finely drawn parallel pleats, with zigzag edges, the hems turned up into fluttering folds. Romanesque figures have been described as "the dream of God on the eve of creation, a terrible first-draft of his plan."

Yet the Vézelay tympanum should not be judged according to a realistic standard; its importance lies in its effectiveness as a symbolic and didactic illustration of Church dogma. Characterized by an exquisite abstract design, this visionary work is populated by figures intended as representations of spiritual characters rather than as illusions of reality.

The Autun Last Judgment.   Closely related in time and style to the sculpture at Vézelay is that at nearby Autun Cathedral. The monumental tympanum on the west facade, carved between 1120 and 1135, is signed *"Gislebertus hoc fecit"* (Gislebertus made it)—an extremely rare example of a signature in medieval art. As in other Romanesque tympana, there is a huge figure of Jesus in the center, surrounded by a mandorla. Flanking Jesus are scenes arranged in different sections. The entire surface is covered with figures.

The tympanum at Autun portrays the *Last Judgment* (fig. 11.19), a very popular subject in Romanesque art,

Figure 11.19 Gislebertus, *Last Judgment*, tympanum, cathedral Saint-Lazare, Autun, ca. 1120–35. Medieval Christians were told, as depicted here, that on the day of judgment one's soul literally "hung in the balance." On the left, the Saved ascend to heaven; on the right, the Damned are consigned to the tortures of hell.

intended to give an image of what awaits the viewer on Judgment Day. The expressive power and impact serve a didactic purpose; people are emphatically, dramatically, reminded to behave themselves while on earth, with the consequences for those who behave badly clearly shown.

In medieval depictions of the Last Judgment the soul literally hung in the balance between heaven and hell. On the right side of Autun's tympanum the Weighing of the Souls is represented literally. On the left, an angel tugs at the basket. On the right, a devil actually hangs from the balance bar. Thus, angel and devil both cheat! The angel wins this particular soul; other saved souls already cling to the angel. Another angel conducts the saved souls to heaven. But what about the damned? Down on the lintel, these unfortunate souls can be seen rising fearfully from the grave. The wicked cringe in agony. A serpent gnaws at the breasts of Unchastity. Intemperance scrapes an empty dish. The claws of the devil close on the head of a sinner. The image is intended to scare people who might otherwise go astray.

DECORATIVE ARTS

Reliquaries and Enamels. One important aspect of participating in a pilgrimage was the possibility of venerating relics that could be found in the churches along the route. The relics were objects connected with sacred figures such as Jesus, the Virgin Mary, or saints, and were believed to have special powers. They might be something the venerated owned, something with which they had contact, or part of their body—including bodily fluids. These relics attracted pilgrims—and their donations—helping to insure a church's prosperity and the town's wealth through tourism. Throughout the Middle Ages, trafficking in stolen and suspect relics was a major enterprise. The great spiritual and commercial value of relics explains why the most precious materials were used to make **reliquaries**, the containers for the relics.

An example is the reliquary coffer shown in figure 11.20, which was made in Limoges in the twelfth century. One of the most important Christian relics was the wooden cross on which Jesus was crucified; many reliquaries were therefore created to house pieces of the cross. The legend of the True Cross tells that the actual cross on which Jesus was crucified was found by the emperor Constantine's mother, Helena, and that most of it was kept in the Church of the Holy Sepulcher in Jerusalem, though part was also kept in Rome. In 614, the Persians conquered Jerusalem and stole the cross. In 630, it was retrieved for Jerusalem by the Byzantine emperor Heraclius, who then took it to Constantinople to protect it from the Arabs. Today, there are over 1100 reliquaries said to contain portions of the True Cross in existence.

The two major areas in Western Europe where enamel work was manufactured are the French city of Limoges, where this coffer was made, and the Mosan area, today part of Belgium. An example of Mosan work is NICHOLAS OF VERDUN's masterpiece, the altarpiece at Klosterneuburg Abbey, near Vienna. This is the most significant piece of enamel work from the twelfth century still in existence. The original altarpiece had forty-five plaques, each depicting a different scene, the figures engraved and gilded on separate enamel plaques.

Figure 11.20 Reliquary coffer, enamel, French, Limoges, twelfth century, now in Saint-Sernin, Toulouse. Elaborate coffers such as this were used to house precious relics: for instance, pieces of Jesus's cross or, perhaps, a piece of silk worn by the Virgin Mary, her milk, or a strand of a saint's hair. Such relics were thought to be endowed with magical powers.

Figure 11.21 Nicholas of Verdun, *Birth of Jesus*, plaque from the *Klosterneuburg Abbey Altarpiece*, 1181, enamel on gold, height 5½" (14 cm), Klosterneuburg Abbey, Austria. By the late twelfth century the Romanesque was being superseded by the Gothic, and evidence of greater interest in recording the visible world appeared. The drapery now reveals the form beneath, clinging and seemingly wet—unlike the flat folds unrelated to the body found in earlier Romanesque art.

The *Birth of Jesus* (fig. 11.21) shows the infant on an altar, a reference to his future sacrifice. He is wrapped in swaddling clothes, as babies customarily were in the Middle Ages. The ox and the ass are traditional inclusions, derived from Isaiah, intended to indicate that even these humble animals recognized Jesus's divinity. In the work of Nicholas of Verdun there is a sense of a three-dimensional body beneath the drapery. The fabric appears to cling, almost as if it were wet—a return to the classical manner of depicting the relationship between the figure and the fabric that covers it. This drapery is not used as a device to create abstract linear patterns, as was characteristic in most of the work of the Romanesque era. After the mid-twelfth century there was a change in artistic representation, indicative of a growing interest in the human figure, in nature, and in the world in general. The art of Nicholas of Verdun is located at this turning point, and is moving out of the Romanesque era and into the Gothic.

THE CHIVALRIC TRADITION IN LITERATURE

With their men off fighting in the crusades, medieval women began to play an increasingly powerful role in everyday life. Many women ran their family estates in their husbands' absence, and, though they had little official or legal status, they promoted a chivalric ideal in which their own position was elevated and the feudal code of stern courage and valiant warfare was displaced in favor of more genteel and refined patterns of behavior.

The Troubadours. Among the most influential proponents of this new chivalric code were the troubadours, poet-musicians who were active in the area of Provence in southern France. Writing in Occitan, the language of southern France at that time, they wrote words to sing to original melodies (as opposed to church composers, who used chant melodies handed down from the past). Troubadours were especially active in aristocratic circles, and sometimes had kings and queens as their patrons. Members of the court themselves composed works too.

The poems these minstrels sang and performed ranged widely in subject from love and morality to war and politics. However, by the middle of the twelfth century, these songs, which were often addressed to court ladies, had taken love, and particularly adulterous passion, as their central theme. Though the works celebrated the chivalric virtues, especially honor, nobility, and commitment to ideals, they were also fully cognizant of the tension between those ideals and the reality of secular love.

Such values were promoted especially by Eleanor of Aquitaine, her daughter Marie of Champagne, and her grand-daughter Blanche of Castille. Eleanor was herself the grand-daughter of one of the first such poets, Duke William IX of Aquitaine, and together with Marie she established a "Court of Love" in Poitiers in 1170. The court was governed by a code of etiquette, which was given written form in *The Art of Courtly Love* (1170–74) by Andreas Cappelanus. Marie commissioned Cappelanus to write and she clearly intended the book to be an accurate portrayal of life in Eleanor's court.

In fact, the court of love was first developed by Eleanor in England before she left Henry II to live with her daughter in Poitiers. Among the poets who wrote for her in England, evidence suggests, was MARIE DE FRANCE (twelfth century), the first woman to write verse in French. Marie de France is best known for her *lais* (lays), narratives of moderate length, which typically involve one or more miraculous or marvelous incidents and adventures concerning romantic love. A number of her *lais* concern the stories of Arthurian legend, including that of Sir Launfal. Marie's treatment of the action is less heroic than it is romantic, the characters less noble than human, the plot less concerned with grave matters of history and state than with the intimate affairs and feelings of a few people.

One of Eleanor's most gifted troubadour poets was BERNART DE VENTADORN [VEN-tuh-DOR] (d. 1195). The following stanza, from a poem apparently addressed to Eleanor herself, gives the modern reader some idea of the freedom of expression the troubadour poet was given:

> Evil she is if she doesn't call me
> To come where she undresses alone
> So that I can wait her bidding

Timeline 11.3 Christianity during the Middle Ages.

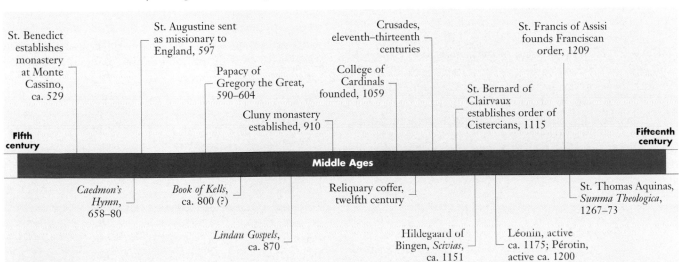

Then & Now

CHANT

*F*or most of its history, chant was the official music of the Catholic Church, just as Latin was its official language. With the Vatican reforms of 1965, however, both the Church's official language and its official music were changed.

The earliest chants were transmitted orally before they were first written down in the ninth century. One explanation for the consistency of these early melodies is that they were the responsibility of a single individual—St. Gregory, who was often depicted with a dove (symbol of divine inspiration) on his shoulder.

Chant suffered a first challenge to its authority as the dominant liturgical musical form in the Reformation of the sixteenth century. Then it was supplanted in Protestant worship by hymns and cantatas such as those composed by J.S. Bach (see Chapters 14 and 15). In the 1960s, chant gave way, even in Catholic worship, to alternative forms of music, including melodies and hymn tunes in popular styles, such as gospel and folk music.

At the end of the twentieth century, however, chant has had a surprising resurgence, less as a form of Catholic liturgy than as a reflection of popular musical taste. In the mid-1990s the CDs *Chant* and *Chant II* exhibited crossover power by heading both the popular and classical music charts. Sung by Spanish monks from the Benedictine abbey of Solesmes, *Chant* inaugurated and reflected a renewed interest in spirituality. The mystical otherworldly character of this ancient music has brought a bit of the Middle Ages into the contemporary world.

Beside the bed, along the edge,
Where I can pull off her close-fitting shoes
Down on my knees, my head bent down:
If only she'll offer me her foot.

There is no direct reference to sexual consummation, though it is implied. Of course, adultery was strictly forbidden by the chivalric code, and though the passions expressed here are strong, they are carefully controlled. Even if in actual court life nobles succumbed to temptation, in poetry at least the notion of *courtoisie*, "courtesy," was always upheld. In the end, much of the pleasure of the poetry of courtly love is derived from the clever word play. The poetry celebrates, in its purest form, the ennobling power of friendship between man and woman.

Chrétien de Troyes. An especially popular literary form depicting the chivalric relations between knights and their ladies was the **romance**, a long narrative form taking its subject matter generally from stories surrounding King Arthur and his Knights of the Round Table. Among the very first writers to popularize the romance was CHRÉTIEN DE TROYES [CRE-tee-EN] (ca. 1148–ca. 1190), whose account of the legend of Lancelot and his adulterous affair with King Arthur's wife Guinevere became a particular favorite. Called "the perfect romance," his *Chevalier de la Charette* expresses the doctrines of courtly love in their most refined form. Identifying Lancelot with Jesus, Chrétien goes so far as to equate Lancelot's noble suffering with Jesus's passion.

MUSIC

Hildegard of Bingen. Only relatively few women, those of the nobility, could enjoy the pleasures of the court of love. Most women worked the fields, at the sides of their husbands, and had the possibility of inheriting the land. Alternatively, women could become nuns and live in convents.

The head of one such convent was HILDEGARD OF BINGEN (1098–1179). Born to noble parents, Hildegard had a mystical vision at the age of five, and when she was eight was put into the care of a small community of nuns attached to the Benedictine monastery outside Bingen, near Frankfurt, Germany. She became a playwright and poet, and composed a cycle of seventy-seven songs in plainchant. She also wrote a book on medicine, and a book of visionary writings.

Hildegard of Bingen's music was written for performance by the nuns of her convent. Her major work, *The Symphony of the Harmony of Celestial Revelations*, which occupied her for much of her creative life, contains some of her finest work. One of her most beautiful compositions, *O Ecclesia*, celebrates St. Ursula who, according to legend, was martyred with eleven thousand virgins at Cologne. Like Hildegard, Ursula had led a company of women and had devoted her life to God. The music for three sopranos is accompanied by an instrumental drone, which serves as a sustained bass over which the voices weave their flowing and undulating chant-like melody.

READINGS

BEOWULF
Prologue

The heroic cast of the story of the Danish king Beowulf, with its dangerous deeds, its ethical prescriptions, and its legendary monsters, makes it both an engaging work and a didactic one. Like Homer, more than 1600 years earlier, the Beowulf poet narrates his story with vivacity and vividness.

Hear me! We've heard of Danish heroes,
Ancient kings and the glory they cut
For themselves, swinging mighty swords!
    How Shild° made slaves of soldiers from every
Land, crowds of captives he'd beaten   *5*
Into terror; he'd traveled to Denmark alone,
An abandoned child, but changed his own fate,
Lived to be rich and much honored. He ruled
Lands on all sides: wherever the sea
Would take them his soldiers sailed, returned   *10*
With tribute and obedience. There was a brave
King! And he gave them more than his glory,
Conceived a son for the Danes, a new leader
Allowed them by the grace of God. They had lived,
Before his coming, kingless and miserable;   *15*
Now the Lord of all life, Ruler
Of glory, blessed them with a prince, Beo,
Whose power and fame soon spread through the world.
Shild's strong son was the glory of Denmark;
His father's warriors were wound round his heart   *20*
With golden rings, bound to their prince
By his father's treasure. So young men build
The future, wisely open-handed in peace,
Protected in war; so warriors earn
Their fame, and wealth is shaped with a sword,   *25*
    When his time was come the old king died,
Still strong but called to the Lord's hands.
His comrades carried him down to the shore,
Bore him as their leader had asked, their lord
And companion, while words could move on
        his tongue.   *30*
Shild's reign had been long; he'd ruled them well.
There in the harbor was a ring-prowed fighting
Ship, its timbers icy, waiting,
And there they brought the beloved body
Of their ring-giving lord, and laid him near   *35*
The mast. Next to that noble corpse
They heaped up treasures, jeweled helmets,
Hooked swords and coats of mail, armor
Carried from the ends of the earth: no ship
Had ever sailed so brightly fitted,   *40*
No king sent forth more deeply mourned.
Forced to set him adrift, floating
As far as the tide might run, they refused
To give him less from their hoards of gold
Than those who'd shipped him away, an orphan   *45*
And a beggar, to cross the waves alone.
High up over his head they flew
His shining banner, then sadly let
The water pull at the ship, watched it
Slowly sliding to where neither rulers   *50*
Nor heroes nor anyone can say whose hands
Opened to take that motionless cargo.

Then Beo was king in that Danish castle,
Shild's son ruling as long as his father
And as loved, a famous lord of men.   *55*

And he in turn gave his people a son,
The great Healfdane, a fierce fighter
Who led the Danes to the end of his long
Life and left them four children,
Three princes to guide them in battle, Hergar   *60*
And Hrothgar and Halga the Good, and one daughter,
Yrs, who was given to Onela, king
Of the Swedes, and became his wife and their queen.
    Then Hrothgar, taking the throne, led
The Danes to such glory that comrades and kinsmen   *65*
Swore by his sword, and young men swelled
His armies, and he thought of greatness and resolved
To build a hall that would hold his mighty
Band and reach higher toward Heaven than anything
That had ever been known to the sons of men.   *70*
And in that hall he'd divide the spoils
Of their victories, to old and young what they'd earned
In battle, but leaving the common pastures
Untouched, and taking no lives. The work
Was ordered, the timbers tied and shaped   *75*
By the hosts that Hrothgar ruled. It was quickly
Ready, that most beautiful of dwellings, built
As he'd wanted, and then he whose word was obeyed
All over the earth named it Herot.
His boast come true he commanded a banquet,   *80*
Opened out his treasure-full hands.
That towering place, gabled and huge,
Stood waiting for time to pass, for war
To begin, for flames to leap as high
As the feud that would light them, and for Herot
        to burn.   *85*
    A powerful monster, living down
In the darkness, growled in pain, impatient
As day after day the music rang
Loud in that hall, the harp's rejoicing
Call and the poet's clear songs, sung   *90*
Of the ancient beginnings of us all, recalling
The Almighty making the earth, shaping
These beautiful plains marked off by oceans,
Then proudly setting the sun and moon
To glow across the land and light it;   *95*
The corners of the earth were made lovely with trees
And leaves, made quick with life, with each
Of the nations who now move on its face. And then
As now warriors sang of their pleasure:
So Hrothgar's men lived happy in his hall   *100*
Till the monster stirred, that demon, that fiend,
Grendel, who haunted the moors, the wild
Marshes, and made his home in a hell
Not hell but earth. He was spawned in that slime,
Conceived by a pair of those monsters born   *105*
Of Cain, murderous creatures banished
By God, punished forever for the crime
Of Abel's death.° The Almighty drove
Those demons out, and their exile was bitter,
Shut away from men; they split   *110*
Into a thousand forms of evil—spirits

---

⁴ *Shild:* A mythological Danish king; Beo's father, Healfdane's grandfather, and Hrothgar's great-grandfather.

¹⁰⁸ *Abel's death:* Genesis 4. In some postbiblical traditions Cain was regarded as the ancestor of monsters and evil spirits of various kinds.

And fiends, goblins, monsters, giants,
A brood forever opposing the Lord's
Will, and again and again defeated.

    Then, when darkness had dropped, Grendel   *115*
Went up to Herot, wondering what the warriors
Would do in that hall when their drinking was done.
He found them sprawled in sleep, suspecting
Nothing, their dreams undisturbed. The monster's
Thoughts were as quick as his greed or his claws: *120*
He slipped through the door and there in the silence
Snatched up thirty men, smashed them
Unknowing in their beds and ran out with their bodies,
The blood dripping behind him, back
To his lair, delighted with his night's slaughter.   *125*

    At daybreak, with the sun's first light, they saw
How well he had worked, and in that gray morning
Broke their long feast with tears and laments
For the dead. Hrothgar, their lord, sat joyless
In Herot, a mighty prince mourning   *130*
The fate of his lost friends and companions,
Knowing by its tracks that some demon had torn
His followers apart. He wept, fearing
The beginning might not be the end. And that night
Grendel came again, so set   *135*
On murder that no crime could ever be enough,
No savage assault quench his lust
For evil. Then each warrior tried
To escape him, searched for rest in different
Beds, as far from Herot as they could find,   *140*
Seeing how Grendel hunted when they slept.
Distance was safety; the only survivors
Were those who fled him. Hate had trimphed.
    So Grendel ruled, fought with the righteous
One against many, and won; so Herot   *145*
Stood empty, and stayed deserted for years,
Twelve winters of grief for Hrothgar, king
Of the Danes, sorrow heaped at his door
By hell-forged hands. His misery leaped
The seas, was told and sung in all   *150*
Men's ears: how Grendel's hatred began,
How the monster relished his savage war
On the Danes, keeping the bloody feud
Alive, seeking no peace, offering
No truce, accepting no settlement, no price   *155*
In gold or land, and paying the living
For one crime only with another. No one
Waited for reparation from his plundering claws:
That shadow of death hunted in the darkness,
Stalked Hrothgar's warriors, old   *160*
And young, lying in waiting, hidden
In mist, invisibly following them from the edge
Of the marsh, always there, unseen.
    So mankind's enemy continued his crimes,
Killing as often as he could, coming   *165*
Alone, bloodthirsty and horrible. Though he lived
In Herot, when the night hid him, he never
Dared to touch king Hrothgar's glorious
Throne, protected by God—God,
Whose love Grendel could not know.

                       But Hrothgar's   *170*
Heart was bent. The best and most noble
Of his council debated remedies, sat
In secret sessions, talking of terror
And wondering what the bravest of warriors could do.
And sometimes they sacrificed to the old
                      stone gods,   *175*
Made heathen vows, hoping for Hell's
Support, the Devil's guidance in driving
Their affliction off.° That was their way,
And the heathen's only hope, Hell
Always in their hearts, knowing neither God   *180*
Nor His passing as He walks through our world, the
                      Lord
Of Heaven and earth; their ears could not hear
His praise nor know His glory. Let them
Beware, those who are thrust into danger,
Clutched at by trouble, yet can carry no solace   *185*
In their hearts, cannot hope to be better! Hail
To those who will rise to God, drop off
Their dead bodies and seek our Father's peace!

    So the living sorrow of Healfdane's son
Simmered, bitter and fresh, and no wisdom   *190*
Or strength could break it: that agony hung
On king and people alike, harsh
And unending, violent and cruel and evil.
    In his far-off home Beowulf, Higlac's°
Follower and the strongest of the Geats—greater   *195*
And stronger than anyone anywhere in this world—
Heard how Grendel filled nights with horror
And quickly commanded a boat fitted out,
Proclaiming that he'd go to that famous king,
Would sail across the sea to Hrothgar,   *200*
Now when help was needed. None
Of the wise ones regretted his going, much
As he was loved by the Geats: the omens were good,
And they urged the adventure on. So Beowulf
Chose the mightiest men he could find,   *205*
The bravest and best of the Geats, fourteen
In all, and led them down to their boat;
He knew the sea, would point the prow
Straight to that distant Danish shore.
    Then they sailed, set their ship   *210*
Out on the waves, under the cliffs.
Ready for what came they wound through the currents,
The seas beating at the sand, and were borne
In the lap of their shining ship, lined
With gleaming armor, going safely   *215*
In that oak-hard boat to where their hearts took them.
The wind hurried them over the waves,
The ship foamed through the sea like a bird
Until, in the time they had known it would take,
Standing in the round-curled prow they could see   *220*
Sparkling hills, high and green,
Jutting up over the shore, and rejoicing

---

[178] *Made heathen … off*: As Christianity was regarded as the only true and valid religion, all other religions and gods were ultimately traceable to the enemy of God, the Devil.   [194] *Higlac*: King of the Geats, a people of southern Sweden. Higlac is both Beowulf's feudal lord and his uncle.

In those rock-steep cliffs they quietly ended
Their voyage. Jumping to the ground, the Geats
Pushed their boat to the sand and tied it   225
In place, mail shirts and armor rattling
As they swiftly moored their ship. And then
They gave thanks to God for their easy crossing.
      High on a wall a Danish watcher
Patrolling along the cliffs saw   230
The travelers crossing to the shore, their shields
Raised and shining; he came riding down,
Hrothgar's lieutenant, spurring his horse,
Needing to know why they'd landed, these men
In armor. Shaking his heavy spear   235
In their faces he spoke:
      "Whose soldiers are you,
You who've been carried in your deep-keeled ship
Across the sea-road to this country of mine?
Listen! I've stood on these cliffs longer
Than you know, keeping our coast free   240
Of pirates, raiders sneaking ashore
From their ships, seeking our lives and our gold.
None have ever come more openly—
And yet you've offered no password, no sign
From my prince, no permission from my people for your
                  landing   245
Here. Nor have I ever seen,
Out of all the men on earth, one greater
Than has come with you; no commoner carries
Such weapons, unless his appearance, and his beauty,
Are both lies. You! Tell me your name,   250
And your father's; no spies go further onto Danish
Soil than you've come already. Strangers,
From wherever it was you sailed, tell it,
And tell it quickly, the quicker the better,
I say, for us all. Speak, say   255
Exactly who you are, and from where, and why."

↤ MEDIEVAL MYSTERY PLAYS
The Chester Pageant of the Deluge

*The biblical Deluge, or Flood, is dramatized in all the surviving
medieval cycles of mystery plays. The following version was performed
in Chester, England, by the guild of the water-leaders and drawers—
the subject of the drama was therefore particularly appropriate to the
profession of the actors. Noah's wife is of especial interest and demonstrates the popular character of these pageants, since in the play she is
far removed from the orthodox Church idea of her as meek and mild.*

GOD   I, God, that all the world have wrought
     Heaven and Earth, and all of nought,
     I see my people, in deed and thought,
     Are foully set in sin.
           My ghost shall not lodge in any man   5
     That through fleshly liking is my fone,°
     But till six score years be gone
     To look if they will blynne.°

     Man that I made I will destroy,
     Beast, worm, and fowl to fly,   10
     For on earth they me annoy,
     The folk that is thereon.
           For it harms me so hurtfully
     The malice now that can multiply,
     That sore it grieveth me inwardly,   15
     That ever I made man.
           Therefore Noah, my servant free,
     That righteous man art, as I see,
     A ship soon thou shalt make thee,
     Of trees dry and light.   20
           Little chambers therein thou make
     And binding slich° also thou take
     Within and out, thou not slake
     To annoint it through all thy might.
           Three hundred cubits it shall be long, 25
     And so of breadth to make it strong.
     Of height so, then must thou fonge,°
     Thus measure it about.
           One window work though thy might;
     One cubit of length and breadth make it,   30
     Upon the side a door shall fit
     For to come in and out.
           Eating-places thou make also,
     Three roofed chambers, one or two:
     For with water I think to stow°   35
     Man that I can make.
           Destroyed all the world shall be,
     Save thou, thy wife, and sons three,
     And all their wives, also, with thee,
     Shall saved be for thy sake.   40
NOAH   Ah, Lord ! I thank thee, loud and still,
     That to me art in such will,
     And spares me and my house to spill
     As now I soothly find.
           Thy bidding, Lord, I shall fulfil,   45
     And never more thee grieve nor grill°
     That such grace has sent me till
     Among all mankind.
           Have done you men and women all;
     Help, for aught that may befall,   50
     To work this ship, chamber, and hall,
     As God hath bidden us do.
SHEM   Father, I am already bowne,°
     An axe I have, by my crown !
     As sharp as any in all this town   55
     For to go thereto.
HAM   I have a hatchet, wonder keen,
     To bite well, as may be seen,
     A better ground one, as I ween
     Is not in all this town.   60
JAPHET   And I can well make a pin,
     And with this hammer knock it in;
     Go and work without more din;
     And I am ready bowne.
NOAH'S WIFE   And we shall bring timber too,   65

---

⁶ *fone:* foe.   ⁸ *blynne:* cease.

⁸ *blynne:* cease. *stow:* hinder, stop. ⁴⁶ *grill:* vex.
⁵³ *bowne:* prepared.

For women nothing else to do
Women be weak to undergo
Any great travail.

SHEM'S WIFE   Here is a good hackstock;
On this you must hew and knock: 70
Shall none be idle in this flock,
Nor now may no man fail.

HAM'S WIFE   And I will go to gather slich,
The ship for to clean and pitch;
Anointed it must be, every stitch,   75
Board, tree, and pin.

JAPHET'S WIFE   And I will gather chips here
To make a fire for you in fear,
And for to dight° your dinner,
Against you come in.   80
*[Here they make signs as though they were working with
divers instruments.*

NOAH   Now in the name of God I will begin,
To make the ship that we shall in,
That we be ready for to swim,
At the coming of the flood.
        These boards I join together,   85
To keep us safe from the weather
That we may roam both hither and thither
And safe be from this flood.
        Of this tree will I have the mast,
Tied with gables that will last   90
With a sail yard for each blast
And each thing in its kind.
        With topmast high and bowsprit,
With cords and ropes, I hold all fit
To sail forth at the next weete°   95
This ship is at an end.
Wife in this castle we shall be kept:
My children and thou I would in leaped!

NOAH'S WIFE   In faith, Noe, I had as lief thou had slept for
all thy frankishfare,°   100
For I will not do after thy rede.°

NOAH   Good wife, do as I thee bid.

NOAH'S WIFE   By Christ not, or I see more need,
Though thou stand all the day and rave.

NOAH   Lord, that women be crabbed aye!   105
And never are meek, that I dare say.
This is well seen of me to-day
In witness of you each one.
        Good wife, let be all this beere°
That thou makest in this place here,   110
For they all ween thou art master;
And so thou art, by St. John!

GOD   Noah, take thou thy company
And in the ship hie that you be,
For none so righteous man to me   115
Is now on earth living.
        Of clean beasts with thee thou take
Seven and seven, or thou seake,
He and she make to make
Quickly in that thou bring.   120

Of beasts unclean two and two,
Male and female, without more;
Of clean fowls seven also,
The he and she together.
        Of fowles unclean two, and no more;   125
Of beasts as I said before:
That shall be saved through my lore
Against I send the weather.
        Of all meats that must be eaten
Into the ship look there be gotten,   130
For that no way may be forgotten
And do all this by deene.°
        To sustain man and beasts therein,
Aye, till the waters cease and blyn.°
This world is filled full of sin   135
And that is now well seen.
        Seven days be yet coming,
You shall have space them in to bring;
After that it is my liking
Mankind for to annoy.   140
        Forty days and forty nights,
Rain shall fall for their unrights;
And that I have made through my might,
Now think I to destroy.

NOAH   Lord, at your bidding I am bayne,°   145
Since none other grace will gain,
It will I fulfil fain,
For gracious I thee find.
        A hundred winters and twenty
This ship making tarried have I: 150
If, through amendment, any mercy
Would fall unto mankind.
        Have done, you men and women all.
Hie you, lest this water fall,
That each beast were in his stall   155
And into ship brought.
        Of clean beasts seven shall be;
Of unclean two, this God bade me;
This flood is nigh, well may we see,
Therefore tarry you nought.   160

SHEM   Sir, here are lions, leopards in,
Horses, mares, oxen, and swine,
Goats, calves, sheep, and kine,
Here sitten° may you see.

HAM   Camels, asses, men may find;   165
Buck, doe, hart and hind,
And beasts of all manner kind.
Here be, as thinks me.

JAPHET   Take here cats and dogs too,
Otter, fox, fulmart also;   170
Hares hopping gaily, can ye
Have kail here for to eat.

NOAH'S WIFE   And here are bears, wolves set,
Apes, owls, marmoset;
Weasels, squirrels, and ferret   175
Here they eat their meat.

SHEM'S WIFE   Yet more beasts are in this house!

---

79 *dight*: prepare.   95 *weete*: tide.   100 *frankishfare*: nonsense.
102 *rede*: advice.   109 *beere*: noise.

132 *by deene*: immediately.   114 *blyn*: stop.   145 *bayne*: ready.
164 *sitten*: settled.

Here cats come in full crowse,°
Here a rat and here a mouse;
They stand nigh together. 180
HAM'S WIFE   And here are fowls less and more,
Herons, cranes and bittern;
Swans, peacocks, have them before!
Meat for this weather.
JAPHET'S WIFE   Here are cocks, kites, crows, 185
Rooks, ravens, many rows;
Cuckoos, curlews, whoso knows,
Each one in his kind.
            And here are doves, ducks, drakes,
Redshanks, running through the lakes, 190
And each fowl that language makes
In this ship men may find.

*[In the stage direction the sons of Noah are enjoined to mention
aloud the names of the animals which enter; a representation of
which, painted on parchment, is to be carried by the actors.*

NOAH   Wife, come in, why standest thou there?
Thou art ever forward, that I dare swear:
Come on God's half, time it were, 195
For fear lest that we drown.
NOAH'S WIFE   Yea, sir, set up your sail
And row forth with evil heale,
For, without any fail,
I will not out of this town. 200
            But I have my gossips every one,
One foot further I will not go;
They shall not drown, by St. John!
If I may save their life.
            They loved me full well, by Christ! 205
But thou wilt let them in thy chest,
Else row forth, Noah, whither thou list,
And get thee a new wife.
NOAH   Shem, some love thy mother, 'tis true;
Forsooth, such another I do not know! 210
SHEM   Father, I shall set her in, I trow,
Without any fail.
            Mother, my father after thee sends,
And bids thee unto yonder ship wend,°
Look up and see the wind, 215
For we be ready to sail.
NOAH'S WIFE   Son, go again to him and say
I will not come therein to-day!
NOAH   Come in, wife in twenty devils' way,
Or else stand without. 220
HAM   Shall we all fetch her in?
NOAH   Yea, sons, in Christ's blessing and mine,
I would you hied you betime,
For of this flood I am in doubt.
JAPHET   Mother, we pray you altogether, 225
For we are here, your children;
Come into the ship for fear of the weather,
For his love that you bought!
NOAH'S WIFE   That I will not for your call, go.
But if I have my gossips all. 230
GOSSIP   The flood comes in full fleeting fast,

On every side it broadens in haste;
For fear of drowning I am aghast:
Good gossip, let me come in!
            Or let us drink ere we depart, 235
For oftentimes we have done so;
For at a time thou drinkst a quart,
And so will I ere that I go.
SHEM   In faith, mother, yet you shall,
Whether you will or not! 240
                                    [*She goes.*
NOAH   Welcome, wife, into this boat!
NOAH'S WIFE   And have them that for thy note!°
            [*Et dat alapam victa.*°
NOAH   Aha! marry, this is hot!
It is good to be still.
My children! methinks this boat removes! 245
Our tarrying here hugely me grieves!
Over the land the water spreads!
God do as he will!
            Ah, great God, thou art so good!
Now all this world is in a flood 250
As I see well in sight.
            This window will I close anon,
And into my chamber will I gone
Till this water, so great one,
Be slaked through thy might. 255

*[Noah, according to stage directions, is now to shut the windows of
the ark and retire for a short time. He is then to chant the psalm,
Salva me, Domine! and afterwards to open them and look out.*

            Now forty days are fully gone.
Send a raven I will anon;
If aught were earth, tree, or stone,
Be dry in any place.
            And if this fowl come not again 260
It is a sign, sooth to say,
That dry it is on hill or plain,
And God hath done some grace.
            [*A raven is now despatched.*
            Ah, Lord! wherever this raven lie,
Somewhere is dry well I see; 265
But yet a dove, by my lewtye°
After I will send.
Thou wilt turn again to me
For of all fowls that may fly
Thou art most meek and hend.° 270

*[The stage direction enjoins here that another dove shall be ready
with an olive branch in its mouth, which is to be dropped by means
of a cord into Noah's hand.*

            Ah Lord! blessed be thou aye,
That me hast comforted thus to-day!
By this sight, I may well say
This flood begins to cease.
            My sweet dove to me brought has 275
A branch of olive from some place;
This betokeneth God has done us some grace,

---

242 *note:* business, occupation.   Stage direction *Et … victa:* And
being conquered she deals a slap.   266 *lewtye:* fidelity.   270 *hend:*
kind.

And is a sign of peace.
　　　　　Ah, Lord! honoured must thou be!
All earth dries now I see;　　　　　　　　　　280
But yet, till thou command me,
Hence will I not hie.
　　　　　All this water is away,
Therefore as soon as I may
Sacrifice I shall do in faye°　　　　　　　　285
To thee devoutly.
GOD　　Noah, take thy wife anon,
And thy children every one,
Out of the ship thou shalt gone,
And they all with thee.　　　　　　　　　290
　　　　　Beasts and all that can flie,
Out anon they shall hie,
On earth to grow and multiply:
I will that it be so.
NOAH　　Lord, I thank thee, through thy might,　　295
Thy bidding shall be done in hight,°
And, as fast as I may dight
I will do thee honour.
　　　　　And to thee offer sacrifice,
Therefore comes in all wise,　　　　　　　300
For of these beasts that be his
Offer I will this stower.°

[Then leaving the ark with his whole family, he shall take the ani-
mals and birds, make an offering of them, and set out on his way.

　　　　　Lord God, in majesty,
That such grace has granted me,
When all was borne safe to be,　　　　　　305
Therefore now I am boune.°
　　　　　My wife, my children, my company,
With sacrifice to honour thee,
With beasts, fowls, as thou may see,
I offer here right soon.　　　　　　　　310
GOD　　Noah, to me thou art full able,
And thy sacrifice acceptable,
For I have found thee true and stable,
On thee now must I myn.°
Curse earth will I no more　　　　　　　315
That man's sin it grieves sore,
For of youth man full of yore
Has been inclined to sin.
　　　　　You shall now grow and multiply
And earth you edify,　　　　　　　　　320
Each beast and fowl that may flie
Shall be afraid for you.
　　　　　And fish in sea that may flitt
Shall sustain you—I you behite°
To eat of them you not lett°　　　　　　325
That clean be you may know.
　　　　　There as you have eaten before
Grasses and roots, since you were born,
Of clean beasts, less and more,
I give you leave to eat.　　　　　　　　330

Save blood and fish both in fear
Of wrong dead carrion that is here,
Eat not of that in no manner,
For that aye you shall lett.
　　　　　Manslaughter also you shall flee,　　335
For that is not pleasant to me
That sheds blood, he or she
Ought where among mankind.
　　　　　That sheds blood, his blood shall be
And vengeance have, that men shall see;　　340
Therefore now beware now all ye
You fall not in that sin.
And forward now with you I make
And all thy seed, for thy sake,
Of such vengeance for to slake,　　　　　345
For now I have my will.
　　　　　Here I promise thee a behest,°
That man, woman, fowl, nor beast
With water while the world shall last,
I will no more spill.　　　　　　　　350
　　　　　My bow between you and me
In the firmament shall be,
By very tokens, that you may see
That such vengeance shall cease.
　　　　　That man, nor woman, shall never more　355
Be wasted by water, as is before,
But for sin that grieveth sore,
Therefore this vengeance was.
　　　　　Where clouds in the welkin
That each bow shall be seen,　　　　　　360
In token that my wrath or tene°
Should never this wroken be.
　　　　　The string is turned toward you,　　—
And toward me bent is the bow,
That such weather shall never show,　　　365
And this do I grant to thee.
　　　　　My blessing now I give thee here,
To thee Noah, my servant dear;
For vengeance shall no more appear;
And now farewell, my darling dear!　　　370

↞ **SONG OF ROLAND**

The Approach of the Saracens

The following excerpt is from the most famous of medieval French
chansons de geste, *the* Song of Roland. *In this section of the poem*
the narrator describes how the French military leader Roland refuses
to sound his ivory horn to call for help in fighting against a much
larger Saracen army.

80

Oliver climbs to the top of a hill,
looks to his right, across a grassy vale,
sees the pagan army on its way there;
and called down to Roland, his companion:
"That way, toward Spain: the uproar I see coming!　5
All their hauberks, all blazing, helmets like flames!

---

²⁸⁵ *faye:* faith　²⁹⁶ *hight:* haste　³⁰² *stower:* steer.　³⁰⁶ *boune:* ready.
³¹⁴ *On thee … myn:* Thee now must I have in mind.　³²⁴ *behite:*
promise.　³²⁵ *lett:* cease.

---

³⁴⁷ *behest:* covenant.　³⁶¹ *tene:* anger.

It will be a bitter thing for our French.
Ganelon knew, that criminal, that traitor,
When he marked us out before the Emperor."
"Be still, Oliver," Roland the Count replies.   10
"He is my stepfather—my stepfather.
          I won't have you speak one word against him."

81

Oliver has gone up upon a hill,
sees clearly now: the kingdom of Spain,
and the Saracens assembled in such numbers: 15
helmets blazing, bedecked with gems in gold,
those shields of theirs, those hauberks sewn with brass,
and all their spears, the gonfanons affixed;
cannot begin to count their battle corps,
there are too many, he cannot take their number.   20
And he is deeply troubled by what he sees.
He made his way quickly down from the hill,
came to the French, told them all he had seen.

82

Said Oliver: "I saw the Saracens,
no man on earth ever saw more of them—   25
one hundred thousand, with their shields, up in front,
helmets laced on, hauberks blazing on them,
the shafts straight up, the iron heads like flames—
you'll get a battle, nothing like it before.
My lords, my French, may God give you
          the strength.   30
Hold your ground now! Let them not defeat us!"
And the French say: "God hate the man who runs!
We may die here, but no man will fail you." AOI.

83

Said Oliver: "The pagan force is great;
from what I see, our French here are too few.   35
Roland, my companion, sound your horn then,
Charles will hear it, the army will come back."
Roland replies: "I'd be a fool to do it.
I would lose my good name all through sweet France.
I will strike now, I'll strike with Durendal,   40
the blade will be bloody to the gold from striking!
These pagan traitors came to these passes doomed!
I promise you, they are marked men, they'll die." AOI.

84

"Roland, Companion, now sound the olifant,
Charles will hear it, he will bring the army back,   45
The king will come with all his barons to help us."
Roland replies: "May it never please God
that my kin should be shamed because of me,
or that sweet France should fall into disgrace.
Never! Never! I'll strike with Durendal,   50
I'll strike with this good sword strapped to my side,
you'll see this blade running its whole length with blood.
These pagan traitors have gathered here to die.
I promise you, they are all bound for death." AOI.

85

"Roland, Companion, sound your olifant now,   55

Charles will hear it, marching through those passes.
I promise you, the Franks will come at once."
Roland replies: "May it never please God
that any man alive should come to say
that pagans—pagans!—once made me sound
          this horn: 60
no kin of mine will ever bear that shame.
Once I enter this great battle coming
and strike my thousand seven hundred blows,
you'll see the bloody steel of Durendal.
These French are good—they will strike like
          brave men.   65
Nothing can save the men of Spain from death."

86

Said Oliver: "I see no blame in it—
I watched the Saracens coming from Spain,
the valleys and mountains covered with them,
every hillside and every plain all covered,   70
hosts and hosts everywhere of those strange men—
and here we have a little company."
Roland replies: "That whets my appetite.
May it not please God and his angels and saints
to let France lose its glory because of me—   75
let me not end in shame, let me die first.
The Emperor loves us when we fight well."

87

Roland is good, and Oliver is wise,
both these vassals men of amazing courage:
once they are armed and mounted on their horses,   80
they will not run, though they die for it, from battle.
Good men, these Counts, and their words full of spirit.
Traitor pagans are riding up in fury.
Said Oliver: "Roland, look—the first ones,
on top of us—and Charles is far away.   85
You did not think it right to sound your olifant:
if the King were here, we'd come out without losses.
Now look up there, toward the passes of Aspre—
you can see the rear-guard: it will suffer.
No man in that detail will be in another."   90
Roland replies: "Don't speak such foolishness—
shame on the heart gone coward in the chest.
We'll hold our ground, we'll stand firm—we're the ones!
We'll fight with spears, we'll fight them hand to hand!"
          AOI.

88

When Roland sees that there will be a battle,   95
it makes him fiercer than a lion or leopard;
shouts to the French, calls out to Oliver:
"Lord, companion: friend, do not say such things.
The Emperor, who left us these good French,
had set apart these twenty thousand men: 100
he knew there was no coward in their ranks.
A man must meet great troubles for his lord,
stand up to the great heat and the great cold,
give up some flesh and blood—it is his duty.
Strike with the lance, I'll strike with Durendal—   105
it was the King who gave me this good sword!

If I die here, the man who gets it can say:
it was a noble's, a vassal's, a good man's sword."

89

And now there comes the Archbishop Turpin.
He spurs his horse, goes up into a mountain,   *110*
summons the French; and he preached them a sermon:
"Barons, my lords, Charles left us in this place.
We know our duty: to die like good men for our King.
Fight to defend the holy Christian faith.
Now you will have a battle, you know it now,   *115*
you see the Saracens with your own eyes.
Confess your sins, pray to the Lord for mercy.
I will absolve you all, to save your souls.
If you die here, you will stand up holy martyrs,
you will have seats in highest Paradise."   *120*
The French dismount, cast themselves on the ground;
the Archbishop blesses them in God's name.
He commands them to do one penance: strike.

90

The French arise, stand on their feet again;
they are absolved, released from all their sins: *125*
the Archbishop has blessed them in God's name.
Now they are mounted on their swift battle horses,
bearing their arms like faithful warriors:
and every man stands ready for the battle.
Roland the Count calls out to Oliver: *130*
"Lord, Companion, you knew it, you were right,
Ganelon watched for his chance to betray us,
got gold for it, got goods for it, and money.
The Emperor will have to avenge us now.
King Marsilion made a bargain for our lives,   *135*
but still must pay, and that must be with swords." AOI.

91

Roland went forth into the Spanish passes
on Veillantif, his good swift-running horse.
He bears his arms—how they become this man!—
grips his lance now, hefting it, working it,   *140*
now swings the iron point up toward the sky,
the gonfanon all white laced on above—
the golden streamers beat down upon his hands:
a noble's body, the face aglow and smiling.
Close behind him his good companion follows;   *145*
the men of France hail him: their protector!
He looks wildly toward the Saracens,
and humbly and gently to the men of France;
and spoke a word to them in all courtesy:
"Barons, my lords, easy now, keep at a walk.   *150*
These pagans are searching for martyrdom.
We'll get good spoils before this day is over,
no king of France ever got such treasure!"
And with these words, the hosts are at each other. AOI.

92

Said Oliver: "I will waste no more words.   *155*
You did not think it right to sound your olifant,
there'll be no Charles coming to your aid now.
He knows nothing, brave man, he's done no wrong;

those men down there—they have no blame in this.
Well, then, ride now, and ride with all your might!   *160*
Lords, you brave men, stand your ground, hold the field!
Make up your minds, I beg you in God's name,
to strike some blows, take them and give them back!
Here we must not forget Charlemagne's war cry."
And with that word the men of France cried out.   *165*
A man who heard that shout: Munjoie! Munjoie!
would always remember what manhood is.
Then they ride, God! Look at their pride and spirit!
and they spur hard, to ride with all their speed,
come on to strike—what else would these men do?   *170*
The Saracens kept coming, never fearing them,
Franks and pagans, here they are, at each other.

✦ MARIE DE FRANCE
The Nightingale

As far as is known, the first woman to write poetry in French was Marie de France. She is best known for her lais, *narratives of moderate length typically involving one or more miraculous or marvelous incidents and other adventures concerning romantic love. "The Nightingale," reflects a few of the conventions of courtly love, medieval guidelines for the behavior of lovers outside marriage.*

The story I shall tell today
Was taken from a Breton lay
Called Laustic in Brittany,
Which, in proper French would be
Rossignol. They'd call the tale   *5*
In English lands *The Nightingale*.
There was, near Saint Malo, a town
Of some importance and renown.
Two barons who could well afford
Houses suited to a lord   *10*
Gave the city its good name
By their benevolence and fame.
Only one of them had married.
His wife was beautiful indeed
And courteous as she was fair,   *15*
A lady who was well aware
Of all that custom and rank required.
The younger baron was much admired,
Being, among his peers, foremost
In valor, and a gracious host.   *20*
He never refused a tournament,
And what he owned he gladly spent.
He loved his neighbor's wife. She knew
That all she heard of him was true,
And so she was inclined to be   *25*
Persuaded when she heard his plea.
Soon she had yielded all her heart
To his real merit and, in part,
Because he lived not far away.
Fearful that they might betray   *30*
The love that they had come to share,
They always took the greatest care
Not to let anyone detect
Anything that might be suspect.
And it was easy enough to hide;   *35*
Their houses were almost side by side

With nothing between the two at all
Except a single high stone wall.
The baron's wife need only go
And stand beside her bedroom window   40
Whenever she wished to see her friend.
They would talk for hours on end
Across the wall, and often threw
Presents through the window too.
They were much happier than before,   45
And would have asked for nothing more;
But lovers can't be satisfied
When love's true pleasure is denied.
The lady was watched too carefully
As soon as her friend was known to be   50
At home. But still they had the delight
Of seeing each other day or night
And talking to their heart's content.
The strictest guard could not prevent
The lady from looking out her window;   55
What she saw there no one could know.
Nothing came to interfere
With their true love until one year
In the season when the summer grows
Green in all the woods and meadows,   60
When birds to show their pleasure cling
To flower tops and sweetly sing.
Then those who were in love before
Do, in love's service, even more.
The baron, in truth, was all intent   65
On love; the messages he sent
Across the wall had such replies
From his lady's lips and from her eyes,
He knew that she felt just the same.
Now she very often came   70
To her window lighted by the moon,
Leaving her husband's side as soon
As she knew that he was fast asleep.
Wrapped in a cloak, she went to keep
Watch with her lover, sure that he   75
Would be waiting for her faithfully.
To see each other was, despite
Their endless longing, great delight.
She went so often and remained
So long, her husband soon complained,   80
Insisting that she must reply
To where she went at night and why.
"I'll tell you, my lord," the lady answered;
"Anyone who has ever heard
The nightingale singing will admit   85
No joy on earth compares with it.
That music just outside my window
Gives me such pleasure that I know
I cannot go to sleep until
The sweet voice in the night is still."   90
The baron only answered her
With a malicious raging laughter.
He wrought a plan that could not fail
To overcome the nightingale.
The household servants all were set   95
To making traps of cord or net;
Then, throughout the orchard, these

Were fixed to hazel and chestnut trees,
And all the branches rimmed with glue
So that the bird could not slip through.   100
It was not long before they brought
The nightingale who had been caught
Alive. The baron, well content,
Took the bird to his wife's apartment.
"Where are you, lady? Come talk to me!"   105
He cried, "I've something for you to see!
Look! Here is the bird whose song
Has kept you from your sleep so long.
Your nights will be more peaceful when
He can't awaken you again!"   110
She heard with sorrow and with dread
Everything her husband said,
Then asked him for the bird, and he
Killed it out of cruelty;
Vile, with his two hands he wrung   115
Its neck, and when he finished, flung
The body at his wife. The red
Drops of blood ran down and spread
Over the bodice of her dress.
He left her alone with her distress.   120
Weeping, she held the bird and thought
With bitter rage of those who brought
The nightingale to death, betrayed
By all the hidden traps they laid.
"Alas!" she cried. "They had destroyed   125
The one great pleasure I enjoyed.
Now I can no longer go
And see my love outside my window
At night the way I used to do!
One thing certainly is true: 130
He'll think that I no longer care.
Somehow he must be made aware
Of what has happened. It will be clear
Then why I cannot appear."
And so she began at once to write   135
On a piece of gold-embroidered samite.
When it couldn't hold another word
She wrapped it around the little bird.
Then she called someone in her service
Whom she could entrust with this,   140
Bidding him take without delay
Her message to her chevalier.
Thus he came to understand
Everything, just as she planned.
The servant brought the little bird;   145
And when the chevalier had heard
All that he so grieved to know,
His courteous answer was not slow.
He ordered made a little case,
Not of iron or any base   150
Metal, but fine gold embossed
With jewels—he did not count the cost.
The cover was not too long or wide.
He placed the nightingale inside
And had the casket sealed with care!   155
He carried it with him everywhere.
Stories like this can't be controlled,
And it was very promptly told.

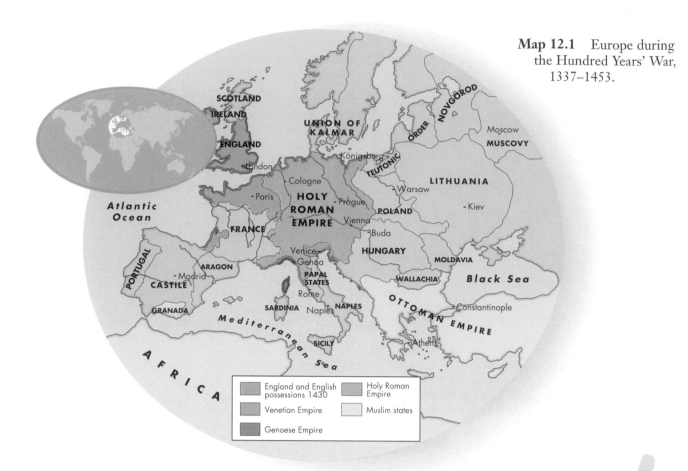

Map 12.1 Europe during the Hundred Years' War, 1337–1453.

England and English possessions 1430

Venetian Empire

Genoese Empire

Holy Roman Empire

Muslim states

THE GOTHIC
AND LATE
MIDDLE AGES

Duccio, *Madonna and Child Enthroned*, 1308–11, Siena, Italy.

THE GOTHIC ERA

PARIS IN THE LATER MIDDLE AGES

No city dominated the later Middle Ages more than Paris. Home to a revival in learning at the newly founded university, Paris was also the seat of the French government, overseen by King LOUIS IX (later St. Louis) (r. 1226–1270). The monarchy had not enjoyed such power and respect since the time of Charlemagne. Louis made a determined effort to be a king to all his people, sending royal commissioners into the countryside to monitor the administration of local government and to ensure justice for all. He outlawed private warfare and abolished serfdom, and granted his subjects the right to appeal to higher courts. Furthermore, he became something of a peacekeeper among the other European powers, and was in most matters more influential than the pope. In short, he became associated with fairness and justice, and France consolidated itself as a nation around him, with Paris as its focal point. Soon all roads led to Paris, as they had once led to Rome.

Louis continued a remarkable building program in Paris. Construction of the cathedral of Notre-Dame had begun in 1163. Under Louis, work progressed, with Paris's approximately 120 guilds all contributing labor and money. The cathedral was, in this sense, not only the center of spiritual life, but also a very real focus for the community. In addition, Louis commissioned the magnificent Sainte-Chapelle, the royal chapel, also on the Île-de-la-Cité, the island in the middle of the Seine River that had been the city center since Roman times. The chapel was built to house the Crown of Thorns, a relic that a French nobleman had given the Venetians as collateral for a loan to support the Fourth Crusade; Louis paid off the debt and returned the relic to Paris. The Sainte-Chapelle was, in effect, its monumental reliquary.

The relative security and productivity of Louis's reign, however, could not long be sustained. In addition to the cost of the building program in Paris, France suffered the crippling expense of fighting what would become known as the Hundred Years' War, which actually began in 1337 and ended in 1453. Ostensibly a fight over the succession to the French throne—none of Louis's successor Philip IV's three sons produced a male heir—it was instigated by Edward III of England (r. 1327–77), who claimed that, as the nephew of the last Capetian king, he was the rightful ruler of France. As the French kings increased taxes to support what was generally a losing battle, and then suffered humiliating defeats at Crécy in 1346 and again at Poitiers in 1356, the general population rebelled.

The English had captured King John II, known as John the Good (r. 1350–64) at Poitiers, and perhaps sensing the weakness of Charles, John's adolescent son, who acted as regent for his father during his captivity in England, the merchant provost Étienne Marcel revolted against the crown. On February 22, 1358, he led a mob into Charles's apartments, slaughtering the regent's counsellors before his eyes. Charles, however, did not surrender, and eventually Marcel was murdered and the revolt crushed.

When Charles came to the throne as CHARLES V (r. 1364–1380), he could not bring himself to live any longer in the buildings where he had witnessed the bloody revolt. Transforming the old palace into his Parliament, or Palace of Justice, as it is known today, he moved across the river onto the right bank, turning old fortifications built by Philip Augustus against the threat of English invasion into the royal residence—the Louvre. In *Les Très Riches Heures* (fig. 12.1), an illuminated

Figure 12.1 Limbourg brothers, *October*, from *Les Très Riches Heures* of the Duke of Berry, French, 1413–16, manuscript illumination, $11\frac{1}{2} \times 8\frac{1}{4}''$ (29.2 × 21 cm), Musée Condé, Château of Chantilly, France. This illustration depicts the Louvre as it appeared in the time of Charles V in a highly realistic manner, containing the first representations of shadows since classical antiquity.

Then & Now

THE LOUVRE

The Louvre today is one of the most famous museums in the world. It is also the largest royal palace in the world, a building that has undergone more redevelopment through the ages than any other building in Europe. The first building on the site was a fortress, erected in 1200 by Philip Augustus, with a keep, the symbol of royal power, surrounded by a moat. Remnants of the moat and keep still exist, and can be viewed on the bottom floor of the museum.

It was Charles V who first used the building as a royal residence, but over the years its galleries and arcades have also served as a prison, an arsenal, a mint, a granary, a county seat, a publishing house, a ministry, the Institute for Advanced Studies, a telegraph station, a shopping arcade, a tavern, and a hotel for visiting heads of state. The expansive and open plan of the Louvre today, with its two great arms extending from the original building west to the Tuileries gardens, is the result of later additions. In the latter part of the sixteenth century, Henry IV added the Grand Galleries, initially conceived as a covered walkway connecting the palace to the garden, and where the Dauphin

would later exercise his camel, riding it up and down their length. In the seventeenth century, Louis XIV closed off the east end, forming the Cour Carrée.

The result of all these various additions and alterations is a building that represents almost every architectural style in the history of the West. A Romanesque fortress forms its basis, and outward from it spread two Gothic and two Renaissance wings. Baroque and Rococo ornamentation can be found throughout, and the closed-off end is Neoclassical. In this spirit of heterogeneity and plurality, architect I.M. Pei designed a glass pyramid (fig. 12.2) to serve as the museum's new entrance in 1988. Set above a network of underground rooms and walkways, Pei's pyramid is 61 feet high and 108 feet wide at the base, and constructed of 105 tons of glass. Beside it are flat triangular pools that reflect the walls of the surrounding palace, bringing the ancient and the modern into harmony.

Figure 12.2 I.M. Pei, Glass Pyramid, addition to the Louvre, Paris, France, 1988. Pei's pyramid was highly controversial at the time of its construction, as Parisians claimed it did not "fit" architecturally into this most eclectic of architectural spaces.

manuscript commissioned by the Duke of Berry and created by the Limbourg brothers in 1413 16, Charles's new palace at the Louvre, with its towers, ramparts, and crenelated walls, is seen in open country just west of the university from a point on the left bank of the Seine. In his new residence Charles installed a library of 973 books, then the largest in France, on cypress-wood shelves (cypress being poisonous to insects). His collection included the texts of Ovid and Livy, works of magic, scripture, bestiaries, and astronomies, and was to eventually form the foundation of the Bibliothèque Nationale, today France's great national library. Charles also erected new walls around the city to the north, anchored to the east by the newly erected Bastille. Within these walls, the population of Paris numbered approximately 150,000, an extremely large city considering that only a few years earlier nearly half its inhabitants had been wiped out by the plague.

GOTHIC ARCHITECTURE

The term **Gothic** refers to the style of visual arts and culture that first developed, beginning about 1140, in the Île de France, and which reached its zenith in the thirteenth century. From the mid-thirteenth through the mid-fourteenth century, Paris was an important source of artistic inspiration for the rest of France, Germany, and England, while Italy remained quite separate aesthetically. By the middle of the sixteenth century, the Gothic style was at an end in France, although aspects of it continued to influence artists in Germany and England until the seventeenth century.

What is now called "Gothic art" was originally called the "French style," and referred to architecture. Architecture, in fact, dominates the era. This is the age of the great cathedrals of northern Europe. However, it was the Italians who gave the style its name. Preferring the classical style, the Italians thought the Gothic barbaric and identified it with the most notorious of the barbarian tribes, the Goths. Thus, the style was labeled "Gothic," with a decidedly derogatory intent.

The Gothic style developed out of the Romanesque. Romanesque buildings, such as the church of Saint-Sernin in Toulouse, are broad and massive, characterized by semi-circular arches, thick walls, and closely spaced supports that create a feeling of security. Solid and heavy, Romanesque buildings seem to be bound to the earth. In contrast, Gothic buildings rise to the heavens. Airy and delicate, they have a soaring quality, for the vertical is constantly emphasized and the walls are thin. Small Romanesque windows give way in Gothic architecture to vast windows of stained glass.

The Gothic was an era of confidence and daring, as its extraordinary architectural accomplishments testify. The tremendous height of the buildings was a reflection of religious ideals and enthusiasm, of inspiration and aspiration. The vast naves of the Gothic cathedrals create an extraordinary atmosphere of spirituality. The chants sung here reverberated from the high vaults.

The important structural innovations (fig. 12.3) that made this new style possible and characterized it included the following:

(1) Pointed arches and vaults, which exert less lateral thrust than the semi-circular Romanesque arches and vaults. The pointed ribbed vault can be constructed in a variety of floor plans and, in theory, built to any height.

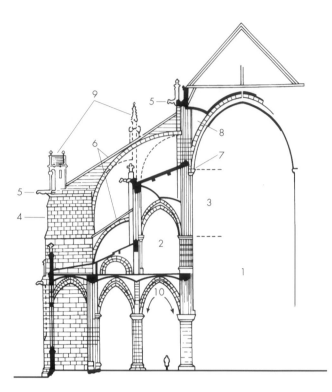

Figure 12.3 The principal features of a Gothic church include (1) the nave; (2) gallery/triforium; (3) clerestory window; (4) buttress; (5) gargoyle; (6) flying buttresses; (7) architectural rib; (8) vault; (9) pinnacles; (10) pointed arch.

Timeline 12.1 France and England during the later Middle Ages.

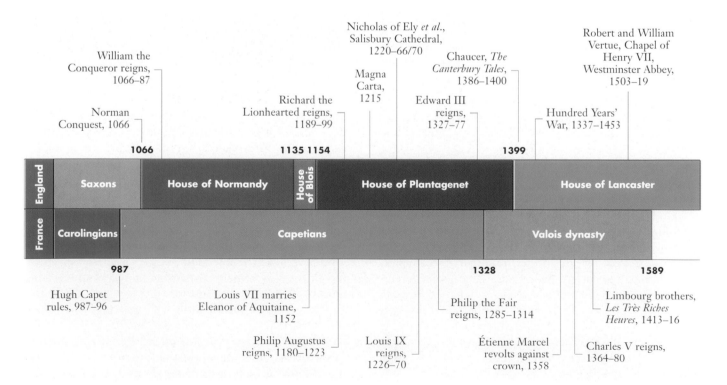

The Gothic system is more flexible than the Romanesque, which cannot attain comparable height and is generally restricted to simpler floor plans.

(2) Ribs, which serve to concentrate the weight of the vault at certain points, making it possible to eliminate the wall between these points.

(3) Flying buttresses, which were introduced in response to the problem created by the lateral thrust exerted by a true vault. The idea of a buttress, a solid mass of masonry used to reinforce a wall, was an old one. But the "flying" part, the exterior arch, was an invention of the Gothic era. Flying buttresses project outward on the exterior of the building and cannot be seen from the inside through the stained glass windows.

Saint-Denis. There is little debate as to where the Gothic style began—the royal abbey of Saint-Denis, located just north of Paris. The first church on the site was erected in 475 in honor of St. Denis, who, as one of

___

Figure 12.4 Royal abbey of Saint-Denis, France. ambulatory, 1140–44. The eccentric and egocentric Abbot Suger initiated the Gothic style of architecture, characterized by a new lightness of proportion and sense of flowing space. The pointed Gothic arches exert less lateral thrust than the Romanesque semi-circular arches, and the ribs reinforce the vaults.

the first of seven bishops sent to Paris around A.D. 250 to convert the Gauls, was rewarded for his efforts by being tortured on a hot grill and then decapitated. St. Denis is said to have picked up his head and walked north to the site where the abbey was subsequently built.

The parts of the abbey of Saint-Denis that herald the beginning of the Gothic were built under Abbot SUGER [SOO-zjay] (1081–1151) around 1140. A Benedictine monk, Suger was also a politician, and he served as advisor to successive kings of France and was even regent of the country during the Second Crusade. He regarded the Church as symbolic of the Kingdom of God on earth and was intent on making Saint-Denis as magnificent as possible. Suger rebuilt the facade, the narthex, and the east end of Saint-Denis. He commissioned a golden altar, jeweled crosses, chalices, vases, and ewers made of precious materials. This richness was in honor of God, France, and possibly also Suger. At a time when humble anonymity was the norm, Suger had himself depicted in stained glass and sculpture, and had his name included in inscriptions.

Of great historical importance as the first large and truly Gothic building, Saint-Denis served as the prototype for other Gothic structures. The facade of Saint-Denis, dated about 1137–40, was the first to synthesize monumental sculpture and architecture. Considered an artistic composition, with rhythm, clarity, and variety, its two towers, **rose window** (a circular window with tracery radiating from its center to form a roselike symmetrical pattern), rows of figures representing Jesus's biblical ancestors, and column figures on the jambs, all became standard features of later Gothic cathedrals. Between 1140 and 1144, when Suger was working on the east end of Saint-Denis, he removed the existing Carolingian apse and built a new choir. Today, the ambulatory and the seven chapels are all that remains of the abbey of Suger's day (fig. 12.4).

In Suger's plan, the divisions between the chapels are almost eliminated. Each chapel has two large windows. This introduction of light was a new concept of architectural space, of light, and of lightness. The space is not divided into distinct units, as it had been in Romanesque architecture. Instead, without the solid walls and massive supports that had characterized the Romanesque, Gothic space flows freely and areas merge with each other.

Notre-Dame, Paris. The celebrated cathedral of Notre-Dame-de-Paris (Our Lady of Paris) (fig. 12.5), located in the heart of Paris on the Île-de-la-Cité, is a major monument in Western architectural history. The spectacular site is the historical center of the city. Gallo-Roman ramparts once fortified it, and earlier churches had been built there as well. Bishop Maurice of Sully, founder of the cathedral, had these removed, however.

Construction of Notre-Dame started in 1163. Work began with the choir—the construction of a church or cathedral usually commences at the choir end, the most significant area for liturgical purposes. The altar is oriented to the east, the entrance toward the west. There are few exceptions to this specific orientation of Christian churches. Notre-Dame was first finished in 1235. Yet a fundamental reconstruction began almost at once. The vaulting of the choir was redone; almost all the clerestory windows were enlarged; the flying buttresses were doubled; the transepts were rebuilt; and work was carried out on over forty chapels. All this remodeling took several decades.

The facade (fig. 12.6) dates, for the most part, from the first half of the thirteenth century. Large amounts of wall are still evident, a holdover from the Romanesque period. At Notre-Dame, a subtle equilibrium of horizontals and verticals creates a masterpiece of balance on an enormous scale. Based on a complex sequence of squares, one inside another, the entire facade is one large square, 142 feet on each side. The towers are one-half the height of the whole solid area—a simple and visually satisfying geometry.

Figure 12.5 Cathedral of Notre-Dame, Paris, France, 1163–ca. 1250, apse, flying buttresses added in the 1180s. Exterior wall buttresses have a long history; innovative are the arch-shaped "flying buttresses," used especially on large multi-storied buildings to absorb the lateral thrust exerted by the vaulting. The solid walls of Romanesque architecture were replaced by the characteristically Gothic flying buttresses.

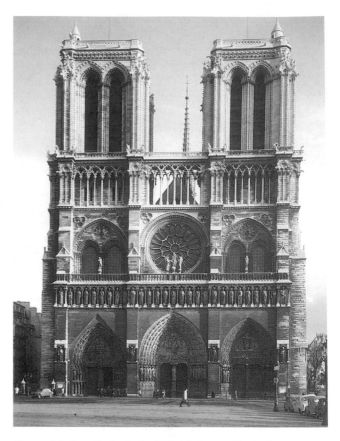

Figure 12.6 Cathedral of Notre-Dame, Paris, France, 1163–ca. 1250, west facade, mostly first half of thirteenth century. This celebrated cathedral is an example of the first phase of the Gothic, referred to as Early Gothic. In Romanesque architecture horizontals dominated; here horizontals and verticals balance; soon the verticals will dominate.

In the 1180s, flying buttresses (see fig. 12.5) were introduced at Notre-Dame to stabilize its great height— the first use of flying buttresses occurred here in Paris. The buttresses are in two parts: the outer buttress is exposed; the inner buttress is hidden under the roof of the inner aisle. From this time forward, flying buttresses would play an important structural and visual role in Gothic architecture.

Notre-Dame, Chartres. The cathedral of Notre-Dame in Chartres (fig. 12.7), a spectacular structure with splendid sculpture and sparkling stained glass, leads into the High Gothic. Earlier Gothic forms are here refined, extended, and made more vertical. The spaces between the buttresses are more open, making the building lighter and airier.

Dedicated to the Virgin Mary, Chartres cathedral was intended to be a "terrestrial palace" for her, built on the highest part of the city in order to bring it closer to heaven. Chartres cathedral possesses an important relic of Mary. Known as the *sancta camisia*, it is a piece of cloth, possibly part of a tunic or veil, said to have been worn by

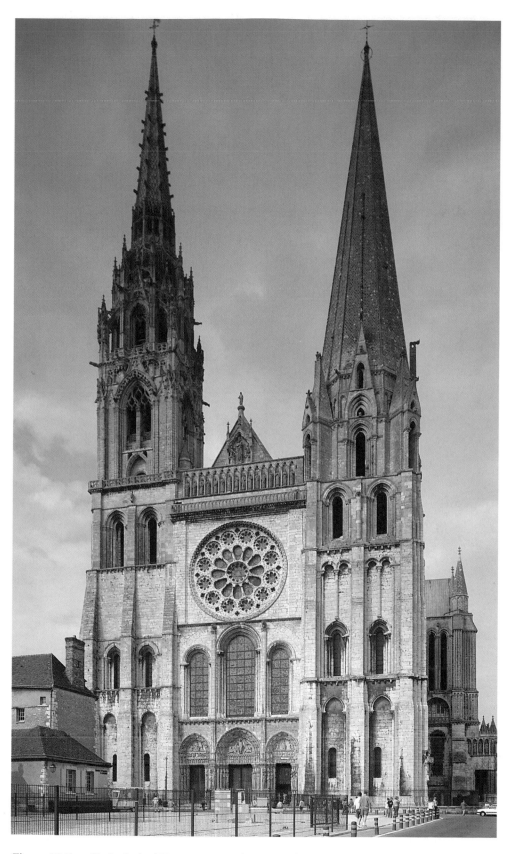

Figure 12.7 Cathedral of Notre-Dame, Chartres, rebuilding 1145–1220; north spire 1507–13. The cathedral dominates the surrounding landscape and is visible for miles around. The Gothic cathedral was routinely built on the highest site available.

Connections

At the cathedral school at Chartres, Plato's theory of the correspondence between visual and musical proportions and the beauty of the cosmos was carefully studied. The number three, also important in Christian theology, seems to have assumed special importance for the builders at Chartres. It symbolized the Holy Trinity and Plato's secular trinity of truth, beauty, and goodness.

The architecture of Chartres is replete with threes—on the exterior a three-step facade is matched by three corresponding internal levels, culminating in the heavenly light of the clere-story. There are three semicircular chapels in the apse, and each clerestory consists of one rose and two lancet windows. The six-petaled rose in the mosaic in the center of the nave represents the sum of one, two and three.

The number nine, associated with the Virgin Mary, is also of special importance. The cathedral, which houses a piece of her veil from the Nativity, celebrates her number. Mary is, as Dante said, "the square of the Trinity." Chartres has nine entrance portals—three times three—and in its original plan it was to have nine towers, two on the facade, two on each of the transepts, two flanking the apse, and one rising over the crossing.

Figure 12.8   Cathedral of Notre-Dame, Chartres, France, rebuilding begun 1145, vault finished by 1220, nave looking toward altar. The first architectural masterpiece of the second phase of the Gothic, known as the High Gothic, Chartres Cathedral was designed from the start to have flying buttresses. In this three-story nave elevation, large clerestory windows allow light to enter directly into the nave, the deep colors of stained glass creating an atmosphere of multi-colored light.

Mary when Jesus was born. Because it had this relic, Chartres was believed to be protected by the Virgin and became an extremely popular pilgrimage site. Although it was believed to have produced many miracles, the relic could not fend off fire, constant enemy of churches during the Middle Ages and the cause of the cathedral's destruction in 1020. Rebuilding began immediately, and by 1024 a new crypt was finished. Known as "Fulbert's Crypt," it was then, and still is, the largest crypt in France. A Romanesque cathedral was then constructed on the site, but in 1134 fire destroyed the town, and the building was damaged. The Royal Portals and the stained glass windows on the west facade were made 1145–55. In 1194 there was yet another fire in which the cathedral suffered great damage. Little more than Fulbert's Crypt and the Royal Portals and windows survived.

Mary's cloth, safe in the crypt, survived the fire of 1194. This was taken as a sign to build a yet more magnificent monument in her honor. The people of Chartres willingly gave money, labor, and time. All social classes participated, from the high nobility to the humble peasantry. Rough limestone was brought from five miles away in carts, an activity referred to as the "cult of the carts." By 1220, the main structure and the vaults were finished, built at great speed yet in a consistent style. In 1260, the cathedral was dedicated. Like the facade of Notre-Dame in Paris, Chartres has four buttresses, three portals, two towers, and one rose window. Yet, at Chartres, the two facade towers are strikingly dissimilar. The south spire is 344 feet high, built at the same time as the rest of the upper facade. But the north steeple of the early sixteenth century, built in a much more "Flamboyant" Gothic style, rises 377 feet. Symmetry was, obviously, not a Gothic aim. Instead, each tower was built in the style popular at the time of its construction. However, the towers are not discordant—it might even be argued that they are twice as interesting as two identical towers.

Chartres is the first masterpiece of the High Gothic, the first cathedral to be planned with flying buttresses

(Notre-Dame in Paris has them, but they are later additions), and to use them for the entire cathedral. The buttresses at Chartres are designed as an integral part of the structure, for they counteract, as discussed above, the lateral thrust of the vault. They join the wall at the critical point of thrust, between the clerestory windows, where there is a minimum of stone and a maximum of glass. Using the flying buttress, it is possible, in theory, to reduce the wall to the point of creating a mere web of stone; flying buttresses also make possible the tremendous height, perpendicularity, and open wall that characterize Gothic religious architecture.

The nave (fig. 12.8) has a sense of soaring verticality, of openness and airiness. Whereas the nave at Notre-Dame in Paris is just over 108 feet high, Chartres's is 121 feet high and 422 feet long. The three-story elevation consists of the arcade; the triforium (although there are four openings in each bay of the *tri*forium); and the clerestory. The lines lead up the wall to the clerestory windows, which are almost the same height as the openings in the nave arcade—about forty-five feet. The openings are tall and narrow, emphasizing the vertical rather than the horizontal. A vast amount of window area is permitted by the exterior buttressing. Yet this was not done to produce a brightly lit interior, as the stained glass prevents much of the natural light from entering.

Instead, stained glass provides colored and changing light in the windows themselves and flickering light over the stone interior.

Notre-Dame, Amiens. The soaring and sophisticated cathedral of Notre-Dame in Amiens (fig. 12.9) represents the climax of the High Gothic style. Like many other French Gothic cathedrals, Amiens Cathedral dominates the city. Building began in 1220 and by 1270 the cathedral was almost finished; only the tops of the towers above the rose window date from the fourteenth and fifteenth centuries. The facade (fig. 12.10) has five parts: (1) the usual three portals on the ground floor, which are exceptionally deep; (2) the gallery; (3) the gallery of kings—twenty-two figures, each fifteen feet high, representing the Kings of Judah, each holding a rod of the Tree of Jesse; (4) the rose window, with sixteenth-century glass; and (5) above this, the fourteenth- and fifteenth-century work. The great height achieved by

Figure 12.10 Robert de Luzarches, Thomas de Cormont, and Renaud de Cormont, Cathedral of Notre-Dame, Amiens, France, begun 1220, west facade. Buildings became ever more delicate during the Gothic era, stone seemingly turned into lace. The height of a city's cathedral was a matter of civic pride—similar to the twentieth-century battle in Manhattan between the architects of the Chrysler Building and those of the Empire State Building to erect "the tallest building in the world."

Figure 12.9 Robert de Luzarches, Thomas de Cormont, and Renaud de Cormont, Cathedral of Notre-Dame, Amiens, France, 1220–70, plan. When building with pointed arches, ribbed vaulting, and flying buttresses, in theory, there is no limit to the height attainable. Soaring heavenward, the nave of Notre-Dame at Paris rises over 108 feet; at Chartres 121 feet; at Amiens 139 feet; yet Beauvais Cathedral, at 158 feet, after it collapsed and was rebuilt, demonstrated the practical limits of the structural system.

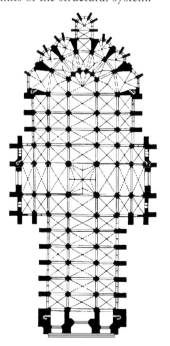

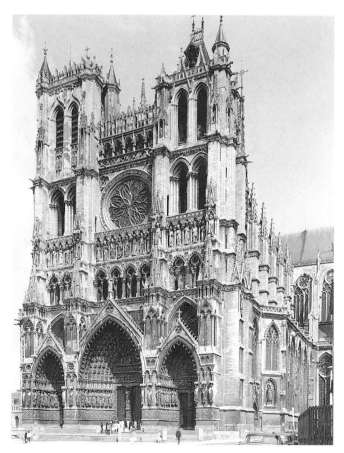

Figure 12.11 Pierre de Montreuil (?), Sainte-Chapelle, Paris, France, 1243–48, upper chapel, looking toward the apse. In this example of the third phase, the Rayonnant Gothic, the amount of masonry is reduced and the building becomes a cage of glass. Standing inside the upper chapel, when sunlight streams through the stained-glass windows, it is as if one is standing inside a sparkling multi-colored, multi-faceted jewel.

medieval masons was a matter of civic pride and a symbol of strength—what might be called "tower power." Each town tried to outdo the others in terms of height. When a conquering army took a defeated city, they destroyed its church or cathedral spire; to lop off the top of the tower was the sign of the city's submission.

Sainte-Chapelle, Paris By the middle of the thirteenth century, a new "Rayonnant" style of Gothic style had begun to emerge. The name "Rayonnant" comes from the French *rayonner*, which means "to shine" or "to radiate." The move to this new phase of the Gothic did not involve a change in basic architectural plan. Rather, it was the result of a changing sense of harmony, and the gradual substitution of window for wall. In this Rayonnant style, stone tracery divisions between the areas of glass in rose windows are made progressively thinner and are formed into ever more intricate patterns.

Paris under King Louis IX was the center for the Rayonnant style. Louis not only acquired a portion of the Crown of Thorns for the Sainte-Chapelle, but purchased many other relics as well, including what was believed to be a piece of Jesus's cross, iron fragments of the Holy Spear that pierced Jesus's side, the Holy Sponge, the robe, the shroud of Jesus, and a nail from the crucifixion. Later, the front part of the skull of St. John the Baptist was purchased (the back was in Amiens). Louis had these relics placed in an ornate shrine in the Sainte-Chapelle which cost at least 100,000 *livres*. While it is difficult to determine what this would equal in today's dollars, some sense of the expense may be had by noting that the chapel itself only cost 40,000 *livres* to build. Nonetheless, 100,000 *livres* for the shrine is somewhat eclipsed by the cost of the Crown of Thorns, for which Louis spent the enormous sum of 135,000 *livres*.

Perhaps the quintessential example of the Rayonnant style, the Sainte-Chapelle looks like an enormous reliquary. Rich and refined, this display of architectural virtuosity was considered a masterpiece as soon as it was built. Its reputation has remained undiminished. Its greatness is not due to great scale; when compared to other Gothic buildings, the Sainte-Chapelle is extremely small. The interior is a mere 108 feet long, and thirty-five feet wide. Divided into a lower and an upper chapel, the lower is only a little under twenty-two feet high, and the upper only just over sixty-seven feet. The upper chapel (fig. 12.11) was dedicated to the Holy Crown of Thorns and the Holy Cross. The plan is extremely simple, consisting of only the nave of four rectangular bays and a seven-sided apse. The walls disappear. The lines soar. The windows are shafts of light. The building is a cage of glass and stone, seemingly weightless, an illusion that relies on extraordinary architectural engineering. The Sainte-Chapelle appears to defy the laws of gravity. The thin piers of stone are hardly noticed. All the space between the piers is given over to huge windows, with more than three-quarters of the walls in this ethereal environment actually being stained glass. The piers actually project inward over three feet, but their bulk is masked by groups of nine colonettes. All other supports are placed outside, leaving the interior a continuous uninterrupted space. In 1323, Master Jean de Jandun described his experience of the chapel in the following way: "On entering, one would think oneself transported to heaven and one might with reason imagine oneself taken into one of the most beautiful mansions of paradise."

The entire scheme of the upper chapel glass relates to the relics of Jesus kept there. The central apse window shows Jesus's passion, introduced by the Old Testament stories in the nave. The cycle begins on the north side with the Book of Genesis. It concludes on the south side with the story of the relics of the passion, especially the Crown of Thorns, and their arrival in Paris. The French king is depicted alongside kings David and Solomon. It has been observed that the windows of the Sainte-Chapelle include a great number of coronation scenes—twenty plus that of Jesus. Could this be interpreted as an attempt to link the crown of France to Jesus's Crown of Thorns, the revered relic in the apse of the Sainte-Chapelle? Is a connection being made between French royalty and biblical royalty?

Saint-Maclou, Rouen. Saint-Maclou in Rouen (fig. 12.12), a small parish church, is the paradigm of the Flamboyant Gothic style, the final phase in the development of Gothic architecture. The church was designed in

Figure 12.12 Pierre Robin, Saint-Maclou, Rouen, France, designed 1434, west facade designed by Ambroise Havel (?) 1500–21. The finest example of the fourth and final phase of the Gothic, the Flamboyant or Late Gothic, this small building has enough decoration to equal that of a huge cathedral. The lacy stone tracery is "flamboyant"—"flamelike"—with its undulating curves.

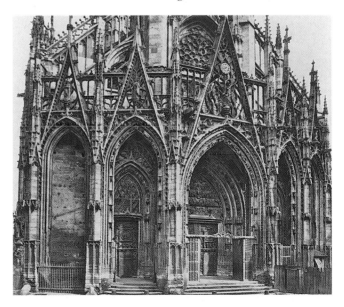

1434 by PIERRE ROBIN, although the facade was probably designed by AMBROISE HAVEL. Perhaps its most striking feature is the porch, which is faceted into three planes and thus bows outward.

The Flamboyant style is so called because of the mesh of flamelike curving stone tracery: *flamboyant* is the French for "flaming." It is a style characterized more by ornament than by structure. There is an identifiable delight in delicacy, a compulsion for complexity. Surfaces become luxurious, covered with a great profusion of lacelike ornament. The skill of the artisans who made it is apparent everywhere, as is their fantasy and, in a sense, ostentation. No large flat wall areas remain. All surfaces are broken.

Indeed, the ornament almost obscures the actual structure beneath it. Complexity is preferred over clarity. The design is exuberant, with interlacing and overlapping planes. The steeply pitched openwork gables are filled with flamelike forms, created by endless curves and countercurves, a surface tangle that is animated by light and shade as the sun moves. This new form of decoration is dynamic, as is the underlying structure that makes it possible.

GOTHIC ARCHITECTURE OUTSIDE FRANCE

Salisbury Cathedral. The French Gothic spread rapidly outside France, each country modifying it for its own needs. In England, the Early Gothic was relatively understated, but the Late Gothic reached extremes of eccentricity beyond anything found in France. Early English Gothic is represented by Salisbury Cathedral (fig. 12.13). The choir, Lady Chapel, transepts, and nave were built between 1220 and 1258 by NICHOLAS OF ELY. Work was finally completed by 1270. The building is not at all compact. The whole structure, which measures 473 by 230 feet, lacks a rounded apse, ambulatory, and radiating chapels, having instead, in typical English Gothic form, a square east end. The long nave has ten bays instead of the seven usually found in France.

The facade of Salisbury Cathedral, although begun in the same year as Amiens Cathedral, has very different proportions. Salisbury is low and wide, as if stretched horizontally, with no particular emphasis on height. The facade is wider, in fact, than the church and is treated as a screen, divided into horizontal bands with importance placed on the sculpture but little on the portals. English cathedrals are usually entered by a porch on the side of the nave or on the transept. Flying buttresses, so characteristic of French Gothic, were used only sparingly in England.

Westminster Abbey, London. After English Gothic architects had thoroughly mastered initial structural problems, they refined and enriched their forms. Vaulting became progressively more adventurous. The

ultimate example of fantastic English vaulting is in Westminster Abbey, London. The enormous interior culminates in the chapel of Henry VII (fig. 12.14). The architects were ROBERT and WILLIAM VERTUE. The tomb of Henry VII is behind a grill at the back of the altar. William Vertue replaced the axial chapel, originally built in 1220, with this one, built 1503–19. The most remarkable feature is the ceiling, a sort of **fan vaulting**, so called because the ribs radiate in a manner similar to those on a fan. But here the idea is carried to an extreme, to become **pendant vaults** hanging down in knobs. Such a structure appears to counter conventional ways of building, in a denial of both logic and gravity. Describing the chapel, one historian noted, "Its extraordinary, petrified foliage gives the impression of some

Figure 12.13 Nicholas Ely *et al.*, Salisbury Cathedral, Salisbury, England, 1220–70, west facade. Typical of early English Gothic, Salisbury is sprawling in plan, surrounded by a green lawn, and makes little use of flying buttresses—as opposed to French Gothic cathedrals, which are typically compact in plan, located in the city center, and rely on flying buttresses for structural support.

Figure 12.14 Robert and William Vertue, Chapel of Henry VII, Westminster Abbey, London, England, 1503–19, interior. The radiating ribs of fan vaulting are taken to an extreme here, becoming pendant vaults that actually hang down into the space of the chapel. The surface dissolves in this late and extreme example of English architectural eccentricity.

Figure 12.15 Arnolfo di Cambio, Francesco Talenti, Andrea Pisano, and others, Florence Cathedral, Florence, Italy, begun 1296; redesigned 1357 and 1366, drum and dome 1420–36; campanile designed by Giotto, built ca. 1334–50. The dome of the cathedral could not be built as originally designed. It was only in the early part of the Renaissance that Filippo Brunelleschi would solve the engineering problems that had prevented its earlier construction (see Chapter 13).

fantastic, luminous grotto encrusted with stalactites." Elaborate designs cover the entire surface, an indication of the English inclination toward the architectural extreme, the eccentric, the intricate, and the opulent.

Florence Cathedral. Italy was only superficially affected by the Gothic style. Instead of the elaborate buttress systems and large windows popular in the north, Italian architects favored large wall surfaces with emphasis on the horizontal, as is evident in the major landmarks of the city of Florence—its cathedral (*duomo*), bell tower or campanile, and baptistery (fig. 12.15).

The single most important construction work carried out during the Gothic era in Florence was that done on the cathedral. The cathedral has an unusually complicated history. There had been an older church on the site, but in 1296 ARNOLFO DI CAMBIO began to build a new cathedral. Work started at the west (entrance) end and proceeded quickly, until Arnolfo's death in 1302, after

which work ground to a halt. In 1343, Francesco Talenti took charge. Work continued over a long period of time, with various architects involved. All of the surfaces are treated to colorful marble incrustation. Italy is wonderfully rich in marbles of many colors, a fine example of which is the Romanesque baptistery, just in front of the cathedral. The decoration is flat, differing from the French love of sculpted surfaces.

The campanile was designed by Giotto and is referred to as "Giotto's Tower." Although the freestanding campanile is typically Italian, it is not an invention of the Italian Gothic; the campanile of Pisa, the famous "Leaning Tower," was built in the Romanesque era (see fig. 11.16). The richly ornamented Gothic campanile of Florence, with its multi-colored marble incrustation and sculpture, served not only as the bell tower but also as a symbol of the sovereignty of the Florence commune.

In 1334, Giotto was appointed architect-in-chief of the building of Florence Cathedral. He received this appointment because he was the most famous Florentine artist of his day. Giotto, however, was a painter who knew little about architectural structure and ended up designing only the campanile. His original drawing of it

Figure 12.16 Milan Cathedral, Milan, Italy, begun 1386, west facade. With its plethora of pinnacles and delicate decoration, Milan Cathedral is the most Gothic example—in the French sense—of cathedral architecture in Italy. Architects came from northern Europe to work on this northern Italian cathedral.

survives, from which it is known that he intended the tower to be topped by a spire. When Giotto died in 1337, only the first floor of the tower was finished. Work was continued by Andrea Pisano among others, and finished by Francesco Talenti in a somewhat different design around 1350–60. The interior of the tower consists of a series of rooms connected by staircases.

Milan Cathedral. The most Gothic of Italian cathedrals, in the French sense, is Milan Cathedral (fig. 12.16), consecrated in 1386 by the ruler of Milan, Gian Galeazzo Visconti, and occupying an impressive site with an enormous piazza in front. The cathedral was built with the support of all classes of Milanese society. Different guilds performed different tasks, each one trying to outdo the others in their contributions. The exterior is covered in Rayonnant ornament, the result of architects from the north coming to Milan to give advice on the cathedral's construction. The building has even been said to have an "over-abundance" of ornament. Certainly, there is an accumulation, all of which seems to compete for the visitor's attention.

Was Italy unreceptive to the Gothic? It has been suggested that there was a conscious resistance to trends in French architecture, with Italian nationalism cited as a possible explanation.

It may be, however, that the reason the French Gothic style never became very popular in Italy had less to do with national pride than with climate. The huge windows that were so desirable in the cathedrals of northern Europe would be extremely impractical in the heat of central or southern Italy, where their effect would be somewhat to cook the congregation. It seems worth noting, in support of this argument, that Milan Cathedral, the most "French" Gothic building to be found in Italy, is in the northern, cooler part of the country.

SCULPTURE

Notre-Dame, Chartres. The logical place to go to find the earliest Gothic sculpture would be Saint-Denis, but the work there has been badly damaged. Fortunately, the sculpture at Chartres Cathedral has fared better. The cathedral has three important triple portals: on the west facade and the north and south transepts, all adorned with magnificent sculpture. On the west, from the early Gothic era, are the Royal Portals (fig. 12.17), dated ca. 1145–55. All the sculpture was once richly painted and gilded; now only the beige stone remains.

Each of the three entrances of the Royal Portal is flanked by statues. These are symmetrical, ordered, and clear—Gothic compositions can typically be grasped at a glance, whereas in the Romanesque era there was a preference for greater complexity. These jamb figures form what is known as a "precursor portal," of a type first seen at Saint-Denis and perhaps started by Abbot Suger. The visitor passes by Old Testament figures to enter the

Figure 12.17 Column figures, ca. 1145–55, stone, flanking the Royal Portals, west facade, Chartres Cathedral, Chartres, France. Early Gothic figures perpetuate the distortion seen in Romanesque figures, but no longer have their frantic animation. Instead, these stiff elongated figures maintain the shape of the column to which they are attached, emphasizing their architectural function.

church. Those without crowns are the prophets, priests, and patriarchs of the Old Testament. They are Jesus's spiritual precursors. Those with crowns are the kings and queens of Judah. They are Jesus and Mary's physical ancestors. Medieval iconography is intentionally complex, with layered meanings, permitting multiple interpretations of these statues. Thus, in addition to being the royal ancestors of Mary and Jesus, the kings and queens of Judah are also associated with the kings and queens of France, joining together religious and secular authority. Further, the church was an earthly version of the heavenly Jerusalem, and these portals were regarded as the "gates of heaven," through which Christians had to pass to enter, making a symbolic spiritual journey through biblical history to arrive at Jesus in the present.

Such jamb figures are also called "column figures," as the shape of the figure follows that of the column. Sculpture here is very closely tied to architecture; columns have been carved to resemble the human form.

Figure 12.18   *Annunciation and Visitation*, ca. 1230–45, stone, west facade, Reims Cathedral, Reims, France. Descendants of column figures, these High Gothic sculptures dominate their architectural setting and have little to do with the columns behind. Characteristic of the increased realism and idealism of the Gothic era, the proportions and movements of these figures are now normal, and they even turn toward one another as if conversing.

Unlike their agitated Romanesque counterparts, these majestic figures are calm and serene, with a noble dignity. They are immobile—there is no twisting, turning, or bending. They do not interact with one another or with the viewer. The drapery, however, still consists of many tiny linear folds that fall into perfect zigzag hems. Obscuring the form of the bodies beneath, it looks much like the fluting of a column, stressing the architectural role of these figures, which are only slightly larger than their columns. The figures are not treated as human bodies with weight, requiring something on which to stand—the feet of these immaterial beings simply dangle.

Notre-Dame, Reims.   The High Gothic figures who act out the *Annunciation and Visitation* (fig. 12.18) on the west facade of Reims Cathedral, dated to the 1230s or early 1240s, are descendants of the column figures at Chartres. Yet at Reims, rather than standing rigidly side by side, unaware of the next figure's presence, they interact. Moreover, the columns from which they extend are less noticeable.

The *Annunciation* depicts the moment when the angel Gabriel tells the Virgin Mary that she will give birth to Jesus. In view of the rather extraordinary nature of the news she has just received, Mary shows surprisingly little emotional response. She is severe, standing erect, her heavy drapery falling in broad sharp folds to completely obscure her legs. But Gabriel is different. He holds his drapery so that it falls diagonally. His slender body forms

an S-curve. He moves gracefully, with a relaxed elegance. And he gives a Gothic grin! The new interest in emotion is a characteristic of the Gothic era.

The *Visitation* shows the meeting of Mary, now pregnant with Jesus, and her cousin Elizabeth, pregnant with John the Baptist. They exchange their happy news. According to the story, Elizabeth is older, and this is correctly shown by the sculptor. Both figures form an S-curve—a revival of the *contrapposto* pose of antiquity. They seem to move in space. Many small drapery folds run on diagonals and horizontals, the complex creases following the outlines of the body.

Notre-Dame-de-Paris.   Medieval art includes a great many images of Mary and the infant Jesus. From the late eleventh century on, there was great popular devotion to the Virgin Mary. Many churches, cathedrals, religious orders, and brotherhoods were dedicated to Mary. Often referred to as "Our Lady" or the "Madonna" (or "My Lady"), she was portrayed as the ideal woman, the second Eve. People of all levels of society participated in the Cult of the Virgin. Images of Mary were commissioned by those who could just barely afford a humble work, and by those who were able to commission a work made in gold by the finest metalworkers and set with glittering gems. Mary's virtues were praised in literature and art, where she was repeatedly portrayed as Queen of Heaven. By the fourteenth century, Mary was often shown being crowned by Jesus and was given

Figure 12.19 *Notre-Dame-de-Paris*, French, early fourteenth century, marble, in the crossing of Notre-Dame cathedral, Paris, France. Gracefully swaying in space, with Jesus on her side, this image of Mary is very different from the stiff unapproachable images of her created during of the Romanesque era. Mary is now shown as an elegant French princess.

comparable status. People appealed to Mary for help as the Madonna of Mercy.

A famous devotional image of the Virgin Mary is known as *Notre-Dame-de-Paris* (Our Lady of Paris) (fig. 12.19), a marble statue that dates from the early fourteenth century and stands in the crossing of Notre-Dame Cathedral in Paris. Graceful and elegant, Mary pulls a garment across her body, increasing the complexity of the pattern of folds, and indicating the body beneath.

Rather than tiny parallel pleats, the drapery now has broader sweeping folds. The silhouette is broken and animated. Rather than sitting rigidly as was the norm in the Romanesque era, the behavior of Jesus is now more appropriate for an infant, for he plays with his mother's clothing. Jesus has finally been portrayed with the bodily proportions of a baby, looking quite different from his portrayal as a little man in the Romanesque era.

Gargoyles. Gargoyles (fig. 12.20) are a special category of medieval sculpture. A multitude of gargoyles glower down from the roof lines of medieval buildings— and on rainy days, they spit! The true **gargoyle**, a characteristic feature of Romanesque and especially Gothic buildings, is a waterspout, a functional necessity turned into a decorative fantasy.

In view of where they are located—often on churches and cathedrals—gargoyles are surprisingly irreverent. The rainwater may issue from a barrel held by a gargoyle in the form of a person, but more often the figure appears to vomit, and some even defecate. Animals, such as dogs or pigs, and more exotic ones like lions or

Figure 12.20 Gargoyle, thirteenth century, stone, west facade, Cathedral of Saint-Pierre, Poitiers, France. Gargoyles, which reached their peak of popularity during the Gothic era, are glorified gutters, typically carved to look like monstrous creatures, the water usually issuing from the mouth. When carving for the gargoyles' aerial realm, sculptors seem to have been exempt from the usual iconographic restraints of medieval art.

monkeys, served as gargoyles as well as human figures. However, the majority of gargoyles are in the form of grotesque fauna, inventions of the fertile medieval imagination: howling monsters or malformed humanoids.

There is great debate over the meaning of the medieval gargoyles. Although they are common on churches and cathedrals, gargoyles do not represent usual religious subjects. It has been suggested that they represent devils and evil spirits who have been excluded from the church, or who have been made to serve the church—as waterspouts. Alternatively, the frequently monstrous physiognomy of the gargoyles may have been intended to scare evil spirits away from the church.

PAINTING AND DECORATIVE ARTS

Manuscript Illumination.   Manuscript illumination reached a peak in the Gothic period. Books were written in finer lettering than ever before, and the size of the books was reduced. After the mid-thirteenth century, painting was greatly affected by stained glass: reds and blues dominate; the figures are outlined in black; the effect is ornamental and flat. A good example is *Joshua Bidding the Sun to Stand Still* (fig. 12.21), a folio in the *Psalter of St. Louis*, made ca. 1260 for King Louis IX of France. Gothic architecture, including rose windows and pinnacles, forms the background in this painting. The two-dimensional buildings contrast with the long, thin, three-dimensional modeled figures.

In the years just before and following 1400, a single style of manuscript illumination was popular throughout Europe, to the extent that it is now referred to as the "International Style." Typical of this International Style are bright contrasting colors, decorative flowing lines, elongated figures, surface patterning, a crowded quality, and opulent elegance. A prime example in northern painting is the celebrated manuscript known as *Les Très Riches Heures* (*The Very Rich Hours*) of the Duke of Berry, which dates from 1413–16 and is the work of the LIMBOURG BROTHERS, POL, HERMAN, and JEAN. They were probably German or Flemish but worked in France for the Duke of Berry, brother of the French king Charles V, and a patron of the arts. *Les Très Riches Heures* is a book of hours or private prayer book. It contains a series of illuminations, one for each calendar month of the year. *June* includes a depiction of the Sainte-Chapelle in Paris, and *October* (see fig. 12.1) shows the Louvre. In both, women and men are shown working in the fields. A different level of society is portrayed in *January* (fig. 12.22), one of several scenes of aristocratic life. The Duke of Berry is hosting a banquet, perhaps in celebration of the New Year, or Twelfth Night, the day the magi, following the star of Bethlehem, arrived to present gifts to the infant Jesus. The Duke sits in front of a large fireplace and is emphasized by the fire screen that creates the effect of a halo around him. Above the head of the man

behind him—some think this is a portrait of Pol de Limbourg—are the words *aproche, aproche,* "come in, come in," signifying the Duke's hospitality. An extraordinary record detailing the many particulars of custom, costume, and consumption that characterized medieval life—note that the dogs are fed on the floor *and* on the table—it underscores a growing interest in everyday life that reflects the teachings of Aquinas and points to the Renaissance celebration of each individual being.

Stained Glass.   Gothic architecture offers the fullest possibilities for stained glass, an important element in the creation of the characteristic atmosphere of Gothic buildings. The solid walls of the Romanesque period were covered with murals simultaneously decorative and didactic. In the Gothic period this dual function passes to stained-glass windows. From the exterior of the building there is little to see in a stained-glass window except the pattern of the stone tracery; stained glass is interior decoration, intended to be seen illuminated from behind by sunlight.

Figure 12.21   *Joshua Bidding the Sun to Stand Still*, from the *Psalter of St. Louis*, French, ca. 1260, manuscript illumination, $5 \times 3\frac{1}{2}''$ (13.6 × 8.7 cm), Bibliothèque Nationale, Paris, France. Manuscript illumination reached a highpoint during the Gothic era, with the finest manuscripts produced in Paris. The elegant, animated, modeled figures are not in scale with the building they enter, and contrast with the flat patterned background, which is based upon contemporary architecture.

Figure 12.22 Limbourg brothers, *January,* from *Les Très Riches Heures* of the Duke of Berry, French, 1413–16, manuscript illumination, $11\frac{1}{2} \times 8\frac{1}{4}''$(29.2 × 21 cm), Musée Condé, Château of Chantilly, France. This famous manuscript includes twelve folios, one for each month of the year, that record how the upper and the lower classes lived, providing details of costume, customs, and climate.

The colored light that floods the interior of Gothic buildings through their stained-glass windows had special religious importance in the Middle Ages. Light was believed to have mystical qualities and was perceived as an attribute of divinity in medieval philosophy. John the Evangelist saw Jesus as "the true light," and as "the light of the world who came into the darkness." St. Augustine called God "light" and distinguished between types of physical and spiritual light.

Chartres Cathedral is famous for its stained-glass windows (fig. 12.23). In addition to the twelfth-century rose window and three lancets on the west facade, there are over 150 early thirteenth-century windows. Local merchants donated forty-two windows, which include over a hundred depictions of their occupations. These windows document medieval tools, materials, and working methods. The masons, for instance, are depicted carving royal

Figure 12.23 *Life of Jesus,* ca. 1150, stained glass, central lancet window, west facade, Chartres Cathedral, Chartres, France. Stained glass was at its peak during the Gothic era, filling the huge windows permitted by the skeletal architectural system, creating constantly changing patterns of colored light flickering over the interiors. Narratives that had been told in paintings on walls and vaults were now told in stained glass windows.

Cross Currents

MUSLIM SPAIN

The great Gothic cathedrals of northern Europe are contemporaneous with one of Spain's most beautiful Islamic buildings, the Alhambra in Granada (see fig. 7.18). Spain was the most multicultural country in Europe, a legacy of the arrival of the first Muslim conquerors in Spain in 711. Spain had been controlled since 589 by Visigoth kings, but by the turn of the eighth century most native Spaniards were no longer willing to serve in the Visigoth army, a duty that the king required of all free men. Furthermore, until 650, Jews had controlled most of the commerce in Spain, but in 694, the Visigoth kings, who had themselves become Christian, enslaved all Jews who would not accept a Christian baptism. Thus most Spaniards, Jews, and Christians alike greeted the Muslim army in 711 as liberators.

And liberators they were. Both the Jews and the Christians were tolerated as "protected" groups. They paid taxes to the Muslim lords, but they were free to practice their own religion and to engage in business as they pleased. Thus Spain became a multicultural country like no other, with Jews, Islamic Moors, and Christians working together in a spirit of *convivencia*, "coexistence." The population consisted of six distinct groups: (1) *Mozárabes*, Christians who had adopted Muslim culture; (2) *Mudéjares*, Moors who were vassals of Christians; (3) *Muladíes*, Christians who had adopted the Islamic faith; (4) *Tornadizos*, Moors who had turned Christian; (5) *Enaciados*, those who sat on the fence between both Islam and Christianity, and who pretended to be one or the other as the occasion warranted; and (6) the large Jewish community.

The cultures seemed to invigorate each other. An older Christian man, writing in 854, lamented the acceptance of Muslim ways by the Christian youth, but his protest reveals much of the culture's vitality:

Our Christian young men, with their elegant airs and fluent speech, are showy in their dress and carriage, and are famed for the learning of the Gentiles; intoxicated with Arab eloquence, they greedily handle, eagerly devour and zealously discuss the books of the Mohammadans ... They can even make poems, every line ending with the same letter, which display high flights of beauty and more skill in handling meter than the Gentiles themselves possess.

The odes of the Islamic poets that the Christian youth were imitating began with an erotic prelude, then moved through a series of conventional themes such as descriptions of camels and horses, hunting scenes, and battles, and then culminated in the praise of a valiant chieftain. The odes soon developed into independent love songs and drinking songs, and it was in fact out of this tradition that the troubadour poets sprang.

Moorish influence on medieval and Renaissance Europe extended beyond this. For instance, it was through Arab scholars that much classical learning passed back into Europe (see Chapter 7). Nonetheless, by 1492 the last traces of this happy cohabitation were erased when Ferdinand and Isabella of Aragon reclaimed Spain for Christianity and expelled the Moors and Jews.

---

figures and show us just how Chartres's sculptures themselves were created.

The Sainte-Chapelle in Paris is a major monument for the study of stained glass. Compare the subject from the Sainte-Chapelle, the *Presentation of Mary at the Temple* (fig. 12.24), with the treatment of the *Annunciation and Visitation* carved out of stone as part of the sculptural architecture at Reims Cathedral (see fig. 12.18). At the Sainte-Chapelle the little figures have a certain vitality and spontaneity about them. The stories are told by gestures and poses. Everything is abbreviated in a highly expressive form of narrative shorthand.

Were these windows created by several workshops, or by several "hands," working under a single master? It is likely that one guiding mind established the program, the iconography, and its sequence of presentation. However, this may not have been the same person who then designed the individual compositions.

Tapestry. Also characteristic of the Gothic era, tapestries were a form of insulation as well as decoration, for these woven wall-hangings helped to keep the cold air out and the cold stone at one remove from the interior living space. They were also luxury items, to be coveted and collected, a significant economic investment.

To produce a tapestry, the artist first makes a small-scale color drawing. This is then copied and enlarged to the dimensions intended for the tapestry on linen or paper. This enlarged design is called the **cartoon**. Next, the weavers translate the cartoon into tapestry. A tapestry is woven on a loom, which is worked by several people sitting side by side. If a set of tapestries was to be produced, as was often the case, several looms were employed. The loom is strung with **warp** threads of tightly twisted wool. The number of warp threads per inch determines how fine the tapestry will be. The warp threads will be hidden by the **weft** threads of wool, silk, and even silver and gold. Tapestries are woven from the back; the finished image is an inversion of the artist's original design. When the design is woven, every change of color requires a change of thread; the weaving of a tapestry is a tedious and exceedingly slow process.

One of the most famous of medieval tapestries is the set known as the *Unicorn Tapestries*, made in Brussels

Figure 12.24 *Presentation of Mary at the Temple*, mid-thirteenth century, stained glass, Sainte-Chapelle, Paris, France. The absence of realism and the decorative quality of this scene are characteristics of stained-glass windows, which are composed of many small pieces of colored glass held together by lead strips. Details of facial features, fingers, and fabric folds are painted onto the glass.

around 1500. These tapestries tell the story of the hunt, capture, and murder of the unicorn. The first and the last tapestry (fig. 12.25) are in the *mille-fleurs* ("thousand-flowers") style, which is characterized by dense backgrounds of plants. Many of these are meticulously observed and can be identified, yet at the same time they represent an unreal realm, an impossible environment in which a variety of plants from different geographic areas and climates are all in bloom simultaneously, the weavers accomplishing what Nature could not. The unicorn, an equally unrealistic figure, is both a religious symbol of Jesus and a secular symbol of a bridegroom.

The tapestries may have been made as a wedding gift. According to religious interpretation, the unicorn represents Jesus at the Resurrection, in a heavenly garden. According to secular interpretation, the unicorn represents the lover, now wearing the *chaîne d'amour* (chain of love) around his neck and surrounded by a fence, perhaps tamed and domesticated by obtaining his lady's affection. Red juice falls on the unicorn's white fur from the pomegranates above. Like the unicorn, the pomegranate can be read in both religious and secular terms. Taken from a religious point of view, the many seeds of the pomegranate represent the unity of the Church and hope for the resurrection. In a secular light, the crown-like finial represents royalty and the many seeds fertility. Here, as elsewhere, the iconography of medieval art is often plural in meaning, with context crucial to the interpretation.

SCHOLASTICISM

Europe was, in fact, ripe for intellectual stimulation. As the Middle Ages progressed, the attitude of the Roman Catholic Church toward secular learning and the wisdom of ancient writers began to change. Assured of its spiritual supremacy, the Church started to lower its opposition to the works of pagan writers. More often than not, the Church simply incorporated into its own teaching the learning it acquired from other cultures, including the literature and philosophy of ancient Greece and Rome, along with the Byzantine and Islamic religious and philosophical traditions. In this more open intellectual climate, forms of secular learning that derived from

Figure 12.25 *The Unicorn in Captivity*, from the *Unicorn Tapestries*, Franco-Flemish, made in Brussels, ca. 1500, wool and silk tapestry, 12'1" × 8'3"(3.68 × 2.51 m), Cloisters Collection, Metropolitan Museum of Art, New York. During the Middle Ages, people believed in the existence of the unicorn, a fabulous animal said to have a single horn in the center of its forehead. When a tapestry is made, the picture is formed as the fabric is woven from colored threads. This type of tapestry is known as *mille-fleurs*—"thousands of flowers," shown scattered over the background.

observation of the natural world rather than the written word of scripture were no longer at odds with a Christian perspective. Such natural knowledge was seen as a necessary foundation for the more advanced states of religious contemplation.

The Growth of the University.

The shift in the Church's intellectual perspective was stimulated by the preservation and translation by Muslim scholars of Aristotle's writings, which passed back into Christian Europe in the twelfth and thirteenth centuries. This appreciation of Aristotle's philosophy was complemented by the rise of the universities, which were evolving into major centers of learning, with the University of Paris leading the way. Cathedral and monastery schools had been obliged, since 1179, to provide an education free of charge to all lay people who wanted to learn, and the University of Paris was the result of the expansion of the cathedral school at Notre-Dame. In turn, the University of Paris gave rise to institutions like Oxford and Cambridge in England, the former being founded by teachers and students who had left Paris, the latter created by a group disenchanted with the Oxford curriculum. Such debate about what should be studied created a climate of intellectual controversy and led to the foundation of more and more universities. Soon universities in Spain, Portugal, and Germany assumed their place among the approximately eighty institutions of higher learning that existed by the end of the Middle Ages.

The university curriculum consisted of the seven original "liberal arts": the *trivium* (grammar, logic, and rhetoric) and the *quadrivium* (arithmetic, astronomy, geometry, and music). Soon degrees were awarded in both civil and canonical law, in medicine, and in theology. And there was a further important change. Prior to the thirteenth century, medieval philosophy had centered on demonstrating the truths of religious faith through reason, but now a new focus on the empirical observation of the natural world began to elevate the importance of rational thinking even when it was divorced from the service of Christian belief. Reason became faith's equal instead of its servant. Predictably enough, with this newfound equality, tensions between faith and reason resulted.

The Synthesis of St. Thomas Aquinas.

Using Aristotle's focus on the natural world to explain how God's wisdom is revealed, the Dominican friar ST. THOMAS AQUINAS [a-QWHY-ness] (1225–1274) effected a synthesis of Aristotelian philosophy and Catholic religious thought. Aquinas, like Aristotle, begins with empirical knowledge. Unlike Aristotle, however, Aquinas then moves from the physical, rational, and intelligible to the divine. Aquinas claimed that the order of nature reflected the mind of God, while being a beautiful harmonious structure in its own right. Thus, he

connected reason with faith in a way that explained how nature revealed divine wisdom.

Aquinas saw no conflict between the demands of reason and the claims of faith. Nor did he see any conflict between the requirements of belief and the inducements of independent thought. In fact, for Aquinas, the exercise of intellectual freedom exemplified an individual's autonomy, which was granted by God according to the divine plan. This freedom was essential not only for defining what makes a person human, but also for presenting the opportunity for every individual to choose or deny God by using the tools of reason.

Unlike his philosophical and theological forebears Plato and Augustine, for whom physical reality and material circumstance were not as real or important as spiritual essences or qualities, Aquinas argued that the soul and body were inextricably interrelated. The body needs the soul to live; the soul needs the body's experience. Each complements and completes the other in a harmonious unity. According to Aquinas, spiritual knowledge and theological understanding require a grounding in the body's experience and in observation of the visible physical world.

In accomplishing this feat of integration, Aquinas showed that philosophy and theology need not be in conflict, and that in fact they could co-exist in mutually supporting ways. Nevertheless, Aquinas's approach was not convincing to all. With the introduction of rational analysis into theological speculation, and the privileging of empirical evidence and material conditions as elements of philosophical thinking, critics of Aquinas's system began to question the validity of his unification of faith and reason.

Duns Scotus and William of Ockham.

Two who refused to accept Aquinas's grand synthesis were DUNS SCOTUS (1265–1308) and WILLIAM OF OCKHAM (1285–1349), both of whom were Franciscan friars. Scotus was a Scotsman who had studied at Oxford and Paris; Ockham was an Englishman, who had also studied at Oxford, and who wound up vilified and excommunicated for what were perceived as heretical views. Duns Scotus, known as "the subtle doctor," reacted against the theological views of both Aquinas and Augustine. In place of Augustine's divine illumination and Aquinas's integration of faith and reason, Scotus posited the central importance of "will," emphasizing the freedom of individuals in their actions. Scotus believed that a person's will is guided on the one hand by what is good for the individual, and on the other by what is good for all, the two being modulated according to a sense of justice.

William of Ockham went beyond Scotus by denying the existence of any correspondence between concrete individual beings or things. He eschewed the notion of universals except as mental concepts. Similarities among individual human beings, or, say, particular dogs or trees, exist strictly in the mind as mental abstractions, as ideas rather than as "real things." For Ockham, the issue of the universal existing beyond the physical was a matter for theology or for logic rather than a concern of philosophy. Thus he rejected Aquinas's notion that the human mind possessed a divine light that guided the intellect toward a proper understanding of reality, and he severed the link between faith and reason that Aquinas had so carefully established. With "Ockham's razor," his principle that the best explanation is the simplest and most direct, Ockham also broke away from the elaborate and subtle explanations of the scholastic philosophers or "schoolmen," whose ideas had dominated medieval philosophical thinking. In doing so, Ockham helped prepare the ground for the developments of Cartesian rationalism and Baconian empiricism (see Chapter 15).

Francis of Assisi.   The intellectualism of scholars like Aquinas was also challenged by the life and teachings of Giovanni Bernadone (1181–1226), nicknamed "Francesco" by his father, who was born in the Italian town of Assisi. Captured as a youth in a battle against the neighboring town of Perugia and held in solitary confinement, FRANCIS OF ASSISI (fig. 12.26), as he came to be known, is said to have decided in prison that real freedom demanded complete poverty. On his release, he consequently gave up all worldly goods and, identifying closely with the passion of Jesus, began to lead the life of a wandering preacher. This lifestyle, which made him wholly dependent on the goodness and generosity of others for his survival, attracted many followers, who came to be known as Franciscans, and who were already a powerful monastic order of the church by the time of Francis's death in 1226.

St. Francis's belief that the average human could share in Jesus's life and example—his own body was said to bear the crucifixion marks, or *stigmata* of Jesus, so close was his identification with the passion—is not entirely incompatible with Aquinas's philosophical position. St. Francis's was a form of intimate knowing, albeit more emotional than intellectual, and his love of creation—the birds and the animals, the poor and the weak—was consistent with Aquinas's belief that the universal and the essential are rooted in the local and the particular.

LITERATURE

Dante's Divine Comedy.   The most celebrated literary work of the Middle Ages is the epic poem *The Divine Comedy* by the Italian poet DANTE ALIGHIERI [DAN-tay] (1265–1321) (fig. 12.27). Born in Florence in 1265, Dante was involved in politics as well as literature. When a rival party seized power in 1302, Dante was exiled from his home city, never to return. *The Divine Comedy* was completed in Ravenna shortly before Dante's death. In the poem, Dante makes numerous

Figure 12.26   *St. Francis of Assisi*, thirteenth century, fresco, Sacro Speco, Subiaco, Italy. The earliest known portrait of St. Francis, this fresco may have been executed during his lifetime. St. Francis founded his own monastic order, the Franciscan order, in 1209, and it had already grown to be a powerful movement within the medieval Church by the time of his death in 1226. One of the most important features of the order was its imposition of poverty on its members.

references to the politics of his day, especially to the rivalry between the Guelphs and the Ghibellines, two opposing Florentine political parties, that left him an exile from this native city.

The Divine Comedy is divided into three parts: *Inferno* (*Hell*), *Purgatorio* (*Purgatory*), and *Paradiso* (*Heaven*). These are the three different places in medieval theology to which the soul can be sent after a person's death. In the poem Dante ascends through Hell and Purgatory to Heaven, guided in the first stages by the pagan poet Virgil and at the end by his beloved, Beatrice. Though deeply indebted to the great classical poetic tradition, *The Divine Comedy* is an explicitly Christian poem. Hence Virgil is not allowed into Heaven with Dante.

The entire poem contains one hundred cantos equally divided among the three sections, with the opening canto of the prologue prefacing the *Inferno*. Dante's attention to organization, especially structural symmetry, is apparent in every aspect of the work, particularly in the use of *terza rima*, a succession of three-line stanzas that rhyme ABA, BCB, CDC, and so on, in which the unrhymed line-ending in each stanza is picked up in the following stanza, where it becomes the principal rhyme. Dante employs this harmonious pattern of interlocked rhyme through the entire length of the work.

One of the most notable features of Dante's *Inferno* is the law of symbolic retribution, which suggests how a punishment should match the sin to which it has been ascribed. In depicting opportunists, for example, Dante positions them outside of Hell proper, in a kind of vestibule. Since they were unwilling to take firm positions in life, they are not completely in or out of Hell after death. And as they were swayed by winds of change and fashion, their eternal punishment is to follow a waving banner that continually changes direction.

Other punishments that seem particularly well suited to their corresponding sins include those who have committed carnal offences, who in life were swayed by sexual passion and in death are swept up in a fiercely swirling wind. Murderers are punished by being immersed in a river of boiling blood, the degree of their immersion determined by the degree of their bloodlust in life. Gluttons are punished by being made to lie in the filthy slush of a garbage dump, while the giant three-headed dog, Cerberus, tears at their flesh with claws and teeth. The souls of those who committed suicide are imprisoned in trees, whose limbs are torn and eaten by giant ugly birds, the fearful Harpies.

This law of symbolic retribution is complemented by another—that the most grievous and heinous of sinners

---

Figure 12.27 Domenico di Michelino, *Dante and His Poem*, 1465, fresco, Florence Cathedral, Florence, Italy. Dante stands holding his poem. To his right is the Inferno, behind him Mount Purgatory, and to his left, representing Paradise, is Florence Cathedral itself, with its newly finished dome by Brunelleschi.

THE GOTHIC AND LATE MIDDLE AGES ← 387

are punished more severely than those who committed less odious crimes in life. Dante's poem is an enormous synthesis of all the learning of his day—astronomy, history, natural science, philosophy—but in this differentiation between sinners it is particularly indebted to the theology of Thomas Aquinas. Dante follows Aquinas, for example, in suggesting that sins of the flesh, such as lust, are not as serious as those of malice or fraud. Thus, lust, gluttony, and anger are punished in the upper portion of Hell, where the punishments are less painful, while sins of violence and fraud are punished in the deeper recesses of the Inferno.

Since deceit and treachery are, for Dante, the most pernicious of sins, these are punished at the very bottom of hell. Dante's scheme is so carefully worked out that he even divides the betrayers into categories—betrayers of their kin, of their country, of their guests and hosts, and, finally, those who betrayed their masters. This last and worst kind of sin Dante represents by the crimes of Brutus and Cassius, who betrayed Julius Caesar; by Judas Iscariot, the betrayer of Jesus; and, worst of all, by Satan, who betrayed God. These sinners are the furthest from God, deep in the cold dark center of Hell. Satan, a three-headed monster, lies encased in ice, while in his three mouths he chews incessantly on the bodies of Brutus, Cassius, and Judas. Many of Dante's political enemies in Florence are discovered by the poet suffering the torments of Hell.

Just as Dante's *Inferno* reflects the type and degree of sinners' guilt, so his *Purgatorio* reflects a similar concern for justice. Dante's Purgatory is a mountain that is also an island. The mountain is arranged in tiers, with the worst sins punished at the bottom, since the sinners punished there are furthest from the Garden of Eden and from the heavens. In ascending order, the sins punished on the mountain of Purgatory are pride, envy, anger, sloth, avarice, gluttony, and lust—roughly the reverse of their positions in the *Inferno*.

Dante's *Paradiso* is based on the seven planets of medieval astronomy—the Moon, Mercury, Venus, the Sun, Mars, Jupiter, and Saturn. Just as the *Inferno* and the *Purgatorio* describe the subject's movement through hell and the purgatorial mountain, Dante's *Paradiso* also describes a journey, this one celestial, from planet to planet and beyond, to the Empyrean, the heavenly abode of God and his saints.

The influence of Dante's *Divine Comedy* can hardly be exaggerated. It was first mentioned in English by Chaucer in the fourteenth century, and in the twentieth century it has continued to influence poets such as T.S. Eliot.

MUSIC

The Notre-Dame School. One of the more elegant features of Gregorian plainchant is the way its single melodic line molds itself to the words of the Latin text. The rounded shape of its vocal melody and the concentrated focus of its single melodic line suit it to the devotional quality of the liturgy. Between the ninth and thirteenth centuries, however, chants began to be composed with multiple voice lines. Those with two voice lines an interval of a fourth, fifth, or octave apart were known as **organum**, the simplest kind of polyphonic, or multi-voiced, musical composition. In organum, the two melodic lines move together, note for note, parallel, and with identical rhythmic patterns. The lower, or bottom, line is the main melody, or **cantus firmus**, above which the second line is composed. Some time during the period from the tenth through twelfth centuries, more elaborate forms of chant polyphony appeared, so that there might be three, four, or even five separate voice parts. Moreover, the melodies for each of the voices differed, with each of the voice lines having an independent quality that simpler forms of parallel-voiced polyphony did not.

The two most prominent chant composers of the twelfth century, LÉONIN [LAY-oh-nan] (ca. 1135–ca. 1200) and PÉROTIN [PEAR-oh-tan] (ca. 1170–ca. 1236), were associated with the cathedral of Notre-Dame in Paris. Though the church was not completed until the 1220s, during the 1180s an altar was consecrated and services were held. Léonin, who was active around 1175, favored a kind of chant for two voices called **organum duplum**, in which the lower-cantus firmus spread slowly over long held notes, while a second voice, scored higher, moved more quickly and with many more notes through the text. This top line was called the **duplum** and the bottom cantus firmus line the **tenor**, from the Latin *tenere*, which means "to hold." (This "tenor" has nothing to do with the later development of "tenor," referring to one of the voice ranges, as in soprano, alto, tenor, and bass.)

Working a generation later, at the turn of the thirteenth century, Pérotin was Léonin's most notable successor in composing polyphonic chants. Pérotin wrote mostly three- or four-voiced chants called respectively **organum triplum** and **organum quadruplum**. Pérotin's more complex polyphony still used the cantus firmus tenor voice, but over it were placed two or three lively voice parts, which the tenor imitated from time to time. An additional distinguishing feature of the polyphonic chants of Léonin and Pérotin was their use of measured rhythm. Unlike the free unmeasured rhythms of plainchant, the polyphonic chants of Léonin and Pérotin had a clearly defined meter with precise time values for each note. Initially, the rhythmic notations for the music were restricted to only certain patterns of notes, with the beat subdivided into threes to acknowledge the Trinity. Later, however, these rules were loosened, and polyphonic chant became even freer in structure and more richly textured.

It has been suggested that the metrical regularity of Léonin's and Pérotin's chants are especially suited to the Gothic cathedral, which by the end of the twelfth century was beginning to supplant the Romanesque, and whose construction had its own architectural rhythms. The repeating and answering patterns of polyphonic chant music have their architectural counterpart in the Gothic cathedral's repetitive patterns of arches, windows, columns, and buttresses, and its visual rhythms.

TOWARD THE RENAISSANCE

As already noted, the eruption of the Black Death in 1347–51, and again in 1388–90, devastated Europe. However, this devastation was almost matched by that wreaked by the Hundred Years' War, which not only brought political and social collapse to much of Europe, but also introduced gunpowder and heavy artillery as agents of destruction for the first time in history. Soldiers died in unprecedented numbers, and many more were crippled in ways hitherto unimaginable.

Conversely, one positive result of both the plague and the war was the rise of modern medicine. In 1390, the medical faculty at the University of Paris invited surgeons to join their ranks. Though no one correctly diagnosed the causes of the plague for centuries, hundreds of theses were published, and the medical community turned its attention away from the mostly philosophical medieval conception of the "humors" —blood, phlegm, yellow bile, and black bile, each of which was related to a specific bodily organ and believed to determine temperament—to questions of diagnosis, treatment, and cure. Perhaps most important of all, the notion of infectious disease began to take hold.

In the midst of these crises, the growing naturalism evident, for instance, in the difference between the sculpture at Chartres and that at Reims (see figs. 12.17 and 12.18), or in the illuminated manuscripts of the Limbourg brothers (see figs. 12.1 and 12.22), became more and more pronounced. In Aquinas's and St. Francis of Assisi's interest in the particulars of nature, we can detect the seeds of scientific inquiry, an urge to know the world in its every detail. Life, more and more people believed, should be an eternal quest for "truth." And the realization of visual and literary truth—the urge to depict or tell things in a manner "true to nature"— began to seem as important a quest as any other. Of

Figure 12.28 Nicola Pisano, *Nativity*, panel on pulpit, 1259–60, marble, $33\frac{1}{2} \times 44\frac{1}{2}''$ (85.1 × 113 cm), Baptistery, Pisa, Italy. Important interests in antiquity and in reviving Italy's cultural past, which were to lead to the Renaissance, are already evident in the sculpture of Nicola Pisano. Ancient Roman sarcophagi reliefs provided inspiration for the classical type of figures.

Figure 12.29 Giovanni Pisano, *Nativity*, panel on pulpit, Pisa Cathedral, Pisa, Italy, 1302–10, marble, $34\frac{3}{8} \times 43''$ (87.2 × 109.2 cm). The greater naturalism of Nicola Pisano's son, Giovanni, when carving the same subject half a century later, is evidenced in his work by less crowding, a greater sense of space, and increased attention to the setting.

course, scholars were increasingly finding what seemed to them to be the "truth" in the writings of antiquity, the classical past. Thus, many reasoned that it might also be appropriate for the arts to reexamine their classical heritage.

NATURALISM IN ART

The Pisanos. Gothic sculpture in Italy differs stylistically from that of the rest of Europe. Italian sculpture is treated separately from the architecture. There is a preference for carving in marble no matter what material is used to construct the building. NICOLA PISANO [pea-SAH-noh] (ca. 1220/25 or before–1284) reintroduced a classical style, as demonstrated by the marble pulpit he made for the baptistery in Pisa, 1259–60, which consisted of a hexagonal structure supported on classical Corinthian columns. He may have studied the ancient Roman sarcophagi preserved in Pisa, for in the panel that portrays the *Nativity* (fig. 12.28) he has carved classical figures and faces. Included are three separate events: the Annunciation on the left; the Nativity itself in the middle; and the Adoration at the top right. Mary appears twice in the center of the composition, once with the angel Gabriel at the Annunciation, and directly below, lying prostrate at the Nativity. She is recognizably the same individual in each instance, though her expression changes. Deeply undercut, solid

and massive, the forms bulge outward from the background. The crowding of the scene is typically Gothic, but the realism and classicism of the figures looks forward to the Renaissance.

Nicola's son GIOVANNI PISANO (ca. 1240/45–after 1314) also carved a *Nativity* for Pisa, this time for the cathedral (fig. 12.29). Executed between 1302 and 1310, the style is different. The figures are slimmer than his father's, and the Mary seems more a young woman than the matronly figure in the earlier work. The drapery that clothes her is more flowing, her body almost substantial beneath its folds. The composition itself is not as crowded as Nicola's, the effect more energetic than serene. Each figure now has a logical amount of space, and the viewer seems to look down from above, thereby making the composition clearer. Giovanni includes more landscape and setting in his depiction than his father, creating a greater sense of depth, and in his sculpting uses even deeper undercutting for a greater play of light and shade.

Duccio and Giotto. Important events occurred in Italian painting at the end of the thirteenth and beginning of the fourteenth century. Two different trends emerged, associated with the rival cities of Siena and Florence. Conservative Siena, represented by the artist Duccio, clung to the medieval and Byzantine traditions, favoring abstract patterns, gold backgrounds, and

Figure 12.30 Duccio, *Madonna and Child Enthroned*, main panel of the *Maestà Altarpiece*, 1308–11, egg tempera and gold on wooden panel, 7′ × 13′ 6¼″(2.13 × 4.12 m), Museo dell'Opera del Duomo, Siena, Italy. The paintings by Duccio of Siena were the final flowering of the medieval Byzantine tradition in Italy. The *Maestà*, which means "majesty" of the Madonna, portrays Mary as extremely elongated, enormous in size, flanked by angels and saints, as if she were a feudal queen holding court. Bright color and flowing outline are stressed rather than three-dimensionality of solid forms in space.

emphasis on line. Progressive Florence, however, represented by the artist Giotto, displayed a greater concern for illusions of reality, three-dimensional space, and emphasis on mass. This is the more naturalistic style that Europe would follow for the next several centuries.

DUCCIO [DUT-cho] (ca. 1255–before 1319) is frequently mentioned in the Sienese archives, not only for his art but also for disturbing the peace, for his many wine bills, and for having borrowed money on more than one occasion. Yet he was a great religious painter, his most famous work being the *Maestà Altarpiece*, 1308–11, on the front of which is the *Madonna and Child Enthroned* (fig. 12.30) (the Italian word *maestà* refers to the "majesty" of the Madonna). Made for the high altar of the cathedral of Siena, it was painted entirely by Duccio (the contract has survived), although the usual practice at this time was for the artist to employ assistants. When it was finished, a feast day was proclaimed in Siena.

In this rigidly symmetrical composition, Mary and the infant Jesus are enthroned, surrounded by tiers of saints and angels. Much larger than any of the other figures, Mary is extremely elongated, ethereal, and immaterial. Her soft drapery has a flowing hemline, the linear quality emphasized by the gold edging. Outline and silhouette play a major role; the effect of shading is minor. The gentle faces are wistful and melancholic, and the angels look tenderly at Mary. The throne appears to be inlaid with multi-colored marbles, much like the architecture of the period. Yet it is not rendered with scientific perspective and does not suggest depth. Duccio represents the culmination of the old Byzantine style rather than the start of a new one.

GIOTTO [JOT-toh] (1267?–1336/7) has an extremely important place in the history of art. He is known primarily as a muralist—the small windows of Italian Gothic architecture left large areas of wall to paint. His naturalism is apparent if we compare his own *Madonna and Child Enthroned* (fig. 12.31) to Duccio's. Both were painted at about the same time. Duccio's Madonna seems like an icon, insubstantial and elongated. Giotto's Mary

Figure 12.31 Giotto, *Madonna and Child Enthroned*, 1310, tempera on panel, 10′8″ × 6′8¼″(3.53 × 2.05 m), Galleria degli Uffizi, Florence, Italy. In contrast to Duccio's slender Mary, Giotto's is solid and appears to sit within the space implied by her throne.

Figure 12.32   Giotto, *Lamentation over the Body of Jesus*, 1305–06, fresco, $6'6\frac{3}{4}'' \times$ $6'\frac{7}{8}''$ (2.00 × 1.85 m), Arena (Scrovegni) Chapel, Padua, Italy. The profound grief of this subject is magnified by the way in which it is depicted by Giotto. The center of attention, usually in the physical center of the composition, is instead low on the left, emotionally "down," and the barren background leads the viewer's eyes down to the heads of Jesus and his mother Mary.

seems, on the other hand, to be a "real" woman. Not only does she appear to sit in real space, but it is as if real bones lie beneath her skin.

Giotto's most famous work is the extensive cycle portraying the lives of Mary and Jesus in the Arena Chapel (Scrovegni Chapel) in Padua, painted 1305–06. In the scene of the *Lamentation ver the Body of Jesus* (fig. 12.32), the composition is used to emphasize the sadness of the subject. Position can be used to convey emotion in art— just as we speak about "feeling down" or say "things are looking up." Here, atypically, the center of attention is low and off-center. Figures bend down to the dead Jesus. The diagonal of the hill leads down to the heads of Mary and Jesus, enhancing the powerful emotional impact characteristic of Gothic art. The figures form a circle around Jesus, leaving a space for one more person—the viewer, who is thereby invited to join in their grieving. Emphasis is on mass rather than line, figures are three-dimensional, solid, and bulky, and an attempt has been

made to place them within the space of an actual landscape. But perhaps most important of all, the mourners appear to convey real emotion, an almost tangible sense of personal grief and loss.

REALISM IN LITERATURE

Boccaccio's Decameron.   If the visual arts were becoming more and more naturalistic by the end of the fourteenth century, literature achieved something of the same effect by forsaking Latin for the spoken language, the **vernacular**, of the day. This is especially true of the work of GIOVANNI BOCCACCIO [bo-CAH-choh] (1313–1375). His most famous prose work, the *Decameron*, has similarities with Chaucer's *Canterbury Tales* and with Dante's *Divine Comedy*, upon which Boccaccio wrote a commentary. However, his interest in classical antiquity, his translations of ancient Greek texts, his Latin writings, and his search for lost Roman works make him, with Petrarch (see Chapter 13), an influential early Italian Renaissance figure.

Boccaccio spent much of his youth in Naples, where his father was a merchant and attorney associated with the powerful Bardi Bank of Florence. Trained in banking himself, Boccaccio nonetheless preferred literature, and spent most of his adult life in Florence pursuing a literary career. *The Decameron* is a collection of a hundred *novelle*, or short stories, told by ten Florentines, who leave plague-infested Florence for the neighboring hill town of Fiesole. Written in the vernacular Tuscan of his time, Boccaccio has each of the work's ten narrators, seven women and three men, tell a tale a day, each through a cycle of ten days. Their tales, mostly comic, center on the lives and fortunes of ordinary people, who are given a voice here for the first time in Western literature. Boccaccio's sharp eye for realistic detail and his ability to present psychologically convincing characters make him a natural storyteller. His wit, frankness, and worldly cynicism are additional attractions of his style.

Chaucer's Canterbury Tales. As a well-educated medieval intellectual, the English poet GEOFFREY CHAUCER [CHAW-ser] (ca. 1342–1400) was, like Boccaccio, familiar with Latin literature, history, and philosophy. He read Ovid and Virgil in their original language, though, like Shakespeare, he did not know much, if any, Greek. Still, Chaucer was familiar with Greek myth, literature, and history through his knowledge of the Latin writers.

The most important influence on Chaucer's work, however, was not Latin but Italian. Chaucer's trip to Italy in 1372 is thought to have been the catalyst for his immersion in Italian literature, especially the works of Dante and Boccaccio. A number of Chaucer's *Canterbury Tales*, as well as the basic narrative structure, derive from Boccaccio's *Decameron*.

Although unfinished at the time of his death in 1400, Chaucer had been working on *The Canterbury Tales*, a collection of stories told by a group of pilgrims traveling from London to Canterbury, for nearly fifteen years. Sometimes described as a medieval portrait gallery, the tales have a tremendous social breadth, including depictions of medieval figures from the highest to the lowest social classes. But *The Canterbury Tales'* distinction lies primarily in its literary art rather than its documentary sense of social history.

Chaucer had originally planned to write 120 tales (or so the Host of the tavern where the pilgrims all first gather tells us in the General Prologue), two for each of his thirty pilgrims to tell on the pilgrimage to Canterbury, and two on the return trip. However, Chaucer only completed twenty-two tales and composed fragments of two others. He also prefaced the tales with a General Prologue, which functions as a framing device for the tales, providing them with an apparent basis in fact—the pilgrimage to the shrine of St. Thomas à Becket at Canterbury. Beyond this important function, the General Prologue also introduces the characters, who later narrate their own tales. Chaucer develops the characterizations of these figures through the tales they then tell. That is, the character of the teller is further revealed by the subject of the tale and the manner in which it is told.

It would seem that Chaucer's attitude toward the various characters depicted in the General Prologue differs widely. Some, such as the Clerk and the Knight, he depicts as models, or ideals, whose behavior is to be emulated; others, such as the Monk and the Pardoner, he portrays as negative models, with their warts (both

Timeline 12.2   The Gothic era.

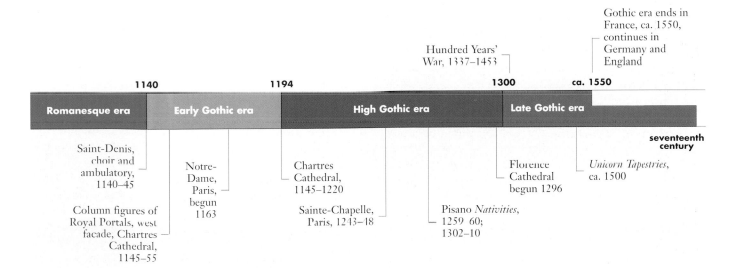

Figure 12.33 *Christine de Pizan Presenting Her Poems to Isabel of Bavaria*, manuscript illumination, British Library, London. The illumination shows the world of women that Christine celebrates in her writing.

literal and figurative) showing. It is through the voice of Chaucer's narrator that the ironic and satiric portraits of the other pilgrims are constructed. Yet this narrator himself is revealed by the author as being slightly naïve: at a number of points in the General Prologue he shows admiration for the Pardoner and the Monk, albeit in ways that differ from his admiration for the Clerk and the Knight. The "naïve" narrator sometimes fails to discriminate between good and evil manifestations of human behavior; he also fails to distinguish between the ideals certain of the characters are supposed to strive for and the less admirable realities they embody—as in the cases of the Monk and the Prioress.

In such instances, Chaucer employs acute irony as an instrument of trenchant satire. His wit and observation are evident throughout the entire work, though perhaps most clearly in the General Prologue. Yet everywhere in the *Tales*, one finds a vitality that reveals a remarkable appreciation of life from its lowest and bawdiest aspects to its most elegant and spiritual manifestations.

Christine de Pizan.   One of the outstanding woman writers of the later Middle Ages, Christine de Pizan [PEA-zan] (1364–ca. 1431) was a scholar and court advisor, as well as a poet and writer of prose pieces (fig. 12.33). Born in Venice, Christine de Pizan moved with her father to France, where he served as court astrologer to the French monarch Charles V. There she learned to write French and Italian as well as to read Latin, an unusual accomplishment for a woman at the time.

At the age of fifteen, she married a court notary, Eugène of Castal, who died four years later in an epidemic. As a widow with three young children, she began writing to support her family. Before long she was a recognized literary luminary, an accomplished poet and the officially sanctioned biographer of Charles V. In her numerous works of prose and poetry, she consistently argued for the wider recognition of women's status and abilities.

Among her many works are a poem about Joan of Arc; a set of letters challenging the depiction of women in the influential medieval poem *The Romance of the Rose*; a book of moral proverbs; a dream vision; a collection of a hundred brief narratives accompanied by their own commentary; a manual of instruction for knights; an admonitory essay on the art of prudence, *The Book of Feats of Arms and Chivalry*; and her best-known work, *The Book of the City of Ladies*. A universal history of women, *The Book of the City of Ladies* includes discussion of pagan as well as Christian women, of those long deceased as well as those of her own time, and of fictional characters as well as actual people. Throughout the book, she attempts to alter the reader's perceptions of women. It is this desire to represent women from a woman's point of view that makes the writing of Christine de Pizan unique. Her book is a refutation of misogynistic images of women constructed by male writers of the past. In particular, she rebuts the images of women portrayed in Giovanni Boccaccio's *De mulieribus claris* (*Concerning Famous Women*). For example, in response to the charge that women are greedy, she states that what appears as greed in women is a prudent and sensible response to male profligacy. Since men squander, women have to protect themselves against such destructive behavior. She counterattacks by arguing that women are fundamentally generous.

Yet even as she argued for enhanced opportunities for women, Christine de Pizan profoundly echoed the ideals of Christian life as espoused in Church teaching. She supported the goals of Christian marriage, in which a moral commitment between spouses enables them to advance in grace and spirituality while fulfilling their roles as husband and wife. To a large extent, she appears to have been an idealist, one who aspired to achieve the highest values articulated in her religious tradition, while ridding it of its entrenched bias against women.

While urging women to accept their place in the hierarchy of the time, she also encouraged them to fulfill their potential—intellectually, socially, and spiritually—by developing nobility of soul, whatever their particular social status or individual circumstances. Nobility, for Christine de Pizan, was a matter of mind, heart, and spirit, rather than of birthright. She believed that through patient and persistent striving, women of her time could become "ladies," noble feminine embodiments of the highest ideals of heart and mind.

SECULAR SONG

Guillaume de Machaut.   In the fourteenth century, medieval music underwent significant changes, including the displacement of church music by secular music. Drinking songs and music that drew on the everyday began to be composed and performed as often as devotional music inspired by religious faith. In addition, a new system of musical notation had developed by the fourteenth century so that composers were now able to spell out the rhythmic values as well as the melodic pitches of notes. Other changes in musical style, such as the use of syncopation (which emphasizes notes "off" the regular beat), became so significant that theorists referred to the new music as *ars nova* (new art) to distinguish it from the *ars antiqua* (ancient or old art) of previous centuries.

One composer who wrote both sacred and secular music in the *ars nova* style was GUILLAUME DE MACHAUT [ghee-OHM duh mash-OH] (1300–1377), the foremost French composer of the time and one of France's leading poets. Like Giotto in painting, Machaut helped to usher in the Renaissance by breaking away from the older medieval style.

Though ordained a priest, Machaut spent most of his life at court. Born in the French province of Champagne, he traveled throughout Europe, and spent his later years in Reims. During his many travels, he presented carefully written and decorated copies of his music and poems to court patrons and foreign nobility. The great care he took in making these copies has ensured their survival.

English Song.   One of the most striking musical works to come out of England during the Middle Ages was the song "Sumer Is Icumen in." The song is unlike anything else that has survived from the thirteenth century in providing a foretaste of musical tendencies and techniques that were to emerge over a century and a half later, in the works of madrigalists such as Thomas Weelkes and Thomas Morley (see Chapter 14).

The words of the text were composed in English, not Latin, and they celebrate nature rather than religion, the physical life of earth rather than the spiritual joys of heaven. The composer set the words to a lively tune, which is sung by all four voice parts in a canon, or round. Each voice enters before the others have finished so that all four sing simultaneously, though they are at different places in the music at any given time.

READINGS
✦

✦ **ST. FRANCIS OF ASSISI**

The Canticle of the Creatures

Francis of Assisi's poem "The Canticle of the Creatures" is among the earliest poems written in the Italian vernacular. It conveys St. Francis's prayerful thanksgiving for the wonders God has provided. His poem reflects the ancient Hebrew tradition of poetic prayer, a psalm of praise that derives from the biblical book of Psalms. Francis's canticle also reflects the humility for which he is famous.

O Most High, Omnipotent, Good Lord; Thine be the praise, the glory and the honor; to Thee be every blessing. To Thee alone, Most Highest, are they due, and there is no man worthy to speak of Thee.

Be praised, O Lord, with all Thy creatures, especially my lord Brother Sun, who gives the day, and by whom Thou showest light. He is beautiful and shining with great splendor; of Thee, Most Highest, he is the symbol.

Be praised, O Lord, for Sister Moon and the stars; Thou hast formed them in the heavens, clear, precious and beautiful.

Be praised, O Lord, for Brother Wind and for air and cloud,

for fair and for all weather by which Thou givest Thy creatures sustenance.

Be praised, O Lord, for Sister Water, the which is so useful, humble, precious and chaste.

Be praised, O Lord, for Brother Fire, by which Thou lightest up the night. He is beautiful and gay, vigorous and strong.

Be praised, O Lord, for our Sister Mother Earth, the which supports and nourishes us and produces diverse fruits, with brilliant flowers and grass.

Be praised, O Lord, for those, who for love of Thee forgive, who bear sickness and tribulation; blessèd those who in peace shall endure, for by Thee, Most High, they shall be crowned.

Be praised, O Lord, for our Sister Death of the Body, from the which no man living may escape; woe to them who shall die in mortal sin and blessèd those who shall be found in Thy most holy will, for the second death shall work them no harm.

Give praises and blessings and render thanks to my Lord, and serve Him with great humility.

↞ ST. THOMAS AQUINAS
from the *Summa Theologica*

In the Summa Theologica, *Aquinas's summation of what can be known about God and human beings, the scholastic philosopher presents his arguments in the form of assertions, objections, and replies to those objections. In the following passage Aquinas analyzes the question of whether people can believe the things they know and know the things they believe, whether, that is, faith and science are about the same things.*

QUESTION I—OF FAITH

FIFTH ARTICLE

Whether Those Things That Are of Faith Can Be an Object of Science?

We proceed thus to the Fifth Article:—Objection 1. It would seem that those things that are of faith can be an object of science. For where science is lacking there is ignorance, since ignorance is the opposite of science. Now we are not in ignorance of those things we have to believe, since ignorance of such things savors of unbelief, according to 1 Tim. i. 13: *I did it ignorantly in unbelief.* Therefore things that are of faith can be an object of science.

Obj. 2. Further, science is acquired by reasons. Now sacred writers employ reasons to inculcate things that are of faith. Therefore such things can be an object of science.

Obj. 3. Further, things which are demonstrated are an object of science, since a *demonstration is a syllogism that pro-*

duces science. Now certain matters of faith have been demonstrated by the philosophers, such as the Existence and Unity of God, and so forth. Therefore things that are of faith can be an object of science.

Obj. 4. Further, opinion is further from science than faith is, since faith is said to stand between opinion and science. Now opinion and science can, in a way, be about the same object, as stated in *Poster.* i. Therefore faith and science can be about the same object also.

On the contrary, Gregory says (*Hom.* xxvi *in Ev.*) that *when a thing is manifest, it is the object, not of faith, but of perception.* Therefore things that are of faith are not the object of perception, whereas what is an object of science is the object of perception. Therefore there can be no faith about things which are an object of science.

I answer that, All science is derived from self-evident and therefore *seen* principles; wherefore all objects of science must needs be, in a fashion, seen.

Now as stated above (A. 4) it is impossible that one and the same thing should be believed and seen by the same person. Hence it is equally impossible for one and the same thing to be an object of science and of belief for the same person. It may happen, however, that a thing which is an object of vision or science for one, is believed by another: since we hope to see some day what we now believe about the Trinity, according to 1 Cor. xiii. 12: *We see now through a glass in a dark manner; but then face to face:* which vision the angels possess already; so that what we believe, they see. In like manner it may happen that what is an object of vision or scientific knowledge for one man, even in the state of a wayfarer, is, for another man, an object of faith, because he does not know it by demonstration.

Nevertheless that which is proposed to be believed equally by all, is equally unknown by all as an object of science; such are the things which are of faith simply. Consequently faith and science are not about the same things.

Reply Obj. 1. Unbelievers are in ignorance of things that are of faith, for neither do they see or know them in themselves, nor do they know them to be credible. The faithful, on the other hand, know them, not as by demonstration, but by the light of faith which makes them see that they ought to believe them, as stated above (A. 4, *ad* 2, 3).

Reply Obj. 2. The reasons employed by holy men to prove things that are of faith, are not demonstrations; they are either persuasive arguments showing that what is proposed to our faith is not impossible, or else they are proofs drawn from the principles of faith, i.e. from the authority of Holy Writ, as Dionysius declares (*Div. Nom.* ii). Whatever is based on these principles is as well proved in the eyes of the faithful, as a conclusion drawn from self-evident principles is in the eyes of all. Hence again, theology is a science, as we stated at the outset of this work (P. I, Q. 1, A. 2).

Reply Obj. 3. Things which can be proved by demonstration are reckoned among the articles of faith, not because they are believed simply by all, but because they are a necessary presupposition to matters of faith, so that those who do not know them by demonstration must know them first of all by faith.

Reply Obj. 4. As the Philosopher says (*loc. cit.*), science and opinion about the same object can certainly be in different men, as we have stated above about science and faith; yet it is possible for one and the same man to have science and faith about the same thing relatively, i.e. in relation to the object, but not in the same respect. For it is possible for the same person, about one and the same object, to know one thing and to think another: and, in like manner, one may know by demonstration the unity of the Godhead, and, by faith, the Trinity. On the other hand, in one and the same man, about the same object, and in the same respect, science is incompatible with either opinion or faith, yet for different reasons. Because science is incompatible with opinion about the same object simply, for the reason that science demands that its object should be deemed impossible to be otherwise, whereas it is essential to opinion, that its object should be deemed possible to be otherwise. Yet that which is the object of faith, on account of the certainty of faith, is also deemed impossible to be otherwise: and the reason why science and faith cannot be about the same object and in the same respect is because the object of science is something seen, whereas the object of faith is the unseen, as stated above.

⤶ DANTE

from *The Divine Comedy*

Throughout The Divine Comedy *Dante creates dramatic scenes, provides numerous comments on the political history of medieval Florence, and describes hundreds of characters—from history, mythology, and religion, as well as from Dante's own world. Saints and sinners, philosophers and heroes, popes and clerics, along with people from all walks of life, make an appearance. In the* Inferno, *Dante selects individual sinners for close-up portrayal. Among the most memorable are the illicit lovers Paolo and Francesca, who are swirled around together in a maelstrom, which represents their passion. Dante the pilgrim pauses to hear Francesca tell their sad story, as Dante the poet characterizes her as she tells it. Also included among numerous close-ups of poets is the Provencal troubadour Bertran de Born, who is placed in hell because he was a sower of discord. Dante's rendition of the scene when he is first noticed is vivid and memorable. Dante's punishment is to sever his head from his body and to have him carry it around with him. These and other characters' stories are told in the* Cantos *from the* Inferno *that follow. The selections below also include representative cantos from the* Purgatorio *and* Paradiso. *The introductions to each canto summarize the action described therein, while the notes gloss historical, biblical, and literary allusions. These aids to reading* The Divine Comedy *make the reader's challenge easier and the poem's rewards even greater.*

INFERNO

CANTO I

The Dark Wood of Error

Midway in his allotted threescore years and ten, Dante comes to himself with a start and realizes that he has strayed from the True Way into the Dark Wood of Error (Worldliness). As soon as he has realized his loss, Dante lifts his eyes and sees the first light of the sunrise (the

Sun is the Symbol of Divine Illumination) lighting the shoulders of a little hill (The Mount of Joy). It is the Easter Season, the time of resurrection, and the sun is in its equinoctial rebirth. This juxtaposition of joyous symbols fills Dante with hope and he sets out at once to climb directly up the Mount of Joy, but almost immediately his way is blocked by the Three Beasts of Worldliness: The Leopard of Malice and Fraud, The Lion of Violence and Ambition, and the She-Wolf of Incontinence. These beasts, and especially the She-Wolf, drive him back despairing into the darkness of error. But just as all seems lost, a figure appears to him. It is the shade of Virgil, Dante's symbol of Human Reason.

Virgil explains that he has been sent to lead Dante from error. There can, however, be no direct ascent past the beasts: the man who would escape them must go a longer and harder way. First he must descend through Hell (The Recognition of Sin), then he must ascend through Purgatory (The Renunciation of Sin), and only then may he reach the pinnacle of joy and come to the Light of God. Virgil offers to guide Dante, but only as far as Human Reason can go. Another guide (Beatrice, symbol of Divine Love) must take over for the final ascent, for Human Reason is self-limited. Dante submits himself joyously to Virgil's guidance and they move off.

Midway in our life's journey,° I went astray
    from the straight road and woke to find myself
    alone in a dark wood. How shall I say
what wood that was! I never saw so drear,
    so rank, so arduous a wilderness!   5
    Its very memory gives a shape to fear.
Death could scarce be more bitter than that place!
    But since it came to good, I will recount
    all that I found revealed there by God's grace.
How I came to it I cannot rightly say,   10
    so drugged and loose with sleep had I become
    when I first wandered there from the True Way.
But at the far end of that valley of evil
    whose maze had sapped my very heart with fear,
    I found myself before a little hill   15
and lifted up my eyes. Its shoulders glowed
    already with the sweet rays of that planet°
    whose virtue leads men straight on every road,
and the shining strengthened me against the fright
    whose agony had wracked the lake of my heart   20
    through all the errors of that piteous night.
Just as a swimmer, who with his last breath
    flounders ashore from perilous seas, might turn
    to memorize the wide water of his death—
so did I turn, my soul still fugitive   25
    from death's surviving image, to stare down
    that pass that none had ever left alive.
And there I lay to rest from my heart's race
    till calm and breath returned to me. Then rose
    and pushed up that dead slope at such a pace   30

---

1 *Midway ... journey:* The biblical life span is three-score years and ten (seventy years). The action opens in Dante's thirty-fifth year, i.e., 1300 A.D.   17 *planet:* The sun. Ptolemaic astronomers considered it a planet. It is also symbolic of God as He who lights the way.

each footfall rose above the last.° And lo!
  almost at the beginning of the rise
  I faced a spotted Leopard, all tremor and flow
and gaudy pelt. And it would not pass, but stood
  so blocking my every turn that time and again   35
  I was on the verge of turning back to the wood.
This fell at the first widening of the dawn
  as the sun was climbing Aries with those stars
  that rode with him to light the new creation.°
Thus the holy hour and the sweet season   40
  of commemoration did much to arm my fear
  of that bright murderous beast with their good omen.
Yet not so much but what I shook with dread
  at sight of a great Lion that broke upon me
  raging with hunger, its enormous head   45
held high as if to strike a mortal terror
  into the very air. And down his track,
  a She-Wolf drove upon me, a starved horror
ravening and wasted beyond belief.°
  She seemed a rack for avarice, gaunt and craving.   50
  Oh many the souls she has brought to endless grief!
She brought such heaviness upon my spirit
  at sight of her savagery and desperation,
  I died from every hope of that high summit.
And like a miser—eager in acquisition   55
  but desperate in self-reproach when Fortune's wheel
  turns to the hour of his loss—all tears and attrition
I wavered back; and still the beast pursued,
  forcing herself against me bit by bit
  till I slid back into the sunless wood.   60
And as I fell to my soul's ruin, a presence
  gathered before me on the discoloured air,
  the figure of one who seemed hoarse from long
    silence.
At sight of him in that friendless waste I cried:
  "Have pity on me, whatever thing you are,   65
  whether shade or living man." And it replied:
"Not man, though man I once was, and my blood
  was Lombard, both my parents Mantuan.
  I was born, though late, *sub Julio*,° and bred
in Rome under Augustus in the noon   70

of the false and lying gods. I was a poet
  and sang of old Anchises' noble son°
who came to Rome after the burning of Troy.
  But you—why do *you* return to these distresses
  instead of climbing that shining Mount of Joy   75
which is the seat and first cause of man's bliss?"
  "And are you then that Virgil and that fountain
  of purest speech?" My voice grew tremulous:
"Glory and light of poets! now may that zeal
  and love's apprenticeship that I poured out   80
  on your heroic verses serve me well!
For you are my true master and first author,
  the sole maker from whom I drew the breath
  of that sweet style whose measures have brought me
    honor.
See there, immortal sage, the beast I flee.   85
  For my soul's salvation, I beg you, guard me from her,
  for she has struck a mortal tremor through me."
And he replied, seeing my soul in tears:
  "He must go by another way who would escape
  this wilderness, for that mad beast that fleers   90
before you there, suffers no man to pass.
  She tracks down all, kills all, and knows no glut,
  but, feeding, she grows hungrier than she was.
She mates with any beast, and will mate with more
  before the Greyhound° comes to hunt her down.   95
  He will not feed on lands nor loot, but honor
and love and wisdom will make straight his way.
  He will rise between Feltro and Feltro, and in him
  shall be the resurrection and new day
of that sad Italy for which Nisus died,   100
  and Turnus, and Euryalus, and the maid Camilla.°
  He shall hunt her through every nation of sick pride
till she is driven back forever to Hell
  whence Envy first released her on the world.
  Therefore, for your own good, I think it well   105
you follow me and I will be your guide
  and lead you forth through an eternal place.
  There you shall see the ancient spirits tried
in endless pain, and hear their lamentation
  as each bemoans the second death° of souls.   110
  Next you shall see upon a burning mountain
souls in fire and yet content in fire,
  knowing that whensoever it may be
  they yet will mount into the blessed choir.
To which, if it is still your wish to climb,   115
  a worthier spirit shall be sent to guide you.
  With her shall I leave you, for the King of Time,

---

31 *each … last:* The literal rendering would be: "So that the fixed foot was ever the lower." "Fixed" has often been translated "right" and an ingenious reasoning can support that reading, but a simpler explanation offers itself and seems more competent: Dante is saying that he climbed with such zeal and haste that every footfall carried him above the last despite the steepness of the climb. At a slow pace, on the other hand, the rear foot might be brought up only as far as the forward foot.   39 *creation:* The medieval tradition had it that the sun was in Aries at the time of the creation. The significance of the astronomical and religious conjunction is an important part of Dante's intended allegory. It is just before dawn of Good Friday 1300 A.D. when he awakens in the Dark Wood. Thus his new life begins under Aries, the sign of creation, at dawn (rebirth) and in the Easter season (resurrection). Moreover the moon is full and the sun is in the equinox, conditions that did not fall together on any Friday of 1300. Dante is obviously constructing poetically the perfect Easter as a symbol of his new awakening.   43-49 *Leopard … him … She-wolf:* These three beasts undoubtedly are take from Jeremiah v, 6. Many additional and incidental interpretations have been advanced for them but the central interpretation must remain as noted. They foreshadow the three divisions of Hell (incontinence, violence, and fraud) which Virgil explains at length in Canto XI, 16–111.   69 *sub Julio:* In the reign of Julius Caesar.

72 *Anchises' noble son:* Aeneas.   95 *The Greyhound … Feltro and Feltro:* Almost certainly refers to Can Grande della Scala (1290–1329), great Italian leader born to Verona, which lies between the towns of Feltre and Montefeltro.   100-101 *Nisus, Turnus, Euryalus, Camilla:* All were killed in the war between the Trojans and the Latins when, according to legend, Aeneas led the survivors of Troy into Italy. Nisus and Euryalus (*Aenid* IX) were Trojan comrades-in-arms who died together. Camilla (*Aeneid* XI) was the daughter of the Latin king and one of the warrior women. She was killed in a horse charge against the Trojans after displaying grewat gallantry. Turnus (*Aeneid* XII) was killed by Aeneas in a dual.   110 *The second death:* Damnation. "This is the second death, even the lake of fire." (*Revelation* xx, 14).

who reigns on high, forbids me to come there
    since, living, I rebelled against his law.°
    He rules the waters and the land and air   *120*
and there holds court, his city and his throne.
    Oh blessed are they he chooses!" And I to him:
    "Poet, by that God to you unknown,
lead me this way. Beyond this present ill
    and worse to dread, lead me to Peter's gate°   *125*
    and be my guide through the sad halls of Hell."
And he then: "Follow." And he moved ahead
in silence, and I followed where he led.

CANTO III

The Vestibule of Hell   The Opportunists

*The Poets pass the Gate of Hell and are immediately assailed by cries
of anguish. Dante sees the first of the souls in torment. They are The
Opportunists, those souls who in life were neither for good nor evil but
only for themselves. Mixed with them are those outcasts who took no
sides in the Rebellion of the Angels. They are neither in Hell nor out
of it. Eternally unclassified, they race round and round pursuing a
wavering banner that runs forever before them through the dirty air;
and as they run they are pursued by swarms of wasps and hornets,
who sting them and produce a constant flow of blood and putrid matter which trickles down the bodies of the sinners and is feasted upon by
loathsome worms and maggots who coat the ground.*

*The law of Dante's Hell is the law of symbolic retribution. As they
sinned so are they punished. They took no sides, therefore they are
given no place. As they pursued the ever-shifting illusion of their own
advantage, changing their courses with every changing wind, so they
pursue eternally an elusive, ever-shifting banner. As their sin was a
darkness, so they move in darkness. As their own guilty conscience
pursued them, so they are pursued by swarms of wasps and hornets.
And as their actions were a moral filth, so they run eternally through
the filth of worms and maggots which they themselves feed.*

*Dante recognizes several, among them Pope Celestine V, but with-
out delaying to speak to any of these souls, the Poets move on to
Acheron, the first of the rivers of Hell. Here the newly-arrived souls
of the damned gather and wait for monstrous Charon to ferry them
over to punishment. Charon recognizes Dante as a living man and
angrily refuses him passage. Virgil forces Charon to serve them, but
Dante swoons with terror, and does not reawaken until he is on the
other side.*

I AM THE WAY INTO THE CITY OF WOE.
    I AM THE WAY TO A FORSAKEN PEOPLE.
    I AM THE WAY INTO ETERNAL SORROW.
SACRED JUSTICE MOVED MY ARCHITECT.
    I WAS RAISED HERE BY DIVINE OMNIPOTENCE,   *5*
    PRIMORDIAL LOVE AND ULTIMATE INTELLECT.

ONLY THOSE ELEMENTS TIME CANNOT WEAR.°
    WERE MADE BEFORE ME, AND BEYOND TIME I STAND.°
    ABANDON ALL HOPE YE WHO ENTER HERE.°
These mysteries I read cut into stone   *10*
    above a gate. And turning I said: "Master,
    what is the meaning of this harsh inscription?"
And he then as initiate to novice:
    "Here must you put by all division of spirit
    and gather your soul against all cowardice.   *15*
This is the place I told you to expect.
    Here you shall pass among the fallen people,
    souls who have lost the good of intellect."
So saying, he put forth his hand to me,
    and with a gentle and encouraging smile   *20*
    he led me through the gate of mystery.
Here sighs and cries and wails coiled and recoiled
    on the starless air, spilling my soul to tears.
    A confusion of tongues and monstrous accents toiled
in pain and anger. Voices harsh and shrill   *25*
    and sounds of blows, all intermingled, raised
    tumult and pandemonium that still
whirls on the air forever dirty with it
    as if a whirlwind sucked at sand. And I,
    holding my head in horror, cried: "Sweet Spirit,   *30*
What souls are these who run through this black haze?"
    And he to me: "These are the nearly soulless
    whose lives concluded neither blame nor praise.
They are mixed here with that despicable corps
    of angels who were neither for God nor Satan,   *35*
    but only for themselves. The High Creator
scourged them from Heaven for its perfect beauty,
    and Hell will not receive them since the wicked
    might feel some glory over them." And I:
"Master, what gnaws at them so hideously   *40*
    their lamentation stuns the very air?"
    "They have no hope of death," he answered me,
"and in their blind and unattaining state
    their miserable lives have sunk so low
    that they must envy every other fate.   *45*
No word of them survives their living season.
    Mercy and Justice deny them even a name.
    Let us not speak of them: look, and pass on."
I saw a banner there upon the mist.
    Circling and circling, it seemed to scorn all pause.   *50*
    So it ran on, and still behind it pressed
a never-ending rout of souls in pain.
    I had not thought death had undone so many
    as passed before me in that mournful train.
And some I knew among them; last of all   *55*
    I recognized the shadow of that soul

---

¹¹⁹ *forbids me to come there since, living, etc.:* Salvation is only
through Christ in Dante's theology. Vergil lived and died
before the establishment of Christ's teachings in Rome, and
cannot therefore enter Heaven.   ¹²⁵ *Peter's gate:* The gate of
Purgatory. The gate is guarded by an angel with a gleaming
sword. The angel is Peter's vicar (Peter, the first Pope, symbolized all Popes; i.e., Christ's vicar on earth) and is entrusted with
the two great keys. Some commentators argue that this is the
gate of Paradise, but Dante mentions no gate beyond this one
in his ascent to Heaven. It should be remembered, too, that
those who pass the gate of Purgatory have effectively entered
Heaven.

---

⁷ *ELEMENTS:* The angels, the Empyrean, and the First Matter are
the elements time cannot wear, for they will last to all time.
Man, however, in his mortal state, is not eternal. The Gate of
Hell, therefore, was created before man.   ⁸ *BEYOND TIME:* So
odious is sin to God that there can be no end to its just punishment.   ⁹ *ABONDON ... HERE:* The admonition, of course, is to the
damned and not to those who come on Heaven-sent errands.

who, in his cowardice, made that Great Denial.°
  At once I understood for certain: these
  were of that retrograde and faithless crew
  hateful to God and to His enemies.   60
These wretches never born and never dead
  ran naked in a swarm of wasps and hornets
  that goaded them the more the more they fled,
and made their faces stream with bloody gouts
  of pus and tears that dribbled to their feet   65
  to be swallowed there by loathsome worms and maggots
Then looking onward I made out a throng
  assembled on the beach of a wide river,
  whereupon I turned to him: "Master, I long
to know what souls these are, and what strange usage 70
  makes them as eager to cross as they seem to be
  in this infected light." At which the Sage:
"All this shall be made known to you when we stand
  on the joyless beach of Acheron." And I
  cast down my eyes, sensing a reprimand   75
in what he said, and so walked at his side
  in silence and ashamed until we came
  through the dead cavern to that sunless tide.
There, steering toward us in an ancient ferry
  came an old man° with a white bush of hair,   80
  bellowing: "Woe to you depraved souls! Bury
here and forever all hope of Paradise:
  I come to lead you to the other shore,
  into eternal dark, into fire and ice.
And you who are living yet, I say begone   85
  from these who are dead." But when he saw me stand
  against his violence he began again:
"By other windings and by other steerage
  shall you cross to that other shore. Not here! Not
    here!
  A lighter craft than mine must give you passage."° 90
And my Guide to him: "Charon, bite back your spleen:
  this has been willed where what is willed must be,
  and is not yours to ask what it may mean."
The steersman of that marsh of ruined souls,
  who wore a wheel of flame around each eye,   95
  stifled the rage that shook his woolly jowls.
But those unmanned and naked spirits there

turned pale with fear and their teeth began to chatter
  at sound of his crude bellow. In despair
they blasphemed God,° their parents, their time on earth
  the race of Adam, and the day and the hour   101
  and the place and the seed and the womb that gave
  them birth.
But all together they drew to that grim shore
  where all must come who lose the fear of God.
  Weeping and cursing they come for evermore,   105
and demon Charon with eyes like burning coals
  herds them in, and with a whistling oar
  flails on the stragglers to his wake of souls.
As leaves in autumn loosen and stream down
  until the branch stands bare above its tatters 110
  spread on the rustling ground, so one by one
the evil seed of Adam in its Fall
  cast themselves, at his signal, from the shore
  and streamed away like birds who hear their call.
So they are gone over that shadowy water,   115
  and always before they reach the other shore
  a new noise stirs on this, and new throngs gather.
"My son," the courteous Master said to me,
  "all who die in the shadow of God's wrath
  converge to this from every clime and country. 120
And all pass over eagerly, for here
  Divine Justice transforms and spurs them so
  their dread turns wish: they yearn for what they fear.°
No soul in Grace comes ever to this crossing;
  therefore if Charon rages at your presence   125
  you will understand the reason for his cursing."
When he had spoken, all the twilight country
  shook so violently, the terror of it
  bathes me with sweat even in memory:
the tear-soaked ground gave out a sigh of wind 130
  that spewed itself in flame on a red sky,
  and all my shuttered senses left me. Blind,
like one whom sleep comes over in a swoon,
I stumbled into darkness and went down.°

CANTO V

Circle Two   The Carnal

The Poets leave Limbo and enter the Second Circle. Here begin the torments of Hell proper, and here, blocking the way, sits Minos, the dread and semi-bestial judge of the damned who assigns to each soul

---

57 *soul ... Denial:* This is almost certainly intended to be Celestine V, who became Pope in 1294. He was a man of saintly life, but allowed himself to be convinced by a priest named Benedetto that his soul was in danger since no man could live in the world without being damned. In fear for his soul he withdrew from all worldly affairs and renounced the papacy. Benedetto promptly assumed the mantle himself and became Boniface VIII, a Pope who became for Dante a symbol of all the worst corruptions of the Church. Dante also blamed Boniface and his intrigues for many of the evils that befell Florence. We shall learn in Canto XIX that the fires of Hell are waiting for Boniface in the pit of the Simoniacs, and we shall be given further evidence of his corruption in Canto XXVII. Celestine's great guilt is that his cowardice (in selfish terror for his own welfare) served as the door through which so much evil entered the Church. 80 *old man:* Charon. He is the ferryman of dead souls across the Acheron in all classical mythology. 90 *A lighter craft:* Charon recognizes Dante not only as a living man but as a soul in grace, and knows, therefore, that the Infernal Ferry was not intended for him. He is probably referring to the fact that souls destined for Purgatory and Heaven assemble not at his ferry point, but on the banks of the Tiber, from which they are transported by an angel.

100 *blasphemed God:* The souls of the damned are not permitted to repent, for repentance is a divine grace. 123 *their dread ... fear:* Hell (allegorically Sin) is what the souls of the damned really wish for. Hell is their actual and deliberate choice, for divine grace is denied to none who wish for it in their hearts. The damned must, in fact, deliberately harden their hearts to God in order to become damned. Christ's grace is sufficient to save all who wish for it. 114 *went down:* This device (repeated at the end of Canto V) serves a double purpose. The first is technical: Dante uses it to cover a transition. We are never told how he crossed Acheron, for that would involve certain narrative matters he can better deal with when he crosses Styx in Canto VII. The second is to provide a point of departure for a theme that is carried through the entire descent: the theme of Dante's emotional reaction to Hell. These two swoons early in the descent show him most susceptible to the grief about him. As he descends, pity leaves him, and he even goes so far as to add to the torments of one sinner. The allegory is clear; we must harden ourselves against every sympathy for sin.

*its eternal torment. He orders the Poets back; but Virgil silences him
as he earlier silenced Charon, and the Poets move on.*

*They find themselves on a dark ledge swept by a great whirl-
wind, which spins within it the souls of the Carnal, those who betrayed
reason to their appetites. Their sin was to abandon themselves to the
tempest of their passions: so they are swept forever in the tempest of
Hell, forever denied the light of reason and of God. Virgil identifies
many among them. Semiramis is there, and Dido, Cleopatra, Helen,
Achilles, Paris, and Tristan. Dante sees Paolo and Francesca
swept together, and in the name of love he calls to them to tell their
sad story. They pause from their eternal flight to come to him, and
Francesca tells their history while Paolo weeps at her side. Dante is so
stricken by compassion at their tragic tale that he swoons once
again.*

So we went down to the second ledge alone;
    a smaller circle° of so much greater pain
    the voice of the damned rose in a bestial moan.
There Minos° sits, grinning, grotesque, and hale.
    He examines each lost soul as it arrives   5
    and delivers his verdict with his coiling tail.
That is to say, when the ill-fated soul
    appears before him it confesses all,
    and that grim sorter of the dark and foul
decides which place in Hell shall be its end,   10
    then wraps his twitching tail about himself
    one coil for each degree it must descend.
The soul descends and others take its place:
    each crowds in its turn to judgement, each confesses,
    each hears its doom and falls away through space.   15
"O you who come into this camp of woe,"
    cried Minos when he saw me turn away
    without awaiting his judgement, "watch where
        you go
once you have entered here, and to whom you turn!
    Do not be misled by that wide and easy passage!"   20
    And my Guide to him: "That is not your concern;
it is his fate to enter every door.
    This has been willed where what is willed must be,
    and is not yours to question. Say no more."
Now the choir of anguish, like a wound,   25
    strikes through the tortured air. Now I have come
    to Hell's full lamentation, sound beyond sound.
I came to a place stripped bare of every light
    and roaring on the naked dark like seas
    wracked by a war of winds. Their hellish flight   30
of storm and counterstorm through time foregone,
    sweeps the souls of the damned before its charge.
    Whirling and battering it drives them on,

and when they pass the ruined gap of Hell°   34
    through which we had come, their shrieks begin
      anew.
    There they blaspheme the power of God eternal.
And this, I learned, was the never ending flight
    of those who sinned in the flesh, the carnal and lusty
    who betrayed reason to their appetite.
As the wings of wintering starlings bear them on   40
    in their great wheeling flights, just so the blast
    wherries these evil souls through time foregone.
Here, there, up, down, they whirl and, whirling, strain
    with never a hope of hope to comfort them,
    not of release, but even of less pain.   45
As cranes go over sounding their harsh cry,
    leaving the long streak of their flight in air,
    so come these spirits, wailing as they fly.
And watching their shadows lashed by wind, I cried:
    "Master, what souls are these the very air   50
    lashes with its black whips from side to side?"
"The first of these whose history you would know,"
    he answered me, "was Empress of many tongues.°
    Mad sensuality corrupted her so
that to hide the guilt of her debauchery   55
    she licensed all depravity alike,
    and lust and law were one in her decree.
She is Semiramis of whom the tale is told
    how she married Ninus and succeeded him
    to the throne of that wide land the Sultans hold. 60
The other is Dido;° faithless to the ashes
    of Sichaeus, she killed herself for love.
    The next whom the eternal tempest lashes
is sense-drugged Cleopatra. See Helen° there,
    from whom such ill arose. And great Achilles,° 65
    who fought at last with love in the house of prayer.
And Paris. And Tristan." As they whirled above
    he pointed out more than a thousand shades
    of those torn from the mortal life by love.
I stood there while my Teacher one by one   70
    named the great knights and ladies of dim time;
    and I was swept by pity and confusion.
At last I spoke: "Poet, I should be glad
    to speak a word with those two swept together

---

² *smaller circle:* The pit of Hell tapers like a funnel. The circles of
ledges accordingly grow smaller as they descend.   ⁴ *Minos:* The
son of Europa and Zeus, who descended to her in the form of a
bull. Minos became a mythological king of Crete, so famous for
his wisdom and justice that after death his soul was made judge
of the dead. Virgil presents him fulfilling the same office at
Aeneas' descent to the underworld. Dante, however, transforms
him into an irate and hideous monster with a tail. The transformation may have been suggested by the form Zeus assumed for
the rape of Europa—the monster is certainly bullish enough
here—but the obvious purpose of the brutalization is to present
a figure symbolic of the guilty conscience of the wretches who
come before it to make their confessions.

---

³⁴ *ruined gap:* ... At the time of the Harrowing of Hell a great
earthquake shook the underworld shattering rocks and cliffs.
Ruins resulting from the same shock are noted in Canto XII,
34, and Canto XXI, 112 ff. At the beginning of Canto XXIV,
the Poets leave the *bolgia* of the Hypocrites by climbing the
ruined slabs of a bridge that was shattered by this earthquake.
⁵³ *Empress:* Semiramis, a legendary queen of Assyria who
assumed full power at the death of her husband, Ninus. ⁶¹ *Dido:*
Queen and founder of Carthage. She had vowed to remain
faithful to her husband, Sichaeus, but she fell in love with
Aeneas. When Aeneas abandoned her she stabbed herself on a
funeral pyre she had had prepared. According to Dante's own
system of punishments, she should be in the Seventh Circle
(Canto XIII) with the suicides. The only clue Dante gives to the
tempering of her punishment is his statement that "she killed
herself for love." Dante always seems readiest to forgive in that
name. ⁶⁴ *Helen:* She was held responsible for the Trojan War;
the wife of King Meneleus of Sparta, she ran away with the visiting Prince Paris from Troy. ⁶⁵ *Achilles:* He is placed among
this company because of his passion for Polyxena, the daughter
of Priam. For love of her, he agreed to desert the Greeks and to
join the Trojans, but when he went to the temple for the wedding (according to the legend Dante has followed) he was killed
by Paris.

so lightly on the wind and still so sad."° 75

And he to me: "Watch them. When next they pass,
call to them in the name of love that drives
and damns them here. In that name they will pause."

Thus, as soon as the wind in its wild course
brought them around, I called: "O wearied souls! 80
if none forbid it, pause and speak to us."

As mating doves that love calls to their nest
glide through the air with motionless raised wings,
borne by the sweet desire that fills each breast—

Just so those spirits turned on the torn sky 85
from the band where Dido whirls across the air;
such was the power of pity in my cry.

"O living creature, gracious, kind, and good,
going this pilgrimage through the sick night,
visiting us who stained the earth with blood, 90

were the King of Time our friend, we would pray His
peace
on you who have pitied us. As long as the wind
will let us pause, ask of us what you please.

The town where I was born lies by the shore
where the Po descends into its ocean rest 95
with its attendant streams in one long murmur.

Love, which in gentlest hearts will soonest bloom
seized my lover with passion for that sweet body
from which I was torn unshriven to my doom.

Love, which permits no loved one not to love, 100
took me so strongly with delight in him
that we are one in Hell, as we were above.°

Love led us to one death. In the depths of Hell
Caïna waits for him° who took our lives."
This was the piteous tale they stopped to tell. 105

And when I had heard those world-offended lovers
I bowed my head. At last the Poet spoke:
"What painful thoughts are these your lowered brow
covers?"

When at length I answered, I began: "Alas!

What sweetest thoughts, what green and young
desire
led these two lovers to this sorry pass." 111

Then turning to those spirits once again,
I said: "Francesca, what you suffer here
melts me to tears of pity and of pain.

But tell me: in the time of your sweet sighs 115
by what appearances found love the way
to lure you to his perilous paradise?"

And she: "The double grief of a lost bliss
is to recall its happy hour in pain.
Your Guide and Teacher knows the truth of this. 120

But if there is indeed a soul in Hell
to ask of the beginning of our love
out of his pity, I will weep and tell:

On a day for dalliance we read the rhyme
of Lancelot,° how love had mastered him. 125
We were alone with innocence and dim time.°

Pause after pause that high old story drew
our eyes together while we blushed and paled;
but it was one soft passage overthrew

our caution and our hearts. For when we read 130
how her fond smile was kissed by such a lover,
he who is one with me alive and dead

breathed on my lips the tremor of his kiss.
That book, and he who wrote it, was a pander.°
That day we read no further." As she said this, 135

the other spirit, who stood by her, wept
so piteously, I felt my senses reel
and faint away with anguish. I was swept

by such a swoon as death is, and I fell,
as a corpse might fall, to the dead floor of Hell. 140

CANTO XII

Circle Seven: Round One   The Violent Against Neighbors

The Poets begin the descent of the fallen rock wall, having first to evade the Minotaur, who menaces them. Virgil tricks him and the Poets hurry by.

Below them they see the River of Blood, which marks the First Round of the Seventh Circle as detailed in the previous Canto. Here are punished the Violent Against their Neighbors, great war-makers, cruel tyrants, highwaymen—all who shed the blood of their fellow-men. As they wallowed in blood during their lives, so they are immersed in the boiling blood forever, each according to the degree of his guilt, while fierce Centaurs patrol the banks, ready to shoot with their arrows any sinner who raises himself out of the boiling blood beyond the limits permitted him. Alexander the Great is here, up to

---

74-75 *those two … sad:* Paolo and Francesca. In 1275 Giovanni Malatesta of Rimini, called Giovanni the Lame, a somewhat deformed but brave and powerful warrior, made a political marriage with Francesca, daughter of Guido da Polenta of Ravenna. Francesca came to Rimini and there an amour grew between her and Giovanni's younger brother Paolo. Despite the fact that Paolo had married in 1269 and had become the father of two daughters by 1275, his affair with Francesca continued for many years. It was sometime between 1283 and 1286 that Giovanni surprised them in Francesca's bedroom and killed both of them. Around these facts the legend has grown that Paolo was sent by Giovanni as his proxy to the marriage, that Francesca thought he was her real bridegroom and accordingly gave him her heart irrevocably at first sight. The legend obviously increases the pathos, but nothing in Dante gives it support. 102 *we are … above:* At many points of *The Inferno* Dante makes clear the principle that the souls of the damned are locked so blindly into their own guilt that none can feel sympathy for another, or find any pleasure in the presence of another. The temptation of many readers is to interpret this line romantically: *i.e.,* that the love of Paolo and Francesca survives Hell itself. The more Dantean interpretation, however, is that they add to one another's anguish (a) as mutual reminders of their sin, and (b) as insubstantial shades of the bodies for which they once felt such great passion. 104 *him:* Giovanni Malatesta was still alive at the writing. His fate is already decided, however, and upon his death, his soul will fall to Caïna, the first ring of the last circle (Canto XXXII), where lie those who performed acts of treachery against their kin.

124-25 *the rhyme of Lancelot:* The story exists in many forms. The details Dante make use of are from an Old French version. 126 *dim time:* The original simply reads "We were alone, suspecting nothing." "Dim time" is rhyme-forced, but not wholly outside the legitimate implications of the original, I hope. The old courtly romance may well be thought of as happening in the dim ancient days. The apology, of course, comes after the fact: one does the possible, then argues for justification, and there probably is none. 134 *that book, and he who wrote it, was a pander:* "Galeotto," the Italian word for "pander," is also the Italian rendering of the name of Gallehault, who in the French Romance Dante refers to here, urged Lancelot and Guinevere on to love.

his lashes in the blood, and with him Attila, The Scourge of God.
They are immersed in the deepest part of the river, which grows shal-
lower as it circles to the other side of the ledge, then deepens again.

The Poets are challenged by the Centaurs, but Virgil wins a
safe conduct from Chiron, their chief, who assigns Nessus to guide
them and to bear them across the shallows of the boiling blood. Nessus
carries them across at the point where it is only ankle deep and imme-
diately leaves them and returns to his patrol.

The scene that opened from the edge of the pit
    was mountainous, and such a desolation
    that every eye would shun the sight of it:
a ruin like the Slides of Mark° near Trent
    on the bank of the Adige, the result of an earthquake 5
    or of some massive fault in the escarpment—
for, from the point on the peak where the mountain split
    to the plain below, the rock is so badly shattered
    a man at the top might make a rough stair of it.°
Such was the passage down the steep, and there   *10*
    at the very top, at the edge of the broken cleft,
    lay spread the Infamy of Crete,° the heir
of bestiality and the lecherous queen
    who hid in a wooden cow. And when he saw us,
    he gnawed his own flesh in a fit of spleen.   *15*
And my Master mocked: "How you do pump your breath!
    Do you think, perhaps, it is the Duke of Athens,
    who in the world above served up your death?
Off with you, monster; this one does not come
    instructed by your sister, but of himself   *20*
    to observe your punishment in the lost kingdom."
As a bull that breaks its chains just when the knife
    has struck its death-blow, cannot stand nor run
    but leaps from side to side with its last life—
so danced the Minotaur, and my shrewd Guide   *25*
    cried out: "Run now! While he is blind with rage!
    Into the pass, quick, and get over the side!"
So we went down across the shale and slate
    of that ruined rock, which often slid and shifted
    under me at the touch of living weight.   *30*
I moved on, deep in thought; and my Guide to me:
    "You are wondering perhaps about this ruin
    which is guarded by the beast upon whose fury
I played just now. I should tell you that when last
    I came this dark way to the depths of Hell,   *35*

this rock had not yet felt the ruinous blast.°
But certainly, if I am not mistaken,
    it was just before the coming of Him who took
    the souls from Limbo, that all Hell was shaken
so that I thought the universe felt love   *40*
    and all its elements moved toward harmony,
    whereby the world of matter, as some believe,
has often plunged to chaos.° It was then,
    that here and elsewhere in the pits of Hell,
    the ancient rock was stricken and broke open.   *45*
But turn your eyes to the valley; there we shall find
    the river of boiling blood° in which are steeped
    all who struck down their fellow men." Oh blind!
Oh ignorant, self-seeking cupidity
    which spurs us so in the short mortal life   *50*
    and steeps us so through all eternity!
I saw an arching fosse that was the bed
    of a winding river circling through the plain
    exactly as my Guide and Lord had said.
A file of Centaurs° galloped in the space   *55*
    between the bank and the cliff, well armed with arrows,
    riding as once on earth they rode to the chase.
And seeing us descend, that straggling band
    halted, and three of them moved out toward us,
    their long bows and their shafts already in hand.   *60*
And one of them cried out while still below:
    "To what pain are you sent down that dark coast?
    Answer from where you stand, or I draw the bow!"
"Chiron° is standing there hard by your side;
    our answer will be to him. This wrath of yours   *65*
    was always your own worst fate," my Guide replied.
And to me he said: "That is Nessus, who died in the wood
    for insulting Dejanira.° At his death

---

⁴ *Li Slavoni di Marco* are about two miles from Rovereto (between Verona and Trent) on the left bank of the River Adige. ⁹ *rough stair:* I am defeated in all attempts to convey Dante's emphasis in any sort of a verse line. The sense of the original: "It might provide some sort of a way down for one who started at the top, but (by implication) would not be climbable from below." ¹² *Infamy of Crete:* This is the infamous Minotaur of classical mythology. His mother was Pasiphaë, wife of Minos, the King of Crete. She conceived an unnatural passion for a bull, and in order to mate with it, she crept into a wooden cow. From this union the Minotaur was born, half-man, half-beast. King Minos kept him in an ingenious labyrinth from which he could not escape. When Androgeous, the son of King Minos, was killed by the Athenians, Minos exacted an annual tribute of seven maidens and seven youths. These were annually turned into the labyrinth and there were devoured by the Minotaur. The monster was finally killed by Theseus, duke of Athens. He was aided by Ariadne, daughter of Minos (and half-sister of the monster). She gave Theseus a ball of cord to unwind as he entered the labyrinth and a sword with which to kill the Minotaur.

³⁶ *ruinous blast:* According to Matthew xxvii, 51, an earthquake shook the earth at the moment of Christ's death. These stones, Dante lets us know, were broken off in that earthquake. We shall find other effects of the same shock in the Eighth Circle. It is worth noting also that both the Upper (See Canto V, 34) and the Lower Hell begin with evidences of this ruin. ⁴³ *chaos:* The Greek philosopher, Empedocles, taught that the universe existed by the counter-balance (discord or mutual repulsion) of its elements. Should the elemental matter feel harmony (love or mutual attraction) all would fly together into chaos. ⁴⁷ *river of boiling blood:* This is Phlegethon, the river that circles through the First Round of the Seventh Circle, then sluices through the wood of the suicides (the Second Round) and the burning sands (Third Round) to spew over the Great Cliff into the Eighth Circle, and so, eventually to the bottom of Hell (Cocytus). ⁵⁵ *Centaurs:* Creatures of classical mythology, half-horse, half-men. They were skilled and savage hunters, creatures of passion and violence. Like the Minotaur, they are symbols of the bestial-human, and as such, they are fittingly chosen as the tormentors of these sinners. ⁶⁴ *Chiron:* The son of Saturn and of the nymph Philira. He was the wisest and most just of the Centaurs and reputedly was the teacher of Achilles and of other Greek heroes to whom he imparted great skill in bearing arms, medicine, astronomy, music, and augury. Dante places him far down in Hell with the others of his kind, but though he draws Chiron's coarseness, he also grants him a kind of majestic understanding. ⁶⁸ *Dejanira:* Nessus carried travellers across the River Evenus for hire. He was hired to ferry Dejanira, the wife of Hercules, and tried to abduct her, but Hercules killed him with a poisoned arrow. While Nessus was dying, he whispered to Dejanira that a shirt stained with his poisoned blood would act as a love charm should Hercules' affections stray. When Hercules fell in love with Iole, Dejanira sent him a shirt stained with the Centaur's blood. The shirt poisoned Hercules and he died in agony.

he plotted his revenge in his own blood.
The one in the middle staring at his chest   *70*
     is the mighty Chiron, he who nursed Achilles:
     the other is Pholus,° fiercer than all the rest.
They run by that stream in thousands, snapping their
        bows
     at any wraith who dares to raise himself
     out of the blood more than his guilt allows."   *75*
We drew near those swift beasts. In a thoughtful pause
     Chiron drew an arrow, and with its notch
     he pushed his great beard back along his jaws.
And when he had thus uncovered the huge pouches   *79*
     of his lips, he said to his fellows: "Have you
        noticed
how the one who walks behind moves what he touches?
That is not how the dead go." My good Guide,
     already standing by the monstrous breast
     in which the two mixed natures joined, replied:
"It is true he lives; in his necessity   *85*
     I alone must lead him through this valley.
     Fate brings him here, not curiosity.
From singing Alleluia the sublime
     spirit° who sends me came. He is no bandit.
     Nor am I one whoever stooped to crime.   *90*
But in the name of the Power by which I go
     this sunken way across the floor of Hell,
     assign us one of your troop whom we may follow,
that he may guide us to the ford, and there
     carry across on his back the one I lead,   *95*
     for he is not a spirit to move through air."
Chiron turned his head on his right breast°
     and said to Nessus: "Go with them, and guide them,
     and turn back any others that would contest
their passage." So we moved beside our guide   *100*
     along the bank of the scalding purple river
     in which the shrieking wraiths were boiled and dyed.
Some stood up to their lashes in that torrent,
     and as we passed them the huge Centaur said:
     "These were the kings of bloodshed and
        despoilment.
Here they pay for their ferocity.   *106*
     Here is Alexander.° And Dionysius,
     who brought long years of grief to Sicily.
That brow you see with the hair as black as night
     is Azzolino;° and that beside him, the blonde,   *110*
     is Opizzo da Esti,° who had his mortal light
blown out by his stepson." I turned then
     to speak to the Poet but he raised a hand:

"Let him be the teacher now, and I will listen."
Further on, the Centaur stopped beside   *115*
     a group of spirits steeped as far as the throat
     in the race of boiling blood, and there our guide
pointed out a sinner who stood alone:
     "That one before God's altar pierced a heart
     still honored on the Thames."° And he passed on.*120*
We came in sight of some who were allowed
     to raise the head and all the chest from the river,
     and I recognized many there. Thus, as we followed
along the stream of blood, its level fell
     until it cooked no more than the feet of the
        damned.
     And here we crossed the ford to deeper Hell.   *126*
"Just as you see the boiling stream grow shallow
     along this side," the Centaur said to us
     when we stood on the other bank, "I would have
        you know
that on the other, the bottom sinks anew   *130*
     more and more, until it comes again
     full circle to the place where the tyrants stew.
It is there that Holy Justice spends its wrath
     on Sextus° and Pyrrhus through eternity,
     and on Attila,° who was a scourge on earth: *135*
and everlastingly milks out the tears
     of Rinier da Corento and Rinier Pazzo,°
     those two assassins who for many years
stalked the highways, bloody and abhorred."
     And with that he started back across the ford.   *140*

CANTO XX

Circle Eight: Bolgia Four   The Fortune Tellers and Diviners

Dante stands in the middle of the bridge over the Fourth Bolgia and looks down at the souls of the Fortune Tellers and Diviners. Here are the souls of all those who attempted by forbidden arts to look into the future. Among these damned are: Amphiareus, Tiresias, Aruns, Manto, Eurypylus, Michael Scott, Guido Bonatti, and Asdente.

     Characteristically, the sin of these wretches is reversed upon them: their punishment is to have their heads turned backwards on their bodies and to be compelled to walk backwards through all eternity, their eyes blinded with tears. Thus, those who sought to penetrate the future cannot even see in front of themselves; they attempted to move themselves forward in time, so must they go backwards through

---

[72] *Pholus:* A number of classical poets mention Pholus, but very little else is known of him.   [89] *spirit:* Beatrice.   [97] *right breast:* The right is the side of virtue and honor. In Chiron it probably signifies his human side as opposed to his bestial side. [107] *Alexander:* Alexander the Great, *Dionysius* Dionysius I (died 367 B.C.) and his son, Dionysius II (died 343), were tyrants of Sicily. Both were infamous as prototypes of the bloodthirsty and exorbitant ruler. Dante may intend either or both.   [110] *Azzolino:* Ezzelino da Romano, Count of Onora (1194–1259). The cruelest of the Ghibelline tyrants. In 1236 Frederick II appointed Ezzelino his vicar in Pádua. Ezzelino became especially infamous for his bloody treatment of the Paduans, whom he slaughtered in great numbers.   [111] *Opizzo da Esti:* Marquis of Ferrara (1264–1293). The account of his life is confused. One must accept Dante's facts as given.

[119-20] *That one … Thames:* The sinner indicated is Guy de Montfort. His father, Simon de Montfort, was a leader of the barons who rebelled against Henry III and was killed at the battle of Evesham (1265) by Prince Edward (later Edward I). In 1271, Guy (then Vicar General of Tuscany) avenged his father's death by murdering Henry's nephew (who was also named Henry). The crime was openly committed in a church at Viterbo. The murdered Henry's heart was sealed in a casket and sent to London, where it was accorded various honors. [134] *Sextus:* Probably the younger son of Pompey the Great. His piracy is mentioned in Lucan (*Pharsalia VI, 420–422*). *Pyrrhus:* Pyrrhus, the son of Achilles, was especially bloodthirsty at the sack of Troy. Pyrrhus, King of Epirus (319–372 B.C.), waged relentless and bloody war against the Greeks and Romans. Either may be intended. [135] *Attila:* King of the Huns from 433 to 453. He was called the Scourge of God. [137] *Rinier … Rinier:* Both were especially bloodthirsty robber-barons of the thirteenth century.

all eternity; and as the arts of sorcery are a distortion of God's law, so are their bodies distorted in Hell.

No more need be said of them: Dante names them, and passes on to fill the Canto with a lengthy account of the founding of Virgil's native city of Mantua.

Now must I sing new griefs, and my verses strain
    to form the matter of the Twentieth Canto
    of Canticle One° the Canticle of Pain.

My vantage point° permitted a clear view
    of the depths of the pit below: a desolation   *5*
    bathed with the tears of its tormented crew,

who moved about the circle of the pit
    at about the pace of a litany procession.°
    Silent and weeping, they wound round and round it.

And when I looked down from their faces,° I saw   *10*
    that each of them was hideously distorted
    between the top of the chest and the lines of the jaw;

for the face was reversed on the neck, and they came on
    backwards, staring backwards at their loins,°
    for to look before them was forbidden. Someone,   *15*

sometime, in the grip of a palsy may have been
    distorted so, but never to my knowledge;
    nor do I believe the like was ever seen.

Reader, so may God grant you to understand
    my poem and profit from it, ask yourself   *20*
    how I could check my tears, when near at hand

I saw the image of our humanity
    distorted so that the tears that burst from their eyes
    ran down the cleft of their buttocks. Certainly

I wept. I leaned against the jagged face   *25*
    of a rock and wept so that my Guide said: "Still?
    Still like the other fools? There is no place

for pity here. Who is more arrogant
    within his soul, who is more impious
    than one who dares to sorrow at God's judgement?*30*

Lift up your eyes, lift up your eyes and see
    him the earth swallowed before all the Thebans,
    at which they cried out: 'Whither do you flee,

Amphiareus?° Why do you leave the field?'
    And he fell headlong through the gaping earth   *35*
    to the feet of Minos, where all sin must yield.

Observe how he has made a breast of his back.
    In life he wished to see too far before him,

and now he must crab backwards round this track.

And see Tiresias,° who by his arts   *40*
    succeeded in changing himself from man to woman,
    transforming all his limbs and all his parts;

later he had to strike the two twined serpents
    once again with his conjurer's wand before
    he could resume his manly lineaments.   *45*

And there is Aruns,° his back to that one's belly,
    the same who in the mountains of the Luni
    tilled by the people of Carrara's valley,

made a white marble cave his den, and there
    with unobstructed view observed the sea   *50*
    and the turning constellations year by year.

And she whose unbound hair flows back to hide
    her breasts—which you cannot see—and who also
      wears
    all of her hairy parts on that other side,

was Manto, who searched countries far and near,   *55*
    then settled where I was born.° In that connection
    there is a story I would have you hear.

Tiresias was her sire. After his death,
    Thebes, the city of Bacchus, became enslaved,
    and for many years she roamed about the earth.   *60*

High in sweet Italy, under the Alps that shut
    the Tyrolean gate of Germany, there lies
    a lake known as Benacus° roundabout.

Through endless falls, more than a thousand and one,
    Mount Appennine from Garda to Val Cammonica *65*
    is freshened by the waters that flow down

into that lake. At its center is a place
    where the Bishops of Brescia, Trentine, and Verona
    might all give benediction with equal grace.

Peschiera, the beautiful fortress, strong in war   *70*
    against the Brescians and the Bergamese,
    sits at the lowest point along that shore.

There, the waters Benacus cannot hold
    within its bosom, spill and form a river
    that winds away through pastures green and gold.   *75*

But once the water gathers its full flow,
    it is called Mincius rather than Benacus
    from there to Governo, where it joins the Po.

Still near its source, it strikes a plain, and there
    it slows and spreads, forming an ancient marsh   *80*
    which in the summer heats pollutes the air.

The terrible virgin, passing there by chance,
    saw dry land at the center of the mire,
    untilled, devoid of all inhabitants.

---

³ *Canticle One:* The *Inferno.* The other Canticles are, of course, the *Purgatorio* and the *Paradiso.*   ⁴ *vantage point:* Virgil, it will be recalled, had set Dante down on the bridge across the Fourth Bolgia.   ⁸ *litany procession:* The litanies are chanted not only in church (before the mass), but sometimes in procession, the priest chanting the prayers and the marchers the reponse. As one might gather from the context, the processions move very slowly.   ¹⁰ *looked down:* A typically Dantean conception. Dante often writes as if the eye pin-pointed on one feature of a figure seen at a distance. The pin-point must then be deliberately shifted before the next feature can be observed. As far as I know, this stylistic device is peculiar to Dante.   ¹⁴ *loins:* General usage seems to have lost sight of the fact that the first meaning of "loin" is "that part of a human being or quadruped on either side of the spinal column between the hipbone and the false ribs." (Webster.)   ³⁴ *Amphiareus:* One of the seven Captains who fought against Thebes. ... Statius (*Thebaid* VII, 690 ff. and VIII, 8 ff.) tells how he foresaw his own death in this war, and attempted to run away from it, but was swallowed in his flight by an earthquake. I have Romanized his name from "Amphiaraus".

---

⁴⁰ *Tiresias:* A Theban diviner and magician. Ovid (*Metamorphoses* III) tells how he came on two twined serpents, struck them apart with his stick, and was thereupon transformed into a woman. Seven years later he came on two serpents similarly entwined, struck them apart, and was changed back.   ⁴⁶⁻⁴⁸ *Aruns:* An Etruscan soothsayer (see Lucan, *Pharsalia*, I, 580 ff.). He foretold the war between Pompey and Julius Caesar, and also that it would end with Caesar's victory and Pompey's death. *Luni:* Also *Luna.* An ancient Etruscan city. *Carrara's valley:* The Carrarese valley is famous for its white (Carrara) marble.   ⁵⁶ *where I was born:* Dante's version of the founding of Mantua is based on a reference in the *Aeneid* X, 198–200.   ⁶³ *Benacus:* The ancient name for the famous Lago di Garda, which lies a short distance north of Mantua. The other places named in this passage lie around Lago di Garda. On an island in the lake the three dioceses mentioned in line 68 conjoined. All three bishops, therefore, had jurisdiction on the island.

There, shunning all communion with mankind,   *85*
   she settled with the ministers of her arts,
   and there she lived, and there she left behind
her vacant corpse. Later the scattered men
   who lived nearby assembled on that spot
   since it was well defended by the fen.   *90*
Over those whited bones they raised the city,
   and for her who had chosen the place before all
      others
   they named it—with no further augury—
Mantua. Far more people lived there once—
   before sheer madness prompted Casalodi   *95*
   to let Pinamonte play him for a dunce.°
Therefore, I charge you, should you ever hear
   other accounts of this, to let no falsehood
   confuse the truth which I have just made clear."
And I to him: "Master, within my soul   *100*
   your word is certainty, and any other
   would seem like the dead lumps of burned out coal.
But tell me of those people moving down
   to join the rest. Are they worth my noting?
   For my mind keeps coming back to that alone."   *105*
And he: "That one whose beard spreads like a fleece
   over his swarthy shoulders, was an augur
   in the days when so few males remained in Greece
that even the cradles were all but empty of sons.°
   He chose the time for cutting the cable at Aulis,   *110*
   and Calchas joined him in those divinations.
He is Eurypylus.° I sing him somewhere
   in my High Tragedy; you will know the place
   who know the whole of it. The other there,
the one beside him with the skinny shanks   *115*
   was Michael Scott,° who mastered every trick
   of magic fraud, a prince of mountebanks.
See Guido Bonatti° there; and see Asdente,
   who now would be wishing he had stuck to his last,
   but repents too late, though he repents aplenty.   *120*
And see on every hand the wretched hags
   who left their spinning and sewing for soothsaying
   and casting of spells with herbs, and dolls, and rags.

95–96 *before … dunce:* Albert, Count of Casalodi and Lord of Mantua, let himself be persuaded by Pinamonte de Buonaccorsi to banish the nobles from Mantua as a source of danger to his rule. Once the nobles had departed, Pinamonte headed a rebellion against the weakened lord and took over the city himself. 109 *Even the cradles were all but empty of sons:* At the time of the Trojan Wars, Greece was said to be so empty of males that scarcely any were to be found even in the cradles. 112 *Eurypylus:* According to Greek custom an augur was summoned before each voyage to choose the exact propitious moment for departure (cutting the cables). Dante has Virgil imply that Eurypylus and Calchas were selected to choose the moment for Agamemnon's departure from Aulis to Troy. Actually, according to the *Aeneid*, Eurypylus was not at Aulis. The *Aeneid* (II, 110 ff.) tells how Eurypylus and Calchas were both consulted in choosing the moment for the departure from Troy. Dante seems to have confused the two incidents. 116 *Michael Scott:* An Irish scholar of the first half of the thirteenth century. His studies were largely in the occult. Sir Walter Scott refers to him in *The Lay of the Last Minstrel.* 118 *Guido Bonatti:* A thirteenth-century astrologer of Forli. He was court astrologer to Guido da Montefeltro … advising him in his wars. *Asdente:* A shoemaker of Parma who turned diviner and won wide fame for his forecastings in the last half of the thirteenth century.

But come: Cain with his bush of thorns° appears
   already on the wave below Seville,   *125*
   above the boundary of the hemispheres;
and the moon was full already yesternight.
   as you must well remember from the wood,
   for it certainly did not harm you when its light
shone down upon your way before the dawn."   *130*
And as he spoke to me, we travelled on.

CANTO XXVI

Circle Eight: Bolgia Eight   The Evil Counselors

Dante turns from the Thieves toward the Evil Counselors of the next Bolgia, and between the two he addresses a passionate lament to Florence prophesying the griefs that will befall her from these two sins At the purported time of the Vision, it will be recalled, Dante was a Chief Magistrate of Florence and was forced into exile by men he had reason to consider both thieves and evil counselors. He seems prompted, in fact, to say much more on this score, but he restrains himself when he comes in sight of the sinners of the next Bolgia, for they are a moral symbolism, all men of gift who abused their genius, perverting it to wiles and stratagems. Seeing them in Hell he knows his must be another road: his way shall not be by deception.

So the Poets move on and Dante observes the Eighth Bolgia in detail. Here the Evil Counselors move about endlessly, hidden from view inside great flames. Their sin was to abuse the gifts of the Almighty, to steal his virtues for low purposes. And as they stole from God in their lives and worked by hidden ways, so are they stolen from sight and hidden in the great flames which are their own guilty consciences. And as, in most instances at least, they sinned by glibness of tongue, so are the flames made into a fiery travesty of tongues.

Among the others, the Poets see a great doubleheaded flame, and discover that Ulysses and Diomede are punished together within it. Virgil addresses the flame, and through its wavering tongue Ulysses narrates an unforgettable tale of his last voyage and death.

Joy to you, Florence, that your banners swell,
   beating their proud wings over land and sea,
   and that your name expands through all of Hell!
Among the thieves I found five who had been
   your citizens, to my shame; nor yet shall you   *5*
   mount to great honor peopling such a den!
But if the truth is dreamed of toward the morning.°
   you shall feel what Prato° and the others

---

124 *Cain … thorns:* The Moon. Cain with a bush of thorns was the medieval equivalent of our Man in the Moon. Dante seems to mean by "Seville" the whole area of Spain and the Straits of Gibraltar (Pillars of Hercules), which were believed to be the western limit of the world. The moon is setting (*i.e.*, it appears on the western waves) on the morning of Holy Saturday, 1300. 7 *truth … morning:* A semi-proverbial expression. It was a common belief that those dreams that occur just before waking foretell the future. "Morning" here would equal both "the rude awakening" and the potential "dawn of a new day." 8 *Prato:* Not the neighboring town (which was on good terms with Florence) but Cardinal Niccolò da Prato, papal legate from Benedict XI to Florence. In 1304 he tried to reconcile the warring factions, but found that neither side would accept mediation. Since none would be blessed, he cursed all impartially and laid the city under an interdict (i.e., forbade the offering of the sacraments). Shortly after this rejection by the Church, a bridge collapsed in Florence, and later a great fire broke out. Both disasters cost many lives, and both were promptly attributed to the Papal curse.

wish for you. And were that day of mourning
   already come it would not be too soon.   *10*
      So may it come, since it must! for it will weigh
      more heavily on me as I pass my noon.
We left that place. My Guide climbed stone by stone
   the natural stair by which we had descended
   and drew me after him. So we passed on,   *15*
and going our lonely way through that dead land
   among the crags and crevices of the cliff,
   the foot could make no way without the hand.
I mourned among those rocks, and I mourn again
   when memory returns to what I saw: *20*
   and more than usually I curb the strain
of my genius, lest it stray from Virtue's course;
   so if some star, or a better thing, grant me merit,
   may I not find the gift cause for remorse.
As many fireflies as the peasant sees   *25*
   when he rest on a hill and looks into the valley
   (where he tills or gathers grapes or prunes his trees)
in that sweet season when the face of him
   who lights the world rides north, and at the hour
   when the fly yields to the gnat and the air grows
      dim—   *30*
such myriads of flames I saw shine through
   the gloom of the eighth abyss when I arrived
   at the rim from which its bed comes into view.
As he the bears avenged° so fearfully
   beheld Elijah's chariot depart—   *35*
   the horses rise toward heaven—but could not see
more than the flame, a cloudlet in the sky,
   once it had risen—so within the fosse
   only those flames, forever passing by
were visible, ahead, to right, to left;   *40*
   for though each steals a sinner's soul from view
   not one among them leaves a trace of the theft.
I stood on the bridge, and leaned out from the edge;
   so far, that but for a jut of rock I held to
   I should have been sent hurtling from the ledge   *45*
without being pushed. And seeing me so intent,
   my Guide said: "There are souls within those flames;
   each sinner swathes himself in his own torment."
"Master," I said, "your words make me more sure,
   but I had seen already that it was so   *50*
   and meant to ask what spirit must endure
the pains of that great flame which splits away
   in two great horns, as if it rose from the pyre
   where Eteocles and Polynices lay?"°
He answered me: "Forever round this path   *55*

Ulysses and Diomede° move in such dress,
   united in pain as once they were in wrath;
there they lament the ambush of the Horse
   which was the door through which the noble seed
   of the Romans issued from its holy source;   *60*
there they mourn that for Achilles slain
   sweet Deidamia weeps even in death;
   there they recall the Palladium in their pain."
"Master," I cried, "I pray you and repray
   till my prayer becomes a thousand—if these souls *65*
   can still speak from the fire, oh let me stay
until the flame draws near! Do not deny me:
   You see how fervently I long for it!"
   And he to me: "Since what you ask is worthy,
it shall be. But be still and let me speak;   *70*
   for I know your mind already, and they perhaps
   might scorn your manner of speaking, since they were
      Greek."
And when the flame had come where time and place
   seemed fitting to my Guide, I heard him say
   these words to it: "O you two souls who pace   *75*
together in one flame!—if my days above
   won favor in your eyes, if I have earned
   however much or little of your love
in writing my High Verses, do not pass by,
   but let one of you° be pleased to tell where he,   *80*
   having disappeared from the known world, went to
      die."
As if it fought the wind, the greater prong
   of the ancient flame began to quiver and hum;
   then moving its tip as if it were the tongue
that spoke, gave out a voice above the roar.   *85*
   "When I left Circe,"° it said, "who more than a year
   detained me near Gaëta long before
Aeneas came and gave the place that name,
   not fondness for my son, nor reverence
   for my aged father, nor Penelope's° claim   *90*
to the joys of love, could drive out of my mind
   the lust to experience the far-flung world
   and the failings and felicities of mankind.
I put out on the high and open sea

---

[34] *he the bears avenged:* Elisha saw Elijah transported to Heaven in a fiery chariot. Later he was mocked by some children, who called out tauntingly that he should "Go up" as Elijah had. Elisha cursed the children in the name of the Lord, and bears came suddenly upon the children and devoured them. (2. Kings ii, 11–24.)   [54] *Eteocles and Polynices:* Sons of Oedipus, who succeeded jointly to the throne of Thebes, and came to an agreement whereby each one would rule separately for a year at a time. Eteocles ruled the first year and when he refused to surrender the throne at the appointed time, Polynices led the Seven against Thebes in a bloody war. In single combat the two brothers killed one another. Statius (*Thebaid* XII, 429 ff.) wrote that their mutual hatred was so great that when they were placed on the same funeral pyre the very flame of their burning drew apart in two great raging horns.

[56] *Ulysses and Diomede:* They suffer here for their joint guilt in counseling and carrying out many stratagems which Dante considered evil, though a narrator who was less passionately a partisan of the Trojans might have thought their actions justifiable methods of warfare. Their first sin was the stratagem of the Wooden Horse, as a result of which Troy fell and Aeneas went forth to found the Roman line. The second evil occurred at Scyros. There Ulysses discovered Achilles in female disguise, hidden by his mother, Thetis, so that he would not be taken off to the war. Deidamia was in love with Achilles and had borne him a son. When Ulysses persuaded her lover to sail for Troy, she died of grief. The third count is Ulysses' theft of the sacred statue of Pallas from the Palladium. Upon the statue, it was believed, depended the fate of Troy. Its theft, therefore, would result in Troy's downfall.   [80] *one of you:* Ulysses. He is the figure in the larger horn of the flame (which symbolizes that his guilt, as leader, is greater than that of Diomede). His memorable account of his last voyage and death is purely Dante's invention.   [86–88] *Circe:* She changed Ulysses' men to swine and kept him a prisoner, though with rather exceptional accommodation. *Gaëta:* Southeastern Italian coastal town. According to Virgil (*Aeneid* VII, 1 ff.) it was earlier named Gaieta by Aeneas in honor of his aged nurse.   [90] *Penelope's:* Ulysses' wife.

with a single ship and only those few souls   95
who stayed true when the rest deserted me.
As far as Morocco and as far as Spain
I saw both shores; and I saw Sardinia
and the other islands of the open main.
I and my men were stiff and slow with age   100
when we sailed at last into the narrow pass
where, warning all men back from further voyage,
Hercules' Pillars rose upon our sight.
Already I had left Ceuta on the left;
Seville now sank behind me on the right.   105
'Shipmates,' I said, 'who through a hundred thousand
perils have reached the West, do not deny
to the brief remaining watch our senses stand
experience of the world beyond the sun.
Greeks! You were not born to live like brutes,   110
but to press on toward manhood and recognition!
With this brief exhortation I made my crew
so eager for the voyage I could hardly
have held them back from it when I was through;
and turning our stern toward morning, our bow toward
     night,
we bore southwest out of the world of man;   116
we made wings of our oars for our fool's flight.
That night we raised the other pole ahead
with all its stars, and ours had so declined
it did not rise out of its ocean bed.   120
Five times since we had dipped our bending oars
beyond the world, the light beneath the moon
had waxed and waned, when dead upon our course
we sighted, dark in space, a peak so tall
I doubted any man had seen the like.   125
Our cheers were hardly sounded, when a squall
broke hard upon our bow from the new land:
three times it sucked the ship and the sea about
as it pleased Another to order and command.
At the fourth, the poop rose and the bow went down 130
till the sea closed over us and the light was gone."

CANTO XXVIII

Circle Eight: Bolgia Nine   The Sowers of Discord

*The Poets come to the edge of the Ninth Bolgia and look down at a
parade of hideously mutilated souls. These are the Sowers of Discord,
and just as their sin was to rend asunder what God had meant to be
united, so are they hacked and torn through all eternity by a great
demon with a bloody sword. After each mutilation the souls are compelled to drag their broken bodies around the pit and to return to the
demon, for in the course of the circuit their wounds knit in time to be
inflicted anew. Thus is the law of retribution observed, each sinner
suffering according to his degree.*

*Among them Dante distinguishes three classes with varying
degrees of guilt within each class. First come the Sowers of Religious
Discord. Mahomet is chief among them, and appears first, cleft from
crotch to chin, with his internal organs dangling between his legs. His
son-in-law, Ali, drags on ahead of him, cleft from topknot to chin.
These reciprocal wounds symbolize Dante's judgement that, between
them, these two sum up the total schism between Christianity and
Mohammedanism. The revolting details of Mahomet's condition
clearly imply Dante's opinion of that doctrine. Mahomet issues an*

*ironic warning to another schismatic, Fra Dolcino. Next come the
Sowers of Political Discord, among them Pier da Medicina, the
Tribune Curio, and Mosca dei Lamberti, each mutilated according to
the nature of his sin.*

*Last of all is Bertrand de Born, Sower of Discord Between
Kinsmen. He separated father from son, and for that offence carries
his head separated from his body, holding it with one hand by the hair,
and swinging it as if it were a lantern to light his dark and endless
way. The image of Bertrand raising his head at arm's length in order
that it might speak more clearly to the Poets on the ridge is one of the
most memorable in the* Inferno. *For some reason that cannot be
ascertained, Dante makes these sinners quite eager to be remembered
in the world, despite the fact that many who lie above them in Hell
were unwilling to be recognized.*

Who could describe, even in words set free
of metric and rhyme and a thousand times retold,
the blood and wounds that now were shown to me!
At grief so deep the tongue must wag in vain;
the language of our sense and memory   5
lacks the vocabulary of such pain.
If one could gather all those who have stood
through all of time on Puglia's° fateful soil
and wept for the red running of their blood
in the war of the Trojans;° and in that long war   10
which left so vast a spoil of golden rings,
as we find written in Livy, who does not err;°
along with those whose bodies felt the wet
and gaping wounds of Robert Guiscard's lances;°
with all the rest whose bones are gathered yet   15
at Ceperano where every last Pugliese
turned traitor;° and with those from Tagliacozzo
where Alardo won without weapons°—if all these
were gathered, and one showed his limbs run through,
another his lopped off, that could not equal   20
the mutilations of the ninth pit's crew.
A wine tun when a stave or cant-bar starts
does not split open as wide as one I saw
split from his chin to the mouth with which man farts.

---

⁸ *Puglia's:* I have used the modern name but some of the events
Dante narrates took place in the ancient province of Apulia.
The southeastern area of Italy is the scene of all the fighting
Dante mentions in the following passage. It is certainly a bloody
total of slaughter that Dante calls upon to illustrate his scene.
¹⁰ *Trojans:* The Romans (descended from the Trojans) fought the
native Samnites in a long series of raids and skirmishes from
343–290 B.C.   ¹⁰⁻¹² *long war ... err:* The Punic Wars (264–146
B.C.). Livy writes that in the battle of Cannae (216 B.C.) so many
Romans fell that Hannibal gathered three bushels of gold rings
from the fingers of the dead and produced them before the senate at Carthage.   ¹⁴ *Robert Guiscard's:* Dante places Guiscard
(1015–1085) in the *Paradiso* among the Warriors of God. He
fought the Greeks and Saracens in their attempted invasion of
Italy.   ¹⁶⁻¹⁷ *Pugliese turned traitor:* In 1266 the Pugliese under
Manfred, King of Sicily, were charged with holding the pass at
Ceperano against Charles of Anjou. The Pugliese, probably
under Papal pressure, allowed the French free passage, and
Charles went on to defeat Manfred at Benevento. Manfred himself was killed in that battle.   ¹⁸ *without weapons:* At Tagliacozzo
(1268) in a continuation of the same strife, Charles of Anjou
used a stratagem suggested to him by Alard de Valéry and
defeated Conradin, nephew of Manfred. "Won without
weapons" is certainly an overstatement: what Alardo suggested
was a simple but effective concealment of reserve troops. When
Conradin seemed to have carried the day and was driving his
foes before him, the reserve troops broke on his flank and rear,
and defeated Conradin's out-positioned forces.

Between his legs all of his red guts hung 25
   with the heart, the lungs, the liver, the gall bladder,
   and the shrivelled sac that passes shit to the bung.
I stood and stared at him from the stone shelf;
   he noticed me and opening his own breast
   with both hands cried: "See how I rip myself! 30
See how Mahomet's mangled and split open!
   Ahead of me walks Ali° in his tears,
   his head cleft from the top-knot to the chin.
And all the other souls that bleed and mourn
   along its ditch were sowers of scandal and schism: 35
   as they tore others apart, so are they torn.
Behind us, warden of our mangled horde,
   the devil who butchers us and sends us marching
   waits to renew our wounds with his long sword
when we have made the circuit of the pit; 40
   for by the time we stand again before him
   all the wounds he gave us last have knit.
But who are you that gawk down from that sill—
   probably to put off your own descent
   to the pit you are sentenced to for your own evil?" 45
"Death has not come for him, guilt does not drive
   his soul to torment," my sweet Guide replied.
   "That he may experience all while yet alive
I, who am dead, must lead him through the drear
   and darkened halls of Hell, from round to round: 50
   and this is true as my own standing here."
More than a hundred wraiths who were marching under
   the sill on which we stood, paused at his words
   and stared at me, forgetting pain in wonder.
"And if you do indeed return to see 55
   the sun again, and soon, tell Fra Dolcino°
   unless he longs to come and march with me
He would do well to check his groceries
   before the winter drives him from the hills
   and gives the victory to the Novarese." 60
Mahomet, one foot raised, had paused to say
   these words to me. When he had finished speaking
   he stretched it out and down, and moved away.
Another—he had his throat slit, and his nose
   slashed off as far as the eyebrows, and a wound 65
   where one of his ears had been—standing with those
who stared at me in wonder from the pit,
   opened the grinning wound of his red gullet
   as if it were a mouth, and said through it:
"O soul unforfeited to misery 70
   and whom—unless I take you for another—
   I have seen above in our sweet Italy;
If ever again you see the gentle plain

that slopes down from Vercelli to Marcabò,°
   remember Pier da Medicina in pain, 75
and announce this warning to the noblest two
   of Fano, Messers Guido and Angiolello:
   that unless our foresight sees what is not true
they shall be thrown from their ships into the sea
   and drown in the raging tides near La Cattolica 80
   to satisfy a tyrant's treachery.°
Neptune never saw so gross a crime
   in all the seas from Cyprus to Majorca,
   not even in pirate raids, nor the Argive time.°
The one-eyed traitor,° lord of the demesne 85
   whose hill and streams one who walks here beside me
   will wish eternally he had never seen,
will call them to a parley, but behind
   sweet invitations he will work it so
   they need not pray against Focara's wind." 90
And I to him: "If you would have me bear
   your name to time, show me the one who found
   the sight of that land so harsh, and let me hear
his story and his name." He touched the cheek
   of one nearby, forcing the jaws apart, 95
   and said: "This is the one; he cannot speak.
This outcast settled Caesar's doubts that day
   beside the Rubicon by telling him:
   'A man prepared is a man hurt by delay.'"
Ah, how wretched Curio° seemed to me. 100
   with a bloody stump in his throat in place of a tongue
   which once had dared to speak so recklessly!
And one among them with both arms hacked through
   cried out, raising his stumps on the foul air
   while the blood bedaubed his face: "Remember, too,
Mosca dei Lamberti,° alas, who said 106
   'A thing done has an end!' and with those words
   planted the fields of war with Tuscan dead."
"And brought about the death of all your clan!"
   I said, and he, stung by new pain on pain, 110
   ran off; and in his grief he seemed a madman.
I stayed to watch those broken instruments,

---

⁷⁴ *Vercelli:* The most western town in Lombardy. *Marcabò* stands near the mouth of the Po. ⁸¹ *tyrant's treachery:* Malatestino da Rimini ... in a move to annex the city of Fano, invited Guido del Cassero and Angioletto da Carignano, leading citizens of Fano, to a conference at La Cattolica, a point on the Adriatic midway between Fano and Rimini. At Malatestino's orders the two were thrown overboard off Focara; a headland swept by such dangerous currents that approaching sailors used to offer prayers for a safe crossing. ⁸³⁻⁸⁴ *Argive time:* The Greeks were raiders and pirates. *Cyprus ... Majorca:* these islands are at opposite ends of the Mediterranean. ⁸⁵ *one-eyed traitor:* Malatestino. ¹⁰⁰ *Curio:* This is the Roman Tribune Curio, who was banished from Rome by Pompey and joined Caesar's forces, advising him to cross the Rubicon, which was then the boundary between Gaul and the Roman Republic. The crossing constituted invasion, and thus began the Roman Civil War. The Rubicon flows near Rimini. ¹⁰⁶ *Mosca dei Lamberti:* Dante had asked Ciacco (Canto VI) for news of Mosca as a man of good works. Now he finds him, his merit canceled by his greater sin. Buondelmonte dei Buondelmonti had insulted the honor of the Amidei by breaking off his engagement to a daughter of that line in favor of a girl of the Donati. When the Amidei met to discuss what should be done, Mosca spoke for the death of Buondelmonte. The Amidei acted upon his advice and from that murder sprang the bloody feud between the Guelphs and Ghibellines of Florence.

---

⁵² *Ali:* Ali succeeded Mahomet to the Caliphate, but not until three of the disciples had preceded him. Mahomet died in 632, and Ali did not assume the Caliphate until 656. ⁵⁶ *Fra Dolcino:* In 1300 Fra Dolcino took over the reformist order called the Apostolic Brothers, who preached, among other things, the community of property and of women. Clement V declared them heretical and ordered a crusade against them. The brotherhood retired with its women to an impregnable position in the hills between Novara and Vercelli, but their supplies gave out in the course of a year-long siege, and they were finally starved out in March of 1307. Dolcino and Margaret of Trent, his "Sister in Christ," were burned at the stake at Vercelli the following June.

and I saw a thing so strange I should not dare
  to mention it without more evidence
but that my own clear conscience strengthens me,   *115*
  that good companion that upholds a man
  within the armor of his purity.
I saw it there; I seem to see it still—
  a body without a head, that moved along
  like all the others in that spew and spill.   *120*
It held the severed head by its own hair,
  swinging it like a lantern in its hand;
  and the head looked at us and wept in its despair.
It made itself a lamp of its own head,
  and they were two in one and one in two;   *125*
  how this can be, He knows who so commanded.
And when it stood directly under us
  it raised the head at arm's length toward our bridge
  the better to be heard, and swaying thus
it cried: "O living soul in this abyss,   *130*
  see what a sentence has been passed upon me,
  and search all Hell for one to equal this!
When you return to the world, remember me:
  I am Bertrand de Born, and it was I
  who set the young king on to mutiny,
son against father, father against son
  as Achitophel set Absalom and David;
  and since I parted those who should be one
in duty and in love, I bear my brain
  divided from its source within this trunk;
  and walk here where my evil turns to pain,
an eye for an eye to all eternity:
thus is the law of Hell observed in me."

Canto XXXII

Circle Nine: Cocytus   Compound Fraud
Round One: Caïna   The Treacherous to Kin
Round Two: Antenora   The Treacherous to Country

At the bottom of the well Dante finds himself on a huge frozen lake. This is Cocytus, the Ninth Circle, the fourth and last great water of Hell, and here, fixed in the ice, each according to his guilt, are punished sinners guilty of Treachery Against Those to Whom They Were Bound by Special Ties. The ice is divided into four concentric rings marked only by the different positions of the damned within the ice.

This is Dante's symbolic equivalent of the final guilt. The treacheries of these souls were denial of love (which is God) and of all human warmth. Only the remorseless dead center of the ice will serve to express their natures. As they denied God's love, so are they furthest removed from the light and warmth of His Sun. As they denied all human ties, so are they bound only by the unyielding ice.

The first round is Caïna, named for Cain. Here lie those who were treacherous against blood ties. They have their necks and heads out of the ice and are permitted to bow their heads—a double boon since it allows them some protection from the freezing gale and, further, allows their tears to fall without freezing their eyes shut. Here Dante sees Alessandro and Napoleone degli Alberti, and he speaks to Camicion, who identifies other sinners of this round.

The second round is Antenora, named for Antenor, the Trojan who was believed to have betrayed his city to the Greeks. Here lie those guilty of Treachery to Country. They, too, have their heads above the

ice, but they cannot bend their necks, which are gripped by the ice. Here Dante accidentally kicks the head of Bocca Degli Abbati and then proceeds to treat him with a savagery he had shown to no other soul in Hell. Bocca names some of his fellow traitors, and the Poets pass on to discover two heads frozen together in one hole. One of them is gnawing the nape of the other's neck.

If I had rhymes as harsh and horrible
  as the hard fact of that final dismal hole
  which bears the weight of all the steeps of Hell,
I might more fully press the sap and substance
  from my conception; but since I must do   *5*
  without them, I begin with some reluctance.
For it is no easy undertaking, I say,
  to describe the bottom of the Universe;
  nor is it for tongues that only babble child's play.
But may those Ladies of the Heavenly Spring°   *10*
  who helped Amphion wall Thebes, assist my verse,
  that the word may be the mirror of the thing.
O most miscreant rabble, you who keep
  the stations of that place whose name is pain,
  better had you been born as goats or sheep!   *15*
We stood now in the dark pit of the well,
  far down the slope below the Giant's feet,
  and while I still stared up at the great wall,
I heard a voice cry: "Watch which way you turn:
  take care you do not trample on the heads   *20*
  of the forworn and miserable brethren."
Whereat I turned and saw beneath my feet
  and stretching out ahead, a lake so frozen
  it seemed to be made of glass. So thick a sheet
never yet hid the Danube's winter course,   *25*
  nor, far away beneath the frigid sky,
  locked the Don up in its frozen source:
for were Tanbernick and the enormous peak
  of Pietrapana° to crash down on it,
  not even the edges would so much as creak.   *30*
The way frogs sit to croak, their muzzles leaning
  out of the water, at the time and season
  when the peasant woman dreams of her day's gleaning°—
Just so the livid dead are sealed in place
  up to the part at which they blushed for shame,   *35*
  and they beat their teeth like storks. Each holds his face
bowed toward the ice, each of them testifies
  to the cold with his chattering mouth, to his heart's grief
  with tears that flood forever from his eyes.
When I had stared about me, I looked down   *40*
  and at my feet I saw two clamped together
  so tightly that the hair of their heads had grown
together. "Who are you," I said, "who lie
  so tightly breast to breast?" They strained their necks,

---

[10] *Ladies of the heavenly spring:* The Muses. they so inspired Amphion's hand upon the lyre that the music charmed blocks of stone out of Mount Cithaeron, and the blocks formed themselves into the walls of Thebes.   [28-29] *Tanbernick ... Pietrapana:* There is no agreement on the location of the mountain Dante called Taubernick. Pietrapana, today known as *la Pania*, is in Tuscany.   [32-33] *time ... gleaning:* The summer.

and when they had raised their heads as if to reply *45*
the tears their eyes had managed to contain
    up to that time gushed out, and the cold froze them
between the lids, sealing them shut again
tighter than any clamp grips wood to wood,
    and mad with pain, they fell to butting heads *50*
    like billy-goats in a sudden savage mood.
And a wraith who lay to one side and below,
    and who had lost both ears to frostbite, said,
    his head still bowed: "Why do you watch us so? *54*
If you wish to know who they are° who share one
    doom,
they owned the Bisenzio's valley with their father,
    whose name was Albert. They spring from one womb,
and you may search through all Caïna's crew
    without discovering in all this waste
    a squab more fit for the aspic than these two; *60*
not him whose breast and shadow a single blow
    of the great lance of King Arthur pierced with light;°
nor yet Focaccia° nor this one fastened so
into the ice that his head is all I see,
    and whom, if you are Tuscan, you know well— *65*
    his name on earth was Sassol Mascheroni.°
And I—to tell you all and so be through—
    was Camicion de' Pazzi.° I wait for Carlin
    beside whose guilt my sins will shine like virtue."
And leaving him,° I saw a thousand faces *70*
    discolored so by cold, I shudder yet
    and always will when I think of those frozen places.
As we approached the center of all weight,
    where I went shivering in eternal shade,
    whether it was my will, or chance or fate, *75*
I cannot say, but as I trailed my Guide
    among those heads, my foot struck violently
    against the face of one.° Weeping, it cried:
"Why do you kick me? If you were not sent
    to wreak a further vengeance for Montaperti, *80*
    why do you add this to my other torment?"

---

⁵⁵ *they:* Allessandro and Napoleone, Counts of Mangona. Among other holdings, they inherited a castle in the Val di Bisenzio. They seemed to have been at odds on all things and finally killed one another in a squabble over their inheritance and their politics (Allessandro was a Guelph and Napoleone a Ghibelline). ⁶¹⁻⁶² *him … light:* Mordred, King Arthur's traitorous nephew. He tried to kill Arthur, but the king struck him a single blow of his lance, and when it was withdrawn, a shaft of light passed through the gaping wound and split the shadow of the falling traitor. ⁶³ *Focaccia:* Of the Cancellieri of Pistoia. He murdered his cousin among others) and may have been the principal cause of a great feud that divided the Cancellieri, and split the Guelphs into the White and Black parties. ⁶⁶ *Sassol Mascheroni:* Of the Toschi of Florence. He was appointed guardian of one of his nephews and murdered him to get the inheritance for himself. ⁶⁸ *Camicion de' Pazzi:* Alberto Camicion de' Pazzi of Valdarno. He murdered a kinsman. *Carlin:* Carlino de' Pazzi, relative of Alberto. He was charged with defending for the Whites the castle of Piantravigne in Valdarno but surrendered it for a bribe. He belongs therefore in the next lower circle, Antenora, as a traitor to his country, and when he arrives there his greater sin will make Alberto seem almost virtuous by comparison. ⁷⁰ *And leaving him:* These words mark the departure from Caïna to Antenora. ⁷⁸ *one:* Bocca degli Abbati, a traitorous Florentine. At the battle of Montaperti … he hacked off the hand of the Florentine standard bearer. The cavalry, lacking a standard around which it could rally, was soon routed.

"Master," I said, "grant me a moment's pause
    to rid my self of a doubt concerning this one;
    then you may hurry me at your own pace."
The Master stopped at once, and through the volley *85*
    of foul abuse the wretch poured out, I said:
    "Who are you who curse others so?" And he:
"And who are *you* who go through the dead larder
    of Antenora kicking the cheeks of others
    so hard, that were you alive, you could not kick
    harder?" *90*
"I *am* alive," I said, "and if you seek fame,
    it may be precious to you above all else
    that my notes on this descent include your name."
"Exactly the opposite is my wish and hope,"
    he answered. "Let me be; for it's little you know *95*
    of how to flatter on this icy slope."
I grabbed the hair of his dog's-ruff and I said:
    "Either you tell me truly who you are,
    or you won't have a hair left on your head."
And he: "Not though you snatch me bald, I swear *100*
    I will not tell my name nor show my face.
    Not though you rip until my brain lies bare."
I had a good grip on his hair; already
    I had yanked out more than one fistful of it, *104*
    while the wretch yelped, but kept his face turned from
    me;
when another said: "Bocca, what is it ails you?
    What the Hell's wrong?° Isn't it bad enough
    to hear you bang your jaws? Must you bark too?"
"Now filthy traitor, say no more!" I cried,
    "for to your shame, be sure I shall bear back *110*
    a true report of you." The wretch replied:
"Say anything you please but go away.
    And if you *do* get back, don't overlook
    that pretty one who had so much to say
just now. Here he laments the Frenchman's price. *115*
    'I saw Buoso da Duera.'° you can report,
    'where the bad salad is kept crisp on ice.'
And if you're asked who else was wintering here,
    Beccheria,° whose throat was slit by Florence,
    is there beside you. Gianni de' Soldanier° *120*
is further down, I think, with Ganelon,°

---

¹⁰⁷ *What the Hell's wrong?:* In the circumstances, a monstrous pun. The original is *"qual diavolo ti tocca?"* (what devil touches, or molests, you?), a standard colloquialism for "what's the matter with you?" A similar pun occurs in line 117: "kept crisp (cool) on ice." Colloquially *"stare fresco"* (to be or to remain cool) equals "to be left out in the cold," i.e., to be out of luck. ¹¹⁶ *Buoso da Duera:* Of Cremona. In 1265 Charles of Anjou marched against Manfred and Naples …, and Buoso da Duera was sent out in charge of a Ghibelline army to oppose the passage of one of Charles' armies, but accepted a bribe and let the French pass unopposed. The event took place near Parma. ¹¹⁹ *Beccheria:* Tesauro dei Beccheria of Pavia, Abbot of Vallombrosa and Papal Legate (of Alexander IV) in Tuscany. The Florentine Guelphs cut off his head in 1258 for plotting with the expelled Ghibellines. ¹²⁰ *Gianni de' Soldanier:* A Florentine Ghibelline of ancient and noble family. In 1265, however, during the riots that occurred under the Two Jovial Friars, he deserted his party and became a leader of the commoners (Guelphs). In placing him in Antenora, Dante makes no distinction between turning on one's country and turning on one's political party, not at least if the end is simply for power. ¹²¹ *Ganelon:* It was Ganelon who betrayed Roland to the Saracens.

and Tebaldello,° who opened the gates of Faenza
    and let Bologna steal in with the dawn."
Leaving him then, I saw two souls together
    in a single hole, and so pinched in by the ice   125
    that one head made a helmet for the other.
As a famished man chews crusts—so the one sinner
    sank his teeth into the other's nape
    at the base of the skull, gnawing his loathsome dinner.
Tydeus in his final raging hour   130
    gnawed Menalippus' head° with no more fury
    than this one gnawed at skull and dripping gore.
"You there," I said, "who show so odiously
    your hatred for that other, tell me why
    on this condition: that if in what you tell me   135
you seem to have a reasonable complaint
    against him you devour with such foul relish,
    I, knowing who you are, and his soul's taint,
may speak your cause to living memory,
    God willing the power of speech be left to me."   140

CANTO XXXIII

**Circle Nine: Cocytus   Compound Fraud
Round Two: Antenora   The Treacherous to
Country
Round Three: Ptolemea   The Treacherous to
Guests and Hosts**

*In reply to Dante's exhortation, the sinner who is gnawing his com-
panion's head looks up, wipes his bloody mouth on his victim's hair,
and tells his harrowing story. He is Count Ugolino and the wretch he
gnaws is Archbishop Ruggieri. Both are in Antenora for treason. In
life they had once plotted together. Then Ruggieri betrayed his fellow-
plotter and caused his death, by starvation, along with his four "sons".
In the most pathetic and dramatic passage of the* Inferno, *Ugolino
details how their prison was sealed and how his "sons" dropped dead
before him one by one, weeping for food. His terrible tale serves only
to renew his grief and hatred, and he has hardly finished it before he
begins to gnaw Ruggieri again with renewed fury. In the immutable
Law of Hell, the killer-by-starvation becomes the food of his victim.*

*The Poets leave Ugolino and enter Ptolemea, so named for the
Ptolomaeus of Maccabees, who murdered his father-in-law at a banquet. Here are punished those who were Treacherous Against the Ties
of Hospitality. They lie with only half their faces above the ice and
their tears freeze in their eye sockets, sealing them with little crystal
visors. Thus even the comfort of tears is denied them. Here Dante
finds Friar Alberigo and Branca D'Oria, and discovers the terrible
power of Ptolemea: so great is its sin that the souls of the guilty fall to
its torments even before they die, leaving their bodies still on earth,
inhabited by Demons.*

The sinner raised his mouth from his grim repast
    and wiped it on the hair of the bloody head
    whose nape he had all but eaten away. At last
he began to speak: "You ask me to renew
    a grief so desperate that the very thought   5
    of speaking of it tears my heart in two.
But if my words may be a seed that bears
    the fruit of infamy for him I gnaw,
    I shall weep, but tell my story through my tears.
Who you may be, and by what powers you reach   10
    into this underworld, I cannot guess,
    but you seem to me a Florentine by your speech.
I was Count Ugolino,° I must explain;
    this reverend grace is Archbishop Ruggieri:
    now I will tell you why I gnaw his brain.   15
That I, who trusted him, had to undergo
    imprisonment and death through his treachery,
    you will know already.° What you cannot know—
that is, the lingering inhumanity
    of the death I suffered—you shall hear in full: 20
    then judge for yourself if he has injured me.
A narrow window in that coop° of stone
    now called the Tower of Hunger for my sake
    (within which others yet must pace alone)
had shown me several waning moons already°   25
    between its bars, when I slept the evil sleep
    in which the veil of the future parted for me.
This beast° appeared as master of a hunt
    chasing the wolf and his whelps across the mountain
    that hides Lucca from Pisa.° Out in front   30
of the starved and shrewd and avid pack he had placed
    Gualandi and Sismondi and Lanfranchi°
    to point his prey. The father and sons had raced
a brief course only when they failed of breath
    and seemed to weaken; then I thought I saw   35
    their flanks ripped open by the hounds' fierce teeth.
Before the dawn, the dream still in my head,
    I woke and heard my sons,° who were there with me,
    cry from their troubled sleep, asking for bread.

---

122 *Tebaldello:* Tebaldello de' Zambrasi of Faenza. At dawn on
November 13, 1280, he opened the city gates and delivered
Faenza to the Bolognese Guelphs in order to revenge himself
on the Ghibelline family of the Lambertazzi, who, in 1274, had
fled from Bologna to take refuge in Faenza. 131 *Menalippus'
head:* Statius recounts in the *Thebaid* that Tydeus killed
Menalippus in battle but fell himself mortally wounded. As he
lay dying, he had Menalippus' head brought to him and fell to
gnawing it in his dying rage.

13 *Ugolino:* Count of Donoratico and a member of the Guelph
family della Gherardesca. He and his nephew, Nino de'
Visconti, led the two Guelph factions of Pisa. In 1288 Ugolino
intrigued with Archbishop Ruggieri degli Ubaldini, leader of the
Ghibellines, to get rid of Visconti and to take over the command
of all the Pisan Guelphs. The plan worked, but in the conse-
quent weakening of the Guelphs, Ruggieri saw his chance and
betrayed Ugolino, throwing him into prison with his sons and
his grandsons. In the following year the prison was sealed up and
they were left to starve to death. 18 *already:* News of Ugolino's
imprisonment and death would certainly have reached Florence.
What you cannot know: No living man could know what happened after Ugolino and his sons were sealed in the prison and
abandoned. 22 *coop:* Dante uses the word *muda,* in Italian signifying a stone tower in which falcons were kept in the dark to
moult. From the time of Ugolino's death it became known as
The Tower of Hunger. 25 *already:* Ugolino was jailed late in
1288. He was sealed in to starve early in 1289. 28 *beast:*
Ruggieri. 29-30 *mountain ... Pisa:* These two cities would be in
view of one another were it not for Monte San Giuliano.
32 *Gualandi and sismondi and L:anfranchi:* Three Pisan nobles,
Ghibellines and friends of the Archbishop. 38 *sons:* Actually two
of the boys were grandsons and all were considerably older than
one would gather from Dante's account. Anselm, the younger
grandson, was fifteen. The others were really young men
and were certainly old enough for guilt despite Dante's charge
in line 90.

You are cruelty itself if you can keep   40
   your tears back at the thought of what foreboding
   stirred in my heart; and if you do not weep,
at what are you used to weeping?—The hour when food
   used to be brought, drew near. They were now awake,
   and each was anxious from his dream's dark mood. 45
And from the base of that horrible tower I heard
   the sound of hammers nailing up the gates:
   I stared at my sons' faces without a word.
I did not weep: I had turned to stone inside.
   They wept. 'What ails you, Father, you look so
     strange.'
my little Anselm, youngest of them, cried.   51
But I did not speak a word nor shed a tear:
   not all that day nor all that endless night,
   until I saw another sun appear.
When a tiny ray leaked into that dark prison   55
   and I saw staring back from their four faces
   the terror and the wasting of my own,
I bit my hands in helpless grief. And they,
   thinking I chewed myself for hunger, rose
   suddenly together. I heard them say: 60
'Father, it would give us much less pain
   if you ate us: it was you who put upon us
   this sorry flesh; now strip it off again.'
I calmed myself to spare them. Ah! hard earth,
   why did you not yawn open? All that day   65
   and the next we sat in silence. On the fourth,
Gaddo, the eldest, fell before me and cried,
   stretched at my feet upon that prison floor:
   'Father, why don't you help me?' There he died.
And just as you see me, I saw them fall   70
   one by one on the fifth day and the sixth.
   Then, already blind, I began to crawl
from body to body shaking them frantically.
   Two days I called their names, and they were dead.
   Then fasting overcame my grief and me."°   75
His eyes narrowed to slits when he was done,
   and he seized the skull again between his teeth
   grinding it as a mastiff grinds a bone.
Ah, Pisa! foulest blemish on the land
   where "si" sounds sweet and clear,° since those
     nearby you
   are slow to blast the ground on which you stand,   81
may Caprara and Gorgona° drift from place
   and dam the flooding Arno at its mouth
   until it drowns the last of your foul race!
For if to Ugolino falls the censure   85

for having betrayed your castles,° you for your part
   should not have put his sons to such a torture:
you modern Thebes!° those tender lives you spilt—
   Brigata, Uguccione, and the others
   I mentioned earlier—were too young for guilt!   90
We passed on further,° where the frozen mine
   entombs another crew in greater pain;
   these wraiths are not bent over, but lie supine.
Their very weeping closes up their eyes;
   and the grief that finds no outlet for its tears   95
   turns inward to increase their agonies:
for the first tears that they shed knot instantly
   in their eye sockets, and as they freeze they form
   a crystal visor above the cavity.
And despite the fact that standing in that place   100
   I had become as numb as any callus,
   and all sensation had faded from my face,
somehow I felt a wind begin to blow,
   whereat I said: "Master, what stirs this wind?
   Is not all heat extinguished here below?"°   105
And the Master said to me: "Soon you will be
   where your own eyes will see the source and cause
   and give you their own answer to the mystery."
And one of those locked in that icy mall
   cried out to us as we passed: "Oh souls so cruel   110
   that you are sent to the last post of all,
relieve me for a little from the pain
   of this hard veil; let my heart weep a while
   before the weeping freeze my eyes again."
And I to him: "If you would have my service,   115
   tell me your name; then if I do not help you
   may I descend to the last rim of the ice."°
"I am Friar Alberigo,"° he answered therefore,
   "the same who called for the fruits from the bad
     garden.
   Here I am given dates for figs full store."   120
"What" Are you dead already?" I said to him.
   And he then: "How my body stands in the world
   I do not know. So privileged is this rim
of Ptolomea, that often souls fall to it
   before dark Atropos° has cut their thread.   125

---

⁷⁵ *fasting overcame my grief and me:* I.e., he died. Some interpret the line to mean that Ugolino's hunger drove him to cannibalism. Ugolino's present occupation in Hell would certainly support that interpretation but the fact is that cannibalism is the one major sin Dante does not assign a place to in Hell. So monstrous would it have seemed to him that he must certainly have established a special punishment for it. Certainly he could hardly have relegated it to an ambiguity. Moreover, it would be a sin of bestiality rather than of fraud, and as such it would be punished in the Seventh Circle. ⁸⁰ *where "si" sounds sweet and clear:* Italy. ⁸² *Caprara and Gorgona:* These two islands near the mouth of the Arno were Pisan possessions in 1300.

⁸⁶ *betrayed your castles.* In 1284, Ugolino gave up certain castles to Lucca and Florence. He was at war with Genoa at the time and it is quite likely that he ceded the castles to buy the neutrality of these two cities, for they were technically allied with Genoa. Dante, however, must certainly consider the action as treasonable, for otherwise Ugolino would be in Caïna for his treachery to Visconti. ⁸⁸ *Thebes:* Thebes, as a number of the foregoing notes will already have made clear, was the site of some of the most hideous crimes of antiquity. ⁹¹ *passed on further:* Marks the passage into Ptolomea. ¹⁰⁵ *heat ... below:* Dante believed (rather accurately, by chance) that all winds resulted from "exhalations of heat". Cocytus, however is conceived as wholly devoid of heat, a metaphysical absolute zero. The source of the wind, as we discover in the next Canto, is Satan himself. ¹¹⁷ *descend ... ice:* Dante is not taking any chances; he has to go on to the last rim in any case. The sinner, however, believes him to be another damned soul and would interpret the oath quite otherwise than as Dante meant it. ¹¹⁸ *Friar Alberigo:* Of the Manfredi of Fenza. He was another Jovial Friar. In 1284 his brother Manfred struck him in the course of an argument. Alberigo pretended to let it pass, but in 1285 he invited Manfred and his son to a banquet and had them murdered. The signal to the assassins was the words: "Bring in the fruit". "Friar Alberigo's bad fruit" became a proverbial saying. ¹²⁵ *Atropos:* The Fate who cuts the thread of life.

And that you may more willingly free my spirit
of this glaze of frozen tears that shrouds my face,
    I will tell you this: when a soul betrays as I did,
    it falls from flesh, and a demon takes its place,
ruling the body till its time is spent.   *130*
    The ruined soul rains down into this cistern.
    So, I believe, there is still evident
in the world above, all that is fair and mortal
    of this black shade who winters here behind me.
    If you have only recently crossed the portal   *135*
from that sweet world, you surely must have known
    his body: Brana D'Oria° is its name,
    and many years have passed since he rained down."
"I think you are trying to take me in," I said,
    "Ser Brana D'Oria is a living man;   *140*
    he eats, he drinks, he fills his clothes and his bed."
"Michel Zanche had not yet reached the ditch
    of the Black Talons," the frozen wraith replied,
    "there where the sinners thicken in hot pitch,
when this one left his body to a devil,   *145*
    as did his nephew and second in treachery,
    and plumbed like lead through space to this dead
        level.
But now reach out your hand, and let me cry."
    And I did not keep the promise I had made,
    for to be rude to him was courtesy.   *150*
Ah, men of Genoa! souls of little worth,
    corrupted from all custom of righteousness,
    why have you not been driven from the earth?
For there beside the blackest soul of all
    Romagna's evil plain, lies one of yours   *155*
    bathing his filthy soul in the eternal
glacier of Cocytus for his foul crime,
while he seems yet alive in world and time!

Canto XXXIV

Ninth Circle: Cocytus   Compound Fraud
Round Four: Judecca   The Treacherous to Their
Masters
The Center: Satan

*"On march the banners of the King," Virgil begins as the Poets face
the last depth. He is quoting a medieval hymn, and to it he adds the
distortion and perversion of all that lies about him. "On march the
banners of the King—of Hell." And there before them, in an infernal
parody of Godhead, they see Satan in the distance, his great wings
beating like a windmill. It is their beating that is the source of the icy
wind of Cocytus, the exhalation of all evil.*

*All about him in the ice are strewn the sinners of the last
round, Judecca, named for Judas Iscariot. These are the Treacherous
to Their Masters. They lie completely sealed in the ice, twisted and
distorted into every conceivable posture. It is impossible to speak to
them and the Poets move on to observe Satan.*

He is fixed into the ice at the center to which flow all the rivers

*of guilt; and as he beats his great wings as if to escape, their icy wind
only freezes him more surely into the polluted ice. In a grotesque parody of the Trinity, he has three faces, each a different color, and in each
mouth he clamps a sinner whom he rips eternally with his teeth.
Judas Iscariot is in the central mouth: Brutus and Cassius in the
mouths on either side.*

*Having seen all, the Poets now climb through the center, grap-
pling hand over hand down the hairy flank of Satan himself—a last
supremely symbolic action—and at last, when they have passed the
center of all gravity, they emerge from Hell. A long climb from the
earth's center to the Mount of Purgatory awaits them, and they push
on without rest, ascending along the sides of the river Lethe, till they
emerge once more to see the stars of Heaven, just before dawn on
Easter Sunday.*

"On march the banners of the King of Hell,"°
    my Master said, "Toward us. Look straight ahead:
    can you make him out at the core of the frozen shell?"
Like a whirling windmill seen afar at twilight,
    or when a mist has risen from the ground—   *5*
    just such an engine rose upon my sight
stirring up such a wild and bitter wind
    I cowered for shelter at my Master's back,
    there being no other windbreak I could find.
I stood now where the souls of the last class   *10*
    (with fear my verses tell it) were covered wholly;
    they shone below the ice like straws in glass.
Some lie stretched out; others are fixed in place
    upright, some on their heads, some on their soles;
    another, like a bow, bends foot to face.   *15*
When we had gone so far across the ice
    that it pleased my Guide to show me the foul
        creature°
    which once had worn the grace of Paradise,
he made me stop, and, stepping aside, he said:
    "Now see the face of Dis! This is the place   *20*
    where you must arm your soul against all dread."
Do not ask, Reader, how my blood ran cold
    and my voice choked up with fear. I cannot write it:
    this is a terror that cannot be told.
I did not die, and yet I lost life's breath: *25*
    imagine for yourself what I became,
    deprived at once of both my life and death.
The Emperor of the Universe of Pain
    jutted out his upper chest above the ice;
    and I am closer in size to the great mountain   *30*
the Titans make around the central pit,
    than they to his arms. Now, starting from this part,
    imagine the whole that corresponds to it!
If he was once as beautiful as now
    he is hideous, and still turned on his Maker,   *35*
    well may he be the source of every woe!
With what sense of awe I saw his head
    towering above me! for it had three faces:
    one was in front, and it was fiery red;

---

¹³⁷ *Brana D'Oria:* A Genoese Ghibelline. His sin is identical in
kind to that of Friar Alberigo. In 1275 he invited his father-in-
law, Michel Zanche (see Canto XXII), to a banquet and had him
and his companions cut to pieces. He was assisted in the butchery by his nephew.

---

¹ *"On … Hell":* The hymn (*Vexilla regis prodeunt*) was written in
the sixth century by Venantius Fortunatus, Bishop of Poitiers.
The original celebrates the Holy Cross, and is part of the service for Good Friday to be sung at the moment of uncovering
the Cross.   ¹⁷ *foul creature:* Satan.

the other two, as weirdly wonderful,   *40*
   merged with it from the middle of each shoulder
   to the point where all converged at the top of the
    skull;
the right was something between white and bile;
   the left was about the color that one finds
   on those who live along the banks of the Nile.   *45*
Under each head two wings rose terribly,
   their span proportioned to so gross a bird:
   I never saw such sails upon the sea.
They were not feathers—their texture and their form
   were like a bat's wings—and he beat them so   *50*
   that three winds blew from him in one great storm:
it is these winds that freeze all Cocytus.
   He wept from his six eyes, and down three chins
   the tears ran mixed with bloody froth and pus.°
In every mouth he worked a broken sinner   *55*
   between his rake-like teeth. Thus he kept three
   in eternal pain at his eternal dinner.
For the one in front the biting seemed to play
   no part at all compared to the ripping: at times
   the whole skin of his back was flayed away.   *60*
"That soul that suffers most," explained my Guide,
   "is Judas Iscariot, he who kicks his legs
   on the fiery chin and has his head inside.
Of the other two, who have their heads thrust forward,
   the one who dangles down from the black face   *65*
   is Brutus: note how he writhes without a word.
And there, with the huge and sinewy arms,° is the soul
   of Cassius.—But the night is coming on°
   and we must go, for we have seen the whole."
Then, as he bade, I clasped his neck, and he,   *70*
   watching for a moment when the wings
   were opened wide, reached over dexterously
and seized the shaggy coat of the king demon;
   then grappling matted hair and frozen crusts
   from one tuft to another, clambered down.   *75*
When we had reached the joint where the great thigh
   merges into the swelling of the haunch,
   my Guide and Master, straining terribly,
turned his head to where his feet had been
   and began to grip the hair as if her were climbing; *80*
   so that I thought we moved toward Hell again.
"Hold fast!" my Guide said, and his breath came shrill°
   with labor and exhaustion. "There is no way
   but by such stairs to rise above such evil."
At last he climbed out through an opening   *85*
   in the central rock, and he seated me on the rim;
   then joined me with a nimble backward spring.
I looked up, thinking to see Lucifer
   as I had left him, and I saw instead
   his legs projecting high into the air.   *90*

Now let all those whose dull minds are still vexed
   by failure to understand what point it was
   I had passed through, judge if I was perplexed.
"Get up. Up on your feet," my Master said.
   "The sun already mounts to middle tierce,°   *95*
   and a long road and hard climbing lie ahead."
It was no hall of state we had found there,
   but a natural animal pit hollowed from rock
   with a broken floor and a close and sunless air.
"Before I tear myself from the Abyss,   *100*
   I said when I had risen, "O my Master,
   explain to me my error in all this:
where is the ice? and Lucifer—how has he
   been turned from top to bottom: and how can the sun
   have gone from night to day so suddenly?"   *105*
And he to me: "You imagine you are still
   on the other side of the center where I grasped
   the shaggy flank of the Great Worm of Evil
which bores through the world—you *were* while I
    climbed down,
   but when I turned myself about, you passed   *110*
   the point to which all gravities are drawn.
You are under the other hemisphere where you stand;
   the sky above us is the half opposed
   to that which canopies the great dry land.
Under the mid-point of that other sky   *115*
   the Man who was born sinless and who lived
   beyond all blemish, came to suffer and die.
You have your feet upon a little sphere
   which forms the other face of the Judecca.
   There it is evening when it is morning here.   *120*
And this gross Fiend and Image of all Evil
   who made a stairway for us with his hide
   is pinched and prisoned in the ice-pack still.
On this side he plunged down from heaven's height,
   and the land that spread here once hid in the sea *125*
   and fled North to our hemisphere for fright;
and it may be that moved by that same fear,
   the one peak° that still rises on this side
   fled upward leaving this great cavern here.
Down there, beginning at the further bound   *130*
   of Beelzebub's dim tomb, there is a space
   not known by sight, but only by the sound
of a little stream° descending through the hollow
   it has eroded from the massive stone
   in its endlessly entwining lazy flow.   *135*
My Guide and I crossed over and began
   to mount that little known and lightless road
   to ascend into the shining world again.
He first, I second, without thought of rest
   we climbed the dark until we reached the point *140*
   where a round opening brought in sight the blest

---

⁵⁴ *bloody froth and pus:* The gore of the sinners he chews, which is mixed with his slaver.   ⁶⁷ *huge and sinewy arms:* The Cassius who betrayed Caesar was more generally described in terms of Shakespeare's "lean and hungry look." Another Cassius is described by Cicero (*Cateline* III) as huge and sinewy. Dante probably confused the two.   ⁶⁸ *night is coming on:* It is now Saturday evening.   ⁸² *breath came shrill:* Cf. Canto XXIII, 85, where the fact that Dante breathes indicates to the Hypocrites that he is alive. Virgil's breathing is certainly a contradiction.

⁹⁵ *middle tierce:* In the canonical day tierce is the period from about six to nine a.m. Middle tierce, therefore, is seven-thirty. In going through the center point, they have gone from night to day. They have moved ahead twelve hours.   ¹²⁸ *one peak:* The Mount of Purgatory.   ¹³³ *stream:* Lethe. In classical mythology, the river of forgetfulness, from which souls drank before being born. In Dante's symbolism it flows down from Purgatory, where it has washed away the memory of sin from the souls who are undergoing purification. That memory it delivers to Hell, which draws all sin to itself.

and beauteous shining of the Heavenly cars.
And we walked out once more beneath the Stars.°

PURGATORIO

Canto I

Ante-Purgatory: The Shore of the Island   Cato of Utica

The Poets emerge from Hell just before the dawn of Easter Sunday (April 10, 1300), and Dante revels in the sight of the rediscovered heavens. As he looks eagerly about at the stars, he sees nearby an old man of impressive bearing. The ancient is Cato of Utica, guardian of the shores of Purgatory. Cato challenges the Poets as fugitives from Hell, but Virgil, after first instructing Dante to kneel in reverence, explains Dante's mission and Beatrice's command. Cato then gives them instructions for proceeding.

The Poets have emerged at a point a short way up the slope of Purgatory. It is essential, therefore, that they descend to the lowest point and begin from there, an allegory of Humility. Cato, accordingly, orders Virgil to lead Dante to the shore, to wet his hands in the dew of the new morning, and to wash the stains of Hell from Dante's face and the film of Hell's vapors from Dante's eyes. Virgil is then to bind about Dante's waist one of the pliant reeds (symbolizing Humility) that grow in the soft mud of the shore.

Having so commanded, Cato disappears. Dante arises in silence and stands waiting, eager to begin. His look is all the communication that is necessary. Virgil leads him to the shore and performs all that Cato has commanded, Dante's first purification is marked by a miracle: when Virgil breaks off a reed, the stalk immediately regenerates a new reed, restoring itself exactly as it had been.

For better waters now the little bark
    of my indwelling powers raises her sails,
    and leaves behind that sea so cruel and dark.
Now shall I sing that second kingdom° given
    the soul of man wherein to purge its guilt   5
    and so grow worthy to ascend to Heaven.
Yours am I, sacred Muses! To you I pray.
    Here let dead poetry° rise once more to life,
    and here let sweet Calliope° rise and play
some far accompaniment in that high strain   10
    whose power the wretched Pierides once felt
    so terribly they dared not hope again.
Sweet azure of the sapphire of the east
    was gathering on the serene horizon
    its pure and perfect radiance—a feast   15
to my glad eyes, reborn to their delight,

as soon as I had passed from the dead air°
    which had oppressed my soul and dimmed my sight.
The planet whose sweet influence strengthens love°
    was making all the east laugh with her rays,   20
    veiling the Fishes, which she swam above.
I turned then to my right and set my mind
    on the other pole, and there I saw four stars°
    unseen by mortals since the first mankind.°
The heavens seemed to revel in their light.   25
    O widowed Northern Hemisphere, bereft
    forever of the glory of that sight!
As I broke off my gazing, my eyes veered
    a little to the left, to the other pole°
    from which, by then, the Wain had disappeared.   30
I saw, nearby, an ancient man, alone.°
    His bearing filled me with such reverence,
    no father could ask more from his best son.
His beard was long and touched with strands of white,
    as was his hair, of which two tresses fell   35
    over his breast. Rays of the holy light
that fell from the four stars made his face glow
    with such a radiance that he looked to me
    as if he faced the sun. And standing so,
he moved his venerable plumes and said: 40
    "Who are you two who climb by the dark stream
    to escape the eternal prison of the dead?
Who led you? or what served you as a light
    in your dark flight from the eternal valley,
    which lies forever blind in darkest night?   45

---

143 *Stars:* Dante ends each of the three divisions of the *Commedia* with this word. Every conclusion of the upward soul is toward the stars, God's shining symbols of hope and virtue. It is just before dawn of Easter Sunday that the Poets emerge.   4 *second kingdom:* Purgatory.   8 *dead poetry:* The verses that sang of Hell. Dante may equally have meant that poetry as an art has long been surpassed by history as the medium for great subjects. Here poetry will return to its classic state.   9 *Calliope:* Muse of Epic Poetry. Dante exhorts Calliope to fill him with the strains of the music she played in the defeat of the Pierides, the nine daughters of Pierius, King of Thessaly. They presumed to challenge the Muses to a contest of song. After their defeat they were changed into magpies for their presumption. Ovid (*Metamorphoses*, V. 294–678) retells the myth in detail.

17 *dead air:* Of Hell.   19 *planet … love:* Venus. Here, as morning star, Venus is described as rising in Pisces, the Fishes, the zodiacal sign immediately preceding Aries. In Canto I of the *Inferno* Dante has made it clear that the Sun is in Aries. Hence it is about to rise.   23 *four stars:* Modern readers are always tempted to identify these four stars as the Southern Cross, but it is almost certain that Dante did not know about that formation. In VIII, 89, Dante mentions three other stars as emphatically as he does these four and no one has been tempted to identify them on the star-chart. Both constellations are best taken as allegorical. The four stars represent the Four Cardinal Virtues: Prudence, Justice, Fortitude, and Temperance. Dante will encounter them again in the form of nymphs when he achieves the Earthly Paradise.   24 *first mankind:* Adam and Eve. In Dante's geography, the Garden of Eden (the Earthly Paradise) was at the top of the Mount of Purgatory, which was the only land in the Southern Hemisphere. All of what were called "the southern continents" were believed to lie north of the equator. When Adam and Eve were driven from the Garden, therefore, they were driven into the Northern Hemisphere, and no living soul since had been far enough south to see those stars. Ulysses and his men (*Inferno*, XXVII) had come within sight of the Mount of Purgatory, but Ulysses mentioned nothing of having seen these stars.   29 *other pole:* The North Pole. The Wain (Ursa Major, i.e., the Big Dipper) is below the horizon.   31 *ancient man:* Marcus Porcius Cato, the younger, 95–46 B.C. In the name of freedom, Cato opposed the policies of both Caesar and Pompey, but because he saw Caesar as the greater evil joined forces with Pompey. After the defeat of his cause at the Battle of Thapsus, Cato killed himself with his own sword rather than lose his freedom. Virgil lauds him in the *Aeneid* as a symbol of perfect devotion to liberty, and all writers of Roman antiquity have given Cato a similar high place. Dante spends the highest praises on him both in *De Monarchia* and *Il Convivio*. Why Cato should be so signally chosen by God as the special guardian of Purgatory has been much disputed. Cato may be taken as representative of supreme virtue short of godliness. He has accomplished everything but the purifying total surrender of his will to God. As such he serves as an apt transitional symbol, being the highest rung on the ladder of natural virtue, but the lowest on the ladder of those godly virtues to which Purgatory is the ascent.

Are the laws of the pit so broken? Or is new counsel
    published in Heaven that the damned may wander
    onto my rocks from the abyss of Hell?"
At that my Master laid his hands upon me,
    instructing me by word and touch and gesture   *50*
    to show my reverence in brow and knee,
then answered him: I do not come this way
    of my own will or powers. A Heavenly Lady
    sent me to this man's aid in his dark day.
But since your will is to know more, my will   *55*
    cannot deny you; I will tell you truly
    why we have come and how. This man has still
to see his final hour, though in the burning
    of his own madness he had drawn so near it
    his time was perilously short for turning.   *60*
As I have told you, I was sent to show
    the way his soul must take for its salvation;
    and there is none but this by which I go.
I have shown him the guilty people. Now I mean
    to lead him through the spirits in your keeping,   *65*
    to show him those whose suffering makes them clean.
By what means I have led him to this strand
    to see and hear you, takes too long to tell:
    from Heaven is the power and the command.
Now may his coming please you, for he goes   *70*
    to win his freedom; and how dear that is
    the man who gives his life for it best knows.
You know it who in that cause found death sweet
    in Utica where you put off that flesh
    which shall rises radiant at the Judgment Seat.   *75*
We do not break the Laws: this man lives yet,
    and I am of that Round not ruled by Minos,°
    with your own Marcia,° whose chaste eyes seem set
in endless prayers to you. O blessed breast
    to hold her yet your own! for love of her   *80*
    grant us permission to pursue our quest
across your seven kingdoms.° When I go
    back to her side I shall bear thanks of you,
    if you will let me speak your name below."
"Marcia was so pleasing in my eyes   *85*
    there on the other side," he answered then
    "that all she asked, I did. Now that she lies
beyond the evil river, no word or prayer
    of hers may move me. Such was the Decree
    pronounced upon us when I rose from there.   *90*
But if, as you have said, a Heavenly Dame
    orders your way, there is no need to flatter:
    you need but ask it of me in her name.
Go then, and lead this man, but first see to it

you bind a smooth green reed about his waist   *95*
    and clean his face of all trace of the pit.
For it would not be right that one with eyes
    still filmed by mist should go before the angel
    who guards the gate: he is from Paradise.
All round the wave-wracked shore-line, there below,   *100*
    reeds grow in the soft mud. Along that edge
    no foliate nor woody plant could grow.
for what lives in that buffeting must bend.
    Do not come back this way: the rising sun
    will light an easier way you may ascend."   *105*
With that he disappeared; and silently
    I rose and moved back till I faced my Guide,
    my eyes upon him, waiting. He said to me:
"Follow my steps and let us turn again:
    along this side there is a gentle slope   *110*
    that leads to the low boundaries of the plain."
The dawn, in triumph, made the day-breeze flee
    before its coming, so that from afar
    I recognized the trembling of the sea.
We strode across that lonely plain like men   *115*
    who seek the road they strayed from and who count
    the time lost till they find it once again.
When we had reached a place along the way
    where the cool morning breeze shielded the dew
    against the first heat of the gathering day,   *120*
with gentle graces my Sweet Master bent
    and laid both outspread palms upon the grass.
    Then I, being well aware of his intent,
lifted my tear-stained cheeks to him, and there
    he made me clean, revealing my true color   *125*
    under the residues of Hell's black air.
We moved on then to the deserted strand
    which never yet has seen upon its waters
    a man who found his way back to dry land.
There, as it pleased another, he girded me.   *130*
    Wonder of wonders! when he plucked a reed
    another took its place there instantly,
arising from the humble stalk he tore
so that it grew exactly as before.

CANTO XXXI

The Earthly Paradise   Lethe; Beatrice, Matilda

Beatrice continues her reprimand, forcing Dante to confess his faults until he swoons with grief and pain at the thought of his sin. He wakes to find himself in Lethe, held in the arms of Matilda, who leads him to the other side of the stream and there immerses him that he may drink the waters that wipe out all memory of sin.

Matilda then leads him to the Four Cardinal Virtues, who dance about him and lead him before the Griffon where he many look into the eyes of Beatrice. In them Dante sees, in a First Beatific Vision, the radiant reflection of the Griffon, who appears now in his human and now in his godly nature.

The Three Theological Virtues now approach and beg that Dante may behold the smile of Beatrice. Beatrice removes her veil, and in a Second Beatific Vision, Dante beholds the splendor of the unveiled shining of Divine Love.

---

77 *Minos:* The Judge of the Damned. The round in Hell not ruled by Minos is Limbo, the final resting place of the Virtuous Pagans. Minos (see *Inferno,* V) is stationed at the entrance to the second circle of Hell. The souls in Limbo (the first circle) have never had to pass before him to be judged. 78 *Marcia:* The daughter of the consul Philippus and Cato's second wife, bearing his three children. In 56 B.C., in an unusual transaction approved by her father, Cato released her in order that she might marry his friend Hortensius. (Hence line 87: "that all she asked I did.") After the death of Hortensius, Cato took her back. 82 *seven kingdoms:* The main divisions of Purgatory according to the seven cardinal, or deadly, sins: Pride, Envy, Anger, Sloth, Avarice, Gluttony, and Lust.

"You, there, who stand upon the other side°—"
  (turning to me now, who had thought the edge
  of her discourse was sharp, the point) she cried
without pause in her flow of eloquence,
  "Speak up! Speak up! Is it true? To such a charge   5
  your own confession must give evidence."
I stood as if my spirit had turned numb:
  the organ of my speech moved, but my voice
  died in my throat before a word could come.
Briefly she paused, then cried impatiently: 10
  "What are you thinking? Speak up, for the waters°
  have yet to purge sin from your memory."
Confusion joined to terror forced a broken
  "yes" from my throat, so weak that only one
  who read my lips would know that I had spoken.   15
As an arbalest will snap when string and bow
  are drawn too tight by the bowman, and the bolt
  will strike the target a diminished blow°—
so did I shatter, strengthless and unstrung,
  under her charge, pouring out floods of tears,   20
  while my voice died in me on the way to my tongue.
And she: "Filled as you were with the desire
  I taught you for That Good beyond which nothing
  exists on earth to which man may aspire,
what yawning moats or what stretched chain-lengths°
    lay
  across your path to force you to abandon   26
  all hope of pressing further on your way?
What increase or allurement seemed to show
  in the brows of others that you walked before them
  as a lover walks below his lady's window?"   30
My breath dragged from me in a bitter sigh;
  I barely found a voice to answer with;
  my lips had trouble forming a reply.
In tears I said: "The things of the world's day,
  false pleasures and enticements, turned my steps   35
  as soon as you had ceased to light my way."
And she: "Had you been silent, or denied
  what you confess, your guilt would still be known
  to Him from Whom no guilt may hope to hide.
But here, before our court, when souls upbraid   40
  themselves for their own guilt in true remorse,
  the grindstone is turned back against the blade.°
In any case that you may know your crime
  truly and with true shame and so be stronger
  against the Siren's song another time,   45
control your tears and listen with your soul
  to learn how my departure from the flesh
  ought to have spurred you to the higher goal.

Nothing in Art or Nature could call forth
  such joy from you, as sight of that fair body   50
  which clothed me once and now sifts back to earth.
And if my dying turned that highest pleasure
  to very dust, what joy could still remain
  in mortal things for you to seek and treasure?
At the first blow you took from such vain things   55
  your every thought should have been raised to follow
  my flight above decay. Nor should your wings
have been weighed down by any joy below—
  love of a maid,° or any other fleeting
  and useless thing—to wait a second blow.   60
The fledgling waits a second shaft, a third;
  but nets° are spread and the arrow sped in vain
  in sight or hearing of the full-grown bird."
As a scolded child, tongue tied for shame, will stand
  and recognize his fault, and weep for it,   65
  bowing his head to a just reprimand,
so did I stand. And she said: "If to hear me
  grieves you, now raise your beard and let your eyes
  show you a greater cause for misery."°
The blast that blows from Libya's hot sand,   70
  or the Alpine gale, overcomes less resistance
  uprooting oaks than I, at her command,
overcame then in lifting up my face;
  for when she had referred to it as my "beard"
  I sensed too well the venom of her phrase.   75
When I had raised my eyes with so much pain,
  I saw those Primal Beings, now at rest,
  who had strewn blossoms round her thick as rain;
and with my tear-blurred and uncertain vision
  I saw Her turned to face that beast which is   80
  one person in two natures without division.°
Even veiled and across the river from me
  her face outshone its first-self° by as much
  as she outshone all mortals formerly.
And the thorns of my repentance pricked me so   85
  that all the use and substance of the world
  I most had loved, now most appeared my foe.
Such guilty recognition gnawed my heart
  I swooned for pain; and what I then became
  she best knows who most gave me cause to smart.   90
When I returned to consciousness at last
  I found the lady who had walked alone°
  bent over me. "Hold fast!" she said, "Hold fast!"
She had drawn me into the stream up to my throat,
  and pulling me behind her, she sped on   95
  over the water, light as any boat.
Nearing the sacred bank, I heard her say
  in tones so sweet I cannot call them back,

---

¹ *other side:* Of Lethe. But also the other side of the immortal
life, i.e., still living. ¹¹ *waters:* Of Lethe. ¹⁸ *diminished blow:*
The figure is a bit confusing. Dante seems to say that the bolt
(corresponding to an arrow) of a crossbow strikes the target with
less force when the bow snaps. He does not stop to consider that
the bolt may miss the target entirely. Nevertheless, the intent of
his figure is clear enough. ²⁵ *moats ... chain-lenghts:* These were,
of course, defensive military measures. The moats guarded castles. The chains were strung to block roads, bridges, and gates.
⁴² *grindstone ... blade:* Turning the grindstone away from the
blade sharpens it. Turning it back against the blade dulls it. Thus
Beatrice is saying that when a soul openly confesses in true
repentance what could not in any case be hidden from God, the
sword of Justice is blunted, i.e., no longer cuts as deeply.

---

⁵⁹ *love of a maid:* Dante mentions another maiden in some of his
songs but in an indefinite way. No specific reference can be
attached to these words. ⁶² *nets:* Sometimes used for trapping
birds. ⁶⁹ *cause for misery:* The sight of her accompanied by the
guilty knowledge that he had turned away from so much beauty and perfection. ⁸¹ *beast ... division:* The Griffon. He is the
masque of Christ and represents His two aspects as man and
God. ⁸³ *first-self:* Her mortal self. ⁹² *lady ... alone:* Matilda,
who appears in Canto XXVIII, having been foreshadowed by
Leah in Dante's dream (Canto XXVII). She may be taken to
symbolize the Active Life of the Soul.

much less describe them here: "*Asperges me*."°
Then the sweet lady took my head between   *100*
    her open arms, and embracing me, she dipped me
    and made me drink the waters that make clean.
Then raising me in my new purity
    she led me to the dance of the Four Maidens;°
    each raised an arm and so joined hands above me. *105*
"Here we are nymphs; stars are we in the skies.
    Ere Beatrice went to earth we were ordained
    her handmaids. We will lead you to her eyes;
but that your own may see what joyous light
    shines in them, yonder Three,° who see more
      deeply,
    will sharpen and instruct your mortal sight." *111*
Thus they sang, then led me to the Griffon.
    Behind him, Beatrice waited. And when I stood
    at the Griffon's breast, they said in unison:
"Look deep, look well, however your eyes may
      smart
    We have led you now before those emeralds° *116*
    from which Love shot his arrows through your heart."
A thousand burning passions, every one
    hotter than any flame, held my eyes fixed
    to the lucent eyes she held fixed on the Griffon. *120*
Like sunlight in a glass the twofold creature
    shone from the deep reflection of her eyes,
    now in the one, now in the other nature.
Judge, reader, if I found it passing strange
    to see the thing unaltered in itself *125*
    yet in its image working change on change.
And while my soul in wonder and delight
    was savouring that food which in itself
    both satisfies and quickens appetite,°
the other Three, whose bearing made it clear *130*
    they were of higher rank, came toward me dancing
    to the measure of their own angelic air.
"Turn, Beatrice, oh turn the eyes of grace,"
    was their refrain, "upon your faithful one
    who comes so far to look upon your face. *135*
Grant us this favor of your grace: reveal
    your mouth to him, and let his eyes behold
    the Second Beauty,° which your veils conceal."
O splendor of the eternal living light!

who that has drunk deep of Parnassus' waters,° *140*
    or grown pale in the shadow of its height,
would not, still, feel his burdened genius fail
    attempting to describe in any tongue
    how you appeared when you put by your veil
in that free air open to heaven and earth *145*
    whose harmony is your shining shadowed forth!

PARADISO

CANTO I

The Earthly Paradise   The Invocation   Ascent to Heaven   The Sphere of Fire, The Music of the Spheres

Dante states his supreme theme as Paradise itself and invokes the aid not only of the Muses but of Apollo.

    Dante and Beatrice are in the Earthly Paradise, the Sun is at the Vernal Equinox, it is noon at Purgatory and midnight at Jerusalem when Dante sees Beatrice turn her eyes to stare straight into the sun and reflexively imitates her gesture. At once it is as if a second sun had been created, its light dazzling his senses, and Dante feels the ineffable change of his mortal soul into Godliness.

    These phenomena are more than his senses can grasp, and Beatrice must explain to him what he himself has not realized: that he and Beatrice are soaring toward the height of Heaven at an incalculable speed.

    Thus Dante climaxes the master metaphor in which purification is equated to weightlessness. Having purged all dross from his soul he mounts effortlessly, without even being aware of it at first, to his natural goal in the Godhead. So they pass through the Sphere of Fire, and so Dante first hears the Music of the Spheres.

The glory of Him who moves all things rays forth
    through all the universe, and is reflected
    from each thing in proportion to its worth.
I have been in that Heaven of His most light,
    and what I saw, those who descend from there *5*
    lack both the knowledge and the power to write.
For as our intellect draws near its goal
    it opens to such depths of understanding
    as memory cannot plumb within the soul.
Nevertheless, whatever portion time *10*
    still leaves me of the treasure of that kingdom
    shall now become the subject of my rhyme.
O good Apollo,° for this last task, I pray
    you make me such a vessel of your powers
    as you deem worthy to be crowned with bay.° *15*
One peak of cleft Parnassus heretofore
    has served my need, now must I summon both°

---

99 *"Asperges me": Asperges me hyssopo, et mundabor; lavabis me, et super nivem dealbabor.* ("Purge me with hyssop, and I shall be clean; wash me, and I shall be whiter than snow.") Psalms li, 7. These are the words the priest utters when he sprinkles holy water over the confessed sinner to absolve him. 104 *Four Maidens:* The Four Cardinal Virtues: Justice, Prudence, Fortitude, and Temperance. In their present manifestation they are nymphs. In another manifestation they are the four stars Dante saw above him when he arrived at the base of the mountain. (I, 23, note.) 110 *Three:* The Theological Virtues: Faith, Hope, and Charity (i.e., Caritas). 116 *emeralds:* The eyes of Beatrice. Dante may have intended to describe them as green (hazel) but more likely his choice of words here is meant only to signify "jewel bright". Green is, of course, the color of Hope, and an allegorical significance may be implied in that. 129 *satisfies and quickens appetite:* "They that eat me shall yet be hungry, and they that drink me shall yet be thirsty." (Ecclesiasticus, xxiv, 21.) 138 *Second beauty:* The smile of Beatrice (Divine Love). Dante was led to the First Beauty by the Four Cardinal Virtues. Now the Three Theological Virtues, as higher beings, lead him to the second, and higher, beauty, which is the joy of Divine Love in receiving the purified soul.

---

140 *Parnassus' waters:* The fountain of Castalia. To drink from it is to receive poetic gifts. To grow pale in the shadow of Parnassus signifies to labor at mastering the art of poetry. 13 *Apollo:* The God of Poetry, and the father of the Muses. Note, too, that Apollo is identified with the Sun and that Dante has consistently used the Sun as a symbol for God. 15 *bay:* The laurel wreath awarded to poets and conquerors. 17 *both:* Parnassus has two peaks: Nisa, which was sacred to the Muses; and Cyrrha, which was sacred to Apollo. Heretofore Nisa has been enough for Dante's need, but for this last canticle he must summon aid from both peaks (i.e., from all the Muses and from Apollo as well).

on entering the arena one time more.
Enter my breast, I pray you, and there breathe
   as high a strain as conquered Marsyas   *20*
   that time you drew his body from its sheath.°
O power divine, but lend to my high strain
   so much as will make clear even the shadow
   of that High Kingdom stamped upon my brain,
and you shall see me come to your dear grove°   *25*
   to crown myself with those green leaves which you
   and my high theme shall make me worthy of.
So seldom are they gathered, Holy Sire,
   to crown an emperor's or a poet's triumph
   (oh fault and shame of mortal man's desire!)   *30*
that the glad Delphic god must surely find
   increase of joy in the Peneian frond°
   when any man thirsts for it in his mind.
Great flames are kindled where the small sparks fly.
   So after me, perhaps, a better voice   *35*
   shall raise such prayers that Cyrrha° will reply.
The lamp of the world rises to mortal view
   from various stations, but that point which joins
   four circles with three crosses, it soars through
to a happier course in happier conjunction   *40*
   wherein it warms and seals the wax of the world
   closer to its own nature and high function.°
That glad conjunction had made it evening here
   and morning there; the south was all alight,
   while darkness rode the northern hemisphere;   *45*
when I saw Beatrice had turned left to raise
   her eyes up to the sun; no eagle ever
   stared at its shining with so fixed a gaze.°

---

²¹ *body from its sheath:* The satyr Marsyas challenged Apollo to a singing contest and was defeated. Ovid (*Metamorphoses*, VI, 382–400) recounts in gory detail how Apollo thereupon punished him by pulling him out of his skin leaving all the uncovered organs still functioning. ²⁵ *groves:* In which grows the sacred laurel, or bay. ³² *Peneian frond:* The laurel or bay, so called for Daphne, daughter of the river god Peneus. Cupid, to avenge a taunt, fired an arrow of love into Apollo and an arrow of aversion into Daphne. Fleeing from the inflamed Apollo, Daphne prayed to her father and was changed into a laurel tree. *The glad Delphic god:* Apollo. ³⁶ *Cyrrha:* Apollo's sacred peak, here taken for Apollo himself. If Apollo does not heed his prayer, Dante will at least show the way, and perhaps a better poet will come after him and have his prayer answered by Apollo, whereby Paradise will at last be well portrayed. ³⁷⁻⁴² *lamp … function:* Short of pages of diagrams, there is no way of explaining Dante's astronomical figure in detail. A quick gloss must do: *The Lamp:* The sun. *Various stations:* various points on the celestial horizon from which the sun rises at various times of the year. *Four circles with three crosses:* The four circles here intended are: (1) the celestial horizon, (2) the celestial equator, (3) the ecliptic, and (4) equinoxial colure—the great circle drawn through both poles and the two equinoxial points. When the sun is in this position, the time is sunrise of the vernal equinox and all four circles meet, each of the other three forming a cross with the celestial horizon. Astrologers took this to be a particularly auspicious conjunction. Its *happier course* (line 40) brings the brighter and longer days of summer. Its *happier conjunction* (line 40) with the stars of Aries brings it back to the sign of the first creation (see *Inferno* I, 38–39, note). And certainly the fact that the diagram forms three crosses would weigh it with the good omens of both the cross and trinity. All would once more be in God's shaping hand. So the *wax of the world* (line 41) is warmed and sealed, in a first sense by the warmth of approaching summer, and in a clearly implicit spiritual sense by the favor of God's will upon His creation. ⁴⁷⁻⁴⁸ *eagle … gaze:* In the Middle Ages men believed that the eagle was able to stare directly into the sun.

And as a ray descending from the sky
   gives rise to another, which climbs back again,   *50*
   as a pilgrim yearns for home; so through my eye
her action, like a ray into my mind,
   gave rise to mine: I stared into the sun
   so hard that here it would have left me blind;
but much is granted to our senses there,   *55*
   in that garden made to be man's proper place,
   that is not granted us when we are here.
I had to look away soon, and yet not
   so soon but what I saw him spark and blaze
   like new-tapped iron when it pours white-hot.   *60*
And suddenly, as it appeared to me,
   day was added to day, as if He who can
   had added a new sun to Heaven's glory.
Beatrice stared at the eternal spheres
   entranced, unmoving; and I looked away   *65*
   from the sun's height to fix my eyes on hers.
And as I looked, I felt begin within me
   what Glaucus felt eating the herb that made him
   a god among the others in the sea.°
How speak trans-human change to human sense?   *70*
   Let the example speak until God's grace
   grants the pure spirit the experience.
Whether I rose in only the last created
   part of my being,° O Love that rulest Heaven
   Thou knowest, by whose lamp I was translated.   *75*
When the Great Wheel that spins eternally
   in longing for Thee,° captured my attention
   by that harmony attuned and heard by Thee,
I saw ablaze with sun from side to side
   a reach of Heaven:° not all the rains and rivers   *80*
   of all of time could make a sea so wide.
That radiance and that new-heard melody
   fired me with such yearning for their Cause
   as I had never felt before. And she
who saw my every thought as well as I,   *85*
   saw my perplexity: before I asked
   my question she had started her reply,
Thus she began: "You dull your own perceptions
   with false imaginings and do not grasp
   what would be clear but for your preconceptions.   *90*
You think you are still on earth: the lightning's spear
   never fled downward from its natural place
   as rapidly as you are riding there."
I grasped her brief and smiling words and shed
   my first perplexity, but found myself   *95*
   entangled in another, and I said:

---

⁶⁸⁻⁶⁹ *Glaucus … sea:* The fisherman Glaucus, noting how his catch revived and leaped into the sea after being laid upon a certain herb, ate some of it and was transformed into a god (Ovid, *Metamorphoses*, XIII, 898–968). ⁷⁴ *part of my being:* The soul, which is created after the body, (see *Purgatorio*, XXV, 37–75.) *O Love that rulest Heaven:* God. *Whose lamp:* Beatrice as the reflector of God's love. ⁷⁶⁻⁷⁸ *Great Wheel … Thee:* Dante says, literally: "The wheel that Thou, in being desired (i.e., loved) by it, makest eternal." The Great Wheel is the Primum Mobile, its motion deriving from the love of God. *That harmony:* the Music of the Spheres. ⁸⁰ *reach of Heaven:* Dante believed that the earth's atmosphere extended as high as the Sphere of the Moon. Beyond the Moon is another atmosphere of fire. This sphere of fire was believed to cause lightning. (See also line 115, "the fire about the moon.")

"My mind, already recovered from the surprise
   of the great marvel you have just explained,
   is now amazed anew: how can I rise
in my gross body through such aery substance?"   *100*
   She sighed in pity and turned as might a mother
   to a delirious child. "The elements
of all things," she began, "whatever their mode,
   observe an inner order. It is this form
   that makes the universe resemble God.   *105*
In this the higher creatures see the hand
   of the Eternal Worth, which is the goal
   to which these norms conduce, being so planned.
All Being within this order, by the laws
   of its own nature is impelled to find   *110*
   its proper station round its Primal Cause.
Thus every nature moves across the tide
   of the great sea of being to its own port,
   each with its given instinct as its guide.
This instinct draws the fire about the moon.   *115*
   It is the mover in the mortal heart.
   It draws the earth together and makes it one.
Not only the brute creatures, but all those
   possessed of intellect and love, this instinct
   drives to their mark as a bow shoots forth its
      arrows.
The Providence that makes all things hunger here   *121*
   satisfies forever with its light
   the heaven within which whirls the fastest sphere.°
And to it now, as to a place foretold,
   are we two soaring, driven by that bow   *125*
   whose every arrow finds a mark of gold.
It is true that oftentimes the form of a thing
   does not matter being deaf to summoning—
just so, the creature sometimes travels wide   *130*
   of this true course, for even when so driven
   it still retains the power to turn aside
(exactly as we may see the heavens' fire
   plunge from a cloud) and its first impulse may
   be twisted earthward by false desire.   *135*
You should not, as I see it, marvel more
   at your ascent than at a river's fall
   from a high mountain to the valley floor.
If you, free as you are of every dross,
   had settled and had come to rest below,   *140*
   that would indeed have been as marvelous
as still flame there in the mortal plain."
So saying, she turned her eyes to Heaven again.

CANTO **XXXI**

The Empyrean   The Mystic Rose, The Angel Host, Beatrice Leaves Dante, St. Bernard

The second soldiery of the Church Triumphant is the Angel Host, and Dante now receives a vision of them as a swarm of bees in eternal transit between God and the Rose.

Dante turns from that rapturous vision to speak to Beatrice and finds in her place a reverend elder. It is St. Bernard, who will

serve as Dante's guide to the ultimate vision of God. Bernard shows Dante his last vision of Beatrice, who has resumed her throne among the blessed. Across the vastness of Paradise, Dante sends his soul's prayer of thanks to her. Beatrice smiles down at Dante a last time, then turns her eyes forever to the eternal Fountain of God.

Bernard, the most faithful of the worshippers of the Virgin, promises Dante the final vision of God through the Virgin's intercession. Accordingly, he instructs Dante to raise his eyes to her throne. Dante obeys and burns with bliss at the vision of her splendor.

Then, in the form of a white rose, the host
   of the sacred soldiery° appeared to me,
   all those whom Christ in his own blood espoused.
But the other host (who soar, singing and seeing
   his glory, who to will them to his love   *5*
   made them so many in such blissful being,
like a swarm of bees who in one motion dive
   into the flowers, and in the next return
   the sweetness of their labors to the hive)
flew ceaselessly to the many-petaled rose   *10*
   and ceaselessly returned into that light
   in which their ceaseless love has its repose.
Like living flame their faces seemed to glow.°
   their wings were gold. And all their bodies shone°
   more dazzling white than any earthly snow.   *15*
On entering the great flower they spread about them,
   from tier to tier, the ardor and the peace
   they had acquired in flying close to Him.
Nor did so great a multitude in flight
   between the white rose and what lies above it   *20*
   block in the least the glory of that light;
for throughout all the universe God's ray
   enters all things according to their merit,
   and nothing has the power to block its way.
This realm of ancient bliss shone, soul on soul,   *25*
   with new and ancient beings, and every eye
   and every love was fixed upon one goal.
O Threefold Light which, blazoned in one star,
   can so content their vision with your shining,
   look down upon us in the storm we are!   *30*
If the barbarians (coming from the zone

° *sacred soldiery:* In XXX, 43 Beatrice promised that Dante would see both hosts of Paradise. The first host is of the sacred soldiery, those who were once mortal and who were redeemed by Christ. They are seated upon the thrones of the Mystic Rose in which are gathered eternally the essences of all those heavenly souls that manifested themselves to Dante in the various spheres below, moved by *caritas* to reveal themselves to Dante at the various levels of his developing understanding. How these souls could be eternally with the Rose while yet manifesting themselves to Dante in the various spheres is, of course, one of the mysteries to be grasped only by revelation. The essential point is that Dante becomes better able to see; the vision of Heaven unfolds to him ever more clearly and ever more profoundly. The second soldiery is of the angels who never left heaven. They soar above the Rose like Heavenly bees, in constant motion between the Rose and the radiance of God. Unlike earthly bees, however, it is from God, the mystical hive of grace, that they bring the sweetness to the flower, bearing back to God, of course, the bliss of the souls of Heaven. (See lines 16–18.) The first host is more emphatically centered on the aspect of God as the Son; the second, on the aspect of God as the Father.   ¹³ *faces seemed to glow:* See the vision of God and Heaven in Ezekiel, I, 14 ff.   ¹⁴ *wings … shone:* See the similar vision in Daniel, x, 4 ff.

---

¹²³ *fastest sphere:* The Primum Mobile.

above which Helice° travels every day
    wheeling in heaven with her beloved son)
Looking at Rome, were stupefied to see
    her works in those days when the Lateran°   *35*
    outshone all else built by humanity;
What did I feel on reaching such a goal
    from human to blest, from time to eternity,
    from Florence to a people just and whole°
By what amazement was I overcome?   *40*
    between my stupor and my new-found joy
    my bliss was to hear nothing and be dumb.
And as a pilgrim at the shrine of his vow
    stares, feels himself reborn, and thinks already
    how he may later describe it°—just so now   *45*
I stood and let my eyes go wandering out
    into that radiance from rank to rank,
    now up, now down, now sweeping round about.
I saw faces that compelled love's charity
    lit by Another's lamp and their own smiles,   *50*
    and gestures graced by every dignity.
Without having fixed on any part, my eyes
    already had taken in and understood
    the form and general plan of Paradise:
And—my desire rekindled—I wheeled about   *55*
    to question my sweet lady on certain matters
    concerning which my mind was still in doubt.
One thing I expected; another greeted me:
    I thought to find Beatrice there; I found instead
    an elder° in the robes of those in glory.   *60*
His eyes and cheeks were bathed in the holy glow
    of loving bliss; his gestures, pious grace.
    he seemed a tender father standing so.
"She—where is she?" I cried in sudden dread.
    "To lead you to the goal of all your wish   *65*
    Beatrice called me from my place," he said;
"And if you raise your eyes you still may find her

in the third circle down° from the highest rank
    upon the throne her merit has assigned her."
Without reply I looked up to that height   *70*
    and saw her draw an aureole round herself
    as she reflected the Eternal Light.
No mortal eye, though plunged to the last bounds
    of the deepest sea, has ever been so far
    from the topmost heaven to which the thunder
        sounds
as I was then from Beatrice; but there   *76*
    the distance did not matter, for her image
    reached me unblurred by any atmosphere.
"O lady in whom my hope shall ever soar
    and who for my salvation suffered even   *80*
    to set your feet upon Hell's broken floor,°
through your power and your excellence alone
    have I recognized the goodness and the grace
    inherent in the things I have been shown.
You have led me from my bondage and set me free *85*
    by all those roads, by all those loving means
    that lay within your power and charity.
Grant me your magnificence that my soul,
    which you have healed, may please you when it slips
    the bonds of flesh and rises to its goal."   *90*
Such was my prayer, and she—far up a mountain,
    as it appeared to me—looked down and smiled.
    then she turned back to the Eternal Fountain.
And the holy Elder said: "I have been sent
    by prayer and sacred love to help you reach   *95*
    the perfect consummation of your ascent.
Look round this garden, therefore, that you may
    by gazing at its radiance, be prepared
    to lift your eyes up to the Trinal Ray.
The Queen of Heaven, for whom in whole devotion *100*
    I burn with love, will grant us every grace
    because I am Bernard, her faithful one."
As a stranger afar—a Croat,° if you will—
    comes to see our Veronica,° and awed
    by its ancient fame, can never look his fill,   *105*
But says to himself as long as it is displayed:
    "My Lord, Jesus Christ, true God, and is this then
    the likeness of thy living flesh portrayed?"—
just so did I gaze on the living love
    of him who in this world, through contemplation, *110*

---

³² *Helice:* The nymph Helice (I am afraid the reader will have to Anglicize her name as HEL-ees [to fit the meter]) attracted Zeus and was turned into a bear by jealous Hera. Zeus translated his nymph to heaven as Ursa Major, the constellation of the Great Bear which contains the Big Dipper. Arcas, her son by Zeus, was translated to Ursa Minor, within which he forms the Little Dipper. The two dippers, being near the pole, are always above the horizon in the northland, the zone from which the barbarians came. ³⁵ *Lateran:* Today a section of old Rome. Here Dante uses it to signify Rome in general. ³⁹ *Florence ... whole:* This is Dante's last mention of Florence. Note that Florence has not improved but that on the universal scale it has become too insignificant for the sort of denunciation he once heaped upon it. ⁴⁵ *later describe it:* It was a custom of the pious, as thanks for an answered prayer, to win forgiveness of sins, or as a testimony of faith, to vow a journey to a stated shrine or temple. Such pilgrimages were often dangerous. Travel was rare in the Middle Ages, and the pilgrim returned from far shrines was much sought after for the hopefully miraculous, and in any case rare, news he brought back. How could Dante, having traveled to the Infinite Summit, fail to think ahead to the way he would speak his vision to mankind? ⁶⁰ *an elder:* St. Bernard (1090-1153), the famous Abbot of Clairvaux, a contemplative mystic and author. Under him the Cistercian Order (a branch of the Benedictines with a stricter rule than the original order) flourished and spread. All Cistercian monasteries are especially dedicated to the Virgin, and St. Bernard is particularly identified with her worship.

⁶⁸ *third circle down:* In the Mystic Rose, Mary sits in the topmost tier, Eve directly below her, Rachel (the Contemplative Life) below Eve. Beatrice sits to the right of Rachel. In Dante, of course, every mention of three must suggest trinity, but the reader is left to decide for himself the significance of the Mary-Eve-Rachel trinity. ⁸¹ *set ... floor:* As she did when she descended to Limbo (as, of course, a manifestation) to summon Virgil. ¹⁰³ *Croat:* Probably used here in a generic sense to signify the native of any far-off Christian land, but Croatia, aside from lying at one of the [then] outer limits of Christianity, was also known for the ardor of its religious belief. ¹⁰⁴ *Veronica:* From *vera icon*, the true image. Certainly the most famous relic in St. Peter's, the Veronica was the handkerchief of the faithful follower ever after known as St. Veronica. She gave it to Jesus to wipe the blood from His face on the road to Calvary, and what was believed to be the true likeness of Jesus was believed to have appeared on what was believed to be the cloth in what was believed to be His own blood.

tasted the peace which ever dwells above.°
"Dear son of Grace," he said, "you cannot know
    this state of bliss while you yet keep your eyes
    fixed only on those things that lie below;
rather, let your eyes mount to the last round   *115*
    where you shall see the Queen to whom this realm
    is subject and devoted, throned and crowned."
I looked up: by as much as the horizon
    to eastward in the glory of full dawn
    outshines the point at which the sun went down.° *120*
By so much did one region on the height
    to which I raised my eyes out of the valley
    outshine the rays of every other light.
And as the sky is brightest in that region
    where we on earth expect to see the shaft   *125*
    of the chariot so badly steered by Phaeton,
While to one side and the other it grows dim—
    just so that peaceful oriflamme lit the center
    and faded equally along either rim.°
And in the center, great wings spread apart,   *130*
    more than a thousand festive angels shone,
    each one distinct in radiance and in art.°
I saw there, smiling at this song and sport,
    her whose beauty entered like a bliss
    into the eyes of all that sainted court.   *135*
And even could my speech match my conception,
    yet I would not dare make the least attempt
    to draw her delectation and perfection.
Bernard, seeing my eyes so fixed and burning
    with passion on his passion, turned his own   *140*
    up to that height with so much love and yearning
That the example of his ardor sent
    New fire through me, making my gaze more ardent.

Canto XXXII

The Empyrean   St. Bernard, The Virgin Mary, The Thrones of the Blessed

His eyes fixed blissfully on the vision of the Virgin Mary, Bernard recites the orders of the Mystic Rose, identifying the thrones of the most blessed.

    Mary's Throne is on the topmost tier of the Heavenly Stadium. Directly across from it rises the Throne of John the Baptist. From her throne to the central arena (the Yellow of the Rose) descends a Line of Christian Saints. These two radii form a diameter that divides the stadium. On one side are throned Those Who Believed in Christ to Come; on the other, Those who Believed in Christ Descended. The lower half of the Rose contains, on one side, the Pre-Christian Children Saved by Love, and on the other, the Christian Children Saved by Baptism.

    Through all these explanations, Bernard has kept his eyes fixed in adoration upon the Virgin Having finished his preliminary instruction of Dante, Bernard now calls on him to join in a Prayer to the Virgin.

Still rapt in contemplation,° the sainted seer
    assumed the vacant office of instruction,
    beginning with these words I still can hear:
"The wound that Mary healed with balm so sweet
    was first dealt and then deepened by that being   *5*
    who sits in such great beauty at her feet.°
Below her, in the circle sanctified
    by the third rank of loves, Rachel is throned
    with Beatrice, as you see, there at her side.
Sarah° and Rebecca and Judith and she°   *10*
    who was the great-grandmother of the singer
    who for his sins cried, 'Lord, have mercy on me!'—
As I go down the great ranks tier by tier,
    naming them for you in descending order,
    petal by petal, you shall see them clear.   *15*
And down from the seventh, continuing from those
    in the first six tiers, a line of Hebrew women
    forms a part in the tresses of the rose.°
Arranged to form a wall thus, they divide
    all ranks according to the view of Christ   *20*
    that marked the faith of those on either side.
On this side, where the flower is in full bloom°
    to its last petal, are arranged all those
    whose faith was founded upon Christ to Come;
on that, where the half circles show the unblended   *25*
    gaps of empty seats, are seated those
    whose living faith was fixed on Christ Descended.
And as, on this side, the resplendent throne
    of Heaven's Lady, with the thrones below it,
    establishes the line of that division;   *30*
so, facing hers, does the throned blessedness

---

111 *tasted ... above:* According to legend, Bernard was rewarded for his holiness by being permitted a vision of Heaven's blessedness while he was yet on earth. 118-20 *horizon ... went down:* The comparison is not, as careless readers sometimes take it to be, between a dawn and a sunset (whose brightnesses would be approximately equal) but between the eastern and western horizons at dawn. Bright as Heaven is, Mary outshines it as the east outshines the west at daybreak. 125-29 *shaft ... rim:* The shaft of the chariot of the Sun would project ahead of the horses. It would, therefore, be the first point of light of the new dawn, that moment when light glows on the eastern rim while the horizon to north and south is still dark. Thus Mary not only outshines all heaven as the east at daybreak outshines the west, but even at the uppermost tier of the blessed, those radiances at either side of her are dim by comparison. 132 *art:* Motion. No two angel beings are exactly equal in their brightness, nor in the speed of their flight. These festive angels are, of course, another manifestation of the Angel Hierarchy.

1-3 *contemplation:* Of the Virgin. His eyes have not left her. Nor do they turn again to Dante. *The vacant office of instruction:* formerly held by Beatrice. *I still can hear:* a rhyme-forced addition, not in Dante's text. 4-6 *wound ... feet:* Mary, Mother of God, sits in the uppermost tier. At her feet in the second tier sits Eve, Mother of Man. *The wound:* original sin. *Balm so sweet:* Jesus. *Dealt:* the first fault, Eve's disobedience. *Deepened:* her seduction of Adam, thus spreading sin to all mankind. *In such great beauty:* Eve, having been created directly by God, was perfect in her beauty. 10 *Sarah:* Wife of Abraham. Hebrews, xi, 11-14, cites her as the mother (by miraculous fertility in her old age) of the Jews who foresaw Christ's coming and believed in him. *Rebecca:* wife of Isaac. *Judith:* She killed Holofernes and freed the Jews. 10-12 *she ... on me!:* Ruth, great-grandmother of David ("the singer"). *Who for his sins:* his lust for Bathsheba, wife of Uriah. In order to marry Bathsheba, David sent Uriah to his death in the first line of battle. David's lament is in Psalm 1. 18 *tresses of the rose:* As if the rose were a head of hair and that vertical row of Hebrew women formed a part in it. In the next line the part becomes a wall. 22 *full bloom:* That half of the rose-stadium that holds the pre-Christian believers would naturally be completely filled. On the other side there are thrones waiting for those who have yet to win salvation through Christ Descended. Dante, in fact, is laboring to earn one of them for himself. The Day of Judgment will be upon mankind when the last throne is filled, for Heaven will then be complete.

424 → CHAPTER 12

of the Great John° who, ever holy, bore
 the desert, martyrdom, and Hell's distress;
and under him, forming that line are found
 Francis, Benedict, Augustine,° and others *35*
 descending to this center round by round.
Now marvel at all-foreseeing profundity:
 this garden shall be complete when the two aspects
 of the one faith have filled it equally.
And know that below that tier that cuts the two *40*
 dividing walls at their centerpoint, no being
 has won his seat of glory by his own virtue,
but by another's, under strict condition;
 for all of these were spirits loosed from flesh
 before they had matured to true volition.° *45*
You can yourself make out their infant graces:
 you need no more than listen to their treble
 and look attentively into their faces.
You do not speak now: many doubts confound you.°
 Therefore, to set you free I shall untie *50*
 the cords in which your subtle thoughts have bound
  you.
Infinite order rules in this domain.
 Mere accidence can no more enter in
 than hunger can, or thirst, or grief, or pain.
All you see here is fixed by the decree *55*
 of the eternal law, and is so made
 that the ring goes on the finger perfectly.
These, it follows, who had so short a pause
 in the lower life are not ranked higher or lower
 among themselves without sufficient cause. *60*
The king in whom this realm abides unchanging
 in so much love and bliss that none dares will
 increase of joy, creating and arranging
the minds of all in the glad Paradise
 of His own sight, grants them degrees of grace *65*
 as He sees fit. Here let the effect suffice.°
Holy Scripture clearly and expressly
 notes this effect upon those twins who fought
 while still within their mother.° So we see

how the Supreme Light fittingly makes fair *70*
 its aureole by granting them their graces
 according to the color of their hair.°
Thus through no merit of their works and days
 they are assigned their varying degrees
 by variance only in original grace. *75*
In the first centuries of man's creation
 their innocence and the true faith of their parents
 was all they needed to achieve salvation.
When the first age of man had run its course,
 then circumcision was required of males, *80*
 to give their innocent wings sufficient force.
But when the age of grace came to mankind
 then, unless perfectly baptized in Christ,
 such innocents went down among the blind.°
Look now on her who most resembles Christ,° *85*
 for only the great glory of her shining
 can purify your eyes to look on Christ."
I saw such joy rain down upon that face°—
 borne to it by those blest Intelligences
 created thus to span those heights of space— *90*
that through all else on the long road I trod
 nothing had held my soul so fixed in awe,
 nor shown me such resemblances to God.
The self-same Love that to her first descended°
 singing *"Ave Maria, gratia plena"* *95*
 stood before her with its wings extended.
Thus rang the holy chant to Heaven's Queen
 and all the blessed court joined in the song,
 and singing, every face grew more serene.
"O holy Father, who endures for me *100*
 the loss of being far from the sweet place
 where fate has raised your throne eternally,
who is that angel who with such desire
 gazes into the eyes of our sweet Queen,
 so rapt in love he seems to be afire?" *105*
Thus did I seek instruction from that Great One
 who drew the beauty of his light from Mary
 as the morning star draws beauty from the sun.
And he: "As much as angel or soul can know
 of exultation, gallantry, and poise *110*
 there is in him; and we would have it so,
for it was he who brought the victory°
 to Mary when the Son of God had willed
 to bear the weight of human misery.
But let your eyes go where my words point out *115*
 among this court, and note the mighty peers
 of the empire of the just and the devout.
Those two whose bliss it is to sit so close
 to the radiance of the Empress of All Joy
 are the two eternal roots of this our rose:° *120*

---

³² *Great John:* The Baptist. He denounced Herod Antipos and was beheaded two years before the Crucifixion. He had to wait in Limbo for two years, therefore, till Christ came for him at the Resurrection. ³⁵ *Francis, Benedict, Augustine:* St. Francis of Assisi (1181?–1226), founder of the Franciscan order; St. Benedict (ca. 480–ca. 547), founder of the Benedictine Order; St. Augustine (354–430). ⁴⁵ *before … volition:* The lower half of the rose-stadium contains the blessed infants, the souls of those who died before they had achieved the true volition of reason and faith. Salvation is granted them not directly through belief in Christ but through the faith and prayers of their parents, relatives, and others of the faithful who interceded for them. ⁴⁹ *many doubts confound you:* The infants are ranked in tiers that indicate degrees of heavenly merit. But if they were saved through no merit of their own, how can one be more worthy than the other? Such is Dante's doubt, which Bernard goes on to set at rest by telling him, in essence, that God knows what He is doing. ⁶⁶ *let the effect suffice:* The cause is buried in God's mind. The effect must speak for itself. ⁶⁸⁻⁶⁹ *twins … mother:* Jacob and Esau. According to Genesis, xvx, 21 ff., they were at odds while still in their mother's womb. (Cf. the legend of Polyneices and Eteocles, twin sons of Oedipus and Jocasta.) Dante follows St. Paul (Romans, ix, 11–13) in interpreting the division between Jacob and Esau as a working of God's unfathomable will. "Even as it is written Jacob I loved, but Esau I hated." Man can note the will of God in such matters ("the effect") but cannot plumb its causes.

⁷² *According … hair:* For what may seem to be superficial reasons. Esau (Genesis, xxv, 25) was red-headed. ⁸⁴ *among the blind:* Among the souls of Hell. Such infants were assigned to Limbo. ⁸⁵ *who most resembles Christ:* The Virgin Mary. ⁸⁸ *face:* Mary's. ⁹⁴ *Love … descended:* The archangel Gabriel, the Angel of the Annunciation. Dante seems to conceive of Gabriel suspended in air before her, repeating the blissful chant of the Annunciation as he had first hymned it in Nazareth. ¹¹² *victory:* (Dante says "the palm.") Of God's election that she bear the promised Messiah. ¹²⁰ *two … rose:* Adam and St. Peter. Adam as Father of Mankind, Peter as Father of the Church. Note that Peter has the place of honor on the right.

the one just to the left of her blessedness
    is the father whose unruly appetite
    left man the taste for so much bitterness;
and on her right, that ancient one you see
    is the father of Holy Church to whom Christ
        gave
    the twin keys to this flower of timeless beauty.   *126*
And that one who in his prophetic sight
    foretold the evil days of the Sweet Bride
    won by the spear and nails,° sits on his right.
While by the other father and first man   *130*
    sits the great leader to whom manna fell
    to feed an ingrate and rebellious clan.°
Across the circle from Peter, behold Anna.°
    She feels such bliss in looking at her daughter
    she does not move her eyes to sing 'Hosanna!'   *135*
And opposite the father of us all
    sits Lucy,° who first urged your lady to you
    when you were blindly bent toward your own fall.
But the time allowed for this dream vision flies.
    As a tailor must cut the gown from what cloth is
        given,
    just so must we move on, turning our eyes   *141*
to the Primal Love, that as your powers advance
    with looking toward him, you may penetrate
    as deep as may be through His radiance.
But lest you should fall backward when you flare   *145*
    your mortal wings, intending to mount higher,
    remember grace must be acquired through prayer.
Therefore I will pray that blessed one°
    who has the power to aid you in your need.
    See that you follow me with such devotion   *150*
your heart adheres to every word I say."
And with those words the saint began to pray.

Canto **XXXIII**

The Empyrean   St. Bernard, Prayer to the Virgin, The Vision of God

St. Bernard offers a lofty prayer to the Virgin, asking her to intercede in Dante's behalf, and in answer Dante feels his soul swell with new power and grow calm in rapture as his eyes are permitted the direct vision of God.

    There can be no measure of how long the vision endures. It passes, and Dante is once more mortal and fallible. Raised by God's presence, he had looked into the Mystery and had begun to understand its power and majesty. Returned to himself, there is no power in him capable of speaking the truth of what he saw. Yet the impress of the truth is stamped upon his soul, which he now knows will return to be one with God's Love.

"Virgin Mother, daughter of thy son;
    humble beyond all creatures and more exalted;
    predestined turning point of God's intention;
thy merit so ennobled human nature
    that its divine Creator did not scorn   *5*
    to make Himself the creature of His creature.
The Love that was rekindled in thy womb
    sends forth the warmth of the eternal peace
    within whose ray this flower has come to bloom.
Here, to us, thou art the noon and scope   *10*
    of Love revealed; and among mortal men,
    the living fountain of eternal hope.
Lady, thou art so near God's reckonings
    that who seeks grace and does not first seek thee
    would have his wish fly upward without wings.   *15*
Not only does thy sweet benignity
    flow out to all who beg, but oftentimes
    thy charity arrives before the plea.
In thee is pity, in thee munificence,
    in thee the tenderest heart, in thee unites   *20*
    all that creation knows of excellence!
Now comes this man who from the final pit
    of the universe up to this height has seen,
    one by one, the three lives of the spirit.
He prays to thee in fervent supplication   *25*
    for grace and strength, that he may raise his eyes
    to the all-healing final revelation.
And I, who never more desired to see
    the vision myself than I do that he may see It,
    add my own prayer, and pray that it may be   *30*
enough to move you to dispel the trace
    of every mortal shadow by thy prayers
    and let him see revealed the Sum of Grace.
I pray thee further, all-persuading Queen,
    keep whole the natural bent of his affections°   *35*
    and of his powers after his eyes have seen.
Protect him from the stirrings of man's clay;°
    see how Beatrice and the blessed host
    clasp reverent hands to join me as I pray."
The eyes° that God reveres and loves the best   *40*
    glowed on the speaker, making clear the joy
    with which true prayer is heard by the most blest.
Those eyes turned then to the Eternal Ray,
    through which, we must indeed believe, the eyes
    of others do not find such ready way.   *45*
And I, who neared the goal of all my nature,
    felt my soul, at the climax of its yearning,
    suddenly, as it ought, grow calm with rapture.
Bernard then, smiling sweetly, gestured to me
    to look up, but I had already become   *50*
    within myself all he would have me be.

127-29 *that one ... nails:* St. John the Evangelist. His *Apocalypse* was received as the prophetic book in which the entire history of the Church is foretold. He sits on Peter's right. 131-132 *great leader ... clan:* Moses. 133-135 *Anna:* Ste. Anna, mother of the Virgin. Her position directly across the circle from Peter's puts her to the right of John the Baptist. *Does not move her eyes to sing 'Hosanna!':* Like all the other heavenly beings, she constantly sings the praise of God. All others, naturally enough, look up as they sing. She, however, is so filled with bliss by the sight of Mary that she does not turn her eyes from her blessed daughter. 137 *Lucy:* See *Inferno*, II, 97-100. It was she who first sent Beatrice to rescue Dante from the Dark Wood of Error. She sits opposite Adam. She would, accordingly, be to the left of John the Baptist. 148 *blessed one:* Mary.

---

35 *Keep ... affections:* Bernard is asking Mary to protect Dante lest the intensity of the vision overpower his faculties. 37 *Protect ... clay:* Protect him from the stirrings of base human impulse, especially from pride, for Dante is about to receive a grace never before granted to any man and the thought of such glory might well move a mere mortal to a hubris that would turn glory to sinfulness. 40 *eyes:* Of Mary.

Little by little as my vision grew
   it penetrated further through the aura
   of the high lamp which in Itself is true.°
What then I saw is more than tongue can say.   *55*
   Our human speech is dark before the vision.
   The ravished memory swoons and falls away.
As one who sees in dreams and wakes to find
   the emotional impression of his vision
   still powerful while its parts fade from his mind— *60*
just such am I, having lost nearly all
   the vision itself, while in my heart I feel
   the sweetness of it yet distill and fall.
So, in the sun, the footprints fade from snow.
   On the wild wind that bore the tumbling leaves *65*
   the Sybil's oracles were scattered so.°
O Light Supreme who doth Thyself withdraw
   so far above man's mortal understanding,
   lend me again some glimpse of what I saw;
make Thou my tongue so eloquent it may   *70*
   of all Thy glory speak a single clue
   to those who follow me in the world's day;
for by returning to my memory
   somewhat, and somewhat sounding in these verses,
   thou shalt show man more of Thy victory. *75*
So dazzling was the splendor of that Ray,
   that I must certainly have lost my senses
   had I, but for an instant, turned away°
And so it was, as I recall, I could
   the better bear to look, until at last   *80*
   my vision made one with the Eternal Good.
Oh grace abounding that had made me fit
   to fix my eyes on the eternal light
   until my vision was consumed in it!
I saw within Its depth how It conceives   *85*
   all things in a single volume bound by Love,
   of which the universe is the scattered leaves;
substance,° accident, and their relation
   so fused that all I say could do no more
   than yield a glimpse of that bright revelation. *90*
I think I saw the universal form
   that binds these things,° for as I speak these words
   I feel my joy swell and my spirits warm.
Twenty-five centuries since Neptune saw
   the Argo's keel have not moved all mankind, *95*
   recalling that adventure, to such awe
as I felt in an instant. My tranced being
   stared fixed and motionless upon that vision,

ever more fervent to see in the act of seeing.
Experiencing that Radiance, the spirit   *100*
   is so indrawn it is impossible
   even to think of ever turning form It.
For the good which is the will's ultimate object
   is all subsumed in It; and, being removed,
   all is defective which in It is perfect. *105*
Now in my recollection of the rest
   I have less power to speak than any infant
   wetting its tongue yet at its mother's breast;
and not because that Living Radiance bore
   more than one semblance, for It is unchanging *110*
   and is forever as it was before;
rather, as I grew worthier to see,
   the more I looked, the more unchanging semblance
   appeared to change with every change in me
within the depthless deep and clear existence *115*
   of that abyss of light three circles shown—
   three in color, one in circumference:
the second from the first, rainbow from rainbow;
   the third, an exhalation of pure fire
   equally breathed forth by the other two. *120*
But oh how much my words miss my conception,
   which is itself so far from what I saw
   that to call it feeble would be rank deception!
O Light Eternal fixed in Itself alone,
   by Itself alone understood, which from Itself *125*
   loves and glows, self-knowing and self-known;
that second aureole which shone forth in Thee,
   conceived as a reflection of the first—
   or which appeared so to my scrutiny—
seemed in Itself of Its own coloration   *130*
   to be painted with man's image. I fixed my eyes
   on that alone in rapturous contemplation.
Like a geometer wholly dedicated
   to squaring the circle, but who cannot find,
   think as he may, the principle indicated— *135*
so did I study the supernal face.
   I yearned to know just how our image merges
   into that circle, and how it there finds place;
but mine were not the wings for such a flight.
   Yet, as I wished, the truth I wished for came *140*
   cleaving my mind in a great flash of light.
Here my powers rest from their high fantasy,
   but already I could feel my being turned—
   instinct and intellect balanced equally
as in a wheel whose motion nothing jars— *145*
by the Love that moves the Sun and the other stars.

---

⁵⁴ *lamp … true:* The light of God is the one light whose source is Itself. All others are a reflection of this.   ⁶⁶ *Sybil's … so:* The Cumean Sybil (Virgil describes her in *Aeneid*, III, 441 ff.) wrote her oracles on leaves, one letter to a leaf, then sent her message scattering on the wind. Presumably, the truth as all contained in that strew, could one only gather all the leaves and put the letters in the right order.   ⁷⁷⁻⁷⁸ *That I … away:* How can a light be so dazzling that the beholder would swoon if he looked away for an instant? Would it not be, rather, in looking at, not away from, the overpowering vision that the viewer's senses would be overcome? So it would be on earth. But now Dante, with the help of all heaven's prayers, is in the presence of God and strengthened by all he sees. It is by being so strengthened that he can see yet more.   ⁸⁸ *Substance:* Matter, all that exists in itself. *Accident:* all that exists as a phase of matter.   ⁹² *these things:* Substance and accident.

✦ BOCCACCIO

from *The Decameron*

The two tales that follow reveal Boccaccio's interest in social mores, legal obligation, and human interaction. In the first tale a woman is at the center of the action in and out of bed. The story reflects fourteenth century Italian customs, including the importance of duty and law, and the legal subservience of women to men. The tale also emphasizes the courage and intelligence of women in the person of the aristocratic protagonist, who not only confesses to her crime of committing adultery, but who also questions the law under which she is to be sentenced. In the second tale, Boccaccio satirizes the behavior of Catholic monks, while portraying the subordinate monk's ingenuity in outsmarting his superior. Like the other tales of the Decameron, these position their author on the brink of new ways of looking at old realities.

First Day, Fourth Tale

… Having completed her story, Filomena fell silent and Dioneo, who was sitting close to her, without awaiting any further order from the Queen (for he realized by the order already begun that he was the next to speak), started speaking in the following manner:

Lovely ladies, if I have understood your intention correctly, we are here in order to amuse ourselves by telling stories, and therefore, as long as we do nothing contrary to this, I think that each one of us ought to be permitted (and just a moment ago our Queen said that we might) to tell whatever story he thinks is likely to be the most amusing. Therefore, having heard how the good advice of Giannotto di Civignì saved Abraham's soul and how Melchisdech defended his riches against the schemes of Saladin, I am going to tell you briefly, without fear of disapproval, how cleverly a monk saved his body from a most severe punishment.

In Lunigiana, a town not too far from here, there was a monastery (once more saintly and full of monks than it now is), in which there lived a young monk whose virility and youth could not be diminished by fasts or by vigils. One day around noon while the other monks were sleeping, he happened to be taking a solitary walk around the church—which was somewhat isolated—when he spotted a very beautiful young girl (perhaps the daughter of one of the local workers) who was going through the fields gathering various kinds of herbs. The moment he saw her, he was passionately attacked by carnal desire.

He went up to her and began a conversation. One subject led to another, and finally, they came to an understanding; he took the girl to his cell without anyone's noticing them. His excessive desire got the better of him while he was playing with the girl, and it happened that the Abbot, who had just got up from his nap, was passing quietly by the monk's cell when he heard the commotion the pair was making. So that he might better recognize the voices, he silently edged up to the entrance of the cell to listen, and it was clear to him that there was a woman inside. At first he was tempted to have them open the door, but then he thought of using a different tactic; so he returned to his room and waited for the monk to come out.

Although the monk was, to his great pleasure and delight, quite occupied with this young lady, he nevertheless suspected something, for he thought he had heard some footsteps in the corridor. In fact, he had peeked out a small opening and had clearly seen the Abbot standing there and listening: he was well aware the Abbot must have realized that the young girl was in his cell, and knowing that he would be severely punished, he was very worried; but without revealing his anxiety to the girl, he immediately began to think of a number of alternative plans, in an attempt to

come up with one which might save him. But then he thought of an original scheme which would achieve the exact end he had in mind, and pretending that he felt they had stayed together long enough, he said to the girl:

"I have to go and find a way for you to leave without being seen, so stay here until I come back."

Having left his cell and locked it with his key, he went immediately to the Abbot's room (as every monk must do before leaving the monastery) and with a straight face he said:

"Sir, this morning I could not bring in all of the firewood that was cut for me; with your permission, I should like to go to the forest to have it carried in."

The Abbot, thinking that the monk did not know he had been observed by him, was happy at this turn of events, and since this offered him the opportunity to get more firsthand information on the sin committed by the monk, he gladly took the monk's key and gave him permission to leave. And when he saw him go off, he began to plan what he would do first: either to open the monk's cell in the presence of all the monks in order to have them see what the sin was—and in doing so prevent any grumbling when he punished the monk—or to hear first from the girl how the affair had started. But then thinking that she might very well be the wife or the daughter of some person of importance and not wanting to shame such a person in front of all his monks, he decided first to see who the girl was and then to make his decision. And so he quietly went to the cell, opened it, entered the room and closed the door.

When the young girl saw the Abbot come in, she became frightened and began to cry out of shame. Master Abbot gave her a quick look and found her to be beautiful and fresh, and although he was old, he immediately felt the warm desires of the flesh, which were no less demanding than those the young monk had felt, and he thought to himself:

"Well, now! Why shouldn't I have a little fun when I can get it? Troubles and worries I can get every day! This is a pretty young girl, and no one knows she's here. If I can persuade her to serve my pleasure, I don't see any reason why I shouldn't! Who will be the wiser? No one will ever know, and a sin that's hidden is half forgiven! This opportunity may never present itself again. I believe it is a sign of great wisdom for a man to profit from what God sends others."

Having thought all this and having completely changed the purpose of his visit, he drew nearer to the girl and gently began to comfort her, begging her not to cry; and, as one thing will lead to another, he eventually explained to her what he wanted.

The young girl, who was by no means as hard as iron or diamond, most willingly agreed to the Abbot's wishes. He took her in his arms and kissed her many times, then lay down on the monk's bed. And perhaps out of concern for the heavy weight of his dignified person and the tender age of the young girl (or perhaps just because he was afraid to lay too much weight on her) he did not lie on top of her but rather placed her on top of him, and there he amused himself with her for quite a while.

Meanwhile, pretending to have gone into the woods, the monk had concealed himself in the dormitory; when he saw the Abbot enter his cell alone, he was reassured that his plan would be successful. And when he saw the Abbot lock himself inside, he knew it for certain. Leaving his hiding place, he quietly crept up to an opening through which he could see and hear everything the Abbot did and said.

When the Abbot decided that he had stayed long enough with the girl, he locked her in the cell and returned to his own room. And after a while, having heard the monk return and believing that he had come back from the woods, he decided that it was time to give him a sound talking to—he would have him locked up in prison in order to enjoy by himself the spoils they had both gained. He had him summoned, and he reprimanded him very severely, and with a stern face he ordered that he be put into prison.

The monk promptly replied:

"But sir, I have not been a member of the Order of Saint Benedict long enough to have had the opportunity to learn every detail of the order's rules. And up until just a moment ago, you never showed me how monks were supposed to support the weight of women a well as fasts and vigils. But now that you have shown me how, I promise you that if you forgive me this time, I shall sin no more in this respect; on the contrary, I shall always behave as I have seen you behave."

The Abbot, who was a clever man, realized immediately that the monk had outsmarted him: he had been witness to what he had done; because of this, and feeling remorse for his own sin, he was ashamed of inflicting upon the monk the same punishment that he himself deserved. And so he pardoned him and made him promise never to reveal what he had seen. They quickly got the young girl out of the monastery, and as one might well imagine, they often had her brought back in again.

Sixth Day, Seventh Tale

In the city of Prato, there was once a statute—in truth, no less harsh than it was worthy of criticism—which, without any extenuating circumstances whatsoever, required that any woman caught by her husband committing adultery with a lover should be burned alive, just the way a woman who goes with a man for money would be. And while this statute was in effect, it happened that a noble lady named Madonna Filippa, who was beautiful and more in love than any woman could be, was discovered in her own bedroom by her husband, Rinaldo de' Pugliesi, in the arms of Lazzarino de' Guazzagliotri, a noble and handsome young man from that city, whom she loved more than herself. When Rinaldo discovered this, he was extremely angry and could hardly restrain himself from rushing at them and murdering them, and had he not been so concerned over what might happen to him if he were to follow the impulse of his anger, he would have done so. While able to restrain himself from doing this, he was, however, unable to refrain from claiming the sentence of Prato's statute, which he was not permitted to carry out by his own hand, that is, the death of his wife.

And so, in possession of very convincing evidence of his wife's transgression, when day broke, without thinking further about the matter, he denounced the lady and had her

summoned to the court. The lady, who was very courageous, as women truly in love usually are, was determined to appear in court, and in spite of the fact that she was advised against this by many of her friends and relatives, she decided that she would rather confess the truth and die with a courageous heart than, fleeing like a coward, live in exile condemned *in absentia* and show herself unworthy of such a lover as the man in whose arms she had rested the night before. Escorted by a large group of women and men, all of whom were urging her to deny the charges, she came before the *podestà* and, with a steady gaze and a firm voice, demanded to know what he wanted of her. Gazing at the lady and finding her to be most beautiful and very well-bred as well as most courageous, indeed, as her own words bore witness, the *podestà* took pity on her and was afraid she might confess to something which would force him, in order to fulfill his duty, to condemn her to death

But since he could not avoid questioning her about what she had been accused of doing, he said to her:

"Madam, as you can see, your husband Rinaldo is here and has lodged a complaint against you, in which he states that he has found you in adultery with another man; and because of this he demands that I punish you by putting you to death in accordance with the statute which requires such sentence here in Prato. But since I cannot do this if you do not confess, I suggest you be very careful how you answer this charge; now, tell me if what your husband accuses you of is true."

Without the slightest trace of fear, the lady, in a lovely tone of voice replied:

"Sir, it is true that Rinaldo is my husband and that this past night he found me in Lazzarino's arms, where, because of the deep and perfect love I bear for him, I have many times lain; nor would I ever deny this; but, as I am sure you know, the laws should be equal for all and should be passed with the consent of the people they affect. In this case these conditions are not fulfilled, for this law applies only to us poor women, who are much better able than men to satisfy a larger number; furthermore, when this law was put into effect, not a single woman gave her consent, nor was any one of them ever consulted about it; therefore, it may quite rightly be called a bad law. And if, however, you wish, to the detriment of my body and your own soul, to put this law into effect, that is your concern; but, before you proceed to any judgment, I beg you to grant me a small favor: that is, to ask my husband whether or not I have ever refused, whenever and however many times he wished, to yield my entire body to him."

To this question, without waiting for the *podestà* to pose it, Rinaldo immediately replied that without any doubt, the lady had yielded to his every pleasure whenever he required it.

"So then," the lady promptly continued, "I ask you, *Messer Podestà*, if he has always taken of me whatever he needed and however much pleased him, what was I supposed to do then, and what am I to do now, with what is left over? Should I throw it to the dogs? Is it not much better to give it to a gentleman who loves me more than himself, rather than let it go to waste or spoil?"

The nature of the case and the fact that the lady was so well known brought almost all of Prato's citizens flocking to court, and when they heard such an amusing question posed by the lady, after much laughter, all of a sudden and almost in a single voice, they cried out that the lady was right and had spoken well; and before they left the court, with the *podestà*'s consent, they changed the cruel statute, modifying it so that it applied only to those women who were unfaithful to their husbands for money. And Rinaldo, confused by the whole mad affair, left the courtroom, and the lady, now free and happy, and resurrected from the flames, so to speak, returned to her home in triumph.

✦ CHAUCER
from *The Canterbury Tales*

The Canterbury Tales is essentially a collection of stories told in rhymed couplets by a group of pilgrims traveling to Canterbury. In the General Prologue, Chaucer includes both generalized and particularized character portrayals of his travelers. Chaucer's type portrayals generalize the qualities of a particular group, usually idealizing it, as in his portrayal of the Clerk and the Knight. Chaucer's individualized portraits, such as those of the Prioress and the Monk, blend attractive and less appealing qualities. The process of characterization is continued in the tales that follow, for the reader learns a good deal about the teller from her or his tale. Moreover, the poet does not neglect the relationships between the pilgrims. These subtle and complex relationships emerge, for example, in the exchange of words between the Host and the Pardoner that precede and follow the Pardoner's Prologue and Tale. Chaucer's presentation of the Host's comments on the tale that precedes the Pardoner's, and Chaucer's description of the Host inviting the next pilgrim to begin his tale, reveal the writer's concern for the thematic and dramatic unity of his work.

The General Prologue

When in April the sweet showers fall
And pierce the drought of March to the root, and all
The veins are bathed in liquor of such power
As brings about the engendering of the flower,
When also Zephyrus with his sweet breath   5
Exhales an air in every grove and heath
Upon the tender shoots, and the young sun
His half-course in the sign of the *Ram* has run,
And the small fowl are making melody
That sleep away the night with open eye   10
(So nature pricks them and their heart engages)
Then people long to go on pilgrimages
And palmers long to seek the stranger strands
Of far-off saints, hallowed in sundry lands,
And specially, from every shire's end   15
Of England, down to Canterbury they wend
To see the holy blissful martyr, quick
To give his help to them when they were sick.
   It happened in that season that one day
In Southwark, at *The Tabard*, as I lay   20
Ready to go on pilgrimage and start
For Canterbury, most devout at heart,
At night there came into that hostelry
Some nine and twenty in a company
Of sundry folk happening then to fall   25

In fellowship, and they were pilgrims all
That towards Canterbury meant to ride.
The rooms and stables of the inn were wide;
They made us easy, all was of the best.
And, briefly, when the sun had gone to rest,   30
I'd spoken to them all upon the trip
And was soon one with them in fellowship,
Pledged to rise early and to take the way
To Canterbury, as you heard me say.
   But none the less, while I have time and space,   35
Before my story takes a further pace,
It seems a reasonable thing to say
What their condition was, the full array
Of each of them, as it appeared to me,
According to profession and degree,   40
And what apparel they were riding in;
And at a Knight I therefore will begin.
There was a *Knight*, a most distinguished man,
Who from the day on which he first began
To ride abroad had followed chivalry,   45
Truth, honour, generousness and courtesy.
He had done nobly in his sovereign's war
And ridden into battle, no man more,
As well in Christian as in heathen places,
And ever honoured for his noble graces.   50
   When we took Alexandra, he was there.
He often sat at table in the chair
Of honour, above all nations, when in Prussia.
In Lithuania he had ridden, and Russia,
No Christian man so often, of his rank.   55
When, in Granada, Algeciras sank
Under assault, he had been there, and in
North Africa, raiding Benamarin;
In Antolia he had been as well
And fought when Ayas and Attalia fell,   60
For all along the Mediterranean coast
He had embarked with many a noble host.
In fifteen mortal battles he had been
And jousted for our faith at Tramissene
Thrice in the lists, and always killed his man.   65
This same distinguished knight had led the van
Once with the Bey of Balat, doing work
For him against another heathen Turk;
He was of sovereign value in all eyes.
And though so much distinguished, he was wise   70
And in his bearing modest as a maid.
He never yet a boorish thing had said
In all his life to any, come what might;
He was a true, a perfect gentle-knight.
   Speaking of his equipment, he possessed   75
Fine horses, but he was not gaily dressed.
He wore a fustian tunic stained and dark
With smudges where his armour had left mark;
Just home from service, he had joined our ranks
To do his pilgrimage and render thanks.   80
   He had his son with him, a fine young *Squire*,
A lover and cadet, a lad of fire
With locks as curly as if they had been pressed.
He was some twenty years of age, I guessed.
In stature he was of a moderate length,   85
With wonderful agility and strength.

He'd seen some service with the cavalry
In Flanders and Artois and Picardy
And had done valiantly in little space
Of time, in hope to win his lady's grace.   90
He was embroidered like a meadow bright
And full of freshest flowers, red and white.
Singing he was, or fluting all the day;
He was as fresh as is the month of May.
Short was his gown, the sleeves were long and wide;   95
He knew the way to sit a horse and ride.
He could make songs and poems and recite,
Knew how to joust and dance, to draw and write.
He loved so hotly that till dawn grew pale
He slept as little as a nightingale.   100
Courteous he was, lowly and serviceable,
And carved to serve his father at the table.
    There was a *Yeoman* with him at his side,
No other servant; so he chose to ride.
This Yeoman wore a coat and hood of green,   105
And peacock-feathered arrows, bright and keen
And neatly sheathed, hung at his belt the while
—For he could dress his gear in yeoman style,
His arrows never drooped their feathers low—
And in his hand he bore a mighty bow.   110
His head was like a nut, his face was brown.
He knew the whole of woodcraft up and down.
A saucy brace was on his arm to ward
It from the bow-string, and a shield and sword
Hung at one side, and at the other slipped   115
A jaunty dirk, spear-sharp and well-equipped.
A medal of St Christopher he wore
Of shining silver on his breast, and bore
A hunting-horn, well slung and burnished clean,
That dangled from a baldrick of bright green.   120
He was a proper forester, I guess.
    There also was a *Nun*, a Prioress,
Her way of smiling very simple and coy.
Her greatest oath was only 'By St Loy!'
And she was known as Madam Eglantyne.   125
And well she sang a service, with a fine
Intoning through her nose, as was most seemly,
And she spoke daintily in French, extremely,
After the school of Stratford-atte-Bowe;
French in the Paris style she did not know.   130
At meat her manners were well taught withal;
No morsel from her lips did she let fall,
Nor dipped her fingers in the sauce too deep;
But she could carry a morsel up and keep
The smallest drop from falling on her breast.   135
For courtliness she had a special zest,
And she would wipe her upper lip so clean
That not a trace of grease was to be seen
Upon the cup when she had drunk; to eat,
She reached a hand sedately for the meat.   140
She certainly was very entertaining,
Pleasant and friendly in her ways, and straining
To counterfeit a courtly kind of grace,
A stately bearing fitting to her place,
And to seem dignified in all her dealings.   145
As for her sympathies and tender feelings,
She was so charitably solicitous

She used to weep if she but saw a mouse
Caught in a trap, if it were dead or bleeding.
And she had little dogs she would be feeding   150
With roasted flesh, or milk, or fine white bread.
And bitterly she wept if one were dead
Or someone took a stick and made it smart;
She was all sentiment and tender heart.
Her veil was gathered in a seemly way,   155
Her nose was elegant, her eyes glass-grey;
Her mouth was very small, but soft and red,
Her forehead, certainly, was fair of spread,
Almost a span across the brows, I own;
She was indeed by no means undergrown.   160
Her cloak, I noticed, had a graceful charm.
She wore a coral trinket on her arm,
A set of beads, the gaudies tricked in green,
Whence hung a golden brooch of brightest sheen
On which there first was graven a crowned A,   165
And lower, *Amor vincit omnia.*
    Another *Nun*, the secretary at her cell,
Was riding with her, and *three Priests* as well.
    A *Monk* there was, one of the finest sort
Who rode the country; hunting was his sport.   170
A manly man, to be an Abbot able;
Many a dainty horse he had in stable.
His bridle, when he rode, a man might hear
Jingling in a whistling wind as clear,
Aye, and as loud as does the chapel bell   175
Where my lord Monk was Prior of the cell.
The Rule of good St Benet or St Maur
As old and strict he tended to ignore;
He let go by the things of yesterday
And took the modern world's more spacious way.   180
He did not rate that text at a plucked hen
Which says that hunters are not holy men
And that a monk uncloistered is a mere
Fish out of water, flapping on the pier,
That is to say a monk out of his cloister.   185
That was a text he held not worth an oyster;
And I agreed and said his views were sound;
Was he to study till his head went round
Poring over books in cloisters? Must he toil
As Austin bade and till the very soil?   190
Was he to leave the world upon the shelf?
Let Austin have his labour to himself.
    This Monk was therefore a good man to horse;
Greyhounds he had, as swift as birds, to course.
Hunting a hare or riding at a fence   195
Was all his fun, he spared for no expense.
I saw his sleeves were garnished at the hand
With fine grey fur, the finest in the land,
And on his hood, to fasten it at his chin
He had a wrought-gold cunningly fashioned pin;   200
Into a lover's knot it seemed to pass.
His head was bald and shone like looking-glass;
So did his face, as if it had been greased.
He was a fat and personable priest;
His prominent eyeballs never seemed to settle.   205
They glittered like the flames beneath a kettle;
Supple his boots, his horse in fine condition.
He was a prelate fit for exhibition,

He was not pale like a tormented soul.
He liked a fat swan best, and roasted whole.   *210*
His palfrey was as brown as is a berry.
    There was a *Friar*, a wanton one and merry,
A Limiter, a very festive fellow.
In all Four Orders there was none so mellow,
So glib with gallant phrase and well-turned speech.   *215*
He'd fixed up many a marriage, giving each
Of his young women what he could afford her.
He was a noble pillar to his Order.
Highly beloved and intimate was he
With County folk within his boundary,   *220*
And city dames of honour and possessions;
For he was qualified to hear confessions,
Or so he said, with more than priestly scope;
He had a special licence from the Pope.
Sweetly he heard his penitents at shrift   *225*
With pleasant absolution, for a gift.
He was an easy man in penance-giving
Where he could hope to make a decent living;
It's a sure sign whenever gifts are given
To a poor Order that a man's well shriven,   *230*
And should he give enough he knew in verity
The penitent repented in sincerity.
For many a fellow is so hard of heart
He cannot weep, for all his inward smart.
Therefore instead of weeping and of prayer   *235*
One should give silver for a poor Friar's care.
He kept his tippet stuffed with pins for curls,
And pocket-knives, to give to pretty girls.
And certainly his voice was gay and sturdy,
For he sang well and played the hurdy-gurdy.   *240*
At sing-songs he was champion of the hour.
His neck was whiter than a lily-flower
But strong enough to butt a bruiser down.
He knew the taverns well in every town
And every innkeeper and barmaid too   *245*
Better than lepers, beggars and that crew,
For in so eminent a man as he
It was not fitting with the dignity
Of his position, dealing with a scum
Of wretched lepers; nothing good can come   *250*
Of commerce with such slum-and-gutter dwellers,
But only with the rich and victual-sellers.
But anywhere a profit might accrue
Courteous he was and lowly of service too.
Natural gifts like his were hard to match.   *255*
He was the finest beggar of his batch,
And, for his begging-district, paid a rent;
His brethren did no poaching where he went.
For though a widow mightn't have a shoe,
So pleasant was his holy how-d'ye-do   *260*
He got his farthing from her just the same
Before he left, and so his income came
To more than he laid out. And how he romped,
Just like a puppy! He was ever prompt
To arbitrate disputes on settling days   *265*
(For a small fee) in many helpful ways,
Not then appearing as your cloistered scholar
With threadbare habit hardly worth a dollar,
But much more like a Doctor or a Pope.

Of double-worsted was the semi-cope   *270*
Upon his shoulders, and the swelling fold
About him, like a bell about its mould
When it is casting, rounded out his dress.
He lisped a little out of wantonness
To make his English sweet upon his tongue.   *275*
When he had played his harp, or having sung,
His eyes would twinkle in his head as bright
As any star upon a frosty night.
This worthy's name was Hubert, it appeared.
    There was a *Merchant* with a forking beard   *280*
And motley dress; high on his horse he sat,
Upon his head a Flemish beaver hat
And on his feet daintily buckled boots.
He told of his opinions and pursuits
In solemn tones, he harped on his increase   *285*
Of capital; there should be sea-police
(He thought) upon the Harwich-Holland ranges;
He was expert at dabbling in exchanges.
This estimable Merchant so had set
His wits to work, none knew he was in debt,   *290*
He was so stately in administration,
In loans and bargains and negotiation.
He was an excellent fellow all the same;
To tell the truth I do not know his name.
    An *Oxford Cleric*, still a student though,   *295*
One who had taken logic long ago,
Was there; his horse was thinner than a rake,
And he was not too fat, I undertake,
But had a hollow look, a sober stare;
The thread upon his overcoat was bare.   *300*
He had found no preferment in the church
And he was too unworldly to make search
For secular employment. By his bed
He preferred having twenty books in red
And black, of Aristotle's philosophy,   *305*
Than costly clothes, fiddle or psaltery.
Though a philosopher, as I have told,
He had not found the stone for making gold.
Whatever money from his friends he took
He spent on learning or another book   *310*
And prayed for them most earnestly, returning
Thanks to them thus for paying for his learning.
His only care was study, and indeed
He never spoke a word more than was need,
Formal at that, respectful in the extreme,   *315*
Short, to the point, and lofty in his theme.
A tone of moral virtue filled his speech
And gladly would he learn, and gladly teach.
    A *Serjeant at the Law* who paid his calls,
Wary and wise, for clients at St Paul's   *320*
There also was, of noted excellence.
Discreet he was, a man to reverence,
Or so he seemed, his sayings were so wise.
He often had been Justice of Assize
By letters patent, and in full commission.   *325*
His fame and learning and his high position
Had won him many a robe and many a fee.
There was no such conveyancer as he;
All was fee-simple to his strong digestion,
Not one conveyance could be called in question.   *330*

Though there was nowhere one so busy as he,
He was less busy than he seemed to be.
He knew of every judgement, case and crime
Ever recorded since King William's time.
He could dictate defences or draft deeds;   335
No one could pinch a comma from his screeds
And he knew every statute off by rote.
He wore a homely parti-coloured coat,
Girt with a silken belt of pin-stripe stuff;
Of his appearance I have said enough.   340
        There was a *Franklin** with him, it appeared;
White as a daisy-petal was his beard.
A sanguine man, high-coloured and benign,
He loved a morning sop of cake in wine.
He lived for pleasure and had always done,   345
For he was Epicurus' very son,
In whose opinion sensual delight
Was the one true felicity in sight.
As noted as St Julian was for bounty
He made his household free to all the County.   350
His bread, his ale were finest of the fine
And no one had a better stock of wine.
His house was never short of bake-meat pies,
Of fish and flesh, and these in such supplies
It positively snowed with meat and drink   355
And all the dainties that a man could think.
According to the seasons of the year
Changes of dish were ordered to appear.
He kept fat partridges in coops, beyond,
Many a bream and pike were in his pond.   360
Woe to the cook unless the sauce was hot
And sharp, or if he wasn't on the spot!
And in his hall a table stood arrayed
And ready all day long, with places laid.
As Justice at the Sessions none stood higher;   365
He often had been Member for the Shire.
A dagger and a little purse of silk
Hung at his girdle, white as morning milk.
As Sheriff he checked audit, every entry.
He was a model among landed gentry.   370
        A *Haberdasher, a Dyer, a Carpenter,*
A Weaver and a Carpet-maker were
Among our ranks, all in the livery
Of one impressive guild-fraternity.
They were so trim and fresh their gear would pass   375
For new. Their knives were not tricked out with brass
Butt wrought with purest silver, which avouches
A like display on girdles and on pouches.
Each seemed a worthy burgess, fit to grace
A guild-hall with a seat upon the dais.   380
Their wisdom would have justified a plan
To make each one of them an alderman;
They had the capital and revenue,
Besides their wives declared it was their due.
And if they did not think so, then they ought;   385
To be called '*Madam*' is a glorious thought,
And so is going to church and being seen
Having your mantle carried, like a queen.
        They had a *Cook* with them who stood alone
For boiling chicken with a marrow-bone,   390
Sharp flavouring-powder and a spice for savour.

He could distinguish London ale by flavour,
And he could roast and seethe and broil and fry,
Make good thick soup and bake a tasty pie.
But what a pity—so it seemed to me,   395
That he should have an ulcer on his knee.
As for blancmange, he made it with the best.
        There was a *Skipper* hailing from far west;
He came from Dartmouth, so I understood.
He rode a farmer's horse as best he could,   400
In a woollen gown that reached his knee.
A dagger on a lanyard falling free
Hung from his neck under his arm and down.
The summer heat had tanned his colour brown,
And certainly he was an excellent fellow.   405
Many a draught of vintage, red and yellow,
He'd drawn at Bordeaux, while the trader snored.
The nicer rules of conscience he ignored.
If, when he fought, the enemy vessel sank,
He sent his prisoners home; they walked the plank.   410
As for his skill in reckoning his tides,
Currents and many another risk besides,
Moons, harbours, pilots, he had such dispatch
That none from Hull to Carthage was his match.
Hardy he was, prudent in undertaking;   415
His beard in many a tempest had its shaking,
And he knew all the havens as they were
From Gottland to the Cape of Finisterre,
And every creek in Brittany and Spain;
The barge he owned was called *The Maudelayne*.   420
        A *Doctor* too emerged as we proceeded;
No one alive could talk as well as he did
On points of medicine and of surgery,
For, being grounded in astronomy,
He watched his patient closely for the hours   425
When, by his horoscope, he knew the powers
Of favourable planets, then ascendent,
Worked on the images for his dependent.
The cause of every malady you'd got
He knew, and whether dry, cold, moist or hot;   430
He knew their seat, their humour and condition.
He was a perfect practising physician.
These causes being known for what they were,
He gave the man his medicine then and there.
All his apothecaries in a tribe   435
Were ready with the drugs he would prescribe
And each made money from the other's guile;
They had been friendly for a goodish while.
He was well-versed in Aesculapius too
And what Hippocrates and Rufus knew   440
And Dioscorides, now dead and gone,
Galen and Rhazes, Hali, Serapion,
Averroes, Avicenna, Constantine,
Scotch Bernard, John of Gaddesden, Gilbertine.
In his own diet he observed some measure;   445
There were no superfluities for pleasure,
Only digestives, nutritives and such.
He did not read the Bible very much.
In blood-red garments, slashed with bluish grey
And lined with taffeta, he rode his way;   450
Yet he was rather close as to expenses
And kept the gold he won in pestilences.

Gold stimulates the heart, or so we're told.
He therefore had a special love of gold.

A worthy *woman* from beside *Bath* city 455
Was with us, somewhat deaf, which was a pity.
In making cloth she showed so great a bent
She bettered those of Ypres and of Ghent.
In all the parish not a dame dared stir
Towards the altar steps in front of her, 460
And if indeed they did, so wrath was she
As to be quite put out of charity.
Her kerchiefs were of finely woven ground;
I dared have sworn they weighed a good ten pound,
The ones she wore on Sunday, on her head. 465
Her hose were of the finest scarlet red
And gartered tight; her shoes were soft and new.
Bold was her face, handsome, and red in hue.
A worthy woman all her life, what's more
She'd had five husbands, all at the church door, 470
Apart from other company in youth;
No need just now to speak of that, forsooth.
And she had thrice been to Jerusalem,
Seen many strange rivers and passed over them;
She'd been to Rome and also to Boulogne, 475
St. James of Compostella and Cologne,
And she was skilled in wandering by the way.
She had gap-teeth, set widely, truth to say.
Easily on an ambling horse she sat
Well wimpled up, and on her head a hat 480
As broad as is a buckler or a shield;
She had a flowing mantle that concealed
Large hips, her heels spurred sharply under that.
In company she liked to laugh and chat
And knew the remedies for love's mischances, 485
An art in which she knew the oldest dances.

A holy-minded man of good renown
There was, and poor, the *Parson* to a town,
Yet he was rich in holy thought and work.
He also was a learned man, a clerk, 490
Who truly knew Christ's gospel and would preach it
Devoutly to parishioners, and teach it.
Benign and wonderfully diligent,
And patient when adversity was sent
(For so he proved in much adversity) 495
He hated cursing to extort a fee,
Nay rather he preferred beyond a doubt
Giving to poor parishioners round about
Both from church offerings and his property;
He could in little find sufficiency. 500
Wide was his parish, with houses far asunder,
Yet he neglected not in rain or thunder,
In sickness or in grief, to pay a call
On the remotest, whether great or small,
Upon his feet, and in his hand a stave. 505
This noble example to his sheep he gave
That first he wrought, and afterwards he taught;
And it was from the Gospel he had caught
Those words, and he would add this figure too,
That if gold rust, what then will iron do? 510
For if a priest be foul in whom we trust
No wonder that a common man should rust;
And shame it is to see—let priests take stock—

A shitten shepherd and a snowy flock.
The true example that a priest should give 515
Is one of cleanness, how the sheep should live.
He did not set his benefice to hire
And leave his sheep encumbered in the mire
Or run to London to earn easy bread
By singing masses for the wealthy dead, 520
Or find some Brotherhood and get enrolled.
He stayed at home and watched over his fold
So that no wolf should make the sheep miscarry.
He was a shepherd and no mercenary.
Holy and virtuous he was, but then 525
Never contemptuous of sinful men,
Never disdainful, never too proud or fine,
But was discreet in teaching and benign.
His business was to show a fair behaviour
And draw men thus to Heaven and their Saviour, 530
Unless indeed a man were obstinate;
And such, whether of high or low estate,
He put to sharp rebuke, to say the least.
I think there never was a better priest.
He sought no pomp or glory in his dealings, 535
No scrupulosity had spiced his feelings.
Christ and His Twelve Apostles and their lore
He taught, but followed it himself before.

There was a *Plowman* with him there, his brother;
Many a load of dung one time or other 540
He must have carted through the morning dew.
He was an honest worker, good and true,
Living in peace and perfect charity,
And, as the gospel bade him, so did he,
Loving God best with all his heart and mind 545
And then his neighbour as himself, repined
At no misfortune, slacked for no content,
For steadily about his work he went
To thrash his corn, to dig or to manure
Or make a ditch; and he would help the poor 550
For love of Christ and never take a penny
If he could help it, and, as prompt as any,
He paid his tithes in full when they were due
On what he owned, and on his earnings too.
He wore a tabard smock and rode a mare. 555

There was a *Reeve*, also a *Miller*, there,
A College *Manciple* from the Inns of Court,
A papal *Pardoner* and, in close consort,
A Church-Court *Summoner*, riding at a trot,
And finally myself—that was the lot. 560

The *Miller* was a chap of sixteen stone,
A great stout fellow big in brawn and bone.
He did well out of them, for he could go
And win the ram at any wrestling show.
Broad, knotty and short-shouldered, he would boast 565
He could heave any door off hinge and post,
Or take a run and break it with his head.
His beard, like any sow or fox, was red
And broad as well, as though it were a spade;
And, at its very tip, his nose displayed 570
A wart on which there stood a tuft of hair
Red as the bristles in an old sow's ear.
His nostrils were as black as they were wide.
He had a sword and buckler at his side,

His mighty mouth was like a furnace door.   575
A wrangler and buffoon, he had a store
Of tavern stories, filthy in the main.
His was a master-hand at stealing grain.
He felt it with his thumb and thus he knew
Its quality and took three times his due—   580
A thumb of gold, by God, to gauge an oat!
He wore a hood of blue and a white coat.
He liked to play his bagpipes up and down
And that was how he brought us out of town.

    The *Manciple* came from the Inner Temple;   585
All caterers might follow his example
In buying victuals; he was never rash
Whether he bought on credit or paid cash.
He used to watch the market most precisely
And got in first, and so he did quite nicely.   590
Now isn't is a marvel of God's grace
That an illiterate fellow can outpace
The wisdom of a heap of learned men?
His masters—he had more than thirty then—
All versed in the abstrusest legal knowledge,   595
Could have produced a dozen from their College
Fit to be stewards in land and rents and game
To any Peer in England you could name,
And show him how to live on what he had
Debt-free (unless of course the Peer were mad)   600
Or be as frugal as he might desire,
And make them fit to help about the Shire
In any legal case there was to try;
And yet this Manciple could wipe their eye.

    The *Reeve* was old and choleric and thin;   605
His beard was shaven closely to the skin,
His shorn hair came abruptly to a stop
Above his ears, and he was docked on top
Just like a priest in front; his legs were lean,
Like sticks they were, no calf was to be seen.   610
He kept his bins and garners very trim;
No auditor could gain a point on him.
And he could judge by watching drought and rain
The yield he might expect from seed and grain.
His master's sheep, his animals and hens,   615
Pigs, horses, dairies, stores and cattle-pens
Were wholly trusted to his government.
He had been under contract to present
The accounts, right from his master's earliest years.
No one had ever caught him in arrears.   620
No bailiff, serf or herdsman dared to kick,
He knew their dodges, knew their every trick;
Feared like the plague he was, by those beneath.
He had a lovely dwelling on a heath,
Shadowed in green by trees above the sward.   625
A better hand at bargains than his lord,
He had grown rich and had a store of treasure
Well tucked away, yet out it came to pleasure
His lord with subtle loans or gifts of goods,
To earn his thanks and even coats and hoods.   630
When young he'd learnt a useful trade and still
He was a carpenter of first-rate skill.
The stallion-cob he rode at a slow trot
Was dapple-grey and bore the name of Scot.
He wore an overcoat of bluish shade   635

And rather long; he had a rusty blade
Slung at his side. He came, as I heard tell,
From Norfolk, near a place called Baldeswell.
His coat was tucked under his belt and splayed.
He rode the hindmost of our cavalcade.   640

    There was a *Summoner* with us at that Inn,
His face on fire, like a cherubin,
For he had carbuncles. His eyes were narrow,
He was as hot and lecherous as a sparrow.
Black scabby brows he had, and a thin beard.   645
Children were afraid when he appeared.
No quicksilver, lead ointment, tartar creams,
No brimstone, no boracic, so it seems,
Could make a salve that had the power to bite,
Clean up or cure his whelks of knobby white   650
Or purge the pimples sitting on his cheeks.
Garlic he loved, and onions too, and leeks,
And drinking strong red wine till all was hazy.
Then he would shout and jabber as if crazy,
And wouldn't speak a word except in Latin   655
When he was drunk, such tags as he was pat in;
He only had a few, say two or three,
That he had mugged up out of some decree;
No wonder, for he heard them every day.
And, as you know, a man can teach a jay   660
To call out 'Walter' better than the Pope.
But had you tried to test his wits and grope
For more, you'd have found nothing in the bag.
Then '*Questio quid juris*' was his tag.
He was a noble varlet and a kind one,   665
You'd meet none better if you went to find one.
Why, he'd allow—just for a quart of wine—
Any good lad to keep a concubine
A twelvemonth and dispense him altogether!
And he had finches of his own to feather: 670
And if he found some rascal with a maid
He would instruct him not to be afraid
In such a case of the Archdeacon's curse
(Unless the rascal's soul were in his purse)
For in his purse the punishment should be.   675
'Purse is the good Archdeacon's Hell,' said he.
But well I know he lied in what he said;
A curse should put a guilty man in dread,
For curses kill, as shriving brings, salvation.
We should beware of excommunication.   680
Thus, as he pleased, the man could bring duress
On any young fellow in the diocese.
He knew their secrets, they did what he said.
He wore a garland set upon his head
Large as the holly-bush upon a stake   685
Outside an ale-house, and he had a cake,
A round one, which it was his joke to wield
As if it were intended for a shield.

    He and a gentle *Pardoner* rode together,
A bird from Charing Cross of the same feather,   690
Just back from visiting the Court of Rome.
He loudly sang '*Come hither, love, come home!*'
The Summoner sang deep seconds to this song,
No trumpet ever sounded half so strong.
This Pardoner had hair as yellow as wax,   695
Hanging down smoothly like a hank of flax.

In driblets fell his locks behind his head
Down to his shoulders which they overspread;
Thinly they fell, like rat-tails, one by one.
He wore no hood upon his head, for fun;   *700*
The hood inside his wallet had been stowed,
He aimed at riding in the latest mode;
But for a little cap his head was bare
And he had bulging eyeballs, like a hare.
He'd sewed a holy relic on his cap;   *705*
His wallet lay before him on his lap,
Brimful of pardons come from Rome, all hot.
He had the same small voice a goat has got.
His chin no beard had harboured, nor would harbour,
Smoother than ever chin was left by barber.   *710*
I judge he was a gelding, or a mare.
As to his trade, from Berwick down to Ware
There was no pardoner of equal grace,
For in his trunk he had a pillow-case
Which he asserted was Our Lady's veil.   *715*
He said he had a gobbet of the sail
Saint Peter had the time when he made bold
To walk the waves, till Jesu Christ took hold.
He had a cross of metal set with stones
And, in a glass, a rubble of pigs' bones.   *720*
And with these relics, any time he found
Some poor up-country parson to astound,
In one short day, in money down, he drew
More than the parson in a month or two,
And by his flatteries and prevarication   *725*
Made monkeys of the priest and congregation.
But still to do him justice first and last
In church he was a noble ecclesiast.
How well he read a lesson or told a story!
But best of all he sang an Offertory,   *730*
For well he knew that when that song was sung
He'd have to preach and tune his honey-tongue
And (well he could) win silver from the crowd.
That's why he sang so merrily and loud.
    Now I have told you shortly, in a clause,   *735*
The rank, the array, the number and the cause
Of our assembly in this company
In Southwark, at that high-class hostelry
Known as *The Tabard*, close beside *The Bell*.
And now the time has come for me to tell   *740*
How we behaved that evening; I'll begin
After we had alighted at the Inn,
Then I'll report our journey, stage by stage,
All the remainder of our pilgrimage.
But first I beg of you, in courtesy,   *745*
Not to condemn me as unmannerly
If I speak plainly and with no concealings
And give account of all their words and dealings,
Using their very phrases as they fell.
For certainly, as you all know so well,   *750*
He who repeats a tale after a man
Is bound to say, as nearly as he can,
Each single word, if he remembers it,
However rudely spoken or unfit,
Or else the tale he tells will be untrue,   *755*
The things pretended and the phrases new.
He may not flinch although it were his brother,

He may as well say one word as another.
And Christ Himself spoke broad in Holy Writ,
Yet there is no scurrility in it,   *760*
And Plato says, for those with power to read,
'The word should be as cousin to the deed.'
Further I beg you to forgive it me
If I neglect the order and degree
And what is due to rank in what I've planned.   *765*
I'm short of wit as you will understand.
    Our *Host* gave us great welcome; everyone
Was given a place and supper was begun.
He served the finest victuals you could think,
The wine was strong and we were glad to drink.   *770*
A very striking man our Host withal,
And fit to be a marshal in a hall.
His eyes were bright, his girth a little wide;
There is no finer burgess in Cheapside.
Bold in his speech, yet wise and full of tact,   *775*
There was no manly attribute he lacked,
What's more he was a merry-hearted man.
After our meal he jokingly began
To talk of sport, and, among other things
After we'd settled up our reckonings,   *780*
He said as follows: 'Truly, gentlemen,
You're very welcome and I can't think when
—Upon my word I'm telling you no lie—
I've seen a gathering here that looked so spry,
No, not this year, as in this tavern now.   *785*
I'd think you up some fun if I knew how.
And, as it happens, a thought has just occurred
To please you, costing nothing, on my word.
Yor're off to Canterbury—well, God speed!
Blessed St Thomas answer to your need!   *790*
And I don't doubt, before the journey's done
You mean to while the time in tales and fun.
Indeed, there's little pleasure for your bones
Riding along and all as dumb as stones.
So let me then propose for your enjoyment,   *795*
Just as I said, a suitable employment.
And if my notion suits and you agree
And promise to submit yourselves to me
Playing your parts exactly as I say
Tomorrow as you ride along the way,   *800*
Then by my father's soul (and he is dead)
If you don't like it you can have my head!
Hold up your hands, and not another word.'
    Well, our opinion was not long deferred,
It seemed not worth a serious debate;   *805*
We all agreed to it at any rate
And bade him issue what commands he would.
'My lords,' he said, 'now listen for your good,
And please don't treat my notion with disdain.
This is the point. I'll make it short and plain.   *810*
Each one of you shall help to make things slip
By telling two stories on the outward trip
To Canterbury, that's what I intend,
And, on the homeward way to journey's end
Another two, tales from the days of old;   *815*
And then the man whose story is best told,
That is to say who gives the fullest measure
Of good morality and general pleasure,

He shall be given a supper, paid by all,
Here in this tavern, in this very hall,   820
When we come back again from Canterbury.
And in the hope to keep you bright and merry
I'll go along with you myself and ride
All at my own expense and serve as guide.
I'll be the judge. and those who won't obey   825
Shall pay for what we spend upon the way.
Now if you all agree to what you've heard
Tell me at once without another word,
And I will make arrangements early for it.'
    Of course we all agreed, in fact we swore it   830
Delightedly, and made entreaty too
That he should act as he proposed to do,
Become our Governor in short, and be
Judge of our tales and general referee,
And set the supper at a certain price.   835
We promised to be ruled by his advice
Come high, come low; unanimously thus
We set him up in judgement over us.
More wine was fetched, the business being done;
We drank it off and up went everyone   840
To bed without a moment of delay.
    Early next morning at the spring of day
Up rose our Host and roused us like a cock,
Gathering us together in a flock,
And off we rode at slightly faster pace   845
Than walking to St Thomas's watering-place;
And there our Host drew up, began to to ease
His horse, and said, 'Now, listen if you please,
My lords! Remember what you promised me.
If evensong and mattins will agree   850
Let's see who shall be first to tell a tale.
And as I hope to drink good wine and ale
I'll be your judge. The rebel who disobeys,
However much the journey costs, he pays.
Now draw for cut and then we can depart;   855
The man who draws the shortest cut shall start.
My Lord the Knight,' he said, 'step up to me
And draw your cut, for that is my decree.
And come you near, my Lady Prioress,
And you, Sir Cleric, drop your shamefastness,   860
No studying now! A hand from every man!
Immediately the draw for lots began
And to tell shortly how the matter went,
Whether by chance or fate or accident,
The truth is this, the cut fell to the Knight,   865
Which everybody greeted with delight.
And tell his tale he must, as reason was
Because of our agreement and because
He too had sworn. What more is there to say?
For when this good man saw how matters lay,   870
Being by wisdom and obedience driven
To keep a promise he had freely given,
He said, 'Since it's for me to start the game,
Why, welcome be the cut in God's good name!
Now let us ride, and listen to what I say.'   875
And at the word we started on our way
And in a cheerful style he then began
At once to tell his tale, and thus it ran.

THE PARDONER'S TALE

The Pardoner's Prologue

'My lords,' he said, 'in churches where I preach
I cultivate a haughty kind of speech
And ring it out as roundly as a bell;
I've got it all by heart, the tale I tell:
I have a text, it always is the same   5
And always has been, since I learnt the game,
Old as the hills and fresher than the grass,
Radix malorum est cupiditas.
    'But first I make pronouncement whence I come,
Show them my bulls in detail and in sum.   10
And flaunt the papal seal for their inspection
As warrant for my bodily protection,
That none may have the impudence to irk
Or hinder me in Christ's most holy work.
Then I tell stories, as occasion calls,   15
Showing forth bulls from popes and cardinals,
From patriarchs and bishops; as I do,
I speak some words in Latin—just a few—
To put a saffron tinge upon my preaching
And stir devotion with a spice of teaching.   20
Then I bring all my long glass bottles out
Cram-full of bones and ragged bits of clout,
Relics they are, at least for such are known.
Then, cased in metal, I've a shoulder-bone,
Belonging to a sheep, a holy Jew's.   25
"Good men," I say, "take heed, for here is news.
Take but this bone and dip it in a well;
If cow or calf, if sheep or ox should swell
From eating snakes or that a snake has stung,
Take water from that well and wash its tongue,   30
And it will then recover. Furthermore,
Where there is pox or scab or other sore,
All animals that water at that well
Are cured at once. Take note of what I tell.
If the good man—the owner of the stock—   35
Goes once a week, before the crow of cock,
Fasting, and takes a draught of water too,
Why then, according to that holy Jew,
He'll find his cattle multiply and sell.
    "And it's a cure for jealousy as well;   40
For though a man be given to jealous wrath,
Use but this water when you make his broth,
And never again will he mistrust his wife,
Though he knew all about her sinful life,
Though two or three clergy had enjoyed her love.   45
    "Now look; I have a mitten here, a glove.
Whoever wears this mitten on his hand
Will multiply his grain. He sows his land
And up will come abundant wheat or oats,
Providing that he offers pence or groats.   50
    "Good men and women, here's a word of warning;
If there is anyone in church this morning
Guilty of sin, so far beyond expression
Horrible, that he dare not make confession,
Or any woman, whether young or old,   55
That's cuckolded her husband, be she told
That such as she shall have no power or grace

To offer to my relics in this place.
But those who can acquit themselves of blame
Can all come up and offer in God's name,   60
And I will shrive them by the authority
Committed in this papal bull to me."
 'That trick's been worth a hundred marks a year
Since I became a Pardoner, never fear.
Then, priestlike in my pulpit, with a frown, 65
I stand, and when the yokels have sat down,
I preach, as you have heard me say before,
And tell a hundred lying mockeries more.
I take great pains, and stretching out my neck
To east and west I crane about and peck   70
Just like a pigeon sitting on a barn.
My hands and tongue together spin the yarn
And all my antics are a joy to see.
The curse of avarice and cupidity
Is all my sermon, for it frees the pelf.   75
Out come the pence, and specially for myself,
For my exclusive purpose is to win
And not at all to castigate their sin.
Once dead what matter how their souls may fare?
They can go blackberrying, for all I care! 80
 'Believe me, many a sermon or devotive
Exordium issues from an evil motive.
Some to give pleasure by their flattery
And gain promotion through hypocrisy,
Some out of vanity, some out of hate;   85
Or when I dare not otherwise debate
I'll put my discourse into such a shape,
My tongue will be a dagger; no escape
For him from slandering falsehood shall there be.
If he has hurt my brethren or me.   90
For though I never mention him by name
The congregation guesses all the same
From certain hints that everybody knows,
and so I take revenge upon our foes
And spit my venom forth, while I profess 95
Holy and true—or seeming holiness.
 'But let me briefly make my purpose plain;
I preach for nothing but for greed of gain
And use the same old text, as bold as brass,
Radix malorum est cupiditas.   100
And thus I preach against the very vice
I make my living out of—avarice.
And yet however guilty of that sin
Myself, with others I have power to win
Them from it, I can bring them to repent; 105
But that is not my principal intent.
Covertousness is both the root and stuff
Of all I preach. That ought to be enough.
 'Well, then I give examples thick and fast
From bygone times, old stories from the past. 110
A yokel mind loves stories from of old,
Being the kind it can repeat and hold.
What! Do you think, as long as I can preach
And get their silver for the things I teach,
That I will live in poverty, from choice? 115
That's not the counsel of my inner voice!
No! Let me preach and beg from kirk to kirk
And never do an honest job of work,

No, nor make baskets, like St Paul, to gain
A livelihood. I do not preach in vain.   120
There's no apostle I would counterfeit;
I mean to have money, wool and cheese and wheat
Though it were given me by the poorest lad
Or poorest village widow, though she had
A string of starving children, all agape. 125
No, let me drink the liquor of the grape
And keep a jolly wench in every town!
 'But listen, gentlemen; to bring things down
To a conclusion, would you like a tale?
Now as I've drunk a draught of corn-ripe ale, 130
By God it stands to reason I can strike
On some good story that you all will like.
For though I am a wholly vicious man
Don't think I can't tell moral tales. I can!
Here's one I often preach when out for winning; 135
Now please be quiet. Here is the beginning.'

The Pardoner's Tale

In Flanders once there was a company
Of youngsters haunting vice and ribaldry,
Riot and gambling, stews and public-houses
Where each with harp, guitar or lute carouses, 140
Dancing and dicing day and night, and bold
To eat and drink far more than they can hold,
Doing thereby the devil sacrifice
Within that devil's temple of cursed vice,
Abominable in superfluity,   145
With oaths so damnable in blasphemy
That it's a grisly thing to hear them swear.
Our dear Lord's body they will rend and tear
As if the Jews had rent Him not enough;
And at the sin of others every tough 150
Will laugh, and presently the dancing-girls,
Small pretty ones, come in and shake their curls,
With youngsters selling fruit, and ancient bawds,
And girls with cakes and music, devil's gauds
To kindle and blow the fires of lechery 155
That are so close annexed to gluttony.
Witness the Bible, which is most express
That lust is bred of wine and drunkenness.
 Look how the drunken and unnatural Lot
Lay with his daughters, though he knew it not; 160
He was too drunk to know what he was doing.
 Take Herod, too, his tale is work pursuing.
Replete with wine and feasting, he was able
To give the order at his very table
To kill the innocent Baptist, good St John. 165
 Seneca has a thought worth pondering on;
No difference, he says, that he can find
Between a madman who has lost his mind
And one who is habitually mellow
Except that madness when it takes a fellow 170
Lasts longer, on the whole, than drunkenness.
O cursed gluttony, our first distress!
Cause of our first confusion, first temptation,
The very origin of our damnation,

Till Christ redeemed us with his blood again!   *175*
O infamous indulgence! Cursed stain
So dearly bought! And what has it been worth?
Gluttony has corrupted all the earth.
　　Adam, our father, and his wife as well,
From Paradise to labour and to Hell   *180*
Were driven for that vice, they were indeed.
While she and Adam fasted, so I read,
They were in Paradise; when he and she
Ate of the fruit of that forbidden tree
They were at once cast forth in pain and woe.   *185*
O gluttony, it is to thee we owe
Our griefs! O if we knew the maladies
That follow on excess and gluttonies,
Sure we would diet, we would temper pleasure
In sitting down at table, show some measure!   *190*
Alas the narrow throat, the tender mouth!
Men labour east and west and north and south
In earth, in air, in water—Why, d'you think?
To get a glutton dainty meat and drink!
How well of this St Paul's Epistle treats!   *195*
'Meats for the belly, belly for the meats,
But God shall yet destroy both it and them.'
Alas, the filth of it! If we contemn
The name, how far more filthy is the act!
A man who swills down vintages in fact   *200*
Makes a mere privy of his throat, a sink
For cursed superfluities of drink!
　　So the Apostle said, whom tears could soften:
'Many there are, as I have told you often,
And weep to tell, whose gluttony sufficed   *205*
To make them enemies of the cross of Christ,
Whose ending is destruction and whose God
Their belly!' O thou belly! stinking pod
Of dung and foul corruption, that canst send
Thy filthy music forth at either end,   *210*
What labour and expense it is to find
Thy sustenance! These cooks that strain and grind
And bray in mortars, transubstantiate
God's gifts into a flavour on a plate,
To please a lecherous palate. How they batter   *215*
Hard bones to put some marrow on your platter,
Spicery, root, bark, leaf—they search and cull it
In the sweet hope of flattering a gullet!
Nothing is thrown away that could delight
Or whet anew lascivious appetite.   *220*
Be sure a man whom such a fare entices
Is dead indeed, though living in his vices.
　　Wine is a lecherous thing and drunkenness
A squalor of contention and distress.
O drunkard, how disfigured is thy face,   *225*
How foul thy breath, how filthy thy embrace!
And through thy drunken nose a stertorous snort
Like 'samson-samson'—something of the sort.
Yet Samson never was a man to swig.
You totter, lurch and fall like a stuck pig,   *230*
Your manhood's lost, your tongue is in a burr.
Drunkenness is the very sepulchre
Of human judgment and articulation.
He that is subject to the domination
Of drink can keep no secrets, be it said.   *235*

Keep clear of wine, I tell you, white or red,
Especially Spanish wines which they provide
And have on sale in Fish Street and Cheapside.
That wine mysteriously finds its way
To mix itself with others—shall we say   *240*
Spontaneously!—that grow in neighbouring regions.
Out of the mixture fumes arise in legions,
So when a man has had a drink or two
Though he may think he is at home with you
In Cheapside, I assure you he's in Spain   *245*
Where it was made, at Lepé I maintain,
Not even at Bordeaux. He's soon elate
And very near the 'samson-samson' state.
　　But seriously my lords, attention, pray!
All the most notable acts, I dare to say,   *250*
And victories in the Old Testament,
Won under God who is omnipotent,
Were won in abstinence, were won in prayer.
Look in the Bible, you will find it there.
　　Or else take Attila the Conqueror;   *255*
Died in his sleep, a manner to abhor,
In drunken shame and bleeding at the nose.
A general should live sober, I suppose.
Moreover call to mind and ponder well
What was commanded unto Lemuel   *260*
—Not Samuel, but Lemuel I said—
Read in the Bible, that's the fountain-head,
And see what comes of giving judges drink.
No more of that. I've said enough, I think.
　　Having put gluttony in its proper setting   *265*
I wish to warn you against dice and betting,
Gambling's the very mother of robbed purses,
Lies, double-dealing, perjury, and curses,
Manslaughter, blasphemy of Christ, and waste
Of time and money. Worse, you are debased   *270*
In public reputation, put to shame.
'A common gambler' is a nasty name.
　　The more exalted such a man may be
So much the more contemptible is he.
A gambling prince would be incompetent   *275*
To frame a policy of government,
And he will sink in general opinion
As one unfit to exercise dominion.
　　Stilbon, that wise ambassador whose mission
Took him to Corinth, was of high position;   *280*
Sparta had sent him with intent to frame
A treaty of alliance. When he came,
Hoping for reinforcement and advice,
It happened that he found them all at dice,
Their very nobles; so he quickly planned   *285*
To steal away, home to his native land.
He said, 'I will not lose my reputation,
Or compromise the honour of my nation,
By asking dicers to negotiate.
Send other wise ambassadors of state,   *290*
For on my honour I would rather die
Than be a means for Sparta to ally
With gamblers; Sparta, glorious in honour,
Shall take no such alliances upon her
As dicers make, by any act of mine!'   *295*
He showed his sense in taking such a line.

Again, consider King Demetrius;
The King of Parthia—history has it thus—
Sent him a pair of golden dice in scorn,
To show he reckoned him a gambler born   *300*
Whose honour, if unable to surmount
The vice of gambling, was of no account.
Lords can amuse themselves in other ways
Honest enough, to occupy their days.

    Now let me speak a word or two of swearing   *305*
And perjury; the Bible is unsparing.
It's an abominable thing to curse
And swear, it says; but perjury is worse.
Almightly God has said, 'Swear not at all',
Witness St Matthew, and you may recall   *310*
The words of Jeremiah, having care
To what he says of lying: 'Thou shalt swear
In truth, in judgement and in righteousness.'
But idle swearing is a sin, no less.
Behold and see the tables of the Law   *315*
Of God's Commandments, to be held in awe;
Look at the third where it is written plain,
'Thou shalt not take the name of God in vain.'
You see He has forbidden swearing first;
Not murder, no, nor other thing accurst   *320*
Comes before that, I say, in God's commands.
That is the order; he who understands
Knows that the third commandment is just that.
And in addition, let me tell you flat,
Vengeance on him and all his house shall fall   *325*
That swears outrageously, or swears at all.
'God's precious heart and passion, by God's nails
And by the blood of Christ that is at Hailes,
Seven's my luck, and yours is five and three;
God's blessed arms! If you play false with me   *330*
I'll stab you with my dagger!' Overthrown
By two small dice, two bitching bits of bone,
Their fruit is perjury, rage and homicide.
O for the love of Jesus Christ who died
For us, abandon curses, small or great!   *335*
But, sirs, I have a story to relate.

    It's of three rioters I have to tell
Who, long before the morning service bell,
Were sitting in a tavern for a drink.
And as they sat, they heard the hand-bell clink   *340*
Before a coffin going to the grave;
One of them called the little tavern-knave
And said 'Go and find out at once—look spry!—
Whose corpse is in that coffin passing by;
And see you get the name correctly too.'   *345*
'Sir,' said the boy, 'no need, I promise you;
Two hours before you came here I was told.
He was a friend of yours in days of old,
And suddenly, last night, the man was slain,
Upon his bench, face up, dead drunk again.   *350*
There came a privy thief, they call him Death,
Who kills us all round here, and in a breath
He speared him through the heart, he never stirred.
And then Death went his way without a word.
He's killed a thousand in the present plague,   *355*
And, sir, it doesn't do to be too vague
If you should meet him; you had best be wary.

Be on your guard with such an adversary,
Be primed to meet him everywhere you go,
That's what my mother said. It's all I know.'   *360*
    The publican joined in with, 'By St Mary,
What the child says is right; you'd best be wary,
This very year he killed, in a large village
A mile away, man, woman, serf at tillage,
Page in the household, children—all there were.   *365*
Yes, I imagine that he lives round there.
It's well to be prepared in these alarms,
He might do you dishonour.' 'Huh, God's arms!'
The rioter said, 'Is he so fierce to meet?
I'll search for him, by Jesus, street by street.   *370*
God's blessed bones! I'll register a vow!
Here, chaps! The three of us together now,
Hold up your hands, like me, and we'll be brothers
In this affair, and each defend the others,
And we will kill this traitor Death, I say!   *375*
Away with him as he has made away
With all our friends. God's dignity! Tonight!'
    They made their bargain, swore with appetite,
These three, to live and die for one another
As brother-born might swear to his born brother.   *380*
And up they started in their drunken rage
And made towards this village which the page
And publican had spoken of before.
Many and grisly were the oaths they swore,
Tearing Christ's blessed body to a shred;   *385*
'If we can only catch him, Death is dead!'
    When they had gone not fully half a mile,
Just as they were about to cross a stile,
They came upon a very poor old man
Who humbly greeted them and thus began,   *390*
'God look to you, my lords, and give you quiet!'
To which the proudest of these men of riot
Gave back the answer, 'What, old fool? Give place!
Why are you all wrapped up except your face?
Why live so long? Isn't it time to die?'   *395*
    The old, old fellow looked him in the eye
And said, 'Because I never yet have found,
Though I have walked to India, searching round
Village and city on my pilgrimage,
One who would change his youth to have my age.   *400*
And so my age is mine and must be still
Upon me, for such time as God may will.
    'Not even Death, alas, will take my life;
So, like a wretched prisoner at strife
Within himself, I walk alone and wait   *405*
About the earth, which is my mother's gate,
Knock-knocking with my staff from night to noon
And crying, "Mother, open to me soon!
Look at me, mother, won't you let me in?
See how I wither, flesh and blood and skin!   *410*
Alas! When will these bones be laid to rest?
Mother, I would exchange—for that were best—
The wardrobe in my chamber, standing there
So long, for yours! Aye, for a shirt of hair
To wrap me in!" She has refused her grace,   *415*
Whence comes the pallor of my withered face.
    'But it dishonoured you when you began
To speak so roughly, sir, to an old man,

Unless he had injured you in word or deed.
It says in holy writ, as you may read,   *420*
"Thou shalt rise up before the hoary head
And honour it." And therefore be it said
"Do no more harm to an old man than you,
Being now young, would have another do
When you are old"—if you should live till then.   *425*
And so may God be with you, gentlemen,
For I must go whither I have to go.'
    'By God,' the gambler said, 'you shan't do so,
You don't get off so easy, by St John!
I heard you mention, just a moment gone,   *430*
A certain traitor Death who singles out
And kills the fine young fellows hereabout.
And you're his spy, by God! You wait a bit.
Say where he is or you shall pay for it,
By God and by the Holy Sacrament!   *435*
I say you've joined together by consent
To kill us younger folk, you thieving swine!'
    'Well, sirs,' he said, 'if it be your design
To find out Death, turn up this crooked way
Towards that grove, I left him there today   *440*
Under a tree, and there you'll find him waiting.
He isn't one to hide for all your prating.
You see that oak? He won't be far to find.
And God protect you that redeemed mankind,
Aye, and amend you!' Thus that ancient man.   *445*
    At once the three young rioters began
To run, and reached the tree, and there they found
A pile of golden florins on the ground,
New-coined, eight bushels of them as they thought.
No longer was it Death those fellows sought,   *450*
For they were all so thrilled to see the sight,
The florins were so beautiful and bright,
That down they sat beside the precious pile.
The wickedest spoke first after a while.
'Brothers,' he said, 'you listen to what I say.   *455*
I'm pretty sharp although I joke away.
It's clear that Fortune has bestowed this treasure
To let us live in jollity and pleasure.
Light come, light go! We'll spend it as we ought.
God's precious dignity! Who would have thought   *460*
This morning was to be our lucky day?
    'If one could only get the gold away,
Back to my house, or else to yours, perhaps—
For as you know, the gold is ours, chaps—
We'd all be at the top of fortune, hey?   *465*
But certainly it can't be done by day.
People would call us robbers—a strong gang,
So our own property would make us hang.
No, we must bring this treasure back by night
Some prudent way, and keep it out of sight.   *470*
And so as a solution I propose
We draw for lots and see the way it goes;
The one who draws the longest, lucky man,
Shall run to town as quickly as he can
To fetch us bread and wine—but keep things dark—   *475*
While two remain in hiding here to mark
Our heap of treasure. If there's no delay,
When night comes down we'll carry it away,
All three of us, wherever we have planned.'

He gathered lots and hid them in his hand   *480*
Bidding them draw for where the luck should fall.
It fell upon the youngest of them all,
And off he ran at once towards the town.
    As soon as he had gone the first sat down
And thus began a parley with the other: *485*
'You know that you can trust me as a brother;
Now let me tell you where your profit lies;
You know our friend has gone to get supplies
And here's a lot of gold that is to be
Divided equally amongst us three.   *490*
Nevertheless, if I could shape things thus
So that we shared it out—the two of us—
Wouldn't you take it as a friendly act?'
    'But how?' the other said. 'He knows the fact
That all the gold was left with me and you;   *495*
What can we tell him? What are we to do?'
    'Is it a bargain,' said the first, 'or no?
For I can tell you in a word or so
What's to be done to bring the thing about.'
'Trust me,' the other said, 'you needn't doubt   *500*
My word. I won't betray you, I'll be true.'
    'Well,' said his friend, 'you see that we are two,
And two are twice as powerful as one.
Now look; when he comes back, get up in fun
To have a wrestle; then, as you attack,   *505*
I'll up and put my dagger through his back
While you and he are struggling, as in game;
Then draw your dagger too and do the same.
Then all this money will be ours to spend,
Divided equally of course, dear friend.   *510*
Then we can gratify our lusts and fill
The day with dicing at our own sweet will.'
Thus these two miscreants agreed to slay
The third and youngest, as you heard me say.
    The youngest, as he ran towards the town,   *515*
Kept turning over, rolling up and down
Within his heart the beauty of those bright
New florins, saying, 'Lord, to think I might
Have all that treasure to myself alone!
Could there be anyone beneath the throne   *520*
Of God so happy as I then should be?'
    And so the Fiend, our common enemy,
Was given power to put it in his thought
That there was always poison to be bought,
And that with poison he could kill his friends.   *525*
To men in such a state the Devil sends
Thoughts of this kind, and has a full permission
To lure them on to sorrow and perdition;
For this young man was utterly content
To kill them both and never to repent.   *530*
    And on he ran, he had no thought to tarry,
Came to the town, found an apothecary
And said, 'Sell me some poison if you will,
I have a lot of rats I want to kill
And there's a polecat too about my yard   *535*
That takes my chickens and it hits me hard;
But I'll get even, as is only right,
With vermin that destroy a man by night.'
    The chemist answered, 'I've a preparation
Which you shall have, and by my soul's salvation   *540*

If any living creature eat or drink
A mouthful, ere he has the time to think,
Though he took less than makes a grain of wheat,
You'll see him fall down dying at your feet;
Yes, die he must, and in so short a while   545
You'd hardly have the time to walk a mile,
The poison is so strong, you understand.'
    This cursed fellow grabbed into his hand
The box of poison and away he ran
Into a neighbouring street, and found a man   550
Who lent him three large bottles. He withdrew
And deftly poured the poison into two.
He kept the third one clean, as well he might,
For his own drink, meaning to work all night
Stacking the gold and carrying it away.   555
And when this rioter, this devil's clay,
Had filled his bottles up with wine, all three,
Back to rejoin his comrades sauntered he.
    Why make a sermon of it? Why waste breath?
Exactly in the way they'd planned his death   560
They fell on him and slew him, two to one.
Then said the first of them when this was done,
'Now for a drink. Sit down and let's be merry,
For later on there'll be the corpse to bury.'
And, as it happened, reaching for a sup,   565
He took a bottle full of poison up
And drank; and his companion, nothing loth,
Drank from it also, and they perished both.
    There is, in Avicenna's long relation
Concerning poison and its operation,   570
Trust me, no ghastlier section to transcend
What these two wretches suffered at their end.
Thus these two murderers received their due,
So did the treacherous young poisoner too.
    O cursed sin! O blackguardly excess!   575
O treacherous homicide! O wickedness!
O gluttony that lusted on and diced!
O blasphemy that took the name of Christ
With habit-hardened oaths that pride began!
Alas, how comes it that a mortal man,   580
That thou, to thy Creator, Him that wrought thee,
That paid His precious blood for thee and bought thee,
Art so unnatural and false within?
    Dearly beloved, God forgive your sin
And keep you from the vice of avarice!   585
My holy pardon frees you all of this,
Provided that you make the right approaches,
That is with sterling, rings, or silver brooches.
Bow down your heads under this holy bull!
Come on, you women, offer up your wool!   590
I'll write your name into my ledger; so!
Into the bliss of Heaven you shall go.
For I'll absolve you by my holy power,
You that make offering, clean as at the hour
When you were born … That, sirs, is how I preach. 595
And Jesu Christ, soul's healer, aye, the leech
Of every soul, grant pardon and relieve you
Of sin, for that is best, I won't deceive you.
    One thing I should have mentioned in my tale,
Dear people. I've some relics in my bale   600
And pardons too, as full and fine, I hope,

As any in England, given me by the Pope.
If there be one among you that is willing
To have my absolution for a shilling
Devoutly given, come! and do not harden   605
Your hearts but kneel in humbleness for pardon;
Or else, receive my pardon as we go.
You can renew it every town or so
Always provided that you still renew
Each time, and in good money, what is due.   610
It is an honour to you to have found
A pardoner with his credentials sound
Who can absolve you as you ply the spur
In any accident that may occur.
For instance—we are all at Fortune's beck—   615
Your horse may throw you down and break your neck.
What a security it is to all
To have me here among you and at call
With pardon for the lowly and the great
When soul leaves body for the future state!   620
And I advise our Host here to begin,
The most enveloped of you all in sin.
Come forward, Host, you shall be the first to pay,
And kiss my holy relics right away.
Only a groat. Come on, unbuckle your purse!'   625
    'No, no,' said he, 'not I, and may the curse
Of Christ descend upon me if I do!
You'll have me kissing your old breeches too
And swear they were the relic of a saint
Although your fundament supplied the paint!   630
Now by St Helen and the Holy Land
I wish I had your ballocks in my hand
Instead of relics in a reliquarium;
Have them cut off and I will help to carry 'em.
We'll have them shrined for you in a hog's turd.'   635
    The Pardoner said nothing, not a word;
He was so angry that he couldn't speak.
'Well,' said our Host, 'if you're for showing pique,
I'll joke no more, not with an angry man.'
    The worthy Knight immediately began,   640
Seeing the fun was getting rather rough,
And said, 'No more, we've all had quite enough.
Now, Master Pardoner, perk up, look cheerly!
And you, Sir Host, whom I esteem so dearly,
I beg of you to kiss the Pardoner.   645
    'Come, Pardoner, draw nearer, my dear sir.
Let's laugh again and keep the ball in play.'
They kissed, and we continued on our way.

↞ **CHRISTINE DE PIZAN**
from *The Book of the City of Ladies*

One of the most important aspects of The Book of the City of
Ladies *is its celebration of learning, particularly its contention that
women are as intellectually able as men. Arguing that the education
of women had long been woefully neglected, Christine de Pizan was
the first woman to insist in writing that women need and deserve to
be educated. Citing examples from history and mythology, including
the Greek poet Sappho and the Roman goddess of wisdom, Minerva,
she illustrates the accomplishments of women and celebrates their*

achievements. Her arguments in support of women provide one of the earliest and strongest counters to the deep male bias against women as she is the first professional woman writer to write from the point of view of women.

Christine asks Reason whether god has ever wished to ennoble the mind of woman with the loftiness of the sciences; and Reasons's answer.

After hearing these things, I replied to the lady who spoke infallibly: "My lady, truly has God revealed great wonders in the strength of these women whom you describe. But please enlighten me again, whether it has ever pleased this God, who has bestowed so many favors on women, to honor the feminine sex with the privilege of the virtue of high understanding and great learning, and whether women ever have a clever enough mind for this. I wish very much to know this because men maintain that the mind of women can learn only a little."

She answered, "My daughter, since I told you before, you know quite well that the opposite of their opinion is true, and to show you this even more clearly, I will give you proof through examples. I tell you again—and don't doubt the contrary—if it were customary to send daughters to school like sons, and if they were then taught the natural sciences, they would learn as thoroughly and understand the subtleties of all the arts and sciences as well as sons. And by chance there happen to be such women, for, as I touched on before, just as women have more delicate bodies than men, weaker and less able to perform many tasks, so do they have minds that are freer and sharper whenever they apply themselves."

"My lady, what are you saying? With all due respect, could you dwell longer on this point, please. Certainly men would never admit this answer is true, unless it is explained more plainly, for they believe that one normally sees that men know more than women do."

She answered, "Do you know why women know less?"

"Not unless you tell me, my lady."

"Without the slightest doubt, it is because they are not involved in many different things, but stay at home, where it is enough for them to run the household, and there is nothing which so instructs a reasonable creature as the exercise and experience of many different things."

"My lady, since they have minds skilled in conceptualizing and learning, just like men, why don't women learn more?"

She replied, "Because, my daughter, the public does not require them to get involved in the affairs which men are commissioned to execute, just as I told you before. It is enough for women to perform the usual duties to which they are ordained. As for judging from experience, since one sees that women usually know less than men, that therefore their capacity for understanding is less, look at men who farm the flatlands or who live in the mountains. You will find that in many countries they seem completely savage because they are so simple-minded. All the same, there is no doubt that Nature provided them with the qualities of body and mind found in the wisest and most learned men. All of this stems from a failure to learn, though, just as I told you, among men and women, some possess better minds than others. Let me tell you about women who have possessed great learning and profound understanding and treat the question of the similarity of women's minds to men's.

She begins to discuss several ladies who were enlightened with great learning, and first speaks about the noble maiden Cornificia

"Cornificia, the noble maiden, was sent to school by her parents along with her brother Cornificius when they were both children, thanks to deception and trickery. This little girl so devoted herself to study and with such marvelous intelligence that she began to savor the sweet taste of knowledge acquired through study. Nor was it easy to take her away from this joy to which she more and more applied herself, neglecting all other feminine activities. She occupied herself with this for such a long period of time that she became a consummate poet, and she was not only extremely brilliant and expert in the learnedness and craft of poetry but also seemed to have been nourished with the very milk and teaching of perfect philosophy, for she wanted to hear and know about every branch of learning, which she then mastered so thoroughly that she surpassed her brother, who was also a very great poet, and excelled in every field of learning. Knowledge was not enough for her unless she could put her mind to work and her pen to paper in the compilation of several very famous books. These works, as well as her poems, were much prized during the time of Saint Gregory and he himself mentions them. The Italian, Boccaccio, who was a great poet, discusses this fact in his work and at the same time praises this woman: 'O most great honor for a woman who abandoned all feminine activities and applied and devoted her mind to the study of the greatest scholars!' As further proof of what I am telling you, Boccaccio also talks about the attitude of women who despise themselves and their own minds, and who, as though they were born in the mountains totally ignorant of virtue and honor, turn disconsolate and say that they are good and useful only for embracing men and carrying and feeding children. God has given them such beautiful minds to apply themselves, if they want to, in any of the fields where glorious and excellent men are active, which are neither more nor less accessible to them as compared to men if they wished to study them, and they can thereby acquire a lasting name, whose possession is fitting for most excellent men. My dear daughter, you can see how this author Boccaccio testifies to what I have told you and how he praises and approved learning in women."

Here she tells of Proba the Roman

"The Roman woman, Proba, wife of Adelphus, was equally outstanding and was a Christian. She had such a noble mind and so loved and devoted herself to study that she mastered all seven liberal arts and was an excellent poet and delved so deeply into the books of the poets, particularly Vergil's poems, that she knew them all by heart. After she had read these books and poems with profound insight and intelligence and had taken pains in her mind to understand them, it occurred to her that one could describe the Scriptures and the stories found in the Old and New Testament with pleasant verses filled with substance taken from these same works. 'Which in itself,' Boccaccio remarked, 'is not just admirable, that such a noble idea would come into a woman's brain, but it is even more marvelous that she could actually execute it.' For then this woman, quite eager to bring her thinking to fruition, set to work: now she would run through the *Eclogues*, then the *Georgics*, and the *Aeneid* of Vergil—that is, she would skim as she read—and in one part she would take several entire verses unchanged and in another borrow small snatches of verse and, through marvelous craftsmanship and conceptual subtlety, she was able to construct entire lines of orderly verse. She would put small pieces together, coupling and joining them, all the while respecting the metrical rules, art and measure in the individual feet, as well as in the conjoining of verses, and without making any mistakes she arranged her verses so masterfully that no man could do better. In this way, starting from the creation of the world, she composed the opening of her book, and following all the stories of the Old and New Testament she came as far as the sending of the Holy Spirit to the Apostles, adapting Vergil's works to fit all this in so orderly a way that someone who only knew this work would have thought that Vergil had been both a prophet and evangelist. For these reasons, Boccaccio himself says that this woman merits great recognition and praise, for it is obvious that she possessed a sound and exhaustive knowledge of the sacred books and volumes of Holy Scripture, as do many great scholars and theologians of our time. This most noble lady wished that this said work, drawn up and composed through her labor, be called the *Cento*. Although the labor demanded by this work, because of its grandeur, would have been enough for one man's lifetime, she spent must less time in devoting herself to its execution, and was also able to compose several other excellent books. One, among others, she composed in verse, also called *Cento* because it contained one hundred lines of verse. She also made use of the poems and verses of the poet Homer, so that in praising her one can conclude that she knew not only Latin literature but also Greek literature perfectly. Boccaccio observes that it should be a great pleasure for women to hear about her and these things."

Here she speaks of Sappho, that most subtle woman, poet, and philosopher

"The wise Sappho, who was from the city of Mytilene, was no less learned than Proba. This Sappho had a beautiful body and face and was agreeable and pleasant in appearance, conduct, and speech. But the charm of her profound understanding surpassed all the other charms with which she was endowed, for she was expert and learned in several arts and sciences, and she was not only well-educated in the works and writings composed by others but also discovered many new things herself and wrote many books and poems. Concerning her, Boccaccio has offered these fair words couched in the sweetness of poetic language: 'Sappho, possessed of sharp wit and burning desire for constant study in the midst of bestial and ignorant men, frequented the heights of Mount Parnassus, that is, of perfect study. Thanks to her fortunate boldness and daring, she kept company with the Muses, that is, the arts and sciences, without being turned away. She entered the forest of laurel trees filled with may boughs, greenery, and different colored flowers, soft fragrances and various aromatic spices, where Grammar, Logic, noble Rhetoric, Geometry, and Arithmetic live and take their leisure. She went on her way until she came to the deep grotto of Apollo, god of learning, and found the brook and conduit of the fountain of Castalia, and took up the plectrum and quill of the harp and played sweet melodies, with the nymphs all the while leading the dance, that is, following the rules of harmony and musical accord.' From what Boccaccio says about her, it should be inferred that the profundity of both her understanding and of her learned books can only be known and understood by men of great perception and learning, according to the testimony of the ancients. Her writings and poems have survived to this day, most remarkably constructed and composed, and they serve as illumination and models of consummate poetic craft and composition to those who have come afterward. She invented different genres of lyric and poetry, short narratives, tearful laments and strange lamentations about love and other emotions, and these were so well made and so well ordered that they were named 'Sapphic' after her. Horace recounts, concerning her poems, that when Plato, the great philosopher who was Aristotle's teacher, died, a book of Sappho's poems was found under his pillow.

"In brief this lady was so outstanding in learning that in the city where she resided a statue of bronze in her image was dedicated in her name and erected in a prominent place so that she would be honored by all and be remembered forever. This lady was placed and counted among the greatest and most famous poets, and, according to Boccaccio, the honors of the diadems and crowns of kings and the miters of bishops are not any greater, nor are the crowns of laurel and victor's palm.

"I could tell you a great deal about women of great learning. Leontium was a Greek woman and also such a great philosopher that she dared, for impartial and serious reasons, to correct and attack the philosopher Theophrastus, who was quite famous in her time."

Here she discusses the maiden Manto

"If women are able to apprehend and fit to learn literary and scientific subjects, I want you to know for certain that the arts likewise are not forbidden to women, just as you will hear. In the ancient cult of the pagans long ago, people would divine the future from the flight of birds, the flames of fire, and the entrails of dead animals. This was an art or science in itself which they held in great respect. The supreme mistress of the art was a maiden, the daughter of Tiresias, who was the high priest of the city of Thebes (or what we would call the bishop, for in other religions priests could marry). This woman, who was named Manto and flourished in the time of Oedipus, king of Thebes, possessed such a brilliant and wide-ranging mind that she was well-versed in the art of pyromancy, that is, divination by fire. The Chaldaeans who invented this art made use of it in very ancient times, though others say that the giant Nimrod discovered it. There was no man in her time who could better discern the movements and colors of flames or the sounds which came out of fire, and who could so brilliantly read the veins of animals, the throats of bulls, and the entrails of beasts; and it was believed that with her arts she often forced spirits to speak in answer to her inquiries. During the lifetime of this lady, Thebes was destroyed as a result of the struggle between the sons of Oedipus the king, so she went to live in Asia and there built a temple to Apollo, which subsequently became quite famous. She ended her life in Italy, and because of her authority a city of that country was, and still is named after this lady, Mantua, where Vergil was born."

She speaks here of Medea and of another Queen, named Circe

"Medea, whom many historical works mention, was no less familiar with science and art than Manto. She was the daughter of Aetes, king of Colchis, and of Persa, and was very beautiful, with a noble and upright heart and a pleasant face. In learning, however, she surpassed and exceeded all women; she knew the powers of every herb and all the potions which could be concocted, and she was ignorant of no art which can be known. With her spells she knew how to make the air become cloudy or dark, how to move winds from the grottoes and caverns of the earth, and how to provoke other storms in the air, as well as how to stop the flow of rivers, confect poisons, create fire to burn up effortlessly whatever object she chose, and all such similar arts. It was thanks to the art of her enchantments that Jason won the Golden Fleece.

"Circe, similarly, was queen of a country on a sea which lay at the entrance to Italy. This lady knew so much about the art of enchantments that there was nothing which she might want to do that she could not accomplish by virtue of the strength of her spells. She knew how to metamorphose the bodies of men into those of wild beasts and animals through the power of a drink which she would administer. In testifying to this power, the story of Ulysses recounts that when he was returning home after the destruction of Troy, intending to go back to his own land in Greece, Fortune and stormy weather drove his ships in all directions, through many tempests, so that they finally arrived in the port of the city of this queen Circe. Since the clever Ulysses did not wish to disembark without the leave and permission of that country's queen, he sent his knights to her in order to find out whether it would please her for them to land. But this lady, thinking they were her enemies, gave the ten knights a drink of her concoction, which immediately changed them into swine. Ulysses quickly went to her, and the men were subsequently changed back to their proper form. Likewise, some say that when Diomedes, another prince of Greece, arrived in the port of Circe, she had his knights changed into birds, which they still remain. These birds are quite large and have a different shape from other birds. The natives are quite proud of them and call them 'Diomedius birds.'

Christine asks Reason whether there was ever a woman who discovered hitherto unknown knowledge

Christine, concentrating on these explanations of Lady Reason, replied to her regarding this passage: "My lady, I realize that you are able to cite numerous and frequent cases of women learned in the sciences and the arts. But I would then ask you whether you know of any women who, through the strength of emotion and of subtlety of mind and comprehension, have themselves discovered any new arts and sciences which are necessary, good, and profitable, and which had hitherto not been discovered or known. For it is not such a great feat of mastery to study and learn some field of knowledge already discovered by someone else as it is to discover by oneself some new and unknown thing."

She replied, "Rest assured, dear friend, that many noteworthy and great sciences and arts have been discovered through the understanding and subtlety of women, both in cognitive speculation, demonstrated in writing, and in the arts, manifested in manual works of labor. I will give you plenty of examples.

"First I will tell you of the noble Nicostrata whom the Italians call Carmentis. This lady was the daughter of a king of Arcadia, named Pallas. She had a marvelous mind, endowed by God with special gifts of knowledge: she was a great scholar in Greek literature and had such fair and wise speech and venerable eloquence that the contemporary poets who wrote about her imagined she was beloved of the god Mercury. They claimed that a son whom she had with her husband, and who was in his time most learned, was in fact the offspring of this god. Because of certain changes which came about in the land where she lived, this lady left her country in a large boat for the land of Italy, and in her company were her son and a great many people who followed her; she arrived at the river Tiber. Landing there, she proceeded to climb a high hill which she named the Palentine, after her father, where the city of Rome was later founded. There, this lady and her son and all those who had followed her built a fortress. After discovering that the men of that country were all savages, she wrote certain laws, enjoining them to live in accord with right and reason, following justice. She was the first to institute laws in that country which subsequently became so renowned and from which all the statutes of law derive. This lady knew through divine inspiration and the spirit of prophecy (in which she was remarkably distinguished, in addition to the other graces she possessed) how in time to come this land would be ennobled by excellence and famous over all the countries of the world. Therefore it seemed to her that once the grandeur of the Roman Empire, which would rule the entire world, had been established, it would not be right for the Romans to use the strange and inferior letters and characters of another country. Moreover, in order to show forth her wisdom and the excellence of her mind to the centuries to come, she worked and studied so hard that she invented her own letters, which were completely different from those of other nations, that is, she established the Latin alphabet and syntax, spelling, the difference between vowels and consonants, as well as a complete introduction to the science of grammar. She gave and taught these letters to the people and wished that they be widely known. This was hardly a minor or unprofitable contribution to learning which this woman invented, nor one for which she merits slight gratitude, for thanks to the subtlety of this teaching and to the great utility and profit which have since accrued to the world, one can say that nothing more worthy in the world was ever invented. The Italians were not ungrateful for this benefit, and rightly so, since for them this discovery was so fantastic that they not only deemed this woman to be greater than any man, but they also considered her a goddess and even honored her during her lifetime with divine honors. After her death they erected a temple to her, built at the foot of the hill where she had resided. To ensure eternal remembrance of this lady, they used many names taken from the science she had discovered and gave her name to many other things, so that the people of this country even called themselves Latins in honor of the science of Latin developed by this lady. Moreover, because *ita*, which means *oui* in French, is the strongest affirmation in Latin, they were not satisfied calling this country the 'Latin land,' but rather they wished that all the country beyond the mountains, which is quite large and contains many diverse countries and dominions, be called *Italy*. Poems were named *carmen* in Latin, after this lady, Carmentis, and even the Romans who lived long afterward, called one of the gates of the city of Rome the *Carmentalis*. Regardless of the prosperity which the Romans enjoyed and the majesty of some of their emperors, the Romans did not change these names, just as it is apparent in the present-day since they still survive.

"What more do you want, fair daughter? Can one say anything more solemn about any man born of woman? And do not think for a minute that she was the only woman in the world by whom numerous and varied branches of learning have been discovered!"

Here she speaks of Minerva, who invented many sciences and the technique of making armor from iron and steel

"Minerva, just as you have written elsewhere, was a maiden of Greece and surnamed Pallas. This maiden was of such excellence of mind that the foolish people of that time, because they did not know who her parents were and saw her doing things which had never been done before, said she was a goddess descended from Heaven; for the less they knew about her ancestry, the more marvelous her great knowledge seemed to them, when compared to that of the women of her time. She had a subtle mind, of profound understanding, not only in one subject but also generally, in every subject. Through her ingenuity she invented a shorthand Greek script in which a long written narrative could be transcribed with far fewer letters, and which is still used by the Greeks today, a fine invention whose discovery demanded great subtlety. She invented numbers and a means of quickly counting and adding sums. Her mind was so enlightened with general knowledge that she devised various skills and designs which had never before been discovered. She developed the entire technique of gathering wool and making cloth and was the first who ever thought to shear sheep of their wool and then to pick, comb, and card it with iron spindles and finally to spin it with a distaff, and then she invented the tools needed to make the cloth and also the method by which the wool should finally be woven.

"Similarly she initiated the custom of extracting oil from different fruits of the earth, also from olives, and of squeezing and pressing juice from other fruits. At the same time she discovered how to make wagons and carts to transport things easily from one place to another.

"This lady, in a similar manner, did even more, and it seems all the more remarkable because it is far removed from a woman's nature to conceive of such things; for she invented the art and technique of making harnesses and armor from iron and steel, which knights and armed soldiers employ in battle and with which they cover their bodies, and which she first gave to the Athenians whom she taught how to deploy an army and battalions and how to fight in organized ranks.

"Similarly she was the first to invent flutes and fifes, trumpets and wind instruments. With her considerable force of mind, this lady remained a virgin her entire life. Because of her outstanding chastity, the poets claimed in their fictions that Vulcan, the god of fire, wrestled with her for a long time and that finally she won and overcame him, which is to say that she overcame the ardor and lusts of the flesh which so strongly assail the young. The Athenians held this maiden in such high reverence that they worshiped her as a goddess and called her the goddess of arms and chivalry because she was the first to devise their use, and they also called her the goddess of knowledge because of her learnedness.

"After her death they erected a temple in Athens dedicated to her, and there they placed a statue of her, portraying a maiden, as a representation of wisdom and chivalry. This statue had terrible and cruel eyes because chivalry has been instituted to carry out rigorous justice; they also signified that one seldom knows toward what end the meditation of the wise man tends. She wore a helmet on her head which signified that a knight must have strength, endurance, and constant courage in the deeds of arms, and further signified that the counsels of the wise are concealed, secret, and hidden.

She was dressed in a coat of mail which stood for the power of the estate of chivalry and also taught that the wise man is always armed against the whims of Fortune, whether good or bad. She held some kind of spear or very long lance, which meant that the knight must be the rod of justice and also signified that the wise man casts his spears from great distances. A buckler or shield of crystal hung at her neck, which meant that the knight must always be alert and oversee everywhere the defense of his country and people and further signified that things are open and evident to the wise man. She had portrayed in the middle of this shield the head of a serpent called Gorgon, which teaches that the knight must always be wary and watchful over his enemies like the serpent, and furthermore, that the wise man is aware of all the malice which can hurt him. Next to this image they also placed a bird that flies by night, named the owl, as if to watch over her, which signified that the knight must be ready by night as well as by day for civil defense, when necessary, and also that the wise man should take care at all times to do what is profitable and fitting for him. For a long time this lady was held in such high regard and her great fame spread so far that in many places temples were founded to praise her. Even long afterward, when the Romans were at the height of their power, they included her image among their gods."

She discusses Queen Ceres, who discovered the art of cultivating the earth and many other arts

"Ceres, who was in ancient times queen of the kingdom of the Sicilians, enjoys the privilege of being the first to discover cultivation and to invent the necessary tools. She taught her subjects to master and tame oxen as well as to train them to the yoke. She also invented the plow and showed her subjects how to plow the earth with plowshares tipped in iron and how to carry out all the accompanying tasks. Afterward she taught them how to cast seed on this ground and cover it over, and later, after the seed had grown and multiplied, she showed them how to reap the grains and how to sift out the ears by beating them with flails. Then she cleverly taught them how to grind the grain between hard stones and in mills and then how to mix the ingredients to make bread. Thus this woman taught and instructed men who had been accustomed, like beasts, to live on acorns, wild grains, and haws, to make use of more convenient foods. This lady did even more: for she had the people of that time gather together in communities. They had traditionally lived scattered here and there in the forest and wilderness, wandering like animals. She taught them to build cities and towns of permanent construction where they could reside together. Thus, thanks to this woman, the world was led away from bestial living conditions to a rational, human life. Poets dreamed up the fable that Ceres' daughter was carried off by Pluto, the god of Hell. And because of the authority of her knowledge and the great good she brought about for the world, the people of that time worshiped her and called her the goddess of grain."

Here she speaks of Isis, who discovered the art of constructing gardens and of planting

"Isis, likewise, was a woman of such great learning acquired through labor that she was not only named the queen of Egypt but also the most singular and special goddess of the Egyptians. The tale has it that Jupiter loved Isis and changed her into a cow and that then she reassumed her original form, all of which signifies her vast knowledge, just as you yourself have touched upon in your *Epistre d'Othea*. She invented a form of shorthand which she taught to the Egyptians and provided them a way to abridge their excessively involved script. She was the daughter of Inachos, king of the Greeks, and sister of the wise Phoroneus. For some reason this lady went from Greece to Egypt with this brother of hers. There, among other things, she taught the Egyptians how to set up vegetable gardens and how to make plantings and grafts from different stalks. She handed down and instituted several good and upright laws; she instructed the people of Egypt, who had, until then, lived like savages without law, justice, or order, to live according to the rule of the law. And to put it briefly, she did so much there that both in her lifetime and after her death they held her in the greatest reverence. Her fame spread everywhere in the world so that temples and chapels were established everywhere. Even at the height of their power, the Romans had a temple in Rome erected in her name where they instituted sacrifices, offerings, and solemn rights in conformity to the custom observed in Egypt.

"The husband of this noble lady was called Apis, who, according to the error of the pagans, was supposed to be the son of the god Jupiter and of Niobe, daughter of Phoroneus, who is mentioned frequently in ancient histories and in the work of ancient poets."

Concerning the great good accrued to the world through these women

"My lady, I greatly admire what I have heard you say, that so much good has come into the world by virtue of the understanding of women. These men usually say that women's knowledge is worthless. In fact when someone says something foolish, the widely voiced insult is that this is women's knowledge. In brief, the typical opinions and comments of men claim that women have been and are useful in the world only for bearing children and sewing."

She answered, "Now you can recognize the massive ingratitude of the men who say such things; they are like people who live off the goods of others without knowing their source and without thanking anyone. You can also clearly see how God, who does nothing without a reason, wished to show men that He does not despise the feminine sex nor their own, because it so pleased Him to place such great understanding in women's brains that they are intelligent enough not only to learn and retain the sciences but also to discover new sciences themselves, indeed sciences of such great utility and profit for the world that nothing has been more necessary. You can therefore see from this Carmentis, whom I just mentioned to you and who invented the Latin alphabet, toward which God has been so favorable and which has spread the skill developed by this lady so that it has even effaced some of the glory of the Hebrew and Greek alphabets, which once enjoyed such great esteem, that all of Europe (which contains a very large part of the world) uses this script, in which practically an endless number of books and volumes have been written and composed, where the deeds of man and the noble and excellent glories of God, as well as the sciences and the arts, have been placed and held in perpetual memory. And let no one say that I am telling you these things just to be pleasant: they are Boccaccio's own words, and his credibility is well-known and evident. Thus you can conclude that the benefits realized by this woman are endless, for, thanks to her, men have been brought out of ignorance and led to knowledge, even if they do not recognize it; thanks to her, they possess the means to send the secrets and meditations of their minds as far away as they want, to announce and to report whatever they wish anywhere, and, by the same token, the means to know the past, present, and future. Moreover, because of this one woman's learning, men can conclude agreements and maintain friendships with distant people and, through the exchange of responses, they can know one another without having seen one another. In short, all the good which comes from the alphabet and thus from books cannot be told; for books describe and facilitate the understanding and knowledge of God, celestial things, the sea, the earth, all people, and all things. Where was there ever a man who did more good?"

On the same topic

"Similarly, where was there ever a man thanks to whom more good came into the world than thanks to this noble queen Ceres whom I have just discussed with you? How could anyone ever acquire a more praiseworthy name than by leading wandering and savage men, living in the woods like cruel beasts without the rule of justice, to reside in cities and towns and by teaching them to make use of law and by securing better provisions for them than acorns and wild apples, that is, grains and cereals? Because of this food, men have more beautiful and more radiant bodies and stronger and more flexible limbs, for this food is more beneficial and useful for humans. And who will ever win more praise for teaching men to beautify the land, which had been overgrown with thistles, thorns, poorly arranged shrubs, and wild trees, to clear it through labor and to sow seed, so that the savage land, thanks to cultivation, became domesticated and ennobled for the common profit of all? Because of this lady, humanity benefited from the transformation of the harsh and untamed world into a civilized and urban place. She transformed the minds of vagabond and lazy men by drawing them to herself and leading them from the caverns of ignorance to the heights of contemplation and proper behavior. By organizing certain men to perform field work, she made it possible for so many cities and towns to be populated and for their residents, who perform the other works necessary for life, to be supported.

"The same holds true for Isis and gardening. Who could sum up the great good she procured for the world by developing a method for taking grafts from trees that bear so many good fruits and spices so useful for human nourishment?

"Minerva, too, from her knowledge provided humanity with so many necessary objects, like woolen clothing for men who had previously worn only animal skins, and solved the problems they had transporting necessities in their arms from one place to another by inventing wagons and carts to help them. For nobles and knights she devised a means of making armor to cover their bodies for greater protection in war and developed better-looking, stronger, and more practical armor than they had had before, which had only consisted of leather from animals."

Then I said to her, "Now, my lady, I indeed understand more than before why you spoke of the enormous ingratitude, not to say ignorance, of these men who malign women, for although it seems to me that the fact that the mother of every man is a woman is reason enough not to attack them, not to mention the other good deeds which one can clearly see that women do for men, truly, one can see here the many benefits afforded by women with the greatest generosity to men which they have accepted and continue to accept. Henceforth, let all writers be silent who speak badly of women, let all of them be silent—those who have attacked women and who still attack them in their books and poems, and all their accomplices and supporters too—let them lower their eyes, ashamed for having dared to speak so badly, in view of the truth which runs counter to their poems; this noble lady, Carmentis, through the profundity of her understanding taught them like a schoolmistress—nor can they deny it—the lesson thanks to which they consider themselves so lofty and honored, that is, she taught them the Latin alphabet!

"But what did all the many nobles and knights say, who generally slander women with such false remarks? From now on let them keep their mouths shut and remember that the customs of bearing arms, of dividing armies into battalions, and of fighting in ordered ranks—a vocation upon which they so pride themselves and for which they consider themselves so great—came to them from a woman and were given to them by a woman. Would men who live on bread, or who live civilly in cities following the order of law, or who cultivate the fields, have any good reason to slander and rebuff women so much, as many do, if they only thought of all the benefits? Certainly not, because thanks to women, that is, Minerva, Ceres, and Isis, so many beneficial things have come to men, through which they can lead honorable lives and from which they live and will live always. Ought not these things be considered?"

"Doubtless, my lady. It seems to me that neither in the teaching of Aristotle, which has been of great profit to human intelligence and which is so highly esteemed and with good reason, nor in that of all the other philosophers who have ever lived, could an equal benefit for the world be found as that which has been accrued and still accrues through the works accomplished by virtue of the knowledge possessed by these ladies."

Glossary

→

Words in **boldface** indicate terms defined elsewhere in the glossary.

abacus A square slab on top of the **capital** of a **column**.

abstraction Art that does not portray the visual reality of an object but reflects an artist's nonrepresentational conception of it.

academy Generally, a society of artists or scholars. The Academy was Plato's school for the study of philosophy.

acanthus A Mediterranean plant whose leaves were often copied as decoration on the **capitals** of **Corinthian columns**.

acropolis Meaning literally "high city," this was the fortified, elevated point in an ancient Greek city. The Acropolis is the specific site in Athens where the Parthenon was built.

aesthetic Related to the appreciation of beauty in the arts.

agora A meeting place in ancient Greece, especially a marketplace.

aisle A long side passageway of a church. Aisles run parallel to the central **nave**.

alap In music, an improvised prelude to an Indian **raga** composition.

allegory A symbolic narrative in which a deeper, often moral meaning exists beyond the literal level of a work.

altar A raised platform or table at which religious ceremonies take place. It is where the Eucharist is celebrated in Christian churches.

altarpiece A painted or carved panel behind or above the **altar** of a church.

alto In music, the range of the lowest female voice.

ambulatory A passageway or **aisle** around the **apse** of a church.

amphitheater An oval or round theater with tiers of seats gradually rising from a central arena.

amphora (AM-fur-uh) A two-handled jar with a narrow neck, used by ancient Greeks and Romans to carry wine or oil.

anagnorisis In drama, the point at which a character experiences recognition or increased self-knowledge.

animal interlace An ornamental pattern of intertwined, elongated animal forms, common in medieval art.

animal style An artistic design popular in ancient and medieval times, characterized by decorative patterns of intricate animal motifs.

anthropomorphism The act of attributing human characteristics to non-human entities, such as gods or animals.

antiphony Vocal or instrumental music in which two or more groups sing or play in alternation.

apse The semi-circular projection at the end of a church sanctuary, often highly decorated; usually the location of the **altar**.

arcade A series of connected **arches**, supported by **columns** or **piers**.

arch In architecture, the curved or pointed structure spanning the top of an open space, such as a doorway, and supporting the weight above it.

Archaic period The Greek cultural and artistic style of about 600–480 B.C., noted for realistic sculptures of the human figure.

Archaic smile An enigmatic facial expression, almost a half-smile, typical in ancient Greek sculpture.

architrave The bottom part of an **entablature**, directly above the **capital**.

archivolt The semi-circular molding outlining an **arch**.

ashlar masonry (ASH-luhr) Masonry of massive dressed or square-cut stones.

assonance Similarity of sound, especially the half-rhyme of words with the same vowel sounds but different consonants, as in *heap* and *leak*.

atlas (plural, **atlantes**) A sculpted male figure used as a supporting **column**.

atrium In architecture, the open room in the center of a Roman house.

axis An imaginary straight line on either side of which components of a piece of art are evenly arranged.

baptistery A small, octagonal structure, usually separated from the main church building, in which baptisms are performed.

bas relief French for "low" relief. In sculpture, **relief** that projects only slightly from its background.

basilica A large rectangular building with a wide central **nave** and an **apse** at one or both ends, originally used in Rome for business and legal meetings, later adapted for Early Christian churches.

basilica plan A building modeled after the rectangular **basilica** floor plan, with a longitudinal **axis**.

bass In music, the range of the lowest male voice.

battered In architecture, sloping inward toward the top, as in a wall.

bay In architecture, a spatial unit that is repeated.

Benedictines Members of the religious order founded by St. Benedict in 529.

bhakti (BUCK-tee) In Hinduism, the expression of personal devotion to a particular deity, especially in the form of poetry.

black-figure style Greek vase painting style featuring black figures painted on a red clay background, with details incised to reveal the red clay below.

blind arcade A decorative **arcade** in which the **arches** and **columns** are attached to the background wall.

bodhisattva (boe-di-SUTT-vuh) In Buddhism, an enlightened being on the brink of buddhahood who forgoes **nirvana** to allow others to attain salvation.

buttress In architecture, a projecting support that reinforces a wall.

Byzantine (BIZ-un-teen) The artistic style of Eastern Europe in the fourth through fifteenth centuries that featured rich colors, Christian imagery, **domed** churches, and **mosaics**.

cabochon (CAB-uh-shawn) A gem that is not cut in facets, but is smoothed and rounded.

caliph One of a succession of leaders who assumed religious and secular control of Islam after Muhammad's death.

campanile (camp-ah-NEE-leh) A bell tower, especially one that stands apart from other main church buildings.

canon In religion, the books of the Bible officially sanctioned by a church as inspired by God.

canto A main division of a poem.

cantus firmus (CAN-tuss FURR-muss) A preexisting melody line around which a new polyphonic composition is constructed.

cap stone The topmost stone in a **corbeled arch** or **dome**, which joins the two sides.

capital The decorative top part of a **column** that supports the **entablature**.

cartoon A full-scale preparatory drawing made for a large work such as a **tapestry** or **mural**.

caryatid (cah-ree-ATT-id) A sculpted female figure used as a supporting **column**.

catacombs Underground cemeteries of Early Christians, especially those on the outskirts of Rome.

catharsis Purging of emotional tension, especially by art; originally described by Aristotle as the effect of **tragic** drama on the audience.

cella (SELL-uh) The inner room of a Greek or Roman temple, where the temple's cult statue was kept.

centering In architecture, a temporary wooden semicircular device used for support during construction of an **arch**, **vault**, or **dome**.

central plan A building having no longitudinal **axis**, such as one with a polygonal or circular floor plan.

cha-no-yu Japanese ritualistic tea ceremony.

chanson de geste (shawn-SAWN duh JZEST) French for "song of deeds." A medieval **epic** poem that celebrates the actions of historical figures or heroes.

chapel A small area for worship, usually set in an alcove of a larger church or within a secular building.

chiton A soft clinging outer garment worn by women in ancient Greece.

chivalry The system of ethical conduct of the Middle Ages based on a blend of Christian and military morals.

choir In architecture, the part of a church where the singers perform, usually between the **transept** and the **apse**.

chorus In ancient Greek drama, the group of actors who spoke or chanted in unison, often while moving in a stylized dance; the chorus provided a commentary on the action. Later, the term was generalized to mean a company of singers.

Cistercians Members of the austere order of monks established by St. Bernard of Clairvaux in 1115.

civilization A culture's development to a stage marked by written language, social organization, and artistic expression.

Classical The artistic style of ancient Greece or Rome that emphasized balance, restraint, and quest for perfection.

classicism Any later artistic style reminiscent of the ancient Greek or Roman **Classical** style and its values of balance, restraint, and quest for perfection.

clerestory (CLEER-story) In church architecture, the upper part of the wall containing a row of windows for light.

cloister A square or rectangular open courtyard surrounded on all sides by covered **arcaded** walkways, and often with a source of water in the center. Generally part of a monastery.

coffer In architecture, a squarish indentation in a **dome** or **vault**.

colonette A small **column**, usually attached to a **pier** in **Gothic** cathedrals.

colonnade In architecture, a row of **columns** placed side by side, usually to support a roof or a series of **arches**.

column A vertical architectural support, usually consisting of a base, **shaft**, and decorative **capital**.

comedy An amusing play or novel with a happy ending, usually including a marriage.

Composite order Roman combination of the Greek **Ionic** and **Corinthian** orders, with a slender **column** and a **capital** with both **acanthus** leaves and a **volute**.

concrete A hard building material made of cement, sand, and gravel; popularized by the ancient Romans.

Confucianism Chinese philosophical perspective based on the teachings of Confucius that emphasized morality, tradition, and ethical behavior.

contrapposto (CONE-truh-POSE-toe) In sculpture and painting, an asymmetrical positioning of the human body in which the weight rests on one leg, elevating the hip and opposite shoulder.

corbel In architecture, a bracket of metal, wood, or stone.

corbeling In architecture, the successive layering of stones, with each layer slightly overlapping the one below it until the stones meet at the top of the opening, such as in an **arch** or **dome**.

Corinthian The most ornate of Greek architectural orders. Featured thin, fluted **columns** and **capitals** elaborately decorated with **acanthus** leaf carvings. See also **Doric**; **Ionic**.

cornice In architecture, a horizontal molding that forms the uppermost, projecting part of an **entablature**.

cosmology Philosophical study of the evolution of the universe.

couplet A unit of poetry consisting of two successive rhyming lines.

covenant In theology, an agreement or contract between God and humans.

crenelated Notched or indented, as at the top of a wall or battlement.

crepidoma; crepis The three visible steps of a **column**'s **platform**.

cromlech (CROM-leck) A prehistoric monument of huge stones arranged in a circle.

crossing The intersection of the **nave** and the **transept** in a cross-shaped church.

crypt An area underneath a church, usually beneath the apse, that is used as a burial place.

culture A group's way of living, including its beliefs, art, and social organization, that is transmitted from one generation to the next.

cuneiform (KYOO-nee-ah-form) The ancient Mesopotamian system of writing that uses wedge-shaped characters.

dharma The Hindu notion of duty or moral responsibility.

Dionysos Greek god of wine (Roman name Bacchus), whose worship developed into an orgiastic cult of fertility and immorality in ancient Rome.

diptych (DIP-tick) A pair of painted or carved panels hinged together.

dome A hemispherical **vault**.

Doric The earliest and simplest of Greek architectural **orders**, featuring short, sturdy **columns**, often unfluted, and a simple **capital** shaped like a square block and a circular cushion. See also **Corinthian**; **Ionic**.

drum In architecture, a circular wall, usually topped by a **dome**.

dualism A religious system that divides the universe into two opposing forces, good and evil, e.g. Zoroastrianism.

duplum The higher pitched of two voice parts in medieval **organum**.

earthenware Pottery made of porous clay fired at a relatively low temperature.

earthwork A large-scale artwork created by altering the land or a natural geographic area.

echinus (ee-KYE-nuhs) The cushionlike molding below the **abacus** of a **Doric capital**.

enamel The artistic technique of fusing powdered colored glass to a metal surface in a decorative pattern, or the object created by this method.

engaged Attached to a background wall, as in a **column**.

engraving A type of print made by cutting an image onto metal or wood and inking the impression.

entablature In architecture, the horizontal structure above the **columns** and **capitals** and below the roof.

entasis (EN-tuh-sis) A slight bulge in the **shaft** of a **column**.

epic An extended narrative poem written in a dignified style about a heroic character or characters.

Epicureanism Greek philosophy founded by Epicurus that held that pleasure, or the avoidance of pain, was the ultimate good.

epistle A book of the New Testament originally written as a letter.

evangelists From the Greek term for "bearer of good news." The name given to Matthew, Mark, Luke, and John, who wrote the gospel books of the New Testament; generally, one who preaches or attempts to spread the gospel.

facade The front face of a building.

faience (FYE-uhns) Lustrous glazed **earthenware**.

fan vaulting A decorative style of **vaulting** with **ribs** radiating like those of a fan.

fang ding A square bronze vessel with four legs, used for storing ceremonial offerings during the Chinese Shang dynasty.

Flamboyant A late stage of **Gothic** architectural style of the fifteenth and sixteenth centuries, characterized by wavy, flamelike **tracery** and elaborate decoration.

fluting In architecture, a decorative motif of a series of parallel vertical grooves, such as on a **column**'s **shaft**.

flying buttress An architectural support consisting of an external **buttress** connected to the main structure by an **arch** which transfers the lateral thrust of the **vaulting** to it; invented and used frequently during the **Gothic** era.

folio A large sheet of paper folded once down the middle, forming two leaves, or four pages, of a book or manuscript; generally, a page in a **manuscript** or book.

foreshortening A painting and drawing technique of shortening the lines of an object to create the illusion of three-dimensional space in a composition.

forum (plural, **fora**) A public square of an ancient Roman town, often used as a marketplace or gathering spot.

Franciscans Members of a Christian order of monks founded by St. Francis of Assisi in 1209; noted for their emphasis on poverty and humility.

fresco A painting style in which pigments are applied to fresh wet plaster, or an artwork created in such a style.

fret A ridge on the fingerboard of a stringed instrument.

friar A male member of certain Christian monastic orders.

frieze A band of ornamental carving, especially the middle section of an **entablature**, between the **architrave** and **cornice**.

gable In architecture, the triangular section at the end of a pitched roof, between the two sloping sides.

gallery In architecture, a long narrow passageway, especially found above the side **aisles** of a church, overlooking the **nave**.

gargoyle A gutter, carved usually in the form of a fantastic creature, the mouth serving as a waterspout. Found especially on Gothic churches and cathedrals.

garth An enclosed garden, especially that within a cloister.

genre (JON-ruh) A category of art, music, or literature.

geoglyph A huge earthen design, such as the Nazca lines.

Geometric period The Greek cultural and artistic style of about 1000–700 B.C., noted for abstract geometric designs, especially on pottery.

glaze A thin, transparent layer of oil paint, usually applied on top of another layer or over a painted surface to achieve a glowing or glossy look.

glissando (plural, **glissandi**) (gli-SAHN-doe) In music, a rapid slide of a succession of adjacent tones.

Gnosticism (NOHS-tih-sizm) The dualistic doctrine of certain pagan, Jewish, and Early Christian sects that redemption is achieved through an occult knowledge of God, revealed to their believers alone.

Golden Section A mathematical formula, developed in ancient Greece, for ideal proportions in fine art. The smaller of two dimensions is the same proportion to the larger as the larger is to the whole work, a ratio of about five to eight.

gospels The first four books of the New Testament (Matthew, Mark, Luke, John), which describe the life and teachings of Jesus.

Gothic The style of architecture and art of the twelfth through sixteenth centuries in Western Europe and revived during the Romantic era. Characterized, especially in churches, by ribbed **vaults**, pointed **arches**, **flying buttresses**, **stained glass**, and high, steep roofs.

Greek cross In architecture, a floor plan having four arms of equal length. Compare with **Latin cross**.

Gregorian chant A **monophonic liturgical** chant, usually sung with no accompaniment; named after St. Gregory, who was pope 590–604. Also called **plainchant**; **plainsong**.

ground bass In music, a phrase in the **bass** that is repeated continually throughout the composition or musical section.

guild An association of people in the same craft or trade, formed during the Middle Ages or Renaissance to give economic and political power to its members and to control the trade's standards.

hadith The Islamic document containing the sayings of Muhammad and anecdotes about him.

harmony In music, playing or singing two or more tones at the same time, especially when the resulting sound is pleasing to the ear; generally, the arrangement of chords.

Hellenic Relating to the culture of **Classical** Greece (from 480 to 323 B.C.).

Hellenistic Relating to the post-**Classical** period in Greek history (after 323 B.C.), during which basic tenets of Classical Greek culture and thought spread throughout the Mediterranean, Middle East, and Asia.

henge A prehistoric circle of stones or posts.

hieroglyphics A writing system, such as that of the ancient Egyptians, that uses pictorial characters to convey sounds or meanings.

Hijrah (or **Hegira**) (hi-JYE-ruh) Muhammad's flight from Mecca to Medina in A.D. 622, which marks the beginning of the Muslim era.

himation A rectangular piece of fabric draped over one shoulder as a garment in ancient Greece.

huaca (WAH-cah) A pyramid made of sun-dried bricks, around which the Moche lived in Peru.

icon A small religious image, such as a figure from the Bible, painted on wood and used as a sacred reminder of important elements of Christianity.

iconoclasm; iconoclastic controversy (eye-KON-o-KLAZ-em) Opposition to the use of religious images; the systematic destruction of religious **icons**.

iconography In visual arts, the symbols used to communicate meaning.

iconophile A lover of artistic images, at odds with iconoclasts in the **iconoclastic controversy** of the Byzantine era.

ideogram A symbol that represents an idea, not just a word or its pronunciation.

illumination The technique of decorating manuscripts and books with richly colored, gilded paintings and ornamental lettering and borders; also, the painting achieved by this method.

imago A Roman death mask.

impost block In architecture, a block placed between the **capital** and the **arch**, used to channel the weight of the arch down onto the **column**.

incarnation Generally, the act of assuming a human body, especially by a god or spirit. In Christian theology, the doctrine of the birth of God in human form as Jesus Christ.

interval In music, the difference between any two pitches.

Ionic Somewhat ornate Greek architectural **order** characterized by its slim, **fluted columns** and **capitals** in the form of spiral scrolls. See also **Corinthian**; **Doric**.

irony Language that states something different from or opposite to what is intended; *dramatic irony* puts characters in a position of ignorance about such an incongruity, while keeping the audience aware of the situation.

Isis The Egyptian goddess of fertility, whose cultlike worship gradually extended throughout the Roman Empire.

jamb The sides of a doorway or window.

ka The ancient Egyptian concept of the human soul or spirit, believed to live on after death.

Kamares Ware Minoan ceramic ware painted white and orange-red on a dark purple-brown background, distinguished by its designs from nature and patterns swirling over the surface of the vessel.

karma The Hindu and Buddhist doctrine that one's moral actions have a future consequence in determining personal destiny.

kiva (KEE-vah) A large underground ceremonial room in a Pueblo village.

Koran See **Quran**.

kore (plural, **korai**) (KOR-ay) **Archaic** Greek statue of a standing clothed female.

kouros (plural, **kouroi**) (KOR-oss) **Archaic** Greek statue of a standing nude male.

krater A large bowl with a wide mouth, used in ancient Greece and Rome for mixing wine and water.

lancet A window with a narrow **arch** shape, used frequently in **Gothic** architecture.

landscape A painting, photograph, or other visual art form that uses a natural outdoor scene as its main subject.

Latin cross In architecture, a floor plan of three short arms and one long one. Compare with **Greek cross**.

lekythos (plural, **lekythoi**) A small cylindrical oil jug with one handle and a narrow mouth, used as a funeral offering in ancient Greece.

lightwell An uncovered vertical shaft that allows light into the lower stories of a building.

linear perspective. See **perspective**.

lintel (LINN-tuhl) In architecture, a horizontal beam above an opening such as a door or window, which usually supports the structure above it.

liturgy A religious rite used in public organized worship.

loggia (LOH-juh) In architecture, a covered, open-air gallery.

logic The study of reasoning, or a particular system of reasoning.

lost-wax process (also known as the "cire-perdue" process) A method of metal casting in which a wax mold is coated with plaster or clay, then heated so the wax melts and runs out of vents in the mold. Molten metal is then poured into the hollow space and, when cooled, the clay or plaster mold is broken, leaving a metal core.

lozenge An ornamental diamond-shaped motif.

lyric poetry Poems that have a songlike quality; usually emotional in nature.

mandorla The almond-shaped area of light shown to surround Jesus or other religious figure.

Manicheism (MAN-i-key-izm) The religious philosophy, founded by the Persian prophet Manes in the third century A.D. and synthesized from elements of Christianity, Gnosticism, and Zoroastrianism, that divided the world between good and evil forces.

manuscript A handwritten book or document.

Mass A central religious ritual, principally in the Roman Catholic church.

mass The musical setting of parts of the **Mass**.

mastaba An ancient Egyptian burial place with a one-story rectangular building, a flat roof, and slanted walls.

mausoleum A monumental tomb, or the building used to store one or more such tombs.

meander An ornamental maze pattern common in Greek art.

megalith A huge stone, especially used as part of a prehistoric monument.

menhir (MEN-hear) A prehistoric monument of a single, huge slab of stone, set in an upright position.

Mesolithic Describing a period between the **Paleolithic** and **Neolithic** periods, about 10,000–8,000 B.C., characterized by domestication of animals and an increasing emphasis on farming.

metope (MET-uh-pee) In **Classical** architecture, a square or rectangular space, often decorated; metopes alternate with **triglyphs** in a **Doric frieze**.

mihrab (ME-rahb) A small niche marking the side of an Islamic **mosque** facing Mecca.

mille-fleurs (meel-FLUHR) French for "a thousand flowers." A background pattern consisting of many flowers and plants, particularly in **tapestry** designs.

minaret (min-uh-RET) In Islamic architecture, a tall slender tower attached to a **mosque**, from which a **muezzin** calls the faithful to prayer.

miniature A detailed, small-scale painting, often on an **illuminated manuscript**.

minstrel A traveling entertainer of the Middle Ages, especially one who performed secular music.

Mithras The Persian god of light and wisdom, whose cultlike worship spread throughout the Roman Empire, eventually rivaling Christianity.

mode The organization of musical intervals into scales, used in ancient and medieval music; later limited to just the major and minor scales.

model In painting, to create the illusion of depth by using light and shadow. In sculpture, to shape a pliable substance into a three-dimensional object.

monastery A residence for monks.

monasticism The life of organized religious seclusion, as in a **monastery** or convent.

monolith A single slab of stone.

monophony Musical texture with a single melody and no accompaniment. Compare **polyphony**.

monotheism Belief in and worship of a single god.

mosaic A design or picture created by inlaying pieces of colored glass, stone, or tile in mortar; mosaics are usually placed on wall, floors, or ceilings.

mosque An Islamic house of worship.

moundbuilders Early Native American cultures in the Mississippi or Ohio river valley noted for their construction of monumental burial mounds.

mudra (moo-DRAH) A symbolic, stylized position of the body or hand in Indian art.

muezzin (myoo-EZ-in) The crier who calls the Muslim faithful to prayer five times a day.

mural A large wall painting.

mystery play A medieval drama form based on biblical narratives.

myth A traditional story, usually featuring heroes, gods, or ancestors, that explains important cultural practices or beliefs.

narthex A rectangular entrance hall or vestibule leading to the **nave** of a church.

natural law A set of rights derived from nature and therefore superior to those established in the civil code.

nave The rectangular central space of a church; it is flanked on both sides by smaller **aisles**.

Neolithic The New Stone Age, about 8000 B.C. to 2000 B.C.; a period characterized by the use of pottery, agriculture, development of early writing, and construction of **megalithic** structures.

Neoplatonism A revival of the philosophy of Plato, developed by Plotinus in the third century A.D. and prevalent during the Renaissance; based on the belief that the psyche is trapped within the body, and that philosophical thought is the only way to ascend from the material world to union with the single, higher source of existence.

neume A basic musical **notation** symbol used in **Gregorian chants**.

niche In architecture, a hollow part in a wall, often used to hold a statue or vase.

nirvana In Buddhism, Hinduism, and Jainism, the state of ultimate bliss.

notation In music, a symbolic method of representing tones.

novella (plural, **novelle**) A short story, usually satirical and with a moral.

octave In music, an eight-note interval; in poetry, an eight-line section of a poem, particularly the first section in a Petrarchan sonnet.

oculus Latin for "eye." In architecture, a circular opening or window, usually at the top of a **dome**.

ode A lyric poem, usually addressed to a person or object and written in a dignified style.

oinoche A Greek wine jug with a pinched lip and curved handle.

oligarchy A form of government in which a few people rule.

olpe A Greek vase or jug with a broad lip.

opera Italian for "a work." Musical form, first introduced in the **Baroque** era, that combines drama, a text set to vocal music, and orchestral accompaniment.

orans In Early Christian art, the pose of a person in prayer, with hands raised to heaven.

order In architecture, a style of architecture, determined by the type of **column** used. See also **Doric**; **Ionic**; **Corinthian**.

organum (ORE-guh-num) Early **polyphonic** music with the voices a fourth, a fifth, or an **octave** apart. The **organum duplum** is such a chant with two voices, with the lower voice holding long notes and the higher voice moving more quickly. Such a chant with three voices is an **organum triplum**; such a chant with four voices is an **organum quadruplum**.

Orientalizing period The Greek cultural and artistic style of about 700–600 B.C. that was influenced greatly by the Near East.

pagoda A Buddhist temple in the shape of a tower, with many stories that each have an upward-curving roof.

Palace Style Minoan ceramic ware painted with dark colors on a light background, distinguished by its designs from nature and patterns that appear to grow up the sides of the vessel.

palaestra (plural, **palaestrae**) A public place in ancient Greece where young men learned to wrestle and box under the guidance of a master.

Paleolithic The Old Stone Age, about 2,000,000–10,000 B.C.; a period characterized by hunting, fishing, the use of stone tools, the increasing dominance of *homo sapiens*, and the creation of the earliest works of art.

palette An artist's choice of colors for a particular work of art, or the surface on which such colors are placed and mixed.

pallium An ancient Roman garment made of a rectangular piece of fabric.

palmette A stylized palm leaf ornament.

pantheon All the gods of a people, or a temple dedicated to all the gods; the Pantheon is the specific circular temple in Rome dedicated to all gods.

parchment Animal skin used to make **manuscript folios**.

patrician A member of the noble family class in ancient Rome that was originally granted special civil and religious rights.

patronage Originally, a system of **patrician** support and protection of a **plebeian** in ancient Rome; later, a system of financially sponsoring art or artists.

pediment In **Classical** architecture, a triangular space at the end of a building, formed by the **cornice** and the ends of the sloping roof.

pendentives Four triangular sections of a large **dome** used as a transition from a square base to the circular rim of a smaller dome above it.

peplos A loose outer garment worn by women in ancient Greece, hanging from the shoulders and belted at the waist.

percussion instrument A musical instrument, such as a timpani or bass drum, played by hitting or shaking.

peripteral Having a single row of **columns** on all sides.

peristyle In architecture, a continuous row of **columns**, forming an enclosure around a building or courtyard.

perspective A method of creating the illusion of three-dimensional space on a two-dimensional surface. Achieved by methods such as *atmospheric perspective*, using slight variations in color and sharpness of the subject, or *linear perspective*, creating a horizon line and orthogonals, which recede toward vanishing points.

piazza (pee-AHT-zuh) A public square in Italy.

pictograph A picture used to represent a word or idea.

pier In architecture, a vertical support structure similar to a **column**, but usually square or rectangular in shape, rather than cylindrical.

pillar A freestanding vertical element, usually used as an architectural support.

plainchant; plainsong In music, the **monophonic**, unmetered vocal music of the Early Christian church, as in **Gregorian chant**.

platform A raised horizontal surface, especially one on which **columns** sit.

Platonism The philosophy of Plato, focusing on the notion that Ideal Forms are an absolute and eternal model that all worldly phenomena strive toward.

plebeian A member of the common lower class in ancient Rome that at first lacked many of the rights that **patricians** enjoyed.

plinth A slab that supports a sculpture or **column**.

podium In architecture, an elevated **platform**; often the foundation of a building, especially an ancient temple.

polis (plural, **poleis**) An independent city-state in ancient Greece.

polyphony The simultaneous playing or singing of several independent musical lines. Compare **monophony**.

polytheism Belief in or worship of more than one god. Compare **monotheism**.

portal In architecture, a grand entrance or doorway.

portico In architecture, a porch or walkway covered by a roof supported by **columns**. It often marks an entrance to the main building.

post and lintel An architectural construction system with two vertical posts supporting a horizontal beam.

potlatch A lavish ceremony among some Native Americans of northwest North America at which the host distributes gifts to guests according to their rank or status.

primary colors The colors red, yellow, and blue. See also **secondary colors**.

pronaos The enclosed vestibule of a Greek or Roman temple, supported by columns.

propylon (plural, **propylaia**) A gateway to a temple or a group of buildings.

pseudo-peripteral Having a single row of **engaged columns** on all sides.

pylon A massive gateway, especially to an Egyptian temple.

qasidah A highly formalized Arabic ode of 30–120 lines, each line ending with the same rhyme. It focuses on the poet's attempt to find his beloved.

qibla (KIB-luh) The direction facing Mecca, to which a Muslim turns when praying.

quadrivium The program of arithmetic, astronomy, geometry, and music in medieval universities.

quatrain A four-line unit of poetry.

Quran; Koran The sacred text of Islam.

radiating chapels Several chapels that are arranged around the **ambulatory** or **apse** of a church.

raga An Indian musical composition, usually partly improvised, that attempts to convey a mood or feeling.

Ramadan The holy ninth month of the Islamic lunar calendar, during which Muslims must fast from sunrise to sunset.

Rayonnant (ray-yo-NAHN) From the French term for "to radiate." The High **Gothic** architectural style of the mid-thirteenth century, noted for its radiating **tracery** patterns and liberal use of **stained glass**.

red-figure style Greek vase painting style featuring red figures surrounded by a black background, with details painted on the surface.

refectory The dining room of a **monastery** or convent.

register system The method of organizing an artistic composition in horizontal bands or rows, each of which depicts a different event or idea.

regular temple Architectural plan for a temple in which the number of **columns** along the sides of the temple is double the number of columns on the ends plus one (e.g. an eight-by-seventeen proportion).

relic A memento or keepsake of religious veneration, especially a body part or personal effect from a saint.

relief In sculpture, a figure projecting from a flat, two-dimensional background; in painting, the *apparent* projection of a figure from its flat background.

relieving triangle In architecture, an opening built into a heavy wall above a **post and lintel** structure that helps to relieve the weight on the **lintel**.

reliquary A container for holding or displaying a **relic**.

repoussé (ruh-poo-SAY) The technique of creating **relief** in metal by hammering out details from the back.

representational Art that attempts to portray the visual reality of an object.

rhyton An ancient Greek drinking horn which may be shaped like an animal head.

rib In architecture, a curved, projecting **arch** used for support or decoration in a **vault**.

romance A long medieval narrative form that related **chivalric** Celtic stories, especially the exploits of King Arthur and his Knights of the Round Table.

Romanesque The style of architecture and art of the eleventh and twelfth centuries in Western Europe. Characterized, especially in churches, by semi-circular **arches**, barrel **vaults**, and thick wall.

rondo form Organizing structure for a musical work in which the main theme repeats itself frequently, with new, contrasting material added between each repetition.

roof comb A crestlike extension along the roof of a Mayan temple that resembles the comb of a rooster.

rose window A round **stained glass** window with **tracery** lines in the form of wheel spokes; a standard feature in the facade of **Gothic** cathedrals.

rosette A roselike ornament that is painted or sculpted.

rotunda A circular building, usually topped by a **dome**.

ruba'i (plural, **ruba'iyat**) A Persian poetry form of four lines with a rhyming pattern of AABA.

sacramentary A **liturgical** book of prayers and rites of the sacraments of the Roman Catholic church.

samsara The Hindu notion of the eternal cycle of birth and death.

samurai Ruler-warriors of Japan, especially during the feudal era.

sarcophagus A stone coffin.

satire Literary or dramatic work that exposes vice or follies with ridicule or sarcasm, often in a humorous way.

satori The Zen Buddhist state of enlightenment.

scale In music, an ascending or descending series of notes.

scroll In Chinese and Japanese art, a painting or text drawn on vertical pieces of silk fabric; the scroll is conventionally kept rolled and tied except on special occasions, when it is hung. Also called *hanging scroll; hand scroll;* Japanese narrative scrolls are called *emaki-mano*.

secondary colors The colors orange, green, and purple, formed when two primary colors (red, yellow, or blue) are mixed. See also **primary colors**.

secular Not sacred or religious.

serdab The cellar of an Egyptian **mastaba**, containing the **ka** statue.

shaft The vertical section of a **column** between the **capital** and the base.

shastras Ancient Hindu texts that describe instructions for various activities, including temple building, cooking, warfare, and music.

Shinto A principal and former state religion of Japan characterized by rituals and venerations for local deities and strong patriotism.

shogun A hereditary military dictator of Japan; originally, commander-in-chief of the **samurai**.

sitar A long-necked, lute-shaped instrument from India.

skene (SKAY-nuh) In Greek theater, a building behind the acting area that functioned as a dressing room and as scenic background.

Skepticism Greek philosophic doctrine that absolute knowledge is not usually possible, and that inquiry must therefore be a process of doubt.

Sophists Ancient Greek philosophers and teachers, less interested in the pursuit of truth than in the use of clever rhetoric and argumentation.

soprano In music, the range of the highest voice of females or young boys.

staff In music, the five horizontal lines and four spaces used in **notation**.

stained glass Artistic technique in which many small pieces of glass are colored with internal pigment or surface paint and then held together with lead strips; used extensively in **Gothic** cathedrals.

statue in the round Sculpture that stands free of a background and is fully formed to be seen from all sides.

stele (STEE-lee) An upright slab of stone that serves as a marker or monument.

stigmata The physical marks or scars on humans that resemble the crucifixion marks of Jesus; said to appear during states of religious ecstasy.

stoa (STO-uh) A covered walk or **colonnade**, which might also house shops in ancient Greece.

Stoicism Greek school of philosophy that held that a spiritual force pervades the universe, and that true happiness is achieved only by aligning one's will with this force and by putting aside indulgence and passion. It was later popular with the Romans and had a strong impact on Early Christian thought.

stupa A **dome**-shaped Indian architectural monument originally for burials and later used by Buddhists for religious **relics**.

stylobate The top step of the **platform** that supports a row of **columns** in a Greek temple.

Sufi An Islamic mystic.

Surah A chapter in the **Quran**.

syllogism A form of deductive reasoning consisting of a major premise, a minor premise, and a conclusion. For example: *All philosophers are mortal; Aristotle was a philosopher; Aristotle was mortal.*

synoptic gospels The **gospels** of Matthew, Mark, and Luke, which are similar. The gospel of John is unique.

tambura An unfretted lute, used to sustain the drone chord in Indian music.

tapestry A heavy piece of fabric used as wall decoration. The design is created as the tapestry is woven.

teleology In philosophy, the study of an end and how it relates to the natural processes leading up to it.

tempera (TEM-purr-uh) Paint made of egg yolk, water, and pigment.

tenor In music, the range of the highest male voice, which usually carries the melody; also, the bottom, slower line of an **organum duplum**.

terra cotta Italian for "baked earth." An orange-red baked clay used for pottery or sculpture.

terza rima (turr-tsah-REE-ma) Poetry form consisting of three-line stanzas in which each stanza's middle line rhymes with the first and third lines of the subsequent stanza (ABA, BCB, CDC, etc).

tessera (plural, **tesserae**) (TESS-ur-ah) A small stone or other material used in making a **mosaic**.

tholos (plural, **tholoi**) Any round building.

thrust In architecture, outward or lateral pressure in a structure.

toga An ancient Roman garment.

tonality In music, the arrangement of all tones of a composition in relation to the central key, or tonic.

Torah Hebrew for "instruction." The first five books of Hebrew scripture.

totem pole A post carved with animal and spirit images and erected by some Native Americans of northwest North America to memorialize the dead.

tracery An elaborate pattern of interlacing stone lines, especially in **Gothic** windows.

tragedy A serious literary or theatrical work about a central character's problems, with an unhappy ending.

transept Either of the two lateral "arms" of a church laid out in a cross pattern; transepts cross the nave at right angles.

treasury A building, room, or box for storing valuables or offerings.

triclinium A dining room in an ancient Roman home, named for the three couches on which the diners reclined.

triforium In **Gothic** architecture, the elevated gallery or **arcade** just below the **clerestory** of a cathedral.

triglyph In Greek architecture, a rectangular block with three vertical grooves; triglyphs alternate with **metopes** in a **Doric** frieze.

triumphal arch A grand freestanding gateway with a large **arch**, which often serves as an urban monument.

trivium The program of grammar, logic, and rhetoric in medieval universities

trope In music, a new word or phrase added to an existing chant as an embellishment.

troubadour (TRUE-buh-door) A poet-musician of medieval southern France.

trumeau A central post or **column** that supports the **lintel** of a large **portal**.

tufa A porous stone that is soft when cut but hardens after exposure to air.

Tuscan order Roman modification of the Greek **Doric order**, but with an unfluted shaft, a base, a plain **architrave**, and an undecorated **frieze**.

tympanum (plural, **tympana**) (TIM-puh-num) The ornamental semi-circular area between an **arch** and the **lintel** above a doorway or window.

vault An arched masonry roof or ceiling. A *barrel* or *tunnel vault* is an uninterrupted semi-circular vault made of a series of **arches**. A *cross* or *groin vault* is created by the intersection of two barrel vaults set at right angles. A *ribbed vault* is a form of groin vault in which the groins formed by the intersection of curved sides are covered with raised **ribs**.

Vedas The oldest sacred Hindu writings, composed 1500–1000 B.C. by the Aryans in present-day India.

vellum The finest quality of **parchment**.

veneer In architecture, a thin layer of high-quality material used as a **facade**, often covering inferior materials.

vernacular The common language spoken in a particular country or region.

vibrato (vi-BRAHT-oh) In vocal or instrumental music, a pulsing effect achieved by slight, rapid variations in pitch.

volute A spiral scroll ornament, as on an **Ionic capital**.

voussoirs (voo-SWAHRS) The wedge-shaped stones or blocks that form an **arch**.

warp The thick threads that run vertically on a loom and provide the structure for a piece of fabric woven of the weft threads.

weft The threads that run horizontally on a loom and usually form the visible pattern on a piece of woven fabric.

westwork The monumental western entryway in a Carolingian, Ottonian, or **Romanesque** church.

white-ground ceramics Ancient Greek pottery ware in which a white matte slip is painted over the surface of a reddish clay vessel, with details painted on the surface with a fine brush.

whole tone; whole step In music, the **interval** between any first and third consecutive keys on the piano; made up of two half steps.

yin and yang The Chinese **dualistic** philosophical image that represents simultaneous contrast and complement. The yin form represents the passive, negative, feminine, dark, earthly; the yang form represents the light, masculine, positive, constructive, and heavenly. The two are in perpetual interplay.

Zen Buddhism Chinese and Japanese form of Buddhism that emphasizes enlightenment achieved by self-awareness and meditation instead of by adherence to a set religious doctrine.

ziggurat An ancient Mesopotamian stepped pyramid temple.

PICTURE CREDITS AND FURTHER INFORMATION

The authors, Calmann & King Ltd, and Prentice Hall wish to thank the institutions and individuals who have kindly provided photographic materials for use in this book. Every effort has been made to contact the copyright holders, but should there be any errors or omissions, the publishers would be pleased to insert the appropriate acknowledgment in any subsequent edition.

Key: A=Alinari, BAL=Bridgeman Art Library, BPK=Bildarchiv Preussischer Kulturbesitz, Berlin, HV=Hirmer Verlag, München, AFK=A.F.Kersting London, S=Scala, TAP=Ministry of Culture, TAP Service, Athens

Introduction/Starter Kit
0.1 © Studio Fotografico Quattrone, Florence; 0.2 © Succession Picasso/DACS 1998; 0.3 Photo: J. Lathion; © Nasjonalgalleriet, Oslo; 0.5 Robert Harding Picture Library, London

Chapter One
1.1 AKG London; 1.2 © YAN, Toulouse; 1.4 Institut Amatller D'Art Hispanic, Barcelona; 1.5 Robert Harding/Adam Woolfitt; 1.6 HV; 1.8 Fletcher Fund 1940; 1.9 Harris Brisbane Dick Fund 1959; 1.11,12+Detail page vi Photo:University of Pennsylvania Museum; 1.15 Gift of John D. Rockefeller Jr. 1932; 1.19 BPK; 1.20 RMN-Hervé Lewandowski; 1.21 © Comstock/Peter Keen 1997; 1.22 Ancient Art & Architecture Collection

Chapter Two
2.1,3 HV; 2.4,5 Spectrum; 2.6,8,9 HV; 2.10 Rogers Fund and Henry Walters Gift 1919; 2.11 AFK; 2.12 HV; 2.14 Lorna Oakes, Hertfordshire; 2.16 Robert Harding; 2.19,20,21 BPK/Margarete Büsing; 2.22 Robert C. Lamm, Scottsdale; 2.23 photo: Stephen Petegorsky

Chapter Three
3.1 Gift of Christos G. Bastis 1968; 3.2 TAP; 3.3,5 Ancient Art & Architecture Collection; 3.6 Spectrum; 3.7,8 TAP; 3.9 C.M. Dixon; 3.10 AFK; 3.12 Ancient Art & Architecture Collection; 3.13 HV; 3.14 TAP; 3.15 Rogers Fund 1914; 3.16 BPK; 3.17 RMN-Hervé Lewandowski; 3.20 Classical Purchase Fund 1978; 3.21+Detail page vii Purchase, Bequest of Joseph H. Durkee, Gift of Darius Ogden Mills and Gift of C. Ruxton Love, by exchange, 1972; 3.23 Fototeca Unione, Rome; 3.24 Robert Harding/Mark Vivian; 3.25 Fletcher Fund 1932; 3.26 Alison Frantz, Princeton NJ

Chapter Four
4.1 Spectrum; 4.4,5+Detail Page vii AFK; 4.8 HV; 4.9 RMN-Hervé Lewandowski; 4.11 World Pictures, London; 4.12 Alison Frantz, Princeton NJ; 4.13 HV; 4.14 Fotografia Foglia, Naples; 4.15 S; 4.16 A; 4.17 Christa Koppermann, München; 4.18 Robert Harding; 4.19 HV; 4.22 AFK; 4.24 BPK; 4.26 BPK/Erich Lessing; 4.27 RMN-Gérard Blot/Jean; 4.28 S

Chapter Five
5.2 S; 5.3 Robert Harding; 5.4 HV; 5.5 A; 5.6 S; 5.7,8,9 AFK; 5.11 D.A.I. Rome; 5.12 Hutchison Library/Bernard Régent; 5.13 AFK; 5.14 AKG London; 5.15 AKG/Erich Lessing; 5.17 A; 5.19 Janetta Rebold Benton; 5.20 A; 5.21+Detail page viii Janetta Rebold Benton; 5.22 © Von Matt; 5.23 Samuel D. Lee Fund 1940; 5.24 Janetta Rebold Benton; 5.25 AFK; 5.26 A; 5.27 S; 5.28 C.M. Dixon; 5.29 Rogers Fund 1903. Photo: Schecter Lee; 5.30 S; 5.31 Fotografia Foglia, Naples

Chapter Six
6.1+Detail page viii Canali Photobank, Rome; 6.5 AFK; 6.7 HV; 6.8, 9 S; 6.10 A

Chapter Seven
7.1 Sonia Halliday; 7.2 AFK; 7.3 4 S; 7.5 © Cameraphoto Arte, Venice; 7.6 Robert Harding/Adam Woolfitt; 7.8,9,10 © Cameraphoto Arte, Venice; 7.11 Andrew Mellon Collection 1937; 7.12 Spectrum; 7.13 Robert Harding/Robert Frerck; 7.15 AFK; 7.16 Sonia Halliday; 7.17 Robert Harding/Robert Frerck; 7.18 Hutchison Library/Patricio Goycoolea; 7.19 The Nasser D. Khalili Collection of Islamic Art (POT 12). Photograph ©NOUR Foundation; 7.21 Francis Bartlett Donation of 1912 and Picture Fund; 7.22+Detail page ix Bodleian Library, Oxford

Chapter Eight
8.1 Dinodia Picture Agency, Bombay; 8.3,4 AFK; 8.5,6 AKG London; 8.7 Dinodia Picture Agency, Bombay; 8.8,9+Detail page ix AFK; 8.11 Redferns

Chapter Nine
9.2 China Pictorial, Beijing; 9.4+Detail page ix BAL; 9.5 Werner Forman Archive; 9.12 Arcaid/Bill Tingey

Chapter Ten
10.1 South American Pictures; 10.2 Comstock/ Georg Gerster; 10.3 Photo:University of Pennsylvania Museum; 10.4 South American Pictures; 10.5+Detail page x Copyright Merle Greene Robertson, 1976; 10.6 South American Pictures; 10.7 Comstock; 10.8 Buckingham Fund,1955.2281 Photo: © 1994 The Art Institute of Chicago. All Rights Reserved; 10.9 Hutchison Library/Robert Francis; 10.10 South American Pictures; 10.11 Royal Anthropological Institute; 10.12 Robert Harding/Tony Waltham; 10.13 Comstock/Georg Gerster

Chapter Eleven
11.5 Dr. H. Busch; 11.8 Pierpont Morgan Library/ Art Resource NY; 11.12 © YAN/Jean Dieuzaide; 11.14 CAISSE © Arch. Phot. Paris SPADEM/ DACS; 11.15 AFK; 11.16 Spectrum; 11.17 S; 11.18,19 © Paul M.R. Maeyaert; 11.20 Ancient Art & Architecture Collection; 11.21 Foto Ritter, Vienna

Chapter Twelve
12.1 BAL; 12.2 Robert Harding; 12.4 HV; 12.5 Spectrum; 12.6 AFK; 12.7 © Angelo Hornak, London; 12.8 AFK; 12.10 © James Austin, 1994; 12.11 Sonia Halliday; 12.12 Giraudon, Paris; 12.13,14 AFK; 12.15 Spectrum; 12.16 AFK; 12.17,18 Janetta Rebold Benton; 12.19 Giraudon, Paris; 12.20 Janetta Rebold Benton; 12.22+Detail page x BAL; 12.23 Sonia Halliday; 12.24 Hutchison Library/ Christine Pemberton; 12.25 Gift of John D. Rockefeller Jr. 1937; 12.26,27,28,29 S; 12.30 © Studio Fotografico Quattrone, Florence; 12.31,32 S

LITERATURE CREDITS

For permission to reprint copyright material the publishers gratefully acknowledge the following:

Aris & Phillips Ltd.: *Pericles' Funeral Oration* from *Thucydides* History II, trans. P.J. Rhodes, by permission of the publisher.
Bantam Doubleday Dell Publishing Group: *The Nightingale* from *Lays of Courtly Love* by Marie de France, trans. Patricia Terry (Anchor Books); from *The Second Teaching* from *Bhagavad Gita*, trans. Barbara Stoler Miller, translation copyright © 1985 by Barbara Stoler Miller by permission of the publisher.
Benziger Pubishing Co.: *Fifth Article* from *Summa Theologica* by St Thomas Aquinas, trans. Father of the English Dominican Province, © 1947.
David Campbell Publishers: *The Chester Pageant of the Deluge* from *Everyman and Other Plays* (1915).
Farrar, Straus & Giroux Inc.: *Then up the ladder of the earth I climbed* from *The Heights of Machu Picchu* by Pablo Neruda, trans. Nathaniel Tarn, translation © 1966 and copyright renewed © 1994 by Nathaniel Tarn, by permission of Farrar, Straus & Giroux Inc. and Random House UK Ltd.
John L. Foster (trans.): *Song of the Harper* and *Hymn to the Sun* from *Echoes of Egyptian Voices* (University of Oklahoma Press), and *Love, how I'd love to slip down to the pond* from *Love Songs of the New Kingdom* (University of Texas Press) by permission of the translator and publisher.
Hackett Publishing Company: from *Confessions* by St. Augustine, trans. F.J. Sheed (1993), by permission of the publisher.
Harcourt Brace & Company: *Oedipus the King* from *Sophocles: The Oedipus Cycle: An English Version* by Robert Fitzgerald and Dudley Fitts.
Harper Collins Publishers: from *The Book of Songs*, trans. Arthur Waley (George Allen & Unwin, 1937), by permission of the publisher.
Alfred A. Knopf Inc.: *The Shell of the Locust*, trans. Edward G. Seidensticker from *The Tale of Genji* by Murasaki Shikibu, copyright © 1976 by Edward G. Seidensticker, by permission of the publisher.
W.W. Norton & Company Inc.: from *The Song of Roland*, trans. Frederick Goldin, copyright © 1978 by W.W. Norton & Company Inc.; from *The Divine Comedy* by Dante Alighieri, trans. John Ciardi, translation copyright 1954, 1957, 1959, 1960, 1961, 1965, 1967, 1970 by the Ciardi Family Publishing Trust; *The Story of the Merchant and the Demon* from *The Arabian Nights: The Thousand and The One Nights*, trans. Husain Haddawy, copyright © 1990 by W.W. Norton & Company, by permission of the publisher.
Oxford University Press: *That man is seen by me as a God's equal* and *We should live, my Lesbia, and love* from *The Poems of Catullus*, ed./trans. Guy Lee, copyright © Guy Lee 1990, by permission of the publisher.
Penguin Books Ltd.: from *The Epic of Gilgamesh*, trans. N.K. Sanders (Penguin Classics); from *The Histories* by Herodotus, trans. Aubrey de Selincourt (Penguin Classics); from *The Canterbury Tales* by Geoffrey Chaucer, trans. Nevill Coghill (Penguin Classics); from *Speaking of Siva*, trans. A.K. Ramanujan (Penguin Classics); from *The Satyricon & Apocolocyntosis* by Seneca, trans. J.P. Sullivan (Penguin Classics); from *The Analects* by Confucius, trans. D.C. Lau (Penguin Classics); from *The Koran*, trans. N.J. Dawood (Penguin Classics).
Penguin USA: from *Beowulf*, trans. Burton Raffel, translation copyright © 1963 by Burton Raffel, Afterword © 1963 by New American Library; from *Decameron* by Giovanni Boccaccio, trans. Bondanella & Musa from *The Italian Renaissance Reader* by Julia Bondanella and Mark Musa copyright © 1987 by Julia Conaway Bondanella and Mark Musa, by permission of Dutton Signet, a division of Penguin Books USA Inc.; *The Coronation* from *The Ramayana*, trans. R.K. Narayan, copyright © 1972 by R.K. Narayan, by permission of Viking Penguin, a division of Penguin Books USA Inc.
Persea Books: from *The Book of the City of Ladies* by Christine de Pizan, trans. Earl Jeffrey Richards, copyright © 1982 by Persea Books.
Prentice-Hall Inc.: from *Nicomachean Ethics* by Aristotle, trans. Martin Ostwald, copyright © 1962 by Martin Ostwald, by permission of Prentice-Hall Inc., Upper Saddle River, NJ.
Random House Inc.: from *The Secret Teachings of Jesus: Four Gnostic Gospels*, trans. Marvin W. Meyer; from *Aeneid* by Virgil, trans. Robert Fitzgerald; from *Iliad* by Homer and *Odyssey* by Homer, trans. Robert Fagles; from *Sappho and the Greek Lyric Poets*, trans. Willis Barnstone.
Simon & Schuster: from *Marcus Aurelius: Meditations*, trans. G.M.A. Grube, copyright © 1963 by The Bobbs-Merrill Company Inc., by permission of Simon & Schuster.
Thelma Sullivan (trans.): *The Midwife Addresses the Newly Delivered Woman*.
Threshold Books: *The Question*, trans. Coleman Barks and John Moyne from Open Secret, originally published by Threshold Books, 139 Main Street, Brattleboro, VT 05301, used by permission.
University of Chicago Press: *The Monk Who Left His Body Behind*, *The Girl Who Married a Snake*, and *Poor Blossom* from *Panchatantra*, trans. Arthur W. Ryder.
University of Oklahoma Press: *With flowers you write ...* and *Oh watcher, watcher from the trees*, trans. Miguel Leon-Portilla from *Pre-Columbian Literatures of Mexico*; *Ah god how they race* from *The Odes of Horace*, trans. Helen Rowe Henze, by permission of the publisher.
Yale University Press: *Yearning* and *Dialogue in the Mountains* by Li Bai from *The Great Age of Chinese Poetry: The T'ang*, trans. Stephen Owen, by permission of the publisher.

INDEX
→

Page numbers in *italics* show specific references to *people, works of art, or major events* in illustrations, maps, timeline diagrams, and extracts from written works.